CHILDREN OF COYOTE,
MISSIONARIES OF SAINT FRANCIS

Published for the Omohundro Institute of
Early American History and Culture, Williamsburg, Virginia,
by the University of North Carolina Press, Chapel Hill

CHILDREN OF COYOTE, MISSIONARIES OF SAINT FRANCIS

INDIAN-SPANISH RELATIONS IN COLONIAL
CALIFORNIA, 1769–1850

◄◄ STEVEN W. HACKEL ►►

The Omohundro Institute of Early American History and Culture is
sponsored jointly by the College of William and Mary and the Colonial
Williamsburg Foundation. On November 15, 1996, the Institute adopted
the present name in honor of a bequest from Malvern H. Omohundro, Jr.

Set in Minion and Othello by Keystone Typesetting, Inc.

Manufactured in the United States of America

Publication of this book was aided by a grant
from the Program for Cultural Cooperation between
Spain's Ministry of Culture and United States Universities.

Library of Congress Cataloging-in-Publication Data

Hackel, Steven W.
Children of coyote, missionaries of Saint Francis : Indian-Spanish
relations in colonial California, 1769–1850 / Steven W. Hackel.
p. cm.
Includes bibliographical references and index.
ISBN 0-8078-2988-9 (cloth: alk. paper)
ISBN 0-8078-5654-1 (pbk.   )
1. Indians of North America—California—Monterey Peninsula—History.
2. Indians of North America—First contact with Europeans—California—
Monterey Peninsula. 3. Indians of North America—Missions—California—
Monterey Peninsula. 4. Franciscans—Missions—California—Monterey
Peninsula—History. 5. Mission San Carlos Borromeo (Carmel, Calif.)—History.
6. Spain—Colonies—America. 7. California—Relations—Mexico.
8. Mexico—Relations—California.
I. Omohundro Institute of Early American History & Culture.   II. Title.
E78.C15H23 2005   979.4'7602—dc22
2005005915

This volume received indirect support from an unrestricted book
publication grant awarded to the Institute by the L. J. Skaggs and
Mary C. Skaggs Foundation of Oakland, California.

CLOTH   09 08 07 06 05   5 4 3 2 1
PAPER   09 08 07 06 05   5 4 3 2 1

For Heidi,
"hand in hand"

PREFACE

I did not intend to write a book on Indians and the California missions. Like so many of the people whose lives I examine here, I set out to do one thing, only to come to the realization, years later, that I had accomplished entirely another. Having immersed myself in the highly polemical scholarship on the missions of colonial California, I envisioned a work that would examine Indians who had remained beyond the reach of missions and presidios and thereby had escaped the domination of Franciscans and soldiers. However, as I engaged with archival materials, I had to rethink my understanding of Alta California and shift the focus of my project. In the archives, I began to uncover, not just collisions, but intersections of Indian and Spanish worlds. These convergences were similar in meaning, if not in content, to those discovered by scholars of other areas of colonial America. Furthermore, I found traces of a coexistence of Indian and Spanish cultures where I had least expected: at the Franciscan missions, I encountered Indians living in their own dwellings, electing their own leaders, and practicing elements of their spiritual beliefs and subsistence economies. Equally surprising to me was the wide range of labor systems Indians participated in throughout colonial California. Indians' economic, political, and cultural systems survived alongside Spaniards and their institutions more than I had believed possible. And I realized, too, that elements of mission life that had proved so destructive to California Indians could sustain a new inquiry. Therefore, what began as an examination of Indians outside the missions and presidios evolved into a reinterpretation of Indian-Spanish relations within those very institutions.

Scholarship on California Indians is vast, diverse, and growing, but I remain convinced of the need for a reinterpretation of Indian-Spanish relations in colonial California, and I am equally committed to rethinking how the people of diverse colonial regions such as the one described here can be brought into our histories of early America. Although this book directly addresses specialists of California's Indians and missions, I hope also to engage general readers, historians, and students of other colonial regions who might incorporate more fully the Spanish colonial frontier and California's native peoples into their understanding of our country's history.

ACKNOWLEDGMENTS

This book could not have been written without the encouragement and enormous assistance of numerous people and institutions. Michael Kammen sparked my interest in colonial history, and Dan Usner gave me the freedom to venture far from what normally passes for early America. Grants from the Phillips Fund of the American Philosophical Society, the Andrew W. Mellon Foundation, the John Randolph Haynes and Dora Haynes Foundation, and the W. M. Keck Foundation enabled me to complete the first stage of research at the Bancroft and Huntington Libraries. The Harry Frank Guggenheim Foundation and the National Endowment for the Humanities (FD-21172-93) funded my initial writing.

The Omohundro Institute of Early American History and Culture gave me two years to chart out and begin revisions. Daily life in Williamsburg and at the Institute in particular helped this book and my intellectual development immeasurably. Since he first invited me to Williamsburg, Ronald Hoffman, Institute Director, has provided steady encouragement, wise counsel, and moral support. Additionally, for many summers, the Henry E. Huntington Library has felt like a second home. Robert C. Ritchie, the W. M. Keck Foundation Director of Research and Education, and the library's staff and collections make the Huntington an ideal place to study California and the West. On two occasions, I had the pleasure of visiting the Centre Roland Mousnier at the Université Paris IV—Sorbonne. Jean-Pierre Bardet, the Director of the center, and Jacques Renard deepened my understanding of historical demography. They did so with patience and hospitality, even as I occasionally descended into a patois of French, English, and Spanish. A faculty fellowship from the Pew Program in Religion and American History gave me a year off from teaching and an opportunity to learn more about Catholicism and Indians' responses to it. At Oregon State University, the Center for the Humanities and the Research Council gave me time to write and resources to purchase microfilm. The skills of my department chairman, Paul Farber, are matched only by his boundless optimism; both made finishing this book easier than it would have been otherwise.

I have been helped by many especially careful readers; here I single out those who read this work in its entirety, at one stage or another. Ramón A. Gutiérrez and David J. Weber forced me to rethink aspects of my interpretation at the outset of my Institute fellowship. Their own work on the borderlands has defined the field and proved indispensable to my own. Albert L. Hurtado read an early revision of the manuscript and helped me to reshape parts of my argument at a crucial moment. His work on early California first attracted me to the field when I was at Cornell. At a later stage, William B. Taylor and Inga Clendinnen told me what worked and what needed more thought. Their deep reading of colonial Latin American history and cultural anthropology as well as their humane approach to scholarship and scholars inspires me.

Over the past decade, other friends and colleagues have improved the book by reading or listening to sections of it. For questions and encouragement, I thank James Axtell, Amy Turner Bushnell, Jon Butler, Charles R. Cutter, Cornelia Hughes Dayton, Ross H. Frank, Robert H. Jackson, Michael McGiffert, James A. Sandos, William S. Simmons, Christopher Tomlins, Jack S. Williams, and Warren Wright, S. J. At Oregon State University, Ben Mutschler, Loren Chavarría, Robert A. Nye, and Jeff Sklansky read portions with characteristic rigor. John R. Johnson read parts of this book and for many years has shared with me his immense knowledge of California Indians and California's anthropological community. In Appendix A, I make clear my large debt to Randall Milliken, whose willingness to share his own research is exemplary. Robert McCaa helped me enter the world of historical demography. Linda Yamane generously shared with me her knowledge of Isabel Meadows. For special acts of kindness and support over these past years, I thank Ramón A. Gutiérrez, Robert C. Ritchie, Jennifer Lundeen, and my colleagues in Milam Hall, especially Robert A. Nye and Mary Jo Nye.

The staffs at many libraries and archives provided indispensable assistance. At the Bancroft Library, Walter Brem steered me to documents, encouraged my pursuits, and facilitated travel to Mexico City and the Archivo General de la Nación. Tony Bliss, Franz Enciso, Bonnie Hardwick, David Kessler, and Bill Roberts answered innumerable questions with enthusiasm. Susan Snyder and James Eason helped me acquire microfilm and photographic reproductions. At the Huntington, Peter Blodgett and Bill Frank directed me to the collections I needed most and then aided my search for additional documents. The staffs at the Academy of American Franciscan History, the Archival Center of the Archdiocese of Los Angeles, the Archive of the Archdiocese of San Francisco, the Santa Barbara Mission Archive-Library, the Santa Barbara Trust for Historic Preservation Presidio Research Center, the San Jose Historical Museum, and the Monterey County Historical Society all furthered my research.

Portions of earlier versions of Chapters 6, 7, and 9 appeared as "The Staff of Leadership: Indian Authority in the Missions of Alta California," *William and*

Mary Quarterly, 3d Ser., LIV (1997), 347–376; "Land, Labor, and Production: The Colonial Economy of Spanish and Mexican California," in Ramón A. Gutiérrez and Richard J. Orsi, eds., *Contested Eden: California before the Gold Rush* (Berkeley, Calif., 1998), 111–146; and "Sources of Rebellion: Indian Testimony and the Mission San Gabriel Uprising of 1785," *Ethnohistory,* L (2003), 643–669.

I am greatly indebted to Fredrika J. Teute for her faith in this project and for her attentive reading of my manuscript revisions. Her sharp questions, incisive comments, and valuable suggestions helped me refine this inquiry and move toward the book I wanted to write. Kathy Burdette copy-edited with great care and thoroughness, skillfully improving both text and notes and making the final stages of this project as smooth and pleasurable as possible.

My family has sustained me while I saw this book through to publication. With their own accomplishments and loving guidance, Jacqueline Hackel, David Rubsamen, Al Hackel, and Brenda Hackel showed me the way and helped me complete this project. Writing has often been a solitary pursuit, but Heidi Brayman Hackel has lived this book with me as she wrote her own. Her keen sense of language and logic strengthened every page. Our walk together that began in the Garden one summer day continues, bringing me the joys of life. Our children, Anna and Gabriel, like their mother, have placed their marks all over this project. Mostly, though, I thank them for reminding me in their own ways of the importance of the present, and just how quickly it becomes the past.

CONTENTS

PART THREE
COLLAPSE OF THE COLONIAL ORDER

ILLUSTRATIONS

TABLES

ABBREVIATIONS AND SHORT TITLES

AGN   Archivo General de la Nación, Mexico City
                AHH (Archivo Histórico de Hacienda)
                CA (Californias)
                Criminal
                DPHM (Documentos Para la Historia de México)
                Indiferente de Guerra
                PI (Provincias Internas)

AHR   *American Historical Review*

APST   Maynard J. Geiger and Clement W. Meighan, eds. and trans., *As the Padres Saw Them: California Indian Life and Customs as Reported by the Franciscan Missionaries, 1813–1815* (Santa Barbara, Calif., 1976)

Bapt. no.   Baptism number

BL   Bancroft Library, University of California, Berkeley
                Archives of Monterey
                Archives of the Missions
                BANC MSS (Bancroft Manuscripts)
                C–A (Archives of California)
                SDC (California Land Grant Case, Southern District Court [San Jose y Sur Chiquito])

Bur. no.   Burial number

CC, I, II David Hurst Thomas, ed., *Columbian Consequences*, 3 vols. (Washington, D.C., 1989–1991), I, *Archaeological and Historical Perspectives on the Spanish Borderlands West,* and II, *Archaeological and Historical Perspectives on the Spanish Borderlands East*

HAHR   *Hispanic American Historical Review*

HL   Henry E. Huntington Library, San Marino, Calif.
                CMRC (California Mission Records Collection)
                David Jacks Collection
                DLG (De la Guerra Collection)
                HM (Huntington Manuscripts)
                Monterey Collection

	SDC (California Land Grant Case, Southern District Court)
	Taylor Coll. (Alexander S. Taylor Collection)
HNAI, VIII, X	William C. Sturtevant, ed., *Handbook of North American Indians*, VIII, *California* (Washington, D.C., 1978), ed. Robert F. Heizer, and X, *Southwest* (Washington, D.C., 1983), ed. Alfonso Ortiz
INAH	Instituto Nacional de Antropología e Historia, Archivo Histórico de la Biblioteca Nacional de Antropología e Historia, Mexico City
JAH	*Journal of American History*
JCB	John Carter Brown Library, Providence, R.I.
Kenneally, ed. and trans., *Writings of Lasuén*	Finbar Kenneally, ed. and trans., *Writings of Fermín Francisco de Lasuén,* 2 vols. (Washington, D.C., 1965)
LDS film	Genealogical Society of the Church of Jesus Christ of Latter-Day Saints, Salt Lake City, Utah, microfilm of California mission sacramental registers San Carlos baptisms (reel 0913159), marriages (reel 0913161), and burials (reel 0913162)
Marr. no.	Marriage number
SBMAL	Santa Barbara Mission Archive-Library, Santa Barbara, Calif. CMD (California Mission Documents)
SCQ	*Southern California Quarterly*
Tibesar, ed. and trans., *Writings of Serra*	Antonine Tibesar, ed. and trans., *Writings of Junípero Serra*, 4 vols. (Washington, D.C., 1955–1966)
WMQ	*William and Mary Quarterly*

INTRODUCTION

Achasta, Tucutnut, Ichxenta, Socorronda, Echilat—it was by village names such as
these that the Children of Coyote knew their respective home ground in the land
the Spanish would call Alta California. In 1769, this province was home to a
diverse population of several hundred thousand Indians, who lived in a multitude of villages throughout the countryside. Soon that would not be so. For,
between 1769 and 1850, the region experienced successive tidal waves of change:
Spain incorporated the land and its people into its realm, Spanish rule gave way
to Mexican independence, Mexico lost California to the United States, and the
territory became the thirty-first state to join the Union. Forever altered by these
momentous developments were the rhythms, practices, and beliefs of native
Californians. In some ways, the changes were so complete that they defy easy
description; in other ways, they were subtle enough to elude easy detection.
Clearly, though, Indians died at an alarming rate, and survivors congregated into
fewer settlements and gradually adopted new forms of language and belief and
different patterns of subsistence, labor, marriage, reproduction, and leadership.
In the midst of these great transformations, Indians pursued a variety of survival
strategies rooted in their cultures. Yet their own designs, although successful in
many ways, often unintentionally reinforced colonists' hold on the region. This
book, then, is an attempt to understand how California Indians contrived to
weather and at times even manage the great upheavals that began with European
colonization as their numbers dwindled and as daily interaction with foreign
institutions and peoples challenged nearly every aspect of their lives.

California, like many colonies, was composed of numerous subregions in which
the same processes played themselves out again and again, each time with only
minor variations, as agents and institutions of European settlement advanced
through new areas. Certainly, each subregion, Indian group, and mission had
its own chronology and trajectory—and therefore its own story. However, this
study's purpose is to explore crucial aspects of Indian-Spanish relations across

Alta California. It examines local developments at particular missions, places those events in the context of the California mission system, and draws comparisons between colonial California and other areas of the Spanish Borderlands, New Spain, and, when pertinent, early modern Europe.[1] Local developments common to all California missions—the incorporation of Indian communities, the Indians' demographic decline, and the conflicts between Indian and Spanish notions of marriage and sexuality—are best examined first at the individual or community level and then set within the broader frame of Alta California. To that end, Mission San Carlos Borromeo serves as a case study. Built in the 1770s just to the south of Monterey, the administrative center of Alta California, this mission often served as the residence of the father president, the Franciscan who set the policies governing all the region's missions. Larger patterns and Spanish systems that shaped California, such as Catholic indoctrination, Indian labor, mission-presidio economic relationships, and military justice, are studied at the regional level; when possible, these discussions are rooted in events at Mission San Carlos.

No single model of cultural interaction can encompass the range of Indian-Spanish relations in colonial California. At times, the goals and practices of Indians and Spaniards so resembled one another that Indian actions and Spanish attempts to influence them dovetailed. Furthermore, the paths to Indians' and Spaniards' separate and perhaps even disparate goals frequently converged. At these times, fundamental aspects of the Indians' economic, political, and social structures remained intact, although in a modified form, providing a measure of coherence and continuity for Indian communities. At other points, however, particularly around matters of sexuality, marriage, and religion, Indian and Spanish cultural practices proved deeply antithetical, and the ensuing conflicts created upheaval and threatened to undo the Spanish colonial project. In many ways, Indian autonomy and Spanish coercion warred within an increasingly confining colonial order.

Wherever they might turn, California Indians grappled with challenges introduced by Spanish colonization, most notably a mission system that itself was anachronistic, self-defeating, and contradictory in its expectations. The inconsistencies contained in and generated by Spain's colonization of California not only complicated the Indians' responses but also destabilized, if not outright doomed, the Spanish colonial project. The missions were rooted in apostolic endeavor yet founded in an age when the Spanish Empire became increasingly secular. Large

---

1. Readers interested in a chronicle of developments in and around the missions, presidios, and pueblos of Alta California may want to turn to Hubert Howe Bancroft's works and the considerable number of books and articles devoted to a particular region or aspect of early California (Bancroft, *History of California,* 7 vols. [San Francisco, Calif., 1884–1890]).

numbers of Indians came to the missions of Alta California, yet this new environment nearly destroyed Indians and their communities. In the missions, Indians entered a distorting world, where, regardless of age, they were treated as juveniles: in the eyes of the Catholic Church, they were "spiritual children"; before the Spanish state and its laws, they were minors. And with that status came both limited protections and extensive discriminations. In the realm of introduced religion, Indians learned a catechism pitched to a child's level of comprehension, yet, when they approached the Catholic sacraments, they found themselves subject to adult standards of comprehension and conduct. In the realm of marriage and sexuality, Indians encountered a Catholic system that insisted upon uncompromising adherence to monogamy and marital fidelity yet contradicted itself in tolerating or pardoning exceptions. In the realm of politics, Indians participated in a system of indirect rule that both missionaries and state officials embraced; this arrangement propped up Spanish control over Indian communities while giving Indians the means to throw off Spanish authority. In the realm of labor and economic exchange, Indians sought labor relationships with soldiers and settlers, but, in so doing, they inadvertently strengthened the colonial order more than they shored up their collapsing communities. And, finally, in the realm of crime and punishment, Indians reacted with violence and disaffection to the corporal punishment padres and soldiers meted out to control them, a response that undermined the stability of the missions and the colonial order upon which it rested.

The chronology, geography, and teleology that have come to define what scholars term early American history have served to exclude colonial California from national historical narratives and larger fields of inquiry.[2] Spain initiated European settlement of Alta California less than a decade before the colonies of British North America declared independence; thus the opening act of California's colonial history coincided with the denouement in orthodox histories of colonial America. California's geographic distance from the English and French colonies of North America compounds this chronological problem. Most important, historians have traditionally read United States history backward; in their desire to explain the origins of the United States' political system, they focused on the

2. Historians have studied Alta California assiduously, but early California history has been largely the terrain of regional specialists, Catholic historians, and cultural anthropologists. Among the most important general works on early California history are Bancroft, *History of California,* I–IV; Charles Edward Chapman, *The Founding of Spanish California: The Northwestward Expansion of New Spain, 1687–1783* (New York, 1916); Chapman, *A History of California: The Spanish Period* (New York, 1921); Maynard J. Geiger, *The Life and Times of Fray Junípero Serra, O.F.M.; or, The Man Who Never Turned Back (1713–1784),* 2 vols. (Washington, D.C., 1959); and Francis F. Guest, *Fermín Francisco de Lasuén (1736–1803)* (Washington, D.C., 1973).

colonies and individuals that played major roles in the American Revolution. Other regions, such as the Spanish Borderlands and New France, and other peoples, namely Indians and African Americans, have only newly begun to receive the attention they deserve.[3]

Generations ago, Herbert Eugene Bolton, the founder of the field of Spanish Borderlands history, envisioned an inclusive and comparative history of the Americas, but his work and that of his many students situated regions like colonial California outside the fields of American colonial history and western American history. To Bolton and his followers, the Spanish Borderlands lacked what seemed to distinguish American history: economic opportunity, which created rugged individualism, and the seeds of political independence, which led to the creation of the United States' political system. In the borderlands, they argued, Spanish absolutism stifled economic opportunity, individual liberty, and self-government.[4] The implicitly negative comparison with archetypal British American frontiers and colonies diminished the history of the Spanish Borderlands and blocked its meaningful incorporation into the main narratives and larger fields of United States history. In accounts devoted to the birth and expansion of what many historians have taken to be a Protestant democracy, Catholic missionaries and Spanish explorers, settlers, and soldiers could have little place, except as cruel or romantic foils.[5] Colonial Latin Americanists have contributed

3. See James H. Merrell, "Some Thoughts on Colonial Historians and American Indians," *WMQ*, 3d Ser., XLVI (1989), 94–119. For a discussion of why early American history has focused almost exclusively on the North Atlantic seaboard, see James A. Hijiya, "Why the West Is Lost," *WMQ*, 3d Ser., LI (1994), 276–292, and a forum of responses at 717–754. For a defense of the orthodox narrative of early American history, see Gordon S. Wood, "A Century of Writing Early American History: Then and Now Compared; or, How Henry Adams Got It Wrong," *AHR*, C (1995), 678–696.

4. Herbert E. Bolton, "Defensive Spanish Expansion and the Significance of the Borderlands," in John Francis Bannon, ed., *Bolton and the Spanish Borderlands* (Norman, Okla., 1964), 32–64; Bannon, *The Spanish Borderlands Frontier, 1513–1821* (New York, 1970). The term and the concept of the Spanish Borderlands have undergone considerable scrutiny since appearing in Bolton's *The Spanish Borderlands: A Chronicle of Old Florida and the Southwest* (New Haven, Conn., 1921). See David Hurst Thomas, "Columbian Consequences: The Spanish Borderlands in Cubist Perspective," in *CC*, I, 1–14; David J. Weber, ed., *The Idea of Spanish Borderlands*, Spanish Borderlands Sourcebooks, I (New York, 1991); Weber, ed., *Myth and the History of the Hispanic Southwest* (Albuquerque, N.Mex., 1988); Weber, *The Spanish Frontier in North America* (New Haven, Conn., 1992), 8. See also Gerald E. Poyo and Gilberto M. Hinojosa, "Spanish Texas and Borderlands Historiography in Transition: Implications for United States History," *JAH*, LXXV (1988–1989), 393–416; and José Cuello, "Beyond the 'Borderlands' Is the North of Colonial Mexico: A Latin-Americanist Perspective to the Study of the Mexican North and the United States Southwest," in Kristyna P. Demaree, ed., *Proceedings of the Pacific Coast Council on Latin American Studies*, IX (San Diego, Calif., 1982), 1–24. For a comprehensive bibliography of scholarship on the Spanish Borderlands and Bolton's approach to the history of the Americas, see Russell M. Magnaghi, *Herbert E. Bolton and the Historiography of the Americas* (Westport, Conn., 1998).

5. On the spotty treatment of the Spanish Borderlands in narratives of American colonial history, see James Axtell, "Europeans, Indians, and the Age of Discovery in American History Textbooks," *AHR*, XCII (1987), 621–632; Michael C. Scardaville, "Approaches to the Study of the Southeastern Borderlands," in R. Reid Badger and Lawrence A. Clayton, eds., *Alabama and the Borderlands: From Prehistory*

to the historiographical isolation of regions like Alta California by generally ignoring the Spanish Borderlands as a serious field of study, considering it a peripheral region of marginal interest, a "subfield within United States history." Historians of early California in particular and those of the Spanish Borderlands in general have inadvertently reinforced this tendency by failing to establish connections between their work and the historiography of colonial Mexico or Latin America.[6]

Through a rich mixture of sources—official correspondence, sacramental registers, and Indian testimony—the main contours and intimate details of Alta California can be brought into full relief and understood as relevant to the larger colonial histories of the United States and Latin America. Doing so strengthens our understanding of Spanish California, draws California more centrally into the study of a broadly conceived American colonial history, and helps to break down the boundaries separating the fields of Latin American history and early American history.[7] Further, the experiences of Indians in Alta California—their

to Statehood (Birmingham, Ala., 1985), 184–196, esp. 188–189; David J. Weber, "John Francis Bannon and the Historiography of the Spanish Borderlands: Retrospect and Prospect," rpt. in Weber, ed., *Myth and the History of the Hispanic Southwest,* 78–79; Poyo and Hinojosa, "Spanish Texas and Borderlands Historiography in Transition," *JAH,* LXXV (1988–1989), 393–416.

6. See Cuello, "Beyond the 'Borderlands' Is the North of Colonial Mexico," in Demaree, ed., *Proceedings,* IX, 1–24, esp. 2, 8. Many borderlands scholars have been trained in Latin American history; see Scardaville, "Approaches to the Study of the Southeastern Borderlands," in Badger and Clayton, eds., *Alabama and the Borderlands,* 184–196, esp. 186.

7. This historiographical transition is already under way. See, for example, Colin G. Calloway, *New Worlds for All: Indians, Europeans, and the Remaking of Early America* (Baltimore, 1997); Alan Taylor, *American Colonies* (New York, 2001); Daniel K. Richter, *Facing East from Indian Country* (Cambridge, Mass., 2001); Joyce E. Chaplin, "Expansion and Exceptionalism in Early American History," *JAH,* LXXXIX (2002–2003), 1431–1455. Among the most influential examinations of Indian-Spanish relations in the colonial period are Charles Gibson, *The Aztecs under Spanish Rule: A History of the Indians of the Valley of Mexico, 1519–1810* (Stanford, Calif., 1964); William B. Taylor, *Drinking, Homicide, and Rebellion in Colonial Mexican Villages* (Stanford, Calif., 1979); Nancy M. Farriss, *Maya Society under Colonial Rule: The Collective Enterprise of Survival* (Princeton, N.J., 1984); Inga Clendinnen, *Ambivalent Conquests: Maya and Spaniard in Yucatan, 1517–1570* (Cambridge, 1987); James Lockhart, *The Nahuas after the Conquest: A Social and Cultural History of the Indians of Central Mexico, Sixteenth through Eighteenth Centuries* (Stanford, Calif., 1992); Ramón A. Gutiérrez, *When Jesus Came, the Corn Mothers Went Away: Marriage, Sexuality, and Power in New Mexico, 1500–1846* (Stanford, Calif., 1991); Steve J. Stern, *Peru's Indian Peoples and the Challenge of Spanish Conquest: Huamanga to 1640,* 2d ed. (Madison, Wis., 1993). William B. Taylor's *Magistrates of the Sacred: Priests and Parishioners in Eighteenth-Century Mexico* (Stanford, Calif., 1996) is an indispensable discussion of priests and Indian parishioners in the late colonial period.

Significant studies of British and French relations with Indians are James Merrell, *The Indians' New World: Catawbas and Their Neighbors from European Contact through the Era of Removal* (Chapel Hill, N.C., 1989); Daniel K. Richter, *The Ordeal of the Longhouse: The Peoples of the Iroquois League in the Era of European Colonization* (Chapel Hill, N.C., 1992); Daniel H. Usner, Jr., *Indians, Settlers, and Slaves in a Frontier Exchange Economy: The Lower Mississippi Valley before 1783* (Chapel Hill, N.C., 1992); Richard White, *The Middle Ground: Indians, Empires, and Republics in the Great Lakes Region, 1650–1815* (Cambridge, 1991).

struggles with disease and death, community formation and collapse, and religious, political, and economic accommodation—shed light on Indian-European relations along other frontiers.

What at first glance seems to set Alta California apart from the well-known regions of colonial North America actually renders the region illustrative of the ways in which Indians experienced colonialism in early America. The absence of a system of treaties and diplomatic relationships between Indians and colonists, the lack of a formalized pattern of trade between Indians and Europeans, and the inability of natives to play one European power off another all establish Alta California as akin to much of colonial America at one time or another. Many Indian peoples were not courted as brothers-in-arms by competing European powers; the multitude of natives did not produce commodities of great value to Europeans. Few were led by men who have captured the attention of historians as did Powhatan, Metacom, Pontiac, and Tecumseh. Ultimately, the greatest number of Indians, like those in Alta California, struggled against the colonial onslaught in relative obscurity and largely alone, bereft of powerful Indian or European allies, unable to find shelter in the interstices of European rivalries, and without the benefits of a European trade that in some regions brought arms and other valued goods.

If Indian-European relations in Alta California seem exceptional given the absence of systems and relationships commonly associated with eastern North America, colonial California may also seem unusual given the presence of Spanish institutions and characters, namely Catholic missions and Franciscans. Yet the Catholic mission, the defining colonial institution of Spanish California, was for a very long while central to many of the border and frontier regions of early America and, of course, to much of the Spanish Borderlands and Latin America. Countless Indians, hundreds of thousands if not millions, first experienced European expansion and colonization through Catholic missions, many of which were administered by Spanish Franciscans. A study of life in and around the missions of Alta California, therefore, can illuminate the experiences of legions of other Indians and the challenges they confronted elsewhere in colonial America. Moreover, the very circumstances of the California mission environment— its close quarters, the intensity of its program, and the type of documents it generated—make colonial California an important and fruitful site for the examination of how natives experienced and managed the disease, population decline, and religious, political, and economic changes that followed encounters with Europeans throughout the New World.

California also offers a compelling model for the study of the dynamics of colonialism. Alta California was, after all, like many regions, a colony of a colony, one that was envisioned and overseen by men who knew much about what they wanted to do but little about those whom they sought to dominate. Spanish officials, therefore, were forced to adapt their plans to Indian initiatives and practices just as California Indians modified their lifeways in response to the Spanish intrusion. Clearly, the Indians' task was the more urgent, but Indians and Spaniards alike played a hand in the evolution of the colonial region and its political, cultural, and economic relations.

The nature of colonization—its systems and key players—dictates the sources available to historians, and in this regard the records of Alta California are unfortunately spotty. The absence of formal treaties or agreements between Indians and Europeans, the lack of an institutionalized pattern of trade between Indians and settlers, the infrequency with which Spanish soldiers recruited Indian auxiliaries, the paucity of literate settlers in the region, the want of vibrant urban settlements, and the nonexistence of a system of Indian land tenure recognized by Spanish law—all of these characteristics mean that historians have not inherited the evidentiary sources that have proved so vital to investigations of other areas of colonial America. Territorial conflicts, reorganizations of colonial documents brought about by changes in national sovereignty, and the disastrous loss of California's principal Spanish archive in the fire following the 1906 San Francisco earthquake have further reduced the historical record.[8]

However, Franciscan missionaries, the region's most active and literate colonial agents, penned a rich, if biased, record in their correspondence. Of equal import, the missionaries left a more even-handed trove of documentation in the missions' birth, marriage, and burial records. (Appendix A discusses these registers and the technique of family reconstitution underlying their analysis.) As will be evident, the interpretation that follows at times relies heavily on these registers and computer manipulation to determine vital rates and population change at Mission San Carlos and to answer a whole range of questions about the religious, sexual, marital, and political lives of Indians in colonial California. Furthermore, these sources, which, after all, capture discrete moments of individual lives, have proved invaluable in writing a book, not about generalized and anonymous mission Indians, but, rather, about individuals, families, and communities.

Spaniards precipitated a rapid acceleration of cultural change among California Indians. The chief indicators of this transformation can be found in the religious beliefs, marital practices, reproductive patterns, and economic, political, and legal institutions that ordered Indians' daily life and defined their very existence. Unfortunately, there are few detailed descriptions of the California Indians' core values or cultural practices before or during the colonial period,

8. Henry Putney Beers, *Spanish and Mexican Records of the American Southwest: A Bibliographical Guide to Archive and Manuscript Sources* (Tucson, Ariz., 1979).

and thus historians of colonial California cannot measure historical change to the same degree as historians of other regions.[9] Nevertheless, the rough outlines of these values and practices and their modification under colonization can be deduced from mission sacramental registers, correspondence of military leaders and Franciscan missionaries, and—most tellingly—impressions of Indians recorded in judicial proceedings. Indian testimony is especially important. Granted, these statements do not begin to approach the detailed narratives embedded in the inquisition records so masterfully exploited by the "microhistorians" who have studied early modern Europe. Nor are they as extensive or varied as those found for other areas of New Spain. Nevertheless, Indian testimony, despite its sparseness, pointedly describes how California Indians grappled with many of the effects of colonization.[10]

Such testimony reinforces the fact that California Indians found Spanish colonization oppressive, disruptive, and at times cruel, but the Indians' recorded words also add detail and subtlety to native experiences that historiography too often has simplified into stereotypes. Native testimony brings to light aspects of Spanish colonization and Indian actions not evident in the Franciscans' correspondence or in the oral traditions of Indians whose ancestors lived in the missions. Indians' descriptions of economic pursuits inside and beyond the missions reveal that the missions as institutions were more porous than scholars have realized. Indian portrayals of the Franciscans' use of corporal punishment and attempts to regulate marriage and sexuality capture the brutal effects of mission policies on the most intimate and personal aspects of the Indians' lives. Indian accounts of conflicts among themselves, both inside and outside the missions, demonstrate that an understanding of California's colonial period rests upon studies not only of Indian-Spanish interactions but of the relations between individual Indians and among groups of Indians as well. Ultimately, colonial

9. Generations of early California historians have relied on the letters, narratives, and reports of the Franciscans, soldiers, and settlers who lived in Spanish and Mexican California. Recently, historians have used the narratives of Indians born in Mexican and American California and the views of Indians alive today. Only Pablo Tac's account, written in the mid-1830s, comes close to describing the imposition of Spanish authority from the perspective of an eyewitness. See Minna Hewes and Gordon Hewes, eds. and trans., "Indian Life and Customs at Mission San Luis Rey: A Record of California Mission Life Written by Pablo Tac, an Indian Neophyte," in Edward D. Castillo, ed., *Native American Perspectives on the Hispanic Colonization of Alta California* (New York, 1992), 35–58.

10. On microhistory, see Carlo Ginzburg, *The Cheese and the Worms: The Cosmos of a Sixteenth-Century Miller,* trans. John Tedeschi and Anne Tedeschi (Baltimore, 1980); Edward Muir and Guido Ruggiero, eds., *Microhistory and the Lost Peoples of Europe* (Baltimore, 1991); Natalie Zemon Davis, *Fiction in the Archives: Pardon Tales and Their Tellers in Sixteenth-Century France* (Stanford, Calif., 1987). Scholars of other regions of New Spain have made good use of the Indian testimony in the criminal record. Among the most important studies are Taylor, *Drinking, Homicide, and Rebellion;* Gutiérrez, *When Jesus Came;* Steve J. Stern, *The Secret History of Gender: Women, Men, and Power in Late Colonial Mexico* (Chapel Hill, N.C., 1995); and Taylor, *Magistrates of the Sacred.*

judicial records reveal multiple Indian perspectives on Spanish colonization and show that, over time, many Indians oscillated between an acceptance and a rejection of the missions.

Catholicism permeated every aspect of the missions' organization, from the codes of behavior the Franciscans tried to impose on Indians to the missions' economic and political ties with the neighboring presidios and pueblos. But California's Franciscans promoted a Catholicism that rested on learned behavior rather than theological complexities, and the record of Indian spiritual beliefs and practices is often too thin to allow for an in-depth study of how Indians wrestled with most Catholic teachings. Indeed, California missionaries rarely bothered to record Indian spiritual beliefs, which they dismissed as dangerous superstitions. Only one missionary, Gerónimo Boscana at San Juan Capistrano, wrote an ethnological treatise of the Indians at his mission, and his account cannot be taken to fully describe the beliefs of Indians at other missions.[11] Thus *Children of Coyote, Missionaries of Saint Francis,* by design and necessity, moves beyond the important but ultimately inscrutable issue of California Indians' receptivity to the intricacies of Catholic doctrine. Instead, it takes as a focus Indian responses to the codes of Catholic behavior the Franciscans prescribed for them—regular attendance at work and at Mass, marital fidelity, and monogamy—and the larger biological, demographic, political, and economic aspects of Spanish colonization that continuously reshaped Indian life.

Since the mid-sixteenth century, the strategies Catholic missionaries used to convert and control Indians have sparked an intense debate that has involved the general public as well as scholars. In California, public interest has focused on the campaign to canonize Father Junípero Serra, the founding father of the California missions, and more generally on Indian-Spanish relations in those missions.[12] The inextinguishable Serra controversy reinforces the fact that, for most

11. For Boscana's account, see Alfred Robinson, *Life in California during a Residence of Several Years in That Territory* . . . (1846; rpt. New York, 1969). Exemplary studies of Indian responses to Catholic doctrine are Louise M. Burkhart, *The Slippery Earth: Nahua-Christian Moral Dialogue in Sixteenth-Century Mexico* (Tucson, Ariz., 1989); Gutiérrez, *When Jesus Came.*

12. The debate over the potential canonization of Serra has been summarized clearly by James A. Sandos, "Junípero Serra's Canonization and the Historical Record," *AHR,* XCIII (1988), 1253–1269. Catholic historians and chroniclers began writing their history of the California missions shortly after Franciscans set foot in the region in 1769. Francisco Palóu's biography of Serra appeared in print in 1787, the year of Serra's death. See Maynard Geiger, ed. and trans., *Palóu's Life of Fray Junípero Serra* (Washington, D.C., 1955). Notable examples of pro-Franciscan interpretations are Zephyrin Engelhardt, *Upper California,* vols. II–IV of *The Missions and Missionaries of California,* 4 vols. (San Francisco, Calif., 1908–1915); Geiger, *Life and Times of Serra;* Francis F. Guest, "An Inquiry into the Role of the Discipline in California Mission Life," *SCQ,* LXXI (1989), 1–68; Guest, "Cultural Perspectives on California Mission Life," *SCQ,* LXV (1983), 1–65. Sherburne F. Cook's essay "The Indian versus the Spanish Mission" still exerts a tremendous influence on California mission studies, and detractors of the missionaries trace much of their critique to his work (originally published in *Ibero-Americana,* XXI

people, the legacy of Spanish settlement in California continues to hinge upon an understanding of such relations. More important, though, the polarizing rhetoric over missionization in general and Serra in particular has at times limited historians' ability to detect nuanced interaction between Indians and Spaniards in California.[13] Anthropologists, who for more than a century have studied California Indians, have contributed the most important modern work on early California, and their techniques and insights, especially those involving mission sacramental registers, suggest innovative methodologies and new avenues for research, some of which have been incorporated into this study.[14]

Part 1 of this study begins with an overview of the Monterey region Indians, the movement of Spanish settlement northward into Alta California, and the missionaries, soldiers, and settlers who comprised the Spanish population of California. Then Part 1 turns to Indian population decline and the transformation of the countryside, dual revolutions that shaped nearly every aspect of colonial California. Given the chasms of time and culture separating today's historians from the Indians of colonial California, the best means to glimpse and interpret how Indians weathered colonial rule rests in moments where events were, in the words of Inga Clendinnen, "writ large or repetitively."[15] Over time, these events tended to accumulate where Indians and Spaniards created recognizable patterns of interaction, where their uneasy overlap left a record of tension, or where their

---

[1943], 1–194, rpt. in Cook, *The Conflict between the California Indian and White Civilization* [Berkeley, Calif., 1976]). See also Rupert Costo and Jeannette Henry Costo, eds., *The Missions of California: A Legacy of Genocide* (San Francisco, Calif., 1987); Robert H. Jackson and Edward D. Castillo, *Indians, Franciscans, and Spanish Colonization: The Impact of the Mission System on California Indians* (Albuquerque, N.Mex., 1995).

13. For exceptions, see James A. Sandos, *Converting California: Indians and Franciscans in the Missions* (New Haven, Conn., 2004); Albert L. Hurtado, *Intimate Frontiers: Sex, Gender, and Culture in Old California* (Albuquerque, N.Mex., 1999); Lisbeth Haas, *Conquests and Historical Identities in California, 1769–1936* (Berkeley, Calif., 1995); Ramón A. Gutiérrez and Richard J. Orsi, eds., *Contested Eden: California before the Gold Rush* (Berkeley, Calif., 1998); George Harwood Phillips, *Chiefs and Challengers: Indian Resistance and Cooperation in Southern California* (Berkeley, Calif., 1975); Russell K. Skowronek, "Sifting the Evidence: Perceptions of Life at the Ohlone (Costanoan) Missions of Alta California," *Ethnohistory*, XLV (1998), 675–708.

14. For a general introduction to the anthropological literature on California Indians, see *HNAI*, VIII. Essential modern anthropological works are Randall Milliken, *A Time of Little Choice: The Disintegration of Tribal Culture in the San Francisco Bay Area, 1769–1810* (Menlo Park, Calif., 1995); Travis Hudson, ed., *Breath of the Sun: Life in Early California as Told by a Chumash Indian, Fernando Librado, to John P. Harrington* (Banning, Calif., 1979); Thomas C. Blackburn, *December's Child: A Book of Chumash Oral Narratives* (Berkeley, Calif., 1975); Lowell John Bean, *Mukat's People: The Cahuilla Indians of Southern California* (Berkeley, Calif., 1972); John R. Johnson, "Chumash Social Interaction: An Ethnohistoric Perspective" (Ph.D. diss., University of California at Santa Barbara, 1988). For a synthetic overview of this recent literature, see Kent G. Lightfoot, *Indians, Missionaries, and Merchants: The Legacy of Colonial Encounters on the California Frontiers* (Berkeley, Calif., 2005).

15. Inga Clendinnen, *Aztecs: An Interpretation* (1991; rpt. Cambridge, 1995), 5.

difference created evidence of hostility and conflict. In Part 2, individual chapters examine five of these principal points of interaction, each proceeding from a different angle and adding a layer to the previous one. With this approach, I analyze crucial aspects of Indian life under Spanish rule: religious indoctrination; marriage and sexuality; politics and leadership; labor and the economy; and crime and punishment. Cumulatively, these chapters suggest that California Indians inhabited a colonial world that was nearly all encompassing. In Part 3, a final chapter and Epilogue discuss the collapse of Spanish authority, the secularization of the missions, and the persistence of Indians in and around Monterey into our times.

The title of this book refers to the Indians of Mission San Carlos and the Monterey region as the Children of Coyote. The phrase evokes an origin myth of the Rumsen Costanoan (San Carlos's first and most numerous Indians) and the myth's narrative of the creation of several other local Indian groups. The title is, therefore, a reminder of the culture and history of the Indians who lived in the Monterey region. At no point does this reference suggest these people to have been children, unable to reason for themselves. Such was the conceit of the missionaries of Saint Francis. Among the Indians and Spaniards discussed here, personal names were vital indicators of culture and identity.[16] In Alta California, missionaries baptized Indians and gave them Spanish names, usually ones rich in Catholic association. In doing so, the Franciscans acted to supplant native identity with one that was at once Catholic and Spanish. To avoid a perpetuation of the displacement and erasure of Indian culture that the Franciscans intended, whenever possible this study employs both Spanish and native names to designate individuals. Although native names rarely occur in the Franciscans' correspondence on mission affairs, some do survive in mission sacramental records. When Indians born outside the mission were baptized as adults, the Franciscans sometimes recorded native names in the baptismal register. And, in the mission's marriage and burial records, the padres now and then continued to use native names as a means to further distinguish between individuals and families. There are no recorded native names for Indians born in the mission, but, on occasion, the Franciscans referred to mission-born Indians by both a Spanish name and a native family name that usually derived from a male ancestor. When Franciscans recorded the Spanish names they gave Indians at baptism, they did not follow

16. The Franciscans realized this, and their own names often reflected chosen identities. Upon his birth and baptism, Father Serra had been given the name Miguel José, after Miguel, one of the four archangels, and José, the husband of Mary, mother of Jesus. But, at seventeen, on the occasion of making his profession to the Franciscan Order, Serra chose a new name, Junípero, in honor of one of the companions of Saint Francis (Geiger, *Life and Times of Serra*, I, 20–21).

consistent rules of spelling. For example, some wrote "Miguel Joseph" where others would write "Miguel José." In this book, I have preserved these variations. As a rule, I have presented Indian names as they first appeared in the individual's baptism record.

Native identity often was obscured not just by given Spanish names but by terms Spanish officials and missionaries used to classify people and establish their place within the colonial order. Specifically, Franciscans and soldiers used the terms *neófito* and *gentil* to distinguish between Indians who had been baptized and those who had not. These words carry misleading assumptions about the significance of baptism, an individual's relationship to Catholicism, and personal identity. They exaggerate differences between groups and create categories that might have had little meaning to those they purport to describe. Nevertheless, sometimes these terms are used here because of the need to discuss the relations between baptized Indians (neophytes), who were affiliated with the mission, and those who remained unbaptized (gentiles) and usually stayed farther away.

The soldiers and settlers of Alta California also used terms that blurred their own social, cultural, and racial origins, often choosing to describe themselves as Spanish—*español* (of pure Spanish descent)—even though they were, in fact, *mestizo* or *mulato*. In this book, "Spanish" and "Spaniard" are used as political and cultural terms to distinguish individuals and policies associated with the colonists from those of native California. Clearly, though, all of these classifications—gentil, neófito, mestizo, mulato, and español, to pick just the most common—separated people into artificial categories that obscured the social and cultural complexities and affinities that extended across these divides. Finally, in recognition of the fact that institutions and customs of Spanish California carried over to the Mexican era as, half a century earlier, Indian ways had carried over into the Spanish period, I write of a Spanish and colonial California as late as the 1830s, more than a decade after 1821, when Mexico, not Spain, claimed sovereignty over Alta California. The persistence of Spanish ways suggests their power and what Indians were up against; this book explores how the Children of Coyote survived.

PEOPLE AND INSTITUTIONS OF COLONIAL CALIFORNIA

1

INDIANS

Long ago, during a catastrophic deluge, the eagle, the hummingbird, and Coyote took refuge on the summit of Pico Blanco, a white-topped mountain of pure limestone that rises more than 3,700 feet above the sea east of Point Sur. These three were not animals but rather First People, mythic, prototypical beings who lived before humans existed. As the floodwaters continued to rise, the eagle, carrying the hummingbird and Coyote, flew inland to the Gabilan mountain range east of Monterey and the Salinas Valley. There the trio stayed until the waters receded. The eagle then sent Coyote down the mountain to see whether the world was dry. When Coyote returned with the news that, yes, the world was dry, the eagle said to him: "Go and look in the river. See what there is there." In the river, Coyote found a beautiful girl, and the eagle told Coyote this girl would be his wife so "people may be raised again."[1]

Coyote had a question for the eagle: "How will my children be raised [created]?" The eagle would not say; he wanted to see whether Coyote was wise enough to know. "Well, I will make them right here in the knee," Coyote said. "No, that is not good," responded the eagle. Then Coyote suggested in the elbow, in the eyebrow, or in the back of the neck, but the eagle counseled him, "No, that is not good either. None of these will be good." Finally, the hummingbird showed Coyote: "This place will be good, here in the belly." The girl, as confused by all of this as Coyote, asked the eagle: "What shall I do? How will I make my children?" Marry the girl, said the eagle to Coyote, and the couple went off together.

---

1. On the figure of Coyote in California Indian mythology, see William Bright, *A Coyote Reader* (Berkeley, Calif., 1993), xi–xiii. For the Rumsen Costanoan myths from which this summary has been constructed, see A. L. Kroeber, *Indian Myths of South Central California,* University of California Publications in American Archaeology and Ethnology, IV (Berkeley, Calif., 1907), 167–250, esp. 199–201; Beverly O. Ortiz, "*Chocheño* and *Rumsen* Narratives: A Comparison," in Lowell John Bean, comp. and ed., *The Ohlone Past and Present: Native Americans of the San Francisco Bay Region* (Menlo Park, Calif., 1994), 99–163, esp. 124–134. The Esselen also took Pico Blanco to have been the center of creation. See "Pico Blanco," in Donald Thomas Clark, *Monterey County Place Names: A Geographical Dictionary* (Carmel Valley, Calif., 1991), 394.

Next, Coyote said to the girl, who was now his wife: "Louse me." The girl complied and found on Coyote a woodtick, which scared her. She threw the woodtick away. Coyote then seized her, ordering her, "Look for it, look for it! Take it! Eat it! Eat my louse! . . . Swallow it, swallow it!" When she swallowed the woodtick, she became pregnant. Afraid, the wife ran to the ocean.

Coyote and his wife soon had a child, but Coyote told her, "We alone cannot have many children." Coyote secured his wife's permission to marry another woman, and Coyote had a total of five children. These children wondered where they would live and whom they would marry. Coyote directed them: "Go out over the world." They then founded five separate village communities in the Monterey region: the Ensen near Salinas; the Rumsen of the Carmel Valley and Monterey; the Kakonta of Big Sur; the Ekkhcya farther south; and the Wacharone near modern Castroville.

Before his death, Coyote provided for his children's well-being. He gave them the bow and arrow to kill rabbits. He taught them how to remove the bitterness from acorns. He instructed them in how to carry wild oat seeds on their backs in baskets. He advised them when to gather abalones and mussels from the sea. And, if these proved scarce, Coyote told the children to gather buckeyes. "Look for these things of which I have told you," Coyote said. "I have shown you what is good. Now I will leave you. You have learned. I have shown you how to gather food, and even though it rains a long time people will not die of hunger. Now I am getting old. I cannot walk. Alas for me! Now I go."

This is a narrative of rebirth and regeneration, one that recounts how the First People were brought to the brink of destruction yet survived to repeople their land. It is a story of setbacks, false starts, doubts, and departures, all on the way to recovery. Thus, it is a most human tale. It was recorded in Monterey a century ago by Alfred L. Kroeber, the pioneering California anthropologist who had become convinced that the Indian communities between San Francisco and Monterey had been reduced to a few dozen survivors who were not long for this world. When an elderly group of three—María Viviena Soto, her niece Jacinta Gonzalez, and her nephew Tom Torres—told Kroeber about the beginnings of their world and of their people, they were, in a sense, describing not only their origins but their present.[2] These three, like Coyote, the eagle, and the hummingbird before them, confronted a world at once rich with possibilities and full of uncertainties. Soto, Gonzalez, and Torres also could have been describing their people's most recent history and in so doing explaining the continued relevance

2. Ortiz, "*Chocheño* and *Rumsen* Narratives," in Bean, comp. and ed., *The Ohlone Past and Present*, 124–125.

into the twentieth century of this brief, powerful narrative. During the colonial period and through the turn of the twentieth century, their ancestors needed this story—and no doubt others like it—as one deluge after another overwhelmed them, thinned their ranks, transformed their world, and forced them repeatedly to relocate and begin anew.

The archaeological record of the Monterey region tells a similar tale of an ancient occupation, a rising sea, and new beginnings. Perhaps as many as twelve thousand years ago, several thousands of years after the end of the last ice age and as humans began to settle elsewhere in the Americas, humans lived along California's coast and in the Monterey region. Little is known about these first Californians, especially those who settled along the coast of central California during what archaeologists term the Early Period, an era that stretched from roughly 10,000 b.c.e. to 500 b.c.e.[3] Because of changes in the earth's climate, sea levels today are some forty-five to sixty meters higher than ten thousand years ago. What we see as the coast of the Monterey region is probably some six or seven miles east of an ancient coastline. Therefore, all but a few of the villages of these first coastal peoples are covered by the ocean or have long since eroded away. What little evidence remains from their early occupation suggests that they lived in small groups and took advantage of a wide variety of resources, especially shellfish and small terrestrial animals. They had few tools and did not exploit either acorns or salmon, both of which were abundant and later became staples.[4]

As sea levels rose, the coastal zone gradually was remade, and these early settlers, just like Coyote, the eagle, and the hummingbird, were forced to venture

3. For a general discussion of California's archaeological record, see Brian M. Fagan, *Before California: An Archaeologist Looks at Our Earliest Inhabitants* (Lanham, Md., 2003). Here I adopt the dates and periodization of Gary S. Breschini and Trudy Haversat, who have done much work on the Monterey region. See Breschini and Haversat, *Baseline Archaeological Studies at Rancho San Carlos, Carmel Valley, Monterey County, California,* Archives of California Prehistory, no. 36 (Salinas, Calif., 1992), 7 n. 3. On dating the Scotts Valley archaeological site (CA–SCR–177) to around 10,000 b.c.e., see Robert Cartier and Victoria Bobo, "Early Peoples of Monterey Bay: The Scotts Valley Site," in Linda Yamane, ed., *A Gathering of Voices: The Native Peoples of the Central California Coast,* Santa Cruz County History Journal, no. 5 (Santa Cruz, Calif., 2002), 109–116. See also the important studies of Elkhorn Slough (CA–MNT–299): Dorothy Patch and Terry Jones, "Paleoenvironmental Change at Elkhorn Slough: Implications for Human Adaptive Strategies," *Journal of California and Great Basin Anthropology,* VI (1984), 19–43, table 1, 26; Terry L. Jones and Deborah A. Jones, "Elkhorn Slough Revisited: Reassessing the Chronology of CA–MNT–229," *Journal of California and Great Basin Anthropology,* XIV (1992), 159–179; and Joseph L. Chartkoff and Kerry Kona Chartkoff, *The Archaeology of California* (Stanford, Calif., 1984), 4.

4. Gary S. Breschini and Trudy Haversat, "Early Holocene Occupation of the Central California Coast," in Jon M. Erlandson and Roger H. Colten, *Hunter-Gatherers of Early Holocene Coastal California,* Perspectives in California Archaeology, I (Los Angeles, 1991), 125–132; Burton L. Gordon, *Monterey Bay Area: Natural History and Cultural Imprints,* 3d ed. (Pacific Grove, Calif., 1996); Chartkoff and Chartkoff, *Archaeology of California,* 38–50.

inland and east to avoid the rising waters. New lagoons formed, freshwater estuaries became saline, and marine life in some areas replaced freshwater species. Beaches came and went, rivers changed course, and inland lakes dried up, as rainfall decreased and evaporation increased. These dramatic transformations mirrored other environmental shifts, and eventually coastal California could support fewer and fewer large animals. As a consequence of all of these changes, the early Indians of the region altered their settlement patterns and widened their subsistence strategies.[5]

Compared to the coastal Indians of the Early Period, those of the Middle Period (500 B.C.E.–1000 C.E.) had a more diversified economy; no single resource was the most important staple. They relied on a wide array of plant foods and smaller animals and practiced seasonal migrations. But constant relocations and cyclical food shortages nevertheless limited their population growth, for these groups could grow no larger than the number that could survive the lean period stretching from late winter to early spring. Perhaps because the diverse and bountiful environment yielded a basic subsistence nearly all of the year, Indians of the Monterey region began to stockpile surplus foods for use during meager times late in their history.[6]

Sometime around one thousand years ago, at the outset of the Late Period (1000 C.E.–1769 C.E.), Indians of the Monterey region modified their subsistence and settlement patterns and began to accumulate large surpluses of food.[7] Unlike elsewhere in the world, where people often turned to animal and plant domestication to overcome seasonal shortages, California Indians seem to have relied more on existing resources that could support larger populations; the key developments, then, were social and technological changes that permitted the

5. Patch and Jones, "Paleoenvironmental Change at Elkhorn Slough," *Journal of California and Great Basin Anthropology,* VI (1984), 19–43; Chartkoff and Chartkoff, *Archaeology of California,* 68–69.

6. Chartkoff and Chartkoff, *Archaeology of California,* 75. Elsewhere in California, at least several thousand years earlier, most likely about four thousand years ago, Indians first began to collect staple foods in great surplus in order to break free from the restrictions on population imposed on them by seasonal scarcities of foods (138–139, 146–149). Because of limits in the archaeological record, it is not exactly clear when this change occurred in the Monterey region. Most of the work on this area discusses when populations characterized by "foraging" were replaced by "collectors." See Stephen A. Dietz, Thomas L. Jackson, et al., *Final Report of Archaeological Excavations at Nineteen Archaeological Sites for the Stage 1 Pacific Grove–Monterey Consolidation Project of the Regional Sewerage System,* II (Berkeley, Calif., 1981), part 2, 700–702; Dietz, William R. Hildebrandt, Terry L. Jones, et al., *Archaeological Investigations at Elkhorn Slough: CA–MNT–229: A Middle Period Site on the Central California Coast,* Papers in Northern California Anthropology, no. 3 (Berkeley, Calif., 1988); Gary S. Breschini and Trudy Haversat, "Archaeological Radiocarbon Dating of a Portion of CA–MNT–103, Monterey, Monterey County, California" (Aug. 4, 2000).

7. Dietz, Jackson, et al., *Stage 1 Pacific Grove–Monterey Consolidation Project,* II, part 2, 692, 700–702; Dietz, Hildebrandt, Jones, et al., *Archaeological Investigations at Elkhorn Slough,* Papers in Northern California Anthropology, no. 3, 424. Dietz and Jackson place this transformation two thousand years ago; Dietz, Hildebrandt, and Jones argue that it occurred more recently, about one thousand years ago.

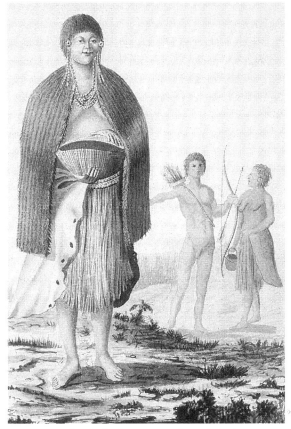

PLATE 1. *India e indio de Monterey*. By José Cardero. 1791.
Courtesy, Museo Naval, Madrid

intensive collection and exploitation of indigenous plants and animals. They dispersed their settlements and occupied more sites seasonally. Their crafts became more specialized, their shell-bead economy more extensive, and their political organization more complex.[8]

The varied topography of the Monterey region, its coastal marshes, inland valleys, hills, and mountains, supported a wide range of plants and animals. During the Late Period, much of the region between the coast and the inland mountains was covered with grasses or woods of oaks, pines, cypresses, willows, and cottonwoods. A Mediterranean climate characterized the region: winters were cool and wet and summers were warm and dry. Soaking rains began in the late fall, in October or November. These storms lasted for several days but were usually

8. Chartkoff and Chartkoff, *Archaeology of California,* 148.

separated by clear, cool breaks. Fall rains brought the germination of annual plants, and winter rains were accompanied by large flocks of waterfowl. In the late spring, rains diminished and days became warmer. Wildflowers bloomed, and rodents, birds, and small mammals nourished themselves on hillsides and grasslands. By May, the rains were infrequent, soils were drying, grasses became dormant, and wildflowers produced their seeds. Throughout these seasonal changes, deer and elk browsed, ranging from valleys to mountains, in pursuit of food. Major climate differences between the coast and the inland valleys enhanced the region's vegetational diversity. On summer days, a coastal strip of land some three to four miles wide was often shrouded in fog; yet, farther inland, up the valleys of the Carmel and Salinas rivers, days were usually warm and clear. In the winter, evening frosts occasionally fell upon inland valleys but not on the coast.[9]

Certainly by 1000 C.E., the Children of Coyote began using a bow and arrow, making baskets and nets, and gathering and processing acorns and buckeyes. They collected a wide range of foods—mammals, birds, fish, shellfish, grasses, and seeds. They lived in stable communities for much of the year, but they also maintained smaller camps, which they used seasonally for food production. They divided their work into small groups and stored meats and acorns for the winter. Most important, production shifted from the household to the community. And, like Indians elsewhere in California, they maximized food sources through burning, irrigation, and pruning. Much of their gathering was gender specific: women collected and processed the acorns, seeds, roots, and berries that constituted the mainstay of the diet; men fished and hunted game, birds, and sea mammals. They also divided their crafts by sex: women wove baskets, clothes, and household articles; men made tools and weapons. Additionally, these Indians carried on an elaborate system of exchange with their neighbors, and shell beads they manufactured were traded and prized as burial goods as far away as the Great Basin.[10]

9. Dietz, Jackson, et al., *Stage 1 Pacific Grove–Monterey Consolidation Project,* II, part 2, 661–666; Gordon, *Monterey Bay Area,* 15–18.

10. On the range of foods, see "Costanoan" and "Esselen," in *HNAI,* VIII, 485–495, 496–499; Robert F. Heizer and Albert B. Elsasser, *The Natural World of the California Indians* (Berkeley, Calif., 1980); Rebecca Allen, *Native Americans at Mission Santa Cruz, 1791–1834: Interpreting the Archaeological Record,* Perspectives in California Archaeology, V (Los Angeles, 1998), 21–22. See also appendixes C–G, in Dietz, Jackson, et al., *Stage 1 Pacific Grove–Monterey Consolidation Project;* Thomas C. Blackburn and Kat Anderson, eds., *Before the Wilderness: Environmental Management by Native Californians* (Menlo Park, Calif., 1993); Edith Wallace, "Sexual Status and Role Differences," in *HNAI,* VIII, 683–684; Nona Christensen Willoughby, *Division of Labor among the Indians of California,* Reports of the University of California Archaeological Survey, no. 60 (Berkeley, Calif., 1963), rpt. in Lowell John Bean and Sylvia Brakke Vane, *Ethnology of the Alta California Indians,* part 1, "Precontact," Spanish Borderlands Sourcebooks, III (New York, 1991), 427–499; James A. Bennyhoff and Richard E. Hughes, *Shell Bead and Ornament Exchange Networks between California and the Western Great Basin,* Anthropological Papers of the American Museum of Natural History, LXIV, part 2 (New York, 1987).

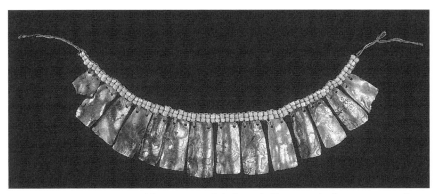

PLATE 2. Costanoan Necklace. Pieces of abalone shell are attached to two rows of white glass beads used as substitutes for shell beads. Necklaces such as these were worn by people of high status during celebrations and festivals.
© The Trustees of The British Museum

By the end of the Late Period, the Children of Coyote were part of a complicated human mosaic that made California into one of the most densely settled areas in all North America. Some 310,000 Indians lived within the boundaries of the present state just before Spanish colonization. Approximately 60,000 Indians existed on the coast between San Diego and San Francisco, where Spain would establish missions, presidios, and civilian settlements. The Tipai and Ipai (Diegueño) peopled the region around San Diego, the Luiseño resided to their immediate north, the Gabrielino occupied the coastal plain of Los Angeles, the Chumash inhabited the Santa Barbara region, the Yokuts lived in the Central Valley, the Salinan, Esselen, and Costanoan settled the central coast between Santa Barbara and the Golden Gate, and the Pomo, Coast Miwok, Wappo, Patwin, and Eastern Miwok claimed the regions immediately north and east of the San Francisco Bay Area. Mission San Carlos gathered peoples from a territory roughly circumscribed by the Salinas River in the east, the Pajaro River in the north, and Vicente Creek in the south. This area was home to between 2,500 and 3,000 Costanoan and Esselen Indians in the first half of the eighteenth century. Costanoans lived in a fifteen-mile-wide coastal strip extending from Point Sur to the Carquinez Straits, just north of San Francisco Bay. The Esselen lived in a smaller, more mountainous area, which included the drainages of the upper Carmel River, the Arroyo Seco, and the upper Salinas Valley.[11]

11. Sherburne F. Cook, *The Population of the California Indians, 1769–1970* (Berkeley, Calif., 1976), 20–43; Peter Gerhard, *North Frontier of New Spain,* rev. ed. (Norman, Okla., 1993), 309. From 1770 to 1808, some 1,525 Indians from the surrounding area attained baptism at San Carlos. Others were also baptized at Mission Soledad, which was founded farther east in 1791. Based upon the number of gentiles baptized in these missions and the assumption that an additional percentage were not baptized, the aboriginal

However, although California supported a large human population, it was no Eden. Human skeletal remains show that prehistoric California was hardly disease-free: streptococcal and staphylococcal infections were common. So were gastrointestinal infections, which often led to dehydration and anemia. Skeletal studies further suggest that tuberculosis and a form of syphilis might also have been present in prehistoric California. In addition, evidence of the disruption of enamel formation on dental remains reveals a prevalence of infectious diseases or malnutrition. Archaeological data also show that those who lived in densely settled areas had high subadult mortality rates. California Indians therefore had a long history of disease well before Spanish colonization. In fact, their health seems to have declined during the Middle and Late periods, as increased sedentation and heightened population densities created new opportunities for the maintenance and spread of disease.[12]

California Indians before Spanish colonization were both numerous and diverse, since language and culture often varied from village to village. As a whole, California comprised six culture areas, seven language stocks, and at least one hundred distinct languages. Trade, marriage, and ritual connected many neighboring communities, but most steadfastly maintained autonomy and protected their areas against encroachment. The Indians of the Monterey region were particularly diverse, since their territory represented the southernmost extent of Costanoan languages and the northern reach of the Esselen linguistic family. Villagers across and sometimes within these language districts spoke mutually

population of the Monterey region seems to have been approximately 2,800 Indians in 1769. Cook's assumption that the ratio of baptisms to the aboriginal population was two to three has been generally accepted (Cook, *Population of the California Indians*, 25–27). This tabulation is based on estimated population totals from the following sources: Randall Milliken, *Ethnohistory of the Rumsen*, Papers in Northern California Anthropology, no. 2 (Berkeley, Calif., 1987), 47–52, orig. publ. as "Ethnohistory of the Rumsen: The Mission Period," in Dietz, Jackson, et al., *Stage 1 Pacific Grove–Monterey Consolidation Project*, I (Berkeley, Calif., 1981), 10–102; Milliken, "Ethnogeography and Ethnohistory of the Big Sur District, California State Park System, during the 1770–1810 Time Period...," California Department of Parks and Recreation and Regents of the University of California, final report, March 1990, 74–76; Milliken, "Ethnographic Context," in Dietz, Hildebrandt, Jones, et al., *Archaeological Investigations at Elkhorn Slough*, 64–66. The Rumsen Indians numbered approximately 500; the Ensen, approximately 300. The Esselen and Sargentaruc together amounted to approximately 1,500; and the Kalendaruc/Locuyusta totaled approximately 500.

12. Phillip L. Walker, Patricia Lambert, and Michael J. DeNiro, "The Effects of European Contact on the Health of Alta California Indians," in *CC*, I, 349–364, esp. 355–357; Lisa Kealhofer, "The Evidence for Demographic Collapse in California," in Brenda J. Baker and Kealhofer, eds., *Bioarchaeology of Native American Adaptation in the Spanish Borderlands* (Gainesville, Fla., 1996), 56–92; Douglas H. Ubelaker, "Patterns of Disease in Early North American Populations," in Michael R. Haines and Richard H. Steckel, eds., *A Population History of North America* (Cambridge, 2000), 51–97. On the California Indians' health before Spanish settlement, see Phillip L. Walker and Russell Thornton, "Health, Nutrition, and Demographic Change in Native California," in Richard H. Steckel and Jerome C. Rose, eds., *The Backbone of History: Health and Nutrition in the Western Hemisphere* (Cambridge, 2002), 506–523.

unintelligible languages. Mission San Carlos itself attracted both Costanoan- and Esselen-speaking peoples, all of whom had extensive repertoires of music, ritual, and dance.[13]

Diversity in the Monterey region was the product of geographic boundaries and a willful separateness. The Costanoan and Esselen rarely intermarried, surely competed for resources in the Monterey region, and perhaps even engaged in periodic hostilities. The few brief accounts of Indian culture in the writings of early European visitors to the Monterey region noted the animosity between Costanoan and Esselen Indians but did not distinguish between their practices. Nor did the Europeans state whether the belief systems of these two groups differed. The Rumsen Costanoan, according to one diarist on a Spanish expedition that stopped in Monterey in 1792, "believed that the sun was of a similar nature to themselves; . . . that he was a man and that he had the power to take their lives." The Esselen held that "after this life everyone was transformed into *teclotes,* or owls, a bird to which they showed a singular veneration."[14]

13. Cook, *Population of the California Indians,* 43; John D. Daniels, "The Indian Population of North America in 1492," *WMQ,* 3d Ser., XLIX (1992), 298–320. On Indian languages in California, see Michael J. Moratto, *California Archaeology* (Orlando, Fla., 1984), 530–574; William F. Shipley, "Native Languages of California," in *HNAI,* VIII, 80–90. See also Chartkoff and Chartkoff, *Archaeology of California,* 203. On village autonomy and regional trade, see Robert F. Heizer and Albert B. Elsasser, *The Natural World of the California Indians* (Berkeley, Calif., 1980); Julia G. Costello and David Hornbeck, "Alta California: An Overview," in *CC,* I, 304–308; James T. Davis, "Trade Routes and Economic Exchange among the Indians of California," *Reports of the University of California Archaeological Survey,* LIV (Berkeley, Calif., 1961).

Costanoan is a Penutian language, whereas Esselen is Hokan. For brief discussions of the linguistic variations among the Indians of California, see Shipley, "Native Languages of California," in *HNAI,* VIII, 80–90; R. B. Dixon and Kroeber, "Linguistic Families of California," in R. F. Heizer and M. A. Whipple, eds., *The California Indians: A Source Book,* rev. ed. (Berkeley, Calif., 1971), 105–111. Sargentaruc was situated between the Costanoan and Esselen territories, and its linguistic affiliation remains a matter of debate. See Sherburne F. Cook, "The Esselen: Territory, Villages, and Population," *Monterey County Archaeological Society Quarterly,* III (1974), 1–12, esp. 6–7, 9; see also Milliken, *Ethnohistory of the Rumsen;* Milliken, "Ethnographic Context," in Dietz, Hildebrandt, Jones, et al., *Archaeological Investigations at Elkhorn Slough;* Milliken, "Ethnogeography and Ethnohistory of the Big Sur District"; and Gary Breschini and Trudy Haversat, *An Overview of the Esselen Indians of Central Monterey County, California* (Salinas, Calif., 1993). Costanoan-speaking tribelets (and villages) baptized at San Carlos: Rumsen (Achasta, Tucutnut, Ichxenta, Socorronda, Echilat); Kalendaruc; Gauchirron (Locuyusta, Culul); Pagsin; and Ensen (Tigirrinta, Pucasta). Esselen-speaking tribelets (and villages) baptized at San Carlos: Excelen (Excelemac, Chelenajan, Capanay); Ecjeajan; Aspasniajan/Ymunajan; and Eslenajan.

14. On the endogamy of the Rumsen Costanoan and the Esselen, see Milliken, *Ethnohistory of the Rumsen,* 73–79. On the violence between the Costanoan and Esselen, see Herbert Ingram Priestley, ed. and trans., *A Historical, Political, and Natural Description of California, by Pedro Fages, Soldier of Spain . . .* (Berkeley, Calif., 1937), 64–65. It should be remembered, however, that Europeans in general almost always viewed Indians prior to their arrival as ravaged by war and famine and that bringing peace to "warring" Indians was one of the apologies frequently offered by Europeans who sought to explain away the disasters that accompanied their expansion to the New World. For Costanoan and Esselen beliefs, see the translation of the manuscript account of the voyage of the *Sutil* and *Mexicana,* in Donald C. Cutter, *California in 1792: A Spanish Naval Visit* (Norman, Okla., 1990), 143.

Indians of the Monterey region lived as tribes or, as conceptualized by Kroeber, "tribelets." This was the most common form of organization among precontact California Indians, and it seems to have arisen only during the Late Period. Tribelets were usually composed of five hundred to one thousand villagers and were frequently aggregates of several settlements. Leaders oversaw these extended communities, but they did not hold absolute authority and were "variously influenced by councils, secret-society officials, shamans and other officials and wealthy men."[15] Precontact social organization is poorly understood, but modern studies suggest that villages—the principal units of organization—were stratified into a ruling elite, commoners, and an underclass. The elite commanded respect and awe from commoners, who had no rank, and from the underclass, who had no formal ties to an intact lineage. Social status was ascribed and authority was distributed hierarchically: elite males inherited political, religious, and economic power through their fathers' lines. Access to power and control of ritual knowledge distinguished the elite, who also wore the finest clothes, inhabited the largest dwellings, and avoided manual labor. The community owned the village land, but the elite determined its use. At the top of the village hierarchy stood a chief, who in counsel with others oversaw the production, allocation, and trade of the community's food and material goods. The Indian groups of California had complex social organizations, but no ethnographic evidence describes the kinship systems of the Indians of the Monterey Bay region or indicates whether their social structures were based upon clans or moieties.[16]

15. Alfred L. Kroeber, "The Nature of Land-holding Groups in Aboriginal California," in Kroeber, ed., *Two Papers on the Aboriginal Ethnography of California,* Reports of the University of California Archaeological Survey, LVI (1962), 19–58; Lowell John Bean, "Social Organization in Native California," in Bean and Thomas C. Blackburn, eds., *Native Californians: A Theoretical Retrospective* (Ramona, Calif., 1976), 99–123. Bean states that, in native California, "the chief was assisted by a managerial or administrative class that was usually associated with the ritual or cult systems, since it was through ritual that many economic and political affairs were articulated. . . . Thus in addition to the obvious administrators such as assistant chief and messenger, there were honorific positions such as dancer or singer" (113).

16. Secondary captains existed among the Costanoans north of Monterey (Priestley, ed. and trans., *Historical Description,* 74). The Sargentaruc—one of the groups baptized at Mission San Carlos—also seem to have had a type of secondary captain, since Nicomedes Joseph Unique is described in his baptismal entry as the "principal confidant" of the Sargentaruc captain Aristeo Joseph Chilichon (Nicomedes Joseph Unique, San Carlos bapt. no. 1074). On village social structures, see Bean, "Power and Its Applications in Native California," "Social Organization," both in Bean and Blackburn, eds., *Native Californians,* 407–420, 673–682; Jeanne E. Arnold, "Complex Hunter-Gatherer-Fishers of Prehistoric California: Chiefs, Specialists, and Maritime Adaptations of the Channel Islands," *American Antiquity,* LVII (1992), 60–84. On the Indians' complex social organization, see Joseph G. Jorgensen, *Western Indians: Comparative Environments, Languages, and Cultures of 172 Western American Indian Tribes* (San Francisco, Calif., 1980). According to John P. Harrington, the Indians of central California had bear and deer moieties, but the evidence is not conclusive (Harrington, *Culture Element Distributions, XIX: Central California Coast,* University of California Publications in Anthropological Records, VII, no. 1 [Berkeley, Calif., 1942], 1–46). A moiety is a form of social organization in which, based on lineage, all members of a group are assumed to belong to one of two categories.

A relatively mild and predictable climate allowed for houses that had a temporary appearance, made as they were of a wooden frame covered by brush roofing. Costanoan and Esselen Indians burned and rebuilt these structures when old ones became unclean or the group decided to relocate with the change of seasons. They made their tools—knives, clubs, drills, needles, to name a few—of bone or stone and obtained their obsidian arrowheads through exchange. California Indians were among the world's most sophisticated basket makers, and the Children of Coyote crafted an enormous variety of fiber baskets for gathering, preparing, and storing food. Since the climate was generally temperate year-round, clothing was minimal: women wore deerskin or fiber skirts; men went naked or wore little clothing, occasionally covering themselves in skins or mud. In the colder months, blankets of rabbit, otter, or deerskin provided warmth and bedding. The Children of Coyote had dark hair and dark eyes. Men stood about five foot six and plucked most of their facial hair with shells or small pieces of wood. They often painted their skin and pierced their ears, and facial tattoos were common.[17]

The lifeways of the Children of Coyote were keyed to the region's rich plant and animal resources and seasonal changes in the climate. In the late summer, they labored intensively to prepare for the winter months. Since their activities and resources were so varied, they seem to have divided themselves into small and temporary groups to allow for a more efficient processing of staples. These smaller groups often relocated for weeks or months at a time to camps along the coast or in the interior, where they collected and processed foods. In the late summer and early fall, groups gathered acorns, harvested grass seeds, and collected buckeyes, nuts, and berries. Some ventured to the shore to gather shellfish; others relocated to rivers and streams to catch steelhead; still others headed farther inland in pursuit of game attracted to dropping acorns. Indians dried shellfish and game meat and stored nuts and seeds. In the fall, they gathered and stored their most important food, acorns, which were a rich source of both carbohydrates and fats. Once the food stores were in place, they set fire to the grasslands. This seasonal burning encouraged the growth of certain plants, protected grasslands from encroaching trees and shrubs, created habitats for large game, and aided in harvesting pine nuts and hunting rabbits.[18]

After the acorn harvest and the burning of the grasslands came a period of comparative inactivity. During the winter months, the Children of Coyote aban-

17. Claude-Nicolas Rollin, "Memoire physiologique et pathologique sur les Américains," Marine, Ser. 3JJ, 387, reel 1, 4–5, Archives nationales, Paris.

18. On California Indians' use of fire to manage the landscape, see Jon E. Keeley, "Native American Impacts on Fire Regimes of the California Coastal Ranges," *Journal of Biogeography,* XXIX (2002), 303–320.

doned coastal and interior camps and returned to their principal villages. Most likely, they marked the transition from fall to winter with ceremonies, which not only punctuated the seasonal change but allowed an exchange and redistribution of foods and goods. For the next four to six months, during the coolest and wettest time of the year, Indians in Monterey collected shellfish and hunted occasionally, but for the most part they subsisted off their stores. With the coming of spring, the pace of life once again quickened. They resumed hunting and collecting in earnest, and, as the weather improved, they dispersed for short periods into small task groups in pursuit of food.[19]

By the middle of the eighteenth century, the Children of Coyote had created a diversified and flexible system. They used hundreds of plants and animals for food and medicinal purposes. They traded with their neighbors to obtain both luxury goods and necessities. They had remade their region, through the use of fire and other techniques, to suit their needs. And, through their adaptable social and political organization, they were able to produce, gather, and accumulate surpluses that allowed them to persist through times of scarcity. Moreover, their skillful use of their environment and the stability of their belief system initially allowed some to maintain a degree of distance from the Spaniards and ultimately gave them the ability to adjust to the Spanish presence. However, with the arrival of Spaniards, crucial aspects of the Indians' way of life became imperiled; many eventually came to an end. Spanish soldiers, missionaries, and settlers brought to California an array of new diseases, plants, and animals, a new religion, new ideas about marriage and sexuality, and new types of political and economic organization. Unlike the ocean's waters, whose gradual ascent in the Early Period had afforded the Indians of Monterey an incremental adaptation over generations, these agents of change flooded in, often unseen, if not wholly unanticipated, and so brought the Children of Coyote to the brink of destruction.

19. Dietz, Jackson, et al., *Stage 1 Pacific Grove–Monterey Consolidation Project*, II, part 2, 657–667.

2

SPANIARDS

On the afternoon of May 31, 1770, the Spanish ship *San Antonio* turned into the harbor of Monterey on the coast of a land known to the Spanish as Nueva or Alta California. Upon seeing the ship, a small party of Spaniards, who had arrived by land a week earlier, set three signal fires. In recognition, the ship fired its cannon and proceeded closer to shore, cautiously following a small launch. The next morning, the men of the land and sea parties embraced and exchanged congratulations for finding the harbor they so ardently desired.[1] On the following Sunday, the men celebrated their arrival and reenacted time-honored European rituals through which they formally took possession of Alta California in the name of the Spanish Crown. Junípero Serra, a Franciscan who had come to New Spain in 1749, led in procession men who had sailed with him on the *San Antonio,* and Gaspar de Portolá, governor of Baja California, headed a second column of those who had marched with him by land from the peninsula. The two groups met on the beach in a place they recognized from the accounts of earlier Spanish explorers. Beneath the branches of an ancient oak, Serra performed a mass, which was punctuated by cannon salvos. He then "sprinkled all the fields and beach of the harbor with holy water, to frighten away the infernal enemies." Having raised a large wooden cross and unfurled a flag of the king, the assembled men shouted in their loudest voices: "Long live the Faith! Long live the king!" In the background, bells rang and rifles fired, and from the *San Antonio* came the thunder and smoke of cannon.[2]

Following these religious and military rituals, Governor Portolá proceeded to the legal formalities of taking possession of the harbor and the surrounding countryside for Spain; he made the "ceremony of throwing earth and stones to the four winds," claimed the territory in the name of Carlos III, and again raised

1. Francisco Palóu, *Historical Memoirs of New California . . .*, ed. and trans. Herbert Eugene Bolton, 4 vols. (1926; rpt. New York, 1966), II, 287–288.

2. Junípero Serra to Juan Andrés, June 12, 1770, Monterey, in Tibesar, ed. and trans., *Writings of Serra,* I, 169.

V. R. DEL V. P. F. JUNIPERO SERRA

hijo de la S.ta Prov.a de N.P.S. Fran.co de la Isla de Mallorca D.y Ex.or de S.col. Comis.o del S.to Oh.o Mis.o del Ap.co Col.o de S.n Fern.do de Mex.co Fund.or y Presid.te de las Mis.es de la Calif.a Septentr.l Murió con gr.e fama de sant.d en la Mis.on de S. Carlos del R.o del N.o Monte-Rey a 28 de Ag.to de 1784. de edad de 70 a.s 9 m.s 4 d.s hab.do gastado la mit.d de su vida en el exerc.o de Mision.o Apost.co

PLATE 3. Woodcut of Junípero Serra. This image appeared in Francisco Palóu's biography of Serra *(Relación histórica de la vida y apostólicas tareas del venerable padre fray Junípero Serra . . .* [Mexico, 1787]). This item is reproduced by permission of *The Huntington Library, San Marino, California*

the royal standard.[3] Later that day, on a plain near the shore, the men got to work constructing the colony: "Hand was put to building a stockade, and inside of it some humble habitations for the royal presidio and mission." Having occupied the harbor, taken possession of Alta California, and established a mission and presidio at Monterey, Portolá sent a messenger to carry the good news to the viceroy in Mexico that he had accomplished his task. A new land had been added to the Spanish realm.[4]

Nearly three centuries passed between the onset of the conquest of the Americas in 1492 and Portolá's act of possession at Monterey; in that time, Spain had extended its New World empire to claim much of the Caribbean, Mexico, Central America, South America, and an expanse of territory that included Florida and stretched from the southern Great Plains, across the Gulf of California, to the peninsula of Baja California. To govern such a vast and diverse territory and the numerous people it encompassed, Spanish officials divided New World conquests into separate viceroyalties, a strategy that had served the Crown well in administering Spain itself. The viceroyalty of New Spain, which was created in 1535, spanned the territories north of Panama far into the present United States, the Caribbean islands, and some of Venezuela; in the 1570s, the Philippines were added. To oversee Panama and all of its South American possessions, Spain created a second viceroyalty in Lima, Peru, in 1544.[5] Soon the Crown recognized that these viceroyalties were too large for effective administration and carved them up into smaller units called *audiencias*. By 1650, the viceroyalties of New Spain and Peru had been divided into ten audiencias. Throughout these vast and populous territories, Spanish exploration, conquest, and colonization were carried out by soldiers and administrators, who scoured frontiers in search of Indian kingdoms to conquer and plunder, and by Catholic missionaries, who were often among the most zealous and intrepid agents of colonial expansion.

It was not until its flood tide, after nearly three centuries of swelling, that the Spanish Empire began to engulf the lands of the Children of Coyote. Yet, long before that day, California Indians knew of Spaniards, as natives throughout the interior of northern New Spain and the peninsula of Baja California encountered Spaniards and spread word to their neighbors of new and menacing strangers.

3. Fernando Boneu Companys, *Documentos secretos de la expedición de Portolá á California* (Lérida, Spain, 1973), 149–153. The quote is from the reproduction of the original text, which has slightly different language from the transcription. Also see Palóu, *Historical Memoirs,* ed. and trans. Bolton, II, 291–292. For rituals through which Europeans claimed the New World, see Patricia Seed, *Ceremonies of Possession in Europe's Conquest of the New World, 1492–1640* (Cambridge, 1995), 1–99.

4. Palóu, *Historical Memoirs,* ed. and trans. Bolton, II, 292.

5. James Lockhart and Stuart B. Schwartz, *Early Latin America: A History of Colonial Spanish America and Brazil* (Cambridge, 1983), 92.

Indians of Baja California first met Spaniards in the 1530s, when Hernán Cortés, fresh from dividing the spoils of Mexico, propelled Spain into the Californias. Like so many *conquistadores*, Cortés dreamed of other Mexicos, territories that might equal or even surpass in riches the lands of the Aztecs. He longed to discover the Strait of Anián, believed to be the direct route through the New World to the Indies. And he sought confirmation of a popular tale that told of California, a craggy island located in the Indies and peopled by Amazonian women, where "gold and precious stones" abounded.[6] With these stories lying like promises in his mind, Cortés dispatched several maritime explorations up the coastlines of Sonora and Sinaloa and Baja California. Much to his disappointment, these voyages unlocked none of the fabled treasures of the north. And, among Indians, they fostered well-founded fears of piratical, dangerous men who came from afar.

To promote his search for the northern treasures, Cortés established a port north of present-day Acapulco in 1522, and his men there quickly began constructing ships for use in future explorations. Despite these feverish early efforts, Spanish explorations of the Pacific stalled at first. It would be a decade before the conquistador sent out Diego Hurtado de Mendoza on a voyage of discovery. And this foray north, driven as it was by avarice, ended quickly, in mutiny. The following year, 1533, Fortún Jiménez, another of Cortés's pilots and himself a mutineer, sailed into a peaceful bay of what he hoped was the long-sought island of California. (Within a decade, Spanish explorations would reveal the land to be the southeastern tip of a peninsula attached to the mainland.) Guaycura warriors, not Amazonian women, greeted Jiménez when he came ashore at the bay he had named La Paz. And, in a fierce and bloody battle, they killed Jiménez and most of his men. The Indians' victory over the Spaniards, however, would prove brief. Survivors of the expedition returned to Mexico and regaled rapt listeners with tales of an island of gold and pearls, and dreams of wealth pushed aside memories of defeat.[7]

Chasing his rainbow, Cortés ventured to La Paz in May 1535. He renamed the bay Santa Cruz and began building a colony with the four hundred Spaniards and three hundred black slaves in his company. But Baja California—like Alta

6. Excerpt from Garcí Ordóñez de Montalvo, *Las sergas de esplandián,* in Charles E. Chapman, *A History of California: The Spanish Period* (1921; rpt. New York, 1939), 57–58.

7. Iris H. W. Engstrand, "Seekers of the 'Northern Mystery': European Exploration of California and the Pacific," in Ramón A. Gutiérrez and Richard J. Orsi, eds., *Contested Eden: California before the Gold Rush* (Berkeley, Calif., 1998), 78–110, esp. 80–81; Chapman, *History of California*, 50; Henry R. Wagner, *Spanish Voyages to the Northwest Coast of America in the Sixteenth Century* ([1929]; rpt. Amsterdam, 1966), 6.

California—would prove hard to settle. Supplies were short, the colony difficult to provision, the land arid and inhospitable. And in this country there was none of the precious yellow metal that would have made the Spaniards' hardships worth enduring. Before long, starving settlers and attacking Indians forced the colony's abandonment. Spaniards left Santa Cruz with little of value other than their own skins and a number of Indians they hoped to use as interpreters in future explorations of the region. Once the Spaniards had gone, the Indians burned the settlement's buildings to the ground. Generations later, they still spoke ill of Cortés and his men, recounting that the invaders had "treated them very badly, killing many of them and setting furious dogs on them."[8]

The Indians of Baja California might not have seen Spaniards again for another thirty or forty years if not for Alvar Núñez Cabeza de Vaca, a survivor of Pánfilo de Narváez's ill-fated expediton to Florida in 1528, who reappeared in northern Mexico in 1536 and rekindled the Spaniards' belief in the Kingdom of Quivira. As a result, another Spanish fleet sailed their way in the summer of 1539. By then, Indians of the peninsula had circulated rumors of their own: threatening men had come from the sea and invaded their lands. Most of the Indians, therefore, fled their houses and abandoned their possessions upon catching sight of Francisco de Ulloa's ships on the horizon. Others attacked his men when they came ashore for water. The Cochimí of Cedros Island so ferociously resisted Ulloa's attempts to land that he concluded that "they wanted to eat us, and, moreover, that they had the power to do so."[9]

The Spaniards' blunt rejection of basic rituals of diplomacy heightened the Indians' wariness and narrowed the possibilities of relations. On one occasion, Ulloa retired to his ship, preferring dinner to "bestiality and barter" with Guaycuras who had offered him a prized possession—a diadem woven of thread and embroidered with red feathers. Ultimately, in a sure sign of his growing impatience with a land and a people he took to be of little value, Ulloa loosed his dogs on those who stood between his men and fresh water. By the spring of 1540, Ulloa had carried his explorations up the Pacific coast to within two hundred miles of what would become known as San Diego Bay and determined that California was not an island. But these discoveries were actually defeats: this California was not the fabled island, and the peninsula held no cities, let alone ones of gold. In the

8. Chapman, *History of California,* 51; William H. Prescott, *History of the Conquest of Mexico,* ed. Wilfred Harold Munro, 3 vols. (1843; rpt. Philadelphia, 1873), III, 320; Engstrand, "Seekers of the 'Northern Mystery,'" in Gutiérrez and Orsi, eds., *Contested Eden,* 81; "The Narrative of Ulloa," "Father Antonio de la Ascención's Account of the Voyage of Sebastian Vizcaíno," both in Wagner, *Spanish Voyages,* 15–46, esp. 17, and 180–272, esp. 194; see also 11.

9. Chapman, *History of California,* 52; "Narrative of Ulloa," in Wagner, *Spanish Voyages,* 27, 41.

hurly-burly of European expansion, men's dreams died hard; for another two centuries, many cartographers would continue to style the peninsula of California, not as it was, but as the island they wanted it to be.[10]

Cortés's efforts to explore the Pacific coast ended with Ulloa, but California Indians' experiences with Spaniards continued as Cortés's rival, Viceroy Antonio de Mendoza, pressed Spanish exploration up the coast and into the lands of Alta California. In June 1542, Juan Rodríguez Cabrillo, a captain of crossbowmen in Cortés's assault on Mexico City, led three small ships out of Navidad, a port north of Acapulco. In September, the fleet entered San Diego Bay.[11]

Given all the Spanish activity in Baja California and central Mexico, one imagines that for many years the Ipai had anticipated the Spaniards' arrival, perhaps even prepared for it. When Cabrillo's men ventured ashore "where there were some people," all but three of the Indians fled. To these three, the Spaniards offered small presents, most likely beads of glass. If the Spaniards hoped to hear news from the Indians of Quivira, they must have been disappointed; the Indians expressed only their anxieties, explaining to Cabrillo that they knew of other Spaniards farther inland.[12] That night, when some of Cabrillo's men came ashore to fish with nets, the Ipai attacked and wounded three. Undaunted, perhaps even eager to avenge the Indians' attack, the Spaniards sailed farther into the harbor the following morning and carried back on board two young boys "who understood nothing by signs." The next day, three Ipai men—perhaps the trio that had stood its ground on the beach—came to the ships and explained that they feared the Spaniards and, no doubt, wished them to leave their land. They showed by signs, one diarist recorded, "that some people like us, that is, bearded, dressed and armed like those on board the vessels, were going about inland." The Ipai suggested that these men "carried cross-bows and swords," and the Ipai "made gestures Uwith the right arm as if using lances, and went running about as if they were going on horseback." Bearded strangers, the Ipai knew, "were killing many of the native Indians." Small presents, mere trifles, then, would do little to ease Ipai concerns. Much to the Ipais' presumed relief, the expedition's ship pointed north three days later, off to explore other lands and waters.[13]

In mid-November 1542, Cabrillo's ships ventured into what would later be known as Monterey Bay, but the mariners dared not go ashore "on account of the

10. "Narrative of Ulloa," in Wagner, *Spanish Voyages,* 34, 42; Engstrand, "Seekers of the 'Northern Mystery,'" in Gutiérrez and Orsi, eds., *Contested Eden,* 82.

11. "Voyage of Cabrillo," in Wagner, *Spanish Voyages,* 79–93, esp. 84–85.

12. Ibid., 85.

13. The Ipai were likely alluding to the expeditions of Francisco Vásquez de Coronado and Hernando de Alarcón, which had tracked over Sonora and Sinaloa and the region of the lower Colorado River in recent years.

great surf." The Children of Coyote might have caught a glimpse of Cabrillo's ships coasting the shore, but most were probably passing the winter inland, in areas more sheltered from the winter fog and rain. Cabrillo chose to winter over on Santa Catalina Island; there he met his fate, suffering a mortal wound while trying to defend his men from an Indian attack. Under the command of Bartolomé Ferrer, the expedition continued to the present California-Oregon border, where furious winds and raging seas proved insurmountable. Thankful to be alive, Ferrer set sail for Mexico. On the return voyage, the Spaniards came back to San Diego Bay, five and a half months after they had departed its waters. Before leaving, they seized two Ipai boys "to carry to New Spain to learn to be interpreters," a final act that could only have deepened California Indians' suspicions.[14]

Cabrillo's expedition lent more credence to the Spaniards' growing realization that the north Pacific coast hid neither an inland passage nor another Mexico. But, after 1565, California Indians continued to see and interact with Spanish mariners because of the region's new importance as a potential military outpost and way station. Spanish vessels returning from the Philippines routinely began to skirt the coast near the end of their months-long transpacific voyage, and English pirates—Francis Drake and Thomas Cavendish—ventured up the Pacific coast in the late 1570s and 1580s. Unlike the Ipai, who had taken Cabrillo's men for what they were—Spaniards, akin to those rumored to be in the interior—the Coast Miwok saw Drake's men as the dead returned. Fearing these men/spirits, the Coast Miwok refused their presents, avoided physical contact with them, and lacerated themselves on various occasions in what might have been a mourning ritual. Why the Coast Miwok would have comprehended these Europeans so differently than coastal Indians to the south is unclear. But, centuries later, some of the Children of Coyote also would see Spanish explorers as the spirits of their ancestors.[15]

The Spanish Crown's response to the growing strategic value of California was halfhearted: it gave to the Manila galleons the added responsibility on the return voyage from the Philippines of charting California's coastal waters. This was a recipe for certain disaster; men who had been at sea for months and had exhausted their supplies lacked the restraint necessary for a peaceful reconnaissance amid peoples who had grown suspicious of them. Predictably, in the fall of 1587, in the vicinity of Morro Bay, a group of Chumash attacked Pedro de Unamuno

14. Ibid., 89–90, 93; Harry Kelsey, *Juan Rodríguez Cabrillo* (San Marino, Calif., 1986), 158–159.

15. David J. Weber, *The Spanish Frontier in North America* (New Haven, Conn., 1992), 83. On Drake's landing in California, see Robert F. Heizer, *Francis Drake and the California Indians, 1579*, University of California Publications in American Archaeology and Ethnology, XLII, no. 8 (Berkeley, Calif., 1947), 251–302. The location of Drake's landing is still debated. In all likelihood, the *Golden Hinde* made landfall just north of San Francisco Bay in the territory of the Coast Miwok.

and killed two of his men after they had spent days on land searching for food. Only after Spaniards opened fire with small arms did the Indians fall back. Seven years later, under the command of Sebastián Rodríguez Cermeño, another galleon made landfall at Drake's Bay. For the most part, Cermeño avoided the conflicts with Indians that had marred Unamuno's voyage, perhaps because he was under strict orders not to venture inland or take anything from the Indians by force.[16]

The experiences of Unamuno and Cermeño suggested that it was far more practical for Spanish mariners to explore the Pacific coast from a base in Acapulco than after a harrowing transpacific voyage. Thus the viceroy of New Spain, the conde de Monterrey, sent out from Acapulco an expedition under Sebastián Vizcaíno, a veteran of several Pacific voyages and architect of another failed colony at La Paz. Vizcaíno's objective: the "discovery and demarkation" of the ports, bays, and inlets between Cabo San Lucas and Cape Mendocino. To avoid conflicts, Vizcaíno was warned "not to allow anyone to go inland in search of Indians, nor even find out if Indians were there, since the intent and principal purposes (of coastal charting and soundings) did not require it."[17]

In early May 1602, Vizcaíno's small fleet—two small ships and a frigate—carrying some two hundred men opened their sails to the breeze in Acapulco and headed for California.[18] Vizcaíno's ships skirted Baja California, making only occasional landfall. Headwinds slowed the expedition's progress, and the ships did not reach the harbor of San Diego until November 10. Five weeks later, on the evening of December 16, Vizcaíno dropped anchor in "the best port that could be desired," which he named Monterey, to honor the viceroy who had sent him on this voyage of exploration. By this time, the Spanish mariners were in terrible shape. Prevailing southerly winds and currents had made the voyage from Acapulco even more demanding than from the Philippines. Seven and a half months at sea had taken its terrible toll. Sixteen of the men died en route; most held only a tenuous grip on life, too weak to continue. Two of the ships' pilots were unable to man their posts. The survivors could only have stumbled ashore, more dead than alive, pitiable indeed. Near "some holes of good water" and beneath a large old oak close to the shoreline, the remnants of Vizcaíno's crew raised a ceremonial arbor to serve as a church. There, friars said Mass and asked their Lord to

16. "Voyage of Unamuno," in Wagner, *Spanish Voyages*, 141–151, esp. 147–149; on Cermeño's experience, see 155, 369 n. 8.

17. Engstrand, "Seekers of the 'Northern Mystery,'" in Gutiérrez and Orsi, eds., *Contested Eden*, 91. Some on the expedition, however, no doubt still held out hope of finding the Strait of Anián and Quivira. See "Ascención's Account," in Wagner, *Spanish Voyages*, 180–181, 265–267.

18. For the number of men, see Donald C. Cutter and Iris H. W. Engstrand, *Quest for Empire: Spanish Settlement in the Southwest* (Golden, Colo., 1996), 60.

give wisdom to the expedition's leaders. Vizcaíno and his men decided that one of the ships would return to New Spain with the gravely ill and carry news of the expedition's progress. Reorganizing the ships necessitated a time-consuming shuffling of crew and supplies and must have occupied all of the men's energies. Nearly two weeks after the ships had sailed into Monterey Bay, the *Almirante* and its sickly cargo departed for Acapulco.[19]

Over the eighteen days Vizcaíno anchored at Monterey Bay, Indians came more than once to the Spaniards' camp. It is not clear what the Children of Coyote made of these intruders, of their weak bodies, endless movements from ship to ship, and chants beneath the arbor. Were they the dead returned or simply sick men from an unknown land? No doubt they had heard stories of bearded men who spread disease, carried powerful weapons, unleashed dogs of war, brazenly took water and wood without offering proper compensation, and even kidnapped children and young men. Yet these Spaniards were pale shadows of those. If the Children of Coyote sensed the Spaniards' plight, they responded little to it, giving them hardly any succor, offering only a few animal skins, not the life-sustaining provisions the Spaniards so badly needed or news of other Mexicos that would make their sufferings tolerable.[20]

Several days after the *Almirante* sailed, the Spaniards who remained at Monterey began to behave in ways that the Children of Coyote might have anticipated. Contravening his orders barring overland exploring, Vizcaíno took ten of his arquebusiers to investigate "the lay of the land and its people and animals." Three miles to the south and east of the Spaniards' encampment, they came across the Carmel River, future site of Mission San Carlos. There, Vizcaíno observed, "no people were found because, on account of the great cold, they were living in the interior." Vizcaíno sent five men to an Indian village farther inland but found it "depopulated." Clearly, the Indians had made themselves scarce, fleeing in advance of the Spaniards. Later that night, Vizcaíno and his expedition sailed on.[21]

Vizcaíno would describe Monterey—the discovery of which was the single achievement of his voyage—in glowing terms. He gave every indication that the harbor would make an ideal way station for Spanish ships: "Besides being sheltered from all the winds, it has many pines for masts and yards, and live oaks and white oaks, and water in great quantity, all near the shore." Moreover, the land and its bounty were ideal to replenish the provisions of hungry sailors: "The land

19. "Diary of Sebastian Vizcaíno, 1602–1603," in Herbert Eugene Bolton, ed., *Spanish Exploration in the Southwest, 1542–1706* (New York, 1916), 52–103, esp. 91–92; "Ascención's Account," in Wagner, *Spanish Voyages*, 244.

20. "Diary of Vizcaíno," in Bolton, ed., *Spanish Exploration*, 92; "Ascención's Account," in Wagner, *Spanish Voyages*, 247.

21. "Diary of Vizcaíno," in Bolton, ed., *Spanish Exploration*, 94.

is fertile, with a climate and soil like those of Castile; there is much wild game, such as harts, like young bulls, deer, buffalo, very large bears, rabbits, hares, and many other animals, and many game birds, such as geese, partridges, quail, crane, ducks, vultures, and many other kinds of birds." To Vizcaíno, the Indians seemed as friendly and inviting as the land: "The land is thickly populated with numberless Indians" who "appeared to be a gentle and peaceable people." So general is this description that it suggests Vizcaíno in fact had little interaction with the Children of Coyote. Surely, the desire to move beyond this vague awareness of the land's inhabitants drove Vizcaíno inland, in search of people. But the Indians had fled before his advance.[22]

Despite Vizcaíno's report urging Spanish settlement of the region, Indians of California would barely be troubled by Spaniards for another 165 years. Vizcaíno had discovered Monterey Bay but little else, and his voyage had cost forty-two of his men their lives. In addition, the year 1603, when Vizcaíno completed his explorations, marked the end of the conde de Monterrey's rule. His immediate successor ridiculed the California project and discouraged further explorations.[23] Moreover, the threat privateers posed to the Manila galleons faded, improvements in ship design and construction made a California way station unnecessary, and no wealthy individual stepped forward, eager to risk fortune and reputation on a California enterprise. Until José de Gálvez arrived in New Spain in 1765, the Spanish Crown would do nothing by way of exploration or settlement to shore up its claim to the Pacific coast north of Baja California.

In the intervening years, Indians of California and the Monterey region likely encountered the odd Spanish barque that pulled ashore in search of water and wood en route from the Philippines to Mexico. In 1783, Juan Francisco Pechipechi, an aged man from a village south of Monterey, remembered "when long ago the ship from China used to make port here"; the Spaniards dealt with the Indians, "giving them beads for otter skins, and on one occasion they left on Cypress Point a cask or barrel that they might make use of the iron of the bands."[24] Pechipechi's recollection suggests that, over the century and a half between Vizcaíno's 1603 exploration and Portolá's 1769 possession of Alta California, Monterey Indians had occasional interactions with Spaniards and came to know them as men, not as spirits or gods. Such contact posed little direct threat to Indians. Spaniards arrived rarely and weakened. And they went on their way quickly, as soon as they had taken on water and wood. But the Spaniards'

22. Ibid., 91–92. Buffalo did not exist in the region, but the other animals Vizcaíno listed did.
23. Cutter and Engstrand, *Quest for Empire*, 61.
24. Juan Francisco Pechipechi, San Carlos bapt. no. 834, Oct. 4, 1783.

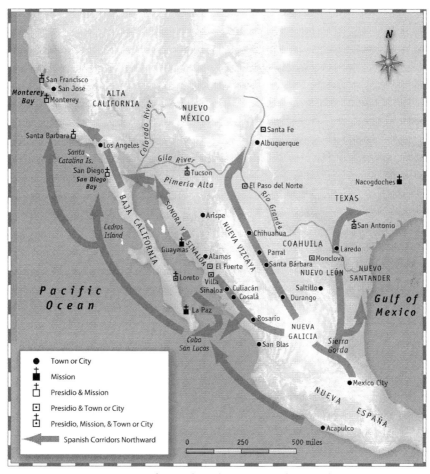

MAP 1. New Spain and Spanish Settlement along the Corridors North,
Late Eighteenth Century. Drawn by Gerry Krieg

periodic landfalls in the Monterey region and the stories California Indians
continued to hear of distant neighbors who suffered plague, invasion, enslavement, kidnapping, beating, and killing, all at the hands of the Spaniards, must
have kept the Children of Coyote keenly aware of the dangers posed by these
seafarers and deeply suspicious of the strangers' ultimate intentions.

Accounts of Spanish depredations rippled toward Alta California for centuries, as legions of Spaniards ventured overland up the interior of New Spain in
a three-pronged advance after the fall of Mexico.[25] Along the Gulf Coast, the
Spanish frontier moved steadily north, eventually as far as Texas. In the west,

25. John Francis Bannon, *The Spanish Borderlands Frontier, 1513–1821* (1963; rpt. New York, 1970), 54.

Spanish settlement expanded through Sonora and Sinaloa and into Baja California. A middle corridor developed north from central Mexico, through the mining areas of Nueva Galicia and Nueva Vizcaya, before it bounded into New Mexico. Large and periodic silver strikes at Zacatecas in the 1540s, Durango in 1563, Santa Bárbara in 1567, Parral in 1631, and finally Chihuahua in the first decade of the eighteenth century gave Spanish settlement north of central Mexico its momentum. On the northern frontier, Spaniards found neither highly concentrated Indian settlements nor the opportunity for easy riches, but they nevertheless established scores of mining and ranching communities that depended upon coerced Indian labor. As the silver frontier expanded north, missionaries often remained behind, attempting to consolidate dispersed and fragmented Indian communities and orient them toward Catholicism, agriculture, and sedentariness. Elsewhere, in the far west and along the Gulf Coast, missionaries were often the vanguard of Spanish advance.

In the 1580s, rumors persisted of the Pueblo Indians' wealth, and Spanish officials believed that a colony in their lands could be supplied from either the Pacific or Atlantic oceans; accordingly, the viceroy of New Spain began a search for someone who would bring these lands into the Spanish realm at little expense to the Crown. Stepping forward was Juan de Oñate, whose father had amassed a fortune in the silver mines of Zacatecas. In 1598, in return for promises from the Crown that he would "receive broad governmental powers" and access to New Mexico's natural resources and Indian labor, Oñate took possession of New Mexico. He was accompanied by ten Franciscan missionaries and an army of some 129 men of fighting age. Relatives of the soldiers, herders, drivers, packers, and servants swelled the expedition's numbers to more than 500.[26]

In their relations with Indians, Oñate and his men were to observe the *Ordinances for the Discovery, New Settlement and Pacification of the Indies* issued by Philip II in 1573. These laws specified that Indians should "of their own will" acknowledge the supremacy of the Spanish monarch and "abandon all that runs contrary" to Catholicism. Specifically, the *Ordinances* endorsed a system of indirect rule: Spaniards were urged to "establish friendship and alliances with the principal lords and head men who would be most useful in the pacification of the land." Indians were promised peace, justice, protection from their enemies, and improvements in their "arts and trades and in their crops and cattle."[27]

26. David J. Weber, *The Spanish Frontier in North America* (New Haven, Conn., 1992), 81–82; Marc Simmons, *The Last Conquistador: Juan de Oñate and the Settling of the Far Southwest* (Norman, Okla., 1991), 93–97.

27. Daniel J. Garr, ed., *Hispanic Urban Planning in North America*, Spanish Borderlands Sourcebooks, XXVII (New York, 1991), 3–33, esp. 29. These regulations replaced the infamous *Requerimiento*

Spanish settlement and colonization in the north rarely if ever followed this blueprint. In New Mexico, Spaniards made themselves unwelcome intruders. They put down Indian resistance with shocking brutality, killing, maiming, or enslaving Indians who defied them. By the early 1600s, Oñate had proved a poor, cruel administrator, and New Mexico had not lived up to its name. Viceroy Luís de Velasco converted New Mexico to a royal colony and recalled Oñate to Mexico City in 1609. Afterward, Spain held the province only in the hopes that it would be a stepping-stone to other conquests, and Franciscan missionaries, who had established missions throughout the region, came to dominate the colonial effort in New Mexico during the seventeenth century.[28]

Along the central corridor as far north as New Mexico, Spanish settlement had been spurred primarily by mineral strikes and the search for easy wealth. To the east of New Mexico, along the Gulf Coast, Spanish expansion was driven by a different motor: the Crown's geopolitical calculations. To protect the important mines of central Mexico from the threat of encroachment by foreign powers—a need that was given urgency in the late seventeenth century by French exploration and tentative settlement of the central Gulf Coast—Spain moved toward establishing a permanent presence in Texas. Once the French set up forts on Biloxi Bay and the Mississippi in 1699 and 1700 and began to use Louisiana as a base for trade with Indians, the viceroy ordered the reoccupation of East Texas. By the end of July 1715, Spain had established a presidio in East Texas and missions among the Hasinai. Three years later, the Spanish governor of Texas created the municipality of San Antonio and a nearby mission and presidio.[29]

To the west of Texas and New Mexico, Spanish settlement slowly crept forward, river valley by river valley, into northern Nueva Vizcaya and the lands adjacent to the Gulf of California. Because the region appeared to offer so few valuable natural resources, it attracted few Spanish settlers, and missionaries put their mark on this frontier by attempting to reorganize Indians into communities according to a Spanish model. This rugged and arid region known to the Spaniards as Sonora and Sinaloa was home to small, autonomous communities of Mayo, Yaqui, Seri, Yuma, Upper Pima, and, farther inland, Tepehuan, Tarahumara, Lower Pima, and Opata. These people, who probably numbered around

---

("requirement"), which had announced to Indians that, if they did not accept subjugation to the Spanish Crown and Roman Catholicism, they would be conquered and perhaps enslaved or even killed. On Oñate, see Weber, *Spanish Frontier*, 77–91; Juan de Oñate, "Act of Obedience and Vassalage by the Indians of Santo Domingo" (1598), in George P. Hammond and Agapito Rey, eds., *Don Juan de Oñate: Colonizer of New Mexico, 1595–1628* (Albuquerque, N.Mex., 1953), part 1, 337–341, esp. 338.

28. Simmons, *Last Conquistador*, 183–185.

29. Weber, *Spanish Frontier*, 161; Bannon, *Spanish Borderlands Frontier*, 115; Jesús F. de la Teja, *San Antonio de Béxar: A Community on New Spain's Northern Frontier* (Albuquerque, N.Mex., 1995).

150,000 prior to Spanish settlement, came into the Spanish colonial world piece-meal, not in large confederations.[30]

In the late seventeenth century, along the edge of the western corridor, Spain opened a related frontier that would be crucial to the eventual settlement of Alta California. Spaniards had known of Baja California since Jiménez's expedition in 1533, but the land's aridity and lack of mineral wealth had discouraged settlement. It would be Jesuit missionaries, the architects of missions in neighboring Sonora and Sinaloa during the seventeenth century, who ultimately brought the Spanish colonial frontier to the barren peninsula. In 1697, the Jesuits began to construct the first of a chain of seventeen missions that eventually stretched from lands south of La Paz to within several hundred miles of the present U.S.–Mexico border. The aridity of the land hindered the growth of missions, and disease rapidly undermined the peninsula's native population, which by the late 1760s had fallen to about seven thousand, less than a fifth of what it had been at the dawn of the eighteenth century.[31]

Across all of these frontiers throughout the seventeenth and eighteenth centuries, the Crown relied on a shifting mixture of religious missions and military fortifications to secure its claim to a wide arc of territory. Yet, by the mid-eighteenth century, this strategy cried out for change as Spain's actual hold on the northern regions remained tenuous. Throughout these lands, missions were in decline, their populations eroded by disease and their padres increasingly eyed with suspicion by the Crown. And military forts, although they had eclipsed Catholic missions as the dominant institution, were poorly staffed and badly organized. Moreover, the few Spanish settlers, soldiers, and priests in the north were greatly outnumbered by natives even after European diseases had thinned their ranks. Nueva Vizcaya, by far the most populous region of northern New Spain, had nearly fifty thousand Hispanic residents in the mid-eighteenth century. In seventeenth-century New Mexico, the number of Spaniards never surpassed 3,000, and they were scattered on small ranches and farms. Not until the late eighteenth century did the non-Indian population of New Mexico approach 20,000, and even then most settlers lived in dispersed river valleys. By the mid-eighteenth century, Sonora's Spanish population hovered around 8,000; all but

30. Edward H. Spicer, *Cycles of Conquest: The Impact of Spain, Mexico, and the United States on the Indians of the Southwest, 1533–1960* (1962; Tucson, Ariz., 1972), 374; Cynthia Radding, *Wandering Peoples: Colonialism, Ethnic Spaces, and Ecological Frontiers in Northwestern Mexico, 1700–1850* (Durham, N.C., 1997), 1–46.

31. Bannon, *Spanish Borderlands Frontier*, 54–60; Harry W. Crosby, *Antigua California: Mission and Colony on the Peninsular Frontier, 1697–1768* (Albuquerque, N.Mex., 1994); Weber, *Spanish Frontier*, 241.

600 of these lived south of today's U.S.–Mexico border. In Texas, in the late eighteenth century, Spaniards numbered only about 2,500. Baja California held only 842 non-Indians in 1790.[32]

Reorganization and renewed attention to the northern rim of New Spain would come only in the wake of Spain's humiliating defeat in the Seven Years' War. England had seized Havana during the war and acquired Florida in the peace settlement of 1763. After the war, Spain needed to protect its newly acquired territory of Louisiana, which it had received from France. As an indication of his resolve, Carlos III sent a special envoy, the marqués de Rubí, to inspect the defenses of the northern frontier and plan their restructuring. Rubí called for a line of evenly spaced presidios—some fifteen in all—to protect the frontier from Indian raids and European rivals. He also proposed administrative reforms to improve military effectiveness and reduce Crown expenditures. His reorganization, however, in particular the shuffling of presidios and their soldiers, served only to further overextend and thus weaken Spanish military defenses. After this failure, Spain sought to accomplish by peace what it could not impose through war. Spanish officials pursued alliances with Comanches and other Indians against the Apaches, and they ultimately tried to win over the Apaches and other Indians of the north through trade, treaties, and gift giving. These policies bore fruit; by the 1780s, a "mantle of peace" had settled over the frontier from Texas to Sonora.[33]

If addressing Indian threats to the security of the northern frontier had demanded bold policy, countering European challenges required bolder plans still. The driving force to protect northern New Spain from rival nations was José de Gálvez, whom Carlos III sent to New Spain in 1765 as his *visitador general,* or inspector general. Skilled and knowledgeable, Gálvez carried enormous authority, surpassing to a degree that of even the viceroy. He and other Spanish officials feared that the English might move west across North America and thereby threaten northern New Spain. The English, they reckoned, might even sail into the Pacific if they found the fabled Northwest Passage. The Russian search for sea otter pelts in the north Pacific and accounts of Russian exploits in that region further alarmed Spanish officials. Gálvez proposed strengthening the military defenses of the western corridor as a base to extend Spain's power farther into the

32. Max L. Moorhead, *The Presidio: Bastion of the Spanish Borderlands* (Norman, Okla., 1975), 1–46. On the population of the provinces of the far north, see Weber, *Spanish Frontier,* 90, 195, 206, 209; Jesús Tamayo Sánchez, *La ocupación española de las Californias (una interpretación del primer impulso urbanizador del noroeste mexicano a partir de algunas fuentes históricas)* (Mexico City, 1992), 68.

33. On Rubí's proposals and their implementation, see Weber, *Spanish Frontier,* 215–222; Moorhead, *Presidio,* 58–61. See also Weber, 224–235, esp. 234.

northwest, and he argued for the incorporation of Sonora, Nueva Vizcaya, and Baja California into one administrative unit. Finally, and most important, he proposed to occupy Alta California.[34]

THE EXPEDITIONS OF GÁLVEZ

In the spring of 1768, Gálvez's desire to plant the Spanish flag in Alta California took on added urgency. Rumor suggested Russian settlement of the region had begun. Taking no chances, the viceroy ordered Gálvez to secure the province. By July, Gálvez had traveled to Baja California to oversee the occupation of Monterey. At that time, the peninsula was in transition, its missions reeling from the Crown's expulsion of the Jesuits from Spain and its colonies. Only recently had missionaries arrived to replace the Jesuits, who had not departed until early in 1768.

Leading the Franciscans into Baja California was Junípero Serra, formerly a university professor in Spain and now a missionary to Indians of the Sierra Gorda. It was there that Serra had won praise as a skilled administrator and ardent missionary. Like Serra, the governor of Baja California, Gaspar de Portolá, was a new arrival to the peninsula. Neither would call Baja California home for long. Both were soon headed to Alta California, Serra to oversee the foundation of missions and Portolá to lead the military expedition that would take the territory for Spain.

Gálvez planned five expeditions from Baja California to Alta California—three by sea and two by land. All were to rendezvous in San Diego; from there, a smaller contingent would continue to Monterey and take possession of the harbor and all of Alta California. Forgotten or ignored were lessons learned centuries earlier by Cabrillo and Vizcaíno about the difficulty of reaching Alta California by sea. The *San Carlos* sailed on January 9, 1769; the *San Antonio* followed five weeks later. Buffeted by heavy seas and contrary winds, the *San Antonio* reached San Diego Bay on April 11, after fifty-five days at sea. Nearly all on board were sick and disabled by the voyage, but no lives had been lost. The men of the *San Carlos* were less fortunate. The ship's water was bad, and the pilot misread his charts and sailed north beyond San Diego. On April 29, 111 days out of La Paz, the *San Carlos* dropped anchor in San Diego Bay. By then, twenty-four of the crew had died of scurvy; the rest were gravely ill. Greater misfortune struck a third Spanish ship sent in support of the original land and sea expeditions. On

34. Bannon, *Spanish Borderlands Frontier*, 153–154.

June 16, the *San José* had sailed from Loreto with men and supplies, never to be seen again.[35]

The overland expeditions fared better. The first arrived at San Diego in the middle of May. The second, commanded by Portolá and including Serra, reached the harbor on July 1, 1769. The march north from Velicatá had taken the expeditions fifty-one and forty-eight days, respectively. When the overland parties arrived at San Diego, they found the Spaniards in desperate condition. The men of the sea expedition were ill and "as good as immobilized." Over the next few months, twenty-nine soldiers would die from illness and be buried on shore. All told, a fourth of the nearly three hundred men who set out for California in 1769 perished. In early July, with only eight of the twenty-eight sailors who had made the voyage to San Diego able to sail, the *San Antonio* returned to San Blas for supplies. The colonists at San Diego—missionaries, soldiers, servants, sailors, and Baja California Indians—now numbered fewer than one hundred.[36]

San Diego was only a stepping-stone to the principal goal of the expeditions: reaching Monterey and taking possession in the name of the king. Thus, on July 14, despite the weakness of his men and their dwindling provisions, Portolá and sixty-two others marched north. Six months later, they straggled back into San Diego, having failed to find the harbor of Monterey.[37]

The search for Monterey was a trial that revealed the Spaniards' growing dependence upon the Indians. Indians along much of the journey largely determined whether and what the men of the expedition ate and drank and where and when they marched and camped. Portolá had departed San Diego with thin provisions, assuming that finding Monterey would prove unproblematic and that he would encounter the *San José* somewhere along the way and thereby resupply his men. The loss of the *San José* doomed the expedition to privation; the elusiveness of the harbor prolonged the men's sufferings by months. Indians, in a range of ways, kept the expedition from disintegrating.

Portolá was in command of the party, but most likely Baja California Indians marched at the head of its long train of soldiers and animals. These men had come north as interpreters, but here, beyond the reach of their languages, they were pressed into service to clear a path for the expedition. To them also fell the

35. Chapman, *History of California,* 221–223; Serra to Francisco Palóu, San Diego, July 8, 1769, in Tibesar, ed. and trans., *Writings of Serra,* I, 141–142; Bannon, *Spanish Borderlands Frontier,* 155. Another account suggests that the ship was damaged by storms, returned to San Blas for repairs, and sailed north from Cabo San Lucas in May 1770 before disappearing.

36. Chapman, *History of California,* 223–224; Fernando Boneu Companys, *Gaspar de Portolá: Explorer and Founder of California,* trans. and ed. Alan K. Brown (Lérida, Spain, 1983), 393; Palóu, *Historical Memoirs,* ed. and trans. Bolton, II, 265.

37. Juan Crespí, "Diary of the First Expedition," in Palóu, *Historical Memoirs,* ed. and trans. Bolton, II, 107.

responsibility of making first contact with local Indian groups, who, in turn, often fed Portolá's men and guided them through their lands. With almost monotonous predictability during the summer months, Indians north of San Diego met the Spaniards as they entered their territory. Warriors came first, bows at hand but unstrung, suggesting peaceful intent but readiness for action. Speeches followed and interactions proceeded peacefully.[38]

To many of the Indians, the interlopers' desires must have seemed clear and manageable, an inconvenience but not a gross imposition; Spaniards wanted food, water, and a place to rest themselves and their animals before moving on. Having deduced the foreigners' intentions, most Indians proved cooperative, showing the way to fresh water, offering foods for purchase, and, most important, suggesting the best route north and out of their lands. Frequently, to the south of the Monterey region, villagers appeared before Portolá with baskets brimming with seeds, fruits, and, occasionally, fish. Sometimes they brought bowls of gruel or soup. These were not gifts, and neither Spaniards nor Indians considered them so. The Indians were demonstrating the bounty of their lands and their ability to manage them, and they expected compensation for what they were ready to offer the Spaniards. Portolá and his men came prepared for just such barter, having brought an abundance of strings of multicolored beads. That the Indians valued these beads is clear: to one diarist, they "yearned" for them, treasured as they were for their color and exchange value within native society. Supplementing their meager food stores through regular if not daily barter with local Indians, Portolá and his men trudged north through July, August, and September.[39]

During the months of summer and early fall, as Indian granaries filled with recently harvested seeds and as people celebrated their plenty through song and dance, the exchange of surplus foods for glass beads proved easy. Later, it became constrained, as fall gave way to winter and as Indians set afire their seed-producing lands and moved inland beyond the reach of the expedition and the coastal fogs. Then most California Indians looked to their surpluses to see themselves through lean months.

At the same time that California Indians were becoming more protective of their own food stores, Portolá's men were growing alarmed at the near exhaus-

38. For such interactions, see the daily log kept by Juan Crespí, Feb. 26, 1769–July 14, 1769, in Alan K. Brown, ed. and trans., *A Description of Distant Roads: Original Journals of the First Expedition into California, 1769–1770* (San Diego, Calif., 2001), 170–257.

39. Ibid., Aug. 31, 1769, 461. For the beads, see the inventories in Boneu Companys, *Documentos secretos,* between pages 16–17 and 64–65. For the general practice of Spanish soldiers' dispensing glass beads to Indians in California, see Dennis H. O'Neil, "The Spanish Use of Glass Beads as Pacification Gifts among the Luiseño, Ipai, and Tipai of Southern California," *Pacific Coast Archaeological Society Quarterly,* XXVIII, no. 2 (Spring 1992), 1–17.

tion of their own provisions. For most of November, the fruitless search for Monterey dragged on, and soldiers were forced to subsist on a daily allotment of five tortillas and "nothing else." Officers and priests subsisted on a daily ration of two tortillas and some dried fish purchased from the Chumash on the march north. Baja California Indians and muleteers, when faced with lesser rations, deserted. By late December, some soldiers had begun to pilfer what provisions remained, leading Portolá to divide the rest among all before it was stolen by a few. An occasional bear or goose the soldiers killed added to the meager diet. Mules, with nothing left to carry, suddenly looked appetizing. Every third day, another was butchered to feed the men. Yet it was food occasionally purchased from local Indians, not the flesh of slain mules, that sustained Portolá and his men as they deliberately marched back to San Diego "in the midst of the utter want of provisions." On January 24, 1770, the party arrived in San Diego. There, Father Juan Crespí, holding a tortilla in his hands, something he "had not had for many a day," forgot all the privations of the journey and sated his hunger. Later, he would pray that all of the country he had traveled through north of San Diego would be "won to the bosom of the Holy Church."[40]

EARLY CONTACTS AND UNDERSTANDINGS

At San Diego during Portolá's absence, keeping locals from attacking the fledgling Spanish settlement had taken precedence over winning them to the Holy Church. On July 16, 1769, two days after the overland party headed for Monterey, Serra had established Mission San Diego, the first Catholic mission in Alta California. The father president, two other missionaries, and a handful of men, when not busy caring for the sick, raised a few humble huts, one of which was to serve as a temporary chapel. But, with the exception of one young boy, upon whom the missionaries lavished attention, the Ipai "manifested great dissatisfaction and ill-will toward" the Spaniards. Sensing the weak pulse of the colonial effort, the Ipai approached the Spaniards' encampment with little apparent fear and with no respect. According to one missionary chronicler, they set about stealing what was not given to them and "greatly disturbing the poor sick men who were lying under the brush shelters." On August 15, some twenty Indians attacked precisely at the moment when the guard had been reduced to only two soldiers, the others being away at the harbor or attending to the horse herd. By then, Spaniards of one stripe or another had been at San Diego for four months. During that time,

40. Crespí, Nov. 28–Dec. 9, Dec. 20, 1769, Jan. 24, 1770, in Brown, ed. and trans., *Description of Distant Roads*, 631, 639, 671.

they had grown steadily less formidable, as illness carried off many and as others sailed south on the *San Antonio* or ventured north with Portolá.[41]

No doubt the Indians' intent in attacking was not to kill but rather to plunder and humiliate. Apparently, the Ipai set about stripping the clothing off the weak and convalescing Spaniards. When two soldiers returned, a fracas broke out. Four soldiers shot three Indians dead; other Ipai fled wounded. One servant boy was killed from an arrow to the throat, and several other Spaniards were injured. After these hostilities and the casualties on both sides, Indians and Spaniards drew inward. The soldiers constructed a wooden defensive stockade around themselves and sought to prevent the approach of any armed Indians. Only the young boy came to the mission, but now less frequently. More hospice for ailing soldiers than mission to the Ipai, Mission San Diego was yet to record its first Indian baptism when Portolá came back from his failed attempt to find Monterey in January 1770.[42]

Returned to San Diego, Portolá's men kept one eye on the Ipai and the other on the horizon, eagerly anticipating the appearance of the *San Antonio* with its promise of flour, corn, beans, dried meat, and other life-sustaining and culturally affirming supplies. From the Ipai, they had received no aid, no trays of seeds or baskets of fish like those other Indians had provided them on the trail to Monterey. Days passed without the ship's arrival. Unbeknownst to the forlorn at San Diego, the *San Antonio* had sailed for Monterey. Portolá contemplated abandoning San Diego just as Cortés had abandoned Santa Cruz more than two centuries earlier, setting March 20, 1770, as the day he and his men would retreat to Baja California unless the *San Antonio* had arrived. They had come to discover, explore, and take possession, he reasoned, not to starve. Father Serra made his own plans to see the undertaking through to the end. On the nineteenth, the appearance of the *San Antonio,* its decks visibly laden with provisions, breathed new life into the fledgling colony. Bad weather prevented the vessel from entering the harbor until the twenty-fourth. Nevertheless, the colony had been saved. On April 17, Portolá set out overland once again in search of Monterey, but this time with only thirty others; the previous day, the *San Antonio* had set sail for the elusive harbor with Serra on board. Six weeks later, Serra and Portolá, together on the beach in Monterey, claimed Alta California as a Spanish possession.[43]

41. Palóu, *Historical Memoirs,* ed. and trans. Bolton, II, 268; Serra to Andrés, Feb. 10, 1770, in Tibesar, ed. and trans., *Writings of Serra,* I, 151.

42. Palóu, *Historical Memoirs,* ed. and trans. Bolton, II, 266–272.

43. On the padres' plans to stay at San Diego, see Brown, ed. and trans., *Description of Distant Roads,* 677. For the number thirty, see AGN, Indiferente de Guerra, CLXI–b, 157a–157b. For the number twenty-nine, see Apr. 16, 17, 1770, in Brown, ed. and trans., *Description of Distant Roads,* 679.

Portolá's two expeditions gave the Children of Coyote extended opportunities to form impressions of Spaniards in the year before the act of possession at Monterey Harbor. To them, the sight of Spaniards inland and on horseback must have been arresting and confusing. But some Indians nevertheless must have found these men familiar, nearly always in need of food to sustain themselves and their animals, and hence still akin to the weak and sick men who had come generations earlier. Clearly, though, most of the Monterey Indians' actions suggest that they found Portolá's men to be an imposition and a frightful appearance.

As summer was giving way to fall, the first Portolá expedition approached and then entered the Monterey region. Through late September and mid-October, the expedition marched north up the Salinas Valley, beyond Monterey, across the Pajaro River, and along the coast toward Santa Cruz. All the while, the expedition's leaders scrutinized Vizcaíno's descriptions of Monterey, knowing that they were near the fabled bay but unable to find it. Two and a half months out of San Diego, the expedition was lost and losing steam by the day. Provisions were running low. Days dawned cold, foggy, and wet. Spirits flagged. And Indian hospitality was fading as fast as summer. On September 26, 1769, east of the Santa Lucia Mountains and at the southern end of the Salinas Valley, Portolá's men were met by a large group of Salinan Indians bearing seeds and pine nuts for barter. Doubtless, they had heard of the group's approach and perhaps even encountered its advance scouts. After an exchange of seeds for beads, the Salinans guided the expedition to a safe crossing of the Salinas River and watched it pass from their lands. That would be the last amicable encounter between Portolá's men and local Indians for nearly a month.[44]

Four days later and farther north, a group of Chalon Indians hunting came upon the Spaniards' encampment. The Chalon resisted entreaties to trade and "commenced to throw handfuls of earth into the air and play on a pipe." This brief act of defiance—one that men like Portolá might have read as the Indians' statement that they possessed this land—shocked Spaniards who had grown accustomed to seeing California Indians approaching, food in hand, at the wave of a white cloth or a string of beads. Some of the Indians' hostility might have been seasonal: now, it was fall, a time to protect the village rather than welcome strangers into it. Markers of the change in the seasons were everywhere to be seen, not just in the Indians' wariness but in the fields, meadows, and grasslands their fires had blackened. With little food to spare, and therefore hardly any inclination to trade, most Indians of the Monterey region avoided the expedition during the winter months. As Portolá's party moved northward through the

---

44. Crespí, Sept. 26, 1769, in Brown, ed. and trans., *Description of Distant Roads*, 525–529.

Salinas Valley in early October, days passed without the Spaniards' seeing one Indian. Well-trod footpaths, however, testified to the natives' presence and their intense use of the land.[45]

Beyond the simple desire to preserve food stores and avoid Spanish requests to barter, the Indians of Monterey probably avoided the expedition out of fear. The soldiers' growing illness and incapacitation would have given the Children of Coyote reason to afford these men a wide berth. Just as Portolá's men entered the Monterey region, some displayed symptoms of advanced scurvy: acute weakness, foul breath, bloody noses, vomiting fits, gaunt features, and pale, bruised, and splotchy skin. On October 8, in the heart of Ensen territory, two soldiers received last rites. Two days later, the group halted on account of "the great many sick men." Then the body of the expedition stalled north of Watsonville for four days so scouts could search for Monterey, the sick could recuperate, and the healthy could construct special saddles with backrests to support men so weakened that they could no longer sit upright. The Children of Coyote might well have concluded that sick, stinking, and bruised men who had to be lifted up into their saddle chairs were well worth avoiding. And the soldiers' ghastly appearances might have even led the Indians to wonder whether these were indeed men or spirits.[46]

From mid-October to mid-November, the Portolá expedition looked for Monterey in the San Francisco Bay Area. On November 11, the group "came head about astern" and traveled south toward Point Piños, reaching San Jose Creek on November 28. By then, the soldiers' scurvy seems to have abated. Now, Portolá's men were in the heart of Rumsen territory, very close to where Mission San Carlos would soon take shape. Exhausted, and so hungry that they set about hunting pelicans and gulls, the soldiers would remain at Carmel Bay until the morning of December 10. Daily, Portolá's scouts tracked through the country in search of clues as to the whereabouts of Monterey Harbor.[47]

During those days, the Rumsen limited their contact with the Spaniards, but

45. Ibid., Sept. 29, 1769, 533–535, esp. 535. The Chalon were a small Costanoan group, probably numbering fewer than a thousand at that time. See Richard Levy, "Costanoan," in *HNAI*, VIII, 485–495, esp. 485. One diarist on the expedition commented, "These are the only people of whom we have observed such behavior along the whole way since San Diego, for all of the ones met with us as far as here have stayed with us, always very friendly and tractable, making us free of whatever they possessed" (Crespí, Sept. 29, 1769, in Brown, ed. and trans., *Description of Distant Roads*, 533–535). On signs of the change in season, see, for example, ibid., Sept. 28, Oct. 16, 27, 1769, 531–533, 563–565, 583–585.

46. For the men's symptoms, see ibid., Oct. 8–15, 1769, 551–563, esp. 557, 561. Days after the two men were given last rites, another three received them. All recovered (559). On scurvy and its symptoms, see "Scurvy," in Kenneth F. Kiple, ed., *The Cambridge World History of Human Disease* (Cambridge, 1993), 1971–1973.

47. Crespí, Nov. 11, 1769, in Brown, ed. and trans., *Description of Distant Roads*, 611; Crespí, Nov. 30, 1769, in Palóu, *Historical Memoirs*, ed. and trans. Bolton, II, 229–230.

their few interactions are revealing and might even have been formative. Immediately upon the expedition's arrival at San Jose Creek, a "good-sized" Indian village nestled along the same stream fled in a panic, "some of them running leaving their fires still burning." A day later, some fifty Indians approached the Spaniards with bows and arrows and baskets of food. Cautiously, a dozen men entered the camp while other villagers remained warily on an adjacent hill. Neither welcoming party nor war party, this was an attempt by the Rumsen to provide the Spaniards with food and to spur their departure. The Rumsen explained that they were encamped a half-league away and had come only to offer food. After exchanging two very large baskets of pinole for beads, the Indians departed, giving the polite but hardly credible excuse that they had far to travel. Years later, a Rumsen boy explained why the Indians had fled and largely stayed away from the Spaniards: elders had told that the Spaniards "had come from below the earth . . . and were the souls of their old gentile ancestors, who had come back in that form." Clearly, these souls from the underworld were to be placated and then avoided.[48]

Two baskets of grain divided among all Portolá's men went quickly, as it was in these days that the expedition subsisted on a small daily ration of thin tortillas. Concluding that Monterey Bay had been hidden or destroyed by the passage of time, the explorers resolved to return to San Diego. Three days later, on December 10, they broke camp. Yet, before leaving, they erected a large wooden cross so that any Spanish ship might know they had been there, and at the foot of the cross they buried a letter in a bottle saying so. A similar cross was raised just north, across Point Piños. The Spaniards were back in Monterey five and a half months later, fewer in number but healthier in body. This time, Portolá and his scouts quickly recognized the harbor of Monterey.[49]

In the months between Portolá's departure and his return, the Rumsen tried to make sense of the large wooden crosses left by the Spaniards. They adorned the arms of one cross with "sardines, small pieces of venison, and feathers," and they placed at its foot "many broken arrows." They did so out of fear, one Rumsen recounted, "to keep it from harming them." Perhaps the Indians had made the connection between the crosses in their midst and the stories of conquest that had come from afar. The Rumsen had come to believe that, at night, the cross rose in the sky, where it shone bright and beautiful, like the sun. No doubt wary

---

48. Crespí, Nov. 29–Dec. 9, 1769, in Brown, ed. and trans., *Description of Distant Roads*, 631. Crespí dates the encounter as Nov. 30 (Palóu, *Historical Memoirs*, ed. and trans. Bolton, II, 228–230). He says it occurred after "four or five days" of the Spaniards' being encamped. For the Rumsen boy's explanation, see Serra to Francisco Pangua, July 18, 1774, in Tibesar, ed. and trans., *Writings of Serra*, II, 112–113 (my trans.).

49. Crespí, Dec. 5, 10, 1769, in Palóu, *Historical Memoirs*, ed. and trans. Bolton, II, 232, 236–239.

of the newly returned and cross-carrying Spaniards, the Rumsen again at first avoided Portolá and his men. Four days after Portolá had reestablished a camp at San Jose Creek, the Rumsen cautiously approached and exchanged grains for beads, but only after the Spaniards had dispersed their horse herd. The Indians pledged to return again in four days with additional food. Two days later, and two days before the ceremony of possession, the Rumsen brought for trade three deer and a sack of pinole. This generosity was most likely in large measure an attempt to urge these souls onward; it did not herald a warming of relations between the Indians and the Spaniards.[50]

Fear and intensive food gathering kept the Children of Coyote away from the Spaniards just as Portolá was performing his ceremony of possession at Monterey Harbor. This momentous event, so pregnant with meaning for the Spaniards, probably passed without the Rumsens' notice, occurring as it did on the beach, a place of little interest to the Indians in early summer. At this time, the Children of Coyote would have been widely dispersed along the coast and in the interior valleys, gathering shellfish, collecting seeds and nuts, hunting deer and rabbits, trading with neighboring groups, beginning the hard work of replenishing stores of food in advance of leaner times.[51]

Had the Indians witnessed the events on the beach, misinterpretation would have been likely. Surely, the Children of Coyote had heard of Spaniards who imposed settlements on Indians, but, other than the soldiers' construction of rude huts near the shore, nothing now suggested that these would do anything other than saddle up or sail away on the ship now in the harbor. The firing of the *San Antonio*'s cannon and guns, the shouting and parading of men up and down the beach, the brandishing of firearms, crosses, flags, and standards, the ringing of bells—all of the actions Spaniards performed to signal their possession of the land could have been read by the Indians as one noisy and smoky prelude to departure.

COLONIZERS

Having taken possession of Alta California, Spanish officials set out to make the land their own. Gálvez's calculation that missions would be less expensive and easier to establish than presidios meant that Alta California would develop along

---

50. For the Indians' decoration of the cross and beliefs surrounding it, see Serra to Pangua, July 18, 1774, in Tibesar, ed. and trans., *Writings of Serra*, II, 112–113 (my trans.). On the Indians' cautious approach, see Crespí, May 24, 29, 31, 1769, in Brown, ed. and trans., *Description of Distant Roads*, 731, 735, 737.

51. On the Indians' absence, see Palóu, *Historical Memoirs*, ed. and trans. Bolton, II, 294–296. The Indians seem to have avoided the Spaniards well into the month of June.

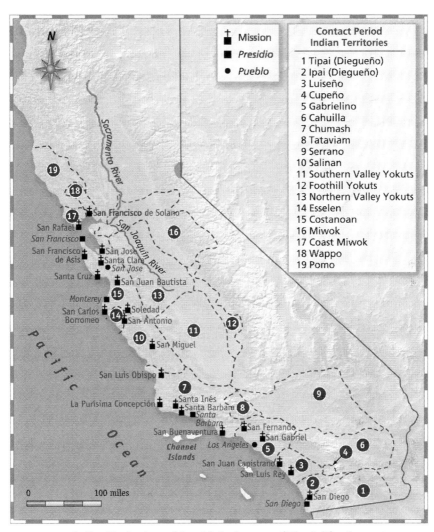

MAP 2. Indian Territories and Spanish Settlements of Alta California, ca. 1823.
Drawn by Gerry Krieg

a familiar trajectory, but one that was now increasingly out of step with developments elsewhere in the Spanish Empire. In Alta California, Spanish colonialism focused on Indians rather than soldiers and settlers, even though during the eighteenth century the Crown had gradually converted most surviving missions in central Mexico and the borderlands to parishes overseen by priests. Under the Bourbon reforms and the policies of men like the marqués de Rubí, the Crown had increasingly emphasized military fortifications, local economic development, and Indian alliances to secure its hold on the northern borderlands. But, to take Alta California quickly and economically, Gálvez needed to act with the tools at his disposal; missions, therefore, not presidios and pueblos, would anchor Spain's colonial effort there. By 1821, when Spanish rule gave way to Mexican independence, more than 70,000 Indians had been baptized in Alta California's twenty missions. Even after more than five decades of demographic disaster brought on by colonization, mission Indians still outnumbered Spanish settlers and soldiers 21,750 to 3,400; missions outnumbered military garrisons by a ratio of five to one and civilian settlements by six to one.[52]

The missionaries who came to dominate so much of Spain's effort in colonial California—all members of the Franciscan order—modeled their lives on that of Saint Francis (1181/82–1226), the son of a wealthy Italian cloth merchant who renounced the high living and concern for social status that had characterized his youth. The Order of Saint Francis (founded in 1209) did not cloister friars in monasteries as monks; rather, it sought to engage the world and reform it by example. By assuming vows of poverty, chastity, and obedience, Franciscans rejected all that was material, corporeal, and individual in an attempt to critique the "vainglories" of the world and "thereby turn society to repentance."[53]

The Children of Coyote remembered their past as marked by advances and retreats. A similar arc characterized the history of the followers of Saint Francis. Early in the conquest of New Spain, Catholic missionaries, in particular the Franciscans, stood at the forefront of the Spanish colonial advance, and they remained active and influential throughout the early colonial period, founding not only numerous missions but apostolic colleges where missionaries trained. Like other Mendicants, such as Augustinians and Dominicans, Franciscans had initially proved attractive to the Crown as it sought to extend its reach in New Spain and live up to its commitment to bring Christianity to the Indians. However, Indian missions were always intended as impermanent, transitional institutions, and as early as 1572 the Crown began to replace the Franciscans in central Mexico with the secular clergy. These efforts reached a peak in the mid-eighteenth century, just before Alta California was established. In 1749, the Crown called for the secularization of all *doctrinas* in the Archdiocese of Mexico. Four years later, the Crown extended this decree throughout Spanish America. For decades, the Franciscans and other missionaries tried to block these royal initiatives, and in

52. David J. Weber, "The Spanish-Mexican Rim," in Clyde A. Milner II, Carol A. O'Connor, and Martha A. Sandweiss, eds., *The Oxford History of the American West* (New York, 1994), 65; Weber, *The Mexican Frontier, 1821–1846: The American Southwest under Mexico* (Albuquerque, N.Mex., 1982), 43–60. Population estimates are for 1820 (Peter Gerhard, *The North Frontier of New Spain* [1982; rpt. Norman, Okla., 1993], 309).

53. Ramón A. Gutiérrez, *When Jesus Came, the Corn Mothers Went Away: Marriage, Sexuality, and Power in New Mexico, 1500–1846* (Stanford, Calif., 1991), 66–71.

some areas they succeeded, but overall these were years of financial crisis and declining influence for the orders. To continue their work among the Indians, the Franciscans were forced to the frontier of the empire, especially its northern periphery, where they moved into all three corridors of the Spanish advance. Alta California would be the Franciscans' final missionary endeavor in New Spain.[54]

Franciscans came to this distant land in relatively small numbers. Nearly all of the 127 Franciscan missionaries who served in Alta California between 1769 and 1833 were born, raised, and educated in Spain. Upon arriving in Mexico, all spent months, if not years, at the College of San Fernando, a Franciscan apostolic college founded in Mexico City in 1734 to recruit, train, and oversee missionaries. These missionaries committed to a minimum of ten years of service, and six in ten would meet or exceed that obligation. Physical hardship and mental illness shortened the terms of some to several years. Many Franciscans, however, served for decades, and they boosted the padres' average length of service in Alta California to almost sixteen years. Fifty-eight Franciscans died in Alta California, two at the hands of California Indians. Others returned to the College of San Fernando, and from there many successfully petitioned to retire in their native land.[55]

For the most part, the Franciscans who created the California mission frontier were themselves new to the colonial enterprise. In a sense, they were novices who came to be surrounded by hundreds and at times thousands of neophytes. As the residence of the father president and the mission closest to the port of Monterey, San Carlos was home, if only briefly, to more than two dozen Franciscans during the colonial period. Of the fifteen who served at Carmel for more than a year, only a few had solid experience as missionaries before coming to California (Table 1). Junípero Serra, chosen by Gálvez as president of the California missions, had already served in that capacity in the missions of the Sierra Gorda, where he had been posted for eight years during the 1750s. José Murguía worked nineteen years in the Sierra Gorda missions and served in Baja California in the aftermath of the Jesuits' expulsion before coming to San Carlos in the mid-1770s. Yet these two were unusual. Most San Carlos missionaries came directly from the

54. William B. Taylor, *Magistrates of the Sacred: Priests and Parishioners in Eighteenth-Century Mexico* (Stanford, Calif., 1996), 84.

55. Only one California missionary was actually born in Mexico. Cantabria, Catalonia, Mallorca, and Aragón sent nearly two-thirds of all the missionaries to Alta California. Spain continued to send large numbers of Franciscans to New Spain through the early nineteenth century; nearly seven hundred came to the viceroyalty between 1790 and 1830. More of these men were affiliated with the College of San Fernando than any other Franciscan institution (Carlos José de Rueda Iturrate, "Envío de misioneros franciscanos a Nueva España, 1790–1830," in *Actas del V congreso internacional sobre los franciscanos en el nuevo mundo [siglos XIX–XX]* [Madrid, 1997], 421–432). For an overview of the Franciscans who served in Alta California, see Maynard Geiger, *Franciscan Missionaries in Hispanic California, 1769–1848: A Biographical Dictionary* (San Marino, Calif., 1969), ix–xi.

TABLE 1. Principal Missionaries of San Carlos

Missionary	Age at Arrival in New Spain	Age at Arrival in Alta Calif.	Years of Missionary Experience before Alta California	Age at Death
Junípero Serra (1713–1784)	35	55	8	70
Juan Crespí (1721–1782)	29	48	15	61
Francisco Dumetz (1734–1811)	36	37	0	77
Fermín Francisco de Lasuén (1736–1803)	23	37	10	67
José Murguía (1715–1784)	n.d.	57	22	68
Matías de Santa Catalina Noriega (1736–1798)	n.d.	43	0	62
José Francisco de Paula Señán (1760–1823)	24	27	0	63
Pascual Martínez de Arenaza (1762–1799)	23	25	0	37
Mariano Payeras (1769–1823)	24	26	0	53
Francisco Pujol (1762–1801)	31	35	0	39
Baltasar Carnicer (1770–n.d.)	23	27	0	n.d.
José Ramón Abella (1764–1842)	31	34	0	77
José Viñals (1759–n.d.)	n.d.	38	0	n.d.
Juan Amorós (1773–1832)	29	30	0	58
Vicente Francisco de Sarría (1767–1835)	37	41	0	67
Average	29	37	n.a.	61

Note: Carnicer, Arenaza, and Noriega returned to Mexico, where they died. All others shown here died in Alta California. Average years of missionary experience before Alta California not calculated, as most Franciscans had none. Missionaries here are in order of arrival in Alta California.

Source: Maynard Geiger, *Franciscan Missionaries in Hispanic California, 1769–1848: A Biographical Dictionary* (San Marino, Calif., 1969), esp. 282–293. Calculations of age and years of missionary experience are my own.

College of San Fernando and in effect learned to be missionaries just as they were teaching Indians how to become Catholic. Despite some differences in age and experience, the Franciscans of colonial California were a homogenous group, sharing a common ideology, religion, training, and upbringing. Of course, they distinguished themselves through temperament and talent, but their strict vows, particularly that of obedience, worked to mute conflict within the order and, by design, to thwart individuality.[56]

By comparison, the soldiers and settlers of Alta California were a diverse and fractious lot. Their origins, economic standing, and social status defy easy characterization. The nine men who ruled Alta California as either *gobernante* or governor were, however, largely of similar background and ideology. All were literate Catholics who, to a varying degree, were regalists: they were protective of the powers of the Spanish Crown, usually to the detriment of the Franciscans' authority. With the exceptions of Fernando de Rivera y Moncada (1774–1777) and José Darío Argüello (1814–1815), who were native to New Spain, all began their careers as young officers and came to the New World in the mid-1760s, in the immediate wake of the Seven Years' War. All but Rivera y Moncada were of noble birth. On average, the gobernantes of Alta California assumed politico-military authority at age fifty following more than a quarter-century of military experience. For all but two, the position came toward the end of both career and life; only Portolá (1769–1770) and Felipe de Neve (1777–1782) achieved promotion after their years in Alta California, and nearly all died within four or five years of the end of their California rule.[57]

Counting soldiers, settlers, and members of their families, probably fewer than a thousand immigrants moved to colonial California, and nearly all of those who did came to the region during its early years. Gálvez's land and sea expeditions left fewer than 100 soldiers in the region; subsequent troop reinforcements increased the number of colonists to some 170 by the end of 1774.[58] Of these 170, 94 lived at the presidio of Monterey or were assigned to the guard at Mission San

56. Geiger, *Franciscan Missionaries in Hispanic California,* app. 2, "List of Franciscan Missionaries Who Served in Upper California, 1769–1848," 282–293. Lasuén and Crespí had also worked in the Sierra Gorda for five and fifteen years, respectively (ibid., 51, 137).

57. As Donald A. Nuttall has explained, "A *gobernante* is an official who is in direct control of a region regardless of his official designation. The term, therefore, is not synonymous with that of governor." Until the capital of the Californias—Baja and Alta—was transferred to Monterey in 1777, the gobernante of Alta California was in theory under the governor, who resided in Loreto; however, in reality the gobernante was independent of him and reported directly to the viceroy. It was not until 1804 that Baja and Alta California had separate governors (Nuttall, "The Gobernantes of Spanish Upper California: A Profile," *California Historical Quarterly,* LI [1972], 253–280, esp. 262 n. 1).

58. William Marvin Mason, *The Census of 1790: A Demographic History of Colonial California* (Menlo Park, Calif., 1998), 19–20, 22, 28. Another 32 Baja California Indians were sent to Alta California in 1772 to help the missionaries.

PLATE 4. *Soldado del presidio de Monterey*. By José Cardero.
1791. Courtesy, Museo de América, Madrid

Carlos. The lack of settlers forced the military to depend on the missions for basic foodstuffs, which in turn led Felipe de Neve to foster agricultural communities in the region, ones that would be populated by Hispanic settlers and provide food for the military. Accordingly, in January 1776, Captain Juan Bautista de Anza, at the behest of Neve, brought some 242 soldiers and settlers to Alta California, including more than 30 families.[59] Their numbers were reinforced in 1781 by a second group of about 230 colonists, recruited by Rivera y Moncada. The first group provided the nucleus for the presidio of San Francisco and Alta

59. Ibid., 28–29. The number of people on the Anza expedition is not agreed upon. Mason places the number at 190 or 191. Here I use the figure stated in Weber, *Spanish Frontier*, 253.

California's first Spanish civilian settlement, San Jose, which was founded in 1777; the second party established the community of Los Angeles in 1781 and the presidio at Santa Barbara the following year. Not until 1819, when an additional 200 soldiers were assigned to Alta California, was there another significant influx of colonists to the region. Thus, nearly all—perhaps 80 percent—of the some 3,500 Hispanic colonists who lived in Alta California in the 1820s descended from those who came to the region between 1769 and 1781.[60]

More than 70 percent of the adult men and women who moved to Alta California originated in the impoverished communities of the northern frontier, specifically in what are now the Mexican states of Sinaloa, Sonora, and Baja California. There was no flow of settlers from Spain; if one excludes the Franciscans, in 1790 there were only ten persons living in California who had been born in Spain, and probably no more than twenty native Spaniards at any time lived in Alta California. One hundred fifteen, or nearly a quarter of the adult colonists in the region in 1790, came from one town, Villa Sinaloa (known today as Sinaloa de Leyva). Roughly ninety more emigrated from the nearby settlements of Alamos, El Fuerte, Culiacán, Cosalá, and Rosario; another fifty-seven came from Baja California. These areas were ripe for an out-migration just as Alta California was in need of settlers. Anza, a presidial soldier who recruited and led many of these settlers overland to California, noted that the inhabitants of Sonora and Sinaloa were "submerged in the greatest poverty and misery."[61] A flood in 1770 had left hundreds, perhaps thousands, homeless in Villa Sinaloa, the mines of the region had been depleted, and Apache and Seri raids restricted the growth of communities across the northwestern frontier. To provide an incentive for potential colonists to relocate to Alta California, the Crown promised a basic subsistence: livestock (mules, horses, and cattle), clothing, two years' pay, and rations for five years. Colonists would be supported at Crown expense as of the day they enlisted, and their transportation to Alta California would also be covered by the Crown.

Ironically, bringing people and animals to Alta California fostered the region's crippling isolation. In 1780, Spaniards had planted two small settlements in the Gila-Colorado junction. In July 1781, Rivera y Moncada, following the route established by Anza only a few years before, escorted a California-bound party of more than two hundred men, women, and children through the region. Just after Rivera y Moncada sent the group ahead, pausing with some of his men to rest

60. For those who arrived in 1781, see Mason, *Census of 1790*, 37–41, 44, 69. There were a few other limited attempts to increase the non-Indian population of Alta California, such as sending convicts, foundlings, or families to the region. Oakah L. Jones, Jr., *Los Paisanos: Spanish Settlers on the Northern Frontier of New Spain*, 218, notes 3 convicts to Monterey in 1791, 22 more in 1798, and 19 orphans in 1800.

61. Mason, *Census of 1790*, 67, 69; Juan Bautista de Anza to Antonio María de Bucareli y Ursúa, Nov. 17, 1774, Mexico, AGN, CA, XXXV, expediente 1, 17.

PLATE 5. *Mujer de un soldado de Monterey (The Wife
of a Monterey Soldier)*. By José Cardero. 1791.
Courtesy, Museo de América, Madrid

their animals, the Yuma rose up over several days, killing Rivera y Moncada,
four missionaries, and most of the soldiers and male settlers living in the recently established communities. The Yuma had begun to chafe under the burden
of Spanish settlement and the pressures of religious missionaries before the
party's passage, but the colonists' demands for food and pasturage seem to have
sparked the revolt. The uprising severed the overland route between California

and Sonora, thereby rendering Alta California in many ways the island that Spaniards in earlier days had believed it to be.[62]

The soldiers and settlers recruited by Anza and Rivera y Moncada were a mixed group, descendants of Indians, Africans, and Spaniards who had worked in the ranches and mines of northern central Mexico. Of the more than two dozen caste terms common to central Mexico's parish records in the colonial period, only five consistently appeared in Alta California: español, mestizo, mulato, *coyote,* and *indio*. In the census of 1790, 46 percent of the non-Indian adults in the region were identified as Spanish, or español, 18 percent as mestizo (half white and half Indian), 17 percent as mulato (half black and half white), 9 percent as indio, and 5 percent as coyote (three-fourths Indian and one-fourth white).[63] Of the 9 percent (forty-five) identified as Indian, twenty-five were from outside Alta California; all but one of the remaining twenty were California Indian women who had married soldiers or settlers (Table 2). These unions were rare and produced very few offspring.[64]

As elsewhere on the northern frontier, Spanish colonial racial and ethnic categories were subjective and the boundaries separating them porous. Men, as they gained promotion in the military or acquired social status, tended to progress from a "darker" caste to a "lighter" one. The changing classifications of Los Angeles's first male settlers were typical: eight appear on the censuses of 1781 and 1790, and seven moved toward a lighter category. Pablo Rodríguez went from indio to coyote, José Antonio Navarro, from mestizo to español; the only man to appear on both lists whose classification did not change was Félix Villavicencio, who was identified on both as español.[65]

In Alta California, being other than español did not carry the same social stigma or legal limitations as in central Mexico. No permanent gulf separated soldiers and settlers identified variously as español, mulato, mestizo, coyote, and indio, although indio was clearly the category to which the least status was attached and not surprisingly one of the least common. Men from all these categories including indio obtained land, served as soldiers, officers, and

62. Bannon, *Spanish Borderlands Frontier,* 185. Weber *(Spanish Frontier,* 257) has the rebellion in June; Mason *(Census of 1790,* 37), Bannon (185), and Chapman *(History of California,* 337) place it in July.

63. Mason, *Census of 1790,* 54. These figures do not include the Franciscans. I have retabulated the information in Mason and have come up with slightly different figures (Mason, 50). Like Mason, I counted the sixteen individuals categorized as *color quebrado, pardo,* and *morisco* as mulato. Color quebrado seems to have been a term used primarily at San Diego. Following Mason, I also considered the three *europeo* individuals as españoles.

64. These totals do not include the several dozen Baja California Indians who lived at the missions and assisted the Franciscans.

65. Mason, *Census of 1790,* 53–54.

TABLE 2. Caste Classifications of Soldiers and Adult Settlers, Alta California, 1790

Caste	TOTAL		MALES		FEMALES	
	No.	% of All	No.	% of Adult Males	No.	% of Adult Females
Español	242	46	161	50	81	41
Mestizo	94	18	61	19	33	17
Mulato	91	17	57	18	34	17
Coyote	25	5	11	3	14	7
Indio						
California	20	4	1	0	19	10
Mexican	25	5	13	4	12	6
Unstated	28	5	21	6	7	4
Total	525	100	325	100	200	102

Note: California *indios* here are those attached to soldier and settler families, usually by marriage. There were 991 individuals in the California census of 1790. I have included only those age thirteen and older. I have not included two Indian prisoners counted in the census. Under the term *mulato*, I have aggregated individuals classified as *color quebrado, pardo,* and *morisco,* since all are variants that refer to persons of African ancestry. I have counted three *europeos* as *español*. The total percentage of adult females is more than 100 percent because of rounding.

Source: The figures here are derived from my tabulation of the transcripts of the 1790 census found in William Marvin Mason, *The Census of 1790: A Demographic History of Colonial California* (Menlo Park, Calif., 1998), 77–105.

municipal officials, and married women of different castes. In day-to-day life, the most important distinction at work in Alta California was cultural rather than racial or ethnic: the division of the population into two groups, Indians and *gente de razón* (literally, "people of reason," as the soldiers and settlers of California called themselves). Mexican Indians and others descended from mixed parentage, who spoke Spanish and dressed and acted more or less as Spaniards, were considered gente de razón, and they achieved rank and status.[66] With the possible exception of the handful who married soldiers and settlers, the Indians of California were seen by the gente de razón as their inferiors, as children, as people unable to reason for themselves. They were relegated to the bottom of the social hierarchy, with all of the discriminations attendant upon that position.

No Hispanic women came to Alta California before 1774, a fact that no doubt contributed to some California Indians' conclusion that the soldiers were the

66. On this point, see Mason, *Census of 1790,* 61.

offspring of their mules. And, long after the arrival of the two groups of settlers in 1776 and 1781, males continued to predominate. In 1790, males constituted 58 percent of the Hispanic population and 62 percent of its adults.[67] The military garrison at Monterey had an even more lopsided ratio of men to women: 65 percent of its adults were men, a figure that would have been even higher had some soldiers not married local Indian women. These numbers suggest that Alta California was among the most masculine of New Spain's northern communities in the late eighteenth century, which is understandable given its recent foundation and the strong presence of the military. In Texas, by comparison, 55 percent of the adult population was male in 1790; in New Mexico at that time, men and women were evenly balanced.[68]

The predominance of men would shape many aspects of life in Alta California for both Indians and colonists. Whereas it was customary in New Spain for Spanish men to marry at a later age than women, in Alta California the excess of men accentuated this trend; it follows that a higher percentage of adult women would be married than adult men. As Table 3 shows, 89.5 percent of adult women in Alta California were married, whereas only 56.6 percent of adult males were married. But there was more at work here than men's simply delaying marriage until they were in their twenties and had achieved a degree of status and economic independence. Brides were in very short supply in Spanish California, as unmarried men outnumbered unmarried women 129 to 12. The shortage of appropriate brides in California meant that women married especially young, just after menarche, and widows remarried quickly unless they were advanced in age. Not all men could marry, therefore, and those who married did so in their mid-to-late twenties or thirties. Although the majority of men eventually married, nearly all remained single through adolescence and much of their early adulthood; fewer than 2 in every 10 men under age twenty-five were married in

67. On the mule offspring theory, see Serra memorandum, June 22, 1774, and Serra to father guardian and discretorium, July 18, 1774, both in Tibesar, *Writings of Serra*, II, 87, 111. I have used Mason's transcription of the 1790 census but have relied on my own tabulations. Thus, the figures on the number of men and women in the region, their marital status, and their racial-ethnic identities are my own. In the following paragraphs, I have asked questions similar to those of scholars who have examined the populations of Texas and New Mexico in the late colonial period; my goal is not only to describe the characteristics of California's colonist population but to do so in a way that facilitates comparison between regions. Most of my comparisons are drawn from Alicia Vidaurreta Tjarks, "Comparative Demographic Analysis of Texas, 1777–1793," rpt. in David J. Weber, ed., *New Spain's Far Northern Frontier: Essays on Spain in the American West, 1540–1821* (Albuquerque, N.Mex., 1979), 137–169; Tjarks, "Demographic, Ethnic, and Occupational Structure of New Mexico, 1790," *The Americas*, XXXV (1978), 45–88.

68. Tjarks, "Comparative Demographic Analysis of Texas," in Weber, ed., *New Spain's Far Northern Frontier*, 144–147, tables 2, 3; Tjarks, "Demographic, Ethnic, and Occupational Structure of New Mexico," *The Americas*, XXXV (1978), 62–66, tables 3, 4, 5.

TABLE 3. Marital Status of Soldier-Settler Population, Alta California, 1790

		MEN					
		Married		Widowers		Unwed	
	No. (N)	No.	% of N	No.	% of N	No.	% of N
California	325	184	56.6	12	3.7	129	39.7
Monterey	72	40	55.6	2	2.8	30	41.7

		WOMEN					
		Married		Widows		Unwed	
	No. (N)	No.	% of N	No.	% of N	No.	% of N
California	200	179	89.5	9	4.5	12	6.0
Monterey	38	34	89.5	3	7.9	1	2.6
Total (Men and Women)	525	363	69.1	21	4.0	141	26.9

Note: Here I include individuals age thirteen and over. I have not included two prisoners and two individuals whose sex was not stated. California totals include Monterey individuals. Because some married men came to Alta California without their wives, there are more married men than women in this table.

Source: The figures here are derived from my tabulation of the transcripts of the 1790 census found in William Marvin Mason, *The Census of 1790: A Demographic History of Colonial California* (Menlo Park, Calif., 1998), 77–105.

1790 (Table 4). These unwed men not only placed sexual demands on California Indian women but came to rely on them as domestic servants as well.[69]

RINGING BELLS AND RISING WATERS

When word of the Spanish occupation of Monterey reached the capital of Mexico in the summer of 1770, these developments and others more dark were still years off. In Mexico City, the news of the taking of Alta California elicited celebrations, and church bells throughout the great city rang out. So that all the inhabitants of New Spain might rejoice in the knowledge that a new province had been added to the Spanish realm, the viceroy ordered the printing of a report on the new foundations in Monterey. This report was a fantasy, a thinly veiled rendering of

69. See Gutiérrez, *When Jesus Came,* 271–281; Colin M. MacLachlan and Jaime E. Rodríguez O., *The Forging of the Cosmic Race: A Reinterpretation of Colonial Mexico,* exp. ed. (Berkeley, Calif., 1990). On the ratio of unmarried men to unmarried women, see Gloria E. Miranda, "Gente de Razón Marriage Patterns in Spanish and Mexican California: A Case Study of Santa Barbara and Los Angeles," *SCQ,* LXIII (1981), 1–21.

TABLE 4. Percentage of Unmarried Men and Women among the Soldier-Settler
Population, Alta California, 1790

	MEN			WOMEN		
Age Group	N	Unmarried	% of N	N	Unmarried	% of N
13–24	94	82	87.2	77	12	15.6
25–39	137	41	29.9	94	2	2.1
40–49	57	9	15.8	19	3	15.8
50+	37	9	24.3	10	4	40.0
Total	325	141	43.4	200	21	10.5

Note: Here I include individuals age thirteen and over. I have not included two prisoners and two individuals
  whose sex was not stated.
Source: The figures here are derived from my tabulation of the transcripts of the 1790 census found in
  William Marvin Mason, *The Census of 1790: A Demographic History of Colonial California* (Menlo Park,
  Calif., 1998), 77–105.

how Spanish officials wished to portray their empire's expansion. Although Indians had been notably absent from the ceremony of possession and the establishment of Mission San Carlos, almost certainly had no sense of the Spaniards'
intent to colonize their lands, and were clearly not always welcoming, the report
proclaimed that the Spanish occupation of Monterey had been of "special satisfaction" to "the innumerable heathen Indians who inhabit all the country." The
Indians reportedly had allowed the Spaniards to feel as safe "as though they were
in the heart" of the Mexican capital and had promised to give their "children to
be instructed in the mysteries" of the Catholic religion. The viceroy's report
neglected the human costs of the expeditions to Monterey, glossing over the fact
that, after the men triumphantly raised the cross and before they said Mass, they
buried another of their own who had died the day before. Nor did the report
point out that other men lay ill or dying farther south, in San Diego, as a result of scurvy and other illnesses they contracted on the lengthy sea voyage to
the region.[70]

But, as surely as the cannon smoke dissipated after the Spanish had taken
possession of Alta California, so too did the promise of easy and rapid conquest.
Indians of California seem to have expressed no enthusiasm for Spanish colonization. Few ever would. At best, some had seemed eager to trade food for beads,
but many, fearing the Spaniards, had steered clear of them and their animals. A
smaller number, like the Ipai, showed no fear and harried and attacked the

70. Donald C. Cutter, "Plans for the Occupation of Upper California: A New Look at the 'Dark Age'
from 1602 to 1769," *Journal of San Diego History,* XXIV (1978), 79–90; Palóu, *Historical Memoirs,* ed.
and trans. Bolton, II, 289, 295–296, 302–303, 305.

Spaniards from their first arrival. In the months and years after the ceremony of possession, Indians of the Monterey region came to interact with Spaniards, learning through daily contact that Spaniards were indeed men, not spirits or the offspring of mules. The Indians' relations with missionaries, soldiers, settlers, and the microbes, crops, animals, and institutions that they brought to California were a world apart from the viceroy's optimistic portrayal. In fact, the crises that followed these potent agents of change bore a resemblance to the nightmare stories of conquest California Indians had heard over generations and through centuries ever since the fall of Mexico. Long before the viceroy's report had been printed and circulated in New Spain, the waters had again begun to rise in the land of Coyote's children.

3

DUAL REVOLUTIONS AND THE MISSIONS
ECOLOGICAL CHANGE AND DEMOGRAPHIC COLLAPSE

In Alta California, there would be no classic military invasion that culminated in the conquest of Indians. Spanish soldiers and Indian warriors did not meet in a climactic battle that decided the fate of the region. Yet the contest for California did involve innumerable battles in villages and throughout the countryside between elements of the Old World and the New. To Alta California, just as elsewhere in New Spain, Spaniards came equipped with unwitting silent armies of pathogens, plants, and animals that rendered them and their institutions nearly invincible. These Old World agents of "ecological imperialism" proved innately suited to the new region and so conquered it with a brutal efficiency, undercutting its peoples and the foods they relied upon through demographic and ecological revolutions that dramatically transformed California's human and natural landscape. At first, these dual revolutions and the Indian response to them precipitated and promoted the efflorescence of Franciscan missions, which initially filled with people and produced surplus foods. But, ultimately, these missions and their Indians would be undone, destroyed by the population collapse that had in part prompted their growth. The story of the rise and fall of the California missions, therefore, suggests the primacy of the biological and ecological forces that to a large degree structured the world in which Indians and Europeans shaped their encounters and communities.[1]

THE ACCIDENTAL GENIUS

European diseases most likely arrived in the Monterey region in the summer of 1769. They might have been first introduced long before, perhaps in 1542 by Juan Rodríguez Cabrillo, in 1602 by Sebastián Vizcaíno, or in the seventeenth or

1. Elinor G. K. Melville, *A Plague of Sheep: Environmental Consequences of the Conquest of Mexico* (Cambridge, 1994), 2; Alfred W. Crosby, *Ecological Imperialism: The Biological Expansion of Europe,*

eighteenth centuries by one of the Manila galleons during an unrecorded stop.[2] But, after the mission and presidio were founded at Monterey in 1770, bringing with them a permanent presence of soldiers and missionaries, pathogens long endemic to Europe easily multiplied and spread through the countryside as they encountered a bountiful population that had no experience with them. These diseases had enormous effects on California Indian communities; they certainly reduced the number of laborers, thinned the leadership ranks, and ultimately forced a change in settlement patterns by helping to push Indians into the missions.[3]

Whether Indians of the Monterey region suffered from epidemic diseases in the first years of Spanish settlement is not clear. However, they came to San Carlos and other missions from villages and communities that were fragmented and frayed, most likely from disease and perhaps from warfare. A significant portion of the young recruits to San Carlos were either orphaned or fatherless; 7.4 percent of those baptized before age fifteen were orphans, and nearly 21 percent were fatherless (Table 5). Every death constituted a tear in the community's social fabric; it was one less parent, one less son or daughter, one less member of a ritual society or clan. Far fewer of the children baptized at Mission San Carlos were motherless than fatherless, a fact that suggests not only that disease and warfare claimed more adult men than adult women but that widows with children especially might have found some aspects of life in the missions preferable to life outside of them. These figures, however, only hint at the social disruption within Indian communities during the early years of Spanish settlement. Many of the Indians' deaths went unrecorded by the Franciscans and are therefore lost to us: children, unmarried adults, and childless widows and widowers—any of these who died without baptism would not have been noted by the Franciscans.

900–1900 (Cambridge, 1986); Jared Diamond, *Guns, Germs, and Steel: The Fates of Human Societies* (New York, 1997). On environmental change in Monterey and Alta California, see Burton L. Gordon, *Monterey Bay Area: Natural History and Cultural Imprints,* 3d ed. (Pacific Grove, Calif., 1996), 56–62; William Preston, "Serpent in the Garden: Environmental Change in Colonial California," in Ramón A. Gutiérrez and Richard J. Orsi, eds., *Contested Eden: California before the Gold Rush* (Berkeley, Calif., 1998), 260–298.

2. Despite a lack of evidence supporting the theory that epidemics preceded Spanish colonization in California, William L. Preston has advanced this hypothesis with vigor and creativity. See his "Portents of Plague from California's Protohistoric Period," *Ethnohistory,* XLIX (2002), 69–121; see also Lisa Kealhofer, "The Evidence for Demographic Collapse in California," in Brenda J. Baker and Kealhofer, eds., *Bioarchaeology of Native American Adaptation in the Spanish Borderlands* (Gainesville, Fla., 1996), 56–92, esp. 56–64.

3. Melville, *A Plague of Sheep,* 5; Alfred W. Crosby, Jr., *The Columbian Exchange: Biological and Cultural Consequences of 1492* (Westport, Conn., 1972); Crosby, "Virgin Soil Epidemics as a Factor in the Aboriginal Depopulation in America," *WMQ,* 3d Ser., XXXIII (1976), 289–299.

TABLE 5. Status of Parents of Gentile Children at Baptism,
Mission San Carlos, 1770–1808

Age Group	Total No. Baptized	FATHER DEAD		MOTHER DEAD		MOTHER AND FATHER DEAD	
		No. Baptized	% of Age Group	No. Baptized	% of Age Group	No. Baptized	% of Age Group
0–9	598	116	19.4	50	8.4	38	6.4
10–14	118	34	28.8	2	1.7	15	12.7
Total	716	150	20.9	52	7.3	53	7.4

Note: I include here only children of Indians of the Monterey region.
Source: Figures are from my database of baptisms, marriages, and burials at San Carlos compiled from the
mission's registers (see Appendix A for methodology).

Although the Franciscans' records only begin to show the losses suffered by Indian communities during colonization, they do allow for a study of the age, sex, and marital status of those who came to the missions. This analysis suggests that a majority of the migrants to Mission San Carlos were perhaps those least confident in their ability to weather the dual revolutions and the sustained upheavals they entailed: the very young, the old, and unmarried women, all of whom comprised more than 70 percent of the gentile baptisms at Mission San Carlos during its decades of recruitment. By and large, the Indians who came to the mission were young: almost half were under age fifteen, and nearly a quarter were under age five (Table 6). Families with many children to feed might have come to rely on mission foodstuffs more rapidly than others. Females constituted about 53 percent of all gentile baptisms and were the majority in nearly every age cohort; males predominated only among Indians between the ages of five and nine, an occurrence perhaps tied to the absence of fathers from many Indian families but also likely related to the Franciscans' intensive recruitment of young boys because of their special importance to the missionary program. Among adults who came to the mission, marriage was a common state, but more so for men than women. Some women might have been widowed and therefore not married at baptism. As in nearly all societies, younger women were more likely to be married than younger men, and older men were more likely to be married than older women (Table 7).

Although the exact date Old World pathogens began to attack the Children of Coyote went unrecorded, the arrival of European animals, namely cattle, mules, horses, and pigs, did not. Spaniards took these from missions in Baja California and brought them on the initial overland expeditions. The presidio at Monterey had horses and mules from its inception in June 1770, and in August 1771 Pedro

TABLE 6. Sex and Marital Status of Gentiles Baptized, Mission San Carlos, 1770–1808

	ALL GENTILES		MALES			
Age Group	No.	%	No.	% of Age Group	No. Married	% Married in Age Group
0–4	349	22.9	165	47.3	0	0.0
5–9	249	16.3	140	56.2	0	0.0
10–14	118	7.7	59	50.0	0	0.0
15–19	151	9.9	73	48.3	8	11.0
20–24	149	9.8	71	47.7	35	49.3
25–29	78	5.1	34	43.6	22	64.7
30–34	86	5.6	36	41.9	22	61.1
35–39	46	3.0	20	43.5	9	45.0
40–44	90	5.9	40	44.4	29	72.5
45–49	29	1.9	14	48.3	9	64.3
50–54	54	3.5	21	38.9	12	57.1
55–59	19	1.2	8	42.1	4	50.0
60–64	56	3.7	23	41.1	11	47.8
65–69	18	1.2	1	5.6	0	0.0
70+	33	2.2	12	36.4	2	16.7
Total	1,525	100.0	717	47.0	163	22.7

Note: Table includes gentiles from the Monterey region baptized at Mission San Carlos through 1808. Table 8 includes all gentiles baptized at Mission San Carlos.

Source: Figures are from my database of baptisms, marriages, and burials at San Carlos compiled from the mission's registers (see Appendix A for methodology).

Fages—the gobernante of Alta California—delivered to the mission a large sow, a large hog, and four piglets.[4] Four months later, the mission accepted eighteen head of cattle, and by then the presidio almost certainly had its own herd. In February 1773, the mission gained twelve mules; six months later it obtained another three mules and eleven horses. Sheep had not been brought to the mission as of 1775, but in all likelihood they were introduced soon thereafter, and, by the end of 1778, there was a small herd of forty-eight sheep at San Carlos. When presented with grasslands containing more food than they had ever needed to maintain their numbers, horses, cattle, and sheep increased in much

4. Francisco Palóu, *Historical Memoirs of New California . . .* , ed. and trans. Herbert Eugene Bolton, 4 vols. (1926; Berkeley, Calif., 1966), I, 50–52; "Libro de cuentas, inventario de la misión," 14a, LDS film 0913303, Mission San Carlos (hereafter cited as San Carlos account book). This document has irregular and at times illegible page numbers. Horses and mules were used for transportation; cattle, for food and labor; and sheep, for wool and food. Pigs were never raised in large numbers at the mission, since the padres considered them dirty and their meat foul.

FEMALES

No.	% of Age Group	No. Married	% Married in Age Group
184	52.3	0	0.0
109	43.6	0	0.0
59	50.0	5	8.5
78	52.0	20	25.6
78	52.3	43	55.1
44	55.7	21	47.7
50	58.1	16	32.0
26	56.5	11	42.3
50	55.5	27	54.0
15	51.7	7	46.7
33	61.1	8	24.2
11	55.6	0	0.0
33	58.9	4	12.1
17	94.4	0	0.0
21	63.6	1	4.8
808	52.8	163	20.2

the same way as would pathogens: they multiplied rapidly and dispersed widely throughout the region. The result was an animal population explosion—an "ungulate irruption"—that emerged from the earliest years of Spanish settlement in Alta California.[5]

By 1783, Mission San Carlos counted some 874 animals: 500 cattle, 110 sheep, 110 goats, 25 pigs, 18 mules, and 111 horses. Indians had built an adobe corral for the sheep and goats and a pen for the pigs, but the larger, more aggressive, and more numerous horses and cattle proved increasingly difficult to contain, and their corrals and stalls were constantly in need of repair and reinforcement. In January 1785, one missionary at San Carlos warned that the cattle herd of 500

5. On the mission's cattle acquisitions, see "Ganado y vacuno," San Carlos account book (no clear page number), and also page 9. On the sheep, see Junípero Serra, Aug. 17, 1775, Monterey, in Tibesar, ed. and trans., *Writings of Serra*, II, 307; Serra, annual report on the missions, Aug. 15, 1779, Mission San Carlos, ibid., III, 355; and see Melville, *A Plague of Sheep*, 6–7, esp. 47–59, for the four stages of the "ungulate irruption." Ungulates are "herbivores with hard horny hooves" (6).

TABLE 7. Indians Married at Baptism, Mission San Carlos, 1770–1808

| | MALES | | | FEMALES | | |
Age Group	No. Baptized	No. Married at Baptism	% Married at Baptism	No. Baptized	No. Married at Baptism	% Married at Baptism
15–24	144	43	30	156	63	40
25+	209	120	57	300	95	32
20–64	267	153	57	340	137	40
15–64	340	161	47	418	157	38

Source: Figures are from my database of baptisms, marriages, and burials at San Carlos compiled from the mission's registers (see Appendix A for methodology).

now posed a threat to the mission's cultivated fields and needed to be reduced.[6] The warning went unheeded and the herd's growth continued unarrested, as did the increase of the mission's holdings of sheep, goats, and horses. As their numbers grew, the animals proved too numerous to keep corralled; most were turned loose to graze the countryside and captured only when needed. The increase went largely unchecked, and for Indians the consequences were dire. Spanish cattle, sheep, and horses not only overran Indian lands, trampling fields and encroaching on villages, but Indians who killed Spanish livestock were themselves punished severely by the padres and soldiers. Soldiers exacerbated the Indians' problems by seeking to eliminate natural predators, such as bears, which occasionally threatened the growing herds.

Cattle and horse herds of the Monterey Presidio also grew unchecked. Soon the padres would complain that the cattle of the soldiers stationed at San Carlos were trampling the mission's corn. Before long, the Monterey Presidio was exporting small numbers of cattle to the rest of the region and beyond. It was able to send surplus cattle to the newly established pueblo of Los Angeles in 1781, provision supply ships with beef and cattle when they stopped at Monterey, reinforce the herds of the other presidios, and provide a daily ration of beef for scores of Indians who labored at the presidio in the late 1780s and 1790s.[7]

6. Serra, report on the missions, July 1, 1784, Monterey, in Tibesar, ed. and trans., *Writings of Serra*, IV, 275; Matías de Santa Catalina Noriega, January 1785, San Carlos account book (no clear page number).

7. Pascual Martínez de Arenaza and José Francisco de Paula Señán, Mission San Carlos annual report for 1787, Jan. 10, 1788, AGN, DPHM, 2d Ser., II, "Misiones de la Alta California," Informes, 1769–1809, Archivo del Colegio de San Fernando, 72a–72b, microfilm, BL; report of Hemenegildo Sal, habilitado [paymaster] of Monterey Presidio, Sept. 30, 1798, Monterey, AGN, CA, XXI, expediente 12, 399a–434a, esp. 408a–411a.

PLATE 6. *View of Monterey Presidio, California* (detail). By José Cardero. 1791.
Sheep, outside the Monterey Presidio, are clearing out native grasses. The
right half of the ground shown has been overgrazed, and the animals are
now at work on the remaining vegetation. BANC PIC 1963.002:1310,
The Bancroft Library, University of California, Berkeley

Just as European diseases radiated from Spanish centers of settlement into remote Indian villages in the years after 1770, so too did environmental degradation,
as Spanish livestock invaded and then exhausted ecological niches farther and
farther from the mission and presidio. Into this disturbed environment came a
host of weeds and plants that Europeans had inadvertently brought with them.
These Old World plants had shown themselves adept at coexisting alongside
European grazing animals elsewhere. They were hardier than native grasses and
bushes and more suited to dry, compacted soil, and, as a result, they succeeded
many indigenous food sources. The near-complete displacement of native plants
by European weeds has been made abundantly clear through analysis of adobe
bricks manufactured in the Monterey region during the 1820s, 1830s, and 1840s:
they contain much higher pollen counts of European weeds than of native plants.[8]
By the turn of the nineteenth century, the hills and valleys of the Monterey region
were covered with alien plants that supported Spanish livestock, but few, if any,
Indian villages remained. In 1800, the mission grazed 4,000 sheep and 1,200 head
of cattle, and the presidio soon counted some 1,275 cattle and more than 7,000
horses. By then, nearly all of the Indians in the area labored for their primary
subsistence in mission fields, not the surrounding countryside.

8. Rebecca Allen, *Native Americans at Mission Santa Cruz, 1791–1834: Interpreting the Archaeological
Record,* Perspectives in California Archaeology, V (Los Angeles, Calif., 1998), 42–43.

The awful, if accidental, genius of Spanish colonization in California, then, was not just in creating a subsistence crisis among Indian communities through introduced diseases, plants, and animals; it was in offering what appeared to be a solution in the form of food Indians raised at the mission. Rumsen Indians had been working for food ever since June 1770, when small groups earned *panocha*, chocolate, flour, and ham for manual labor they performed at the presidio.[9] Spaniards had brought these goods north from Mexico, and in the early 1770s Indians used them to supplement a diet still largely gathered from beyond the mission; it would be another decade until Indians at the mission had cleared enough land and planted enough crops to sustain large numbers of villagers.

The Franciscans had come to California with the seeds and tools—hoes, plows, shovels, and picks—they needed to transform the land. At first, they had little success. In the year after Mission San Carlos was established, Rumsen field hands, under the directions of the missionaries, planted "all kinds of seeds" in a little enclosed garden. But nothing came of these efforts, for, as Father Junípero Serra wrote, the land was occasionally "washed over by the salt water of the estuary" and so was "fit for nothing but nettles and reeds." Later that year, in the summer of 1771, because of the bad soil—and his deteriorating relationship with Fages— Serra moved the mission several miles southwest to its present location, farther from the presidio and closer to Rumsen laborers and fresh water. Even at the new location, Serra continued to despair about the mission's progress: "With regard to crops nothing worthy of the name has as yet been achieved . . . as regards spiritual matters, much could have been accomplished if only there were some-thing to eat."[10]

Not until the winter of 1772 did Indians plant crops at the new location on land that was, in one padre's words, "half dug and half cleared." The wheat and barley, however, yielded only small harvests, and the corn and beans were damaged by a late frost. Serra lamented: "Finding ourselves unable to give [the neophytes] food and keep them with us, we baptized very few, except when necessity demanded." Missionaries were forced to subsist on what little remained from the supplies brought north, and the few Indians at the mission relied on gathered food. Two years after its establishment, the mission owed its continued existence to the

9. Account of rations distributed at Monterey, June–August 1770, AGN, Indiferente de Guerra, legajo 161b, 160b–161a.

10. San Carlos account book, 8. The mission received additional agricultural implements and seeds when the *San Antonio* arrived again in May 1771. See Serra, memorandum, June 20, 1771, Junípero Serra to Francisco Palóu, June 21, 1771, Serra to Rafael Verger, Aug. 8, 1772, all in Tibesar, ed. and trans., *Writings of Serra*, I, 227–235, 240–241, 257 (my trans.).

neighboring gentile Indians, who, Serra wrote, "are the main supporters of our people." But, over time, just as the dual revolutions were eroding native communities and remaking the countryside, mission fields worked by Rumsen hands began to support an increasing number of natives. Thus, Indians not only responded to changes in their world; they accelerated them.[11]

In 1774, the mission's garden, which by then had been itself blessed in honor of Saint Joseph and was referred to as a *milpa*, yielded a large and diverse crop: 225 bushels of corn, 187 bushels of wheat, 30 bushels of barley, 7.5 bushels of kidney beans, and another 1.5 bushels of broad beans. And this was only the beginning. New baptisms continued to add laborers to the mission while taking them away from native villages, and the padres found agricultural varieties suited to Monterey's soil and climate that furthered the displacement of indigenous plants. In 1775, Indians and missionaries added peas, garbanzos, and lentils to the garden, in addition to planting three different varieties of wheat. Altogether that year, Indians harvested 885 bushels of produce at the mission. In 1781, Indians spent seven months working on an irrigation system, which was largely completed by December, and they kept clearing new fields for more crops, a task that proved arduous, given that the land had been "covered with long tough grasses and thickets but also with great trees, willows, alders, and so forth."[12]

By 1783, Indians working the mission's irrigated fields, which might have comprised some 155 acres of what once was native terrain, were producing a significant surplus of food.[13] The padres boasted of a "sizeable walled garden [which produces] abundant vegetables and some fruit." In that year, Indians harvested some 4,500 bushels, a huge figure that no doubt explains why 166 gentiles came to the mission for baptism—more than in any other year. So abundant was the crop that Serra sent nearly 200 bushels of wheat to the soldiers at the presidio. More tellingly, though, the padres "gave," in their words, some 375 bushels of grain to villagers of Sargentaruc and Excelen who had worked in the mission's fields during the harvest; these more remote villages by the early 1780s were beginning to see their own numbers and economies undercut by the dual

11. San Carlos account book, 16; Serra to Palóu, Aug. 18, 1772, Serra to Antonio María de Bucareli y Ursúa, May 21, 1773, both in Tibesar, ed. and trans., *Writings of Serra*, I, 265, 353.

12. San Carlos account book, 15a, 15b; Serra, report on the missions, July 1, 1784, in Tibesar, ed. and trans., *Writings of Serra*, IV, 269, 273.

13. In consultation with faculty at Oregon State University's College of Agriculture, I determined this figure by multiplying the harvest of the principal crops by estimated harvest per acre. Wheat harvest of 835 fanegas (1.5 bushels per fanega) at 20 bushels an acre equals 62.6 acres. Corn harvest of 971 fanegas at 40 bushels an acre equals 36.4 acres. Barley harvest of 740 fanegas at 20 bushels an acre equals 55.5 acres for a total of 154.5 acres cultivated. This does not include any of the vegetables or fruit grown at the mission (San Carlos account book, 17a).

revolutions, and they were increasingly looking to the mission for subsistence. The more than 600 Indians already at the mission, according to Serra, were maintained "without any scarcity."[14]

THE CONQUEST OF THE COUNTRYSIDE

The Indians' decision to migrate to the missions generated a momentum all its own. In electing to move, Indians made choices for themselves and their families, but their decisions worked against others who might have wanted to stay away. The migrations could only have accelerated the collapse of villages and subsistence economies that had become unable, it seems, to support even the declining number of people living in them. Simultaneously, the Indians provided more labor for the missions' fields, which in turn then produced more crops and in so doing bolstered the missions' appearances as places of refuge, as sources of food and shelter and community.[15]

Earlier and elsewhere in colonial America, as in northeastern North America, many Indian groups had responded to the shocks of colonization by launching wars on their Indian neighbors to secure access to European trade and captives, replacing those lost to disease or war. In Alta California, as in some other parts of northern New Spain, however, Indians instead generally came to missions; they were compelled by the upheaval of the dual revolutions and lured still by the material (in this case, food, not muskets or alcohol) and the hope of community regeneration through association with other remnant, refugee groups. Thus, what the Franciscans set out to establish as Catholic missions, California Indians originally must have viewed as resources oriented around agricultural production. In this regard, in becoming places of congregation for Indians, the California missions were unusually successful. In Baja California, by comparison, only the demographic revolution took hold: missions proved hotbeds for contagion but were unable to support the plants and animals upon which the growth

14. Serra, report on the missions, July 1, 1784, in Tibesar, ed. and trans., *Writings of Serra*, IV, 271, 273; San Carlos account book, 17a. Nearly all of the harvest was in corn, wheat, and barley. The majority of gentiles that year attained baptism in late summer, fall, and early winter, during and after the harvest.

15. For the primacy of disease in the movement of Indians to Spanish missions, see Daniel T. Reff, *Disease, Depopulation, and Culture Change in Northwestern New Spain, 1518–1764* (Salt Lake City, Utah, 1991); Reff, "The Jesuit Mission Frontier in Comparative Perspective: The Reductions of the Río de la Plata and the Missions of Northwestern Mexico, 1588–1700," in Donna J. Guy and Thomas E. Sheridan, eds., *Contested Ground: Comparative Frontiers on the Northern and Southern Edges of the Spanish Empire* (Tucson, Ariz., 1998), 16–31. Reff pays far more attention to disruptions originating in disease than to changes in the environment caused by the introduction of new plants and animals.

of most borderlands missions so depended. This was also largely the case in Texas and Sonora, where missions rarely counted large numbers of Indian residents.[16]

This movement to the missions began almost as soon as Spaniards and their silent weapons arrived in Monterey. All told, the Children of Coyote came to Mission San Carlos from many outlying villages over nearly four decades, and, when each village is viewed separately, the distribution over time of its members' baptisms conforms to several patterns. Every *ranchería*, or village, had one or two years in which many more individuals joined the mission than in other years; in no instance did all the residents of a single village attain baptism in fewer than five years. Even in years when large numbers of Indians from one village came, their baptisms were usually spread out over several months. The gradual rate of baptisms from each village reveals that, throughout the period 1770 to 1808, individuals and family units came steadily to Mission San Carlos. Whole villages were not forced into the mission during a short period of time as some scholars have asserted; they were driven by a different sort of occupying force than one of soldiers bearing guns and lances.[17]

Indians came to the mission in what now appear as four distinct waves spread out over the thirty-nine-year period from 1770 to 1808. Each successive wave involved villages located a greater distance from Mission San Carlos. The period

16. Daniel K. Richter, *Facing East from Indian Country: A Native History of Early America* (Cambridge, Mass., 2001); Harry W. Crosby, *Antigua California: Mission and Colony on the Peninsular Frontier, 1697–1768* (Albuquerque, N.Mex., 1994), 209–221; Robert H. Jackson, *Indian Population Decline: The Missions of Northwestern New Spain, 1687–1840* (Albuquerque, N.Mex., 1994), 69–83; Mardith Keithly Schuetz, "The Indians of the San Antonio Missions, 1718–1821" (Ph.D. diss., University of Texas, Austin, 1980); Schuetz, "Demography of the Mission Indians," in Clark Spencer Larsen, ed., *Native American Demography in the Spanish Borderlands,* Spanish Borderlands Sourcebooks, II (New York, 1991), 206–231. On population decline in the missions of Sonora, see Jackson, *Indian Population Decline,* 61–69; on the economy of the missions, see Cynthia Radding, *Wandering Peoples: Colonialism, Ethnic Spaces, and Ecological Frontiers in Northwestern Mexico, 1700–1850* (Durham, N.C., 1997).

17. The first converts from virtually every ranchería were usually children and older women. Children, who required less instruction, were baptized much more quickly than adults. Language difficulties and the padres' need to instruct Indians in the basics of Catholic doctrine prevented the Franciscans from rapidly baptizing all of the gentiles who desired it. The catechism of Indians in preparation for baptism is discussed below in Chapter 4.

For two extreme and divergent positions on the role of Spanish coercion in Indian baptisms in Alta California, see Sherburne F. Cook, *The Conflict between the California Indian and White Civilization* (Berkeley, Calif., 1976); Francis F. Guest, "An Examination of the Thesis of S. F. Cook on the Forced Conversion of the Indians in the California Missions," *SCQ,* LXI (1979), 1–77. There is no evidence to suggest that the Indians of the Monterey Bay region were forcibly relocated to Mission San Carlos or baptized under duress at other Franciscan missions in California. Scholars might have confused the Spaniards' policy of compelling Indians upon baptism to reside at the missions with coerced relocation. The clearest argument that cultural pressures left Indians with no alternative other than movement to the nearest mission is presented in Randall Milliken, *A Time of Little Choice: The Disintegration of Tribal Culture in the San Francisco Bay Area, 1769–1810* (Menlo Park, Calif., 1995). See also John R. Johnson, "The Chumash and the Missions," in *CC,* I, 365–375.

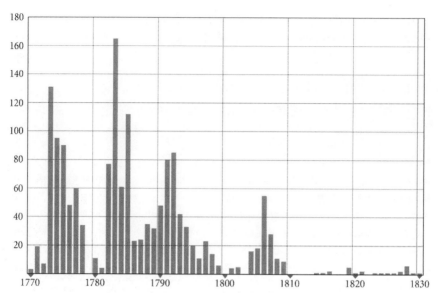

FIGURE 1. Annual Baptisms of Gentiles, Mission San Carlos, 1770–1831. Drawn by Rebecca L. Wrenn. Figures are from my database of baptisms, marriages, and burials at San Carlos compiled from the mission's registers (see Appendix A for methodology)

from 1773 to 1778 represented the first major wave of gentiles: 454 were baptized during these years, roughly 30 percent of all the 1,525 gentiles baptized at the mission through 1808. Through 1778, 417 Rumsen Indians from Achasta and Tucutnut, the closest villages to the newly established mission, and Ichxenta, Socorronda, and Echilat, located up the river valleys, were christened at San Carlos.[18] During the 1770s, only a few dozen Indians from the more distant Excelen, Ensen, and Sargentaruc attained baptism. The majority of the last of the local Rumsen Indians were baptized in 1778; after that, only fifteen gentiles joined the mission in 1779, 1780, and 1781.

The period 1782–1785 constituted the second major migration of gentiles to the mission. In these years, the Franciscans expanded their reach to groups beyond the immediate vicinity: the Excelen, Eslenajan, Ecjeajan, Sargentaruc, Kalendaruc, and Ensen. From these groups, about 400 gentiles attained baptism,

18. For these Indians' villages and political affiliations, see Randall Milliken, *Ethnohistory of the Rumsen,* Papers in Northern California Anthropology, no. 2 (Berkeley, Calif., 1987), 43–58, orig. publ. as "Ethnohistory of the Rumsen: The Mission Period," in Dietz, Jackson, et al., *Stage 1 Pacific Grove–Monterey Consolidation Project,* I (Berkeley, Calif., 1981), 10–102. The villages of Achasta, Tucutnut, Ichxenta, Socorronda, and Echilat were located in the valleys of the Carmel River and San Jose Creek, both of which flow into the sea adjacent to Mission San Carlos.

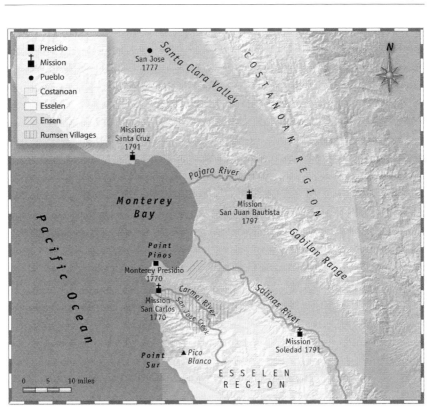

MAP 3. Indian Territories and Spanish Settlements of the Monterey Region,
Late Eighteenth Century. Drawn by Gerry Krieg

approximately 26 percent of all the gentile baptisms that would occur at the mission. The third movement of gentiles to San Carlos occurred in 1790–1792, when 213 were baptized, 78 from the Costanoan group Ensen. The drop-off in baptisms between 1796 and 1803, when only 63 gentiles were baptized, can probably be explained by the Franciscans' changing leadership at the mission and the terrible epidemic that struck Mission Carmel in 1802. The last major wave took place in 1805–1807, when the final outlying villagers came into the mission.

Although certainly not exact—and only one part of a very complicated story—there is a rough correlation between when individuals from specific villages attained baptism and when cattle and other livestock spread into their territory. This relationship appears weakest in the early years of colonization, when livestock totals were lowest, and more pronounced in the years when Spanish herds multiplied. The first movements to San Carlos involved Indians from five associated Rumsen villages situated within ten miles of Mission San Carlos in the hills and valleys of the Carmel River and San Jose Creek, all early grazing areas of mission and presidio livestock. In the second half of the 1770s, Indians came to Mission San Carlos from the upper Carmel River valley and the Salinas River valley, just as these areas were becoming important sources of pasturage for European cattle. In the early 1780s, Spanish livestock extended their grazing farther up the Salinas Valley, into the upper Carmel River valley, and farther south to the Big Sur region, forcing Indians into San Carlos from the Esselen territories of Sargentaruc, Excelen, and Eslenajan. These villages were all some twenty to thirty-five miles from San Carlos. In the late 1780s and the 1790s, large numbers of Indians ventured to San Carlos and Mission Soledad from throughout the greater Monterey region as the intruding livestock expanded dramatically in number and range and remade the landscape a considerable distance from the missions. In these years, Indians moved in large numbers from the Ensen villages of the Salinas Valley—then a prime area for mission and presidio cattle—and the Esselen villages of Imunahan and Aspasniajan, both of which were situated to the south of recently established Mission Soledad and located in the valleys and canyons where its own herds grazed. By the early 1800s, after a fourth and final wave composed largely of elderly holdouts, seemingly all the Indians of the region had relocated to one of the Franciscan missions.

The missionaries and soldiers misunderstood the relationship between the spread of their diseases, animals, and plants and the mounting number of baptisms at the missions: they saw the growth of agriculture and a pastoral economy as drawing Indians to the missions rather than pushing them there. But they were fully aware by the mid-1790s that the Monterey region's natural environment was in a period of transformation and crisis. In the early 1790s, the number of cattle and sheep kept by San Carlos nearly doubled, increasing from 1,082 cattle and 900 sheep in 1790 to 2,300 and 1,577, respectively, in 1794. And, by that same year, Missions Santa Cruz and Soledad (both founded in 1791) together held nearly 700 cattle and 900 sheep. Furthermore, the presidio's horses and cattle numbered in the thousands. When drought gripped the overgrazed region in 1793, 1794, and 1795, suddenly there was inadequate pasture to support the steadily increasing herds. Soon, the royal herd of cattle grazed in the lower Salinas Valley was declining in numbers and producing far fewer calves, a sure sign of its malnourishment. The resulting diminution in the presidio's herd prompted an investigation by the governor. Soldiers, who doubled as cowherds and shepherds, all described a region that had not seen rain in years, where the pasturage had become "infinitely" reduced. By the mid-1790s, the native vegetation of the region had been severely damaged, if not totally destroyed, by the introduced animals and the lack of rain. Sheep and their ability to eat grasses down to the ground proved especially damaging to the pasturage in and around Monterey. What the livestock had not eaten, they had trampled.[19]

Ironically, the environmental crisis of the mid-1790s served only to complete the ungulates' dominance of the land. Thousands of horses, cattle, and sheep ranged farther and farther in search of pasture, scouring the valleys and hills, rooting out any remaining pockets of native grasses. Indians who had not yet moved to San Carlos, Santa Cruz, or Soledad, and therefore still relied upon the countryside for their subsistence, were hit especially hard. Suffering from what the soldiers described as their great "hunger" as a result of the disappearance of the acorns and other seeds, Indians increasingly turned to cattle as a source of food. Soldiers asserted that their own horses were simply too weak and too scrawny to allow them to look after so many animals and prevent Indians from attacking them.[20]

Spanish livestock recovered quickly after the drought; native vegetation and the Indians who depended upon it could not. Once rains returned, as in 1798, nonnative grasses and introduced livestock solidified their hold, and by then nearly all the Indians of the region had relocated to one of its missions. Now it became a pastoral paradise, with its mild climate, its wet but cool winters, and its rich covering of grasses well adapted to both drought and aggressive grazing. In 1800, Missions Santa Cruz, San Carlos, Soledad, and San Juan Bautista grazed some 3,811 cattle, 11,082 sheep, and 2,678 horses; two decades later, they counted nearly three times as many animals—some 22,000 cattle, 23,200 sheep, and 2,533 horses. This process played itself out throughout the rest of Spanish California in the decades after 1770, as more missions and their animals came to dominate and then transform the countryside. Herds of horses increased so rapidly that, by 1805, Father President Estevan Tapis was asking the governor to slaughter them. One visitor to Monterey in 1806 reported that the governor had recently sent out a party of soldiers to kill 20,000 head of cattle "wherever they found them, because he feared that they would multiply to the point that there would not be enough pasture to feed them." Such practices reduced for a moment the number

19. Letter of Joseph María Beltrán, May 2, 1798, testimony of soldiers, Dec. 1–2, 1798, Monterey Presidio, both in AGN, CA, XXI, expediente 12, 400a–401b, 414a–419a. By the mid-1790s, when the drought struck, the animals' needs exceeded the land's carrying capacity. The crash that ensued conforms to Stage 3 of the cycles of ungulate irruptions described by Melville, *A Plague of Sheep*, 53–55. On variability of climate in California and its potentially drastic impact upon native subsistence, see Lester B. Rowntree, "Drought during California's Mission Period, 1769–1834," *Journal of California and Great Basin Anthropology*, VII (1985), 7–20; H. C. Fritts and G. A. Gordon, "Reconstructed Annual Precipitation for California," in M. K. Hughes et al., *Climate from Tree Rings* (New York, 1982), 185–191; Daniel O. Larson, "California Climatic Reconstructions," *Journal of Interdisciplinary History*, XXV (1994), 225–253.

20. Testimony of soldiers, Dec. 1–2, 1798, Monterey Presidio, AGN, CA, XXI, expediente 12, 414a–419a.

of cattle in the region, but, by the end of the Spanish period, missions in California collectively held some 193,234 sheep, 149,730 cattle, and 19,830 horses. The presidios, a small number of private ranchos, and numerous wild herds held countless more.[21]

CONTINUITY AMID CHANGE

Faced with declining numbers and an inability to maintain their annual subsistence, California Indians elected to move to missions such as San Carlos Borromeo because doing so at first allowed them to survive and to hold on to crucial elements of their culture. When Indians left their villages, they brought to missions many things, including their music, dances, architecture, and what remained of their subsistence economies. Although the Franciscans objected to dances that brought men and women together after dark, they rarely prevented those that occurred in broad daylight, and thus they signalled to Indians that important native practices were compatible with life at the missions. Dancers at San Carlos with some regularity painted their bodies, donned regalia, and came together as they created spectacles for themselves and foreign visitors to the region.[22]

When Georg Heinrich von Langsdorff came to Mission San Jose in 1806, Father Pedro de la Cueva gave the Indians the day off from mission work to prepare a dance in honor of the visitor. To secure the participation of the mission's best dancers, De la Cueva gave them "finery." The morning of the dance, the men gathered beyond the mission, by a creek, where some decorated themselves "with cinders, red clay, and chalk." Others painted figures on their chests, stomachs, thighs, and backs. Several covered their naked bodies with down. Women adorned themselves with "mussels, feathers, and coral." For the better part of the day, the Costanoan of Mission San Jose danced for Langsdorff and themselves, "jumping rhythmically and making all kinds of body movements and grimaces" as they portrayed "scenes from war and domestic life with the help of bows and arrows and with feathers held in their hands and on their heads." The women had their own songs and way of dancing, hopping near the men and

21. Estevan Tapis to José Joaquín de Arrillaga, cited in Robert Archibald, *The Economic Aspects of the California Missions* (Washington, D.C., 1978), 180. During the drought and the following decade, nearly eight hundred Indians came to the Franciscan missions of the region, and more than a third of those went to Mission San Carlos. For animal counts, see Archibald, *Economic Aspects,* 179–181. For quote, see Georg Heinrich von Langsdorff, *Remarks and Observations on a Voyage around the World from 1803 to 1807,* ed. Richard A. Pierce, trans. Victoria Joan Moessner, 2 vols. (Kingston, Ont., 1993), II, 99.

22. Raymundo Carrillo, Oct. 13, 1802, Santa Barbara, AGN, PI, CCXVI, expediente 1, 104b–111a, esp. 109a–109b.

PLATE 7. *An Indian Dance at the Mission of San Jose, in New California*. By Georg Heinrich von Langsdorff. 1806. "The last dancer had an original idea. He has painted his naked body so that he looks like a Spanish soldier in uniform with collar, cuffs, boots, stockings, breeches, etc. Next to the Indians at the foot of a tree is a fire. From time to time, the dancers take burning coals from it and swallow them" (Langsdorff, *Remarks and Observations on a Voyage around the World from 1803 to 1807*, ed. Richard A. Pierce, trans. Victoria Joan Moessner, 2 vols. [Kingston, Ont., 1993], II, 272). BANC PIC 1963.002:1023, The Bancroft Library, University of California, Berkeley

"sliding their thumb and index finger rhythmically from one side to the other of their abdomens." As rich as this description is of the Indians' music, costumes, and preparations, elements of these dances must have spoken uniquely to the Indians' beliefs and concerns. Clearly, though, Indian dances at the missions were elaborate affairs through which participants told stories of their history and affirmed native beliefs and hierarchies.[23]

Although modern reconstructions of Spanish missions give the impression that all baptized Indians resided within a closed quadrangle under the padres' surveillance, from 1770 until 1807 Indians at San Carlos inhabited a village of

23. Langsdorff, *Remarks and Observations,* ed. Pierce, trans. Moessner, II, 114–116.

their own construction on a bluff just beyond the main buildings. Pedro Fages observed in 1773 that the village was "built after the manner of the country": it was composed of huts clustered together and made of thatch and straw.[24] The French naval explorer Jean-François de Galaup de la Pérouse, who visited the mission in 1786, left a vivid description of the ranchería:

> The Indian village is on the right, consisting of some 50 huts housing the seven hundred and forty individuals of both sexes (including the children) who make up the Mission of St Carlos or Monterey.
>
> These huts are the most wretched one can find anywhere; they are round, 6 feet in diameter by 4 in height; a few stakes the thickness of an arm stuck into the ground and joined to form a vault at the top make up their frame; eight or ten bundles of straw roughly arranged on these stakes more or less protect the inhabitants from rain or wind, and more than half this hut remains open when the weather is fine; their only precaution is to keep two or three bundles of hay in reserve near their huts.

The entrance to these huts was low and narrow; a small hearth stood in the middle of the structure, and smoke escaped through a small hole in the roof. For decades, the desires of the Indians to remain in their own lodgings overrode the missionaries' plans to place Indian families in separate adobe cabins. In 1792, one of the diarists of a Spanish naval expedition reported that the Franciscans had offered to help the Indians build Spanish-style houses, but "they just continued not wanting to live in them, preferring to live in the open."[25]

The Indians' decision to remain in their own huts testifies to their affinity for their own architecture, a style that reflected their way of life: families overlapped, slept as one on pelts on the ground; villagers came and went; and villages relocated as seasons changed.[26] La Pérouse had counted about fifty huts that together accommodated some 740 persons in 1786, suggesting that each structure could house about fifteen residents—clearly more than a small nuclear family. The Indians' preference for their own huts also suggests a desire to maintain distance between themselves and the Franciscans, who were not welcome inside. Virtually

24. For Fages's quote, see Herbert Ingram Priestley, ed. and trans., *A Historical, Political, and Natural Description of California, by Pedro Fages, Soldier of Spain* ... (Berkeley, Calif., 1937), 64–65. Fages stated that there were 151 Indians at the mission, and the sacramental registers suggest that this must have been in the fall of 1773.

25. John Dunmore, ed. and trans., *The Journal of Jean-François de Galaup de la Pérouse, 1785–1788*, 2 vols. (London, 1994–1995), I, 179; Claude-Nicolas Rollin, "Memoire physiologique et pathologique sur les Américains," Marine, Ser. 3JJ, 387, reel 1, file 7, 13, Archives nationales, Paris (hereafter cited as Rollin, "Memoire physiologique"); Donald C. Cutter, *California in 1792: A Spanish Naval Visit* (Norman, Okla., 1990), 134. On Rollin, see Dunmore, ed. and trans., *Journal of La Pérouse*, I, lxxxi–lxxxiii.

26. Rollin, "Memoire physiologique," 13–14.

PLATE 8. *Vista del convento, yglecia, y rancherias de la mision del Carmelo*. By José Cardero. 1791. This early view of Mission San Carlos clearly shows the Indians' *ranchería* in the background. Just behind the village is the mission's corral. In the right foreground, missionaries greet members of the Malaspina expedition. Courtesy, Museo Naval, Madrid

all the Franciscan and military officials who traveled throughout Alta California stated that the Indians did not allow them to enter their homes.

What convinced the Indians to abandon their straw huts is unclear, but in 1806 and 1807 they built ninety-three small adobe houses as part of the quadrangle adjacent to the mission church.[27] Perhaps the grasses and brush were not so readily available in the transformed landscape. And, similarly, the expertise necessary to build these huts might also have been scarce in an Indian community increasingly composed of those raised in and around the mission. The completion of the last of the adobes in 1807 was followed a year later by the baptism of the Monterey region's last gentile Indians. By 1806, Indians must have realized that the mission was to be their home year-round for the foreseeable future; permanent lodgings therefore would have had an appeal and logic not present decades earlier. Significantly, by then the Indians' numbers and families were smaller, and perhaps the family unit had taken on a more nuclear structure. The mission's population in 1807 was approximately 562. Each of the newly con-

27. James Culleton, *Indians and Pioneers of Old Monterey* (Fresno, Calif., 1950), 171. Culleton puts the number of new houses at eighty-nine. For a report of ninety-three houses constructed over two years, see Robert H. Jackson and Edward D. Castillo, *Indians, Franciscans, and Spanish Colonization: The Impact of the Mission System on California Indians* (Albuquerque, N.Mex., 1995), app. 3, 146–147.

structed houses, therefore, could have held a family of six, a family unit far smaller than the extended households living together in the brush huts. The movement into the adobes, therefore, came only after decades of gradual change and adaptation.

Just as it was many years before Indians at Mission San Carlos abandoned straw huts for adobe lodgings, Indians in general only gradually gave up their lives outside the missions. In particular, they continued subsistence gathering, hunting, and related activities even though they depended upon such practices for sustenance less and less each year. At some times, the Indians' continuation of these habits was rooted in a need to overcome temporary shortages of food, especially in the missions' first years. Franciscans encouraged Indians to fend for themselves during times of need: "It may be necessary," Serra stated during one very lean time, "to send the greater part, or all, of our new Christians who can do so to look for food in the mountains, or on the beach, as they did not so many years ago."[28] What the Franciscans viewed as a necessity in times of shortfall was in all likelihood seen by the Indians as an affirmation that the missions represented a blending of old and new practices. Moreover, Indians might have even seen their settlement in the missions as the padres saw the Indians' continued subsistence gathering: as a temporary strategy to weather a crisis.

Even when not driven by necessity, Indians persisted in leaving the missions to gather plants and hunt animals, many of which were important for cultural and religious practices. Furthermore, gathering provided an occasion to renew and create ties with others beyond the missions, and it allowed Indians to affirm autonomy, community, and cultural identity, especially as these became imperiled. So strong were the Indians' desires to combine life at the missions with occasional forays outside of them that Father President Fermín Francisco de Lasuén remarked, "If we absolutely denied them the right to go the mountains, I am afraid that they would riot." The depth of the neophytes' commitment to life beyond the mission was revealed by one man who had participated in an attack on Mission San Diego in 1775. He had done so after he became concerned that "all the gentiles were going for baptism, and that as a consequence there would be no one to greet him when he went to the countryside to take time off and enjoy himself." For this neophyte and for many others, life in the mission was intolerable if it was not coupled with life beyond it. The Franciscans eventually granted baptized Indians a few weeks' leave each year from the missions to gather native foods, visit family members, and travel to distant villages. This system not only

28. Serra to Fernando de Rivera y Moncada, Oct. 24, 1775, Monterey, in Tibesar, ed. and trans., *Writings of Serra*, II, 367 (my trans.). See also Serra to Bucareli, May 21, 1773, ibid., I, 347. Later that year, Palóu noted that the food shortage was so severe that the Indians could not stay at the mission (Palóu, *Historical Memoirs*, ed. and trans. Bolton, III, 230–231).

allowed the missionaries to prevent food shortages by encouraging a sizable portion of the mission population to fend for itself, but it helped Indians to equate elements of their lives at the missions with those they had lived previously.[29]

The amount of time the Indians spent away from the missions varied: at Mission San Diego, perhaps the least agriculturally productive of the California missions, the vast majority spent only a week or two a year at the mission; at San Carlos Borromeo, by contrast, most Indians left for only two weeks a year. At Santa Barbara, at least in 1800, one-fifth of the mission population was usually away on *paseo*. Every Sunday after Mass in front of the church, the padres would read the names of the fifth of the community that would be allowed to leave. Indians from distant villages would take two weeks; those from nearby would go for a week. Only during the wheat harvests did missionaries deny Indians leaves, and, once the harvest was completed in the summer, everyone was given two weeks off. Clearly, by the early 1800s, in the face of the Indians' continued insistence on leaving, the Franciscans realized that more than hunger lay behind the Indians' desires. In one revealing exchange, Father Lasuén responded with annoyance when Indians who he believed were well fed said they were hungry and therefore needed to leave the mission for a week to gather foods. "Why, you make me think that if one were to give you a young bull, a sheep, and a *fanega* of grain every day you would still be yearning for your mountains and beaches," Lasuén responded. Then, "the brightest of the Indians who were listening to me said, smiling and half ashamed of himself, 'What you say is true, Father. It's the truth.' "[30]

Significantly, it was not just in leaving the missions for days or weeks that Indians stuck to activities that had long been meaningful to them. Late summer months were a time when the Rumsen customarily gathered at the seashore, collected sardines, hunted birds, and socialized, and Indians continued these get-togethers after they had moved to Mission San Carlos. In the summers of the mid-1770s, baptized Indians divided their time between harvesting wheat from the mission fields and gathering sardines from the shore. Father Serra described this symbiosis of Indian and Spanish worlds:

> The said reaping began July 18 and had to be continued until August 12, because as soon as it began, great schools of sardines appeared near the beach, close to the mission. So the arrangement was that, until noontime,

29. Fermín Francisco de Lasuén, "Refutation of Charges," June 19, 1801, Monterey, AGN, PI, CCXVI, expediente 1, 72a, and in Kenneally, ed. and trans., *Writings of Lasuén*, II, 215.

30. Tapis and Juan Cortés to Lasuén, Oct. 30, 1800, Mission Santa Barbara, AGN, PI, CCXVI, expediente 1, 82b; Lasuén, "Refutation of Charges," June 19, 1801, Monterey, AGN, PI, CCXVI, expediente 1, 69b, and in Kenneally, ed. and trans., *Writings of Lasuén*, II, 203–204.

we harvested wheat, and in the afternoon caught sardines. This lasted fully twenty days without a break. . . . After two weeks of fish eating, on the Sunday following, leaving the sardines in peace, they went hunting for the nests of sea birds that live in the rocks and feed on fish. They caught a lot of young birds which were, generally speaking, as big as a good-sized chicken. And so they passed Sunday camping on the Carmel beach, divided into countless groups, each with its fire, roasting and eating what they had caught. . . . The harvesting of the wheat, thus interrupted by the fishing, lasted twenty-five days.[31]

As Serra's description shows, the Indians split their time on a given day between the pursuit of still-viable, time-honored subsistence activities and the production of crops that the Franciscans had introduced. Both baptized and nonbaptized Indians congregated on the beach, a mixing that was emblematic of the openness of California Indian communities during times of particular plenty. Serra and other missionaries were fascinated by the large congregation by the shore; Serra went to watch the gathering along with two other missionaries, and he considered it "good theatre," an unusual comment from a man who habitually cast nearly all Indian activities outside of Catholic devotion in a negative light. Serra probably hoped that this intermingling might in some way lead to the eventual baptism of the gentiles. In supporting these activities, the Franciscans showed their understanding that the fledgling mission would rest upon both Indian and European patterns of production, a belief upon which the Children of Coyote had staked their survival.[32]

The seemingly smooth "arrangement" likely masked a crucial fact: even after they moved to the missions, Indians still gave a higher priority to many of their accustomed activities and beliefs than those introduced by the missionaries. In particular, Indians harvested sardines and gathered birds over many Sundays, thereby withdrawing from and in essence subverting Catholic observances. Missionaries did not see a religious component in the Indians' gatherings by the beach; if they had, they in turn would have subverted the Indians' observances.

---

31. Serra to Bucareli, Aug. 24, 1774, in Tibesar, ed. and trans., *Writings of Serra*, II, 145.

32. Ibid., 144–145 (my trans.). When the same events occurred the following year, Serra saw an opportunity to recruit gentiles to the mission; he remarked, "It is most appropriate that we turn our hands to fishing for souls" (Serra to Bucareli, Aug. 17, 1775, in Tibesar, ed. and trans., *Writings of Serra*, II, 305). In other instances, Indians less immediately affected by colonization gave their own customary economic activities priority over those introduced by Spaniards. In the mid-1780s, Spanish officials in Los Angeles had great difficulty persuading gentile Indians to help with the harvest even after they paid Indians to work their fields. Only after completing their own round of subsistence gathering did the Gabrielino devote their time and energy to the pueblo's harvest (Steven W. Hackel, "Land, Labor, and Production: The Colonial Economy of Spanish and Mexican California," in Gutiérrez and Orsi, eds., *Contested Eden* [Berkeley, Calif., 1998], 111–146, esp. 127–128).

PLATE 9. *Jeu des habitants de Californie*. By Louis Choris. 1816. Choris et al., *Voyage pittoresque autour du monde*, part 3 (Paris, 1822), plate 4. This lithograph of Choris's watercolor shows Indians at Mission San Francisco engaging in games of chance. California Historical Society; FN–30509

To the missionaries, the issue seemed to be how to manage the disruption of the harvest all this entailed. Serra's likening the Indians on the beach to "theatre" is a clue to the Franciscans' own distance from the Indians during the early years of colonization: clearly, the missionaries were spectators, separated from the Indians not just by physical space but by a cultural gulf. In supporting activities, the full import of which they did not wholly grasp and which they were often powerless to prevent, missionaries left alone the social and economic web undergirding indigenous culture. Camping on the beach, divided into groups, each around a fire, roasting and eating what they had caught, Indians engaged in more than the spectacle that Serra saw: they celebrated the land and its bounty and reaffirmed elements of harmony, continuity, and community in what to them must have been an increasingly disharmonious and chaotic world.

Extended leaves from the missions, like these late-summer hunts, occurred annually. Yet throughout the year Indians ventured out in pursuit of traditional foods. When La Pérouse visited Mission San Carlos in 1786, he observed that Indian men continued "to fish and hunt on their own account." In the year of La Pérouse's visit, around 700 Indians lived at San Carlos, and the mission harvested 440 fanegas of wheat, 969 of barley, 167 of corn, 79 of beans, and 72 of peas for a total of 2,868 bushels.[33] In 1792, a diarist from the Malaspina expedition was surprised to see an Indian girl at San Carlos eating one of the local plants, which was prepared in the Indians' customary manner: "Those who are in the mission have not yet lost fondness for such [native] foods, for we have seen a girl chew with considerable pleasure stalks of the most tasteless plants; and despite being aided by those provided by the mission, they gather a great quantity of the seeds to which they are accustomed. The one they like the best is the one they call *teda*. To eat those that they use in place of bread, they toast them in trays by throwing heated stones over the seeds and mixing these with them until they get them to the proper point."[34]

A unique view of the persistence of customary Indian activities long into the mission period was recorded in the testimony of several baptized Chumash who testified in the murder of an Indian from Mission San Luis Obispo in the summer of 1796. For days before the murder, Indians had traveled through the mountains, hills, and coastal areas miles from the mission. Some gathered *quiotes* (yucca stalks); others, clams. They killed and processed deer, gathered wood, and visited relatives left behind in native villages. All of this, the wide-ranging travel, the eating of familiar foods, the sleeping outdoors, the renewal of family relationships, sustained the Indians' social and cultural networks and the value system that lay beneath them.[35]

Just as neophytes headed to the countryside to pursue supplemental gathering and familiar activities, gentiles opportunistically came to the missions to augment their diet with mission-produced foods. Perhaps more Indians did not move to Mission San Carlos in the mid-1770s because of the ease with which gentiles could take advantage of the mission's economic production and maintain social contacts with baptized Indians without assuming the yoke of Catholicism. In an intersection of multiple economic and social systems, gentile Indians purchased part of the mission harvest directly from the baptized Indians. With the rise of the missions, a frontier exchange economy—one no doubt embedded in both evolving and collapsing social ties and communication networks—developed in which mission Indians peddled wheat, corn, or barley for beads. According to Father Lasuén: "Our neophytes sell one measure of wheat, or corn, etc., (it is true; they sell them, and they even keep them in order to sell them) for four strings of beads. They can buy a like quantity of seeds from the countryside for just two. The

33. Dunmore, ed. and trans., *Journal of La Pérouse,* I, 184; Zephyrin Engelhardt, *Mission San Carlos Borromeo (Carmelo): The Father of the Missions* (Santa Barbara, Calif., 1930), 244.

34. Cutter, *California in 1792,* 140. For more on Indians' subsistence practices at other missions, see Tapis to Lasuén, Oct. 13, 1800, Mission Santa Barbara, AGN, PI, CCXVI, expediente 1, 82b; *APST,* 168 n. 79; response of the missionaries of San Buenaventura to question 17, in *APST,* 86.

35. See "Causa criminal contra Silverio y Rosa . . . ," AGN, CA, LXV, expediente 6, 241a–301b.

Indians themselves have established this rate of exchange; and they are in the habit of saying that among the wild seeds there are none equal to our barley." At Mission San Buenaventura, large groups of Indians from the surrounding villages came and purchased various seeds and grains from mission Indians. Apparently, in one year, Indians from the Channel Islands off the coast of Santa Barbara came to the mission and left with some eleven canoes full of food purchased from mission Indians. The trade went both ways; mission Indians not only purchased goods from the gentiles with mission-produced foods, but they also acquired food from gentiles by using as exchange the glass beads they obtained from the padres and the soldiers.[36]

Trade between mission Indians and gentiles certainly undermined the Franciscans' goal of using food as a means of attracting Indians to Catholicism and simultaneously detaching them from indigenous society and customs. But, without this trade, the missions themselves and the supply of Indian labor upon which they depended would have been weakened. Moreover, the neophyte-gentile exchange networks were as crucial to the survival of the neophytes as they were beneficial to the gentiles. Among the native groups of Alta California, as with virtually all peoples, trade was a sign of the absence of hostility. Mission Indians' refusal to trade with gentiles might have precipitated an attack on the mission. In fact, a rupture in relations between mission and gentile Indians had led Indians to attack Mission San Gabriel in its first years. Thus, what at first appears to have been a simple economic exchange of barley for beads between different Indian groups might have been an indication of lasting social bonds and the establishment of an economic and political equilibrium between Indians at and beyond the missions.[37]

Eventually, though, over a period of decades, this blending of multiple economies—this increasingly tenuous social, economic, and political symbiosis—dissolved as the environment changed, Indians' numbers declined, and Indian customs altered. In some areas more rapidly than others, Indians at the missions came to depend almost completely on mission-produced foods just as they finally abandoned their brush huts for adobe cabins. Indications of the degree to which

36. Lasuén, "Refutation of Charges," June 19, 1801, Monterey, AGN, PI, CCXVI, expediente 1, 67b–68a, and in Kenneally, ed. and trans., *Writings of Lasuén*, II, 200–202; Señán and Vicente de Santa María, response to question no. 6, AGN, PI, CCXVI, expediente 1, 92b–93b. Lasuén does not specifically refer to the Indians of Mission San Carlos in his statement; he speaks of "our" Indians, which could mean all the Indians under the control of the Franciscans or those at Mission San Carlos. When he was at San Diego years earlier, he had noted a similar exchange between neophytes and gentiles. For a full investigation of a "frontier exchange economy," see Daniel H. Usner, Jr., *Indians, Settlers, and Slaves in a Frontier Exchange Economy: The Lower Mississippi Valley before 1783* (Chapel Hill, N.C., 1992).

37. Serra to Bucareli, May 21, 1773, Mexico City, in Tibesar, ed. and trans., *Writings of Serra*, I, 359–361.

Old World plants and animals had actually come to replace the Indians' traditional diets exist in plant and animal remains unearthed at the missions by archaeologists. For example, at Mission Santa Cruz, less than 10 percent of the vegetal remains recovered from Indian housing came from plants native to the region. Hazelnuts were the most common nonintroduced plant recovered in the mission but constituted only 8 percent of all vegetal remains. By comparison, corn and wheat—the staple of mission agriculture—constituted nearly two-thirds of the recovered remains.[38]

Animal remains show a similar reliance by mission Indians upon nonnative livestock. Archaeological work suggests that beef and mutton made up at least 80 percent of the meat consumed by Indians in some missions. The grazing habits of domesticated livestock, together with the Spaniards' policy of punishing Indians who set fire to fields—a practice that formerly had increased the browse for deer—combined to reduce the deer population. Not surprisingly, therefore, the bones of the deer, which had been the primary source of meat for Indians before colonization, were comparatively rare among excavated remains. The only native animals that remained undiminished by European colonization and a steady part of mission Indians' diets were shellfish—most importantly clams and mussels—and fish, but these had never been the Indians' main sources of food, merely a supplement to the seeds, grasses, nuts, and deer upon which subsistence in the Monterey region had formerly rested.[39]

FUGITIVISM

Scores of thousands of California Indians left their native villages for Franciscan missions during the colonial period. For all Indians, the movement to the missions and the acceptance of baptism were to place one foot in a completely different world. After baptism, some found they could not straddle both worlds, and they tried to retrace their steps back to their previous villages and lives. Others came to envision their lives as a more fluid continuum between missions and rancherías, and they intended to leave the missions only briefly. Franciscans had trouble distinguishing between Indians who had completely rejected the missions and those who saw their absences as temporary. In what constituted an important but exaggerated polarization, the Franciscans mistakenly interpreted all unpermitted Indian absences from the missions as a rejection of Catholicism and a challenge to their authority. Branding all absentee Indians as *huidos,* or

38. Allen, *Native Americans at Mission Santa Cruz,* 43–47. No similar archaeological studies were undertaken for Mission San Carlos.

39. Ibid., 55–61.

PLATE 10. *Portrait Heads of Indians of California.* By Louis Choris. 1816. Choris et al.,
Voyage pittoresque autour du monde, part 3 (Paris, 1822), plate 7. This lithograph of
Choris's watercolor captures the clothing, hairstyles, tattoos, and perhaps despair of
men who had only recently moved to the mission. BANC PIC 1963.002:0365, The
Bancroft Library, University of California, Berkeley

fugitives, Franciscans called upon soldiers and trusted Indians to bring them
back, and they flogged Indians who repeatedly left without permission.[40]

Disease, hunger, punishments—usually inflicted after Indians fled in search of
food and other comforts—and a general unhappiness with the constraints of life
cumulatively drove many Indians from the missions. Only on rare occasions were
the Indians' motivations investigated by Spanish officials. After at least 280 Indians abandoned Mission San Francisco in the spring of 1795 (approximately a
third of the mission's Indian population), the governor launched an inquiry into
the causes of this mass desertion. Twenty-three male adult Indians from the East
Bay were brought back to the mission and asked why they had fled.[41] The record

40. On the missionaries' justifications of these punishments, see Chapter 8, below.

41. For a discussion of the events surrounding this mass flight from the mission, see Milliken, *A Time
of Little Choice,* 137–146. Soldiers stated that too much work, too much punishment, and too much
hunger had caused the Indians to flee the mission. On the twenty-three adult Indians, see testimony of
runaway Indians, Aug. 12, 1797, San Francisco Presidio, AGN, CA, LXV, expediente 2, 108a–109a.
Milliken, in *A Time of Little Choice,* has provided a translation of the Indians' testimony (299–303). I
have consulted the original for my quotations and used Milliken for the Indians' native names and
biographical information.

of testimony is spare, usually not more than a sentence or two, but, when read in the context of events, it offers insight into how Indians did and did not adjust to the missions and how and when they sought to assert autonomy and independence within a controlling system.

Put simply, for many the specter of death and illness hung over the missions. Half of the Indians cited their own sickness, the death of a family member, or a fear of death as a reason for flight. Marciano Muiayaia, a forty-three-year-old Huchiun, "offered no other reason for having fled than that he had become sick." A close look at the mission's burial register suggests that no other reason would have been necessary. In the spring of 1795, an epidemic of unknown cause struck Mission San Francisco, and Indian deaths rose dramatically. Two hundred twenty-four neophytes died in 1795, 74 in March and April alone, compared to 123 in all of 1794 and 101 in all of 1796. Thus, people like Marciano Muiayaia had good reason to flee Mission San Francisco in 1795: it was an exceptionally unhealthy place that year.[42]

Eleven of the others explained that they left because of hunger. Per capita agricultural production at Mission San Francisco did decline in 1794 and 1795 as a result of drought, but not one of the Indians testified that there was not enough food. To the contrary, two acknowledged that mission-produced food might not have been bountiful in 1795 but was certainly available. Many Indians, however, especially those most recently baptized, did not consider the mission as their only source of food. For those new to the missions, the repetitive diet of corn and grain soups offered by the Franciscans was a poor and unpalatable substitute for the traditional variety to which their bodies were accustomed. Recent migrants to the missions would indeed be hungry. In fact, hunger as a stated motive for leaving correlates inversely with time spent in the mission. Of the twenty-three fugitive men who testified, thirteen had been baptized only a few months before their flight, and, of these thirteen, eleven stated hunger as a reason for their abandonment.[43]

42. Testimony of Marciano Muiayaia, Aug. 12, 1797, San Francisco Presidio, AGN, CA, LXV, expediente 2, 108a; Mission San Francisco de Asís libro de difuntos, 1776–1809, BL. In 1795, the crude death rate at Mission San Francisco was 250 (Milliken, *A Time of Little Choice*, app. 2, 266).

43. On the Costanoans' diet, see Richard Levy, "Costanoan," in *HNAI*, VIII, 491. See also Milliken, *A Time of Little Choice*; Robert F. Heizer and Albert B. Elsasser, *The Natural World of the California Indians* (Berkeley, Calif., 1980). Paleopathological studies do suggest that some Indians in the missions might have suffered from nutritional deficiencies (Phillip L. Walker, Patricia Lambert, and Michael J. DeNiro, "The Effects of European Contact on the Health of Alta California Indians," in *CC*, I, 352–355). The link between population change and nutrition and the degree to which malnutrition increases the human body's susceptibility to disease is not as clear as it once appeared. See Massimo Livi-Bacci, *Population and Nutrition: An Essay on European Demographic History* (Cambridge, 1990). Indians who had been at the mission for several years suggested that it was the padres' corporal punishment that led them to flee.

When Indians were denied the opportunity to leave, or when they were punished for leaving against the padres' wishes, they often fled. Indian testimony
clearly reveals that many found it difficult to balance the work the padres required of them with their desire to continue elements of their lives outside the
missions. At San Francisco, for example, Milan Alas stated that he had been
whipped by Father Antonio Dantí one afternoon after "he left work [in the
tannery] to look for clams to feed his family." And Prospero Chichis claimed that
he was punished by the same padre after "he had gone one night to the lagoon to
hunt ducks for food."[44] Significantly, this food gathering seems to have focused
on waterfowl and marine life, two sources of food that would have been minimally affected by the spread of European plants and animals. The efforts of these
men to supplement their diets are useful reminder of the risky yet pragmatic
flexibility of Indian food gathering at the missions; it stood in stark contrast to
the Franciscans' rigid agrarian and pastoral practices.

The Indians' testimony further suggests that these men relied on their families
and in particular on their wives, not on the missionaries or their functionaries, to
procure and prepare some of their food. Much of the gathering and the carrying
of customary foods back to the mission seems to have been the responsibility of
women. In 1801, thirty years after Mission San Carlos was founded, it was still
common for Indian women to return from the beach or the hills weighted down
with fish, shellfish, or seeds. At Mission San Francisco, Roman Ssumis, a fifty-
year-old man, stated that, after his wife and son left the mission, "he did not have
anyone to give him food." Otolon Eunucse, aged twenty-four, left Mission San
Francisco in part "because his wife did not care for him or give him food." And
Patabo Guecuéc, aged forty-three, claimed that, after his wife and two children
died, "he had no one to care for him."[45] Indian hunger and the fugitivism it
generated, therefore, were related to the disintegration in the missions of the
family networks and relationships Indians depended upon for gathering and
food preparation.

Although it is difficult to determine how many and how often baptized Indians
fled from the missions, the absolute number of permanent fugitives has been
historically overestimated, if Mission San Carlos is typical. The difference between the number of Indian baptisms minus Indian deaths and the resident
mission population should approximate the maximum number of Indians who

44. Testimony of Milan Alas and Prospero Chichis, Aug. 12, 1797, San Francisco Presidio, AGN, CA,
LXV, expediente 2, 108b–109a; Indian names from Milliken, *A Time of Little Choice,* 302–303.

45. Lasuén, "Refutation of Charges," June 19, 1801, Mission San Carlos, in Kenneally, ed. and trans.,
Writings of Lasuén, II, 209; testimony of runaway Indians (Roman Ssumis, Otolon Eunucse, and Patabo
Guecuéc), Aug. 12, 1797, San Francisco Presidio, AGN, CA, LXV, expediente 2, 108a–108b; Indian names
from Milliken, *A Time of Little Choice,* 300–302.

fled and never returned. This calculation suggests that, at Mission San Carlos, the maximum number of permanent fugitives through 1817 was 218, or 8.4 percent of the Indians baptized through that year. Through the end of 1831, the number was 298, or roughly 10.5 percent of the 2,844 Indians baptized at the mission. At least 80 San Carlos neophytes moved to other missions, where they died and were buried, bringing the number of permanent fugitives down to around 218, or about 7.7 percent of the Indians baptized at the mission through 1831, a figure far below the 15.6 percent suggested by previous historians.[46]

The letters of the padres and notations they left in the sacramental registers also can be used to estimate the total number of Indians who abandoned Mission San Carlos at one time or another. Some of those listed might have been coerced into returning; others likely were not so much fugitives as individuals trying to live a transient, coexistent life between missions and native villages. Thirty-nine Indians appear in the Franciscans' correspondence as huidos from San Carlos. Many of these, however, did return after an extended period away. Others lived out their days in their native rancherías. The baptismal and burial registers also reveal other Indians who left the missions, both temporarily and permanently. Sixteen neophytes were born while their parents were classified by the missionaries as fugitives, but most of these thirty-two parents came back. Sixty-eight Indians died away from the mission, most in a distant village. Some of these may safely be considered permanent fugitives, but others might have died suddenly while on paseo, on what they intended as a temporary absence, or on flights prompted by a sense of imminent death. These different sources suggest that 139 (4.9 percent of total mission baptisms) would be a conservative estimate of the number of permanent fugitives during the period 1770 through 1831.

Missionaries occasionally provided the military with lists indicating the names of absent Indians. These suggest rates of fugitivism from specific missions in a given year. One such list from San Carlos indicates a minimum rate of 1.3 percent

46. Sherburne F. Cook was the first scholar to attempt to calculate the number of fugitives from the missions (Cook, "Population Trends among the California Mission Indians," *Ibero-Americana,* XVII [1940], 399–446, esp. 425–526, rpt. in Cook, ed., *Conflict*). Cook revisited the issue of Indian fugitivism in "The Indian versus the Spanish Mission," *Ibero-Americana,* XXI (1943), 1–194, esp. 51, rpt. in Cook, ed., *Conflict.* He asserted that approximately 10 percent of the total mission population in Alta California permanently fled and that Mission San Carlos had the highest overall rate of neophyte fugitivism at 15.6 percent *(Conflict,* 59–61). He drew his conclusions from a transcription of a document that purports to list for each mission the number of Indians baptized, the number buried, the total alive, and the count of fugitives at the end of 1817 (see Archives of California, C–A 50, 356, BL). This document is misleading; its figures include Indians, soldiers, settlers, and anyone else who was baptized or buried at the mission. Cook believed that, at San Carlos, more than 3,000 Indians had been baptized through 1817, although the correct figure is fewer than 2,600. The number of Indians recorded in the death register of the mission through 1817 is also far fewer than believed by Cook; he posited more than 2,200, when the number is below 2,000.

in 1799.[47] Surviving lists from 1818 and 1819 show that rates varied from mission to mission but were normally very low, except in highly unusual circumstances, such as at San Francisco in 1795. In 1818, 4.5 percent of the Indians at San Fernando and 9.1 percent of those at Soledad were absent; yet, at Santa Barbara, the rate of fugitivism was 1.1 percent. Similarly, in 1819, less than 1 percent of the neophytes at Mission San Jose had fled. That same year, only 1.3 percent of the Indian population at Mission San Gabriel were missing; at Santa Clara, the rate was 1.8 percent. Hence the historical estimate of a fugitivism rate of 10 percent of all Indians baptized in the missions throughout the colonial period is too high; a figure of 5 percent may be more accurate, although rates fluctuated from year to year and mission to mission.[48]

Because most mission-born Indians did not live to adulthood, and life outside required skills that many mission-born Indians did not have, fugitives were far more likely to have been baptized as adults. This, of course, is not to imply that adult mission-born Indians were more content than those who came to the missions as adults; it does, however, suggest their limited options, because life in the countryside was simply not a viable option for the mission born, especially since, by the time they came of age, the natural landscape had been transformed into one more hospitable to livestock than Indians. Of the twenty-three men who fled Mission San Francisco in 1795 and later gave testimony about their motivations, at least twenty-one were baptized as adults. Similarly, most of the forty-seven fugitives from Mission San Fernando whom the padres identified by age in 1818 had been baptized as adults. Their average age when they fled was thirty-nine, and the group included thirteen men and women over age fifty, who, like the rest, must have had extensive experience living outside the mission.

47. The list from 1799 is incomplete, since the padres only listed those Indians whose whereabouts were known (Baltasar Carnicer and Francisco Pujol to Diego de Borica, Apr. 3, 1799, Taylor Coll., doc. 207, HL).

48. Marcos Antonio de Vitoria to José Antonio de la Guerra, June 3, 1818, San Fernando, DLG, folder 1016, HL; Antonio Ripoll, June 16, 1818, Santa Barbara, ibid., box 18, folder 827; Antonio Jayme to Pablo Vicente de Solá, Dec. 9, 1818, Taylor Coll., doc. 962, HL; Narciso Durán to governor, Dec. 31, 1819, Taylor Coll., doc. 964, HL; José María Zalvidea to Solá, Oct. 13, 1819, Taylor Coll., doc. 978, HL; José Viader to Solá, Nov. 1, 1819, Santa Clara, Taylor Coll., doc. 958, HL; Jayme to Solá, Dec. 9, 1818, Taylor Coll., doc. 962, HL; Cook, *Conflict*, 59–61.

Ironically, although scholars have actually overstated the number and percent of Indians who fled the missions, they have also most likely proposed rates of fugitivism that understate flight as an Indian response to the missions. Measuring fugitives as a percentage of the Indians baptized over the life of a mission or as a proportion of the annual mission population are valuable ways to compare missions and different moments in early California history. But these two methods create artificially low measures of Indian fugitivism, and neither can be fully adjusted to consider only Indians able to flee. Very high infant and childhood mortality dramatically reduced the number of mission-born Indians who could ever become permanent fugitives. And the inclusion of Indians too young or too old to flee in measuring fugitives as a percentage of a mission's annual population creates a misleadingly low rate of fugitivism.

At San Carlos, Indian fugitivism seems to have peaked in the early 1790s, when the mission's population was at its historic high and imperiled by an epidemic.[49] In subsequent years, flight—especially that which was intended as permanent— just does not seem to have been a feasible solution for even the most discontented. By then, few Indians lived removed from missions in the Monterey region. Trade networks through which Indians had acquired many of their staple foods had been thoroughly disrupted or even eliminated by the establishment of missions to the north, south, and east of San Carlos. And, by the early 1800s, most adults at the mission had been born there. These mission born were almost certainly less skilled than earlier generations in constructing brush huts, cultivating wild plants, and wringing an existence out of the countryside, especially one that now had grown stingy. Gradually, therefore, as the world changed around them and Indians transformed their world by relocating to the missions, they lost the ability and perhaps even the desire to balance older customary activities outside the mission with life inside it. Certainly, many Indians wanted a life away from the missions, but, increasingly during the 1810s and 1820s, Indians left, not for the countryside, but to work on a Spanish ranch or in one of California's growing pueblos, where they could ply skills or trades taught by the Franciscans or Spanish artisans. These late-colonial "fugitives," then, were not so much the displaced orphans of Spanish colonization and the dual revolutions as had been their parents and grandparents—but rather their most assimilated offspring.

DISEASE AND POPULATION DECLINE

Flight was in general an option taken by only a minority of Indians, and it only slightly reduced the size of mission communities. The majority of Indians who went to the missions stayed at the missions and tried to continue as before where possible; thus most looked back but did not go back, and they remained at places like San Carlos, where they died of disease or suffered drastically reduced fertility long before they could replenish their numbers and reestablish their communities. Mission populations were to prove incapable of surviving in California, as they struggled everywhere in northern New Spain, perhaps even less viable than the deteriorating village communities Indians had left behind. At Mission San Carlos, for example, the population rose for a quarter of a century after 1770— swelled as it was by a stream of adults and children from neighboring villages—

---

49. I base this conclusion in part on the fact that after 1795 no Indians baptized at San Carlos were born while their parents were fugitives.

but then dropped, steadily and seemingly irreversibly, once high mortality and low fertility undermined natural increases and the mission had drained its pool of local gentile Indians. There, in a nutshell, is a short history of all the California missions. They offered the promise of individual and community salvation, but they destroyed nearly all those they intended to save.

Then as now, the Indians' population collapse commanded attention—not just because it affected all aspects of colonial California, both Indian and Spanish, but because this catastrophe raised profound issues about the efficacy and morality of the Franciscan enterprise, leading contemporaries to fight over the causes and significance of the Indians' decline. Soldiers blamed missionaries. Missionaries at first blamed soldiers and Indians. And Indians, it seems, blamed missionaries and other Indians for the calamitous diseases that overtook them. In some areas of colonial America, disease and Indian depopulation had played into the hands of colonists and missionaries, who pointed to the ineffectiveness of native shamans and collective wisdom as proof of the justness of their colonial enterprise. But this does not seem to have been the case in Alta California, where padres acknowledged the utility of some Indian cures and admitted the failure of their own, and consistently high rates of Indian mortality led Indians to distrust missionaries and Franciscans to question openly the legacy of their endeavor.

Scholars have long observed that native Americans experienced a drastic population decline following European contact and colonization.[50] In the mission communities of Alta California, the decline of the Indians was documented in greater detail and with greater accuracy than nearly anywhere else in North America during the colonial period. Annual aggregate totals of births and deaths recorded by the Franciscans at Mission San Carlos and elsewhere reveal the inability of the Indian population to sustain itself through natural increase in the face of extremely high mortality. The annual crude death rate at Mission San Carlos averaged 79 deaths per thousand between 1784 and 1831 (Table 8). By our standards today, these are very high, but even for the eighteenth century this was

---

50. For modern introductions to the literature on Indian depopulation, see Nicolás Sánchez-Albornoz, coord., special issue of *Revista de Indias,* LXIII, no. 227 (January–April 2003); Russell Thornton, "Population History of Native North Americans," in Michael R. Haines and Richard H. Steckel, eds., *A Population History of North America* (Cambridge, 2000), 9–50; Thornton, "Health, Disease, and Demography," in Philip J. Deloria and Neal Salisbury, eds., *A Companion to American Indian History* (Malden, Mass., 2002), 68–84; see also John W. Verano and Douglas H. Ubelaker, eds., *Disease and Demography in the Americas* (Washington, D.C., 1992); Kenneth F. Kiple and Stephen V. Beck, eds., *Biological Consequences of European Expansion, 1450–1800* (Hampshire, 1997); Ann F. Ramenofsky, *Vectors of Death: The Archaeology of European Contact* (Albuquerque, N.Mex., 1987). A particularly useful examination of Indian population change in the missions of Texas is Mardith Keithly-Schuetz, "Demography of the Mission Indians," in Larsen, ed., *Native American Demography in the Spanish Borderlands,* Spanish Borderlands Sourcebooks, II, 206–231.

TABLE 8. General Population Table, Indians at Mission San Carlos, 1770–1831

Years	Gentile Baptisms	Births	Total Baptisms	Deaths	CBR	CDR	Mission Pop.
1770	3	0	3	0	—	—	—
1771	19	0	19	1	—	—	—
1772	7	1	8	2	—	—	—
1773	131	3	134	2	—	—	154
1774	95	4	99	17	20	85	244
1775	90	7	97	20	—	—	—
1776	47	14	61	3	—	—	—
1777	60	15	75	15	—	—	—
1778	31	19	50	22	—	—	—
1779	0	24	24	40	—	—	487
1780	11	19	30	41	—	—	—
1781	4	16	20	47	—	—	—
1782	77	21	98	67	—	—	—
1783	165	12	177	30	—	—	614
1784	61	29	90	44	46	70	645
1785	112	35	147	65	52	96	711
1786	23	28	51	69	40	98	694
1787	24	31	55	36	44	51	707
1788	34	32	66	53	45	74	720
1789	32	34	66	44	47	61	732
1790	48	33	81	101	46	140	712
1791	80	34	114	61	46	82	770
1792	85	29	114	77	37	98	800
1793	42	36	78	41	44	50	835
1794	33	48	81	55	57	65	861
1795	20	43	63	55	50	63	876
1796	11	18	29	59	21	69	835
1797	23	26	49	51	31	61	832
1798	14	37	51	44	47	56	738
1799	6	28	34	41	38	56	720
1800	0	37	37	18	50	25	747
1801	4	22	26	51	30	70	705
1802	5	16	21	79	23	113	688
1803	0	21	21	51	33	80	591
1804	16	15	31	45	25	76	591
1805	18	21	39	41	36	70	587

TABLE 8. *Continued*

Years	Gentile Baptisms	Births	Total Baptisms	Deaths	CBR	CDR	Mission Pop.
1806	55	15	70	76	26	134	550
1807	28	19	47	37	34	67	562
1808	11	28	39	51	50	92	550
1809	9	20	29	41	37	76	533
1810	0	18	18	42	34	80	511
1811	0	23	23	43	46	86	485
1812	0	17	17	42	36	89	455
1813	0	19	19	28	42	62	448
1814	1	15	16	32	34	73	431
1815	1	25	26	32	59	75	423
1816	2	18	20	35	43	85	405
1817	0	26	26	28	64	69	402
1818	0	19	19	29	48	73	390
1819	5	30	35	22	76	56	397
1820	1	16	17	34	41	87	381
1821	2	19	21	24	50	64	374
1822	0	12	12	44	34	123	341
1823	1	20	21	32	61	97	317
1824	1	18	19	28	58	90	306
1825	1	17	18	28	57	93	295
1826	1	19	20	17	66	59	277
1827	2	13	15	15	47	54	275
1828	6	12	18	55	47	216	234
1829	1	14	15	16	60	69	233
1830	1	15	16	16	65	69	229
1831	0	9	9	8	41	37	209
Total	1,560	1,284	2,844	2,343			
Avg.					45	79	

Note: The table is designed to show shifts in population at the mission, and thus it includes the occasional baptisms and burials of Indians not native to the Monterey region. It does not include 52 or so Indians baptized at San Carlos who came to the mission with soldiers after Spain gave up Nootka Sound. The crude birth rate (CBR) is the live births in a year over the midyear population multiplied by the constant 1,000. The crude death rate (CDR) is the deaths in a year over the midyear population multiplied by the constant 1,000.

Source: Gentile baptisms, births, and deaths: figures are from my database of baptisms, marriages, and burials at San Carlos compiled from the mission's registers (see Appendix A for methodology). Annual population totals are from the annual reports of the mission in SBMAL; and Zephyrin Engelhardt, *Mission San Carlos Borromeo (Carmelo): The Father of the Missions* (1934; rpt. Ramona, Calif., 1973), app. B, "Spiritual Results," 243.

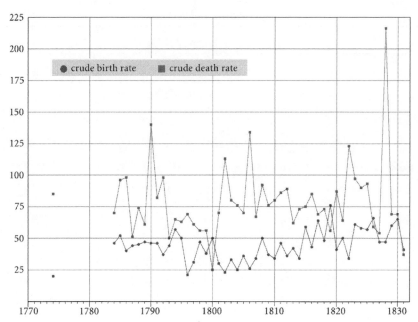

FIGURE 2. Annual Crude Birth and Death Rates, Indians, Mission San Carlos, 1770–1831. Drawn by Rebecca L. Wrenn. The mission population is not known in 1770–1772, 1775–1778, or 1780–1782. Figures are from my database of baptisms, marriages, and burials at San Carlos compiled from the mission's registers (see Appendix A for methodology)

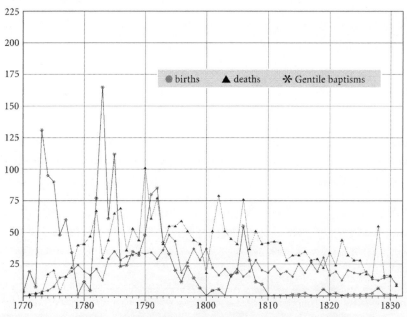

FIGURE 3. Annual Births, Deaths, and Gentile Baptisms, Mission San Carlos, 1770–1831. Drawn by Rebecca L. Wrenn. Annual totals of births, deaths, and gentile baptisms are from my database compiled from the mission's registers (see Appendix A for methodology)

FIGURE 4. Annual Population, Mission San Carlos, 1770–1831. Drawn by Rebecca L. Wrenn.
The mission population is not known in 1770–1772, 1775–1778, or 1780–1782. Annual popu-
lation totals are from annual reports of the mission, in SBMAL; and Zephyrin Engelhardt,
Mission San Carlos Borromeo (Carmelo): The Father of the Missions (1934; rpt. Ramona,
Calif., 1973), app. B, "Spiritual Results," 243

extraordinary. For example, in England between 1730 and 1820, the crude death
rate dropped from 31 to 24 per thousand. During epidemics, the crude death rate
at Mission San Carlos surpassed 100, and, in 1828, when nearly a quarter of the
Indians at the mission died, it reached a staggering 216 per thousand. The least
healthy season was winter, when rain, wind, and fog rendered the mission cold,
damp, and especially lethal (Tables 9, 10). Since morbidity—the incidence of
disease in a population—is normally greater than mortality (unless everybody
dies), in a year in which between 5 and 10 percent of the mission population
succumbed to disease, a far greater percentage would have been sick and possibly
incapacitated by illness. Significantly, the average annual crude death rate at the
mission was nearly double the average annual crude birth rate of 45 births per
thousand. Thus, in nearly every year of the mission's existence, the Indian population was failing to reproduce itself. During the mission's first decades, this
population collapse was masked by new arrivals, but, once the influx began to
taper off in the early 1790s, the population peaked at 876 and then went into

TABLE 9. Monthly Distribution of Births and Conceptions, Indians,
Mission San Carlos, 1770–1834

	J	F	M	A	M	J	J	A	S	O	N	D	
	MONTH OF BIRTH												
	A	M	J	J	A	S	O	N	D	J	F	M	Total
	MONTH OF CONCEPTION												
No. of births	124	116	117	85	96	96	97	87	88	64	97	77	1,144
Proportion	128	131	121	90	99	102	100	90	94	66	103	79	1,203

Note: Table includes Indians only, not the *gente de razón*. The proportion is a figure that takes into account
the number of days in each month, thereby compensating for the unequal length of the months. To arrive
at the proportion, for each month the number of births is divided by the number of days. The resulting
figures are replaced by proportional numbers such that all total 1,200. If births were not seasonal, each
month would be represented by a proportional value of 100. The total of all twelve values may be slightly
above or below 1,200 because of rounding.

Source: Figures are from my database of baptisms, marriages, and burials at San Carlos compiled from the
mission's registers (see Appendix A for methodology). Calculations performed by CASOAR Program CG4.

steady decline. By 1821, the last year of Spanish rule in California, the mission
population stood at 374; a decade later, it was fewer than 210.[51]

Although aggregate annual statistics and crude birth and death rates allow for
an observation of gross population trends, the use of nominal records and the
technique of family reconstitution provide the means for an analysis of population change. Once families have been reconstituted and the life course of individuals has been charted, this method can yield evidence as to how the high mortality at Mission San Carlos was distributed among age groups and whether it was
concentrated among the very young or very old. In particular, family reconstitution is useful in measuring mortality during infancy and childhood, the periods
of early life when death is most likely. Similarly, estimates of the rates of fertility—
or the number of births per woman—across different age cohorts can determine
the degree to which the low number of births at the mission was related to
individual women's having few children or to a low number of women of reproductive age.[52]

51. There is an extensive literature on Indian population decline in Alta California. Among the most
important works are Cook, *Conflict*; Cook, *The Population of the California Indians, 1769–1970* (Berkeley, Calif., 1976); Jackson, *Indian Population Decline*. The crude death rate (CDR) is the number of
deaths in a year divided by the total population at midyear and multiplied by 1,000. The crude birth
rate (CBR) is the births in a year divided by the total population at midyear and multiplied by 1,000.

52. This is not to discount the merits of inverse or back projection, but family reconstitution can
provide for a much fuller demographic analysis. The reconstitution of the Mission San Carlos Indian
community and the population analysis derived from it are discussed in Appendix A, below. The full
demographic analysis presented here is supported by preliminary work on population change at
Missions San Diego and San Gabriel that yielded similar results. My study of population change at San
Diego and San Gabriel has been undertaken with data compiled under my supervision by the staff of

An analysis based on family reconstitution shows that infant mortality was extremely high at Mission San Carlos. Eleven percent of all infants died in the first month of life, and nearly all these deaths occurred in the first two weeks after delivery (Table 11). These rates suggest that many infants arrived prematurely, suffered from congenital birth defects, had a very low birth weight, or contracted a lethal infection at birth or during a difficult delivery. Infants whose births followed that of an older sibling by nine to fifteen months—and therefore might have been premature—were twice as likely to die in the first month of life as those whose mothers had a longer interval between births. At the mission, infant mortality declined over the first five months of life, but it increased around the twelfth month, perhaps due to weaning, teething, and the introduction of solid foods. Many Indian women nursed their children for eighteen or twenty months, but the onset of weaning would have deprived infants of some of the immunities they received from nursing; teething and open gums would have made them more susceptible to infection; and infection might have been introduced when they began to eat solid foods and drink water.[53]

All told, 37 percent of babies born at Mission San Carlos died before their first birthday. Infant mortality was a burden shared equally by both sexes: 39 percent of males and 35 percent of females died in the first year of life (Table 12). The rate varied a bit with the seasons; infants born in the winter and spring had a slightly higher mortality than those born in the summer or fall.[54] Infant mortality, however, did vary by decade, and therefore it seems to have been related to both the size of the mission population—which would have had an impact on sanitary conditions—and the type of structures the Indians lived in. Infant mortality at the mission was at its highest in the 1780s, when the population surpassed seven hundred Indians, most of whom lived in the straw-hut village. The rate was at its lowest in the 1820s, when the population dipped below three hundred and all of the Indians lived in adobe structures that provided some warmth and protection from the elements. (The infant mortality rate for the 1770s is deceptive, given the small number of births at the mission in that decade.) (Table 13) Indian housing was not inherently unhealthful, but, under normal circumstances,

---

the Early California Population Project. There have been no previous analyses of population change in the missions according to the standard guidelines of family reconstitution as currently practiced by European historical demographers; thus I draw my comparisons between the mission and seventeenth- and eighteenth-century Europe. On the lack of family reconstitution studies for colonial Mexico, see Robert McCaa, "The Peopling of Mexico from Origins to Revolution," in Richard Steckel and Michael Haines, eds., *The Population History of North America* (Cambridge, 2000), 241–304.

53. Josep Bernabeu-Mestre, "Problèmes de santé et causes de décès infantiles en Espagne (1900–1935)," *Annales de démographie historique* (1994), 61–77, esp. 70. On the Indians' nursing customs, see Rollin, "Memoire physiologique," 27.

54. Although more infants died in December, January, February, and March than other months, more were also born in those months.

TABLE 10. Monthly Distribution of Deaths, Indians, Mission San Carlos, 1770–1834

Age at Death		MONTH OF DEATH								
		J	F	M	A	M	J	J	A	S
0–12 mos.	No.	69	71	84	63	56	59	50	53	52
	Proportion	112	127	137	106	91	99	81	86	87
1–4 yrs.	No.	48	44	30	18	19	23	21	14	26
	Proportion	170	171	106	66	67	84	75	50	95
5–19 yrs.	No.	32	26	38	24	21	10	15	16	20
	Proportion	141	125	167	109	92	45	66	70	91
20–59 yrs.	No.	100	69	106	71	71	65	44	50	50
	Proportion	144	109	152	106	102	97	63	72	74
60+ yrs.	No.	7	4	9	5	8	12	6	8	8
	Proportion	91	57	117	67	104	161	78	104	107
All deaths	No.	256	214	267	181	175	169	136	141	156
	Proportion	135	124	141	99	92	92	72	74	85

Note: Table includes Indians only, not the *gente de razón*. The proportion is a figure that takes into account the number of days in each month, thereby compensating for the unequal length of the months. To arrive at the proportion, for each month the number of deaths is divided by the number of days. The resulting figures are replaced by proportional numbers such that all total 1,200. If deaths were not seasonal, each month would be represented by a proportional value of 100. The total of all twelve values may be slightly above or below 1,200 because of rounding.

Source: Figures are from my database of baptisms, marriages, and burials at San Carlos compiled from the mission's registers (see Appendix A for methodology). Calculations performed by CASOAR Program CG4.

Indians of the Monterey region had seasonal encampments, moving from place to place and constantly rebuilding their villages. Most villages were not inhabited year-round. This, however, was not the case with Indian brush huts at the mission, and, over time, the Indian village at Mission San Carlos appears to have become unhealthful.

San Carlos's infant mortality rate of 366 per thousand is consistent with estimated infant mortality at other California missions. Moreover, it is consistent with the highest rates in many preindustrial communities of the past. In the late 1800s, infant mortality in Europe varied from around 100 in Norway and Sweden to 250 in Germany, Austria, and Russia. And, in the seventeenth and eighteenth centuries, many European communities experienced rates on a level with those at Mission San Carlos. In England between 1580 and 1750, roughly 10 percent of all babies died in the first month; the same was true at San Carlos. In London in the 1730s and 1740s, infant mortality was above 300 per thousand. In the French countryside during the first half of the eighteenth century, the infant mortality rate fluctuated between 120 and 360 per thousand; and, in a sample of Italian towns of the early eighteenth century, infant mortality was consistently above 320

O	N	D	Total
48	48	72	725
78	81	117	1202
36	29	24	332
128	106	85	1203
23	20	23	268
101	91	101	1199
58	44	91	819
83	65	131	1198
7	7	10	91
91	94	129	1200
172	148	220	2235
91	81	116	1202

per thousand. In some regions of eighteenth-century Spain, infant mortality was well above 200 and even topped 300 per thousand in some communities. Thus, infant mortality at Mission San Carlos is best understood as being roughly equivalent to that which characterized the most unhealthful communities in Europe through the seventeenth and eighteenth centuries. And, in all likelihood, the high infant mortality at Mission San Carlos was not a dramatic increase from rates commonly experienced by California Indians before Spanish colonization.[55]

55. Phillip L. Walker and John R. Johnson, "For Everything There Is a Season: Chumash Indian Births, Marriages, and Deaths at the Alta California Missions," in D. Ann Herring and Alan C. Swedlund, eds., *Human Biologists in the Archives: Demography, Health, Nutrition, and Genetics in Historical Populations* (Cambridge, 2003), 53–77; Johnson, "The Chumash and the Missions," in *CC*, I, 365–375, esp. 372; Carlo A. Corsini and Pier Paolo Viazzo, "Recent Advances and Some Open Questions in the Long-term Study of Infant and Child Mortality," in Corsini and Viazzo, eds., *The Decline of Infant and Child Mortality: The European Experience, 1750–1990* (The Hague, 1997), xiii; E. A. Wrigley, R. S. Davies, J. E. Oeppen, and R. S. Schofield, *English Population History from Family Reconstitution, 1580–1837*, 226, table 6.4; John Landers, *Death and the Metropolis: Studies in the Demographic History of London, 1670–1830* (Cambridge, 1993), 192; Jacques Dupâquier, "La France avant la transition démographique," Guiliano Pinto and Eugenio Sonnino, "L'Italie," both in Jean-Pierre Bardet and Dupâquier, eds., *Histoire des populations de l'Europe: Des origines aux prémices de la révolution démographique*, I

TABLE 11. Infant Mortality Rates by Season and Age, Indians, Mission San Carlos, 1770–1834

Age (Mos.)	SEASON OF BIRTH				
	Winter (Jan–Mar)	Spring (Apr–Jun)	Summer (Jul–Sep)	Fall (Oct–Dec)	Year (Jan–Dec)
0	122	118	99	96	111
1	56	55	45	82	58
2	51	53	47	91	59
3	21	23	11	29	20
4	21	17	23	7	18
5	9	6	18	23	13
6	4	42	18	24	20
7	22	13	6	32	18
8	18	6	12	0	11
9	19	6	13	0	11
10	33	26	19	17	25
11	40	14	26	68	36

Note: This table shows rates of infant mortality, not numbers of deaths. Each figure expresses the rate of mortality per 1,000 infants in that age group. For example, 122 of every 1,000 infants born in winter died in the first month of life. Similarly, 55 of every 1,000 infants born in spring who survived the first month died in the second month of life; 47 of every 1,000 infants born in summer who survived the first two months of life died during the third month; and so on.

Source: Figures are from my database of baptisms, marriages, and burials at San Carlos compiled from the mission's registers (see Appendix A for methodology). Calculations performed by CASOAR Program CD2.

Childhood mortality—deaths between the ages of one and five—was a different story. In most societies studied by historical demographers, the rate of childhood mortality is considerably lower than that of infant mortality. But, at Mission San Carlos, the infant mortality rate of 366 per thousand was surpassed by a childhood mortality rate of 427 per thousand (see Table 12). In other words, 37 percent of all newborns died in the first year, and 43 percent of those who survived the first year died before their fifth birthday. The rate of childhood mortality at Mission San Carlos was nearly four times that of England in the

(Paris, 1997), 452, 501; David Sven Reher, *Town and Country in Pre-industrial Spain: Cuenca, 1550–1870* (Cambridge, 1990), 111, table 3.20; Reher, Vicente Pérez-Moreda, and Bernabeu-Mestre, "Assessing Change in Historical Contexts: Childhood Mortality Patterns in Spain during the Demographic Transition," in Corsini and Viazzo, eds., *Decline of Infant Mortality,* 39, table 2.1. See also Johnson, "Chumash Social Organization: An Ethnohistoric Perspective" (Ph.D. diss., University of California, Santa Barbara, 1988), 143–146, tables 5.2, 5.3, 5.4.

TABLE 12. Mortality Rates of Indians Age 0–14, Mission San Carlos, 1770–1834

Age (Years)	All	Males	Females	Survivors (Male and Female)
0	366	385	349	634
1	213	236	194	499
2	107	108	106	446
3	125	139	113	390
4	68	84	56	363
5	37	46	31	350
6	33	43	27	338
7	56	63	51	319
8	51	94	24	303
9	61	48	68	285
10	33	56	19	275
11	54	37	64	260
12	16	0	25	256
13	18	0	29	252
14	62	0	100	236
1–4	427	462	394	
5–9	217	262	156	
10–14	171	91	119	

Note: This table shows rates of mortality, not numbers of deaths. Each figure expresses the rate of mortality per 1,000 individuals in that age group. For example, 213 of every 1,000 children who survived their first year would die before their second birthday. Two hundred thirty-six of 1,000 boys born at the mission who survived their first year would die before their second birthday. Survivors are the number of original 1,000 births still living. Thus, of 1,000 live births at the mission, 366 would die in the first year, leaving 634 to live beyond their first birthday; of these, 213 per thousand would die (135 of the 634 survivors), leaving 499 to survive after their second birthday.

Source: Figures are from my database of baptisms, marriages, and burials at San Carlos compiled from the mission's registers (see Appendix A for methodology). Calculations performed by CASOAR Program CD1.

seventeenth and eighteenth centuries, and nearly double that of Spain in the eighteenth century.[56]

As with infant mortality, both of the sexes suffered very high childhood mortality rates: 46 percent of boys and 39 percent of girls died between ages one and five. This meant a very low expectation of life at birth: 11.2 years. At Mission San Carlos, the healthiest years of life were those between early childhood and adult-

56. Wrigley, Davies, Oeppen, and Schofield, *English Population History,* 250–251, table 6.10; Reher, *Town and Country in Pre-industrial Spain,* 111, table 3.21; Reher, Pérez-Moreda, and Bernabeu-Mestre, "Assessing Change in Historical Contexts," in Corsini and Viazzo, eds., *Decline of Infant Mortality,* 39, table 2.1.

TABLE 13. Mortality Rates of Indians Age 0–9 by Decade, Mission San Carlos, 1770–1829

	DECADE					
Age	1770s	1780s	1790s	1800s	1810s	1820s
0	106	432	407	404	341	302
1–4	245	422	454	496	369	571
5–9	141	243	252	283	191	91

Note: This table shows rates of mortality, not numbers of deaths. Each figure expresses the rate of mortality per 1,000 individuals in that age group. For example, in the 1780s, 432 of every 1,000 live births died before their first birthday; the survivors died at a rate of 422 per thousand between their first and fifth birthdays.
Source: Figures are from my database of baptisms, marriages, and burials at San Carlos compiled from the mission's registers (see Appendix A for methodology). Calculations performed by CASOAR Program CD1.

hood, yet the risk of dying between ages five and fifteen was still three to four times greater than in England during the seventeenth and eighteenth centuries. Less than 25 percent of Indians born at Mission San Carlos lived to age fifteen.[57]

The comparatively healthy years that Indians enjoyed at Mission San Carlos between ages five and fifteen did not herald the onset of a long adult life. Mortality rose dramatically for men and women during the early adult years, when they became sexually active and were exposed to a host of diseases. Mortality remained high throughout adult life and increased steadily with age (Table 14). Although both sexes suffered similarly high rates of mortality as infants, children, and adolescents, the dangers of childbearing led the mortality of adult women to far outstrip that of adult men. These risks were extreme during and after the first pregnancy; nearly one in three married women who survived to age fifteen died before age nineteen. For most age cohorts, adult mortality at Mission San Carlos was two to three times that found in seventeenth- and eighteenth-century England. These exceptionally high rates, in particular among women, must have contributed to the rates of infant and childhood mortality, for the death of one or both parents could have had serious consequences for the nutrition and health of children born at the mission. Furthermore, the high mortality rates among women of reproductive age lowered the crude birth rate by reducing the number of women of childbearing age.

Decades of elevated mortality among adult women created an abnormal population structure at San Carlos. In 1780, when the mission was largely composed of recently arrived villagers, the population, when distributed by age and sex, resembled a pyramid, with women between ages twenty to forty outnumbering their male counterparts. Forty years later, however, the natural pyramidal shape

57. Wrigley, Davies, Oeppen, and Schofield, *English Population History,* 250–251, table 6.10.

TABLE 14. Mortality Rates of Adult Indians by Age Group and Sex, Mission San Carlos, 1770–1834

Age Group	MALE		FEMALE		BOTH SEXES	
	Pessimistic	Optimistic	Pessimistic	Optimistic	Pessimistic	Optimistic
15–19	149	158	316	336	235	249
20–24	178	173	182	185	179	179
25–29	168	165	312	304	230	225
30–34	180	175	285	276	223	217
35–39	218	221	314	298	257	252
40–44	237	224	174	173	214	204
45–49	223	220	345	328	273	263
50–54	258	241	459	444	342	324
55–59	421	404	184	184	325	317
60–64	487	489	677	677	600	592
65–69	470	421	600	600	540	512
70–74	800	800	500	500	615	615

Note: There are two sets of results, pessimistic and optimistic, according to whether the end of observation is the earliest or latest possible. This table shows rates of mortality for married adults, not numbers of deaths. Each figure expresses the rate of mortality per 1,000 individuals in that age group. For example, individuals in the age group 45 to 49 experienced a rate of mortality of 263 or 273 per thousand; men in that age group experienced a rate of mortality of 220 or 223 per thousand.

Source: Figures are from my database of baptisms, marriages, and burials at San Carlos compiled from the mission's registers (see Appendix A for methodology). Calculations performed by CASOAR Program CD6.

of the population had been destroyed, and men outnumbered women in every age group between fifteen and sixty-four.

The high mortality rates at Mission San Carlos among all age groups, and in particular among adult married women, provide only a partial explanation of the rapid collapse of the Indian population at San Carlos and throughout Alta California. Ultimately, the constant inability of Indians to offset their deaths by births doomed them. To better understand the reasons behind population growth or decline, historical demographers frequently measure the number of children produced in a community by calculating age-specific marital fertility rates.[58] At Mission San Carlos, the age-specific marital fertility rate for women aged twenty

58. This measure has the advantage of relating births registered in a community, not to the overall population of the community, as with the crude birth rate, but rather only to those women at risk of having those births. In other words, the age-specific marital fertility rate measures the number of children produced by women at different periods in their reproductive life, commonly accepted as between the ages fifteen and forty-nine. The rate is calculated by dividing the number of births occurring to women in a particular age cohort by the number of years women of that age cohort were exposed to the risk of bearing a child. For example, between the ages twenty and twenty-four, a married

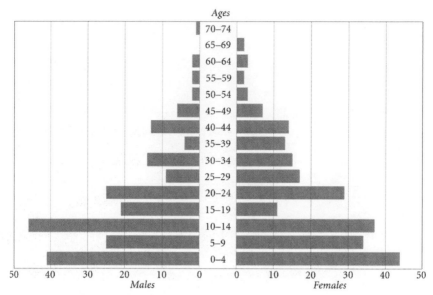

FIGURE 5. Population Pyramid, Mission San Carlos, 1780. Population totals for each age group are from my database of baptisms and burials at San Carlos compiled from the mission's registers (see Appendix A for methodology). Drawn by Rebecca L. Wrenn

to twenty-four was 287 per thousand, suggesting that most women between those ages would have given birth to only one child during those five years (Table 15). By this measure, the fertility of women at Mission San Carlos was low, lower than that in contemporary Spain, France, England, and Germany, where women would have most likely given birth to two children between the ages twenty and twenty-four. In fact, the fertility of women at the mission was low enough that it could only have reproduced a population that experienced very low rates of mortality. Low marital fertility rates at Mission San Carlos do not seem to have been the result of the Indians' own attempts at contraception, for the Indians' fertility patterns conform to that of a population that did not practice it.[59]

---

woman will have five years of exposure to the risk of having a child. If, during those five years, she has one child, her marital fertility rate will be 200 per 1,000 (1/5 × 1,000).

59. Dupâquier, "La France avant la transition démographique," in Bardet and Dupâquier, eds., *Histoire des populations de l'Europe*, 453; John E. Knodel, *Demographic Behavior in the Past: A Study of Fourteen German Village Populations in the Eighteenth and Nineteenth Centuries* (Cambridge, 1988), 257; Reher, *Town and Country in Pre-industrial Spain*, 92; Wrigley, Davies, Oeppen, and Schofield, *English Population History*, 355. It is unlikely that an underregistration of births at the mission explains the low age-specific marital fertility rates at Mission San Carlos, and the rates have been calculated using Louis Henry's method designed to compensate for underregistration of births. Indian women at San Carlos measured .004 on the Coale-Trussel Index, where a value greater than 0.20 suggests that birth control is likely and a value greater than 0.30 suggests it is certain.

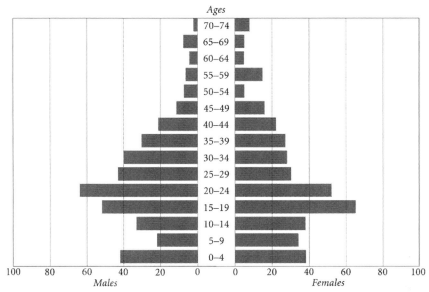

FIGURE 6. Population Pyramid, Mission San Carlos, 1800. Population totals for each age group are from my database of baptisms and burials at San Carlos compiled from the mission's registers (see Appendix A for methodology). Drawn by Rebecca L. Wrenn

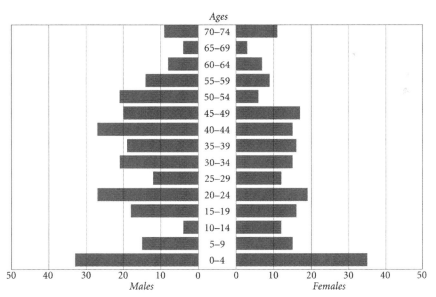

FIGURE 7. Population Pyramid, Mission San Carlos, 1820. Population totals for each age group are from my database of baptisms and burials at San Carlos compiled from the mission's registers (see Appendix A for methodology). Drawn by Rebecca L. Wrenn

TABLE 15. Age-Specific Marital Fertility Rates, Indians, Mission San Carlos, 1770–1834

Age at Marr.	ACTUAL AGE						
	15–19	20–24	25–29	30–34	35–39	40–44	45–49
15–19	250	303	237	245	130	69	107
20–24		249	299	217	231	311	0
25–29			230	222	201	143	0
30–34				241	129	26	0
35–39					195	142	44
40–44						72	26
45–49							73
Overall	250	287	254	231	164	119	42

Note: Figures in this table are not actual births but the births per 1,000 women for each age group. For exam-ple, if 1,000 women married at age fifteen and stayed married for the next five years, they would have pro-duced 250 children before they were twenty years old.

Source: Figures are from my database of baptisms, marriages, and burials at San Carlos compiled from the mis-sion's registers (see Appendix A for methodology). Calculations performed by CASOAR Program CF1A.

To estimate the number of children a woman would have had if her childbear-ing experience replicated that of all women in each specific age group, one can sum the age-specific fertility rates and arrive at what demographers call the average total marital fertility rate. By this measure, married women at Mission San Carlos who lived to age fifty and stayed married would have given birth to 6 children during their reproductive lives. By modern standards, this figure may seem high, but it is low compared to societies of the past. English women gave birth on average to 7.5 children during the seventeenth and eighteenth centuries, and French women gave birth to more than 8. And, in the nineteenth century, the average total fertility of the Euromestizo elite of Mexico City was 8.5.[60]

At Mission San Carlos, however, most Indian women gave birth to far fewer than the 6 children suggested by the rate of total fertility. The average age of first marriage for mission-born women was fifteen, the average interval between marriage and the birth of the first child was a long forty-six months, and the average interval between births was thirty-three months.[61] Women who were still married at age fifty gave birth to their last child on average at age forty-one. But less than 10 percent of women who married at the mission were alive and married

60. Robert McCaa, "The Peopling of Mexico from Origins to Revolution," in Richard Steckel and Michael Haines, eds., *The Population History of North America* (Cambridge, 2000), 250.

61. Forty-six months is a long interval, suggesting that many young women lost their first child. For women who delivered in the first thirty-six months after marriage—and most likely therefore would have not lost a first pregnancy—the interval between marriage and the birth of the first child was twenty-two months.

at fifty. When high adult female mortality is factored into the low fertility of women at the mission, the "true" total fertility of women at Mission San Carlos plummets to a meager 1.9 children, obviously below the necessary figure of 2.6 or 2.7 sufficient to reproduce the population. Thus, although very high mortality at the mission among infants, children, and women of reproductive age was the principal cause of the population collapse at Mission San Carlos, low fertility accelerated the decline of the Indians' numbers; it meant that surviving women were producing unusually few children at a time when the community was suffering a mortality crisis. Padres and Indians, no doubt, struggled to grasp the enormity of this problem. At San Buenaventura, from 1811 to 1815, missionaries recorded the names of pregnant women and whether the women delivered a living child. Tragically, they found that nearly one in four pregnancies ended in miscarriage or stillbirth. At La Purísima, the crisis was even more severe: in 1810, the majority of pregnant women, especially the youngest, had stillborns, according to the missionaries.[62]

Excessively high mortality and low fertility throughout Alta California were largely the result of a host of chronic infectious diseases introduced to the region by the Spaniards. Close quarters, little shelter from wind, rain, or fog, and bad water, in all likelihood fouled by Spanish livestock or the Indian village itself, proved especially lethal at San Carlos. Clearly, epidemics also exacted a terrible toll: in at least nine years between 1770 and 1831, the crude death rate approached or surpassed 100 per thousand at the mission. Through 1808, when the last gentiles attained baptism, most of these epidemics—revealed through a surge and decline in the crude death rate—coincided with the arrival of large numbers of gentiles from the surrounding area. But it is not clear whether soaring death rates were the result of previously healthy Indians' living in overcrowded conditions at the mission or whether sick Indians from the countryside came to the mission after epidemics tore through their villages. In all likelihood, both scenarios reinforced one another, and the health of Indians in and out of the missions probably deteriorated in tandem.[63]

The most detailed description of the illnesses that plagued Mission San Carlos was recorded by Claude-Nicolas Rollin, who served as surgeon to the La Pérouse expedition. Rollin was to be granted a pension if he could keep the mortality rate

62. Cf. Cook, *Conflict*, 415–416; and see "Book of Clothing Distribution to Indians, Mission San Buenaventura, 1806–1815," Archival Center of the Archdiocese of Los Angeles (this record appears on the last page of the book); Mariano Payeras to Tapis, Jan. 13, 1810, La Purísima, in Donald C. Cutter, ed. and trans., *Writings of Mariano Payeras* (Santa Barbara, Calif., 1995), 50. Only 37 of the 390 families remained under observation when the woman reached age fifty.

63. Of course, not all premature deaths were the result of disease. Mission burial registers record that Indians throughout Alta California died after bear attacks, insect bites, and acts of violence; some suffered fatal injuries when they were gored by cattle, crushed by wagons, or thrown from horses.

of the *Boussoule* under 3 percent, and, in keeping with the spirit of the expedition, he was to examine the bodies of the Indians he encountered and investigate their maladies and cures. When Rollin visited the mission in 1786, he interviewed a surgeon from the presidio, a resident Franciscan, and several neophytes. Moreover, hundreds of Indians separated by sex assembled in the mission plaza and stood for inspection. Rollin learned that, in the winter, these Indians suffered from throat and lung infections; in the spring, they endured fever and digestive ailments. Summer brought dysentery. Poor care compounded ailments such that they became grievous and lethal. Failed pregnancies were common, and infants often suffered from convulsions, whooping cough, strabismus, and diarrhea.[64]

Missionaries and government officials in California had none of Rollin's training and did little more than guess at the identity of the diseases that erupted in their midst. Their accounts, however, suggest that diphtheria, dysentery, measles, influenza, and tuberculosis were the most prevalent and dangerous illnesses in the missions. In 1802, diphtheria and pneumonia were the likely culprits in an epidemic that killed 11 percent of the Indians at San Carlos. In 1806, measles carried off another 13 percent. Both of these epidemics exacted a similarly high toll at other California missions. In July 1806, Father Mariano Payeras lamented that, at Mission La Purísima, where the disease killed 150 Indians, "the measles with the consequences has cleaned out the mission and filled the cemeteries." Smallpox, the most lethal of the diseases that scourged the Indians of the New World during the colonial period, most likely did not take hold in Alta California until the late 1820s and seems not to have hit Mission San Carlos until the 1840s. Measles might have been the cause of an epidemic that killed more than 20 percent of the Indians at San Carlos in 1828.[65]

Although deadly epidemics periodically erupted in the mission, endemic disease exacted a higher cumulative toll. So many Indians died from disease every year that even in nonepidemic years the crude death rate was disastrously high. Dysentery and other waterborne illnesses were ever present. Overcrowding and the housing of single and widowed women in a cramped separate dormitory must have aided the spread of infection. Furthermore, venereal diseases, notably gonorrhea and syphilis, both highly infectious, not only contributed to the high

64. Rollin, "Memoire physiologique," 18, 27.
65. Cook, *Conflict*, 17–30; Milliken, *A Time of Little Choice*, 172–176, 193–200; Phillip L. Walker and John R. Johnson, "Effects of Contact on the Chumash Indians," in Verano and Ubelaker, eds., *Disease and Demography*, 127–139, esp. 133–135; Mariano Payeras to Josef Vinalls [sic], July 2, 1806, La Purísima, in Cutter, ed. and trans., *Writings of Mariano Payeras*, 34; Cook, "Smallpox in Spanish and Mexican California, 1770–1845," *Bulletin of the History of Medicine*, VII (1939), 153–191. See also Robert M. Moses, "Smallpox Immunization in Alta California: A Story Based on José Estrada's 1821 Postscript," *SCQ*, LXI (1979), 125–145.

PLATE 11. *Reception of La Pérouse at Mission San Carlos.* By José Cardero. 1791. La Pérouse and his officers, including the ship's doctor, Claude-Nicolas Rollin, tour the mission in 1786. Missionaries greet the Frenchmen, and Indian men and women are lined up in separate rows for review. In the left background is the Indian *ranchería* and to the right are the mission's bells, which called Indians to prayer and work. Cardero created this drawing from an original sketch at San Carlos. Courtesy, Museo Naval, Madrid

mortality but almost certainly contributed to the low fertility that prevented the mission population from stabilizing between epidemics.[66]

Until the middle of the nineteenth century, gonorrhea was confused with syphilis or assumed to be a different manifestation of the same illness. And syphilis itself was very difficult to diagnose until modern times, as its symptoms closely resemble those of dozens of other diseases. The Franciscans, military officers, and visitors to the region, however, were convinced that syphilis was endemic to Indians in the missions; and, although their conviction that Indians lived as sexual libertines predisposed them to see syphilis in many of the Indians' ailments, their correspondence makes a powerful case that syphilis—and in all likelihood gonorrhea—were indeed prevalent among Indians in colonial California. These Indians might have first contracted a virulent form of the diseases from Portolá's expeditionary force; one account suggests that Anza brought

66. Joseph A. McFalls, Jr., and Marguerite Harvey McFalls, *Disease and Fertility* (Orlando, Fla., 1984); David E. Stannard, "Disease and Infertility: A New Look at the Demographic Collapse of Native Populations in the Wake of Western Contact," in Kiple and Beck, eds., *Biological Consequences of European Expansion,* 297–322.

syphilis to the province in 1776. Although the exact date will never be known, soldiers stationed at the missions and those who traveled between the presidios had ample opportunities to infect the native population and also to become infected themselves.[67]

In health reports, the Franciscans consistently suggested that syphilis was the most serious disease afflicting the Indians. Some described conditions consistent with the symptoms of the malady: visible ulcers, coughing up blood, trouble voiding. Rollin, in 1786, found syphilis to have spread widely at San Carlos. He examined Indians who suffered from lesions, ulcers, and inflammations of the lymph glands. Some missionaries went so far as to suggest that the disease was destroying the Indian population. Typical were the comments of the Franciscans at Mission San Miguel: "The dominant malady among them is venereal disease which is carrying them to the grave rapidly. . . . now for every three births there are four deaths. I do not believe there is an effective remedy for the said malady." From the early 1790s through the 1830s, the governors of the region also noted the terrible toll that venereal diseases were taking on the mission Indians. One of the most detailed descriptions of the symptoms was provided by Langsdorff:

> The most terrible of all diseases, known world wide as syphilis, is found here in all of its variations. It is common among the Spanish and the Indians and causes even greater devastation, because absolutely no medical measures are taken to prevent it. The usual results are spots on the skin, horrible rashes, persistently running sores, painful aches in the bones, throat infections, loss of the nose, deformities and death.

Langsdorff also observed among Indians "ophthalmia, rheumatism, virulent abscesses at the corners of the mouth and chronic diseases of various types," all of which he attributed to syphilis. Ophthalmia—or irritation of the eyes—can have many origins, but syphilis is not typically one of them. It is, however, one of the primary maladies suffered by children born to mothers with gonorrhea.[68]

Gonorrhea, like syphilis, is easily transmitted through sexual contact, and it

67. "Gonorrhea," in Kenneth F. Kiple, ed., *The Cambridge World History of Human Disease* (Cambridge, 1993), 759–760; McFalls and McFalls, *Disease and Fertility,* 310; Cook, *Conflict,* 23. The missionaries and soldiers commonly identified syphilis as *gálico,* after the *morbus gallicus* known to Europe since the late fifteenth century. See, for example, Antonio Grajera to Borica, Aug. 14, 1795, San Diego, Archives of California, C–A 7, 355, BL; Arrillaga, June 19, 1797, Archives of California, C–A 55, 102, BL; Luis Argüello, Oct. 31, 1807, San Francisco, Archives of California, C–A 16, 306, BL; Ramón Abella to Solá, Jan. 29, 1817, Mission San Francisco, Taylor Coll., doc. 698, HL; Abella to Solá, July 31, 1817, Mission San Francisco, Taylor Coll., doc. 727, HL.

68. *APST,* 71–80, esp. 75–76; Abella to Solá, July 31, 1817, Mission San Francisco, Taylor Coll., doc. 727, HL; Cook, *Conflict,* 26–27; Rollin, "Memoire physiologique," 23. Langsdorff quote in Langsdorff, *Remarks and Observations,* ed. Pierce, trans. Moessner, II, 125.

most likely played a significant role in Indian suffering and population decline at Mission San Carlos. After one or two acts of coitus with an infected partner, 20–30 percent of men and 50–70 percent of women will contract the disease. Previous infection offers little or no resistance to reinfection. Gonorrhea does not kill adults, but the disease drastically reduces the health of fetuses and newborn infants: up to a third of all infected pregnant women will spontaneously abort the fetus; and up to two-thirds of infants born to infected mothers will be premature and therefore less likely to survive the first month of life. Most important, pelvic inflammatory disease (acute salpingitis), which results when gonorrhea spreads into the uterus and fallopian tubes, can often lead to sterility. Of women with untreated gonorrhea, 15 to 20 percent develop pelvic inflammatory disease, and 60 to 70 percent of those women will be completely unable to conceive a child. Gonorrhea can also destroy the fertility of men. In the era before antibiotics, the disease probably rendered sterile up to half of its male victims. Gonorrhea, therefore, almost certainly played a large role in depressing fertility and thereby hastening the decline of Indians at Mission San Carlos.[69]

During syphilis's primary and secondary phases, which can last four years after the initial exposure, the disease is highly contagious; 10–50 percent of persons exposed to it will become infected, and pregnant women can transmit it to the fetus. Over time, usually five to twenty years after exposure to the disease, the infected individual will develop what is known as late syphilis, which is not infectious but kills or incapacitates half of its victims. Syphilis does not impair conception, but it can lead to pregnancy loss. A woman who has primary or secondary syphilis is unlikely to deliver a normal-term infant: at least 30 percent of pregnancies of women with syphilis will abort spontaneously; 20 percent of infants born to women with infectious syphilis are likely to die shortly after birth. The remainder can be born with or develop lesions in the first six months of life and subsequently suffer the effects of congenital syphilis. According to the Franciscans at Mission San Gabriel, many Indians were in fact born with indications of congenital syphilis: "Many of the children at birth give evidence immediately of the only heritage their parents give them. As a result of every four children born, three die in their first or second year, while of those who survive the majority do not reach the age of twenty-five." Furthermore, syphilitic women

69. Here I follow the lead of other scholars and assume that the modern-day progression of disease is similar to that of the past. See McFalls and McFalls, *Disease and Fertility*, 260, 262, 276–277; Paolo Miotti and Gina Dallabetta, "The Other Sexually Transmitted Diseases," in Marie-Louise Newell and Jonas McIntyre, eds., *Congenital and Perinatal Infections: Prevention, Diagnosis, and Treatment* (Cambridge, 2000), 278–279. When not treated with antibiotics, gonorrhea in men progressed to epididymitis in 58 percent of untreated cases, and 50–85 percent of those men became sterile (McFalls and McFalls, 298–299).

who have spontaneous abortions may be vulnerable to sterilizing infections. Perhaps this is one reason why about half of all Indian couples at San Carlos had no children. Transmission of syphilis to the fetus is very rare after the fourth year of maternal infection, so, in an otherwise healthy population, endemic syphilis would not have a dramatic impact on fertility and population levels, for it would most likely cost women the first, and maybe even the second, of seven or eight eventual pregnancies. But, in colonial California, where adult women rarely lived long enough to have more than one or two pregnancies, syphilis would have had a devastating effect on the population's ability to reproduce itself. When one considers that gonorrhea and syphilis often accompanied one another, the low fertility rates at the mission become understandable.[70]

When Indians left the mission and returned to their native villages, they often carried infections with them, and as a result low fertility also seems to have characterized many Indian women well before they moved to the mission. One Franciscan near the end of the Spanish period claimed that it was generally agreed upon that gentile Indian women had few children. "Young [gentile] women," observed Father Ramón Abella after two decades at Mission San Francisco, "never bring children [to the mission]," women in their late twenties rarely brought two or three, and it was quite rare for women to have five or six children, "as is common with the gente de razón."[71]

LOCAL UNDERSTANDINGS

There is little in the historical record suggesting how Indians in colonial California understood the diseases that were overwhelming them. Some Indians, according to one missionary, attributed the deaths of so many to herbal poisons that the Indians gave one another. Short of abstaining from sexual contact with one another or with soldiers, the Indians at the missions could do little to prevent the spread of venereal diseases among themselves. But they must have realized that their numbers were thinning, and, in an attempt to stabilize their population, they might have increased their sexual activities and thereby the likelihood of contracting infection. Furthermore, although lifelong monogamy had never been the rule in precontact California, and it certainly was not in the California

70. McFalls and McFalls, *Disease and Fertility,* 323, 333, 336; "Syphilis," in Kiple, *Cambridge World History of Disease,* 1029; *APST,* 105. See also Stannard, "Disease and Infertility," in Kiple and Beck, eds., *Biological Consequences of European Expansion,* 340.

71. Abella to Solá, July 31, 1817, Mission San Francisco, Taylor Coll., doc. 727, HL. Given the large number of Indians baptized at the missions and the Franciscans' awareness about when they had baptized complete villages and the last Indians from certain villages, it seems unlikely that women with children simply stayed away from the missions.

missions, the high adult mortality and the frequency with which widows remarried increased the likelihood that adult Indians would have more than one sexual partner and therefore eventually contract syphilis or gonorrhea. Franciscans almost always associated venereal diseases with sexual promiscuity, yet they acknowledged that marriage—not just extramarital relations—helped to spread syphilis: "All are infected with it for they see no objection to marrying another infected with it. As a result births are few and deaths many so that the number of deaths exceeds births by three to one."[72]

At best, Indians could treat only some of the skin disorders that accompanied syphilis. At Mission San Carlos, men daily repaired to a sweat lodge, where they perspired so profusely that upon leaving they gave the "appearance of having bathed." For men, this was as much a social as a medicinal activity. And, at first, the missionaries tried to stop this practice, but they relented when they realized its medicinal value. When the men at the mission "betook themselves to the *temescal* again scarcely a man was found afflicted with the itch." Women and children, however, did not make use of this therapy, even though, once infected, they suffered from similar skin disorders. Other curatives regularly practiced by the Indians at San Carlos and throughout Alta California—such as bloodletting and the sucking of blood out of an infected body part—were perceived by the Indians as beneficial, but they might have been detrimental to the health of the sick and even hastened the transmission of contagious diseases to the healthy. Indians at San Carlos also drank herbal infusions intended to induce vomiting or sweating.[73]

Missionaries incorrectly believed that Indians rejected any sort of special food or medicine they offered, fearing that it was poison. Father President Narciso Durán observed that sick Indians would drink a cup of broth he or the soldiers' wives gave them. But, to his dismay, Durán "had often seen them, when they had finished drinking it, turn their backs, put feathers in their mouths, and not stop until they had regurgitated it." Indians did the same thing with laxatives the padres gave them. Rather than trying to rid themselves of the padres' cures, these Indians probably took them as emetics. At San Carlos, Indians commonly applied a paste of crushed plants to the chest of those suffering respiratory ailments.

72. Ibid.; *APST,* 74.

73. *APST,* 77. Fever therapy can arrest the syphilitic infection and reduce its virulence, but only once it has progressed to late syphilis (McFalls and McFalls, *Disease and Fertility,* 347). It is not clear exactly what disease the padres were referring to here when they mentioned "the itch." Perhaps they saw only the symptoms of an unknown disease. In addition to syphilis, the itch could have been scabies. Regarding the Indians' curatives, current medical science would suggest that bloodletting and -sucking did not improve the health of the sick. But Indians believed in them, and they might indeed have had some sort of salutary effect. See also Rollin, "Memoire physiologique," 18, 23–24, for the Indians' curatives and method of preparing a sweat lodge.

Topical medicines offered by the missionaries—salves, poultices, and ointments—were of no use in either preventing or limiting the effects of venereal diseases, and nothing the padres did could avert pregnancy loss or stillbirths among infected women. Indian women, in addition to suffering the losses of their stillborn children, had blame heaped upon them by missionaries: "In the beginning it was attributed to incontinence. In order to prevent it, precautions were taken; they were taught, preached to, and perhaps even punished (tactfully); but up to now it has all been in vain, and we have not yet been able to discern the origin and cause of such deplorable events." One missionary went so far as to publicly humiliate and punish a childless couple, demanding to know from the Indian woman: "Why don't you bear children?" After she responded "Who knows!" and desperately resisted the Franciscan's attempts to examine her reproductive organs, he had her flogged and publicly humiliated for being childless.[74]

As early as the 1810s, Franciscans in California began to suggest that venereal diseases were not just symptomatic of the Indians' unchastity but, in fact, if left unchecked, would depopulate the missions. At San Luis Obispo, the Franciscans observed that venereal disease "puts an end to men as well as women" and warned, "If no steps are taken to check these effects this conquest will soon come to an end." Those at San Gabriel were even more direct: "If the government does not supply doctors and medicine Upper California will be without any Indians at all." However, before the discovery of penicillin in the early twentieth century, there was no effective cure for either syphilis or gonorrhea, so any medicine sent to the missions would have probably done more harm than good. In any event, during Mexico's struggle for independence between 1810 and 1821, virtually no supplies of any kind were sent from central Mexico to the missions of Alta California. This neglect would not prove salutary.[75]

In 1820, on sending to his superiors in Mexico the annual population totals from all the missions, which continued to show that deaths outnumbered births for the most part, Father President Mariano Payeras wrote a most thoughtful reflection on the legacy of a half century of Spanish and Franciscan rule in Alta California. Having served in Alta California since 1793, Payeras wrote from experience, which gave his letter a mournful quality that is in marked contrast to the optimism that characterized nearly all the Franciscans' reports to their superiors

74. Durán, May 22, 1826, Mission San Jose, Academy of American Franciscan History, archive translation; original at AGN, DPHM, 2d. Ser., IV, 178–183; Milliken, *A Time of Little Choice*, 173; Payeras to Tapis, Jan. 13, 1810, La Purísima, in Cutter, ed. and trans., *Writings of Mariano Payeras*, 50. See also *APST*, 106. On the padre's punishment of the childless woman, see Lorenzo Asisara, in Edward D. Castillo, "The Native Response to the Colonization of Alta California," in *CC*, I, 377–394, esp. 380.

75. *APST*, 105. Mercury was the most common treatment in the eighteenth and nineteenth centuries, but it was highly toxic. Treatment of pelvic inflammatory disease that results from gonorrhea is still quite complicated (McFalls and McFalls, *Disease and Fertility*, 282–283).

in Mexico. Payeras reported that, after fifty-one years of work, the Franciscans had baptized all the Indians between San Diego and an area just north of San Francisco. The missionaries had expected their efforts to lead to a "beautiful and flourishing church and some beautiful towns which could be the joy of the sovereign majesties of heaven and earth." But instead they found themselves "with missions or rather with a people miserable and sick, with rapid depopulation of rancherías which with profound horror fills the cemeteries." Previously healthy Indians, once baptized and resident at the missions, became feeble, lost weight, and sickened and died. This was particularly true, Payeras noted, of women, "especially those who have recently become pregnant."[76]

The missionaries had believed initially that Indians died at the missions because of the "change of home, climate, food, customs, and ideas," and they consoled themselves "with the idea that the sons of the mission or those born in it, having been raised in its rule and customs, would be different and would keep their normal health and constitution." But a half century of "sad experience" had demonstrated that they had "erred" in their "calculation" and that the mission born "are consumed indiscriminately and are rapidly vanishing." As an example, Payeras pointed to Mission San Carlos, which had 835 inhabitants in 1796 but only 390 in 1818, despite the steady baptisms of gentiles from the surrounding region and "but two epidemics in 24 years." By 1820, Mission Soledad, where Payeras had been stationed in the early 1800s, had been reduced to "a skeleton of a mission with an unbalanced society made up of a group of 200 (or close to it) of either widowers or single men without one woman to whom to marry them, nor even the hope of doing it."[77]

To arrest the spread of disease and to care for the sick, the missions had built infirmaries and acquired medicines, but, Payeras lamented, all had been in vain. Like most Franciscans before and after, he concluded that the Indians' ill health was owing to their unrestrainable sexual promiscuity and that there was "no human recourse" left other than to alert his superior in Mexico that Alta California was a dying province, which would soon be "deserted and depopulated of Indians within a century of its discovery and conquest by the Spaniards." In closing his letter, Payeras expressed his plea that perhaps his superior or even the viceroy might take some unspecified measures to free the Franciscans from the "undeserved reproach" that future generations were likely to visit upon the missionaries for their role in the decimation of the Indians. Mexican independence and the end of Spanish rule in 1821 rendered any viceregal intervention

76. Payeras to [Baldomero López], Feb. 2, 1820, La Purísima, in Cutter, ed. and trans., *Writings of Mariano Payeras*, 225–228, esp. 225.

77. Ibid., 225–227.

impossible, and, by 1820, when Payeras wrote his letter, it was too late anyway to reverse the population decline initiated by Spanish colonization.[78]

WIDER UNDERSTANDINGS

The transformation of places like Mission San Carlos from growing centers of Indian congregation to "skeleton" communities is especially important because of the sheer magnitude of the American Indians' decline during European expansion. The picture of population collapse I have just sketched shows in detail only one of twenty-one missions in California. But what happened at Mission San Carlos was representative of what occurred at twenty other Alta California missions and in countless villages throughout the countryside. And it is suggestive of the demographic processes set in motion whenever and wherever Europeans attempted to colonize the native peoples of the Americas. All European colonists, however, did not react alike to the Indians' destruction. For the Franciscans, without Indians alive, working, and undergoing a process of civilization, the conquest had lost its object and could even be deemed a failure. In this regard, the views of California missionaries and those elsewhere in the Spanish Borderlands differed sharply from those of contemporary Anglo-Americans during and after the colonial period. On the frontiers in British North America, where few Europeans could ever really imagine or work toward a world with Indians meaningfully included, the demise of Indians was welcomed as progress hastened.[79]

California missions by the end of the Spanish period had become places of grief for Indians and missionaries. Payeras was haunted not only by the sheer number of Indians who had died in the missions but by the memory of those he had known personally. It was "horrible to go through the missions now," Payeras confessed, "especially those of the north and ask after the many robust and young neophytes who lived there twenty years ago" when in most there was not "one or two" living whom he could remember. Although Payeras's own horror at what the missions had wrought was no doubt profound, his sadness might have been unusual among California missionaries, and in any event it can only hint at the emotions Indians themselves experienced as they buried their own, tended to the

78. Ibid., 226–228. The viceroy had been alerted to the prevalence of unchecked diseases in the California missions as early as 1805; see José Vicuña Muro to José de Iturrigaray, May 10, 1805, Mexico, Archives of California, C–A 12, 62–64, BL; Iturrigaray to Arrillaga, June 6, 1805, Mexico, Archives of California, C–A 12, 64, BL.

79. Richter, *Facing East from Indian Country*; Gregory Evans Dowd, *War under Heaven: Pontiac, the Indian Nations, and the British Empire* (Baltimore, 2002).

sick, and continued to live in and around the missions—places that had appeared initially as centers of refuge but had in reality proved to be graveyards for their kin.[80]

A glimpse of the emotional despair that overcame many Indians in the wake of the illnesses and deaths of so many—and one Franciscan's intolerance of such grief—was recorded by Spanish military officials who asked some of the Indians who had abandoned Mission San Francisco in 1795 and later returned why they had fled. The Indians' words are clear and direct. Their answers, in their likely acceptability to Spanish interrogators, suggest just how notorious the missions had become as maelstroms of destruction. Bridging the colonial gulf, Indians presented a litany of grief arising out of the dislocation and disorientation that accompanied the high mortality, plunging fertility, and fraying of family and kinship networks in the missions.

Tiburcio Obmusa: "He explained that after his wife and daughter died, because he was crying, on five separate occasions Father Dantí ordered him whipped. For these reasons he fled."

Homobono Sumipocsé: "His motive for having fled was that his brother had died on the other shore and when he cried for him they whipped him in the mission."

Liborato Yree: "He fled because of the deaths of his mother, two brothers, and three nephews."

Nicolás Ennót: "He explained that he ran away only because his father had died. He had no other motive."

And Macario Uncatt: "He testified that, because of the deaths of his wife and one child, he fled, no other motive than that."[81]

80. Payeras to José Gasol, Feb. 2, 1820, La Purísima, in Cutter, ed. and trans., *Writings of Mariano Payeras*, 227.

81. Testimony of runaway Indians, Aug. 12, 1797, San Francisco Presidio, AGN, CA, LXV, expediente 2, 108a–109a. I have consulted the original for my quotations and used Milliken, *A Time of Little Choice*, for the Indians' native names.

INTERACTION

4

INDIANS AND THE FRANCISCAN
RELIGIOUS PROGRAM

What Indians had hoped to find in the missions—sustenance, community life, and support for their imperiled way of life—Franciscans considered primarily as a means to something wholly opposite: the Indians' conversion to Catholicism and adoption of what they considered a "civilized" life. Indians might not have been aware of the gulf between their intentions in moving to the missions and the Franciscans' own designs. Missionaries, however, were, and they consciously offered Indians one thing as a means to another. In the words of Rafael Verger, the father guardian of the College of San Fernando, Indians ventured to missions for food, and thus food had to be central to appeals to gentiles: "Experience has taught, and it shows us daily, that the foremost Sermon with which these unfortunate savages can be reduced to our Holy Faith, and to the Obedience of our Catholic Monarch, is food, and clothing, with which they can cover their shameful nakedness; one could say, that with them to some extent, *faith enters through the mouth*." The padres, therefore, were conscious to always approach the Indians with "bread in hand." They realized that the spirit of Christ, his teachings, and the Host would have to wait.[1]

Evangelism, however, would not have to wait long, as the missionaries quickly joined their efforts to feed and clothe Indians with attempts to convert them. Indians, therefore, from their first days at the missions, encountered an extensive religious program, one that was highly scripted and showed only minor variations between missions and over time. Indians, through their study of basic Catholic prayers before baptism, subsequent daily catechism, exposure to liturgical art and music, and subjection to an intrusive annual confession, experienced the Franciscans' unstinting efforts to hammer away at their beliefs. In this highly charged context, the Children of Coyote and other California Indians experi-

---

1. Rafael Verger, Nov. 15, 1772, College of San Fernando, Mexico City, Fondo Franciscano, CXXII, rollo 41, par. 3, 38b–39a, INAH (emphasis added).

mented with Catholicism, perhaps with a desperation fitting their circumstances. Some took to it, whole or in part, finding in this new religion a familiar path to the sacred. Others rejected it, believing that it offered no way to salvation, let alone comfort from the bitter realities of the dual revolutions and mission life. In the early decades of the California missions, meaningful conversions to Catholicism by Indians must have been rare; syncretism, a stable synthesis of Indian and Catholic religious views, seems highly improbable. Not until the 1830s and 1840s, when the missions themselves were collapsing and undergoing secularization and the recruitment of new converts had largely ended, can a strong union of the beliefs of Monterey Indians and Franciscans be detected, but by then the social, economic, and political foundation of this new spiritual equilibrium was crumbling, threatening anew the few surviving Children of Coyote.[2]

In some regions of colonial America, it seems Indians were attracted to Catholicism in the hopes that its priests and prayers might offer what native religion could not: protection from calamitous disease. But this does not seem to have been the case in Alta California. There is no indication that Indians came to or stayed in the missions because of a desire for Catholic protection from disease. Moreover, disease in fact might have reduced Catholicism's appeal to Indians; it certainly hobbled the Franciscan religious program and impeded Indian attempts to wrestle with its content. The high mortality in the missions not only depleted the ranks of adults, some of whose understanding and faith in Catholicism might have been growing, but it swept away children who, had they lived, might have grown to accept some Catholic beliefs. In addition, the deaths of so many neophytes spurred the Franciscans to prop up the missions through more recruits, nearly all of whom the dual revolutions had pushed into the padres' hands. These Indians brought with them their own spirituality, little knowledge of Catholicism, and different languages, all of which forced the Franciscans to begin anew the difficult and time-consuming process of language acquisition and religious indoctrination. Clearly, these factors undermined the growth of communities of Catholic Indians at the missions. So, too, did contradictions within the Franciscan approach. In essence, missionaries taught Indians only the rudiments of Catholicism but required of them a deep and enduring faith. Moreover, the Franciscans' inclusive conceptualization of the sacrament of baptism created an illusion of steadily growing Catholic Indian communities in the missions, as more

2. Fermín Francisco de Lasuén, memorandum, July 8, 1789, Mission San Carlos, in Kenneally, ed. and trans., *Writings of Lasuén*, I, 193–194; Inga Clendinnen, "Ways to the Sacred: Reconstructing 'Religion' in Sixteenth[-]Century Mexico," *History and Anthropology*, V (1990), 105–141; William B. Taylor, *Magistrates of the Sacred: Priests and Parishioners in Eighteenth-Century Mexico* (Stanford, Calif., 1996), 47–62. On recent formulations of religious syncretism, see Taylor, 53–62.

and more Indians attained baptism and came to participate in many aspects of the missions' religious life. However, the administration of Holy Communion in the missions reveals a different image, one in which few Indians gave themselves over to Catholicism and most Franciscans denied them full participation.

EIGHTEENTH-CENTURY FRANCISCANS AND THE INDIANS' "SPIRITUAL APTITUDE"

The religious program at Mission San Carlos was the product of the Franciscans' long historical experience. Franciscan missionaries, just like microbes and live-stock, had been reshaping Indian communities in New Spain for centuries by the time Gaspar de Portolá took possession of Alta California and Junípero Serra initiated a chain of coastal missions. To the first generation of Catholic mission-aries in New Spain, the legitimacy of the Spanish conquest rested upon the obligation of the Spanish Crown to propagate the Catholic faith, and the padres' authority in the New World derived directly from the pope, who had ruled that Indians were rational human beings created in the image of God and capable of church membership and redemption.[3] Although the earliest Franciscans to the New World concluded that Indians were in bondage to the devil, they were nevertheless encouraged by the Indians' worship of gods, their construction of dense, urban settlements, and their tolerance of material impoverishment—all of which suggested that Indians had a capacity for spirituality, civilization, and an ascetic existence. Furthermore, the Franciscans believed God had brought them to the New World and was working to effect the Indians' salvation. In the six-teenth century, missionaries held that converting Indians to Catholicism re-quired a basic understanding of native culture and language, and they devoted themselves to the study of Indian beliefs and practices. This hard-earned knowl-edge became an important weapon against native religion; missionaries used it to launch destructive campaigns against idols, temples, and religious practices and to translate Catholic catechisms, prayers, and confessionals into Indian lan-guages. Because linguistic barriers often proved formidable—and because mis-

---

3. Edwin Edward Sylvest, Jr., *Motifs of Franciscan Mission Theory in Sixteenth Century New Spain: Province of the Holy Gospel* (Washington, D.C., 1975), 19, 44, 77. The literature on the early missionaries is enormous. Among the most important works are Robert Ricard, *The Spiritual Conquest of Mexico: An Essay on the Apostolate and the Evangelizing Methods of the Mendicant Orders in New Spain, 1523–1572* (Berkeley, Calif., 1966); John Leddy Phelan, *The Millennial Kingdom of the Franciscans in the New World* (Berkeley, Calif., 1970); Sylvest, *Motifs*; Lino Gómez Canedo, *Evangelización y conquista: Experi-encia franciscana en Hispanoamérica* (Mexico City, 1977); Inga Clendinnen, *Ambivalent Conquests: Maya and Spaniard in Yucatan, 1517–1570* (Cambridge, 1987).

sionaries sought to couple their attack on native culture with gentle forms of persuasion that appealed to the senses of the Indians—the early Franciscans also deployed music, drama, and artistic representations to impress upon the Indians the fundamentals of Catholicism. However, when these means failed and Indians resisted Christianity, Franciscans relied on physical coercion and force to punish Indians for their sinful disobedience.[4]

As we shall see, California missionaries inherited many of these beliefs and methods, but there were differences between the experiences of early colonial Franciscans and those of the late colonial period.[5] In New Spain, during the seventeenth and eighteenth centuries, the political climate within which missionaries worked shifted dramatically, as the Crown curtailed their authority and converted missions to parishes overseen by diocesan priests.[6] The attitudes of the Franciscans who came to California were shaped by this epic struggle and their failure to win it. They knew that, even as they established a new mission frontier in California, elsewhere in New Spain their power was on the wane. Many had witnessed the expulsion of the Jesuits from the Spanish Empire in 1767 and realized that, just as they were setting foot in California, diocesan priests were preparing to assume control of the missions in the Sierra Gorda, where they and many of their brethren had labored for years. And all were aware that royal officials were contemplating stripping them of control over the social, economic, and political affairs of mission communities and restricting Franciscan authority to spiritual affairs, the saying of Mass and the administering of the sacraments.

4. Sylvest, *Motifs*, 103–107. The missionaries found justification for their use of force in what they saw as their paternal relationship to the Indians. See ibid., 118; Inga Clendinnen, "Disciplining the Indians: Franciscan Ideology and Missionary Violence in Sixteenth-Century Yucatán," *Past and Present*, no. 74 (February 1982), 27–48.

5. There is a very extensive literature on the Franciscan missionary approach in California. Most of this work has been written by Franciscan historians. See, for example, Francis F. Guest, "Cultural Perspectives on California Mission Life," *SCQ*, LXV (1983), 1–65; Guest, "An Examination of the Thesis of S. F. Cook on the Forced Conversion of the Indians in the California Missions," *SCQ*, LXI (1979), 1–77; Guest, "An Inquiry into the Role of the Discipline in California Mission Life," *SCQ*, LXXI (1989), 1–68; Guest, "The California Missions Were Far from Faultless," *SCQ*, LXXVI (1994), 255–307. The best work on the life of the founding father of the California missions is Maynard J. Geiger, ed. and trans., *The Life and Times of Fray Junípero Serra, O.F.M.; or, The Man Who Never Turned Back (1713–1784)*, 2 vols. (Washington, D.C., 1959). For a sharp counterpoint to the Franciscan perspective, see Rupert Costo and Jeannette Henry Costo, eds., *The Missions of California: A Legacy of Genocide* (San Francisco, Calif., 1987).

6. This was part of a larger movement within Spanish society, and clerics came to see themselves as under attack from a variety of forces (William J. Callahan, "The Spanish Church," in Callahan and David Higgs, eds., *Church and Society in Catholic Europe of the Eighteenth Century* [Cambridge, 1979], 34–50, esp. 48–50). See also Callahan, *Church, Politics, and Society in Spain, 1750–1874* (Cambridge, Mass., 1984), 73–185; Charles C. Noel, "Missionary Preachers in Spain: Teaching Social Virtue in the Eighteenth Century," *AHR*, XC (1985), 866–892, esp. 887.

Out of the dramatic decline of their fortunes in New Spain emerged, first, the missionaries' inclination to see in every challenge to their authority a mortal threat to their lifework and, second, their intention not to provide their secularist foes with yet more proof that they had outlived their usefulness.

Beyond the declining power of the religious orders within the Spanish realm, changes in Franciscan attitudes toward Indians further distanced the California missionaries from their sixteenth-century forebears. By the late eighteenth century, the Franciscans' zeal and optimism for the conversion of the Indians had been punctured, and their concern with the extirpation of Indian idols had given way to a belief of Indian sinfulness as rooted in superstition and ignorance, not in a willful rejection of God or the intervention of the devil. Moreover, by 1769, Franciscan attempts at comprehending and ultimately overturning the Indians' inner spirituality had been supplanted by a strategy of monitoring the externalities of religious behavior. This shift coincided with and was reinforced by the Franciscans' work in far northwestern New Spain. In Sonora, Texas, and Baja California, the Indians' diffuse settlements led Spaniards increasingly to see natives as primitive, unintelligent, bereft of religion, and unable to comprehend more than the most basic rites and rituals of Catholicism.[7]

Given the California Franciscans' lack of interest in studying Indian culture, their weakening position within the viceroyalty of New Spain, and their sense that California Indians were primitive, it comes as little surprise that they shaped a religious program around assumptions that California Indians had attained only a minimal level of social, cultural, and religious development and that converting them would take a long time. In 1772, Rafael Verger explained to the viceroy that, whereas Hernán Cortés had "found cities and pueblos, well formed, civilized, and provisioned with everything necessary," whose inhabitants only lacked "knowledge of the True God and the Holy Law," missionaries in California had found Indians who "lack all of the aforementioned qualities and for the most part go naked and wander in their remote hills and valleys." These Indians, Verger believed, "do not grow crops but live off the wild grasses and fruits of the trees, and their hunting, with arrows, differs little from that of irrational brutes." Thus, in addition to making Indians into Catholics, the padres would also have to "civilize" them, something that Verger concluded would not be achieved "as quickly as one would like." Decades later, in 1801, Father President Fermín Francisco de Lasuén echoed Verger's comments when he wrote that the "greatest

---

7. Taylor, *Magistrates of the Sacred,* 48–49; Fernando Cervantes, *The Devil in the New World: The Impact of Diabolism in New Spain* (New Haven, Conn., 1994), esp. 149–154; Sabine MacCormack, " 'The Heart Has Its Reasons': Predicaments of Missionary Christianity in Early Colonial Peru," *HAHR,* LXV (1985), 443–466.

trouble" confronting the California missionaries was the transformation of a "savage" people "into a society that is human, Christian, civil, and industrious."[8]

In seeing Indians as primitives lacking both civilization and Christianity, missionaries initially took them to be prelapsarian innocents. Serra wrote of a group of Cochimí he encountered during his overland journey: "They were entirely naked, as Adam in paradise before sin." Similarly, the Franciscans described California Indians as a living embodiment of the values to which they had dedicated themselves upon joining the Order of Friars Minor: obedience, charity, humility, compassion, generosity, and meekness, all in the face of a life lived in poverty and hardship. But, once the Indians showed themselves to be unreceptive or hostile to the padres' teachings, the Franciscans saw them as a pitiful, childlike people of slow intelligence who were overcome by their *rudeza,* or rude ignorance. Even worse, they were a savage people of "brutal appetites," prone to the vices of promiscuity, thievery, mendacity, drunkenness, and idleness.[9]

Franciscans, whether they saw Indians as innocents or savages, perceived little in native culture upon which they could build a belief in Catholicism, and they concluded that Indian culture had been fertile ground for superstitious beliefs and practices that had to be eliminated before Christianity could take root.[10] Where Indians smoked, fasted, painted their bodies, consumed special foods and drinks, worshiped and sacrificed large birds, and adorned tall wooden prayer poles with offerings of food and feathers, the padres saw superstition. They also saw it in the credence Indians gave to their dreams and in the offering of seeds and other foods to old men and women, who the Indians believed controlled the growth of plants and the arrival of rain. Men, according to the padres, never consumed animals they personally caught for fear that doing so would prevent

8. Verger, Nov. 15, 1772, Fondo Franciscano, CXXII, rollo 41, par. 15, 44b–45a; Lasuén, "Refutation of Charges," June 19, 1801, Monterey, AGN, PI, CCXVI, expediente 1, 68a, and in Kenneally, ed. and trans., *Writings of Lasuén,* II, 202.

9. Junípero Serra, diary of the expedition from Loreto to San Diego, Mar. 28–July 1, 1769, entry for May 15, 1769, in Tibesar, ed. and trans., *Writings of Serra,* I, 62 (my trans.); responses of missionaries to question no. 9, in *APST,* 43–45; Serra to Antonio María de Bucareli y Ursúa, Aug. 24, 1775, Monterey, in Tibesar, ed. and trans., *Writings of Serra,* II, 150–151. For Indians' rudeza, see Verger, Nov. 15, 1772, Fondo Franciscano, CXXII, rollo 41, par. 12, 42b–43a; Vicente Francisco de Sarría, circular letter, June 22, 1813, Mission San Carlos, libro de patentes, par. 16, 17, 20, LDS film 0913303 (hereafter cited as Sarría, circular letter); Lasuén, "Refutation of Charges," June 19, 1801, Monterey, AGN, PI, CCXVI, expediente 1, 68a, 73b, and in Kenneally, ed. and trans., *Writings of Lasuén,* II, 202, 220; responses of the missionaries to question no. 25, in *APST,* 107–108.

10. See Serra to Francisco Pangua and discretorium, in Tibesar, ed. and trans., *Writings of Serra,* II, 115; responses of the missionaries to question no. 35, in *APST,* 43–46. Father President Lasuén's dismissal of Indian culture was sweeping and influential. He saw them as "a people without education, without government, religion, or responsibility, who shamelessly pursue without restraint whatever their brutal appetites suggest to them" (Lasuén, "Refutation of Charges," June 19, 1801, Monterey, AGN, PI, CCXVI, expediente 1, 73b, and in Kenneally, ed. and trans., *Writings of Lasuén,* II, 220).

them from hunting successfully. And husbands abstained from "touching" their wives until after a newborn child could stand or walk, lest he be prevented from fathering another. The padres did not blame these and other beliefs on the devil, nor did they consider them a willful rejection of Christianity; rather, they attributed such behaviors to ignorance and errors inherited from ancestors and elders. To combat the superstition that seemed to taint all aspects of the Indians' lives, the Franciscans preached against it, pressured and humiliated Indians who persisted, and ultimately drew strength from their sense that in time such practices would vanish with the older generations.[11]

The Franciscans' own belief in what others could have termed superstitions gave them confidence that they eventually would convert the California Indians to Christianity. Franciscans believed that they were sent by God as his servants to work in California's missionary field. Their faith was strengthened further by their conviction that God's work in California had long preceded their own. Specifically, Franciscans who served in Alta California knew about the seventeenth-century Franciscan nun, María de Jesús de Agreda, who claimed to have been transported numerous times by angels to preach among the Indians of New Mexico, a province believed to be not far from Alta California. María de Agreda had been declared venerable shortly after her death in 1665, and missionaries carried her book, *The Mystical City of God*, to the California missions.[12] Some Franciscans reported Indian accounts that an "alien woman" had come to California long ago, confirming that María de Agreda had also been to Alta California, where she had preached among the Indians. Other Franciscans found verification of María de Agreda's assertion that Saint Francis had brought "to these northern nations two friars of his Order to preach the faith of Jesus Christ." At Mission San Antonio, Father Francisco Palóu had been told, an Indian woman believed to be more than one hundred years old stated that she desired baptism because in her childhood "she heard her father say that a priest who wore the same habit as we, had come to this land, not traveling on horseback or on foot,

---

11. Responses of the missionaries to question no. 10, *APST,* 47–51.

12. Sylvia M. Broadbent, comp., shelf list of Carmel Mission library, Jan. 25, 1956, C–C 218, BL. Serra included three copies of *The Mystical City of God* in his inventory of Mission San Luis Obispo (Serra to Bucareli, report on spiritual and material status of California missions, Feb. 5, 1775, Monterey, in Tibesar, ed. and trans., *Writings of Serra,* II, 235); Lasuén noted four volumes of the same work and "one volume with Notes, critical Prologue, and Life of the Venerable Mother, Sister Mary of Jesus, of Agreda," in the library at Mission San Diego in 1783 (Lasuén, inventory of San Diego Mission library, May 4, 1783, Mission San Diego, in Kenneally, ed. and trans., *Writings of Lasuén,* I, 91–92). On the Franciscans' belief in María de Agreda, see Sarría, circular letter, par. 48; David J. Weber, *The Spanish Frontier in North America* (New Haven, Conn., 1992), 99; William H. Donahue, "Mary of Agreda and the Southwest United States," *The Americas,* IX (1953), 291–314; Clark Colahan, *The Visions of Sor María de Agreda: Writing Knowledge and Power* (Tucson, Ariz., 1994).

but flying; and that he preached to them the same as they were now preaching, and that remembering this caused her to be a Christian." Other Indians at the mission told the same story, and, as word of these seemingly miraculous events spread among the Franciscans, they found "hope for great conversions in this immense body of heathen."[13]

As proof of the holiness of their calling, the Franciscans also pointed to portentous natural wonders that they believed had signaled their own arrival in Alta California. Serra recounted that, in April 1769, months before he first set foot in San Diego and established Alta California's first mission, the "inanimate creatures of heaven and earth began to preach in a most marvelous way to these poor wretched gentiles." On the day that the supply ship *San Antonio* carrying Franciscans and their provisions dropped anchor in the port of San Diego, an earthquake and an eclipse of the sun, which according to the Franciscans were experienced only by the natives of the region, alerted the Indians that "there was some great event about to take place." At Monterey, upon first seeing the Spaniards coming through the fields, the Indians "saw a great multitude of birds of beautiful colors, such as they had never seen before." "The birds came down from the heavens, and they stayed in the air just ahead of them singing, as if they had come to greet and welcome these new guests in this land." Such events made a lasting impression on the Franciscans, giving them greater faith that they would in fact win over California's Indians.[14]

LINGUISTIC BARRIERS

Missionaries knew that the Indians' conversion would involve numerous steps and depend upon instruction more than miracles. The first step was the Indians' acceptance of the basic beliefs of Catholicism and a commitment to cast off native custom; the second was baptism; and the third, daily religious instruction and observance of church obligations. The Mexican synod of 1555 had forbidden the baptism of adult Indians without basic religious instruction, and in 1585 another synod directed that preliminary religious teaching had to occur in the

---

13. "Alien woman": responses of Marcelino Marquínez and Jayme Escudé of Mission Santa Cruz to questions no. 12 and no. 35, Apr. 30, 1814, in *APST,* 60, 145. On the Indians' verifications of Agreda's visit, see Francisco Palóu, report to the viceroy, Nov. 10, 1773, Mission San Carlos, in Palóu, *Historical Memoirs of New California . . .* , ed. and trans. Herbert Eugene Bolton, 4 vols. (1926; rpt. New York, 1966), III, 227–228.

14. Serra to Bucareli, May 21, 1773, Mexico City, and memorandum, June 22, 1774, Monterey, both in Tibesar, ed. and trans., *Writings of Serra,* I, 367, II, 88 (my trans.); see also Serra to Pangua and discretorium, July 18, 1774, Monterey, ibid., I, 115.

Indians' own languages.[15] Thus, in contrast to the first missionaries in New Spain, who baptized thousands of Indians in a single day, Franciscans in Alta California did not immediately baptize healthy adult Indians. Only children under the age of nine or adults on the verge of death could be baptized without an understanding and acceptance of the basic tenets of Catholicism.[16]

Prebaptismal religious instruction required that the Franciscans—or their assistants—have a basic command of the Indians' languages. Franciscans believed that Indians, if taught the fundamental Catholic prayers and beliefs solely in Castilian, would commit them to memory without understanding them.[17] In 1813, soon after his election as the first commissary prefect of Alta California, Father Vicente Francisco de Sarría wrote what amounted to the most thorough summary guide to the Franciscan program in California. Sarría compared the Indians' minds to "rebellious stomachs that resisted certain nourishments"; no matter how much effort was expended, the "daily bread of Christian doctrine," if presented in Castilian, "will not be digested." Moreover, a partial knowledge of the Indians' languages for missionaries would run the risk of mistranslation and the introduction of errors that would prove extremely difficult to eradicate. According to Alonso de la Peña Montenegro's influential guide, the *Itinerario para*

15. Ricard, *Spiritual Conquest,* 83. The Council of Trent and the First, Second, and Third Mexican Provincial Councils, all of which convened during the sixteenth century, established the guidelines for the form and content of the Catholicism preached and practiced in the California missions as well as throughout all of New Spain. The laws and customs pertinent to the administration of religious missions were synthesized in numerous missionary guidebooks, the most influential of which was Alonso de la Peña Montenegro's *Itinerario para párrocos de indios*. Most of the California missions had a copy of the *Itinerario* in their library, as did Mission San Carlos Borromeo. First published in 1668, the *Itinerario* circulated widely in the Spanish Borderlands. In five volumes, it covered nearly all missionary responsibilities, including conditions under which Indians could receive sacraments (Taylor, *Magistrates of the Sacred,* 152–162). For a modern printing of this text, see De la Peña Montenegro, *Itinerario para párrocos de indios,* ed. C. Baciero et al., Consejo Superior de Investigaciónes Científicas, Corpus Hispanorum de Pace, 2d Ser. (Madrid, 1995). At the Huntington Library, I examined a 1726 edition printed in Antwerp (rare book no. 44457). All citations to the *Itinerario* are to the modern printing. Of much less direct influence on the religious program in the California missions was the Fourth Mexican Provincial Council that met just as the first missions in California were being founded; nevertheless, the religious program of the California missions was largely consistent with its doctrine. See Luisa Zahino Peñafort, *El cardenal Lorenzana y el IV concilio provincial mexicano* (Mexico City, 1999).

16. Clendinnen, *Ambivalent Conquests,* 48–49. According to Father José Gasol, the father guardian of the College of San Fernando, once Indians were nine years old, they could no longer be baptized as *párvulos* (small, innocent children). Gasol referred directly to a 1775 letter by one of his predecessors, Francisco Pangua (copy of circular letter of Gasol, "Libro patente," Mission San Carlos, par. 2, LDS film 0913303.

17. Serra to Teodoro de Croix, Apr. 26, 1782, Santa Barbara, in Tibesar, ed., *Writings of Serra,* IV, 117; Sarría, circular letter, par. 7. Father presidents in California and their superiors at the College of San Fernando were following a long line of missionaries and clerics who had counseled for more than two centuries that an understanding of native languages lay at the heart of conversion. See De la Peña Montenegro, *Itinerario,* ed. Baciero et al., libro 1, tratado 10, sects. vi–vii, 332–335, esp. 334. De la Peña Montenegro cited as his authority Romans 10:17: "So then faith *comes* by hearing, and hearing by the word of God."

párrocos de indios (1668), teaching Indians in their own idioms was so important that all missionaries had to make every effort to learn the Indians' languages, even though doing so would cost them "sleepless nights and much sweat." The challenge was great; yet it was a task so essential to the spiritual conquest that De la Peña Montenegro suggested that missionaries who devoted their lives to the study of Indian languages surpassed in valor the efforts of the king's soldiers on the battlefield and would therefore "merit the highest rewards in heaven."[18]

For all their acknowledgment of the indispensability of teaching Indians in their own tongues, most missionaries in California were not up to the task; they found the multitude of unfamiliar languages confusing and too difficult. Only a minority devoted "sleepless nights and much sweat" to the effort. Serra, after a year at San Carlos, knew little Rumsen. And, after seven years in Alta California and three at Mission San Diego, Lasuén expressed a lingering frustration that must have been shared by many other Franciscans: he wrote that he was "perturbed" that he had difficulty with the inflections of the local dialect and could not "grasp its syllables."[19] The multiplicity of dialects compounded the Franciscans' problems. In 1782, Serra despaired that in no two of the nine California missions did the Indians speak the same language. As the padres established new missions, their linguistic challenges multiplied. In 1795, Lasuén reported that Indians between San Diego and San Francisco conversed in at least seventeen or eighteen languages; by 1814, the number of languages in the missions had more than doubled as new groups arrived. Indians at Mission San Luis Obispo spoke more than fifteen languages, the missionaries claimed. In the face of this linguistic diversity, many Franciscans found themselves overwhelmed and were slow to acquire more than an elemental knowledge of the Indians' words.[20]

Because of their troubles with native languages, missionaries turned to local Indians, hoping they would learn Spanish and serve as their interpreters. The padres looked to Indian children, particularly young boys, whom they believed were able and willing to learn Spanish and would ultimately be potent allies in

18. Sarría, quoting Granados's 1790 letter, in circular letter, par. 7. The position of commissary prefect outranked that of father president, from whom he took over the general supervision of the missionaries in the province. For his duties, see Maynard Geiger, *Franciscan Missionaries in Hispanic California, 1769–1848: A Biographical Dictionary* (San Marino, Calif., 1969), 228–229. For De la Peña Montenegro's views, see his *Itinerario,* ed. Baciero et al., libro 1, tratado 10, sect. vii, par. 2, 334, par. 5, 335.

19. Serra to Palóu, June 21, 1771, Monterey, in Tibesar, ed., *Writings of Serra,* I, 241. See also Serra to Rafael Verger, June 20, 1771, Monterey, ibid., I, 225; Lasuén to Pangua, Nov. 6, 1780, San Diego Mission, in Kenneally, ed. and trans., *Writings of Lasuén,* I, 77–78. Missionaries like Serra and Lasuén might have had the most difficulty with native languages; they shouldered considerable administrative responsibilities and were among the first to attempt to learn the languages at their respective missions.

20. Serra to Croix, Apr. 26, 1782, Santa Barbara, in Tibesar, ed. and trans., *Writings of Serra,* IV, 117; Lasuén, "Biennial Report for the Years 1793 and 1794," Mar. 11, 1795, San Carlos Mission, in Kenneally, ed. and trans., *Writings of Lasuén,* II, 380; responses of the missionaries to question no. 3, *APST,* 19–21.

their struggle against the Indians' superstitious beliefs. Of Indian adults and their ability to learn Spanish, the missionaries had only disparaging words. According to the padres at San Francisco: "The natives who have reached the age of thirty years and more never learn another language than their own." Although this is doubtless an overstatement, adult Indians' resistance to Spanish, just like their hesitation to trade their brush huts for adobe houses, indicates one more native attempt to limit the changes associated with life at the missions.[21]

At San Carlos, Serra tried to teach Castilian to a few Rumsen boys, but they were slow to pick up the language. In a letter to his friend and colleague Francisco Palóu, he explained:

Four big boys, Francisco, Buenaventura, Fernando, and Diego, are beginning to understand Castilian, but as yet they do not speak it. But we have quite an idea we are going to try out. Two of the boys, Buenaventura and Fernando, one about eight, the other about ten years old, will go with the boat, so attached to it have they become. One will be put in [the] charge of the Captain, the other of the Quartermaster, on the understanding that they are to be returned without fail when the boat comes back. The whole idea is that by the time they return they will both speak Spanish like natives. God grant it turn out well.

Buenaventura and Fernando seem to have survived their immersion into Spanish language and culture and returned to San Carlos, but two young boys could not compensate for the padres' persistent inability to master local languages.[22]

Two years after Mission San Carlos had been established, the Franciscans had not yet baptized any adults, and the incapacity of Indians and Franciscans to effectively communicate became the Franciscans' excuse for their larger failures to attract Indians to their way of life. Serra observed, "If, at the present time, they are not as yet all Christians, it is, in my judgement, only for want of a knowledge of their language." Serra also blamed the Indians, who were slow to pick up Spanish. "In countries like these, where it is impossible to get hold of an interpreter, or anybody who can act as an instructor, until someone from the locality

21. On the Franciscans' particular interest in young boys, see Ramón A. Gutiérrez, *When Jesus Came, the Corn Mothers Went Away: Marriage, Sexuality, and Power in New Mexico, 1500–1846* (Stanford, Calif., 1991), 75–81; Richard C. Trexler, "From the Mouths of Babes: Christianization by Children in Sixteenth Century New Spain," in J. Davis, ed., *Religious Organization and Religious Experience* (New York, 1982), 115–135. On Indian adults and Spanish, see responses of the missionaries of San Francisco to question no. 3, Ramón Abella and Juan Sainz de Lucio, Nov. 11, 1814, in Geiger and Meighan, *APST*, 21. On young boys as interpreters, see Serra to Verger, Aug. 8, 1772, Monterey, in Tibesar, ed. and trans., *Writings of Serra*, I, 259; Lasuén, memorandum, Feb. 28, 1792, Mission San Diego, in Kenneally, ed. and trans., *Writings of Lasuén*, I, 216.

22. Serra to Palóu, June 21, 1771, Monterey, in Tibesar, ed. and trans., *Writings of Serra*, I, 241–243.

can learn Spanish, it is unavoidable that some time should be required [before the Indians' conversion]." In the summer of 1773, three years after Mission San Carlos was founded, Franciscans were still "preparing some boys to be interpreters." In these early years, before a group of interpreters had emerged, the padres relied upon Cypriano Rivera, one of the Baja California Indians who had come to Alta California with them. Rivera had learned Spanish as a boy in Mission San Borja and apparently was able to attain a "good knowledge" of Rumsen in the early 1770s.[23]

Eventually, some of the children baptized at San Carlos became proficient speakers of Spanish, and over many years at least fourteen local Indians served as interpreters. Eight spoke Costanoan, the language of the majority of Indians at the mission; six spoke Esselen, the language of the next largest group (Table 16). Half of these interpreters were among the very first Indians baptized at the mission. All but one were born outside the mission, and all but two came to San Carlos before age thirteen. Eleven attained baptism between ages six and twelve, when they were old enough to have begun mastering their native tongue but still young enough to take quickly to Spanish. The Franciscans might have had unusual access to these young children, which may further explain their emergence as interpreters. Most were baptized months if not years before their parents; some of their parents never attained baptism. The existence of only one mission-born interpreter, Maximiano Joseph, testifies to the high infant and childhood mortality at San Carlos and reflects the likelihood that those born at the mission were not as proficient in native languages as those born outside it. Moreover, mission-born children might not have been as culturally adept in mediating between two worlds as those who had earlier lived in native villages. Maximiano Joseph brought to the position his own special qualifications as a cultural broker and linguistic mediator: he was the son of Cypriano Rivera, who long enjoyed the Franciscans' confidence and had himself been an interpreter. Maximiano Joseph's mother, María Antonia Solol, was from the Rumsen village of Achasta and was one of only three women who served as interpreters at San Carlos.

A linguistic divide continued to separate Franciscans and Indians long into the colonial period. New arrivals, especially adults, often showed little interest in learning Spanish, and the missionaries had to find new interpreters and grasp new dialects. Such was the case at Mission San Carlos after the mid-1770s, when disease carried off nearly all the mission-born children and the dual revolutions brought in hundreds of Esselen-speaking Indians. As of 1792, more than twenty years after the mission's establishment, Father President Lasuén had compiled

---

23. Serra to Palóu, Aug. 18, 1772, Monterey, Serra to Miguel de Petra, Aug. 4, 1773, Mexico City, both in Tibesar, ed. and trans., *Writings of Serra*, I, 267, 393; Serra, memorandum, June 22, 1774, Monterey, ibid., II, 89.

TABLE 16. Indian Interpreters at Mission San Carlos

Spanish name	Bapt. No.	Sex	Age at Bapt.	Birth	Origin	Death
Buenaventura	0003	M	8	1762	Achasta	1781
Francisco Joseph	0010	M	10	1761	Achasta	1806
Juan Evangelista Joseph	0015	M	9	1762	Achasta	1778
Fernando Joseph	0016	M	8	1763	Tucutnut	1780
Diego Joseph	0017	M	6	1765	Ichxenta	1774
María Antonia Solol	0030	F	12	1760	Achasta	1830
Miguel Berardo Murcschu	0035	M	7	1766	Tucutnut	1802
Jacinta María	0195	F	7	1767	Tucutnut	1787
Joseph María	0425	M	8	1768	Excelen	1826
Juan de Ducla	0460	M	20	1757	Excelen	1800
Maximiano Joseph	0540	M	2 days	1778	Mission	—
Romualda María	0609	F	20	1760	Ichxenta	1816
Misael Joseph Apajachiqui	1143	M	7	1778	Excelen	1837
Oresio Antonio Sichon	1509	M	7	1783	Eslenajan	1818

Source: Mission San Carlos baptismal and burial registers.

only a brief list containing some 120 terms, encompassing the most basic words: numbers, family relations, foods, and body parts. Although this vocabulary did not represent the totality of the Franciscans' comprehension of the native languages at San Carlos, its brevity suggests that the padres had not progressed much beyond a rudimentary understanding of Rumsen and Esselen. Similarly, many Indians who had been at the mission for years had only limited facility with Spanish. In 1791, when Estanislao Joseph Tupag was called to testify on charges that he had committed murder, he was interrogated through an interpreter even though he had been at the mission since his baptism in 1777 at age nine.[24]

PREBAPTISMAL INSTRUCTION

Franciscans cultivated interpreters for many reasons, but primarily so that they could prepare gentiles for baptism. Little is known about the precise content of the California Indians' prebaptismal instruction, but what is known suggests that

24. "Dictionary of the Runsien and Eslen Languages," in Donald C. Cutter, *California in 1792: A Spanish Naval Visit* (Norman, Okla., 1990), 147–149. The transcript of the murder case is in the Taylor Coll., HL. An unnumbered document, its internal pages are 63-2a–63-10a. For the testimony of Estanislao, see 63–8r; Estanislao Joseph Tupag (San Carlos bapt. no. 459, June 28, 1777).

in many aspects it was superficial and varied only slightly from mission to mission and from decade to decade. Father President Lasuén insisted that Indians did not attain baptism unless they first had "the necessary grasp of the articles" of the Catholic religion. José Francisco de Paula Señán, who later served twice as father president of the missions, stated that catechumens did not need to know by heart all the articles of faith. Rather, all they needed to know in their own language was the Our Father, the Ave María, and the Ten Commandments. Señán held out the hope that, despite what he saw as the Indians' inability to learn and their simplicity and lack of motivation, over time they would eventually understand the "Holy Mysteries and Precepts" upon which Catholicism rested.[25]

Father Juan Cortés, who worked at Santa Barbara from 1798 to 1805, prepared a statement that seems to have been read to many Indians just before their baptism. This brief exhortation suggests that Cortés wanted to be sure that adult Indians had a basic understanding of the fundamental beliefs of Catholicism. For them to be baptized and die well, they had to know and believe with all their hearts

> that there is only one true God, the creator of all the things that we see and of all those we do not see; and that God has always existed and no one created him; that God is the Most Holy Trinity, God the Father, God the Son, and God the Holy Spirit, three distinct Persons, and only one true God; also that God the Son, who is also called Jesus Christ, became man in the Womb of Mary Most Holy, Ever a Virgin, with whom no man ever was; and that he suffered and died, nailed to the Cross, in order to forgive us our sins and to take us to Heaven; and also that God is a just payer, who gives to all according to their works: for those who are good and do what God commands, Heaven, where all good things abide; for those who are wicked and commit sin, Hell, where all is wickedness and eternal fire; and that when Men die, only the body dies, the soul does not die; and that the soul of the just goes to Glory and that of the wicked to Hell.[26]

Cortés then reminded the Indians that it was not enough merely to understand these ideas but they had to believe them. Yet it is likely that Indians under Cortés's tutelage as well as those at other California missions attained baptism with only a

25. Lasuén, "Refutation of Charges," June 19, 1801, Mission San Carlos, in Kenneally, ed. and trans., *Writings of Lasuén,* II, 200; Vicente de Santa María and José Francisco de Paula Señán, Mission San Buenaventura, Oct. 2—, 1800, AGN, PI, CCXVI, expediente 1, 91b.

26. Harry Kelsey, ed. and trans., *The Doctrina and Confesionario of Juan Cortés* (Altadena, Calif., 1979), 93, original at SBMAL.

scant understanding or weak commitment to Catholicism. Cortés's prebaptismal exhortation is written in Spanish only, which raises the probability that his catechumens neither understood the statement nor held the beliefs that it required them to affirm. This declaration may reveal the Franciscans' hope of what Indians knew at baptism—or more likely what the very best-prepared Indian catechumens knew at baptism—but it yields nothing about most Indians' actual comprehension of or commitment to Catholicism.

In most cases, a simple statement by Indians of their faith in Catholicism and its Mysteries was sufficient for baptism. In his summary guide to all the missionaries of California, Commissary Prefect Sarría emphasized that, in the final days of their preparation for baptism, Indian catechumens needed to renounce "the disorders and chaos of their pagan ways" and show "themselves to be obedient and prepared to forever observe the obligations of Christians." For the majority of California missionaries, therefore, perhaps the most important achievement necessary for baptism was an Indian's commitment to casting off native behaviors and customs. Although Sarría's standard clearly allowed the baptism of Indians who knew little of the intricacies of Catholic doctrine, it reaffirmed the Franciscans' own commitment to transforming native behavior and custom, a goal that was not readily apparent to Indians who came to the missions as a strategy to weather the dual revolutions.[27]

The steady growth in the proficiency of interpreters and the Franciscans' limited but gradual acquisition of more of the Indians' languages meant that prebaptismal instruction required less time as the mission period progressed. The Franciscans' growing awareness of their limited ability to communicate with Indians and carefully instruct them in Catholicism might also have helped to shorten the length of time Indians studied before attaining baptism. In the 1770s, Indians might have prepared intermittently over months if not years before baptism. In the winter of 1774, about one hundred Indians were under instruction for baptism at Mission San Carlos. Although it is not clear how long these particular Indians were studying—and some might have died or simply left Mission San Carlos without baptism—it was not until the spring of 1776 that an additional one hundred adults had attained the sacrament. Decades later, the process was much more rapid. On the same day Franciscans founded Mission San Luis Rey in 1798, twenty-three adults began prebaptismal instruction in their native language. After a little more than two weeks of instruction, morning and evening, all were granted baptism. Similarly, at San Buenaventura in 1800, nearly twenty years after it was founded, Indians spent only two to three weeks in

27. Sarría, circular letter, pars. 16, 17.

prebaptismal instruction. By 1801, at most missions, adult Indians passed between two weeks and a month in preparation for baptism. Lasuén noted, "Very rare are those who have been baptized after only a week of instruction. Usually, one devotes fifteen, twenty, thirty, or more days to it, according to what one observes of their aptitude and other circumstances." Mission baptismal registers also reveal a decrease over decades in the length of time Indians studied Catholicism before baptism. Occasionally, when the Franciscans baptized a child, they would note whether the child's parents were catechumens at the mission. The time lag between the child's and the parents' baptisms provides a rough indication of the length of time that the Franciscans devoted to preparing adults for baptism.[28] During the 1770s, most of the parents listed as catechumens in their children's baptismal entries were not baptized until many years after their children. This time lag decreased throughout the 1770s, 1780s, and 1790s; at first, it could be measured in years and months, then weeks, and finally in days.[29]

Nothing in the historical record suggests that this shortening of the time required for prebaptismal instruction should be read as a manifestation of a rising enthusiasm by Indians for life at the missions or an increasing understanding of Catholicism on their part. Rather, the ensuing conflicts between missionaries and many of the Indians they baptized suggest something quite different: that successive California Indian groups actually might have known less of what the padres ultimately expected of them when they joined the mission community than their predecessors had known. Ironically, the initial building of linguistic bridges between Indians and missionaries in California, to the extent that it accelerated Indian baptisms, might have only fostered greater misunderstandings down the line. To be sure, later groups of gentiles baptized at the missions must

28. Serra to Pangua and discretorium, Jan. 8, 1775, Monterey, and Serra to Bucareli, detailed report of the spiritual and material status of the California missions (hereafter cited as "detailed report"), Feb. 5, 1775, Monterey, both in Tibesar, ed. and trans., *Writings of Serra,* II, 207, 247; Lasuén to Diego de Borica, June 20, July 1, 1798, in Kenneally, ed. and trans., *Writings of Lasuén,* II, 86–87; Lasuén, "Refutation of Charges," June 19, 1801, Monterey, AGN, PI, CCXVI, 67a, and in Kenneally, ed. and trans., *Writings of Lasuén,* II, 200; Vicente de Santa María and José Séñan, Oct. 2–, 1800, Mission San Buenaventura, AGN, PI, CCXVI, expediente 1, 91b.

Childless catechumens would not be part of this sample. The time periods suggested here could be over- or underestimated because of two factors: adults who became catechumens before their child's baptism would have a period of catechistical training longer than that revealed by this study, and adults who left the mission for an extended period of time after their child's baptism would have a shorter real catechistical period.

29. In the 1770s, the lag in days between the baptism of a child and a parent was 902.1 (N = 30); 1780s, 24.4 days (N = 16); and, in the 1790s, 3.7 days (N = 9). Thirteen catechumens listed in November 1774, for example, were baptized between February 1776 and October 1783. Five catechumens listed in 1775 were baptized after less than a year. Seventeen catechumens listed from 1776 to 1783 were baptized after approximately five weeks. And seventeen of the eighteen catechumens listed after November 1783 were baptized within fifteen days or fewer of their children.

have heard from others that the Franciscan establishments were indeed places of conflict, illness, and death, just as they must have known that Spanish depredations had overturned other native communities beyond their lands for generations. But, as their awareness of the threats posed by the missions was spreading, so, too, were the dual revolutions. The continual baptism of Indians testified to both the superficiality of prebaptismal instruction and the limited choices available to Indians in colonial California.

CATECHISM AND DAILY RELIGIOUS INSTRUCTION

Since, for California missionaries, the minimum goal of prebaptismal instruction was to wash away native behaviors and customs, the Indians' religious indoctrination intensified after baptism, an act that in the eyes of the Franciscans constituted the Indians' irrevocable commitment to a Catholic life.[30] To facilitate the neophytes' study of Catholicism, Franciscans and native interpreters translated into the Indians' vernacular catechisms and basic prayers—known together as the doctrina, or *rezo*—that baptized Indians recited daily. Some missionaries, in their words, devoted "indescribable labor and patience" to the task. Father Felipe Arroyo de la Cuesta went so far as to title his little handwritten manual containing his extensive translations of catechisms and prayers the "Oro molido." In its prologue, he explained: *oro* (gold) because the book was worth more than even gold, and *molido* (grounds) in memory of the countless "hardships and tribulations he had undertaken to attain its little pieces, all of which are of the greatest importance." They were important, Arroyo de la Cuesta concluded, because the Indians "understood no Spanish and even less about the Divine."[31]

30. This was in marked contrast to the Puritan missions of New England, where Indians attained baptism only after years of religious instruction and demonstrations of their knowledge of Protestantism. The literature on the Praying Towns is enormous. Among the most important works are Alden T. Vaughan, *New England Frontier: Puritans and Indians, 1620–1675* (Boston, 1965); Francis Jennings, *The Invasion of America: Indians, Colonialism, and the Cant of Conquest* (Chapel Hill, N.C., 1976); Susan L. MacCulloch, "A Tri-partite Political System among the Christian Indians of Early Massachusetts," *Kroeber Anthropological Society Papers*, XXXIV (1966), 63–73; Kenneth M. Morrison, "'That Art of Coyning Christians': John Eliot and the Praying Indians of Massachusetts," *Ethnohistory*, XXI (1974), 77–92; Neal Salisbury, "Red Puritans: The 'Praying Indians' of Massachusetts Bay and John Eliot," *WMQ*, 3d Ser., XXXI (1974), 27–54; James Axtell, *The Invasion Within: The Contest of Cultures in Colonial North America* (New York, 1985); James Holstun, *A Rational Millennium: Puritan Utopias of Seventeenth-Century England and America* (New York, 1987).

31. Responses of the missionaries of San Gabriel and San Buenaventura to question no. 11, in *APST*, 53; Felipe Arroyo de la Cuesta, cuaderno, 1810–1819, C–C 60, 7, 8, BL. The most accomplished linguist among the California Franciscans was Arroyo de la Cuesta, who served at Mission San Juan Bautista from 1808 to 1832. He composed a guide to the language of the mission that contained some 2,884

Even though Franciscans like Arroyo de la Cuesta viewed Indians as children, they did not rely upon the widely adopted Ripalda catechism that had been compiled centuries earlier expressly for Spanish children but instead chose an even more simplified one written in 1644 by the Jesuit Bartolomé Castaño for the missions of Sonora. Castaño's "Catecismo breve" was composed of just twenty-four questions and answers. Together, they affirmed the central beliefs of Catholicism: there is one all-powerful and -knowing God, who made heaven, earth, and all things; this God is manifested in the Holy Trinity, God the Father, God the Son, and the Holy Spirit; God the Son, Jesus Christ, was created in the womb of the Virgin Mary by the work of the Holy Spirit; Jesus Christ was made a man by God to cleanse the souls of man; he suffered persecution, crucifixion, and death, was buried and resurrected, and ascended to heaven, where he now sits at the right hand of God the Father; Jesus Christ died as a man, and, when a man dies, his body dies but not his soul; on Judgment Day, when body and soul are reunited, those who follow the commandments of God and the pope will go to heaven forever; those who do not will go to hell forever. The brief catechism also stressed the importance of confession and Communion.[32]

By 1776, many baptized Indians up and down the coast of California recited a version of this catechism. At San Diego, Indian boys committed it to memory and then began to preach it in surrounding villages. To Serra, the indoctrination of adults through their own children seemed as natural as a babe suckling milk from a mother's breast. In 1795, to speed the assimilation of Indians into Spanish society, the Crown forbade Franciscans or their assistants from instructing Indians in New Spain exclusively in their native tongues. Subsequently, Indians recited the catechism, mornings and evenings, once in Spanish and once in their own language. As new groups of Indians came to the missions, Franciscans prepared additional translations. In 1798, Father Juan Cortés began to translate

---

phrases in Mutsun, and he also composed a similar guide to the language of the "Tulareños." In his time, Arroyo de la Cuesta was highly regarded for his linguistic talents. Sarría wrote in 1817: "He applied himself most assiduously to learning the respective languages with such success that I doubt whether there is another who has attained the same proficiency in understanding and describing its intricate syntax. He even reduced to some sort of rules the confusing formation of its verbs, adverbs and the rest of the parts of speech which I understand may serve likewise for the other missions; for notwithstanding that their languages are very different, and that many of them have two or three idioms in the same district, they preserve their analogy with regard to expressing their ideas. I have animated him to compose a work on the subject. He has labored, as I understand, with good success, wherefore he may succeed in the work" (Geiger, *Franciscan Missionaries in Hispanic California,* 19–20). For Arroyo de la Cuesta's observation, see Felipe Arroyo de la Cuesta, cuaderno, 1810–1819, C–C 60, 80, BL.

32. The Ripalda catechism was published in 1591 in Burgos and prepared by the Jesuit missionary Gerónimo Ripalda (Ricard, *Spiritual Conquest,* 102). I have used a microfilm copy of the Castaño catechism ("Actos de fé, esperanza, y charidad; ..." [Mexico, 1778], Medina Coll., HA–M 81–5, Medina, 6059, Brown University, Providence, R.I.).

the catechism into the Chumash language spoken at Mission Santa Barbara, and in 1801 this catechism and another one like it were used by Indians at Santa Barbara and San Buenaventura. By 1814, Indians at the nineteen missions as yet established recited the "Catecismo breve" in Spanish and their local dialects.[33]

The few catechisms that survive from California's colonial period vary somewhat in complexity and reflect local missionaries' modifications in response to Indian belief and practice. Indians at San Carlos and Santa Barbara committed to memory a catechism that adhered closely to Castaño's form; yet Yokuts at Mission Santa Cruz studied only the first fourteen of Castaño's twenty-four questions. Left out from their recitations were discussions of the immortality of the soul, the presence of Jesus Christ in the Holy Sacrament, and the importance of confession and Communion. Significantly, Indians at Mission San Juan Bautista also studied a simplified version of the Castaño catechism, even though one of their missionaries, Arroyo de la Cuesta, was, among all the Franciscans to serve in Alta California, perhaps the most fluent in the native languages spoken at his mission. Indians under Arroyo de la Cuesta's tutelage did not memorize that God had made heaven, earth, and everything. They did not learn the Spanish name for the Holy Trinity, although they did wrestle with the Spanish belief that God was composed of three distinct persons. Arroyo de la Cuesta's catechism did not speak of the immortality of the soul; it stated that Christ died to cleanse Indians' sins rather than their sinful souls. Furthermore, Indians at Mission San Juan Bautista did not grapple with the vexing question: "When man dies, does his soul die or only his body?" Nor did they have to see the Holy Spirit as an agent in the immaculate conception of Christ, something that might have been difficult to accept. And they did not speak in their catechesis of Pontius Pilate, Judgment Day, and the authority of the pope, all concepts and people foreign to native belief. Arroyo de la Cuesta's deep understanding of Indian languages and culture leaves little doubt that his simplification of the catechism came after his realization that some

33. Diary of Pedro Font, Jan. 5, 1776, in Herbert Eugene Bolton, ed. and trans., *Anza's California Expeditions*, 5 vols. (1930; rpt. Berkeley, Calif., 1966), IV, 181. When Alejandro Malaspina's naval expedition visited Monterey in 1791, the padres at San Carlos had a written translation of the Castaño catechism in the two languages of the mission (Cutter, *California in 1792*, 151–155). See also Serra to Pangua, Oct. 7, 1776, San Diego, in Tibesar, ed. and trans., *Writings of Serra*, III, 70–71; Lasuén to the missionaries, Feb. 23, 1795, Mission San Carlos, in Kenneally, ed. and trans., *Writings of Lasuén*, I, 329–330; Kelsey, ed. and trans., *Doctrina and Confesionario*, 3, 6. Between 1804 and 1810, Mariano Payeras, working with the mission's interpreters, wrote a catechism for La Purísima Concepción, a mission that was not founded until 1797 (Payeras, Jan. 13, 1810, La Purísima, in Donald C. Cutter, ed. and trans., *Writings of Mariano Payeras* [Santa Barbara, Calif., 1995], 49). See also Vicente de Santa María and José Francisco de Paula Señán, Oct. 2—, 1800, San Buenaventura, AGN, PI, CCXVI, expediente 1, 91a–91b; responses of the missionaries to question no. 11, *APST*, 53–55; and see Trexler, "From the Mouths of Babes," in Davis, ed., *Religious Organization and Religious Experience*, for children and catechism.

doctrinal points would either confuse or alienate Indians. More than most missionaries, Arroyo de la Cuesta would have been aware which issues would be sticking points for Indians and which ones would be familiar and unproblematic and therefore conducive to Indians' apprehension of Catholicism.[34]

Commissary Prefect Sarría, on the other hand, sought to adjust the catechism, not through doctrinal editing, but by appending to it more questions and answers that emphasized rudimentary Catholic concepts of behavior. What had God demanded of them? That they love God above all else and love others as they loved themselves. And how would they do this? By not committing murder, having bad intentions toward anyone, stealing another man's wife, committing injury to anyone, or lying. And, if they had bad thoughts, what were they to do? Ask God to remove the bad thoughts from their minds. Would God give them what they asked for? Yes, if they asked with sincerity and prayed for the intervention of Mary or one of the saints. Sarría's belief that Indians at all missions needed to reiterate such fundamental tenets of Catholicism every day long after they had been baptized suggests the tenacity with which some Indians held to native understandings of their relationship to the supernatural and the intervention of deities in their lives.[35]

Catechism was the centerpiece of the Indians' religious indoctrination, but they were to learn further Catholic beliefs by memorizing and reciting the acts of faith, hope, charity, and contrition, the Apostles' Creed, the sign of the cross, and fundamental prayers, such as the Our Father, the Hail Mary, and the Salve Regina. The Ten Commandments, which mission Indians also committed to memory, dictated the essentials of human conduct and presented a foundation for Christian morality. In addition, Indians were to learn by rote the five commandments of the church that provided order and discipline to their communal worship: Indians were to hear Mass on Sundays and holy days of obligation, confess their sins at least once a year during Lent, receive Communion at Easter, fast when commanded to by the church, and pay tithes and firstfruits to the church. Finally, the Indians committed to memory the seven sacraments of the

34. The San Carlos catechism is published in Cutter, *California in 1792*, 151–155; the Santa Barbara catechism of Juan Cortés can be found in Kelsey, ed. and trans., *Doctrina and Confesionario*, 52–59, 103–106. A microfilm copy of the *Llanos,* or Santa Cruz catechism, is at the BL at the conclusion of BANC MSS 70/63c. This document is of uncertain provenance; an original is now at the SBMAL. The San Juan Bautista catechism by Arroyo de la Cuesta is available in manuscript form only, filed as "1816—Compendio de doctrina christiana en Ausaima," at SBMAL. Arroyo de la Cuesta prepared others, but they are only in native languages and currently defy analysis.

35. I examined a copy of Sarría's catechism at the SBMAL. It is an extract in the hand of Arroyo de la Cuesta of a catechism circulated to all the California missions by Sarría in November 1818.

church through which Catholics experienced the love and power of God: baptism, confirmation, penance, Communion, matrimony, extreme unction, and Holy Orders.

Indians recited this doctrina communally twice a day as part of their instruction; perhaps to increase attendance and participation, the padres often coupled recitations with morning and evening meals. The Franciscans also required baptized Indians who did not live at the missions to demonstrate their knowledge of basic Catholic prayers. Indians at outlying cattle ranches were required to return to the missions every two weeks to recite the doctrina. Franciscans asserted a paternal right and obligation to punish their spiritual children if they strayed, and, as we will see, they resorted to physical coercion and violence when neophytes failed to attend religious instruction.[36]

By the time Franciscans came to Alta California, two and a half centuries of conversion attempts had predisposed them to assume that Indians were capable of only a child's comprehension of Catholicism, and experience had taught them to let go of prayers and concepts that impeded the Indians' acceptance of Catholicism. Moreover, mounting political pressure against the Franciscans had led them to insist time and time again that Indians needed their spiritual guidance at every point of their lives; no doubt these endless self-justifications heightened the missionaries' sense that Indians were able to ingest only small pieces of Catholic doctrine and prayer. Thus, although it consisted of a lengthy set of prayers and statements of faith, the doctrina California Indians learned was less comprehensive than what Indians confronted in earlier missions elsewhere in New Spain. In central Mexico in the sixteenth century, Indians were to memorize the venial and mortal sins and the seven deadly sins, in addition to the basic doctrine taught in Alta California. And, in the seventeenth-century missions of Florida, Indians also committed to memory the seven virtues, the seven capital sins, the seven corporal works of mercy, the enemies of the soul, the beatitudes, and the answers to a catechism of thirty-three, not twenty-four, questions. In New Mexico in the seventeenth century, the religious education of the Indians was modeled largely on Father Alonso de Molina's "Doctrina christiana," which required Indians to memorize a much wider range of dogma than in Alta California.[37]

36. Lasuén, memorandum, July 8, 1789, Mission San Carlos, in Kenneally, ed. and trans., *Writings of Lasuén,* I, 193; Payeras to Estevan Tapís, Jan. 13, 1810, La Purísima, in Cutter, ed. and trans., *Writings of Payeras,* 52. See Chapter 8, below, for a discussion of the Franciscans' use of corporal punishment in the missions.

37. Ricard, *Spiritual Conquest,* 101; Amy Turner Bushnell, *Situado and Sabana: Spain's Support System for the Presidio and Mission Provinces of Florida* (Athens, Ga., 1994), 95–97; Gutiérrez, *When Jesus Came,* 81.

BEYOND WORDS

The Children of Coyote did not learn about Catholicism through words alone. Like Indians elsewhere in Spanish missions, their memorization of the doctrina was supplemented by liturgical art—religious paintings, portable canvases, and mass-produced prints—intended to display the glory and power of the church. At first, much of the art Indians gazed upon in the missions was that which had been taken from Baja California. From the mission church of Loreto, the father president chose "eight medium sized prints, with their tortoise-shell frames, of the Mysteries of Most Holy Mary and of Saint Joseph," and he requested that other paintings as well be sent north.[38] In 1770, Indians at San Diego conducted their morning and evening prayers in front of one such borrowed image, a painting of the Virgin. To overcome an initial shortage of liturgical art in the missions, Serra included a petition for religious paintings or printed images in virtually every request he sent to Mexico for supplies. And, when he returned to Mexico City to meet with Viceroy Antonio María de Bucareli y Ursúa in the early 1770s, the father president commissioned more art. Visual images of Catholicism proved so indispensable to native indoctrination that missionaries on occasion tore images out of their missals and displayed them in front of assembled Indians.[39]

The liturgical art of the missions, just like the Catholic prayers Indians recited, was the product of Franciscan scrutiny. The exacting requests that Serra made for paintings of the missions' patron saints suggest the Franciscans' concern over the details of the visual embodiments of their teachings. These paintings were to be liturgically correct and varied in color so as to catch the Indians' attention. In 1771, Serra insisted that Saint Louis, the bishop, was to be painted "with his episcopal insignia, showing below the level of his rochet, the Franciscan habit and cord plainly to be seen, a mitre on his head, the cope decorated with flowers, and his royal crown and sceptre at his feet." Indians were to see Saint Clare with

38. On the placement of this art in the mission church, see James L. Nolan, "Anglo-American Myopia and California Mission Art," *SCQ*, LVIII (1976), part 1, 1–44, part 2, 143–204, and part 3, 261–331; cf. Norman Neuerburg, "The Angel on the Cloud, or 'Anglo-American Myopia' Revisited: A Discussion of the Writings of James L. Nolan," *SCQ*, LXI (1980), 1–48. In all likelihood, liturgical dramas also reinforced the catechism. Alfred Robinson witnessed one such drama, *Los Pastores,* acted by the Indians of Mission San Diego in 1841 (Robinson, *Life in California . . .* [1846; New York, 1969], 195–196). Little is known, however, about the performance of these dramas in California by Indians or for Indians during the colonial period; see Neuerburg, "Anglo-American Myopia," 1–44. On the Baja paintings, see Serra to Palóu, May 8, 1779, Mission of Santa María de los Angeles, in Tibesar, ed. and trans., *Writings of Serra,* I, 125–131, esp. 125. The eight prints were lost when the supply ship *San José* disappeared at sea.

39. Serra to José de Gálvez, July 2, 1770, Monterey, in Tibesar, ed. and trans., *Writings of Serra,* I, 188–189. Serra recalled how, when he visited San Gabriel before the mission had a painting of its patron saint, he found placed over the altar a page from the missal the missionaries "had torn out from a Mass for the first Sunday of Advent, so as to have a picture of the holy Archangel" (Serra to Pangua and discretorium, Apr. 13, 1776, Monterey, in Tibesar, ed. and trans., *Writings of Serra,* II, 431).

her veil "falling on the shoulders, as she is painted in Europe." And Serra specified that Saint John Capistran's "habit should not be blue, as in other pictures
which have come here," and that "the saint should have a handsome, resolute and
devout appearance" and "not be painted by [just] any kind of painter." Serra
wanted the painting done by José de Páez, a prolific Mexican artist, and the
canvas still hangs in Mission San Juan Capistrano. When the missions' resources
were more limited, the Franciscans' procurator in Mexico was encouraged to
purchase devotional paintings and religious images at auction sales in the capital.
These paintings need not be fine art, one missionary observed, but, in acknowledgment of his own standards and perhaps the Indians' aesthetic predilections,
they should be "neither crude nor ridiculous."[40]

Throughout the colonial period, Indians at San Carlos observed a substantial
and expanding array of devotional paintings. In 1774, the mission received a
painting of its patron saint along with others depicting Saint Bonaventure, Saint
Louis, the glory of heaven, the horrors of hell, and the death of Saint Joseph;
engravings of Our Lady of Sorrows, the crucifixion, and the tree of the Franciscan order; and collections of prints of Franciscan saints, popes, cardinals, and
generals. In 1791, the mission acquired an additional 229 religious engravings.
Many of the paintings were large, usually five or six feet tall and supported by a
rod across the back, which might have allowed them to be moved about during
instruction and worship. The mission also had several very portable large roll-up
canvases—like *The Divine Shepherdess*—that came attached to hinged, wooden
storage tubes.[41]

These paintings and engravings were intended to present Indians with dramatic visual representations of Catholic belief. And they must have had quite an
effect upon those who did in fact reflect upon them. *The Horrors of Hell*, which
hung in the mission across from *The Glory of Heaven*, was a gruesome depiction
of eternal suffering, showing the condemned "enclosed in the expanded jaws of a
dragon" and hell as "swarming with devils, who tormented their victims with
spears and pitchforks." In *The Glory of Heaven*, also by Páez and still hanging at
San Carlos, Indians observed a rich tableau vividly illustrating Saint John the
Baptist, Adam and Eve, the Triune God, Moses with the Ten Commandments,

40. Serra to Verger, June 20, 1771, Monterey, Serra to Pangua, Aug. 22, 1775, Monterey, both in
Tibesar, ed. and trans., *Writings of Serra*, I, 221, II, 319; Señán to Tomás de la Peña Saravia, Feb. 4, 1806,
Mission San Buenaventura, Señán to José Viñals, Nov. 5, 1806, College of San Fernando, both in Lesley
Byrd Simpson, ed., *The Letters of José Señán, O.F.M., Mission San Buenaventura, 1796–1823*, trans. Paul
D. Nathan (San Francisco, Calif., 1962), 17, 22–23. For what little is known about José de Páez, see
Martin J. Morgado, *Junípero Serra's Legacy* (Mount Carmel, Calif., 1987), 204.

41. Serra to Bucareli, detailed report, Feb. 5, 1775, Monterey, in Tibesar, ed., *Writings of Serra*, II, 243;
Norman Neuerburg, "The Function of Prints in the California Missions," *SCQ*, LXVII (1985), 263–280,
esp. 267.

PLATE 12. *San Juan Bautista*. By José de Paez. 1775. A wooden tube at the top of the rolled-up canvas protected it, making the painting portable and ideal for the mission frontier. Mission San Luis Obispo Sacristy, San Luis Obispo, Calif. Photograph used by permission of Patrick Tregenza Photography

Joseph and Mary, Saint Francis, and the archangels Gabriel, Michael, and Raphael. Significantly, several of the martyrs in the painting seem to be Indian, and they appear to be wearing the loose-fitting coarse cotton clothing common to mission Indians. Such representations—although possibly inadvertent—might have encouraged the Indians' belief that the gates of heaven were open to them and that they too could achieve salvation through Catholicism.[42]

Inventories and annual reports suggest that Indians at all the missions were widely exposed to liturgical paintings and prints. Among the most common devotional and instructional images in the California missions were representations of the *vía crucis*, or the stations of the cross, which concentrate on fourteen scenes from Christ's Passion.[43] These visual representations of the condemnation, humiliation, crucifixion, death, and burial of Christ—events absolutely central to Christian theology—were often displayed prominently in the mission churches. Although most of the visual art dealt with the basic religious themes and stories covered in the doctrina, some was specifically requested in response to conditions in the missions. In March 1807, just after a measles epidemic had ravaged the region, the padres at San Buenaventura requested a painting of Saint Roque, who had been canonized for giving his life for the victims of the plague in Italy.[44]

Liturgical art served as more than a backdrop to the Indians' religious indoctrination and communal prayers. Many Indians might actually have possessed their own Catholic imagery. Mission San Diego, for example, received one thousand engravings in 1791. The sheer quantity of prints sent to the California missions suggests that the Franciscans might have distributed them directly to the Indians, either as rewards for good behavior or as a means to stir devotion and assist memorization of the catechism. Serra, as a young man in Mallorca, was known to have distributed small devotional engravings of Saint Francis as he walked the streets of Palma.[45]

Indians at all the missions were exposed to sculptural representations of major Catholic figures, but imported statuary played a less important role in their indoctrination than paintings and prints. Mission San Carlos had statues of the

---

42. On the artistic traditions of California Indians, see Georgia Lee and Norman Neuerburg, "The Alta California Indians as Artists before and after Contact," in *CC*, I, 467–480. *Horrors of Hell*: Bayard Taylor, quoted in Morgado, *Junípero Serra's Legacy*, 158 n. 76. This painting must have been transferred from the mission to the presidio chapel.

43. Mission San Diego had a set as early as 1770. Mission San Carlos repeatedly requested a vía crucis but did not receive its set of prints of the stations of the cross until 1809 (Norman Neuerburg, "The Indian Via Crucis from Mission San Fernando: An Historical Exposition," *SCQ*, LXXIX [1997], 348).

44. Señán to Viñals, Mar. 4, 1807, Mission San Buenaventura, in Simpson, ed., *Letters of Señán*, trans. Nathan, 26. The request was not honored, and Señán renewed his demand ten years later (list of supplies for 1817, Nov. 6, 1816, San Buenaventura, ibid., 95).

45. Neuerburg, "Function of Prints," *SCQ*, LXVII (1985), 267, 268.

Virgin of Bethlehem, Saint Joseph, and the mission's patron saint, Saint Charles of Borromeo. Near the altar at San Diego, a carved statue of Mary with a silver crown stood upon an octagonal cedar pedestal, covered by a muslin baldachin. The mission also held a statue of the infant Jesus, which had survived the mission's destruction in 1775. And Santa Barbara displayed a sculpture of its own patron saint. Statues such as these, however, were expensive and difficult to bring to California. And, perhaps, because missionaries found so few Indian sculptures there, and almost none that they considered idols, they devoted comparatively little time or expense trying to acquire and display their own.[46]

Baptized Indians rehearsed Catholic prayers in churches and baptistries adorned with visual representations of church teachings, and they witnessed the sumptuously attired Franciscans preside over Mass or administer the sacraments. Franciscan vestments themselves were not a direct extension of the doctrina, but they were intended to demonstrate the power, majesty, and tradition of the Catholic Church, and therefore they played a central role in the Indians' indoctrination. Of course, colorful, shiny, and exotic clothing must have served as a spectacle and, therefore, to some degree, attracted Indians. According to Father Palóu, the visitador general José de Gálvez made an explicit connection between the beauty of the padres' vestments and the likelihood of Indian conversions. Gálvez therefore wanted only the finest for the California missions so that the Indians "might see how God our Lord was worshipped, and with what care and purity the Holy Sacrifice of the Mass was said, and how the house of God our Lord was adorned, so that by this means they might be induced to embrace our Holy Faith."[47]

Although Indians could not see church history depicted in Franciscan vestments, the padres' ceremonial clothing suggested the progression of the liturgical year, which retold the story of Christ and the saints. The padres wore white on Easter and during the Christmas season, red on Passion Sunday, Good Friday, and Pentecost, violet during Lent and Advent, green during Ordinary Time, and black for funeral services. Indian boys who assisted in church services also wore special colorful clothing: at Mission San Antonio, for instance, Indian sacristans typically wore blue cassocks, and, on Catholic feast days, they wore red.[48]

46. Lasuén, inventory of the Mission San Diego church and sacristy, Apr. 30, 1783, San Diego Mission, in Kenneally, ed. and trans., *Writings of Lasuén*, I, 88–91. For goods damaged in transit, see Señán to Viñals, Nov. 3, 1808, San Buenaventura, in Simpson, ed., *Letters of Señán*, trans. Nathan, 34; Payeras to Josef Guilez, Oct. 5, 1810, La Purísima, in Cutter, ed. and trans., *Writings of Payeras*, 54.
47. Gálvez, paraphrased by Palóu, *Historical Memoirs*, ed. and trans. Bolton, I, 57.
48. For lists of the padres' extensive vestments, see Serra, memorandum to Bucareli, June 4, 1777, Monterey, in Tibesar, ed. and trans., *Writings of Serra*, III, 149; Lasuén, status of Mission San Diego at the end of December 1782, Dec. 31, 1782, Mission San Diego, in Kenneally, ed. and trans., *Writings of*

If the padres' clothing did not catch the Indians' eyes and attention, certainly the items used for religious services did. Every mission needed at least fifty different objects for the performance of Catholic rites and administration of sacraments. No neophyte could have missed the mission's large iron cross, which symbolized the church, Christ's crucifixion, and the redemptive promise of Christianity. More mysterious would have been the consecrated altar stone that was intended to suggest the holiness of the church and its historical connection to the lives of the saints. Elaborate candlesticks held burning candles to remind the Indians of the presence of Christ. Further, every mission had bells to call Indians to worship, lanterns to illuminate liturgical processions, silver shells to hold baptismal water, a silver chalice and cruets for the celebration of the Eucharist, a silver aspergillum to sprinkle the holy water, a ciborium to hold hosts for Communion, a monstrance to display the consecrated host, a stand for the missal, a boat containing incense, and a censer to hold hot coals to burn the incense. So substantial were the religious paraphernalia at San Diego in 1775 that, after the Indians burned the mission to the ground, the padres recovered more than seventeen pounds of melted silver from the church's smoldering ruins.[49]

All of these items were intended to be beautiful, but for Franciscans their principal value resided in their ability to capture the Indians' attention and bring the Holy Spirit and the body of Christ into their lives. Serra, therefore, was particularly concerned, deeply pained, in fact, by the absence of a monstrance in the newly established mission of San Francisco, and he asked Viceroy Bucareli to provide one so that the Franciscans would "be able to expose the Blessed Sacrament, in front of that immense multitude of gentiles in whose midst they live." In July 1778, when the elaborate new monstrance arrived at San Carlos along with a painting of Our Lady of Sorrows, the missionaries staged an elaborate celebration involving the Indians. Franciscans displayed the consecrated Host in the new monstrance before the Indians, and, in the "presence of Our Most Sacramental Lord," sang Mass and fired salutes with small bronze guns they used for such celebrations. Furthermore, to emphasize the glory of the day and the sacredness of the monstrance and the image of the Virgin, the padres gave all the Indians a special portion of meat along with their regular ration of food. Although Serra had requested the monstrance for Mission San Francisco, it carried

Lasuén, II, 357. For colored clothing for sacristáns, see Serra to Bucareli, detailed report, Feb. 5, 1775, Monterey, in Tibesar, ed., *Writings of Serra*, II, 237, 243.

49. Serra to Bucareli, list of church furnishing requested for Mission San Diego, May 30, 1777, Monterey, and memorandum to Bucareli, June 4, 1777, both in Tibesar, ed., *Writings of Serra*, III, 135–137, 149–151. See also Amy Turner Bushnell, "The Sacramental Imperative: Catholic Ritual and Indian Sedentism in the Provinces of Florida," in *CC*, II, 475–490; Serra to Pangua, Sept. 24, 1776, San Diego, in Tibesar, ed., *Writings of Serra*, III, 29.

an inscription around its base stating that it was for the use of the Carmel mission. Serra kept the new monstrance at Carmel and sent the mission's older one to San Francisco, leaving both missions, in his words, "better off and happy about it."[50]

MUSIC, PROCESSIONS, AND CELEBRATIONS

In California, Indians learned devotional songs and catechetical hymns as part of their indoctrination. In spite of the Indians' playing flutes and drums and singing chants and songs before the Spaniards arrived, the Franciscans believed they had no knowledge of music. The young boys whom the Franciscans trained to sing in choirs and play in small orchestras took quickly to Catholic songs and musical instruments. Choristers learned an extensive repertoire of liturgical music in both Spanish and Latin. In at least one mission—San Juan Bautista—they even sang Catholic devotional music in their native language. At San Buenaventura, Indians sang hymns of praise or the Salve Regina after reciting the catechism. And Indian choristers throughout California sang or chanted specific hymns appropriate to Mass and the principal feasts of the year. Indians at Santa Clara formed an accomplished band of musicians, attired in uniforms that the padres purchased from a French whaler. By the 1830s, many missions had extensive collections of musical instruments that allowed large numbers to participate in religious services. In 1834, Mission Santa Barbara, for instance, had four flutes, three clarinets, two trumpets, two bass viols, three drums, twenty violins, and three triangles, in addition to four music stands and uniforms for the musicians.[51]

Although the words, melodies, and instruments introduced by the Franciscans were new, Indians likely found in them a familiar way to the sacred. Father Narciso Durán of Mission San Jose was among the most devoted of the California missionaries when it came to musical instruction. In 1813, in a prologue to an

50. Serra to Pangua, June 27, Sept. 24, 1776, Aug. 19, 1778, Monterey, all in Tibesar, ed., *Writings of Serra*, III, 13, 29, 229.

51. Responses of the missionaries to question no. 33, in *APST*, 133–137; photograph of Arroyo de la Cuesta's musical notebook in Mary Dominic Ray and Joseph H. Engbeck, *Gloria Dei: The Story of California Mission Music* (Sacramento, Calif., 1974), 17; Vicente de Santa María and Señán, Oct. 2—, 1800, Mission San Buenaventura, AGN, PI, CCXVI, expediente 1, 91b; Payeras to Tapis, Jan. 13, 1810, La Purísima, in Cutter, ed. and trans., *Writings of Payeras*, 50; Marguerite Eyer Wilbur, ed. and trans., *Duflot de Mofras' Travels on the Pacific Coast* (Santa Ana, Calif., 1937), I, 221; Edith Buckland Webb, *Indian Life at the Old Missions* (1952; rpt. Lincoln, Neb., 1982), 252. For useful works on California mission music, see James A. Sandos, *Converting California: Indians and Franciscans in the Missions* (New Haven, Conn., 2004), 128–153; Owen da Silva, *Mission Music of California: A Collection of Old California Mission Hymns and Masses* (1941; rpt. Los Angeles, Calif., 1954); Ray and Engbeck, *Gloria Dei*; Webb, *Indian Life at the Old Missions*, 245–258.

extensive choir book he composed, Durán argued that it had been a mistaken assumption that the Indians "did not possess the ability to take up singing." However, like the missionaries elsewhere in California, he restricted his musical training to young boys, who he was convinced could learn "two or three entire masses." Durán stated that in the past a small number of especially gifted Indians at many of the missions had memorized the sacred chants of the Mass. But, when these select few were ill or away and therefore unable to lead the choir, the sacred music was reduced to a "ridiculous" "clamour." To rectify the choirs' dependence on a few Indians with especially good memories, Durán designed rules and principles that he used to teach Indians to read music. Within a few years, choristers, playing musical instruments, accompanied the religious services. Eventually, the extensive repertoire of the Indian choir included several masses, numerous hymns, and plainchant propers for some thirty-two feast days. At San Jose, Indians not only sang the Mass, but thirty played violins, trumpets, and drums.[52]

On days of special religious import to the Franciscans, such as Palm Sunday, the feast of Corpus Christi, or the day devoted to honoring a mission's patron saint, Indians participated in solemn processions that drew upon all the missions' liturgical tools. To celebrate the feast of Corpus Christi, Indians lined up behind missionaries, who no doubt were dressed in their finest vestments. All— missionaries, soldiers, and Indians—then wended their way around the mission and into the church, accompanied by the pealing of bells, the firing of cannons, and the singing and chanting of Catholic songs. This pageantry was intended to glorify the body of Christ and make his presence real to the Indians. Furthermore, the participation of the soldiers, the beating of drums, the fire and smoke of luminaria, the thunderclap of cannons, the streaming of banners—all of these evoked warfare and reminded the Indians of their certain defeat at the hands of the Catholic Spaniards.[53]

Such elaborate processions provided regular occasions for Indian participation in dramatic displays of Catholic pageantry and liturgy. More spectacular still, yet much less frequent, were church dedications. Throughout the colonial period, as rain, floods, wind, fire, and overcrowding rendered existing churches

---

52. Da Silva, *Mission Music of California,* 29–33, esp. 30, 31. For a list of the contents of Durán's compilation, see 126–127.

53. See Maynard J. Geiger, ed. and trans., *Palóu's Life of Fray Junípero Serra* (Washington, D.C., 1955), 30–33, for descriptions of the processions that Serra organized in the Sierra Gorda before he came to Alta California. For descriptions of the music that accompanied these celebrations, see Webb, *Indian Life at the Old Missions,* 255. On the larger meaning of these dramatic events in colonial New Mexico, see Gutiérrez, *When Jesus Came,* 83–84. For colonial Mexico, see William H. Beezley, Cheryl English Martin, and William E. French, eds., *Rituals of Rule, Rituals of Resistance: Public Celebrations and Popular Culture in Mexico* (Wilmington, Del., 1994).

unstable and unusable, Indians constructed new ones under Franciscan direction. Scholars have estimated that Indian laborers built as many as sixty-eight churches at the region's twenty-one missions between 1769 and the 1830s.[54] In May 1784, Fathers Serra, Palóu, and Tomás de la Peña, the governor of California, and the commander of the San Francisco Presidio all gathered at Santa Clara to dedicate the recently completed church. When the Indian crossbearer, acolytes, and torchbearers had assembled, Serra, in a public expression of church-state unity, handed the key of the new church to the governor. All the assembled— Franciscans, soldiers, and neophytes—processed into the church in order of rank, amid ringing bells and cannon- and gunfire. The blessing of the church concluded with Indians' and others' reciting the Te Deum Laudamus, a prayer that praised God and reinforced the central teachings of the church.

Thirty-five years later, in September 1820, in honor of the dedication of its new church building, Mission Santa Barbara hosted a three-day celebration that was by day a solemn religious occasion and by night a raucous public fiesta. Franciscans and Indian musicians and dancers came to Santa Barbara from neighboring missions, soldiers ventured over from the nearby presidio, and the governor traveled all the way from Monterey for the occasion. All of those amassed chanted the Te Deum followed by the Compline in front of the illuminated altar. Once the religious service was over, Indians saw the mission and its church lit up in dramatic fashion:

> In succession, were illuminated the (*azoteas*) housetops, the corridors, and the tower, the last named having many flags of all colors. Immediately the musicians of the three Missions passed through the corridors, where they played with a will for about two continuous hours. Meanwhile, rockets, serpents, firecrackers, were fired *(tirandose en estas cohetas, buscapies, carretillas)*, followed at once by the *castillo de fuego artificial* (castle of artificial fire). Then came bull-baiting, the baitors having the same artificial fire, which caused the greatest fun and diversion. All this was repeated on the two following nights.[55]

On occasions of this grandeur and drama, which drew hundreds if not thousands of Indian participants and others from many stations of life, processions and celebrations showed the living church following its Lord. Events such as these demonstrated to Indians the hierarchy of colonial society and the church and religion that stood at its center.

54. Robert H. Jackson and Edward D. Castillo, *Indians, Franciscans, and Spanish Colonization: The Impact of the Mission System on California Indians* (Albuquerque, N.Mex., 1995), 142.

55. Francisco Suñer, Sept. 13, 1820, quoted in Webb, *Indian Life at the Old Missions*, 280 (emphasis added).

THE *PRECEPTO ANUAL*

Much of the Indians' indoctrination into Catholicism and participation in the life of the church—reciting the doctrina, attending Mass, marching in processions, and celebrating church dedications—was public and communal. But, during the most intense period in the Catholic liturgical calendar, the Easter season, Indians were to approach the Franciscans alone, just as Christ had died on the cross. They were to confess, perform penance, and ultimately receive Communion, the most holy of the Catholic sacraments. In general, Indians, as well as most other Catholics, performed these religious obligations once a year. Doing so allowed them to reconcile with God and the community they had sinned against. During the confession that necessarily preceded penance, Indians had their consciences probed for sin and their minds tutored in basic Catholic beliefs. The Indians' inability to comprehend and embrace fundamental Catholic beliefs gave the Franciscans pause about whether neophytes understood the sacrament of penance and could be trusted to give a full and sincere confession. Ultimately, however, missionary guides like De la Peña Montenegro's *Itinerario* counseled that an Indian who knew enough Catholic doctrine for baptism knew enough for confession and could not be denied the opportunity for reconciliation.[56]

At baptism, the Franciscans believed, Indians had taken on the responsibility to confess annually. Few neophytes, however, submitted to the confession voluntarily, and missionaries ascribed this resistance to primitiveness. But Indians must have found distasteful the Franciscans' intrusiveness into their personal beliefs and private behaviors, and they might not have had any experience with a religion that promised reconciliation through prayer to an Almighty rather than through gifts to the injured or aggrieved. Moreover, Indians might have found alienating a religion that purported to judge them as individuals, not as members of a family, clan, or village. Most Indians who balked at fulfilling the *precepto anual,* however, ultimately were compelled to confess by the Franciscans. At San Carlos between 1808 and 1830, almost three-quarters of all Indians confessed, and in some years it appears that all adults did so (Table 17).[57]

Typically, at Mission San Carlos, the Children of Coyote confessed to a padre who was seated in a booth that had been fashioned out of Mexican cedar packing

56. Lasuén, memorandum, July 8, 1789, Mission San Carlos, in Kenneally, ed. and trans., *Writings of Lasuén,* I, 193. On whether neophytes could be trusted to give a sincere confession, see Sarría, circular letter, par. 21.

57. Sarría, circular letter, par. 19. Beginning in 1808, the Franciscans kept records of how many Indians confessed annually at the California missions. Children under the age of reason—age nine in the missions—were considered too young to understand sin and therefore too young for confession. When the population is reduced by those too young to confess, it becomes clear that the Franciscans at San Carlos were successful in compelling nearly all adult Indians to confess.

TABLE 17. Confessions by Indians, Mission San Carlos, 1808–1830

Year	Indian Pop.	# Indians Who Confessed	% Indians Who Confessed	Adult Indian Pop.	% Adult Indians Who Confessed
1808	550	300	55	462	65
1809	533	300	56	447	67
1810	511	350	68	451	78
1811	485	400	82	424	94
1812	455	400	88	395	101
1813	448	400	89	374	107
1814	431	380	88	369	103
1815	423	370	87	347	107
1816	405	330	81	334	99
1817	402	335	83	327	102
1818	390	310	79	310	100
1819	397	314	79	305	103
1820	381	300	79	290	103
1821	374	300	80	286	105
1822	341	280	82	266	105
1823	317	205	79	241	104
1824	306	196	64	233	84
1825	295	204	69	209	98
1826	277	180	65	193	93
1827	275	150	55	193	78
1828	234	180	77	179	101
1829	233	—	—	176	—
1830	229	125	55	177	71
Total	8,692	6,354	73	6,988	91

Note: The Franciscans' annual reports for Mission San Carlos indicate the number of adults and children at the mission. In some years, the proportion of Indian adults who confessed is greater than 100 percent. Perhaps, in these years, the Franciscans compelled children to confess, or the missionaries included the confessions of *gente de razón* in some of their tabulations. The number of confessions at Mission San Carlos in 1829 is not known.

Source: Annual reports of Mission San Carlos, in SBMAL; and Zephyrin Engelhardt, *Mission San Carlos Borromeo (Carmelo): The Father of the Missions* (1934; rpt. Ramona, Calif., 1973), app. B, "Spiritual Results," 243.

crates and California redwood. During the confession, Indians responded to a battery of prepared questions, propounded in either Spanish or an Indian language, and focused on beliefs and behaviors Franciscans considered sinful and dangerous. At the outset, Indians were asked a simple question calculated to determine their most basic knowledge of Catholicism: "Do you know how to pray?" If their answer revealed an unfamiliarity with basic Catholic prayers, they were admonished: "Look here: try to learn how to say prayers, for every Christian must know whatever is required to get to heaven." Then they were told to affirm the central teachings of the catechism. These confessions must have been frightening and isolating, a time when many Indians learned what Catholicism promised them: to burn in hell if they did not repent and express sincere remorse for sins they committed.[58]

After the confession, Indians were lectured further in the central teachings of the doctrina: the immortality of the soul, the horrors of damnation, and the glories of salvation. Although Indians were to accept these tenets of Catholicism through faith, the tenets were described to the Indians through images drawn from the hardships of daily life at the missions. At Santa Barbara, Indians were told to sin no more, for,

> when you die, only your body dies; the soul cannot die. And if you die in sin, your soul goes to Hell to suffer forever from every ill and every infirmity, much hunger, much thirst, much coldness, eternal darkness, and you will be there burning like a tile in the furnace, suffering such as I am unable to describe. But if you are good and do not sin, you will go to Heaven with God for eternity, where all the good things and all the sweet things and all the beautiful things are. There, best of all things, you will see God, Jesus Christ, Blessed Mary, and your soul will be more beautiful than the Sun, and always very happy and very content.

In essence, Indians were taught that to avoid sin would be to earn forever a world beyond the dual revolutions, for, in heaven, Indians heard, "one has everything

---

58. The confessional booth that still survives is first noted by Serra in the mission inventory of 1774 (Serra to Bucareli, detailed report, Feb. 5, 1775, Monterey, in Tibesar, ed., *Writings of Serra*, II, 243). On the effort expended to translate the confessional into native languages, see Payeras to Tapis, Jan. 1, 1810, La Purísima, in Cutter, ed. and trans., *Writings of Payeras*, 49. "Pray": Kelsey, trans. and ed., *Doctrina and Confesionario*, 107; "Look here": Madison S. Beeler, ed., *The Ventureño Confesionario of José Señán, O.F.M.*, University of California Publications in Linguistics, XLVII (Berkeley, Calif., 1967), 13. At Santa Barbara, the catechism began, "Tell me Brother, how many Gods are there? Where is God? Who made heaven, earth, and all things?" The mission's confession began with the same concepts: "Tell me now: Do you believe with your heart that there is only one true God, creator of heaven, and of earth?" (Kelsey, trans. and ed., *Doctrina and Confesionario*, 102, 103 [my trans.]). The confession continued in that manner, affirming every doctrinal concept in the mission's catechism.

PLATE 13. Confessional of California redwood and Mexican cedar, constructed at
Mission Carmel before 1775. Mission Carmel Museum, Carmel, Calif.
Photograph used by permission of Patrick Tregenza Photography

one wants; there is no sickness, nor cold, nor heat, nor hunger, nor thirst, nor anything bad."[59]

Sinful Indians might still get to heaven if they performed repetitious penitential acts, ones that again inculcated central church teachings. Although it was up to individual missionaries to determine the exact penance, manuals such as the *Itinerario* reminded them not to be excessive in their demands, as God does not request more from an ignorant people than they can achieve. Other manuals explicitly reminded missionaries when determining penance to take into account the "status, condition, sex, age, and also the disposition of the Penitent." One manual, written expressly for the Franciscan missions of Texas, recommended that missionaries perform the assigned penance along with the penitent, lest the Indian become confused or forget to complete it. Attached to confessionals were usually lists of numbers and discussions of how to express still-higher numbers in local Indian languages; these gave the Franciscans the ability to finely calibrate penitential acts to the severity of the Indians' sins. In the California missions, the Indians' penance typically ranged from three recitations of the Lord's Prayer to repeating the Lord's Prayer four times a day for eight days, to praying the Holy Rosary every Sunday for a month. Penance, however, did not guarantee reconciliation with the church. Father Sarría stated that Indians with little knowledge of Catholicism could be granted the sacrament of penance, but he advised missionaries not to grant such Indians absolution, a precondition for Communion. Here, as we shall see, it seems that the church resisted inclusiveness as much as many Indians resisted Catholicism, for the Indians' infrequent receipt of the sacrament of Communion demonstrated the degree to which most remained marginalized within the Catholic faith.[60]

SYMBOLS OF CONFLATION

Describing the Indians' participation in their own religious indoctrination is easier than measuring their commitment to it, for they responded in myriad ways to Catholicism, and their reactions were individual, idiosyncratic, and often

59. Kelsey, trans. and ed., *The Doctrina and Confesionario,* 80 (my trans.).

60. De la Peña Montenegro, *Itinerario,* ed. Baciero et al., libro 3, tratado 3, sect. 7, par. 5, 87; Miguel Venegas, *Manual de parrochos, para administrar los santos sacramentos, y executar las demas sagradas funciones de su ministerio . . . ,* 2d ed. (Mexico City, 1766), 102 (my trans.), copy at the Archive of the Archdiocese of Orange County, Mission San Juan Capistrano; Bartholomé García, *Manual para administrar los santos sacramentos de penitencia, eucharistia, extrema-uncion, y matrimonio . . .* (Mexico City, 1760), 1; Beeler, ed., *Ventureño Confesionario,* 74–79. The San Carlos vocabulary also had a similar list of numbers (Cutter, *Monterey in 1792,* 147). For Sarría's advisory on absolution, see Sarría, circular letter, par. 21.

grounded in experimentation and ambivalence. Through the simplified catechism, daily prayer, displayed ritual, and rigorous annual confession, Indians encountered an extensive and all-encompassing cluster of Catholic beliefs: mono-
theism, the Trinity, the immortality of the soul, the eternal glories of heaven and
the torments of hell, the importance of Jesus and Mary, and the need for the
sacraments, ritual redemption, and intercession with God. Over and over again,
in a variety of forms, Indians heard Franciscans insist upon these fundamental
beliefs. But what Indians memorized through song and prayer was not necessarily learned, and what they viewed in art and spectacle was not necessarily
understood or believed. Doubtless, some accepted Catholicism on terms approaching the Franciscans'. Yet, of the motivations and thoughts of these individuals—like the vast majority of California Indians—we know little. They moved
with the Franciscan flow and therefore left few ripples in the historical record
outside of their names in the sacramental registers.

Although the Indians' receipt of various sacraments revealed little about their
interior world, the Franciscans saw Indian participation in the religious life of the
missions as a hopeful sign of their movement toward Catholicism. In June 1774,
Serra shared with the viceroy his satisfaction with what he took to be the Children of Coyote's spiritual progress: in San Carlos, Serra found, "where but yester-
day there had never been pronounced the name of God nor of Jesus Christ,
[there are] more than two hundred souls, counting Christians and catechumens." "Three times a day they eat from what we provide them; they pray, sing
and work." Thirty-five years later, when the missions were more firmly established, Father Mariano Payeras wrote with satisfaction: "We hear them pray, sing
(this year another beautiful Mass with much music was created) and play, as
proficient musicians and singers." In fact, after Indians had been emancipated
from the missions during the 1820s and 1830s, many continued to return to the
mission and its Catholic rituals. Romualda Tiguis and her husband, Caio Cristiano of Mission Soledad, had their son Miguel, who was born next to the levee of
the Monterey River, baptized at San Carlos soon after his birth. Additionally,
Benvenuta Puntcans and Macedonio Chuguis of San Carlos had a son born in a
distant rancho, and they brought their child, Juan Evangelista, to the mission
for baptism.[61]

What lay behind these Indians' seeming embrace of Catholicism is not clear.
Some apparently observant Indians might have been raised at the missions from
birth as practicing Catholics, but others, especially those baptized as adults, were

61. Serra to Bucareli, June 21, 1774, Monterey, in Tibesar, ed., *Writings of Serra,* II, 79; Payeras to Tapis,
Jan. 13, 1810, La Purísima, in Cutter, ed. and trans., *Writings of Payeras,* 50; Romualda Tiguis (San Carlos
bapt. no. 2800); Miguel (San Carlos bapt. no. 3758); Benvenuta Puntcans (San Carlos bapt. no. 2997);
Macedonio Chuguis (San Carlos bapt. no. 3005); Juan Evangelista (San Carlos bapt. no. 3820).

likely drawn to experiment with Catholicism because some of its symbols and rituals reflected and resembled in form if not in content those they held. In Alta California, as throughout Christendom, the cross was the most visible symbol of the Catholic religion and the Spanish conquest. Upon their arrival and during the foundation of the missions, soldiers and Franciscans raised tall wooden crosses to mark their possession of the land and its sanctity. Spanish soldiers and missionaries also wore crosses on their bodies and clothing, and they made the sign of the cross before and after they prayed, when they approached a Catholic place of worship, and when they feared for their lives. To the Indians of colonial New Mexico, the cross appeared as a Pueblo Indian prayer stick. And the Maya also analogized the Catholic cross to their own prayer sticks. Similarly, California Indians might have seen in the Spaniards' large wooden crosses a variant of the symbol they had long used to mark their lands as sacred and settled.[62]

Throughout California, Indians had raised tall wooden poles to honor deities and claim territories. When the Franciscans and soldiers first arrived at Monterey, they did the same thing, setting up two large crosses to mark the land as Spanish and Christian. Predictably, Indians decorated these crosses as if they were their own prayer poles, hanging from one of them strings of sardines and pieces of deer meat and placing at its foot "many broken arrows." One Rumsen boy years later explained that the Indians " 'had done so, that the cross'—*porpor* was the name they gave it—'might not be angry with them.' " The conflation of the Christian cross with Indian prayer poles must have been common in Alta California. According to missionaries at Santa Inés, Chumash prayer poles had dotted the landscape and indicated sacred areas: "When the villages were still inhabited by pagans one could see at various places bunches of feathers fixed to a pole and these could be called their places of worship." At Santa Cruz, just north of Mission San Carlos, Indians congregated to "raise a long stick crowned by a bundle of tobacco leaves or branches of trees or some other plant." And, at San Juan Bautista, to the east of San Carlos, locals marked their places of worship with "a stick painted red, white and black with some arrows attached or hanging jars and other things." "Other arrows they place at the foot of another stick which they call *chochon* and there they also placed pinole, beads and a pouch of tobacco." It is not just the similarities in the shape of the cross and poles that are important but rather that both Indians and Spaniards symbolized and invoked their deities in similar ways, through inanimate wooden structures that symbolized deeper beliefs.[63]

62. Gutiérrez, *When Jesus Came*, 82; Clendinnen, *Ambivalent Conquests*, 174–175.

63. Serra, memorandum, June 22, 1774, Monterey, and Serra to Pangua and discretorium, July 18, 1774, both in Tibesar, ed., *Writings of Serra*, II, 89, 113. If the arrows were indeed "shot" at the cross, that

The Children of Coyote's ability to see one of their own sacred symbols in the Christian cross—and their apparent comfort with the cross as a way of invoking or placating a deity—facilitated their acceptance of this central Catholic symbol, but the Franciscans were not about to allow prayer poles to serve as surrogate crosses. Missionaries worked to replace the poles, and crosses soon became as common on the California landscape as the Indians' poles had been. At each mission, Franciscans placed a large wooden cross that dominated the interior grounds. And the padres did not confine Catholic crosses to mission quadrangles; they placed them along the paths and roads of Alta California soon after their arrival. At San Buenaventura in Chumash territory, the stations of the cross marked a path from the mission to a chapel at the beach. And, at Monterey, crosses came to mark the road between the mission and the presidio. Whereas the Spaniards considered the displacement of the Indians' prayer poles an indication of the triumph of Christianity over superstition, Indians most likely, unbeknownst to the missionaries, long into the colonial period continued to associate the crosses with aspects of their native beliefs, not those introduced by the Franciscans.[64]

Like the cross, the Virgin Mary was a central icon in the Indians' indoctrination, and Mary was among the first and most common images of the church California Indians saw. Mary's image figured prominently in the foundation ceremonies of most missions, and every mission had an image of the Virgin in its altarpiece. Through the catechism and especially the Hail Mary, Indians were taught to revere the Blessed Virgin as a symbol of fertility and motherhood ("blessed is the fruit of thy womb, Jesus") and as an intercessor between humanity and God ("Mary, Mother of God, pray for us sinners, now and at the hour of our death"). By many accounts, neophytes did develop a strong devotion to Mary. Nearly 20 percent of all Indian women born at San Carlos were given some form of the name María.[65]

As with the cross, the Indians' devotion to Mary might also have been an extension of earlier beliefs and the embrace of a familiar type of symbol. The Gabrielino, for example, believed in a virginal woman named Chukit, who gave

might suggest an altogether different interpretation. But broken arrows, it would seem, could not have been shot; most likely they were broken and placed at the foot of the cross. On the prayer poles, see responses of the missionaries of Missions Santa Inés, Santa Cruz, and San Juan Bautista to question no. 10, and responses of the missionaries of San Juan Bautista to question no. 35, in *APST,* 48, 50, 145.

64. On the disappearance of the Indians' prayer poles, see the responses of the missionaries of Santa Inés to question no. 10, in *APST,* 48. On the placement of crosses, see Webb, *Indian Life at the Old Missions,* 270–271.

65. Nolan, "Anglo-American Myopia and California Mission Art," *SCQ,* LVIII (1976), part 2, 272–273; tabulation of "María" from database of San Carlos baptismal register. On naming practices in Bourbon Mexico, see Taylor, *Magistrates of the Sacred,* 288–291, 685–686 nn. 132, 133. Whether Indians chose these names or Franciscans picked them for Indians is not clear.

birth to the Son of God after being impregnated by lightning. And, long before and long after the Franciscans came, California Indians revered certain women in their communities who they believed controlled fertility and rain. At San Carlos, old Indian women often claimed that they were the ones who caused fruits and seeds to grow. In return, neophytes gave them gifts every year.[66]

In a possible extension or displacement of this practice, many Indians in the missions bestowed gifts directly upon images of Mary. Soon after San Gabriel was founded in September 1771, the Gabrielino gave offerings to a painted image of the Virgin in the crudely constructed church. After seeing the image, the Gabrielino women "went to their homes and came back loaded down with seeds and provisions, which they offered to the holy image, leaving their offerings in front of the altar."[67] By the 1820s and 1830s, the role of the Virgin as intercessor on behalf of mission crops was explicit. When drought gripped the Santa Barbara region and threatened the community's corn, beans, wheat, and pasturage, the mission community called upon Mary to intercede. Alfred Robinson described the Indians' procession from the mission to the beach and back again: "First, came the priest in his church robes, who, with a fine clear voice, led the Rosary. On each side of him were two pages, and the music followed; then, four females, who supported on their shoulders a kind of litter, on which rested a square box containing the figure of the Holy Virgin. Lastly, came a long train of men, women and children, who united in the recital of the sacred mysteries . . . accompanied by violins and flutes." The reverence of the Virgin Mary as intercessor and controller of fertility might have found a deep resonance in Indians' pre-Catholic beliefs and customs. Their acceptance of Mary might have been accelerated by the deaths and growing infertility of the women in their own communities: as more and more women died from illness and as syphilis and other venereal diseases undermined the reproductive health of female survivors, Indian women might have lost their ability to assert credibly that they did have reproductive powers and therefore influence over rain and the growth of plants. The Virgin Mary, ever present in the church, untainted by intercourse yet Mother of God, was a plausible substitute for these beliefs.[68]

---

66. Susanna Bryant Dakin, *A Scotch Paisano in Old Los Angeles: Hugo Reid's Life in California, 1832–1852, Derived from His Correspondence* (1939; rpt. Berkeley, Calif., 1978), letter no. 14, 249–250; Edward D. Castillo, "Gender Status Decline, Resistance, and Accommodation among Female Neophytes in the Missions of California: A San Gabriel Case Study," *American Indian Culture and Research Journal*, XVIII (1994), 67–93, esp. 70; responses of the missionaries of San Carlos to question no. 10, in *APST*, 49–50.

67. Serra to Bucareli, May 21, 1771, Mexico City, in Tibesar, ed., *Writings of Serra*, I, 359. Palóu says that this event occurred earlier, in 1769, just before the mission was founded. Zephyrin Engelhardt, *San Gabriel Mission and the Beginnings of Los Angeles* (San Gabriel, Calif., 1927), 4, places the event before the mission's establishment. The altar would have been a portable one.

68. Robinson, *Life in California*, 149–150.

Resemblances between Catholic and Indian religious ceremonies and cultural rituals facilitated the Indians' apparent acceptance of many other aspects of Catholic worship as they continued to seek out familiar ways to the sacred during this period of intense upheaval. Although native religions differed from region to region and group to group, certain ceremonial practices were common throughout Indian California, and many of these were similar in form to Catholic ones.[69] In the California missions, the padres used shells made of silver to hold the holy water before baptism. Indians up and down the coast might have found this practice familiar and disarming, since they were used to harvesting shellfish and manufacturing money, jewelry, and regalia from seashells. In most Indian groups, an elite male priesthood controlled religious ceremony and held exclusive rights to sacred knowledge. Native religious leaders adorned themselves with special clothes and remained aloof from the group when they led communal worship. Among some peoples, religious leaders even spoke a special language. California Indians expressed their religions ceremonially through processions, music, song, dance, fasting, and feasting. And many native groups began their ceremonial year at the December solstice. These Indians found parallels or imperfect reflections in Catholic rituals, where missionaries spoke Latin, adorned themselves in extravagant clothing, led communal song and music, and performed rites and rituals exclusive to the priesthood.

Although the record of Indian religious belief in precontact and colonial California is disappointingly thin, it is clear that Indian and Catholic spirituality occasionally overlapped in content, not just symbol and form. Only one missionary, Gerónimo Boscana of San Juan Capistrano, wrote an ethnographic treatise of the Indians at his mission, and regional variations within native California were too great for his study to represent the beliefs of Indians at other missions. Nevertheless, Boscana's narrative suggests significant points of similarity between Luiseño religious beliefs—and perhaps those of other California Indians—and those taught by the Franciscans. Some Luiseños believed that rocks and stones, trees and shrubs, herbs and grass, and animals and man were created over six days. The Luiseño knew their just and omniscient god, Chinigchinich, who had ascended to the heavens after his death, by three distinct names. According to Boscana and his Luiseño informants, Chinigchinich told his people, "When I die, I shall ascend above, to the stars, and from thence, I shall always see you; and to those who have kept my commandments, I shall give all they ask of me; but those who obey not my teachings, nor believe them, I shall punish severely." Thus, when the Luiseño heard the Franciscans speak of the creation of the world in six

69. Joseph G. Jorgensen, *Western Indians: Comparative Environments, Languages, and Cultures of 172 Western American Indian Tribes* (San Francisco, Calif., 1980), 262–268.

days, of a just god, of the Holy Trinity, and of the Ascension of Christ after his death, they must have recognized concepts they already accepted. Furthermore, the familiarity of these ideas and the translators' reliance on Luiseño words or the substitution of Spanish loanwords without any context might have meant that the Franciscans' teachings reinforced old notions rather than introduced new ones.[70]

The ability of Indians to see themselves and their spirituality as compatible with or part of a Catholic cosmology and worldview—and the limitations the Franciscans tried to place on such conceptions—found no better expression than in the liturgical art Indians created occasionally for the missions. Because there were usually no Spanish or Mexican artists in Alta California and it was often difficult for the missions to acquire liturgical art from Mexico, the Franciscans taught a handful of Indians to paint Catholic images in European styles. In some instances, native art and Mexican baroque so resembled one another that it is not clear whether mission Indian artists were inspired by their own artistic traditions or followed those introduced by the Franciscans.[71] For example, native artists painted the interior of one chapel with geometric images that, according to one art historian, could be derived from Indian or European culture or a combination of the two. Furthermore, Indian images of symbols or animals cover many of the interiors of the missions. However, the overwhelming majority of the surviving liturgical art in the missions appears to be devoid of Indian influence. Missionaries discouraged Indians from representing themselves and their beliefs in Christian iconography; the goal of mission art was, after all, to teach Indians about Catholicism, not to commemorate or to validate Indian beliefs.[72]

The most extensive surviving example of Catholic liturgical art created by Indian hands is the Mission San Fernando *vía crucis*, which in form and content is clearly of Catholic origin. Perhaps because of the increasing difficulty of transporting goods and art to California in the early 1800s after the onset of the

70. Gerónimo Boscana, *Chinigchinich; a Historical Account . . .* (New York, 1969), in Robinson, *Life in California*, 243, 256. Of course, it is possible that Boscana's description of Indian religious belief reflects postcontact rather than precontact understandings.

71. Neuerburg, "Indian Via Crucis," *SCQ*, LXXIX (1997), 329–382, esp. 353. Indians, to a much lesser extent, were also taught to carve statues of central Catholic figures (Neuerburg, "Indian Carved Statues at Mission Santa Barbara," *The Masterkey*, LI, no. 4 [October/December 1977], 147–151). On baroque architecture in Mexico and its reception among Indians, see Elizabeth Wilder Weismann, *Art and Time in Mexico: Architecture and Sculpture in Colonial Mexico* (New York, 1985), 44–66.

72. The geometric images were painted in the *asistencia* of Pala, which was essentially a satellite chapel associated with the larger mission of San Luis Rey (Lee and Neuerburg, "Alta California Indians as Artists," in *CC*, I, 477); Neuerburg, *The Decoration of the California Missions* (Santa Barbara, Calif., 1987), 7 (on Indian symbols or animals covering the mission interiors, see 3, 7, 8, 12, 23, 25, 32, 36); Neuerburg, "Indian Pictographs at Mission San Juan Capistrano," *The Masterkey*, LVI, no. 2 (April/June 1982), 55–58; Neuerburg, "More Indian Sculpture at Mission Santa Barbara," *The Masterkey*, LIV, no. 4 (October/December 1980), 150–153.

struggle for Mexican independence, Indians at Mission San Fernando, most likely working from a set of engravings, painted fourteen panels representing the stations of the cross. To many scholars, the fourth station is the most interesting and least orthodox of the panels, for the unusually prominent and oversize figure with the red cap in the foreground helping Christ carry the cross may actually be a self-portrait of one of the Indian painters.[73]

A painting of Saint Raphael, the guardian angel of humanity, at Mission Santa Inés is the only other surviving Catholic liturgical image in the missions attributed to a local Indian. For California Indians, the conflation of their beliefs with Catholicism occurred in the fleeting realm of ideas and thoughts, as they sought to understand and assimilate new images and concepts. Rarely was such an emotional and spiritual act crystallized as in this painting of Raphael as a young Chumash man. The image blends native and Catholic images and represents a previously unappreciated melding of Indian beliefs with Catholicism that was common elsewhere in New Spain. The fish held by Raphael seems unusual, perhaps inspired by the artist.[74] The wings of Raphael are muscular and realistic; they may represent those of the California condor, a bird of great spiritual import to the Chumash (Chumash leaders often adorned their capes with condor feathers). Tellingly, this Raphael does not so much hold a staff as stand his ground. Through his stern and unwavering facial expression, he seems to make a clear and defiant statement: the Chumash interpreted Catholicism and mission life through their own cultural conventions, and elements of Catholic belief could be assimilated into a Chumash worldview. One wonders, therefore, how the Franciscans at Santa Inés understood and justified the placement of this Raphael within the mission. If it reminds us today of the persistence of Chumash culture, how must it have appeared to the Franciscans who struggled daily to convert Indians? Did they accept the painting because it seemed to suggest that Indians could find a place within Catholic iconography and therefore within the life of the church? Perhaps for the missionaries it was vital that this Raphael bear the correct Catholic emblems and icons; he carries a staff and a fish and stands above the clouds. But, most important of all, a cross crowns his headband. Raphael

73. The most exhaustive study of the San Fernando vía crucis has been done by Neuerburg ("Indian Via Crucis," *SCQ*, LXXIX [1997]); cf. George Harwood Phillips, "Indian Paintings from Mission San Fernando: An Historical Interpretation," *Journal of California Anthropology*, III, no. 3 (Summer 1976), 96–114; Edward D. Castillo, "The Other Side of the 'Christian Curtain': California Indians and the Missionaries," *The Californians: The Magazine of California History*, X (1992), 8–17.

74. Lisbeth Haas, "Images and Iconography of Spanish and Mexican California," paper delivered at the Twenty-first Annual Meeting of the Society for Historians of the Early American Republic, Lexington, Kentucky, 1999. Yet the fish also bears a striking resemblance to one held by a Rafael in a painting at nearby Mission Santa Barbara. See Kurt Baer, *Painting and Sculpture at Mission Santa Barbara* (Washington, D.C., 1955), 99.

PLATE 14. *Archangel Raphael.* Painted by a Chumash neophyte at Mission Santa Inés, early nineteenth century. Photo courtesy of Old Mission Santa Inés, Santa Inés, Calif.

thereby embodies the primary teaching of the missionaries at Santa Inés: Catholicism was to dominate and triumph over the minds and bodies of the Chumash. However, the miniature cross on Raphael's headband, because of its resemblance in shape to a prayer pole and perhaps a Chumash leadership symbol, could have been read by Indians as one more affirmation that the mission could be a place where their spirituality, just like their foods and structures, could coexist alongside Catholicism and Spanish lifeways.

REJECTION AND RESISTANCE

For some Indians, the similarities in form and content between their indigenous religion and that introduced by the Franciscans led to an acceptance of elements of Catholicism or at least a fleeting experimentation with Christianity. Other Indians, however, who perhaps associated Catholicism with all they disliked about mission life and the convulsions of the dual revolutions, showed little interest in Catholicism or even outright hostility to the Franciscan religious program. By their own admission, the Franciscans found it extremely difficult to persuade adult Indians to accept any aspects of Catholicism. Long after they attained baptism, many neophytes believed that an invisible being or a particular person—not the Triune God—caused rain or sickness and had created the ocean. At San Juan Capistrano in 1821, baptized Indians saw a comet as the return of one of their village chiefs. Sometimes native beliefs directly challenged the Franciscan religious program: in 1801, for instance, a woman at Santa Barbara dreamed that the Chumash being Chupu had told her that, to avoid death, all gentiles must resist baptism and all neophytes must renounce Christianity, present offerings to Chupu, and cleanse their heads with special water. The Chupu prophecy quickly took hold in the mission community and beyond. Nearly all Indians at the mission went to the house of the prophet, showered her with gifts of beads and seeds, and renounced Christianity. Three days after the Chupu revelation, a neophyte informed the Franciscans of the movement, and the cult was suppressed. Nevertheless, the Indians' rapid acceptance of the Chupu prophecy signals the depths of indigenous spiritual belief at Mission Santa Barbara even among a community of the baptized.[75]

When Indians whom the padres had indoctrinated as children did survive diseases and reach adulthood, they usually assumed positions of authority within the religious hierarchy. From these mission-born survivors emerged the sacristans,

75. Responses of the missionaries to question no. 10, in *APST*, 47–51; Boscana, *Chinigchinich*, in Robinson, *Life in California*, 320; Robert F. Heizer, "A Californian Messianic Movement of 1801 among the Chumash," *American Anthropologist*, XLIII (1941), 128–129.

pages, interpreters, *fiscales,* and *alcaldes* who helped administer the sacraments and run the missions. Yet even many of these Indians frequently rejected the Franciscan religious program. For instance, the alcaldes at Santa Barbara took part in the Chupu cult instead of denouncing it. Father Gerónimo Boscana—perhaps one of the most careful, if not the most generous, observers of Indians in colonial California—believed that the neophytes had become expert at "dissimulation." He despaired that they "easily gain our confidence, and at every pass we are deluded." And he concluded that the most intelligent Indians, who were entitled to the Franciscans' greatest confidence, were "the least to be trusted."[76]

Nevertheless, it was rare for baptized California Indians to so explicitly reject Catholicism as they did in the Chupu prophecy. Most regularly attended Mass, observed feast days, and participated in sacramental life; yet, like many Catholics during the early modern era, they did so with only a partial understanding of the doctrine that lay behind the rituals and rites. For the majority of neophytes—the men, women, and children who were not part of an elite priesthood and who came from traditions that restricted most ritual knowledge to a select few—religion had largely been practiced through participation and observation rather than by subscription to specific doctrinal beliefs. But, for the California Franciscans, even though they taught Indians a religion that was grounded in ritual and observance, Indians' joining in the daily life of the church could be no substitute for belief and faith in Catholic dogma. Ultimately, then, Franciscans dismissed as secondary, even as misleading, the Indians' daily participation in the religious life of the mission, especially when those same Indians could not or would not demonstrate a devotional commitment to religious beliefs the Franciscans held dear.[77]

The gulf between how Franciscans and most Indians ultimately understood and experienced Catholicism is evident in the recorded disparity between the size of the mission community and the number of Indians in it who took Communion. Communion was to be the final act in the fulfillment of the precepto anual. To qualify for the Eucharist, Indians had not only to have confessed and performed penance, but they had to have left behind their previous customs, shown an active knowledge of Catholicism, and demonstrated the following: an understanding that the consecrated Host was the body of Christ, an awareness not to spit after receiving the Host in case a small part of it remained in their mouths, a

76. Boscana, *Chinigchinich,* in Robinson, *Life in California,* 328. For a full discussion of the extent to which Indian officials often turned against the missions, see Steven W. Hackel, "The Staff of Leadership: Indian Authority in the Missions of Alta California," *WMQ,* 3d Ser., LIV (1997), 347–376. See also Chapter 6, below.

77. On religious practice in eighteenth-century Spain, see Callahan, *Church, Politics, and Society in Spain,* 52–54.

comprehension of all the points of the catechism, and a knowledge of all that was contained in the credo. Most Indians did not attain or put to use this level of understanding, and consequently few took Communion.[78] Franciscans did not hesitate to distinguish Indians by their level of Catholic piety, and they eagerly separated what they saw as the Christian wheat from the superstitious chaff, deeming most Indians unfit for the Eucharist. But Indians, for their part, might have spurned Communion or been content to have it withheld from them. Not partaking in the sacrament demonstrated distance from Catholicism and per-haps even affirmed native beliefs, for Indians must have been aware that taking Communion—a ritual that likely had no analogy in native religion—symbolized an acceptance of the major tenets of Catholicism.

At San Carlos, on average, less than half (47 percent) of all adult Indians took annual Communion between 1808 and 1830. And only slightly more than half (51 percent) of the adult Indians who confessed proceeded to Communion (Table 18). Between 1814 and 1819, the only years for which the padres kept such aggre-gate statistics for all of the missions, roughly 70 percent of the adult population received annual Communion. But, in many other missions during those years, less than 5 percent of adult Indians received annual Communion, and on average only 9 percent received the sacrament (Table 19).[79] Most likely, missions with the lowest rates of annual Communion were recruiting new groups of gentiles, for these populations were more likely to have children who would not qualify for Communion as well as significant numbers of recently baptized adults, individ-uals whom the Franciscans would have considered unfit to receive Communion and who simply might not have accepted many of the missionaries' teachings.

Adult Catholics were to receive Communion during the precepto anual and when they were in danger of death. Although the *Itinerario* advised missionaries to deny annual Communion to Indians who appeared deficient in their faith, it recommended a far more lenient standard in granting the *Viático* ("food for the journey"), or final Communion, which was to be administered to persons near death. To De la Peña Montenegro, a missionary committed a mortal sin by not

78. De la Peña Montenegro, *Itinerario,* ed. Baciero et al., libro 4, tratado 4, sect. 3, par. 15, 381–382. Jake Ivey has found that missionaries in northwestern New Spain more than a century earlier granted Communion to few Indians. He argues that these restrictions were in part a result of the fact that many missions did not have the sacred paraphernalia needed to administer Communion. Some missions in New Mexico, for example, lacked tabernacles or irons to bake the Hosts. These factors, however, do not seem to apply to the missions of California, which, at least according to mission inventories, were far more equipped to provide the sacrament of Communion than those in seventeenth-century New Mexico. See Jake Ivey, "*Ahijados*: The Right of Communion and Mission Status on the North-ern Frontier in the Seventeenth Century," *Catholic Southwest: A Journal of History and Culture,* XI (2000), 7–26.

79. Figures for all missions include Mission San Carlos.

granting the sacrament to a dying Indian who was capable of absolution and who believed that Christ was in the consecrated Host. Yet, even as Indians approached death, the Franciscans in California were ever mindful to distinguish the smaller community of the faithful from the larger community that seemed at best to have a weak embrace of Catholicism.[80]

Missionaries at San Carlos gave nearly all adult Indians who died at the mission the sacraments of penance (reconciliation with the church) and/or extreme unction (anointment of the dying), but considerably fewer of those same Indians received the Viático. By comparison, nearly all adult gente de razón who received extreme unction and the sacrament of penance took the Viático. Not one Indian at San Carlos received final Communion during Serra's tenure there, which ended with his own Viático and death in August 1784. It was not until the fall of 1787, after the padres had buried more than five hundred Indians at the mission, that Jacinta María, a twenty-four-year-old Rumsen who had been baptized more than thirteen years earlier and served as an interpreter, became the first Indian at Carmel to receive the sacrament. Before 1799, less than 5 percent of Indians buried at the mission who received the last rites of penance and/or extreme unction obtained final Communion (Table 20). How many others simply refused the Viático or desired it but were deemed unworthy is not known; yet the very low figure further underscores both the limits of the Franciscan religious program and the weakness of many Indians' embrace of Catholicism.[81]

Clearly, for some Indians, impending death and Franciscan concern provoked a need to affirm either Catholic beliefs or native spirituality, and, much to the Franciscans' disappointment, many Indians' seeming commitment to Catholicism melted away as their lives ebbed. In 1808, at Mission La Purísima, a twenty-three-year-old man, whom the padres had raised and indoctrinated from infancy, "instructed in every thing appertaining to religion," and relied upon as an interpreter, became deathly ill, yet he refused to confess and die "like a Christian." Only after a native curer had concluded that the man's allegiance to the Franciscans had led his own god to forsake him and condemn him to death did he relent to the Franciscans' pressure and utter his half-hearted confession. Ten years later, a terminally ill man at San Juan Capistrano, whom the padres had carefully

80. De la Peña Montenegro, *Itinerario,* ed. Baciero et al., libro 4, tratado 4, sect. 3, par. 8, 379; Sarría, circular letter, pars. 28–31. As the *Itinerario* stated and Father Sarría reiterated later, "At the time of death, one must dispense with many things that in other times one would not . . . and therefore, the sufficiency that is required to be absolved in the sacrament of penance will be enough for the sacred communion" (libro 4, tratado 4, sect. 3, par. 12, 380).

81. Jacinta María was baptized on July 27, 1774 (San Carlos bapt. no. 195); she died on Oct. 27, 1787 (San Carlos bur. no. 571).

TABLE 18. Indian Communicants at Mission San Carlos, 1808–1830

Year	Indian Population	No. of Indians Who Took Communion	% of Indians Who Took Communion
1808	550	230	42
1809	533	230	43
1810	511	240	47
1811	485	250	52
1812	455	230	51
1813	448	250	56
1814	431	230	53
1815	423	200	47
1816	405	150	37
1817	402	147	37
1818	390	130	33
1819	397	112	28
1820	381	145	38
1821	374	113	30
1822	341	102	30
1823	317	92	29
1824	306	80	26
1825	295	90	31
1826	277	70	25
1827	275	50	18
1828	234	50	21
1829	233	—	—
1830	229	70	31
Total	8,692	3,261	38

Note: The number of Indians who confessed and took Communion at Mission San Carlos in 1829 is not known.

Source: Annual reports of Mission San Carlos, in SBMAL; and Zephyrin Engelhardt, *Mission San Carlos Borromeo (Carmelo): The Father of the Missions* (1934; rpt. Ramona, Calif., 1973), app. B, "Spiritual Results," 243.

Adult Indian Population	% of Adults Who Took Communion	% of Adults Who Confessed and Took Communion
462	50	77
447	51	77
451	53	69
424	59	63
395	58	58
374	67	63
369	62	61
347	58	54
334	45	45
327	45	44
310	42	42
305	37	36
290	50	48
286	40	38
266	38	36
241	38	37
233	34	41
209	43	44
193	36	39
193	26	33
179	28	28
176	—	—
177	40	56
6,988	47	51

TABLE 19. Annual Indian Adult Communions, Alta California Missions, 1814–1819

Mission	Avg. Indian Population	Avg. Est. Adult Indian Population	Avg. Est. % of Indian Adults Who Took Communion
San Diego	1,431	1,145	15
San Luis Rey	2,121	1,697	0
San Juan Capistrano	1,155	924	6
San Gabriel	1,656	1,325	11
San Fernando	1,031	825	5
San Buenaventura	1,230	984	7
Santa Barbara	1,231	985	2
Santa Inés	673	538	0
La Purísima	967	774	11
San Luis Obispo	581	465	18
San Miguel	1,032	826	15
San Antonio	971	777	22
Soledad	499	399	38
San Carlos	408	326	70
San Juan Bautista	602	482	2
Santa Cruz	386	309	2
Santa Clara	1,320	1,056	1
San Jose	1,479	1,183	0
San Francisco	1,118	894	1
Total average	1,047	838	9

Note: The base figure for the average population of each mission is the actual average population of the mission. The estimated average adult population is the base figure multiplied by .80; I arrived at this multiplier by calculating the average number of Indian children as a percentage of the annual population at Mission San Carlos. In their annual reports, the missionaries provided population counts of both adults and children. Of course, adult-to-children ratios differed from mission to mission, so these figures are just rough estimates, since I applied the San Carlos multiplier to all missions.

Source: Annual Communion totals for these years can be found in the annual reports in possession of the Archdiocese of Orange County, Mission San Juan Capistrano; annual reports of Mission San Carlos, in SBMAL; J. N. Bowman, "The Resident Neophytes (Existentes) of the California Missions, 1769–1834," *Historical Society of Southern California Quarterly,* XL (1958), 143–148.

TABLE 20. Indian *Viático* Recipients, Mission San Carlos, 1770–1829

Years	All Deaths of Indians at San Carlos	Deceased Who Received a Sacrament	Deceased Who Received *Viático*
1770–1779	122	39	0
1780–1789	496	207	3
1790–1799	585	190	17
1800–1809	490	206	24
1810–1819	333	182	111
1820–1829	293	137	73
All	2,319	961	228
1770–1799	1,203	436	20
1800–1829	1,116	525	208

	PROPORTION		
Years	Deceased Who Received a Sacrament	Deceased Sacrament Recipients Who Received *Viático*	Deceased Who Received *Viático*
1770–1779	32.0%	0.0%	0.0%
1780–1789	41.7	1.4	0.6
1790–1799	32.5	8.9	2.9
1800–1809	42.0	11.7	4.9
1810–1819	54.7	61.0	33.3
1820–1829	46.8	53.3	24.9
All	41.4	23.7	9.8
1770–1799	36.2	4.6	1.7
1800–1829	47.0%	39.6%	18.6%

Note: Children and those who died away from the mission are included in the total deaths at San Carlos and the proportion of the deceased who received the *Viático*. Indians younger than nine years old would have been considered too young for the Eucharist.

Source: Figures are from my database of baptisms, marriages, and burials at San Carlos compiled from the mission's registers (see Appendix A for methodology). When they recorded burials at the mission, Franciscans specified whether they had administered last rites.

instructed, refused extreme unction, horrifying the padres. When the Franciscans persisted, he responded in anger, "If I have been deceived whilst living, I do
not wish to die in the delusion!"[82]

After the early 1800s, the taking of the Viático by Indians at San Carlos gradually became more common, but generally only by the small number of Indians
who had wrestled long with Catholicism, having lived at the mission on average
for 25.7 years before death. A larger number of adult Indians received only
penance and/or extreme unction; they had been at the mission on average for
13.5 years before their death. Adults who died without any sacrament had lived at
the mission the least amount of time, just under 11 years.[83] Not only had the
Indians who received the Viático been at the mission for decades, but most had
grown up with Catholicism, as nearly all had been baptized as young children,
and they therefore had lived their lives under Franciscan instruction. More than a
third of the Indians who received the Viático were baptized before their first
birthday, whereas less than a tenth of those who died without it had been baptized at such a young age. The median age at baptism for those who received the
Viático was three years old; it was twenty for those who died after receiving only
penance and/or extreme unction.

Indians who took the Viático, who we may cautiously assume were the most
ardent of Indian adherents to Catholicism, constituted less than 10 percent of
baptized Indians—children and adults—who died at Mission San Carlos before
1830 and less than a quarter of Indians who died with sacraments (Table 20). Data
on the administration of the Viático at other missions as well supports these
observations. Between 1814 and 1819, less than 13 percent of all Indians who died
at the missions received the Viático (Table 21). In each year between 1814 and 1819,
ten or fewer Indians received the Viático in thirteen of Alta California's nineteen
established missions (Table 22). During these years, therefore, it would appear
that hardly any Indians who died had lived as Catholic converts. At San Carlos,
where there was only a small influx of gentiles after the 1790s, the proportion of
Indians attaining the Viático between 1814 and 1819 was higher; nearly 33 percent
of all Indians died having received final Communion.

Everywhere in Alta California, neophytes rejected Catholicism by refusing
final Communion or by learning so little of Catholicism that the missionaries
denied them the Eucharist. Some Indians went beyond personal acts of resistance
to Catholicism and mocked those who lived by it. After shooting the Spanish

---

82. Boscana, *Chinigchinich*, in Robinson, *Life in California*, 325–327.

83. The Franciscans recorded the deaths of hundreds of adult Indians who died without any sacraments. Many Indians did not alert the Franciscans about their illnesses. Others died in their ancestral
villages or in the countryside surrounding the mission. In certain rejection of Catholicism, a few died
away from the mission and were cremated according to Indian custom.

TABLE 21. Cumulative Totals of Indian *Viático* Recipients, All Alta California Missions, 1814–1819

Years	All Deaths of Indians	# Deceased Who Received *Viático*	% Deceased Who Received *Viático*	% Deceased at San Carlos Who Received *Viático*
1814	1,395	177	12.7	34.4
1815	1,714	215	12.5	25.0
1816	1,690	219	13.0	42.9
1817	1,695	192	11.3	28.6
1818	1,673	231	13.8	37.9
1819	1,475	193	13.1	22.7
1814–1819	9,642	1,227	12.7	32.6

Note: Indian children and those who died away from the missions are included. Indians younger than nine years old would have been considered too young for the Eucharist.

Source: Annual reports in possession of the Archdiocese of Orange County, Mission San Juan Capistrano; annual reports of Mission San Carlos, in SBMAL. Figures are from my database of baptisms, marriages, and burials at San Carlos compiled from the mission's registers (see Appendix A for methodology).

mission foreman Pedro Miguel Alvarez full of arrows in revenge for a chain of abuses, three Indian shepherds from San Diego prepared to smash his skull. Realizing his grim fate and fearing for the state of his soul, Alvarez pleaded with his assailants: "Men, don't kill me, let me confess!" Fermín, however, who had been repeatedly beaten and cuckolded by Alvarez, responded with derision: "I will confess you now, you son of a bitch!" whereupon he crushed Alvarez's skull with a large wooden stick.[84] At the moment of the murder, the shepherds not only revealed their contempt for the *mayordomo* but, in mocking his final wish, they showed their understanding of the importance of confession before death to Catholics. In denying it to Alvarez, the shepherds knew they were increasing not only Alvarez's emotional suffering but perhaps also the tribulations of his soul. In another act of violence and defiance, Indians at Mission San Diego not only killed one of the missionaries but were reported to have scorned his final words. Just before he was beaten to death, Father Luís Jayme apparently exclaimed: "Children, love God!" The Indians' retort: "No longer is there any love for God."[85]

84. "Causa criminal contra tres indios neófitos de la misión de San Diego por la muerte que dieron a su mayordomo," 1809, AGN, CA, LXII; declaration of Fermín, 22–28, esp. 27.

85. "Hijos, amar a Dios!" and "Ya, no hay amar a Dios." These words were written by an unidentified hand and attached to the end of a letter Jayme wrote in 1772. This is my translation of a facsimile in Maynard J. Geiger, ed. and trans., *Letter of Luís Jayme, O.F.M.: San Diego, Oct. 17, 1772,* Baja California Travel Series, XXII (Los Angeles, Calif., 1970), 49, 66.

TABLE 22. Annual Indian *Viáticos*, Alta California Missions, 1814–1819

Mission	Average Indian Population	Average No. of *Viáticos*
San Diego	1,431	5
San Luis Rey	2,121	7
San Juan Capistrano	1,155	20
San Gabriel	1,656	45
San Fernando	1,031	7
San Buenaventura	1,230	27
Santa Barbara	1,231	10
Santa Inés	673	0
Purísima	967	14
San Luis Obispo	581	14
San Miguel	1,032	8
San Antonio	971	20
Soledad	499	2
San Carlos	408	10
San Juan Bautista	602	2
Santa Cruz	386	10
Santa Clara	1,320	0
San Jose	1,479	6
San Francisco	1,118	3
Total	1,047	11

Source: Annual totals for these years can be found in the annual reports in possession of the Archdiocese of Orange County, Mission San Juan Capistrano.

Although Indians in Alta California encountered a program of religious indoctrination that was largely characterized by uniformity, they responded variously as they struggled to make sense of their changing world. Unlike the padres, who saw Indian "superstition" as antithetical to Christian ideals, many Indians saw a reflection of their own rituals and practices in the central symbols of the church. The form of the Franciscans' religious program, oriented as it was toward the cross, the Virgin Mary, and an elite priesthood, accompanied by music and song, offered Indians a familiar way to the sacred. But few adult Indians traveled far down this road. Although the Franciscans might have had more success indoctrinating the young than the old, the overwhelming majority of baptized Indians died of disease long before they reached adulthood or embraced Catholicism. To compensate for their deaths, the Franciscans continually sought new recruits from among Indian populations farther and farther from the established missions. Time and time again they found willing souls among ever more distant groups overturned by the dual revolutions. Yet the padres' un-familiarity with their languages complicated their indoctrination, and their firmly held beliefs nearly always proved resistant to Catholicism. Ultimately, the Franciscans at San Carlos and elsewhere in colonial California responded to what they considered the Indians' persistent depravity, not with more rigorous indoc-trination or new techniques, but by "taking advantage of every incident and occurrence" to instruct the Indians "in their Christian duties" and by enforcing a rigid code of conduct that came to define nearly all aspects of the Indians' lives, especially marriage and sexuality. It is these most intimate aspects of Indian experience in the missions that are the subject of the following chapter.[86]

86. Lasuén, memorandum, July 8, 1789, Mission San Carlos, in Kenneally, ed. and trans., *Writings of Lasuén*, I, 193.

5

MARRIAGE AND SEXUALITY

Most neophytes quickly found that, although missionaries might tolerate, even support, some of their behaviors, in matters of marriage and sexuality, Franciscans demanded complete and immediate compliance with Catholicism. Thus conditions were established for a terrific and tragic conflict, one that was as predictable as it was inevitable. Wherever they had worked in New Spain, missionaries had provoked anger and frustration among Indians when they sought to regulate the most intimate aspects of the Indians' lives.[1] Not surprisingly, the Children of Coyote had very different views of sexual relations than did the Franciscans. They occasionally practiced polygyny, now and then engaged in extramarital sexual relations, and from time to time dissolved their marriages, all actions at odds with Roman Catholicism.[2] Among Indians and Franciscans alike,

---

1. In general, the Spanish state was interested in controlling sexuality and marriage so as to ensure the legality of inheritance among surviving family members. Among mission Indians, however, who were seen by the law as minors and whose real land and resources were administered by the missionaries, the state had no stake in regulating Indian sexuality or marriage (Asunción Lavrin, "Sexuality in Colonial Mexico," in Lavrin, ed., *Sexuality and Marriage in Colonial Latin America* [Lincoln, Neb., 1989], 3). Much of the recent work on marriage, sexuality, and gender in New Spain has examined the concepts of honor and shame. See, for example, Ramón A. Gutiérrez, *When Jesus Came, the Corn Mothers Went Away: Marriage, Sexuality, and Power in New Mexico, 1500–1846* (Stanford, Calif., 1991); Steve J. Stern, *The Secret History of Gender: Women, Men, and Power in Late Colonial Mexico* (Chapel Hill, N.C., 1995); Ann Twinam, *Public Lives, Private Secrets: Gender, Honor, Sexuality, and Illegitimacy in Colonial Spanish America* (Stanford, Calif., 1999); Patricia Seed, *To Love, Honor, and Obey in Colonial Mexico: Conflicts over Marriage Choice, 1574–1821* (Stanford, Calif., 1988). James F. Brooks expansively explores the intersection of marriage, slavery, and exchange across the cultures of the Southwest in *Captives and Cousins: Slavery, Kinship, and Community in the Southwest Borderlands* (Chapel Hill, N.C., 2002).

2. There is an extensive literature on gender, sexuality, and marriage in Alta California. The most important works are Albert L. Hurtado, *Intimate Frontiers: Sex, Gender, and Culture in Old California* (Albuquerque, N.Mex., 1999); Virginia Marie Bouvier, *Women and the Conquest of California, 1542–1840: Codes of Silence* (Tucson, Ariz., 2001); Antonia I. Castañeda, "Engendering the History of Alta California, 1769–1848: Gender, Sexuality, and the Family," in Ramón A. Gutiérrez and Richard J. Orsi, eds., *Contested Eden: California before the Gold Rush* (Berkeley, Calif., 1998), 230–259. See also Edward D. Castillo, "Gender Status Decline, Resistance, and Accommodation among Female Neophytes in the Missions of California: A San Gabriel Case Study," *American Indian Culture and Research Journal,*

there was little room for compromise on matters of such import, and few worked toward it. The same dynamics that had hindered the Indians' religious indoctrination—the low survival rate of the mission born and the steady influx of adults—all but ensured that missions would have large numbers of adults who found alien and objectionable many Catholic precepts governing marriage and sexuality. Notably, in 88 percent of Indian marriages at San Carlos, the groom was not mission born; in 83 percent of marriages, the bride was not mission born. In only 6 percent of marriages were both bride and groom mission born and therefore raised from birth within the compass of Franciscan teaching and supervision (see Table 28, below).[3] For the missionaries' part, nothing in their training or belief rendered them flexible in such intimate areas, particularly given their own vows of celibacy. Aware of the gulf between their beliefs and the Indians', missionaries acted quickly to enforce Catholic precepts and condemn and punish Indians for sinful behavior, doing so with a commitment they reserved for what they considered the most visible reminders of the Indians' depravity. In their zeal, Franciscans brought not only confusion and conflict to Indians but change to native patterns of intimacy, union, and reproduction. The tensions in the Indian community that emerged from the padres' aggressive enforcement of Catholic precepts were exacerbated by the Franciscans' mixed messages about Indian unions and by a soldier-settler population that, especially during the early years of conquest, consistently preyed upon native women.

INDIAN PRECONTACT MARRIAGE PATTERNS

Historians and anthropologists have only a partial understanding of the precontact marriage practices of California Indians. Clearly, though, marriage was a basic institution, one that structured society and personal and group relations. Closely regulated and the basis of economic and political alliances, marriage mattered to families and often required the subordination of individual to group

---

XVIII (1994), 67–93; Gloria E. Miranda, "Gente de Razón Marriage Patterns in Spanish and Mexican California: A Case Study of Santa Barbara and Los Angeles," *SCQ*, LXIII (1981), 1–21; Miranda, "Racial and Cultural Dimensions of Gente de Razón Status in Spanish and Mexican California," *SCQ*, LXX (1988), 265–278; Salomé Hernández, "No Settlement without Women: Three Spanish California Settlement Schemes, 1790–1800," *SCQ*, LXXII (1990), 203–324; Miroslava Chavez, " 'Pongo Mi Demanda': Challenging Patriarchy in Mexican Los Angeles, 1830–1850," in Valerie J. Matsumoto and Blake Allmendinger, eds., *Over the Edge: Remapping the American West* (Berkeley, Calif., 1999), 272–290.

3. For a pioneering quantitative approach to the study of marriage and sexuality in the missions, see Sherburne F. Cook and Woodrow Borah, "Mission Registers as Sources of Vital Statistics: Eight Missions of Northern California," chap. 3 in Cook and Borah, *Essays in Population History*, III, *Mexico and California* (Berkeley, Calif., 1979), 117–311.

needs.[4] In all of these ways, Indians viewed marriage much as did Spaniards. Moreover, to the Spaniards' surprise, California Indians, like Roman Catholics, prohibited unions of siblings and marriages between children and parents. Father Luís Jayme, who served at Mission San Diego from 1769 until his death at the hands of the Diegueño in 1775, burst into tears of joy when the first adults he baptized told him that they "do not marry relatives" and that "the married men sleep with their wives only" and considered adultery to be "very bad." Furthermore, "if a man plays with any woman who is not his wife, he is scolded and punished by his captains." But, for many other California Indians, sexual relations and marriage were not inextricably linked; premarital sex does not seem to have been forbidden, and marriage was neither indissoluble nor strictly monogamous.[5]

Costanoan and Esselen women seem to have entered marriage for the first time between the ages of eighteen and twenty; men married later, at about age twenty (Tables 23, 24).[6] For both sexes, marriage usually occurred several years after puberty and, in all likelihood, after the beginning of sexual activity. As in most societies, men not only married later than women but usually married women about five years their junior (Table 25). Some men came to Mission San Carlos with spouses ten or twenty years younger. The difference in age between husband and wife increased with the man's age; most likely, many widowers married much younger women so as to increase the chance of offspring (Table 26). The age differential between husband and wife also might have been related to the man's political status. Such was probably the case with the village captain Aristeo Joseph Chilichon, who had a wife twenty-seven years younger than he.[7] Not all men married younger women; 15 percent of the married men baptized at

4. Lowell John Bean, "Social Organization in Native California," in Bean and Thomas C. Blackburn, eds., *Native Californians: A Theoretical Perspective* (Ramona, Calif., 1976), 99–123, esp. 106–109.

5. Maynard J. Geiger, ed., *Letter of Luís Jayme, O.F.M.: San Diego, October 17, 1772*, Baja California Travel Series, XXII (Los Angeles, Calif., 1970), 41–42. Franciscans despaired at these aspects of the Indians' sexual and marital practices and their own inability to eradicate them. The padres became convinced that California Indians were prone to lust, unchastity, fornication, and immorality and, in the words of Father President Lasuén, inclined to "lasciviousness." See Lasuén, June 19, 1801, Mission San Carlos, AGN, PI, CCXVI, expediente 1, 73a, for the original Spanish. See also missionaries' responses to question no. 24, in *APST*, 105–106.

6. The age at which Indians in Monterey first married before Spanish settlement is impossible to determine precisely. Nevertheless, baptism and marriage records kept by the Franciscans provide the material for an estimation of age at first marriage for men and women of the Monterey region before Spanish colonization. Two kinds of marriages are recorded in the sacramental registers: renewals of unions contracted before baptism and standard marriages contracted after. The contrast between these two sets reveals the contours—if not the details—of precontact marriage patterns. Of course, only the ages of Indians born at the mission are known with precision. The ages of Indians born in native villages who attained baptism as children or adults are approximate, based as they are on information the padres gathered when they baptized these Indians. The clustering of ages around multiples of five suggests that the Franciscans sometimes estimated Indians' ages.

7. San Carlos marr. no. 293.

TABLE 23. Baptized Female Indians Age 10–40, Age and Marital Status,
Mission San Carlos, 1773–1808

Age at Baptism	No. Baptized	No. Married at Baptism	% of Baptized Women Already Married
10	14	0	0
11	7	1	14
12	8	0	0
13	11	2	18
14	19	2	11
15	14	0	0
16	13	3	23
17	5	1	20
18	37	12	32
19	9	4	44
20	52	29	56
21	2	1	50
22	14	8	57
23	1	1	100
24	9	4	44
25	26	12	46
26	5	5	100
27	2	0	0
28	7	2	29
29	4	2	50
30	35	12	34
31	0	0	0
32	7	3	43
33	5	1	20
34	3	0	0
35	16	7	44
36	6	2	33
37	0	0	0
38	2	1	50
39	2	1	50
40	38	19	50
Total	373	135	36

Source: Figures are from my database of baptisms, marriages, and burials at San Carlos compiled from the mission's registers (see Appendix A for methodology).

TABLE 24. Baptized Male Indians Age 10–40, Age and Marital Status,
Mission San Carlos, 1773–1808

Age at Baptism	No. Baptized	No. Married at Baptism	% of Baptized Men Already Married
10	20	0	0
11	8	0	0
12	11	0	0
13	5	0	0
14	15	0	0
15	13	0	0
16	12	1	8
17	8	0	0
18	31	6	19
19	9	1	11
20	42	23	55
21	3	2	67
22	17	6	35
23	4	1	25
24	5	3	60
25	19	14	74
26	7	5	71
27	2	0	0
28	4	3	75
29	2	0	0
30	21	15	71
31	1	1	100
32	3	3	100
33	4	1	25
34	7	2	29
35	11	5	45
36	4	2	50
37	2	1	50
38	2	0	0
39	1	1	100
40	32	23	72
Total	325	119	37

Source: Figures are from my database of baptisms, marriages, and burials at San Carlos compiled from the mission's registers (see Appendix A for methodology).

TABLE 25. Marriage Renewals and Age Difference between Spouses,
Mission San Carlos, 1773–1808

Years	No. of Renewals	Husband's Avg. Age	Wife's Avg. Age	Age Difference (Yrs.)
1773–1779	64	32.7	28.8	3.9
1780–1789	60	35.1	28.8	6.3
1790–1799	29	36.5	30.9	5.6
1800–1808	10	44.6	40.7	3.9
Total	163	35.3	29.9	5.4

Note: There were no marriage renewals before 1773 or after 1808 at Mission San Carlos.
Source: Figures are from my database of baptisms, marriages, and burials at San Carlos compiled from the mission's registers (see Appendix A for methodology). Ages are derived from Mission San Carlos baptism records.

San Carlos had older wives. But, when women married younger men, the age difference was only a few years.

In California, Indian marriages were embedded in rituals of exchange, celebration, and compensation. Before the wedding, the groom gave gifts to the bride's family to demonstrate his wealth, acknowledge her family's status, and compensate for her family's loss of her labor. Gift giving, feasting, singing, and dancing followed the wedding. Friends and relatives congregated from different villages, and each presented a small gift to the new couple. Festivities could last days, with guests even bringing their own supplies of food. Since the bride and groom were frequently from different villages, these gatherings celebrated and created social, economic, and political ties between families and across settlements.[8]

Divorce was an option that either the husband or the wife could initiate. However, because marriage had strong implications for the family and community, divorce was frowned upon. A man could divorce because of "sterility, laziness, or infidelity"; a woman could do so if her husband or his family was cruel. Scholars estimate that, among the Chumash, roughly one in five marriages ended in divorce. Whereas broken marriages might have been relatively common, remarriage was more restricted. Among some Chumash, the divorced could remarry only a widow or widower, and, among others, men could not divorce but could remarry if widowed. These rules underscored the important role that marriage played in maintaining stability in Indian society. Husbands and wives, therefore, did not separate and remarry upon a whim, as the Franciscans charged, and in all likelihood they responded to communal pressures that reduced the incidence of

8. Herbert Ingram Priestley, ed. and trans., *A Historical, Political, and Natural Description of California by Pedro Fages, Soldier of Spain* . . . (Berkeley, Calif., 1937), 75.

TABLE 26. Married Indians at Baptism by Age Group and Average Age of Spouses, Mission San Carlos, 1773–1808

	HUSBANDS			WIVES	
Age Group	No.	Avg. Age of Wife	Age Group	No.	Avg. Age of Husband
10–14	0	—	10–14	5	21.3
15–19	8	20.6	15–19	20	26.7
20–24	35	19.6	20–24	43	26.5
25–29	22	23.6	25–29	21	27.5
30–34	22	27.6	30–34	16	37.3
35–39	9	32.4	35–39	11	37.5
40–44	29	33.2	40–44	27	45.0
45–49	9	34.0	45–49	7	47.4
50–54	12	43.3	50–54	8	56.0
55–59	4	46.3	55–59	0	—
60+	13	48.6	60+	5	62.0
Total	163		Total	163	

Source: Figures are from my database of baptisms, marriages, and burials at San Carlos compiled from the mission's registers (see Appendix A for methodology). Ages are derived from Mission San Carlos baptism records.

divorce. On occasion, California Indians permitted extramarital relations. Husbands were usually compensated by the spouse's partner, but it is not clear whether a wife received any sort of indemnity if her husband had an affair.[9]

Although divorce was an option for nearly all in precontact California, polygyny—the practice of having more than one wife or mate at one time—was solely for the men of the leadership class. Apparently only in the San Diego area did village chiefs keep just one wife; Gabrielino village captains had two wives, and Chumash leaders often had three. Polygyny was also common farther north in the San Francisco region, where missionaries baptized one Costanoan man who

9. John R. Johnson, "Chumash Social Interaction: An Ethnohistoric Perspective" (Ph.D. diss., University of California at Santa Barbara, 1988), 167; Priestley, ed. and trans., *Historical Description*, 33, 48; Bean, "Social Organization," in Bean and Blackburn, eds., *Native Californians*, 108–109. The Franciscans believed that California Indians dissolved their marriages easily and with little thought as soon as the couple had any sort of disagreement or the husband or wife desired someone else. Father Francisco Palóu wrote dismissively that the Indians' marriages lasted "until there is a quarrel, when they separate, and join with another" (Maynard J. Geiger, ed. and trans., *Palóu's Life of Fray Junípero Serra* [Washington, D.C., 1955], 194). Payments to cuckolded husbands had their origin long before Spanish settlement, and they persisted into the missions. This may be why confessionals urged the Franciscans to ask married men whether they had provided their wives to other men. See the appropriate sections in *HNAI*, VIII, 186, 209, 239, 498. See also Albert L. Hurtado, "Sexuality in California's Franciscan Missions," *California History*, LXXI (1992), 371–385, 451–453.

was married to three sisters and their mother.[10] Leaders in the Monterey region also had multiple wives. The captain of Sargentaruc came to San Carlos along with three wives, two of whom were sisters. By marrying sisters, a practice known as sororal polygyny, leaders sought to ensure their links to other powerful families. These marriages also allowed co-wives to share household duties with a relative rather than with someone unrelated to them. Sororal polygyny was common enough in native California to be embodied in kinship terms; among some groups, the mother and the mother's sister were known by the same word. Similarly, a husband often called his wife and her sister by the same term.[11]

FRANCISCAN UNDERSTANDINGS

Franciscans brought to California their own guidelines for marriage and sexuality, as codified in the mid-sixteenth century by the Council of Trent (1545–1563). When the council convened, its participants did not have in mind Indians who were being indoctrinated to Catholicism; rather, in the wake of the Protestant Reformation, they sought to regulate and reform European Catholicism and to ensure social stability. One of the council's principal aims was to eliminate clandestine marriages and unions the church deemed inappropriate. The council restricted the sacrament of marriage to Catholics who did not have close blood, marriage, or spiritual ties and decreed that marriage could be conferred only by

10. Priestley, ed. and trans., *Historical Description*, 11, 21, 33. All three sisters had given birth to a child of his within a few months of one another. Palóu noted that, upon his baptism, the man had taken as his Catholic wife the oldest sister, who was his first wife, and that the other sisters had married neophytes at the mission after their baptisms (Geiger, ed. and trans., *Palóu's Life of Serra*, 194).

11. Aristeo Joseph Chilichon, San Carlos bapt. no. 1072. See also San Carlos marr. nos. 293, 297. Evidence from the baptismal records of Aristeo Joseph's children confirms his polygyny. He fathered at least five children with three different women between 1777 and 1784. María Teresa, his Catholic wife, was the mother of only the fourth child; the first and last were born to Aurora María and the second and third to Natalia María (San Carlos bapt. nos. 712, 739, 696, 691, 1065). After Aristeo Joseph's baptism and Catholic marriage to María Teresa, Father Mathías Antonio de Santa Catalina performed a marriage between one of Aristeo Joseph's previous wives, Aurora María, and Vicente Marinero, a widower. In recording this marriage, the padre noted that Aurora María had been "the principal gentile wife of the captain Aristeo" but that Aristeo Joseph "had repudiated her, choosing the younger María Teresa" instead (San Carlos marr. no. 297). If a man had more than one wife, or if he had a series of wives, Alonso de la Peña Montenegro's *Itinerario* stated that the wife who was baptized alongside the man became his legitimate wife, even if she was not his first (De la Peña Montenegro, *Itinerario para párrocos de indios*, ed. C. Baciero et al., Consejo Superior de Investigaciónes Científicas, Corpus Hispanorum de Pace, 2d Ser. [Madrid, 1995], libro 3, tratado 9, sect. 5, par. 2, 273). The First Mexican Provincial Council suggested that the first gentile wife was the valid wife. Furthermore, if, at the time of baptism, a man was baptized alongside his second or third wife, the couple had to renew its vow for the marriage to be valid. For, if a previous spouse was living, the contract of the gentile matrimony was null and void because he or she could actually still be married to the original spouse. Co-wives: Bean, "Social Organization," in Bean and Blackburn, eds., *Native Californians*, 108.

the church through a priest. In an attempt to block unlawful marriages, the officiating priest was to announce on three successive feast days the intent of a couple to marry, and he would also conduct a prenuptial investigation to reveal impediments. After the wedding, the priest was to write down and register in a book the names of the husband and wife and the date and place the sacrament was granted. These records not only served as proof that the couple had been lawfully wedded, but they allowed priests to keep track of closely related individuals and thereby prevent marriages between them.[12]

Catholic doctrine considered marriage both a contract and a sacrament. The contractual aspect was valid only if the betrothed entered into the marriage willingly. And, according to church law, sexual activity outside the contract was sinful, since the fundamental purpose of marriage was procreation and the stabilization of the community and the social order. Marital vows exchanged in the church did not simply join the couple; they symbolized and embodied the steadfastness of Christian love, the betrothed's love for Christ, and the covenant between God and his people. A Catholic marriage, therefore, once consecrated and consummated, could be dissolved only through the death of a spouse or a church-sponsored annulment.[13]

MARRIAGE RENEWALS AND DISSOLUTIONS

The Children of Coyote, of course, had their own institutions of marriage, and roughly 40 percent of the adults who came to Mission San Carlos already were married by Indian custom at the time of their baptism. The Franciscans formally recognized most of these unions through ceremonies of renewal. The most notable exceptions were marriages involving polygyny, unions where there was no chance that both husband and wife would accept baptism, and marriages lacking mutual consent of the betrothed. Most marriage renewals occurred just after the couple had attained baptism, but, in the earliest years of a mission, it was not uncommon for a husband and wife to have been baptized weeks or even months apart. In these instances, their marriage was almost always renewed within a day of the trailing spouse's baptism.[14]

12. Lavrin, "Sexuality in Colonial Mexico," in Lavrin, ed., *Sexuality and Marriage in Latin America*, 4–6; *The Canons and Decrees of the Council of Trent*, sect. 24 (London, 1637), rare book no. 443992, 123–124, HL. By "spiritual ties," I mean those created between godparents and their godchildren and marriage witnesses and brides and grooms.

13. Lavrin, "Sexuality in Colonial Mexico," in Lavrin, ed., *Sexuality and Marriage in Latin America*, 27.

14. De la Peña Montenegro, *Itinerario*, ed. Baciero et al., libro 3, tratado 9, sects. 2–6, 268–275. Here I define "adult" as age fifteen and higher. In seven northern California missions (including San Carlos)

Indians who renewed their unions in Roman Catholicism experienced different procedures than those who contracted marriage after baptism. In a marriage renewal, since the couple was already joined in the eyes of the community, a public notification of their intent to marry through the reading of the banns was not necessary. Furthermore, since the church imposed fewer restrictions on Indians who renewed marriages than on others it married, there was no formal prenuptial investigation. When Indians came to missions already married, only impediments rooted in natural law, such as prohibitions against marriages between siblings and between parents and children, could render the union null and void and lead the Franciscans to prevent its renewal.[15] This comparatively relaxed standard allowed the easy renewal of nearly all gentile marriages, perhaps giving Indians the impression that Catholicism was not inconsistent with their understanding of this important native institution. Yet the Franciscans' subsequent refusal to allow those same Indians to live according to the rules and customs that had governed marriages before their Catholic renewal—and the padres' later insistence on who was and who was not an appropriate marriage partner—must have precipitated misunderstanding and frustration.

Perhaps adding to the Indians' frustration and consternation was a Catholic provision known as the Pauline Privilege. Even though the church recognized the contractual validity of gentile marriages founded upon mutual consent and did not allow those it married to divorce, the Privilege provided for the dissolution of a gentile marriage when a spouse of a neophyte resisted the Catholic faith and was unlikely to attain baptism. In these instances, the gentile marriage dissolved at the moment that the baptized convert contracted a new marriage with a Catholic. The marriage register of San Carlos contains only a few examples of neophytes' dissolving their gentile marriages and marrying new partners, and these cases all involve women whose husbands had refused baptism.[16] Yet, from

---

studied by Cook and Borah, renewals totaled 31 percent of all Indian marriages between 1770 and 1834 (Cook and Borah, "Vital Statistics," chap. 3 in *Essays in Population History,* III, *Mexico and California,* table 3.9, 282).

15. Ecclesiastical impediments imposed by the church, such as the prohibition against marriages between persons related by blood or marriage up to the fourth degree, did not apply to the renewal of gentile Indian marriages (De la Peña Montenegro, *Itinerario,* ed. Baciero et al., libro 3, tratado 9, sects. 2–6, 268–275). Since California Indians also had a taboo against these unions, it seems unlikely that the padres would have found cause not to renew any gentile marriages because of the couple's blood or marriage ties to each other.

16. De la Peña Montenegro, *Itinerario,* ed. Baciero et al., libro 3, tratado 9, sect. 5, 272–274. In a marriage among the unbaptized, if only one spouse accepted baptism, in the eyes of the Catholic Church there could be no sacramental marriage (ibid., sect. 3, 270). At Mission San Carlos, the Franciscans seem to have only granted the Pauline Privilege to Indian women; women, however, not men, came to the mission with children, the most visible reminders of their past marriages and relationships. Only because the Franciscans asked these women pointed questions in an attempt to determine the identity and whereabouts of the fathers of their children do we know they were married

these exceptions, Indians might have come to wonder why the Franciscans insisted that no marriages were dissoluble and that divorce was not an option for either the husband or the wife within Catholicism.

**PRELIMINARIES TO MARRIAGES OF
SINGLE AND WIDOWED MEN AND WOMEN**

Renewals constituted most of the first marriages at the California missions, but only a small percentage of all the marriages at the missions were renewals. At San Carlos, for example, nearly 80 percent of all Indian marriages over the life of the mission involved partners who contracted marriage after baptism (Table 27). Similarly, in the seven northern California missions studied by Sherburne F. Cook and Woodrow Borah, roughly 70 percent of all weddings between 1770 and 1834 were new, or standard, marriages. These Indians had to submit to a *diligencia matrimonial,* or matrimonial investigation, for the identification of any canonical impediments that could prevent a sacramental marriage. During the investigations, both the bride and groom had to attest to their free consent to the marriage. To that end, the groom first answered three simple questions: "Do you want to marry? With whom do you want to marry? Are you marrying because you are afraid of someone or because you want to marry?"[17] Then the groom had to state whether he had promised another woman that he would marry her. The bride faced analogous questions. Since differences between the Indians' kinship categories and those of the Franciscans often complicated the search for impediments, the bride, groom, and their relatives often had to answer a battery of questions designed to clarify their relationships: Is this your father? Your son? Your maternal grandfather? Your brother? Your maternal uncle? Your father-in-law? Fornication also created ties of affinity, and both the groom and the bride would have to say whether they had had sexual relations with the brother or sister

---

before their baptism. Men, it seems, either did not tell the Franciscans about their living gentile wives, or, as was the case with many adult Indians, they came to the missions after their gentile spouses had died.

17. Cook and Borah, "Vital Statistics," chap. 3 in *Essays in Population History,* III, *Mexico and California,* table 3.9, 282. In matrimonial investigations of Indians—unlike those of the gente de razón—missionaries kept no record of the questions they asked or the responses they received (copy of letter of José Gasol, father guardian of the College of San Fernando, to the missionaries, "Libro patente," Oct. 1, 1806, par. 6, 22b, LDS film 0913303). The padres merely noted in the marriage register that an investigation had taken place on a certain day before the wedding. The contemporary missionary manual prepared by Father Bartholomé García, a Franciscan who spent decades in the missions of Texas and the Southwest, suggests the questions' probable focus and tenor. See Bartholomé Garcia, *Manual para administrar los santos sacramentos de penitencia, eucharistia, extrema-uncion, y matrimonio . . .* (Mexico City, 1760), 1, 76.

TABLE 27. Marriage of Indians by Type and Decade, Mission San Carlos, 1772–1832

Years	All Marriages (N)	Renewals	New Marriages	New Marriages (% of N)
1772–1779	135	64	71	53
1780–1789	214	60	154	72
1790–1799	171	29	142	83
1800–1809	147	10	137	93
1810–1819	71	0	71	100
1820–1829	41	0	41	100
1830–1832	15	0	15	100
1772–1799	520	153	367	71
1800–1832	274	10	264	96
Total	794	163	631	79

Note: There were no Indian marriages at San Carlos before 1772. Franciscan record keeping at the mission was less reliable after 1832, as secularization approached.

Source: Figures are from my database of baptisms, marriages, and burials at San Carlos compiled from the mission's registers (see Appendix A for methodology).

of their intended spouse. Questions such as these must have at times made marrying a humiliating and bewildering experience.[18]

Witnesses to these investigations helped missionaries unravel family relationships and verify that the bride and groom were being truthful and understood the questions. Soldiers and Baja California Indians served in this capacity during the first decades of the missions, but eventually local Indians who the Franciscans believed understood both Spanish and Catholicism stood witness. The missionary instructed the witnesses that he had called them to tell the truth, and, if they were to lie, "the devil will take them to hell." Then witnesses answered a litany of similar questions—whether they were related to either the bride or groom, whether the bride or groom had promised to marry someone else, whether either one was already married, and, if so, whether the husband or wife was already dead.[19]

18. García noted that, in missions, "the means with which these Indians explain their family relationships is very diffuse" *(Manual,* 77). Father José Francisco de Paula Señán at San Buenaventura had a similar lament: "It is very difficult to understand the relationships of these people, who give the name brothers [and sisters], without any distinction, to any first or second cousins, even distant relatives, and perhaps even to those whose relationship is neither real nor true" (Madison S. Beeler, ed., *The Ventureño Confesionario of José Señán, O.F.M.,* University of California Publications in Linguistics, XLVII (Berkeley, Calif., 1967), 40 (my trans.). For sample questions, see García, *Manual,* 76–81.

19. García, *Manual,* 82–84, esp. 82. At San Carlos by the mid-1790s, it was common for two Indians from the community to appear as marriage witnesses, and by the later 1790s Indians always served as witnesses at marriages of Indians at the mission. Fernando Joseph (San Carlos bapt. no. 16), Juan

Beyond the matrimonial investigation, to further ensure that closely related individuals did not marry, the priest was to proclaim to the community on three successive feast days the couple's intent to wed. Yet, despite the importance of the banns to the Franciscans' search for impediments and therefore to the sacramental nature of the marriage, the missionaries did not always read the banns three times. In 9 percent of the Indian marriages at San Carlos before 1805, the Franciscans proclaimed the banns only once or twice, and, in some cases, not at all. In most of these instances, the padres merely noted in the marriage register that they had dispensed with the proclamations for "just" or "urgent" cause. On one occasion, the officiating priest noted that he had not read all the banns because of the proximity of Lent, the solemn forty-day period between Ash Wednesday and Easter Sunday in which the Catholic Church allowed only for a far simpler wedding ceremony. To the Franciscans, dispensing with the banns was preferable to postponing marriage. The Indians' annual summer leave from the mission also forced the padres to occasionally skip a complete reading of the banns. Again, Franciscans concerned with the prospect of Indians' living in sin probably reasoned that it made the most sense to allow those who were already betrothed to marry right away rather than after they had returned weeks or even months later. Perhaps aware of the padres' inconsistent readings, the father guardian of the College of San Fernando reminded his California missionaries in October 1806 that a full reading of the banns was indispensable.[20]

Indians were surely confused by these different Roman Catholic procedures and their varied implementation by the Franciscans. At San Carlos, where nearly all marriage renewals occurred during the first decades of the mission and none took place after 1808, the Franciscans' double standards regarding Indian marriages contracted outside the mission and those contracted inside applied largely to different generations of Indians, many of whom were not contemporaries. But, at other missions, large numbers of gentiles attained baptism well into the

Evangelista Joseph (San Carlos bapt. no. 15), Miguel Berardo Murcschu (San Carlos bapt. no. 35), Oresio Antonio Sichcon (San Carlos bapt. no. 1509), Juan de Ducla (San Carlos bapt. no. 460), and Maximiano Joseph (San Carlos bapt. no. 540), all of whom were variously identified as interpreters, served repeatedly as marriage witnesses. Many of the other marriage witnesses also served as alcaldes, *regidores,* or sacristáns. Either Miguel Berardo Murcschu or Maximiano Joseph stood witness at nearly every Indian marriage at San Carlos between 1781 and 1822.

20. For banns not read at standard marriages, see San Carlos marr. nos. 65, 70, 71, 297, 302, 304, 353, and 651. For banns read once, see San Carlos marr. nos. 62, 88, 186, 191, 205, 209, 254, 289, and 667. For banns read twice, see San Carlos marr. nos. 14, 18, 19, 25, 26, 104, 116, 165, 193, 208, 217, 252, 307, 315, 335, 402, 412, 424, 486, and 669. On March 3, 1783, Junípero Serra noted that he read the banns only once before marrying Pasqual María Finigè and Caridad María because there were no more feast days between the baptism of Caridad María on March 1 and Ash Wednesday on March 5 (San Carlos marr. no. 209). After José Gasol's policy directive, there are no more recorded cases of the San Carlos Franciscans' dispensing with any of the banns. See copy of letter of Gasol to the missionaries, Oct. 1, 1806, "Libro patente," par. 6, 22b, LDS film 0913303.

1820s; some couples would have seen their marriages renewed with little scrutiny where others were carefully investigated and publicly announced on repeated occasions.[21] To many, therefore, the Franciscans' management introduced not only new ideas about the meaning and permanence of marriage but what must have seemed an inconsistent, if not capricious, application of processes designed to regulate when marriages could occur and who was and who was not an appropriate marriage partner.

THE MARRIAGE CEREMONY

Whether they were renewals or new marriages, virtually all weddings at San Carlos took place within the mission church. Only occasionally—perhaps when the building was under construction or repair—did weddings occur in the church atrium or the adjacent cemetery. Missionaries oversaw all these ceremonies in strict accordance with Catholic rules, since the church forbade innovation in the administration of the sacraments. At the wedding, a second set of witnesses, increasingly composed of Indians, observed the ceremony and testified to its execution. For Franciscans, wedding ceremonies, beyond bestowing the sacrament, provided another opportunity to indoctrinate Indians into Catholic marriage; for Indians, however, especially the majority who might not have grasped the import of the padres' words and the meaning of the Latin liturgy, the ritualistic and symbolic aspects of the ceremony likely held the most significance.[22]

Today, the sacramental rite of marriage occurs during the Mass, after the Gospel and the homily. But, before the reforms of the Second Vatican Council, that was not the case. Once the couple, the witnesses, and any other attendees had assembled, the padre would lecture the couple about the origin and meaning of the marriage sacrament. One missionary guide suggested a brief and pointed exhortation:

21. At Mission Santa Clara, for example, renewals constituted at least 25 percent of all Indian marriages in every five-year period between 1778 and 1829. See Cook and Borah, "Vital Statistics," chap. 3 in *Essays in Population History,* III, *Mexico and California,* table 3.9, 285.

22. Atrium: San Carlos marr. no. 548. Burial ground: San Carlos marr. nos. 531–537. In all likelihood, the weddings of Indians at San Carlos, and in the other missions of Alta California, resembled the simple ceremony recommended by García, but they might have followed the more elaborate and customary ceremony outlined in Father Miguel Venegas's manual. García's manual was specifically to guide missionaries in the administration of the sacraments to Indians, but the Venegas guide—which Franciscans certainly used at San Carlos—was not directed solely to missionaries or those who ministered to Indians. Mission San Carlos, although primarily an Indian mission, also served as the local church for the soldiers and settlers of Monterey. See García, *Manual,* 84–87; Miguel Venegas, *Manual de parrochos, para administrar los santos sacramentos, y executar las demas sagradas funciones de su ministerio* . . . (Mexico City, 1766), 409–426. I examined the San Carlos copy of this volume at the Archives of the Archdiocese of Orange County, Mission San Juan Capistrano.

You, who we would like to marry, know that Our Father Jesus Christ created the Holy Sacrament of Matrimony, so that the husband does not sin with another woman who is not his; and so that the wife does not sin with another man who is not hers.

He also made this Holy Sacrament so that when you have children you will teach them the things that God demands. If you do this, God will help you, and bring you to Heaven; but we advise you, that you should gather all your sins, so that you confess, and with a clean soul be married.[23]

Before Indians married at Mission Santa Barbara, the bride and groom received a careful admonishment from Father Juan Cortés that they were always to love one another and that a Catholic marriage was a different kind of union: "Now look, you must marry like Christians and not like the gentiles; the husband must always love his wife and she her husband, and you must go now and do it and receive the holy sacrament that is called matrimony." Cortés must have been aware that the betrothed might not comprehend his words, for he concluded his admonition thus: "Now do you understand this?" After the exhortation, the bride and then groom answered two questions: "Do you want to marry —— who is here, as commanded by God and our Holy Mother Church?" and "Do you now take him [or her] as yours?" If both answered in the affirmative, the husband would place his right hand on the wife's, and the couple would be enjoined: "What God has joined, let no man separate: I join you in Matrimony, in the name of the Father, the Son, and the Holy Spirit." They would then receive a sprinkling of holy water. [24]

An additional and highly symbolic ritual, the blessing and veiling of the bride, followed in a little more than half of all Indian marriages at San Carlos. Only if the bride had not been married before as a Catholic would the couple participate in the acts. The bride would place a ring on the groom's thumb, index finger, middle finger, and finally the ring finger, saying, "In the name of the Father, the Son, and the Holy Spirit. Amen." In the same manner, the husband would place a ring on his wife's fingers.[25] Next, the husband would give to his wife the *arras,* or thirteen ceremonial coins, which the padres kept on hand and recovered after the ceremony. The missionary would place the arras in the hand of the husband, who, before he gave them to his wife, would say: "My wife, I give you this ring

23. García, *Manual,* 84–85.

24. Harry Kelsey, ed. and trans., *The Doctrina and Confesionario of Juan Cortés* (Altadena, Calif., 1979), 36 (my trans.); García, *Manual,* 86–87.

25. On the restriction of the nuptial blessing to a woman's first Catholic marriage, see Venegas, *Manual de parrochos,* 424–425; for the ring ceremony, see 414–420. On the symbolism of this ceremony, see Gutiérrez, *When Jesus Came,* 267.

and these coins so that you will see that I am married to you, as commanded by God and our Holy Mother Church." The wife was to acknowledge the gift, saying, "Thus, I accept them." The couple would kneel before the altar, and the missionary would place a veil over the shoulders of the husband and the head of the wife. In some areas of New Spain, priests would draw around the couple a belt or a rope known as a *yugo* (yoke), symbolizing their ties to one another and the yoke of Catholicism that bound them together and to the church. While the couple knelt before the altar, the missionary continued to recite the Mass in Latin. Once the nuptial Mass was complete, the veil and yoke would be removed, and the couple would hear a further admonishment that they had received the blessing of the church and must be faithful, love one another, and fear God. After delivering the right hand of the bride to the groom, the missionary dismissed the newly-weds, reminding the groom to love his wife as Christ loves his church. These very public rituals—the groom's giving his bride tokens of value and receiving her hand—echoed native traditions in which the groom gave gifts to his bride's family before marriage to compensate them for the loss of her labor. Also, the symbolic binding together of bride and groom with a yoke must have been an especially clear statement of union.[26]

Yet brides renewing unions as well as widows remarrying would have wedded in a far simpler ceremony, one that did not carry such obvious symbolism. These women might have wondered why their second wedding differed ritualistically from the first when the rules governing it were the same. On the other side of the aisle, men who married only widows would never have had their marriages so blessed. Still other grooms, those very few who married single women time and again, would have participated in the rituals of rings, arras, and yugos over and over. These anomalies and the ensuing confusion for brides, grooms, and observers were magnified because so many marriages of Indians at the missions were renewals or involved widows remarrying after their husbands had died prematurely from disease.[27]

The suffering and hardship these confusions created for Indians in colonial California are exemplified by the case of an Indian woman named Yumen, who was born around 1765 in a village near what would become Mission Santa Clara.

26. Venegas, *Manual de parrochos,* 420, 423; García, *Manual,* 87.

27. The seasons of Advent and Lent further complicated matters. Canon law prohibited imparting the nuptial blessing during these solemn periods when Catholics were to dedicate themselves to contemplating the Incarnation and the Resurrection. Indians, however, could still marry in the church during these seasons as long as they did so with "modesty" and without "pomp." Compared to other periods in the year, marriages were rarely performed at Mission San Carlos during Lent, but the Franciscans do not seem to have observed any sort of prohibition on marriages during Advent. See Venegas, *Manual de parrochos,* 405–406.

She hoped to marry Sebastian Alvitre, a troublesome character who came to the region in 1769 from Villa Sinaloa. As early as 1781, the two had professed their desire to marry, but they had been rebuffed by Father Tomás de la Peña of Mission Santa Clara. De la Peña believed that Yumen was married already. Yumen, however, insisted that she had divorced her gentile husband, Pedro Pablo Huajolis, and her parents delivered the same message directly to De la Peña. De la Peña nevertheless told Alvitre that allowing the couple to marry would serve as a bad example and undermine the church position that the "matrimonial knot was indissoluble." At this time, Yumen was working in the pueblo of San Jose as a domestic servant, and her employer, Gertrudis Pacheco, as well as Alvitre, had convinced her that, if she attained baptism without Huajolis, she then (according to the Pauline Privilege) could marry Alvitre. So, in February 1785, Yumen came to Mission Santa Clara, asked for baptism, and took the name Pelagia María. De la Peña knew what the couple intended, and he did not approve. He hounded Alvitre and Pelagia María Yumen such that they fled to the countryside and then on to San Francisco, hoping to find another missionary who would marry them. When the couple arrived at the San Francisco Presidio, Alvitre was promptly arrested for taking the woman from Santa Clara; she, in turn, was sent back to the mission, where she was confined and flogged.[28]

During all of this, Huajolis was nowhere to be seen. But, in late June, he apparently became gravely ill and hovered near death. In accordance with canon law, the missionaries baptized him with urgency, without his having undergone proper religious instruction at the mission. Remarkably, Huajolis recovered immediately, and, within days, he and Pelagia María Yumen were taken to the church at Santa Clara, where the missionaries renewed the couple's gentile marriage.[29] Afterward, Pelagia María Yumen refused to live with Huajolis, and for that De la Peña ordered her confined and flogged again. Meanwhile, Alvitre escaped from the San Francisco Presidio and whisked away Pelagia María Yumen and her three-year-old daughter, intending to appeal directly to the governor for justice. After three months, the couple was recaptured and arrested. Pelagia María Yumen testified that she did not consider herself married to Pedro Pablo Huajolis because their wedding had not included the nuptial blessing or the exchange of arras and rings. She claimed that De la Peña had, in fact, tricked her

28. Pelagia María Yumen, Santa Clara bapt. no. 714, Feb. 18, 1785, in Mission Santa Clara Baptisms, book 1, SBMAL. The case is at AGN, PI, CXX, BL. See also Tomás de la Peña to Pedro Fages, May 25, 1785, Santa Clara, AGN, PI, CXX, 49a–50b; declaration of "María Indian neófita de la misión de Santa Clara," Mission San Gabriel, Mar. 27, 1786, ibid., 54a–56b; declaration of Sebastian Alvitre, Apr. 4, 1786, Santa Barbara Presidio, ibid., 58b–59b.

29. Pedro Pablo Huajolis, Santa Clara bapt. no. 738, June 30, 1785, CMRC, MSS film 528:11, reel 1, HL; Santa Clara marr. no. 102, July 2, 1785, ibid.

into remarrying her ex-husband, and she described in great detail the renewal, which she regarded as creating no bonds of marriage:

> On the day that the soldier Manuel Mendoza married Gregoria, she [María] was taken to the church at the same time so she would marry Pedro Pablo. And although the padre asked her questions, she did not respond. She saw the ceremonies that they did to marry the soldier Manuel Mendoza, and they did none of that for her. They did not exchange the arras or rings or anything. And afterward, they sent her to live with Pedro Pablo, telling her that he was her husband, but because neither she nor he wanted this, he [Pedro Pablo] went off with his gentile wife, and she slept in the house of her relatives. Shortly thereafter, the padre came to lock her up.... She added that she never wanted Pedro Pablo as a husband, and as she saw that they did not make for her the same ceremonies as with the soldiers, she believed that she was not married.[30]

Pelagia María Yumen not only criticized the padres for forcing her to marry Huajolis and for performing an incomplete ceremony, but she argued that her church wedding was invalid, even by the Franciscans' own standards. Neither she nor he had consented to it. They had not exchanged gifts before or during the ceremony. And their union had not been consummated: after the wedding, he returned to his gentile wife, and she to her family.

Pelagia María Yumen's testimony conveys one California Indian woman's perceptions of the Catholic rite of marriage. But, in all likelihood, the misunderstandings that surrounded her wedding were not unique to her situation and were a result of what to many California Indians must have appeared as the padres' arbitrariness. The anomalies in the marriage ceremonies probably rendered Franciscan management and intrusion all the more objectionable; to Indians who took as an arrogation the Franciscans' attempts to regulate and monitor their marital and sexual lives, the inconsistencies spawned skepticism, disbelief, and further incentive for resistance.

FRANCISCAN ATTEMPTS TO CONTROL INDIAN SEXUALITY

To Franciscans, marriage and sexuality were inseparable. In daily religious instruction, prenuptial investigations, and postmarital exhortations, missionaries taught Indians that neither could properly exist without the other. During the

30. Declaration of "María India neófita," Mission San Gabriel, Mar. 27, 1786, AGN, PI, CXX, 54a–56b.

annual Lenten confession, the Franciscans went to extra lengths to affirm this relationship when they scrutinized Indians' sexuality and marital fidelity.[31] The confessional guides used by California missionaries underscore the Franciscans' concern with the sixth and ninth commandments, which prohibit fornication, adultery, and lust. One guide composed at San Carlos and circulated to all the missions by Father President Vicente Francisco de Sarría in 1818 devoted nearly a third of its more than 120 questions to uprooting sexual sin. The tallies kept by the Franciscans after 1807 suggests that a majority of adults experienced some aspects of these troubling interrogations annually (see Table 17, above).[32]

The most exacting of the guides began, "Are you married?" and then continued with a presumption of guilt: "With how many women have you sinned?" "Tell me how many times you sinned [with each] one?" "Is she married?" Indians then would be asked whether their sinful relationship had also been incestuous: "Is she your relative?" "Is she a very close relative of yours?" "Is she your sister?" At this point, differences in kinship classifications complicated the questioning. But, because missionaries needed to distinguish between fornication, adultery, and incest, the interrogation continued: "Do you and she have the same father and the same mother?"[33]

In the prenuptial investigation, as during the Lenten confession, the Franciscans were concerned with uncovering consanguineous, marital, and spiritual ties, but here the focus was on ferreting out sin, not impediments. "Let me know whether the woman with whom you sinned is married, or if she is related to you or to your wife, . . . or whether you have taken her child to baptism or confirmation, or whether she is a gentile," Father José Francisco de Paula Señán stated in his guide. If the sinful relationship was current, the Franciscans were prepared to break off the interrogation, deny penance and absolution, and demand that the neophyte return only after mending his or her ways. "Look here," the padres were to admonish sinful Indians, "if you wish in [your] heart for God to pardon you,

31. James A. Sandos, "Levantamiento! The 1824 Chumash Uprising," *The Californians: The Magazine of California History,* V (1978), 8–20; Serge Gruzinski, "Individualization and Acculturation: Confession among the Nahuas of Mexico from the Sixteenth to the Eighteenth Century," Lavrin, "Sexuality in Colonial Mexico," both in Lavrin, ed., *Sexuality and Marriage,* 46–95, esp. 48–54, and 96–117; Monica Barnes, "Catechisms and Confesionarios: Distorting Mirrors of Andean Societies," in Robert V. H. Dover, Katharine E. Seibold, and John H. McDowell, eds., *Andean Cosmologies through Time* (Bloomington, Ind., 1992), 67–94.

32. I examined a copy of this confessional at the SBMAL. It is an extract in the hand of Felipe Arroyo de la Cuesta, written June 1818 and circulated by Sarría in November 1818. Señán's confessional (Beeler, ed., *Ventureño Confesionario*) included more than 150 questions, and more than 60 relate to the sixth and ninth commandments alone. Counts: Zephyrin Engelhardt, *Mission San Carlos Borromeo (Carmelo): The Father of the Missions* (1934; rpt. Ramona, Calif., 1973), table B, 243.

33. Beeler, ed., *Ventureño Confesionario,* 38–41 (my trans.).

do not sin with this woman anymore. . . . Think about God for two weeks, and pray often Jesus Christ my Father etc., and from now on do not sin with this woman. At the end of two weeks, return to confess again, and I will forgive you, and God will forgive you if you have taken the sin from your heart."[34]

The missionaries intended to compel Indians to confine their sexuality to marriage, but they also wanted to monitor and control behaviors within those marriages. Roman Catholicism deemed sinful sexual acts that did not lead to conception, and the padres sought to root them out. "Have your ever handled a woman?" "Have you ever handled yourself?" "How many times have you spilled the [seed of your bo]dy?" Indians also had to explain whether they had had intercourse when their spouses requested, whether they had coupled "improperly" to avoid pregnancy, or whether they had given their spouse to another. Missionaries were also concerned with any sexual acts that might have crossed the Indians' minds or passed before their eyes. "Have you ever dreamed evil things about women?" "Have you thought about or desired women . . . [or] ever watched with pleasure persons or animals sinning?" One confessional even asked Indians whether they had sung lewd songs. Another queried men whether they had committed rape or sinned with a *joya* (transvestite) or a man. Finally, since the Franciscans sought to regulate sexual relations of all community members, Indians were to state whether they had allowed others beyond their family to have intercourse in their houses.[35]

That the Franciscans were prepared to ask all adults about fornication and homosexuality does not, of course, mean that all Indians engaged in these behaviors, nor should it lead us to conclude that Franciscans suspected all Indians of participating in them. Doing so would force us to conclude that all Indians were suspected of murder, since the Franciscans were equally ready to ask them whether they had violated the fifth commandment. Clearly, these guides took their form and content from standard manuals published in Mexico, and they therefore reflected the fears and anxieties of the Catholic Church more than the actual behavior of California Indians. Nevertheless, the padres' questions had a clear goal: to uncover sins so that they could prescribe proper penance and lead the Indians to absolution. But the church's willingness eventually to "forgive and forget" violations of the rules it insisted must never be abrogated can

34. Ibid., 44–45 (my trans.). If a man admitted that he had tricked a young woman into a sinful relationship with a promise of marriage, Señán ordered the man, "Fulfill your promise, or do what you said, and marry the woman" (46–47) (my trans.).

35. Ibid., 46–53; Sarría confessional, circ. Nov. 13, 1818, SBMAL. In California, the Spanish used the term *joya* for male Indians who dressed as women. Indians held these individuals in high esteem; some married women and fathered children. Missionaries saw the joyas as prostitutes and sodomites.

only have compounded the confusion and resentment of the Indians who were daily warned against the perils of sin.[36]

Franciscan control over Indian sexuality depended upon more than daily persuasion and annual interrogation; it found expression in the architecture and living arrangements of the missions. Each mission had a special dormitory for widows and single women over age eleven, and some had similar buildings for unmarried men. These buildings were the result of a pervasive Spanish ideology that not only placed a premium on female virginity and chastity but also exalted male sexual conquest. All women were assumed to be the weaker sex, and any self-respecting man protected his daughter, wife, and mother from sexual assault. The seclusion of unmarried women that resulted was common throughout the communities of the borderlands. In California, therefore, the construction of dormitories for unmarried women was not an innovation but an extreme attempt by missionary "fathers" to protect the purity of their spiritual daughters.[37]

As early as 1772, Franciscans locked up unmarried women at night in a dormitory at Mission San Carlos. In 1801, Father President Lasuén described this building as a large, secure structure: "It is sixteen *varas* in length, more than six in width, and the same in height. The walls are an adobe-and-a-half thick, finished in mortar and whitewashed. There is a firm platform along the two sides and along the front [for the women to sleep on]; it is one vara high. There are three large windows with lattices on the one side, and on the other are four lancet windows. The toilets are separate. The entire structure is of good-quality beams covered with coarse lumber. The roof is of tile." Lasuén insisted that "all possible care is taken so that nothing will be prejudicial to their health." But these buildings were crowded, therefore unhealthful, and confinement itself would have been detrimental to the Indians' well-being. In 1798, three years before Lasuén described the *monjerío* at San Carlos, some forty-eight single women—not counting widows—between the ages of twelve and twenty-two lived at the mission. These women, identified in a mission census as *solteras,* or unmarried women, most likely would have been confined at night to the monjerío. If only

---

36. Lavrin, "Sexuality in Colonial Mexico," in Lavrin, ed., *Sexuality and Marriage,* 8–9.

37. Zephyrin Engelhardt, *Mission La Concepción Purísima de María Santísima* (1932; Santa Barbara, Calif., 1986), 42. James A. Sandos, "Between Crucifix and Lance: Indian-White Relations in California, 1769–1848," in Gutiérrez and Orsi, eds., *Contested Eden,* 196–229, esp. 206, says the dormitories were for all females over age seven. On women's seclusion in the borderlands, see Gutiérrez, *When Jesus Came,* 208, 213–214, 235–238. Mission San Carlos did not have a dormitory for young, unmarried men. Of course, the ideology that women were weaker than men and objects of sexual conquest was not unique to Spain or its colonial regions.

half of them actually slept in the dormitory, they still would have been crowded in a room that was only roughly fifty by twenty feet.[38]

One wonders how Indians understood the segregation of their unmarried women, or whether they even could within the context of their belief systems. Many California Indian groups had strong cultural barriers separating men and women, and some exiled menstruating women from their villages, but the women's dormitories were far different in their design, intent, and function. Locking up single women severely restricted courtship and ceremonial practices, and it certainly fomented anger and dismay, if not illness and premature death. One night in 1799, two unmarried men, Modesto and Ciriaco Joseph Esparza, sneaked into the girls' dormitory. What the men did there is not known, but the Franciscans considered it a grave enough offense to put the two in shackles.[39]

INDIAN RESISTANCE AND FRANCISCAN PUNISHMENT

Through exhortations, interrogations, and actual physical confinement, Franciscans sought to restrict Indians to a heterosexual, procreative, married model. When these efforts failed, as they often did, missionaries forced adherence to the model through assaults on the Indians' bodies. An unmarried woman of San Carlos, Victoria María, was caught one afternoon outside the mission having sex with Simón Carpio, a muleteer from Mission San Antonio. Serra locked up Victoria María and asked the governor to apprehend Simón Carpio at the presidio. When Indians like Victoria María refused to live up to the Franciscans' expectations even after being chastised, the missionaries sent them to the presidio for an added dose of "correction." The padres sent one such unfortunate, Tito, an unmarried and recently baptized man from San Juan Bautista, to the Monterey Presidio because they had been powerless to prevent him from living "scandalously" with a married mother of five children. The governor was to punish Tito in such a way that, when he returned to the mission, he would need no additional correction.[40]

38. Serra to Verger, Aug. 8, 1772, Monterey, in Tibesar, ed. and trans., *Writings of Serra,* I, 257; Lasuén, "Refutation of Charges," June 19, 1801, Mission San Carlos, in Kenneally, ed. and trans., *Writings of Lasuén,* II, 206–207; Macario de Castro, Jan. 3, 1798, San Carlos, Archives of the Missions, C–C 4–5, folder 20, BL.

39. Francisco Pujol and Baltasar Carnicer to Diego de Borica, Apr. 3, 1799, Mission San Carlos, Taylor Coll., doc. 207, HL. The arrested were Modesto (San Carlos bapt. no. 773) and Ciriaco Joseph Esparza (San Carlos bapt. no. 602). Modesto's late father, Theodosio Jutis (San Carlos bapt. no. 896) had been an Esselen village leader.

40. Estevan Tapis and Juan Cortés, Oct. 30, 1800, Mission Santa Barbara, AGN, PI, CCXVI, expedi-

Many Indians continued their illicit relationships nonetheless. Antonio Pablo, recently widowed, had been living "obscenely" for years with Felicitas, a married woman. The padres at San Juan Capistrano in 1807 complained that they had done everything in their power to prevent this, yet the couple persisted. Indeed, "every day" Antonio Pablo's "rebelliousness" grew greater, stirring up the missionaries' fears about political and social instability. The Franciscans saw no option but to break up the offending couple, and they proposed that the governor exile Antonio Pablo to a distant presidio, Monterey or San Francisco, for two or three years. Only such a separation, claimed the missionaries, would put an end to the couple's "blind passion."[41]

Juan Pedro, a thirty-year-old weaver from Mission San Miguel, also refused to mend his ways. The missionaries had dispatched him for punishment several times to the presidio and, by 1833, considered him incorrigible. Accused of living in concubinage, he was put on trial in Monterey. In his own testimony, Juan Pedro admitted that on at least two occasions he had fled San Miguel with married women. But he denied that he had lived adulterously at the mission. When asked to clarify the apparent discrepancy—how he could have fled the mission with married women but not lived adulterously—he replied that it was true that he had "gone with women," but he added that he had never done so "in the mission." Juan Pedro, and perhaps many other Indians as well, might have believed that Catholic mores were not binding in areas beyond Franciscan control. This distinction, however, did not impress the municipal officials of Monterey, who found Juan Pedro guilty and sentenced him to labor in shackles for three years.[42]

Examples such as these, of Indians' being punished for expressing their sexuality, abound in the historical record. To most Indians, elements of the Franciscans' definition of marriage and appropriate sexual behavior were at minimum alien, not anchored in native systems of belief. Some Indians might also have been ignorant of them at the time they received the Catholic sacrament of marriage, given the difficulty of translating Catholic ideals into Indian languages, the brevity of the religious instruction offered before baptism, and the inconsistencies in

ente 1, 85a; Gregorio Fernández, La Purísima Concepción, Nov. 11, 1800, AGN, PI, CCXVI, expediente 1, 90a; Victoria María, San Carlos bapt. no. 94; Serra to Fernando de Rivera y Moncada, Jan. 22, 1775, Carmel, in Tibesar, ed., Writings of Serra, IV, 421; Estevan Tapis to Luís Argüello, May 20, 1823, San Juan Bautista, Taylor Coll., doc. 1448, HL.

41. Antonio Pablo was baptized at San Juan Capistrano on Feb. 8, 1793 (bapt. no. 1220, LDS film 0913316). See also José Faura and Juan Norberto de Santiago, July 6, 1807, San Juan Capistrano, Taylor Coll., doc. 321, HL. Furthermore, the padres wanted Antonio Pablo exiled because they feared that Felicitas's husband, who had fled the mission, might eventually return and punish her.

42. "Sumaria de vagos contra el neófito de la misión de San Miguel Juan Pedro por amaciato" (1833), Archives of Monterey, C–A 150, I, reel 1, 734–748, BL.

TABLE 28. Marriages and Marriage Partners of the Mission Born,
Mission San Carlos, 1772–1832

Period	All Marriages of Inds.	Groom MB	Bride MB	Groom and Bride Both MB	Groom *Soltero* and MB	Bride *Soltera* and MB	*Soltero* and *Soltera* both MB
1772–1779	135	0%	0%	0%	0%	0%	0%
1780–1789	214	0	1	0	0	1	0
1790–1799	171	10	13	3	10	12	2
1800–1809	147	15	27	5	9	19	2
1810–1819	71	30	46	11	21	32	10
1820–1829	41	49	63	39	37	39	29
1830–1832	15	87	93	80	53	87	53
Total	794	12%	17%	6%	9%	13%	4%

Note: MB = Mission Born. *Solteras* and *solteros* are women and men never married before at the mission.
Source: Figures are from my database of baptisms, marriages, and burials at San Carlos compiled from the mission's registers (see Appendix A for methodology).

the administration of the preliminaries and rituals of the ceremony. Not until the early 1830s, when the missions collapsed and Franciscan authority waned, did most marriages join brides and grooms who had been exposed throughout their lives to Spanish and Catholic traditions and teachings. Until then, most marriages wed those who came to the mission as adults. As noted earlier, in only 6 percent of all marriages were both bride and groom born at the mission (Table 28). And in only 26 percent of marriages did both bride and groom move to the mission and attain baptism before age ten (Table 29). Although many individuals born to Catholicism or raised under Catholic tutelage have not subscribed to the ideal of monogamy and the prohibition of sex outside marriage, the small percentages of marriages joining the mission born or the mission raised underscore why so many could have chafed under Franciscan control. It is no surprise that most Indians—either willfully or out of ignorance of the padres' teachings—did not adhere to the Catholic model of sexuality and marriage and that missionaries subsequently went to great lengths to prohibit and punish their rebelliousness.

Oppression often prompts violence among and between the colonized. Such was the case in California, where Indians chastised for violating Catholic marital and sexual values occasionally became so frustrated that they assaulted and even killed their spouses. Some neophytes did so with the hope that, once they were widowed, they would be able to marry again, or at least that is how they explained their crimes. A case of spousal homicide at Mission San Carlos provides one glimpse of Indians' sexual involvement outside of marriage and suggests that

TABLE 29. Marriages and Marriage Partners of the Mission Raised,
Mission San Carlos, 1772–1832

| | | | | PROPORTION OF N | | | |
Period	All Marriages of Inds.	Groom MR	Bride MR	Groom and Bride Both MR	Groom *Soltero* and MR	Bride *Soltera* and MR	*Soltero* and *Soltera* both MR
1772–1779	135	8%	16%	6%	8%	15%	6%
1780–1789	214	23	24	14	18	18	9
1790–1799	171	36	40	22	32	36	18
1800–1809	147	50	54	37	29	35	20
1810–1819	71	70	75	52	42	49	27
1820–1829	41	80	80	71	39	41	34
1830–1832	15	93	100	93	53	87	53
Total	794	37%	41%	26%	25%	30%	16%

Note: MR = All Indians baptized before their tenth birthday, including the mission born. *Solteras* and *solteros* are women and men never married before at the mission.
Source: Figures are from my database of baptisms, marriages, and burials at San Carlos compiled from the mission's registers (see Appendix A for methodology).

the desire to escape an unhappy union and make way for entrance into a new one could be a credible motive for murder. In July 1791, the body of Francisca María Chalc, who had been missing for weeks, was found partially eaten by animals in the woods adjacent to Mission San Carlos. Military officials, after interviewing several Indians, accused Francisca María's husband, Estanislao Joseph Tupag, of murder. The contours of the couple's lives together resembled those of many others at San Carlos. Both were Costanoan; she was born in the village of Tucutnut, he in Ensen. Both were baptized in the mid-1770s, she at age seven, he at age nine. They married in 1780, when they were in their early teens. The couple had two children; the first died in infancy, the other at age two.[43]

At the heart of Francisca María and Estanislao Joseph's troubles was their desire to be with others. During his testimony, Estanislao Joseph revealed that Francisca María was having an affair with another man, Eliseo Joseph Cachirro, and that, when she was missing, so was he. Estanislao's mother, Josefa Neve Tuyoschiris, stated that she was certain her son had killed Francisca María so that

43. The transcript of this case is in the Taylor Coll. in an unnumbered document, pages 63-2a–63-10a, HL. The soldiers believed that Estanislao Joseph Tupag's three brothers were his accomplices. The four were arrested and imprisoned at the Monterey Presidio, where the military quickly set out to determine the cause of Francisca María's death and the culpability of the accused. See Estanislao Joseph, San Carlos bapt. no. 459, June 28, 1777; Francisca María, San Carlos bapt. no. 61, Feb. 14, 1773, and marr. no. 158, May 23, 1780; Phelipe Neri, San Carlos bapt. no. 998, May 28, 1784, and bur. no. 373, June 21, 1784; Ybon Francisco, San Carlos bapt. no. 1285, May 20, 1787, and bur. no. 651, June 30, 1789.

he could marry his mistress, Anastacia María, an unmarried woman who had been widowed twice at San Carlos. Brought to the presidio, Anastacia María testified that "one night Estanislao was in her house, and the deceased [Francisca María] came to get him from there; they began to fight, and they left, and she saw that they were headed to the corral, and afterwards he came back alone, and took some beads that he kept in her house and went away. . . . She never saw the deceased again." A few days later, Anastacia María asked Estanislao Joseph whether he had killed his wife. He had told her that, "yes, it was true that he had killed her because she was involved with Eliseo." Anastacia María admitted her involvement with Estanislao Joseph, but she claimed she did not want to marry him.[44]

Confronted with these testimonies, Estanislao Joseph Tupag confessed. It was true that his wife had fetched him from Anastacia María's home and that, when he admitted the affair, he and his wife had quarreled. The following day, away from the mission, they had fought again. This time, though, Estanislao Joseph hit and kicked her in the chest. Francisca María became sick and too weak to return to the mission. Estanislao Joseph claimed that he had left to make her a fire, but, when he returned, she was gone, never to be seen alive again. Estanislao Joseph said that he had never intended to kill her, only to punish her because he "loved her with his heart." Spanish officials were unable to determine whether Estanislao Joseph or wild animals had killed Francisca María, and after a year in prison Estanislao Joseph was freed. But the testimony constitutes an enduring record of the violence that could accompany marriages and extramarital affairs in the California missions. Perhaps, had Estanislao Joseph and Francisca María not been living under the watchful eyes of the Franciscans and their rigid precepts, they would have dissolved their marriage and peacefully pursued others.[45]

If Estanislao perhaps killed his wife to marry his mistress, other men seem to have beaten and killed their spouses because the cost of carrying on an illicit relationship in the missions was simply too high. In the late 1790s, at Mission San Juan Capistrano, such a tragedy unfolded when one couple—Aurelio Jujuvit and Tomasa Coroni—found themselves unhappily married. Aurelio and Tomasa's marital discontent and lack of sexual interest in one another had become apparent: they did not care for one another, they did not eat together, and they did not always sleep under the same roof. By the spring of 1797, Aurelio had been carrying on for a long time with Benedicta, a married woman. Tomasa had a lover of

44. "First Confession of the Principal Offender," July 22, 1791, Monterey Presidio, Taylor Coll., 63-5b–63-6b, HL; Eliseo Joseph Cachirro, San Carlos bapt. no. 882, Dec. 1, 1783; testimony of Anastacia María, July 22, 1791, Monterey Presidio, Taylor Coll., 63-6a–63-7a. See also Anastacia María, San Carlos bapt. no. 98, Apr. 10, 1773; San Carlos marr. no. 9, Apr. 10, 1773; San Carlos marr. no. 179, Dec. 10, 1781.

45. "Second Confession of the Principal Offender," July 23, 1791, Monterey Presidio, Taylor Coll., 63-8a–63-9a, HL.

her own, Juan José Echvich, who had been paying Aurelio in beads, cigars, and other goods so that he could be with Tomasa. Through their extramarital affairs, and the required reciprocal payments, Aurelio, Benedicta, Tomasa, and Juan José had made their lives under Catholic rule both more bearable and more familiar. In many ways, like most migrants to the missions, these men and women for a time managed their relations as they might have done outside the mission.[46]

But the Franciscans' discovery of Tomasa's and Aurelio's relationships put an end to these arrangements. On two separate occasions, Bruno, the mission alcalde, had punished Tomasa and Juan José for merely talking alone. After Benedicta, Aurelio's lover, had been chastised, she tried against Aurelio's wishes to break off their relationship. And, after Juan José had been punished "so much" by the padres, he had ended—also against Aurelio's wishes—his relationship with Tomasa and cut off his payments to Aurelio. In a very short period of time, therefore, Aurelio, through the intervention of the Franciscans, had had his personal life overturned. He found himself not only with a wife whom he could not divorce and who neither respected nor cared for him but estranged from his mistress, who was now afraid even to see him and could certainly not marry him. Moreover, he had been denied a source of income and compensation for his wife's extramarital affair.[47]

One Friday evening around sunset, Aurelio finished his day's work as a mission *vaquero* (cowherd), rode back to the mission, and carried Tomasa away on horseback, after telling his sister-in-law that they were going to sleep in the hills. When Aurelio returned alone, he was asked where his wife was and offered that "maybe she had fled." Bruno the alcalde noticed her absence all the next week but claimed that he was too busy to investigate. The following Sunday after Mass, Aurelio remained in church long after everyone else had exited. When Bruno asked him what was wrong, Aurelio revealed that he had killed his wife. Soon thereafter, Tomasa's badly beaten body was found buried a league from the mission. During the criminal investigation, Aurelio asserted that he had never intended to kill her, but he had kicked and hit her because "she was a bad wife." If Tomasa was a "bad wife," it was clear Aurelio was a worse husband, yet the

46. For more on Aurelio Jujuvit and Tomasa Coroni, see San Juan Capistrano marr. no. 290, May 30, 1791; San Juan Capistrano bapt. nos. 777, Aug. 16, 1787 (Aurelio Jujuvit), and 280, May 30, 1791 (Tomasa María Coroni); and San Juan Capistrano bur. no. 618, Mar. 5, 1797, all in CMRC, MSS film 528:4, reels 1–3, HL. For the case, see declarations of Camilo and Juan José, "Criminal contra Aurelio Jujuvit indio natural de la misión de San Juan Capistrano, acusado de haver dado muerte a su muger Tomasa Coroni india de dicha misión en 5 de marzo 1797," AGN, CA, LXV, expediente 8, 335a–370a, esp. 340b–342b, 349b. In all likelihood, when Tomasa Coroni and Juan José became involved, Juan José was a widower, since his wife María Ygnacia was dead by 1797 (San Juan Capistrano bur. no. 538, Feb. 3, 1796).

47. Declarations of Bruno, Benedicta, and Juan José, all in "Criminal contra Aurelio Jujuvit," AGN, CA, LXV, expediente 8, 345b, 347b, 348b.

frustrations that he took out on her body may be attributable in part to the inflexible rules of the mission and Aurelio's inability to circumvent them without risking his own physical punishment.[48]

Estanislao Joseph beat his wife and Aurelio beat and killed his, but, in another case, a wife murdered her husband out of marital and sexual frustration. In December 1800, Eulalia of Mission San Antonio reported that Juan, her husband, had choked to death while smoking tobacco. Years before, Eulalia had married Juan, a Baja California Indian. Cayetano Espinosa, the leader of the guard at the mission, suspected foul play and placed several under arrest, including Eulalia. The subsequent investigation and trial revealed that Eulalia, along with her lover Primo and his brother Bentura, had attacked Juan in his sleep during the middle of the night, while Eulalia and Juan were encamped about a league from the mission. Primo, Bentura, and Eulalia were aware of the Catholic rules of marriage, and they no doubt understood that divorce and remarriage were simply not options. Eulalia had gone to confession, learned the doctrina, and understood the Ten Commandments. So had Bentura, who claimed to have been to confession on three separate occasions. Primo had been baptized six years before the crime and had "always confessed." But he did not know the Ten Commandments and had not been tutored in the doctrina: "The little he knew of it, he had learned on the occasions that he had gone to pray in the church with the community." Despite Primo's weak understanding of Catholicism, after six years in and around the mission he must have realized—as his accomplices would have—that his own marriage as well as Eulalia's constituted an almost insurmountable barrier to their desire to be together.[49]

At the time of Juan's murder, Eulalia and Primo had been having an affair for five years. This was common knowledge at the mission, and, after they had been "caught in the act," the padres had given Primo "many lashes" and cut Eulalia's hair. These punishments had not ended the couple's interest in each other; Primo asserted that he loved Eulalia. But the disciplinary measures had begun to take their toll on the couple's relationship. At the time of the murder, according to Primo, the two—much like Tomasa and Juan José and Benedicta and Aurelio— had broken things off for fear of additional beatings and humiliations.[50]

Those who testified in the investigation offered several possible motivations

48. Declarations of Camilo and Bruno and confession of Aurelio, ibid., 341a–341b, 345a, 351a. Amazingly, Aurelio Jujuvit remarried twice after killing Tomasa. See San Juan Capistrano marr. nos. 574, Dec. 14, 1803, and 883, Jan. 16, 1814.

49. Declarations of Eulalia, Bentura, and Primo, "Proceso contra los neófitos de la misión de San Antonio llamados Primo, Bentura, y Eulalia . . . ," and letter of Calletano Espinosa, Jan. 5, 1811, both in AGN, PI, VI, expediente 3, 44a–85b, esp. 45a, 51b, 53b, 56a.

50. Declarations of Juan Nepomuceno, Santos Clavil, Eulalia, and Primo, in "Proceso contra los neófitos de la misión de San Antonio," ibid., 50a, 51a, 52b–53a, 56b.

for the murder, and all linked the crime to the frustrations of the accused with Franciscan supervision of their intimate and personal lives. Although Primo denied that he had killed Juan so that he could marry Eulalia, others testified differently: Eulalia stated that Primo had "blindly insisted that he would marry her [by] killing his own wife and her husband." Bentura testified that, just after they had killed Juan, Primo confided in him that he wanted to let a little time go by before he murdered his wife and married Eulalia. Primo, however, denied that he had ever planned a double murder, but he did acknowledge somewhat coyly that "if he were not married it could be that he would want to [marry Eulalia] since she did not have a husband."[51]

In his defense, Primo asserted that Eulalia had told him to kill Juan and that he had done so only because Juan had repeatedly abused and mistreated Eulalia. Eulalia's contempt for Juan and her desire to have Primo kill him might have resulted from his mistreatment of her and from the fact that, through a marriage that seemed indissoluble, Juan had acquired control over her. Perhaps this explains Eulalia's unusual assault on Juan the night of the murder. While Primo and Bentura strangled him, Eulalia pulled on Juan's testicles "until he was dead." Pedro, another of the Indians who testified, claimed that, after the three killed Juan, the assailants partially severed Juan's testicles, "leaving them hanging." Spousal homicides and sexual assaults were not unique to the missions in California, and the murder of Juan may reflect the persistence of precontact behaviors as much as a response to the mission environment. But the rigid enforcement of Catholic norms, in particular the missionaries' refusal to allow unhappy Indians to separate, divorce, and remarry and the corporal punishment meted out, could only have inflamed marital tensions and driven Indians like Primo and Eulalia to desperation and violence.[52]

Whereas Primo and Eulalia apparently murdered Juan in the hope that they would soon marry, in another case, a man murdered his wife so that he could wed his widowed lover before the Franciscans pressured her into another union. Thus, not only the Franciscans' enforcement of the indissolubility of marriage but their aggressive matchmaking precipitated tragedy at San Luis Obispo. When Rebecca died in June 1796 at the hands of her husband Silverio, they had been married for fifteen years. At some point, their marriage soured, the two began to fight in public, and Silverio became involved with Rosa, a widow. Shortly before her death, Rebecca seems to have grown especially fearful of Silverio. Tiburcio, a blacksmith at the mission, reported that one day he had seen Silverio, Rebecca, and her mother gathering seeds. Silverio hit Rebecca and told his mother-in-law,

51. Testimonies of Eulalia, Bentura, and Primo, ibid., 52b–53a, 55b, 57a.
52. Testimony of Pedro, ibid., 47b.

when she tried to intervene, that he would kill Rebecca since she did not have any relatives to defend her. When Rebecca's mother said she would protect her daughter, Silverio struck her as well.[53]

Later that month, when Silverio told Rebecca that they would be joining a group that was heading to the countryside for a while to gather seeds, Rebecca became suspicious and concluded that she might never return. She tearfully asked her cousin Pomposa to care for her two children. While she and Silverio were away, Rebecca implored her friend Edicta not to leave them alone because she feared that Silverio would kill her. One day after Silverio and Rebecca became separated from the others, Silverio came running into the Indians' encampment, crying that a bear had killed Rebecca. His tale fooled no one. Rebecca's injuries resembled wounds inflicted by a knife, not an animal. Silverio's affair with Rosa was common knowledge, and he had not kept secret his intention to slay Rebecca. When confronted with this evidence, Silverio admitted his crime, but he blamed Rosa for ordering him to murder his wife. Rosa denied this, claiming she slept in the monjerío, not with him, and offered in her defense a sharp understanding of gender relations inside and outside of marriage in Spanish California: she stated that, "without being his wife, she could not have ordered him to do anything."[54]

Silverio, it seems, killed Rebecca when he did because he feared that very soon the padres were going to facilitate a marriage between Rosa and a recently widowed man, Anselmo Lapiquia. If Silverio and Rosa's affair was as widely known to the Franciscans as it was to the rest of the community, perhaps the missionaries hoped to end it by finding a spouse for the widowed Rosa. In fact, Rosa claimed that, before Silverio killed Rebecca, he had told her he was so upset about the possibility of her marrying someone else that he had been unable to sleep. And he had confided in Rosa that, if the padres "gave her a[nother] husband," it would end their relationship: "no longer would he come to see her, nor would he come to her house." Moreover, according to Silverio, on several occasions Rosa

53. See "Causa criminal contra Silverio y Rosa . . . ," AGN, CA, LXV, expediente 6, 241a–301b; for Tiburcio's testimony, see 256a–258b. Pedro Fages asserted that, at Mission San Luis Obispo, by Indian standards, men could not remarry until they were widowed. Thus the Indians' own restrictions on remarriage, not just those introduced by the Franciscans, might have contributed to the motivations behind this case of spousal homicide. Rebecca had been baptized and married to Silverio in 1781, the year she turned sixteen; by 1796, the couple had had five children born at the mission, but only two, Silveria and Silverio, survived childhood illnesses (personal communication with John R. Johnson). For more about Rebecca and Silverio, see San Luis Obispo bapt. nos. 504, July 23, 1781 (Rebecca), and 524, Nov. 8, 1781 (Silverio), in San Luis Obispo Baptisms, 1772–1821, LDS film 0913300; San Luis Obispo marr. no. 113, Dec. 10, 1781, and San Luis Obispo bur. no. 523, June 17, 1796 (Rebecca), in CMRC, MSS film 528:15, reels 2, 3, HL.

54. Declarations of Tiburcio, Rosa, Edicta, Dalmas Estumo, and Silverio, all ibid., 248b, 257a, 260a, 260b, 266b, 267a, 269b–270b.

had urged him to kill Rebecca and had begun to doubt that he had the nerve to do it. Silverio, therefore, might have concluded that he needed to do away with Rebecca quickly, before Rosa completely lost faith in him and before she was forced into another marriage. Perhaps he feared falling into a situation like the one that had afflicted Aurelio Jujuvit and Benedicta at San Juan Capistrano. For Silverio to carry on a clandestine relationship as a married man under the watchful eyes of the Franciscans must have been complicated and dangerous, but, if Rosa married Anselmo, he would have had greater problems not just with Rosa's husband but with the Franciscans as well.[55]

The padres' strict enforcement of Catholic precepts not only led to violence against and between Indians but also against the Franciscans and their mission system. In 1812, Father Andrés Quintana of Mission Santa Cruz died under mysterious circumstances. An initial investigation found that Quintana had died of natural causes, but years later several Indians asserted they had killed Quintana because of his cruel punishments, and a subsequent inquiry implicated eight Indians in the murder, five of whom received harsh retributions for the crime. The manner in which the attackers claimed to have mutilated and murdered Quintana suggests that they wanted to take revenge on him for his interference in their sexual relations, particularly his readiness to flog them for what he took to be sinful behavior. After nearly strangling Quintana, the assailants "took" one of his testicles, and, hours later, when he appeared to be regaining consciousness, "they crushed the Father's other testicle." After the murder, Donato, who had been whipped severely by Quintana, apparently "walked around the room with the plural results of his operation in hand saying, 'I shall bury these in the outdoor privy.'" In the hours after Quintana's death, the assailants unlocked the dormitories of the single men and single women, and "the young people of both sexes got together and had their pleasure." This oral history of the murder of Quintana was narrated in 1877 by Lorenzo Asisara, who was born at Mission Santa Cruz in 1820. Although some of the details of this account have a folkloric dimension, the narrative—and the murder it describes—suggests the depth of the Indians' resentment and its persistence within the Indian community for generations, long after the Franciscans had left the region.[56]

In 1824, a decade after the death of Father Quintana, Chumash Indians at three

55. Declaration of Rosa, "Causa criminal contra Silverio y Rosa," AGN, CA, LXV, expediente 6, 267b. For more on Anselmo Lapiquia, see San Luis Obispo bapt. no. 184, May 7, 1776. Anselmo's wife, Casilda, had died on Apr. 6, 1796. See San Luis Obispo bur. no. 513.

56. Maynard Geiger, *Franciscan Missionaries in Hispanic California, 1769–1848: A Biographical Dictionary* (San Marino, Calif., 1969), 204–206; Edward D. Castillo, ed. and trans., "The Assassination of Padre Andrés Quintana by the Indians of Mission Santa Cruz in 1812: The Narrative of Lorenzo Asisara," *California History*, LXVIII, no. 3 (Fall 1989), 116–125, 150–152, esp. 122.

missions rebelled, ostensibly in response to the whipping of a La Purísima neo-phyte at Mission Santa Inés. But the Indians' sexual license outside the mission after the uprising suggests other motivations. The Indians who rebelled against and fled from the Santa Barbara missions left behind the sexual segregation, the prohibitions against premarital sex and adultery, and the disallowal of marriage between the baptized and unbaptized that dominated their lives. According to five Indian men who testified later, men and women, married and unmarried, gentiles and neophytes, all lived together outside the mission. Zenen asserted that "the married and single men lived all mixed up and did what they wished with all the women, regardless of their marital status." Fernando Huililiaset revealed that "he noticed the married couples consorting with one another, but no one knew who was married and who was not for they were all mixed up." And Leopoldo explained "that the Christians exchanged their women with the heathen, and vice versa, likewise the unmarried girls were all interchanged."[57]

Only a handful of California Indians responded to sexual and marital con-straints by murdering their spouses, assaulting the Franciscans, or organizing large-scale rebellions. Some, no doubt, submitted to Catholicism and abided by its rules and precepts; rather than flee or commit acts of violence, most Indians tried to make the best of a difficult situation and furtively sought happiness with partners other than their spouses. Nevertheless, the travails and acts of Donato at Santa Cruz, Aurelio and Tomasa of San Juan Capistrano, and the rest call atten-tion to the fundamental differences between Indian and Franciscan perceptions of marriage and sexuality and the tension and violence that often ensued.

Further evidence of the Franciscans' unceasing surveillance of the Indians' sexuality may be found in the rarity of bridal pregnancies (births by the start of the eighth elapsed month following marriage) and the few illegitimate births to baptized Indians at Mission San Carlos (Table 30). In the first decade of the mission, only 3 percent of babies were in fact conceived or born out of wed-lock.[58] In the 1790s, the incidence rose to 5 percent. Overall, of the 1,260 Indian

---

57. On the rebellion, see Hubert H. Bancroft, *History of California,* 7 vols. (San Francisco, Calif., 1884–1890), II, 527–537; James A. Sandos, "Levantamiento! The 1824 Chumash Uprising Reconsidered," *SCQ,* LVII (1985), 109–133. Sandos suggests that the revolt might have been sparked by several events, in particular the appearance of a comet and the rigor of the Lenten confession. But the rebellion began in February, a full month before the onset of Lent, when the padres heard confessions. On the men and women's living together outside the mission, see testimony given at Santa Barbara Presidio, June 1, 1824, in Sherburne F. Cook, *Expeditions to the Interior of California: Central Valley, 1820–1840,* University of California Anthropological Records, XX, no. 5, 151–214, esp. 153–154.

58. In some areas of eighteenth-century New Spain, illegitimacy rates reached nearly 50 percent of recorded births. See, for example, Thomas Calvo, "The Warmth of the Hearth: Seventeenth-Century Guadalajara Families," in Lavrin, ed., *Sexuality and Marriage,* 287–312; Twinam, *Public Lives, Private Secrets,* 12. Following a standard practice, when the Franciscans baptized a newborn infant, they would note whether the child was the legitimate offspring of sacramentally married parents. Not all children

TABLE 30. Bridal Pregnancies and Illegitimate Births, Indians, Mission San Carlos, 1772–1829

Period	Births (N)	BRIDAL PREGNANCIES		ILLEGITIMATE BIRTHS		BRIDAL PREGNANCIES AND ILLEGITIMATE BIRTHS	
		No.	% of N	No.	% of N	No.	% of N
1772–1779	87	0	0	3	3	3	3
1780–1789	257	1	0	5	2	6	2
1790–1799	332	5	2	11	3	16	5
1800–1809	214	3	1	2	1	5	2
1810–1819	210	0	0	2	1	2	1
1820–1829	160	0	0	2	1	2	1
1772–1799	676	6	1	19	3	25	4
1800–1829	584	3	1	6	1	9	2
Total	1260	9	1	25	2	34	3

Note: A bridal pregnancy is a birth that occurs by the start of the eighth elapsed month following marriage.
Source: Figures are from my database of baptisms, marriages, and burials at San Carlos compiled from the mission's registers (see Appendix A for methodology).

births to baptized parents recorded at San Carlos between 1772 and 1829, only 34, or 2.7 percent, were conceived out of wedlock. For the non-Indian population, the figure is slightly higher: 2.8 percent. Of the 34 Indian instances, 9 consisted of cases where the bride was pregnant at marriage. In another 14 recorded births, the mother was not married, and the identity of the father remained unknown to the Franciscans. Eight Indian births were clearly the result of extramarital affairs, and 3 were instances of sex between the unmarried.[59]

---

baptized at the mission were legitimate, and the recorded Indian births at the mission fell into four major categories. Legitimate children were classified as *hijo legitimo*. If the father was known and the mother was not married to him, the child was recorded as *hijo natural*. If the mother was not married and the father was not known, the child was *padre no conocido*. Finally, in some instances, the Franciscans simply noted that the newborn was *hijo de*, or "child of," and the parents were then listed. I cross-checked these parents with the marriage register and determined that some were not married; therefore, I counted their children as illegitimate even though they were not explicitly recorded by the Franciscans as such. For those children identified as *hijo de*, by comparing the children's birth dates to the parents' date of baptism and marriage, I determined whether they had been conceived out of wedlock. In two cases, when children were conceived before both parents were baptized, I did not count these births as out-of-wedlock conceptions.

59. Bridal pregnancies: San Carlos bapt. nos. 1287, 1496, 1552, 1589, 1790, 1999, 2309, 2684, 2744. Hijo natural: San Carlos bapt. nos. 962, 986, 1374, 1849, 2110, and 3249. Hijo de: San Carlos bapt. nos. 440, 567, 590, 1067, 1405, 1600, 1602, 1637, 1695, 1717, 1773, 1887, 2010, 2252, 2337, 2414, 2908, 2924, and 3216.

Obviously, not all pre- or extramarital sex culminated in pregnancy, birth, and baptism. Indians must have practiced their own methods of birth control, and there might have been an underregistration of illegitimate births. Offspring of adulterous affairs could have been invisible as children of the violated marriage. Clearly, though, recorded out-of-wedlock conceptions and births by baptized parents were quite rare at Mission San Carlos, and almost all occurred before 1800, when the population was increasing steadily with the recruitment of gentiles from the surrounding areas. Therefore, after the mid-1790s, when births at the mission began to consistently outnumber adult baptisms and when a greater percentage of the Indians of childbearing age were either mission born or longtime residents there, recorded out-of-wedlock conceptions and births became even more exceptional. Although we will never know for certain why the overall rates of illegitimacy were so low at San Carlos, the phenomenon does suggest that the Franciscans were increasingly successful—either by instruction or by punishment—in enforcing their own notions of marriage and sexuality at Mission San Carlos. Or, perhaps just as likely, Indians simply became more skilled at hiding or masking their intimate lives.[60]

CHANGES IN AGE AND MARITAL STATUS OF MARRIAGE PARTNERS

The missionaries and the environment they fostered also seem to have effected equally important but far less visible changes in marriage patterns. Clearly, men and women at the mission often married at an earlier age than most in premission society. At San Carlos, the average age of first marriage for mission-born women was about fifteen; more than half married at age fifteen or younger. By comparison, outside of the mission, few had married before age sixteen: one younger than thirteen renewed a marriage, and only four of forty-four women baptized between ages thirteen to fifteen were already married.

Indian women born in native villages but raised at the mission also married younger than those who lived beyond San Carlos. And the padres quickly forced their model of marriage on women who came to the mission as adults; nearly all married within four months of baptism, just about enough time for Franciscans to find them a partner, perform the premarital investigations, and read the banns three times. For men, the story is the same, although in every category of analysis men married for the first time later than women.

The low age of first marriage in the mission compared to outside may have

---

60. Of course, the low rate of illegitimacy must also be related to Indian notions of marriage and sexuality.

TABLE 31. Marital Status of Indian Brides and Grooms,
Mission San Carlos, 1772–1832, Part 1

Period	No. Marrying	Renewing Marriages	Solteras and Solteros Marrying	Viudas and Viudos Marrying
1772–1779	270	128	120	22
1780–1789	428	120	202	106
1790–1799	342	58	208	76
1800–1809	294	20	138	136
1810–1819	142	0	70	72
1820–1829	82	0	34	48
1830–1832	30	0	21	9
1772–1799	1,040	306	530	204
1800–1832	548	20	263	265
Total	1,588	326	793	469

Note: Solteras and solteros are men and women never married before at the mission. Viudas and viudos are
widows and widowers.
Source: Figures are from my database of baptisms, marriages, and burials at San Carlos compiled from the
mission's registers (see Appendix A for methodology).

several causes. Franciscans no doubt pressured the young to marry early so as to prevent premarital sexual relations and out-of-wedlock births. Yet more than Franciscan pressure was probably at work. The exceptionally high mortality of women increased competition among men for brides and thereby drove down the age of first marriage for women. The young marriage age for women might also have been an explicit response to the instability of the mission population. Some might have taken spouses at a tender age after disease had left them orphaned or with little extended family. Moreover, perhaps Indians were coupling younger to knit together the imperiled village communities that now lived closely with one another at the mission and to overcome the high mortality and low fertility that were eroding those same communities. Such a strategy, however, might have been counterproductive, since pregnant young women often develop complications that impair, if not destroy, their ability to conceive.

The missionary program and Indians' high rate of mortality also altered the composition of couples. At San Carlos, high adult mortality meant that unions did not last very long; the average duration was just eight years. As diseases held down the number of children who survived to marriageable age, the number of single Indians entering wedlock further decreased. Therefore, marriages increasingly involved widowers and widows, not single men and single women. In marriages between 1772 and 1779, the previously unmarried outnumbered the wid-

TABLE 32. Marital Status of Indian Brides and Grooms,
Mission San Carlos, 1772–1832, Part 2

			MARITAL STATUS OF GROOM AND BRIDE			
Period	All Marriages of Indians (N)	Renewal of Gentile Marriages	*Soltero-Soltera*	*Viudo-Soltera*	*Soltero-Viuda*	*Viudo-Viuda*
			Proportion of N			
1772–1779	135	47%	41%	5%	2%	4%
1780–1789	214	28	32	17	13	10
1790–1799	171	17	46	19	11	7
1800–1809	147	7	36	16	6	35
1810–1819	71	0	32	20	14	34
1820–1829	41	0	34	7	7	51
1830–1832	15	0	53	33	0	13
1772–1799	520	29	39	15	9	8
1800–1832	274	4	36	16	8	36
Total	794	21%	38%	15%	9%	17%

Note: Solteras and *solteros* are women and men never married before at the mission. *Viudas* and *viudos* are widows and widowers. Percentages may total less than 100 percent because of rounding.

Source: Figures are from my database of baptisms, marriages, and burials at San Carlos compiled from the mission's registers (see Appendix A for methodology).

owed by nearly 6:1. Between 1790 and 1799, the ratio dropped to almost 3:1 (Table 31). From 1800 to 1809, a nearly equal number of single and widowed Indians married, but, in the following two decades, more widows and widowers wedded than singles. Clearly, adult human relationships at the missions in the wake of the dual revolutions were increasingly short-lived, temporary, and unstable.

All of these changes diversely affected the sexes and successive generations. First of all, more widowers than widows remarried, and more widowers remarried single women than widows remarried single men (Table 32). And more single women than single men married, despite their even number. At San Carlos, 41 percent of all new marriages involved widowers; only 33 percent involved widows (Table 33).[61] Since women were far more likely than men to die in early

61. At the end of 1796, there were seventy-five single men and seventy-three single women, according to a list of Indians at the mission; see Macario de Castro, comp., *Padrón,* Dec. 31, 1796, LDS film 0909228. For the seven northern California missions (including San Carlos) studied by Cook and Borah, the figures are similar: 41 percent of all new marriages involved widowers, and only 30 percent involved widows ("Vital Statistics," chap. 3 in *Essays in Population History,* III, *Mexico and California,* table 3.10a, 288).

TABLE 33. Marital Status of Indian Brides and Grooms,
Mission San Carlos, 1772–1832, Part 3

	GROOMS				
Period	No. Marrying (N)	Renewing Marriages (% of N)	Solteros and Viudos Marrying (n)	Solteros (% of N/ % of n)	Viudos (% of N/ % of n)
1772–1779	135	47	71	43/82	10/18
1780–1789	214	28	154	45/62	27/38
1790–1799	171	17	142	57/68	26/32
1800–1809	147	7	137	42/45	51/55
1810–1819	71	0	71	46/46	54/54
1820–1829	41	0	41	41/41	59/59
1830–1832	15	0	15	53/53	47/47
1772–1799	520	29	367	48/68	22/32
1800–1832	274	4	264	44/45	53/55
Total	794	21	631	47/59	33/41

	BRIDES				
Period	No. Marrying (N)	Renewing Marriages (% of N)	Solteras and Viudas Marrying (n)	Solteras (% of N/ % of n)	Viudas (% of N/ % of n)
1772–1779	135	47	71	46/87	7/13
1780–1789	214	28	154	50/69	22/31
1790–1799	171	17	142	65/78	18/22
1800–1809	147	7	137	52/55	41/45
1810–1819	71	0	71	52/52	48/48
1820–1829	41	0	41	41/41	59/59
1830–1832	15	0	15	87/87	13/13
1772–1799	520	29	367	54/76	17/24
1800–1832	274	4	264	52/54	44/46
Total	794	21	631	53/67	26/33

Note: Solteras and solteros are men and women never married before at the mission. Viudas and viudos are widows and widowers.

Source: Figures are from my database of baptisms, marriages, and burials at San Carlos compiled from the mission's registers (see Appendix A for methodology).

TABLE 34. Remarriage according to Age of *Viudas* and *Viudos* at Death of Spouse, Indians, Mission San Carlos, 1772–1832

Age of *Viudas* and *Viudos* at Death of Spouse	FREQUENCY OF REMARRIAGE PER 1000	
	Men	Women
to 30 years	752	288
30–39	823	462
40–49	550	286
50–59	231	286
60–69	300	333
70+	0	0
Total	664	329

Note: Viudas and *viudos* are widows and widowers. This table shows rates of remarriage by age group, not actual numbers of viudos and viudas who remarried. For example, viudos ages twenty-nine and under remarried at a rate of 752 per thousand, whereas viudas ages sixty to sixty-nine remarried at a rate of 333 per thousand.

Source: Figures are from my database of baptisms, marriages, and burials at San Carlos compiled from the mission's registers (see Appendix A for methodology). Calculations performed by CASOAR Program CM4.

adulthood—given the dangers associated with pregnancy—it makes sense that there would be more men remarrying than women. As a result, single men competed for brides (it seems often unsuccessfully) against older widowers, whose age and status might have given them an advantage. In native society, junior men had probably always fared poorly against seniors for brides, especially with the existence of polygyny for the powerful. Senior men of high status who somehow survived diseases might have gained several wives, but only serially; in the missions, the most they could hope for was a quick remarriage after they were widowed. For junior men in the missions, the prospect of never marrying was especially real, since so many women were dying young. Spanish customs and Franciscan practices, and perhaps Indian beliefs as well, discriminated against older women, especially those at the end of or beyond childbearing age. At San Carlos, only 33 percent of widows remarried, whereas 66 percent of widowers did so (Table 34). All of these patterns—notably, the very low age of first marriage, the increasing number of unions composed of widows and widowers, and the greater competition for brides—are as ironic as they are unfortunate, given the Franciscans' belief that instituting missions and enforcing Catholic notions of marriage and sexuality would bring enduring relationships and stable communities.

CROSS-CULTURAL SEXUAL RELATIONS

In colonial California, as in other regions of New Spain, marriage and sexuality crossed community, racial, and ethnic boundaries and encompassed relations between Indian women and Spanish soldiers and settlers. In understanding these mixed unions, it is worth remembering that they brought together individuals more alike than racial or ethnic categories might suggest. Nearly all the gente de razón who married Indian women were themselves offspring of mixed unions. Yet, in Alta California, interracial or interethnic relationships nonetheless often emerged out of a range of conflicting and inconsistent motivations and were sometimes characterized by stealth, coercion, and violence.

The Children of Coyote had frequently looked outside of their own villages or communities for marriage partners, and the motivations of women for wedding soldiers might have been consistent with the precontact practice of marrying for political or economic reasons. In marrying soldiers, Indian women might have hoped to create kinship ties that could provide access to Spanish goods and soften the harsh realities of conquest. Some San Carlos women who married soldiers were from leadership families, and their unions might have helped their families maintain positions of authority. Of the eleven weddings at San Carlos before 1800 that joined soldiers and Indian women, at least three involved sisters or daughters of Indian officials or village captains. Three more involved sisters-in-law of mission Indian officials, and one, a woman who was a more distant relative of an Indian official. Franciscans sometimes encouraged these marriages to prevent illicit sexual relations between soldiers and Indians and promote community stability.[62]

Soldiers most likely married Indian women for economic reasons and because there were few other available women. Soldiers who married neophytes could acquire land and animals to support their families and gain permanent assign-

---

62. On precontact marriage patterns, see Randall Milliken, "Monterey Region Ethnography," chap. 2 in Stephen A. Dietz, Thomas L. Jackson, et al., *Final Report of Archaeological Excavations at Nineteen Archaeological Sites for the Stage 1 Pacific Grove–Monterey Consolidation Project of the Regional Sewerage System,* I (Berkeley, Calif., 1981), esp. 80–86. On rates of intermarriage in Alta California, see Castañeda, "Engendering History," in Gutiérrez and Orsi, eds., *Contested Eden,* 230–259, esp. 238–241. The three high-status marriages are Athanasio Joseph's daughter Cathalina María Islas (San Carlos bapt. no. 29) to Joseph Joachim de Espinosa (San Carlos marr. no. 154) and then to the soldier Antonio María Alegre (San Carlos marr. no. 197); and Felis Juan Ranchero's daughter María Beatris (San Carlos bapt. no. 63) to the soldier José Vicente Gonzales (San Carlos marr. no. 405). The soldier Domingo Aruz married María Seraphina (San Carlos bapt. no. 69), a distant relative of Nestor José (San Carlos bapt. no. 1729, marr. no. 181); soldier Antonio Yorba married María de Gracia (San Carlos bapt. no. 99), who was a sister-in-law of Baltazar (San Carlos bapt. no. 268, marr. no. 182); the sailor/servant Tomás María Camacho married Tecla María (San Carlos bapt. no. 82), a sister-in-law of Carlos Juan (San Carlos bapt. no. 79, marr. no. 183); and the soldier Marcos Villela married Viridiana María, the sister-in-law of Eusebio Joseph Saueyom (bapt. no. 731, marr. no. 334).

ment to their wife's mission. This policy was in effect by the early 1770s, when six of the first eleven soldiers who married at Monterey took Indian brides. Importantly, there were no Hispanic women in Alta California before 1774. And, for decades, non-Indian women were in short supply: there were seven unmarried men for every unmarried Hispanic woman in 1790. Moreover, of the twenty-one unmarried adult women in Spanish California in 1790, not all were suitable mates: four were only fourteen years old and twelve were widows, seven of whom were older than forty.[63]

For some Indian women, marriage into soldier society brought great complications, further discontinuities, and, one imagines, few benefits. Cathalina María of San Carlos experienced the extreme disruption that could accompany this type of union. She was baptized at San Carlos in 1772, when she was fifteen years old. Two weeks later, she married Fernando Joseph, a young orphan from the village of Tucutnut whom Serra was grooming as an interpreter. Their marriage—odd as it must have seemed to all—was the first Catholic marriage performed at San Carlos. Four years later, the couple had a child, but Fernando Joseph died in the spring of 1780. Two months later, Cathalina María married a soldier, Joseph Joachim de Espinosa from Sinaloa. Espinosa, however, lived only long enough for the couple to produce a child. In September 1782, shortly after Espinosa's death, Cathalina María married Antonio María Alegre, a forty-two-year-old soldier born in Italy. By 1790, the couple, along with their daughter Vicenta Anastacia, was living in San Jose. But it seems that their marriage was less than perfect. In early 1790, Cathalina María had taken up with Francisco Avila, a widowed soldier who also lived in the pueblo. Avila, however, spent most of 1790 in jail not only because of his dalliance with Cathalina María but because the authorities accused him of a "bestial" crime.[64]

In August 1775, after six soldiers had married women from San Carlos and produced children, Serra wrote with enthusiasm that these families formed the

63. Serra to Antonio María de Bucareli y Ursúa, Mar. 13, 1773, Mexico City, in Tibesar, ed., *Writings of Serra*, I, 325. These marriages occurred between 1773 and 1779. Bucareli sent word that he approved the granting of land and animals to soldiers who married local Indian women (Bucareli to commander of Monterey, Sept. 21, 1774, Archives of California, C–A 1, 91, BL). For figures, see Tables 2 and 3. On the small numbers of Spanish and Mexican women in Alta California, see Castañeda, "Engendering History," in Gutiérrez and Orsi, eds., *Contested Eden*, 238–241; Hernández, "No Settlement without Women," *SCQ*, LXXII (1990), 203–233.

64. Cathalina María Islas, San Carlos bapt. no. 29; Fernando Joseph, San Carlos bapt. no. 16; San Carlos marr. nos. 1 (Nov. 10, 1772), 154 (May 8, 1780), and 197 (Sept. 30, 1782); William Marvin Mason, *The Census of 1790: A Demographic History of Colonial California* (Menlo Park, Calif., 1998), 100; Fages, inspection of California presented to José Antonio Roméu, Feb. 26, 1791, Archives of California, C–A 6, 152–169, esp. par. 21, BL. Despite his tender age, Fernando was one of the oldest males baptized at San Carlos at that time, and, despite her relative youth, Cathalina María was the oldest local Indian at the mission. On Fernando Joseph's age (eleven or twelve), see Serra to Palóu, June 21, 1771, Monterey, in Tibesar, ed. and trans., *Writings of Serra*, I, 241–243.

"beginnings of a town." Yet, despite the number of unions between soldiers and Indian women in the first decade of Spanish colonization, they proved exceptional during the colonial period. And the communities that eventually emerged in Monterey, San Jose, Los Angeles, and elsewhere in California were not the product of such intermarriages. At Mission San Carlos, for example, between 1770 and 1833, there were only thirteen marriages between soldiers and mission women. Most took place in the first fifteen years of the mission, when there were few unmarried Spanish women and definite economic incentives for soldiers to marry Indians. By 1790, the padres seem to have scuttled their earlier plan, as Father Lasuén made clear in his opposition to the retired soldier Francisco Cayuelas's receiving mission land after he married a woman from San Luis Obispo. Soldiers who married Indian women could no longer expect land or animals to help them support themselves. With the removal of incentives for intermarriage, followed by the presence of more single Spanish women after the mid-1790s, marriages between Indians and soldiers all but disappeared. Between 1797 and 1823, there were none at San Carlos and only two between 1824 and 1833. Less than 10 percent of all soldier marriages during the mission period at San Carlos involved Indians, and, of course, an even smaller percentage of all Indian marriages involved soldiers.[65]

More common than marriage between soldiers and Indian women was illicit sex. Indian women might have slept with soldiers for the same reasons that they married them: to create advantageous kinship ties and to improve their family's economic lives. On occasion, they went to the presidios to have sex and receive food or other goods in return. In some cases, these women were married, and their husbands were well aware of this sexual commerce. One Spaniard observed that some men had "become pimps, even for their own wives, for any miserable profit." Although the Franciscans branded as prostitutes Indian women who traded sex for material goods and considered such activities an indication of depravity, the Indians' encounters are more appropriately understood as a measure of their material impoverishment and the desperate conditions they faced in the missions.[66]

In 1808, one such extramarital sexual relationship with an important variation came to light at Mission San Diego. During the investigation of the murder of the

---

65. Serra to Bucareli, Aug. 24, 1775, Monterey, in Tibesar, ed., *Writings of Serra*, II, 151. At the mission, another twelve marriages joined Baja California Indian men and San Carlos women. For Lasuén's comments, see Lasuén to Fages, July 26, 1790, Mission San Antonio de Padua, in Kenneally, ed. and trans., *Writings of Lasuén*, I, 205–207. See also José Pérez-Fernández to Borica, Apr. 30, 1795, San Francisco, Archives of California, C–A 7, 369, BL.

66. Lesley Byrd Simpson, ed. and trans., *Journal of José Longinos Martínez: Notes and Observations of the Naturalist of the Botanical Expedition in Old and New California and the South Coast, 1791–1792* (San Francisco, Calif., 1961), 55. For padres' comments branding these Indian women as depraved, see Tapis and Cortés, Oct. 30, 1800, Mission Santa Barbara, AGN, PI, CCXVI, expediente 1, 84b.

mission's cruel Spanish labor foreman, numerous Indians testified that the mayordomo had repeatedly given María Cecilia, an Indian woman at the mission— not her husband—watermelon, meat, and corn flour in return for sexual favors. María Cecilia's husband, Fermín, who had been beaten by the mayordomo and participated in his murder, approved of this arrangement. According to María Cecilia, Fermín not only told her when to go to the mayordomo but witnessed and profited from their sexual encounters, eating with his wife "all that the mayordomo had given her." María Cecilia, in accepting payments from the soldier, transformed what would previously have been her husband's expected compensation into an economic asset for the household. This traditional practice of indemnities persisted into the mission period, as revealed in the previously examined case where Juan José paid Aurelio so that he could carry on an affair with Tomasa, Aurelio's wife. But, when soldiers were involved in casual and illicit sexual relations with married Indian women, the terms of the equation shifted, and the payment went to the wife, not the cuckolded husband. Such an exchange brought more than food into the home of María Cecilia and Fermín; it challenged household boundaries, certainly as they were constructed by the Franciscans who married the Indian couple and perhaps also as they would have normally been seen by the Indians themselves. One can see in María Cecilia's sexual relations with the mayordomo a desperate attempt to forge a kinship bond between her family and the labor foreman, a tie that she and Fermín perhaps thought would lead to an end of the soldier's abuse of her husband. When the mayordomo continued his beatings in spite of María Cecilia's overtures, Fermín and several others shot him full of arrows and bludgeoned him to death.[67]

The governors repeatedly issued regulations criminalizing illicit sexual relations between Indians and soldiers, but the paucity of non-Indian women all but ensured that soldiers would seek out Indians for sex. In the early 1770s, any soldier who had an *acto carnal* with an Indian woman, even if she consented, could be forced to perform extra burdensome guard duty for nine consecutive days. And soldiers were repeatedly forbidden to go to native villages without permission. Decrees, however, did not prevent rogues from venturing into Indian villages for sexual liaisons or from having sexual relations with women at the missions. The shortage of unmarried female gente de razón through the close of the eighteenth century meant that not all soldiers could marry, and even those who did remained single through adolescence and much of their early adulthood. Marriage was exceptional for soldiers and male settlers under age twenty-

67. Testimony of María Josefa, "Causa criminal contra tres indios neófitos de la misión de San Diego por la muerte que dieron a su mayordomo," 1809, AGN, CA, LXII, 60. Three Indian men were convicted of the murder, one of whom was María Cecilia's husband, who stated that it was the mayordomo's beatings, not his sexual contact with María Cecilia, that led them to kill.

five; fewer than two in every ten were married in 1790. Given this situation, for most soldiers, having sex meant doing so outside of marriage.[68]

On occasion, Spanish officials punished soldiers and servants who had illicit relationships with neophyte women. In 1774, the soldier Agustín Castelo was arrested and shipped to the port of San Blas, charged with dereliction of duty and having a relationship with a married woman at San Carlos. As we shall see, Castelo already had a record as a sexual predator. In this case, he denied shirking his duties but admitted the relationship. Castelo, however, claimed that he was being singled out for retribution and that other soldiers had suffered only a week in prison for similar deeds. In 1777, after a successful appeal to the viceroy, Castelo was vindicated of all charges except the liaison, and he returned to California and regained his previous rank. Castelo, however, was warned that he would be severely punished if he did it again.[69]

Although Castelo's ordeal might have led some to hesitate before becoming involved with Indian women, his ultimate vindication suggests that soldiers' illicit sexual relations were not taken very seriously by authorities. Spanish officials continued to issue prohibitions of illicit acts, yet the activities continued, and only rarely were soldiers punished. In July 1785, Governor Pedro Fages reissued an order that soldiers must not behave scandalously and that those who did must be "severely punished." And, in 1796, because of the ineffectiveness of previous regulations, the governor increased the punishment to several months' hard labor. This decree, too, was flouted, and in 1802 another soldier was put in shackles because he had abandoned his post for an Indian village adjacent to the mission.[70]

The governors' tough talk must have been viewed with mounting skepticism by soldiers, especially after Governor Fages's own wife accused him of an affair with a

68. One of the most common punishments for soldiers was the wearing of multiple *cueras*, the thick leather jackets that they wore for protection against the Indians' arrows. See, for example, the instructions signed by Governor Fages for soldiers at San Diego, 1773, AGN, PI, CCXI, 341a–344b; Fages, "General Orders to be Observed by the Sergeant of the Guard at the New Mission of Purísima Concepción," Apr. 7, 1788, San Gabriel, Archives of California, C–A 4, 206–211, BL. The prohibition of soldiers from entering villages was reiterated throughout the colonial period. See, for example, Felipe de Neve's "Instructions to the Commander of the Presidio of Santa Barbara and the Sergeant of the Escorts of Purísima Concepción and San Buenaventura," San Gabriel, Mar. 6, 1782, AGN, CA, LXI, 106a–116b, esp. 110b–111a. In 1790, 90 percent of adult women in Alta California were married (Table 3), whereas only 57 percent of adult males were married. Here, "adult" is defined as "age thirteen and older."

69. "Expediente formado a consecuencia de las diligencias practicadas por el capitán don Fernando de Rivera y Moncada contra el soldado Agustín Castelo. . . ," AGN, Criminal, CCCLXXVIII, expediente 2, 27a–43a; Bucareli to Felipe de Neve, Mar. 5, 1777, Mexico, Archives of California, C–A 1, 222, BL. Castelo spent three years trying to recover his post and his personal belongings, seized upon his arrest. On the Spanish practice of confiscating a defendant's goods to ensure payment of any fines or court fees, see Charles R. Cutter, *The Legal Culture of Northern New Spain, 1700–1810* (Albuquerque, N.Mex., 1995), 119.

70. Fages to José Joaquín de Arrillaga, July 1, 1785, Monterey, California File, HM, doc. 16581, HL; [Borica] to the presidial commanders, Apr. 11, 1796, Monterey, Archives of California, C–A 23, 421–422, BL; extract of diary of Raymundo Carrillo, May 17, 1802, Monterey, Archives of California, C–A 11, 205, BL.

young Indian girl. In the fall of 1784, Fages and his wife Eulalia had begun to feud over whether they would reside permanently in California. To punish Fages and persuade him to take her and her children out of California, Eulalia had banished him from their bedroom. After several months of sleeping away from Eulalia, Fages showed no signs of capitulating, and Eulalia became suspicious that he was taking someone else to bed. Early one morning, Eulalia claimed to have caught him about to engage in sex with a young Yuman servant girl who was living in their home at the presidio. Enraged, Eulalia told everyone within earshot of her husband's infidelities. Surely such a spectacle undermined the governor's half-hearted attempts to prevent such behavior among his own troops.[71]

Whereas some women, like María Cecilia, extracted payment from soldiers and settlers in return for sexual favors, others were simply raped. In the early 1770s, at the very outset of the colonial period, three soldiers at San Diego—Agustín Castelo, Juan María Ruiz, and José Marcelino Bravo—raped several women and then tried to purchase their silence and that of José Antonio, a witness, with tortillas and ribbons. Farther north, just after the establishment of Mission San Gabriel in the fall of 1771, soldiers raped the wife of a Gabrielino chief. Indian women and their communities responded in various ways to these assaults. In the early 1770s, having heard about the soldiers' attacks, all but the most aged Indians of the San Diego region abandoned their villages when the Franciscans and their military escort approached. Doubtless, most cases of rape went unreported, but, in a risky move, some Indians brought these crimes to the attention of the Franciscans. After the rapes in San Diego, the victims and the witness told Father Luís Jayme what had happened. In an act of revenge and in an attempt to prevent José Antonio from telling his story again, the soldiers placed him in the stocks until Jayme could win his release.[72]

Rape and the fear of it were yet another terrible burden for women and their families, all of whom were already struggling to make order out of the chaos that accompanied Spanish settlement. According to Hugo Reid, an Anglo-American settler who married a woman from Mission San Gabriel in the late 1830s, the effects of the soldiers' attacks lingered for years. Indian women "became accustomed to these things, but their disgust and abhorrence never left them till many years after." Some who became pregnant had to confront not only the trauma of the assault but the shame they associated with bearing a child out of wedlock. Catholicism's strict linking of marriage and sexuality could have only

71. Bancroft, *History of California,* I, 389–393; Donald Nuttall, "The Señoras Gobernadoras of Spanish Alta California, a Comparative Study," Santa Barbara Trust for Historic Preservation, Occasional Papers (Santa Barbara, Calif., 1998), 17–25. It is likely that the young girl was María del Carmen, a Yuman who married at San Carlos during the crisis (San Carlos marr. no. 290, Mar. 2, 1785).

72. Geiger, ed., *Letter of Luís Jayme,* 40, 46–48; William McCawley, *The First Angelinos: The Gabrielino Indians of Los Angeles* (Novato, Calif., 1996), 189–190.

intensified the emotional burdens that accompanied rape. Some women, to the horror of the Franciscans, tried to abort these pregnancies; if their efforts failed, some committed infanticide rather than raise these unwanted children.[73]

Although many attacks on women went unpunished, military officials did not always look the other way. In the spring of 1773, Governor Fages pressed charges against three soldiers for raping three gentile girls, one of whom died afterward. But the prosecution of the crime was lackluster, and the case fell apart when the governor found the investigation deficient because the victims had not testified and the accused had not received adequate legal counsel. Decades later, the military investigated charges by Veneranda, a woman from Mission Soledad who testified that she had been imprisoned at the Monterey Presidio and raped daily by members of the infantry. According to Egidio, who was imprisoned in an adjacent cell, Veneranda told him that the commander of the presidio had informed her that he was selling her to the soldiers. Eventually, with the help of Egidio, Veneranda escaped. The two made their way back to Mission Soledad, where they took refuge in the mission church and related her terrible ordeal. The historical record is silent on whether the infantrymen were found guilty of assaulting Veneranda and, if so, what sort of punishments they received.[74]

Military regulations prescribed a death sentence for a soldier who raped a woman who was "honorable, married, widowed, or a maiden." However, Indian women, in the eyes of many Spaniards, had no honor to lose. Therefore, on the rare occasions when gente de razón were found guilty of raping Indian women, they faced far less severe punishment than if their victims had been gente de razón. In 1789, a settler spent just twenty days in prison for raping a gentile woman and for neglecting his fields; it is not clear which crime the authorities considered more serious. Similarly, Serapio Zuñiga, the son of a mulato from Guadalajara and a neophyte from San Juan Capistrano, was sentenced to only six months for raping an Indian girl. And military authorities at San Diego sentenced José Antonio Tapia to just six months' labor at the presidio for raping a married Indian woman. Clearly, this leniency did little to discourage soldiers' attacks and only reinforced the belief that crimes against Indian women were not serious.[75]

73. Robert F. Heizer, ed., *The Indians of Los Angeles County: Hugo Reid's Letters of 1852*, Southwest Museum Papers, no. 21 (Los Angeles, 1968), 70; Geiger, ed., *Letter of Luís Jayme*, 42–44.

74. "Representación de don Pedro Fages sobre el estupro violento que cometieron los tres soldados," Apr. 14, 1773, San Diego, and "Causa criminal contra Francisco Abila, Sebastian de Alvitre y Mateo de Zoto . . . ," AGN, CA, II, part 1, expedientes 6, 7, 243a–252b, 253a–292b; fragment of military investigation, 1820, Taylor Coll., doc. 1112, HL.

75. Félix Colón de Larriátegui, *Juzgados militares de España y sus indias*, 4 vols. (Madrid, 1797), IV, 362; Gutiérrez, *When Jesus Came*, 176–240; Felipe Goycoechea to Fages, May 7, 1789, Santa Barbara, Archives of California, C–A 5, 109–110, BL; [Arrillaga] to presidial commander at Santa Barbara, Feb. 15, 1805, Loreto, Archives of California, C–A 26, 105–106, BL; Santiago Argüello, juez fiscal, July 14, 1818, San Diego, Archives of California, C–A 17, 250–252, BL.

Sexual assaults on Indian women must be viewed within a larger cultural context in which Spanish men frequently took sexual liberties with most women. Soldiers in California, therefore, did not limit their illicit sexual relationships or assaults to Indian women. Once there were other women in California and once soldiers began to raise families, some had sex with the wives and daughters of their comrades.[76] And, throughout the Spanish and Mexican periods, some soldiers beat and sexually assaulted their own wives and daughters. Not surprisingly, military officials punished these crimes more severely and prosecuted the offenders more thoroughly than if their victims had been Indian. Perversely, female Indians might have been the beneficiaries of the sexual aggression upon Spanish women: if the Franciscans' correspondence and the surviving judicial records from the colonial period are any indication, the soldiers' sexual assaults on native women were far more common at the outset of colonial rule than during its wane. Thus, by the 1820s, Indian and Spanish lives were deeply intertwined even at these most intimate and tragic moments.[77]

76. Gutiérrez, *When Jesus Came,* 208–226; Castañeda, "Engendering History," in Gutiérrez and Orsi, eds., *Contested Eden,* 232. See also the following instances of adultery: (Marcelo Pinto) José Darío Argüello to Fages, Nov. 26, 1788, San Francisco, Archives of California, C–A 4, 250, BL; (Mariano Castro) José Moraga to Fages, Dec. 23, 1784, San Francisco, Archives of California, C–A 3, 112, BL; (Luís Peralta) Fages to Moraga, Sept. 17, 1783, San Francisco, Archives of California, C–A 23, 202, BL; (Cabo José Castillo) [Pablo Vicente de Solá] to Captain Moraga, Sept. 11, 1821, Monterey, C–A 26, 68, BL; (unnamed soldier) [Arrillaga] to commander of Santa Barbara Presidio, June 7, 1803, Loreto, C–A 26, 96, BL; (Salvador Amesquita) [Arrillaga] to commander at Monterey, Nov. 15, 1809, C–A 26, 219, BL; (Ventura and Juan Manuel Zuñiga) Javier Alvarado, Oct. 3, 1806, Los Angeles, C–A 16, 301, BL; (Anastacia Zuñiga and José Antonio Ramirez) Solá to José de la Guerra, Oct. 3, 1818, Monterey, C–A 17, 205–206, BL; (Domingo Peralta) *sumaria* signed by Solá, Dec. 6, 1821, Monterey, C–A 17, 334, BL; (José Higuera) causa criminal, Antonio Buelna, fiscal, Jan. 3, 1824, San Jose, C–A 18, 113, BL.

77. Regarding harsher punishments for crimes against Spanish women: the soldier José Ignacio Lugo was sentenced to two years' hard labor for merely attempting to sexually assault an eight-year-old Spanish girl (José Joaquín Maitorena, juez, July 12, 1821, Santa Barbara, Archives of California, C–A 17, 349, BL). José Castillo was sentenced to six years' presidial labor for the rape of his sister-in-law (Ignacio Martínez, fiscal, May 5, 1821, Archives of California, C–A 17, 348–349, BL).

Castañeda suggests that there was a "low incidence of sexual violence toward Spanish and mestiza women in colonial California" and calls for more research on the issue ("Engendering History," in Gutiérrez and Orsi, eds., *Contested Eden,* 251). For examples that suggest otherwise, see the following cases. Rape: (José J. Contreras accused of raping wife of soldier J. Maldonado) Borica to commander of San Francisco Presidio, June 9, 1796, Archives of California, C–A 24, 88, BL; (Hilario García accused of raping a married woman) Ignacio del Valle, "Causa por violación de una casada," Apr. 24, 1839, Santa Barbara, Archives of California, C–A 20, 364, BL; (Ignacio Herrera accused of raping a five-year-old girl) Luís Antonio Argüello, commander of San Francisco Presidio, to José María de Echeandía, Archives of California, C–A 18, 407–414, BL. Incest: (Bernardo Ramírez) José Joaquín Maitorena, "Causa criminal de un soldado inválido por incestuoso con su hija," Feb. 12, 1810, Archives of California, C–A 17, 30–31, BL; (José Rosalino Fernández) Goycoechea to [Borica], Jan. 22, 1799, Santa Barbara, Archives of California, C–A 54, 123, BL; (Ventura Zuñiga) Solá to Lieutenant Manuel Gómez, June 12, 1822, Monterey, Archives of California, C–A 18, 8–65, BL; (Vicente Quijada) trial by José Raymundo Carrillo, commander of Santa Barbara Presidio, Nov. 28, 1806, Archives of California, C–A 16, 342–356, BL. Chavez examines patriarchy and violence toward women in Mexican Los Angeles in " 'Pongo Mi Demanda,' " in Matsumoto and Allmendinger, eds., *Over the Edge,* 272–290.

6

SOCIAL CONTROL, POLITICAL
ACCOMMODATION, AND INDIAN REBELLION

In colonial California, the Children of Coyote and the missionaries of Saint Francis could not reconcile their understandings of marriage and sexuality, and the result was frustration, resistance, and, in some cases, even violence. But a different and countervailing process unfolded in the realms of social control and political organization: native leaders and institutions actually meshed with colonial practices and imperatives as Indian leaders helped to hold the missions together. The filterings, accommodations, and negotiations of power that would characterize politics in the missions were not in play when Gaspar de Portolá and Junípero Serra reached Monterey in 1770 and claimed authority over California and its people through European rituals of possession. But, later, when Spanish military and religious officials exercised authority over Indians, they could not afford to rely upon ceremony and proclamation alone, even in the wake of the dual revolutions' upending of native society. Their small numbers and limited resources drove them to more practical and cooperative measures, for each mission had on average two missionaries and a military guard of four or five soldiers. Spaniards, therefore, looked to established Indian leaders to help organize and regulate the missions' life and work just as some Indian leaders stepped forward in an attempt to shape the emerging colonial system.[1]

By the late eighteenth century, Indians' enlistment in their own subjugation

---

1. When they first reached the Indies, Spaniards sought legitimacy by unfurling banners carrying the symbols of the Kingdom of Castile and the pope. Later, from 1513 to 1573, they read to uncomprehending New World peoples the *Requerimiento,* a brief statement that gave Indians the option of recognizing the supremacy of Castile and accepting Christian missionaries or facing warfare and enslavement. For the text of the *Requerimiento,* see Charles Gibson, ed., *The Spanish Tradition in America* (New York, 1968), 58–60. In 1573, after decades of debate about the violent nature of Spanish expansion, the *Requerimiento* was replaced by the *Ordinances for the Discovery, New Settlement and Pacification of the Indies,* a document that spoke of pacification, not conquest. A translation of these regulations can be found in Daniel J. Garr, ed., *Hispanic Urban Planning in North America,* Spanish Borderlands Sourcebooks, XXVII (New York, 1991), 3–33.

dovetailed with the Bourbon state's desire to allow them a measure of self-governance within the Spanish colonial order. Indians chose their own officials through annual elections, instituted and directed by Spaniards, thereby enabling Spanish authorities to rule Indians through Indians. This pattern is visible at Mission San Carlos and demonstrates a complex interplay of Indian and Spanish priorities. Though hierarchical in form, the system was flexible in operation and based upon mutual accommodation. Indian officials not only served the needs of missionaries and military leaders, but they also protected the interests of their own communities and, in some cases, rebelled against the Spanish order. For, as the padres quickly learned, Indian leaders could modify and subvert colonial objectives as well as implement them. Thus the Spaniards' use of and dependence on Indian officials reveal a paradox: indirect rule not only allowed Spaniards to reshape Indian lives, but it also provided Indians with the means and the personnel to retain control over certain aspects of their communities, in some areas long after the collapse of colonial rule.[2]

SPANISH MUNICIPAL GOVERNMENT AND THE "REPUBLIC OF INDIANS"

The political system Indians encountered in California missions emerged during Spain's reconquest of the Iberian peninsula and over two and a half centuries of New World colonization. In the reconquest, the *municipio* (township) became the principal vehicle through which new territories were settled and secured, and, in the New World, it became the primary form of local Spanish political organization.[3] In areas settled by Spain, formal attachment to a municipality was not an

2. Scholars have maintained that Indian officials in California derived their authority from the Spaniards, not from their own people, and acted as overseers, not community representatives; they have interpreted the actions of Indian officials with little knowledge of who they were or how they fitted into their native communities. In their work, the identities of officials often become insignificant because the mission is described as a polarized "plural institution," composed of two antagonistic groups: Indians and Spaniards. See, for example, George Phillips, "The Alcaldes: Indian Leadership in the Spanish Missions of California," in *The Struggle for Political Autonomy: Papers and Comments from the Second Newberry Library Conference on Themes in American Indian History* (Chicago, 1989), 83–89; Edward D. Castillo, "The Other Side of the 'Christian Curtain': California Indians and the Missionaries," *The Californians: The Magazine of California History*, X (1992), 8–17; Robert L. Hoover, "Spanish-Native Interaction and Acculturation in the Alta California Missions," in *CC*, I. For an alternate view, see Steven W. Hackel, "The Staff of Leadership: Indian Authority in the Missions of Alta California," *WMQ*, 3d Ser., LIV (1997), 347–376.

3. On the municipio as a colonial institution, see Lyle N. McAlister, *Spain and Portugal in the New World, 1492–1700* (Minneapolis, 1984), 133–152; Mario Góngora, *Studies in the Colonial History of Spanish America*, trans. Richard Southern (Cambridge, 1975), 98–107; John E. Kicza, "Patterns in Early Spanish Overseas Expansion," *WMQ*, 3d Ser., XLIX (1992), 233. For an introduction to the literature on

option but a legal requirement and considered one of the conditions for a productive and civilized life. As early as 1501, Ferdinand and Isabella instructed Nicolás de Ovando, the first royal governor of Hispaniola, to ensure that none of that island's Christian inhabitants "lives outside the communities that are to be made on the said island." Within a few years, the monarchs extended a similar law to Indians: in 1503, they ordered Ovando to gather the Indians into towns to facilitate their economic integration and religious instruction. This policy of *congregación* was a basic Spanish strategy for the organization and social control of native communities throughout New Spain, and Indians proved less resistant to it after the dual revolutions had decimated their villages and populations.[4]

Officials in New Spain used the Castilian *cabildo* (town council) as a model for the political organization of Indian communities as well as for their own. In Spain, most towns were governed by a council composed of six to twelve *regidores* (councilmen). Regidores usually represented the economic interests of the most important families, and they served long tenures, sometimes for life. Two alcaldes served ex officio on the town council, but, unlike regidores, who were their social superiors, they rotated off the cabildo after a single year in office.[5] A *corregidor,* a crown-appointed outsider who represented both the town and the central government, presided over the cabildo. True to this model, most Spanish towns in the Americas were administered by four to eight regidores, two alcaldes, and various minor officials, all governing in concert with an *adelantado* or a governor. These New World cabildos, whose members were usually *encomenderos,* or Spaniards with aristocratic pretensions, had authority over the basics of urban life: they drafted ordinances, punished wrongdoing, and regulated the local economy.[6]

Spanish town planning in North America, see Dora P. Crouch, Daniel J. Garr, and Axel I. Mundigo, *Spanish City Planning in North America* (Cambridge, Mass., 1982); and, for the borderlands, see Garr, ed., *Hispanic Urban Planning,* Spanish Borderlands Sourcebooks, XXVII, 37–132.

4. "Royal Instructions to Ovando" (1501), in Gibson, ed., *Spanish Tradition in America,* 55–57, esp. 56. On congregación, see Robert Ricard, *The Spiritual Conquest of Mexico: An Essay on the Apostolate and the Evangelizing Methods of the Mendicant Orders in New Spain, 1523–1572,* trans. Lesley Byrd Simpson (Berkeley, Calif., 1966), 136–137; McAlister, *Spain and Portugal in the New World,* 170–173. The English and French also wanted Indians to settle into compact towns, but their attempts were neither as far-reaching nor as effective. See James Axtell, *The Invasion Within: The Contest of Cultures in Colonial North America* (New York, 1985), 43–70, 131–178.

5. For the Iberian origins of cabildos in New Spain, see James Lockhart, *The Nahuas after the Conquest: A Social and Cultural History of the Indians of Central Mexico, Sixteenth through Eighteenth Centuries* (Stanford, Calif., 1992), 36; J. H. Elliott, *Imperial Spain, 1469–1716* (1963; rpt. New York, 1990), 93–97.

6. An adelantado was a royal deputy; the title was granted by the Spanish Crown to the conquerors and founders of new colonies. Encomenderos were Spaniards who received allotments of tribute-paying Indians in return for services rendered to the Crown. They were to protect and convert Indians. On the creation of cabildos in the New World, see McAlister, *Spain and Portugal in the New World,* 135; Góngora, *Studies in the Colonial History of Spanish America,* 100–102; C. H. Haring, *The Spanish Empire in America* (1947; rpt. New York, 1963), 147–165.

As a conquered people, Indians rarely served on Spanish cabildos, but they retained a measure of control over their communities through annual election of their own cabildos. Known collectively as the *República de Indios* (Republic of Indians), these councils by the late seventeenth century were regulated by laws (codified in 1681 in the *Recopilación de leyes de los reynos de las Indias)*, which prescribed the frequency of elections and the number of officials. Selected by Indian electors, most cabildos consisted of a governor, several regidores and alcaldes, and various lesser officials, such as scribes, all in numbers proportional to the population of the settlement.[7]

The Republic of Indians drew on the Spanish notion of the republic, which originated in Saint Augustine's *City of God*. Augustinian theory held that a republic consisted of and provided order to society's various peoples, all of whom suffered "the exigencies of life on this earth." In a republic, order prevented contention and allowed all to serve God's purpose: harmony and justice. Clearly, the Republic of Indians was no republic in the sense that Anglo-Americans would come to understand the term during the last decades of the eighteenth century, as a polity founded on representative government and devoted to the protection of individual liberty. Rather, it was one characterized by rigid social orders—the clergy, nobility, and commoners—each of which had its own juridical status and was subordinate to the monarchy. Only Christians were members of the republic. Jews and Muslims were excluded and tolerated only as long as they paid tribute to the monarch.[8]

Spaniards sought to institute this social order in the Indies, with conquerors and encomenderos forming a nobility, clerics constituting the second estate, and *vecinos* (settlers and townsfolk), the third. During the early decades of discovery and conquest, Spaniards stumbled over the place of Indians in the republic. What they saw as the natives' manifest inferiority and secret worship of Satan led them to brand Indians as dangerous and hostile, even antithetical to the aims of the republic. As such, Indians, therefore, would be relegated to a separate Republic of Indians, an intellectual construct that segregated them and allowed them to be discriminated against and treated paternalistically. Early missionaries supported, even promoted, the Republic of Indians as a bulwark against the rapaciousness of

---

7. Góngora, *Studies in the Colonial History of Spanish America*, 110, 116–119; McAlister, *Spain and Portugal in the New World*, 395–396; Amy Turner Bushnell, "Ruling 'the Republic of Indians' in Seventeenth-Century Florida," in Peter H. Wood, Gregory A. Waselkov, and M. Thomas Hatley, eds., *Powhatan's Mantle: Indians in the Colonial Southeast* (Lincoln, Neb., 1989), 134–150, esp. 137–139. For the regulations governing cabildo elections, see *Recopilación de leyes de los reynos de las Indias . . .* , 4 vols. (Madrid, 1681), libro 6, título 3, law 15. For an English translation of this law, see S. Lyman Tyler, *The Indian Cause in the Spanish Laws of the Indies,* Western Civilization and Native Peoples Occasional Papers, no. 16 (Salt Lake City, 1980), 115.

8. McAlister, *Spain and Portugal in the New World,* 24–33.

the Spanish conquest. Separate and protected from most Spaniards, Indians could be safely and gradually educated in Catholicism and tutored in the rudiments of civilization.[9]

Throughout New Spain, native forms of social and political organization, if not preexisting leaders themselves, influenced the establishment and rule of Indian cabildos within the Republic of Indians.[10] The Nahuas of central Mexico had built the most hierarchical and complex of all of the New World societies encountered by Spaniards. For centuries, the Nahuas had lived in cities as they built a civilization upon wealth extracted from subject peoples. In this context, cooperative preconquest dynastic rulers often gained appointment as Indian governors.[11] The jurisdiction of these governors remained what it had been before conquest: the preexisting ethnic states or communities *(altepetl)*. As the number of Indians who could assert lineage to the preconquest nobility dwindled, a seat on the cabildo became an avenue to social distinction and the object of bitter competition between remaining nobles and ascendant commoners. Dependence upon Spanish officials was the price survivors paid for their status in the colonial order. Despite the fact that Indian officials had to answer to Spanish authorities for their behavior, through the cabildos, indigenous communities retained continuity with the past and some control over their future.[12]

In central Mexico, newly appointed Indian governors carried on in the roles of preconquest rulers: they had judicial and financial responsibilities and oversaw the use of land. Specifically, they protected the community from the Spaniards'

9. Ibid., 177–181.

10. On the persistence of Indian sociopolitical structures under Spanish rule, see Robert Haskett, *Indigenous Rulers: An Ethnohistory of Town Government in Colonial Cuernavaca* (Albuquerque, N.Mex., 1991); Lockhart, *The Nahuas after the Conquest,* 28–58; William B. Taylor, *Landlord and Peasant in Colonial Oaxaca* (Stanford, Calif., 1972), 35–66; John K. Chance, *Conquest of the Sierra: Spaniards and Indians in Colonial Oaxaca* (Norman, Okla., 1989), 123–150; Ronald Spores, *The Mixtecs in Ancient and Colonial Times* (Norman, Okla., 1984), 165–186; Nancy M. Farriss, *Maya Society under Colonial Rule: The Collective Enterprise of Survival* (Princeton, N.J., 1984), esp. 86–114, 231–237. For Florida, see Bushnell, "Ruling 'the Republic of Indians,' " in Wood, Waselkov, and Hatley, eds., *Powhatan's Mantle,* 134–150; John H. Hann, *Apalachee: The Land between the Rivers* (Gainesville, Fla., 1988), 102.

For the blending and transformation of Indian and Spanish elements of governance, see Pedro Carrasco, "The Civil-religious Hierarchy in Mesoamerican Communities: Pre-Spanish Background and Colonial Development," *American Anthropologist,* n.s., LXIII (1961), 483–497. Charles Gibson argued that the Spanish municipal system displaced Indian leadership lineages in *The Aztecs under Spanish Rule: A History of the Indians of the Valley of Mexico, 1519–1810* (Stanford, Calif., 1964), 166–193, esp. 191; Gibson, "Rotation of Alcaldes in the Indian *Cabildo* of Mexico City," *HAHR,* XXXIII (1953), 212–223.

11. Elsewhere, uncooperative Indian leaders often suffered a brutal fate. In the more isolated Sierra Zapoteca district during the 1520s and 1530s, Indian *caciques* held less control over their people and land than their counterparts in central Mexico, and thus they were more expendable to Spaniards. When Indian leaders did not cooperate, they were hanged, burned, or thrown to the dogs. See Chance, *Conquest of the Sierra,* 18.

12. Ibid., 135–137.

more excessive demands as they continued to collect rents, oversee the community treasury, confirm elections of lesser officials in subject cities, allocate land, and hear minor cases "concerning debts, petty theft, assault, and the local market." These governors also took on new duties: they assisted in the collection of tribute, marshaled military support for the Spaniards, and promoted the spread of Catholicism. Through their cooperation, they retained or increased their sizable landholding and its attached economic advantages. Although their participation in the collection of taxes and in the exploitative *encomienda* (royal grant of Indian tribute and labor) and *repartimiento* (labor draft) led to frequent disputes with their communities, Indian governors could limit the Spaniards' demands through litigation. The duties of Indian alcaldes and regidores in central Mexico also blended Indian leadership responsibilities with Castilian political forms. These lesser officials collected tribute and organized labor, handled land transactions, oversaw the apprehension of criminals, supported the local church, and, through litigation, tried to protect the interests of the community.[13]

Along with the governor, alcaldes, and regidores, most Indian cabildos included a religious official known as a *fiscal*. Because there were so few missionaries in New Spain, fiscales held wide-ranging civil and religious responsibilities. Elected or occasionally appointed by priests, they helped to manage local church finances, rang bells for Mass, and gathered parishioners for religious celebrations. At a minimum, fiscales were "church constables" who punished villagers for violating Catholic teachings, but usually they were full members of the cabildo; most had previously served as regidores or alcaldes. Together in the late colonial period, Indian cabildo officials formed an elite that controlled many important aspects of Indian community life in New Spain.[14]

In some of the northernmost regions of New Spain—Nueva Galicia, Nueva Vizcaya, Baja California, and Sonora—cabildos played a central role in Indians' daily lives.[15] This was especially true in the communities that emerged as Indians

13. On the roles of alcaldes and regidores, see Haskett, *Indigenous Rulers,* 99–102, 104–107, 114–116. For enrichment of governors, see Taylor, *Landlord and Peasant,* 39. Indian governors imitated or threatened court cases over "land usurpation, boundary conflicts, water-rights struggles, and rental disputes" (Haskett, *Indigenous Rulers,* 101). For legal channels open to Indians in New Spain, see Woodrow Borah, *Justice by Insurance: The General Indian Court of Colonial Mexico and the Legal Aides of the Half-Real* (Berkeley, Calif., 1983).

14. Haskett, *Indigenous Rulers,* 95–123; Chance, *Conquest of the Sierra,* 154.

15. Indian officials in these regions donned the following titles: *gobernador, teniente de gobernador, capitán, sargento, alférez* (ensign), *alcalde, regidor, fiscal, alguacil* (constable), *tópil* (minor official), *sacristán,* and *cantor* (singer). For an overview of Spanish governmental systems in the northern borderlands, see Edward H. Spicer, *Cycles of Conquest: The Impact of Spain, Mexico, and the United States on the Indians of the Southwest, 1533–1960* (Tucson, Ariz., 1962), 289–291, 303–304, 328, 388–395. Nueva Vizcaya: Susan M. Deeds, "Indigenous Responses to Mission Settlement in Nueva Vizcaya," in Erick Langer and Robert H. Jackson, eds., *The New Latin American Mission History* (Lincoln, Neb., 1995), 82–83, 88–89; William B. Griffen, *Indian Assimilation in the Franciscan Area of Nueva Vizcaya*

responded to the dual revolutions and Spaniards pursued the policy of con-gregación. Yet many factors limited the full development of Indian cabildos in the north: the loose organization of Indian settlements, the resistance of many Indians to Spanish intrusion, the waning of the encomienda and repartimiento, and the priorities of the missionaries who oversaw the appointment and election of Indian officials.[16] Although Indian officials rarely sat on full-blown cabildos in the northern regions, they nevertheless held a wide range of offices, many of which were tied to the mission church. The flexibility of the Spanish sys-tem in response to Indian political structures is most clear in New Mexico, where Indians had a very long history of electing large governing councils. In the pueblo of Jémez, Spanish officials at the close of the seventeenth century recog-nized twenty Indian elected officials.[17] Through the elections across the northern borderlands, Indians bound themselves to their leaders; these leaders, in turn, through their oaths of office, submitted the entire Indian community to Spanish authority. And, as Spain advanced into Alta California during the late eighteenth century, it continued to use the cabildo as a model for the political organization of new communities. Significantly, though, by the time Alta California was colo-nized, Spanish royal officials had come to see in the establishment of Indian cabildos another means to challenge the missionaries' jurisdiction over Indi-ans. The election of Indian officials in the missions, therefore, opened up con-flicts between the governors, the Franciscans, and the Indians they both sought to control.

(Tucson, Ariz., 1979), 45. Sonora: John L. Kessell, *Friars, Soldiers, and Reformers: Hispanic Arizona and the Sonora Mission Frontier, 1767–1856* (Tucson, Ariz., 1976), 71–72; Evelyn Hu-DeHart, *Missionaries, Miners, and Indians: Spanish Contact with the Yaqui Nation of Northwestern New Spain, 1533–1820* (Tucson, Ariz., 1981), 32–36; Cynthia Radding, *Wandering Peoples: Colonialism, Ethnic Spaces, and Ecological Frontiers in Northwestern Mexico, 1700–1850* (Durham, N.C., 1997), 67–68. Texas: Mardith Keithly Schuetz, "The Indians of the San Antonio Missions, 1718–1821" (Ph.D. diss., University of Texas, Austin, 1980), 254–267.

16. On Spanish labor institutions in northern New Spain, see José Cuello, "The Persistence of Indian Slavery and Encomienda in the Northeast of Colonial Mexico, 1577–1723," *Journal of Social History,* XXI (1987–1988), 683–700; Susan M. Deeds, "Rural Work in Nueva Vizcaya: Forms of Labor Coercion on the Periphery," *HAHR,* LXIX (1989), 425–449.

17. In New Mexico, officials remained under the authority of the civilian government, not the clerics. See Ramón A. Gutiérrez, *When Jesus Came, the Corn Mothers Went Away: Marriage, Sexuality, and Power in New Mexico, 1500–1846* (Stanford, Calif., 1991), 156–161. On their election, see Diego de Vargas, "Extracts from Governor Vargas's Journal on the Reestablishment of the Missions, September 18–October 7 and November 1–December 21, 1694," in J. Manuel Espinosa, ed. and trans., *The Pueblo Revolt of 1696 and the Franciscan Missions in New Mexico: Letters of the Missionaries and Related Documents* (Norman, Okla., 1988), 98–99. So tight was this interweaving of Indian and Spanish systems that elements of it endured in the pueblo of San Juan well into the twentieth century: Indians con-tinued to appoint among their fourteen leadership positions a governor, two lieutenants, an alguacil, and four fiscales; see Alfonso Ortiz, *The Tewa World: Space, Time, Being, and Becoming in a Pueblo Society* (Chicago, 1969), 61–67.

CREATING INDIRECT RULE IN ALTA CALIFORNIA

In December 1778, Alta California's governor, Felipe de Neve, ordered that mission Indians elect their own alcaldes and regidores. Neve based his decree on historical precedent and his interpretation of the *Recopilación*. As governor, he sought to implement the imperial policy of assimilating Indians into the Spaniards' political system. In Neve's words: "With the elections and the appointment of a new republic [Indian cabildos], the will of His Majesty will be fulfilled in this region, and under our direction, in the course of time, he will obtain in these Indians useful vassals for our religion and state."[18] Neve and his successors believed that extending to Indians the rudiments of municipal government would teach them a civics lesson that was at least equal in importance to the catechism. Missions San Diego (1769) and San Carlos Borromeo (1770) were to proceed with the election of two alcaldes and two regidores; neophytes at smaller, more recently founded missions, such as San Antonio (1771), San Gabriel (1771), and San Luis Obispo (1772), were to elect one alcalde and one regidor. The newly established missions of San Francisco (1776), San Juan Capistrano (1776), and Santa Clara (1777) were exempt from the governor's orders. Upon election, each official was to report to the nearest military garrison, where the commander would install him in office in the name of the king. The official then would take from the presidial commander the certificate he needed to exercise his powers; alcaldes also were to receive a large wooden staff of leadership.[19]

Despite the established presence of mission Indian officials elsewhere in New Spain, the Franciscans bitterly opposed the elections. Their resistance emerged, not from objections to indirect rule, but from a power struggle between secular and religious authorities that deepened during the late eighteenth century. Church and state officials held opposing views about the origin of civil authority, and each claimed ultimate jurisdiction over Indians. State jurists increasingly insisted that the king was the vicar of Christ and that the power to oversee the church and instruct Indians therefore resided, first and foremost, with the king and his representatives. Clerics and canon lawyers maintained that the king was a vicar of the pope and that the church was therefore the principal protector and

18. Felipe de Neve to Junípero Serra, quoted in Serra to Neve, Jan. 7, 1780, Mission San Carlos, in Tibesar, ed. and trans., *Writings of Serra*, III, 410 (my trans.).

19. The only record of Neve's original order is Fermín Francisco de Lasuén's response, Jan. 25, 1779, in Kenneally, ed. and trans., *Writings of Lasuén*, I, 75–77. Neve notified Teodoro de Croix, commandant general of the Interior Provinces, of his directive (Feb. 24, 1779 [copy certified in Monterey, Nov. 15, 1796], AGN, CA, LXV, expediente 7, 303a). Croix sent his approval (July 28, 1779, AGN, CA, LV, expediente 7, 304a). Regidores apparently did not carry a staff; see Serra to Lasuén, [Mar. 29], 1779, Monterey, in Tibesar, ed. and trans., *Writings of Serra*, III, 295.

instructor of Indians. These disputes intensified under the Bourbon ascendancy: they became urgent after Spain's defeat in the Seven Years' War, when Carlos III (1759–1788) and his ministers set out to bolster royal authority by curtailing the powers of the Catholic Church and strengthening the economy of New Spain.[20]

As agents of Bourbon reform, the first military and civil administrators of Alta California brought to their posts an official hostility to religious orders in general and missions in particular. In 1767, just two years before the Franciscans moved into Alta California, Carlos III expelled the Jesuits from New Spain because he feared they would use their wealth and independence to obstruct his secular reforms. Gaspar de Portolá oversaw the Jesuits' removal from Baja California, and Neve himself directed their ouster from the mining center of Zacatecas.[21] The Bourbon reforms not only heightened the general suspicion with which the clergy and royal officials looked at one another; they also increased the role that non-Indians played in Indian elections in New Spain. Bourbon election reform laws emerged out of the pessimistic conclusion that Indians, left to their own devices, had proved incapable of conducting valid elections. But the new laws also were moved by a countervailing assumption that Indians, with proper guidance, would be able to profit from municipal elections and limited self-rule.[22]

The Bourbons' inclusive political vision and extension of royal power were challenged by the Franciscans' restrictive religious agenda. The friars wanted absolute control over the missions and the Indians who lived in them, and they believed that natives so recently subjugated to the church and the Crown could not possibly be ready for a measure of institutionalized self-governance, no matter how elementary its form. And the Franciscans rightly feared that Indian officials would use their elevated political status to pursue their own goals. Moreover, they did not want Indians to learn that the Spanish governor, not the Franciscans, had ultimate civil and judicial authority over Indians.

But there was much more at stake in this dispute than the degree to which Franciscans would be able to control mission Indians: the definition and therefore the very function of California's Franciscan establishments hung in the balance. Governor Neve had provoked Serra's anger by insisting that there were

20. On these rivalries, see Nancy M. Farriss, *Crown and Clergy in Colonial Mexico 1759–1821: The Crisis of Ecclesiastical Privilege* (London, 1968); Ramón A. Gutiérrez, "Church and State: Spanish," in Jacob Ernest Cooke, ed., *Encyclopedia of the North American Colonies* (New York, 1993), III, 520–528; Christon I. Archer, *The Army in Bourbon Mexico, 1760–1810* (Albuquerque, N.Mex., 1977).

21. On the removal of the Jesuits, see Magnus Mörner, ed., *The Expulsion of the Jesuits from Latin America* (New York, 1965); David J. Weber, *The Spanish Frontier in North America* (New Haven, Conn., 1992), 242; Edwin A. Beilharz, *Felipe de Neve, First Governor of California* (San Francisco, Calif., 1971), 9–13.

22. Haskett, *Indigenous Rulers*, 54–55.

no missions, only doctrinas, in Alta California.[23] Doctrinas were in essence secularized missions, self-supporting parishes that fell under the jurisdiction of a
bishop, not a religious order or missionary college. Missions had always been
envisioned by the Crown and the regular orders as temporary establishments
that were necessary to introduce Catholicism to the Indians. And, by the time
Alta California became a Spanish province, nearly all the missions of New Spain
had been converted to doctrinas or parishes. Moreover, the conversion was an
integral part of the Bourbon agenda to reduce the power of independent religious orders and to centralize its political authority. Thus, by invoking the
Recopilación, calling for elections, and speaking of doctrinas, Neve was challenging the very nature of the Franciscan enterprise in California. Predictably, the
Franciscans responded that they themselves were apostolic missionaries, not
parish priests; therefore, the *Recopilación* did not apply, and the governor's order
of elections had no foundation in law.[24]

At San Diego, the governor's insistence in 1779 on elections prompted the
Franciscans to threaten resignation lest their acquiescence be interpreted as proof
that they were in fact parish priests. Serra called on the governor to suspend the
elections in the designated missions. The conflict came to a climax just before
Mass on Palm Sunday, when Neve and Serra exchanged bitter words. Later that
evening, overcome with agitation and unable to rest, Serra cried out: *"¿Qué es
esto Señor?"* ("What is the meaning of it, Lord?") Serra was calmed by a voice
from within that repeated one of Christ's admonitions to the apostles: "Be pru-
dent as serpents and simple as doves." Reassured, Serra decided to go along with
the governor's orders but only in ways that would not "cause the least change
among the Indians or in the mode of governing" established by Franciscans.
Serra believed that, with God's help, he could join the simplicity of the dove with
the cunning of the serpent to outmaneuver the governor.[25]

As Serra intended, the Franciscans quickly asserted a large degree of control
over the elections. They convinced Neve that only with their guidance would
Indians and Spaniards profit from the process. At several of the missions, accord-

23. On Governor Neve's failed efforts to convert the missions in California to doctrinas, see Beilharz,
Felipe de Neve, 118–120; Serra to father guardian and discretorium, Aug. 13, 1778, Monterey, in Tibesar,
ed. and trans., *Writings of Serra,* III, 215–225.

24. For the different terms used by Spaniards to describe mission settlements, see Amy Turner Bushnell, *Situado and Sabana: Spain's Support System for the Presidio and Mission Provinces of Florida*
(Athens, Ga., 1994), 20–23; David J. Weber, *Bárbaros: Spaniards and Their Savages in the Age of Enlight-
enment* (New Haven, Conn., 2005). For Lasuén's insistence that the padres were not parish priests, see
Lasuén to Neve, Jan. 25, 1779, San Diego, in Kenneally, ed. and trans., *Writings of Lasuén,* I, 75–77.

25. Serra to Lasuén, [Mar. 29], 1779, Monterey, in Tibesar, ed. and trans., *Writings of Serra,* III, 294
(my trans.). Serra's biblical references are to Matt. 10:16, and Gen. 2:4.

ing to Serra, the first Indian officials had committed crimes or behaved ar-
rogantly, acting as if they were "gentlemen." By January 1780, when the second
annual elections were to take place, several of the officials had abandoned their
missions, whereas others had been overcome by disease and were too ill to vote.
Consistent with Spanish law, Neve specified that only former Indian officials
could act as electors, but he increased the missionaries' role in the elections,
relying on them to ensure "success" or "appropriateness." The Franciscans did so
by controlling the nomination of candidates, as Pedro Fages, Neve's successor as
governor, described:

> It has been established that each mission at the completion of [its first] five
> years must elect one or two alcaldes and the same number of regidores
> according to the number of individuals in the mission who have been
> reduced. They are to make these appointments successively, at the begin-
> ning of the year, with the assistance and intervention of the respective
> missionaries, who propose three of the least unqualified. A plurality of
> votes decides the elected, [whose names] are submitted to the governor
> who approves or disapproves them according to his criteria, in the name of
> His Majesty.

By narrowing the field of candidates, the Franciscans guaranteed the election of
men whom they expected to facilitate their control of the mission.[26]

A limitation on the number of candidates was not unique to California missions, nor did it apply only to Indians. During the early 1780s in San Jose, officials
restricted municipal elections after the settlers chose men who proved unwilling
or unable to control the community. The governor appointed a *comisionado*
(town commissioner) and an alcalde to supervise the town. Later, the outgoing
alcalde submitted three names to the comisionado; if he approved, the three
nominees cast lots. The winner was named alcalde, and the other two regidores.
As in the missions, the governor had to approve these appointments, and he
occasionally rejected them and selected new officials.[27]

In addition to securing a large measure of control over the elections, Serra

26. Serra to Lasuén, Aug. 16, 1779, Monterey, in Tibesar, ed. and trans., *Writings of Serra*, III, 364–369;
Pedro Fages, general report on the missions, [1787], par. 32, Archives of California, C–A 52, 121–151, esp.
144, BL. Neve's instructions to Serra have not survived, but they were paraphrased in Serra to Neve, Jan.
7, 1780, Monterey, in Tibesar, ed. and trans., *Writings of Serra*, III, 409. The restriction of the franchise
to a select few was consistent with practices in Spain and its colonies; see Haskett, *Indigenous Rulers*,
29–30.

27. Francis F. Guest, "Municipal Government in Spanish California," *California Historical Society
Quarterly*, XLVI (1967), 307–335, esp. 312–313; Guest, "Municipal Institutions in Spanish California,
1769–1821" (Ph.D. diss., University of Southern California, 1961), 202, 227–229. For a description of
similar electioneering in the Indian towns of Cuernavaca, see Haskett, *Indigenous Rulers*, 55.

tried to prevent Indian officials from learning that the military constituted a secular power that rivaled Franciscan authority. Serra instructed his trusted subordinate at San Diego, Lasuén, to speak to the presidio officer whose responsibility it was to confirm the Indians in office: "Ask him to carry out this function so that, without failing in the slightest degree in his duty toward his superior officer, the Indians may not be given a less exalted opinion of the fathers than they have had until now." Furthermore, Serra preferred that the Indian officials remain ignorant of the responsibilities with which the military charged them. "The document that is used in conferring these offices on them," Serra advised Lasuén, "may be as powerful as they wish, provided Your Reverences are the only ones to receive it and read it." Even after these precautions, the Franciscans resisted sending newly elected Indians to the presidios for installation. An inquiry in the mid-1790s by the governor revealed that none of the current presidio commanders had ever been called on to give Indians their oaths of office.[28]

Serra further counseled Lasuén to obstruct the governor's plan that elections be held on the first day of every new year: "Pretend that you do not understand—with the pretext that a year had not been completed [since the last elections] and that you are still awaiting a response from the letter you sent him via the lieutenant . . . [and] if the governor sends a letter requesting elections, include all you have said to him in the above mentioned letter." Such behavior as this led Governor Neve to conclude, "There is no mischief these religious will not attempt if exasperated, such is their boundless unbelievable pride. My politeness and moderation over more than four years have not been enough to turn them from the hostility with which they engage in surreptitious conspiracies against the government and its laws. There is no means whatsoever they would scorn." Although the Franciscans' grumbling continued until 1797, when Viceroy Miguel de la Grúa Talamanca y Branciforte put an end to the padres' resistance, elections of Indian officials occurred annually in the largest and oldest California missions after the early 1780s.[29]

28. Serra to Lasuén, [Mar. 29], 1779, Monterey, in Tibesar, ed. and trans., *Writings of Serra*, III, 296 (my trans.); Diego de Borica to commanders of San Francisco, Monterey, Santa Barbara, and San Diego presidios, and their responses, Mar. 2–30, 1796, AGN, CA, LXV, expediente 7, 307a–314b.

29. Serra to Lasuén, Aug. 16, 1779, Mission San Carlos, in Tibesar, ed. and trans., *Writings of Serra*, III, 367 (my trans.); Neve to Croix, Mar. 26, 1781, Monterey, quoted in Beilharz, *Felipe de Neve*, 153–155. By January 1783, Fages had ordered the Franciscans at Missions San Francisco, San Juan Capistrano, and Santa Clara to oversee Indian elections. At Mission San Diego, the Franciscans recognized local village captains as alcaldes. In ending the missionaries' challenge, Branciforte did not side with the earlier position of the governor of California that the missions were in fact doctrinas, but he did agree that the Indian officials should be elected in the missions, subject to royal authority, and remain somewhat independent from the Franciscans. The viceroy concurred with his adviser, who asserted, "The last motive [of the Crown] would be to create men independent from the obedience and vassalage of the sovereign, to whom all must be subject and acknowledge its greatness and absolute sovereignty and

THE ROLES AND RULE OF INDIAN OFFICIALS IN
THE CALIFORNIA MISSIONS

The cabildos elected by California Indians had fewer officials and responsibilities and less autonomy than their contemporaries in central Mexico. Rarely did a California mission have more than two alcaldes and two regidores.[30] Indian scribes were not a part of the cabildo: few California Indians were literate in Spanish; the Franciscans and governors, not the Indian officials, kept the community archives; and Indian officials rarely met as a council. Furthermore, because California Indians were never subject to repartimiento or encomienda, the office most often associated with these outlawed labor institutions, the Indian *gobernador,* was conspicuously absent. Throughout the missions of northern New Spain, the duties of church and secular Indian officials overlapped, but, in California, perhaps to a greater extent than elsewhere in the Spanish Borderlands, Indian alcaldes and regidores served as assistants to the missionaries, much like fiscales in central Mexico.

The Indian officials' intended subordination to the Franciscans was made clear in 1787 by Governor Fages: "Although these authorities are granted some powers, they are necessarily dependent on the missionaries, without whose direction they would not be able to exercise them." Indian officials faced the same heavy-handed paternalism that characterized all the Indians' interactions with missionaries. Officials were subject to corporal punishment at Franciscan hands, and they could not bring charges against the missionaries, although on occasion they did testify against them in cases brought by others. This disability set them apart from their counterparts in central Mexico, who, as noted above, frequently employed the legal system to claim that their curates manipulated elections, misappropriated communal funds, and imposed excessive labor demands.[31]

Even though they worked under Franciscan supervision and exerted influence within a circumscribed arena, Indian officials in California had wide-ranging authority over other Indians, and therefore they helped determine the tenor of

---

power, without anyone's being exempt from it" (opinion of the *Fiscal de lo Civile,* Mexico City, May 31, 1797, AGN, CA, LXV, expediente 7, 302a–334b, esp. 326b–328a).

30. Mission San Luis Rey might have had seven alcaldes. See Minna Hewes and Gordon Hewes, eds. and trans., "Indian Life and Customs at Mission San Luis Rey: A Record of California Mission Life Written by Pablo Tac, an Indian Neophyte," in Edward D. Castillo, ed., *Native American Perspectives on the Hispanic Colonization of Alta California* (New York, 1992), 35–58, esp. 51. For politics in Mission San Luis Rey, see Florence Connolly Shipek, "A Strategy for Change: The Luiseño of Southern California" (Ph.D. diss., University of Hawaii, 1977), 145–154.

31. Pedro Fages, general report on the missions, [1787], par. 33, Archives of California, C–A 52, 121–151, esp. 144–145, BL. For Serra's argument that the Franciscans flogged Indian officials, see Serra to Neve, Jan. 7, 1780, in Tibesar, ed. and trans., *Writings of Serra,* III, 407–417, and Serra to Lasuén, Apr. 25, 26, 1780, ibid., IV, 3–11.

daily life in the missions. Crucially, though, these men did not set policy; they could never shake the Franciscans' perception of them as inferiors, nor could they separate the missionaries from their conviction that they always knew what was best for their charges. But, in frontier California, there was stated colonial policy, and then there was colonial policy as implemented; and the difference between the two often could be measured in the intentions of Indian officials, who, because they served as intermediaries between Franciscans and Indians, could shape and manipulate Franciscan directives and initiatives.

Pablo Tac, a Luiseño who, at age ten in 1832, was taken from California to Europe by a Franciscan, was one of a handful of Indians who provided a description of the officials' responsibilities.[32] According to Tac, one of the alcaldes' main functions was to speak in the Indians' language for the Franciscans: "In the afternoon, the alcaldes gather at the house of the missionary. They bring the news of that day, and if the missionary tells them something that all the people of the country ought to know, they return to the villages . . . [and] each one of the alcaldes wherever he goes cries out what the missionary has told them, in his language, and all the country hears it." Given the alcaldes' roles in conveying Franciscan directives, Tac's statement that officials "knew how to speak Spanish more than the others" comes as no surprise. According to the *Recopilación*, the officials also were charged with ensuring that neophytes attended Mass and remained sober. In the words of Serra, they were to "make the rounds of the Indian village at night, lead the people to prayer and work, and thereby allow us some relief."[33]

Perhaps because of their language skills, and certainly because of their prominence, Indian officials were among the few Indians to participate in the administration of the sacraments of baptism and marriage as godparents and witnesses. Their very presence helped to connect Catholic rituals to the Indians of the mission. And they often translated Catholic rites into terms that were comprehensible to their people. The content of these unrecorded mediations is unknown, but, in trying to explain Catholic rituals to often uncomprehending neophytes, they might well have invoked familiar concepts and colored the padres'

32. Pablo Tac's narrative was written after the end of the Spanish period, and it is problematic as a source for mission life before 1821. Tac was born in 1822, after the collapse of Spanish authority; furthermore, he was anything but an independent or objective informant. His account was penned by an Italian linguist in Rome, where Tac had been taken in 1832 by one of the Franciscans for priestly instruction, and it was only later assembled into its current form. Nevertheless, the narrative is a very valuable source, especially since it is confirmed by other evidence. For microfilm of the original Tac manuscript, see MS film 255, HL.

33. Hewes and Hewes, eds. and trans., "Indian Life and Customs at Mission San Luis Rey," in Castillo, ed., *Native American Perspectives*, 51; *Recopilación*, libro 6, título 3, law 16; Serra to Neve, Jan. 7, 1780, in Tibesar, ed. and trans., *Writings of Serra*, III, 406 (my trans.).

words and actions with Indian meaning. Indian officials might also have helped translate and thereby shape catechisms and confessional manuals that the Franciscans used to prepare Indians for baptism, penance, and Communion.

With mixed results, Franciscans enlisted Indian officials in their project of controlling sexual behavior. Alcaldes were to keep unmarried men and women in the single-sex dormitories and prevent them from having illicit contact. As we have seen, most missions had special lodgings for the unmarried women. Mission Santa Cruz even had one alcalde to police the men and another to oversee the women.[34] In these responsibilities, many alcaldes placed other desires above the Franciscans' demands. In 1779, officials at San Luis Obispo and San Gabriel apparently committed adultery and "supplied" women to the soldiers. These sorts of activities continued over decades, and Franciscans replaced many officials for what they considered sexual offenses and indiscretions. In 1821, Modesto, an alcalde at Mission San Juan Bautista, took advantage of the illness of one of the Franciscans and "delivered" the single women to the men. He was quickly suspended from office and replaced by Francisco Sevilla, a former alcalde who had "taken good care of the single women." Modesto, too, might have plausibly asserted that he had acted in the women's best interests, liberating them from their confinement.[35]

Alcaldes played a crucial but somewhat ambiguous role in structuring the Indians' daily routines, primarily through a rigid labor regime. Pablo Tac recounted how officials circulated through the villages telling people when and where to report for work: "Tomorrow the sowing begins and so the laborers go to the chicken yard and assemble there." When their calls went unheeded, officials beat those who they or the Franciscans believed were shirking. In 1797, Claudio Ssojorois declared that one of the reasons he had run away from Mission San Francisco was that the alcalde Valeriano "made him go to work" when he was sick. Homobono Sumipocsé, who also fled, declared that Valeriano "hit him with

34. Manuel Fernández to Borica, Dec. 12, 1797, Taylor Coll., doc. 120, HL; see also Juan Bautista de Alvarado, "Historia de California" (1876), 5 vols., I, 69–70, C–D 1, BL (English trans.).

35. On alcaldes' not regulating sexuality as the padres desired, see Serra to Neve, Jan. 7, 1780, Monterey, in Tibesar, ed. and trans., *Writings of Serra*, III, 415; Borica to the Franciscans at San Diego, Jan. 7, 1797, Monterey, Archives of California, C–A 24, 502, BL. One alcalde used his own power to sexually assault a woman: in 1798, Antonio de Padua of Mission Soledad told a married woman that the padre wanted to see her. But, according to Father Antonio Jayme, Padua instead dragged the woman into an arbor, where he assaulted her. Father Jayme told the governor that Antonio "was not good for alcalde" and then proceeded with a new election. See Jayme to Pablo Vicente de Solá, Mar. 25, 1798, Mission Soledad, Taylor Coll., doc. 130, HL. On Modesto, see Estevan Tapis to Solá, Feb. 24, 1821, Mission San Juan Bautista, Taylor Coll., doc. 1200, HL. For other examples of Indian officials' going against the Franciscans' wishes and courting dismissal, see Jayme to Solá, May 9, 1817, Mission Soledad, Taylor Coll., doc. 794, HL; Juan Bautista Sancho to Solá, Mar. 3, 1819, Mission Soledad, Taylor Coll., doc. 1070, HL; Sancho to Solá, Mar. 18, 1820, Mission Soledad, Taylor Coll., doc. 1126, HL.

a heavy cane for having gone to look for mussels at the beach," an outing that most likely took him away from his work. Not all officials, however, could be counted on to enforce the Franciscans' work schedules. Other alcaldes at San Francisco frequently rebuffed the padres' demands that they supervise work, choosing instead to pursue different activities in the countryside. They were not just flouting Franciscan authority but using their own to sanction other behaviors, ones that they and their followers considered appropriate but the padres took as subversive.[36]

Indian officials also administered a share of the corporal punishment that the Franciscans considered necessary for the Indians' souls. Foreign visitors and Anglo-American immigrants emphasized that alcaldes "did a great deal of chastisement, both by and without [Franciscan] orders." Frederick Beechey, an English sea captain who visited Mission San Francisco in 1826, claimed that officials used goads to keep fellow Indians kneeling during Mass, for "goads were better adapted to this purpose than the whips, as they would reach a long way, and inflict a sharp puncture without making any noise." Hugo Reid, a Scot who married a Gabrielina, later wrote that alcaldes carried "a wand to denote their authority, and what was more terrible, an immense scourge of rawhide, about ten feet in length, plaited to the thickness of an ordinary man's wrist!" Although these descriptions may well be exaggerations motivated by religious and national difference, Indian complaints substantiate the basic claim of alcalde violence.[37]

In addition to being the intelligible voice and occasional strong arm of the Franciscans, Indian officials were to be the military's eyes and ears. Military officials expected alcaldes to investigate and report crimes. When Aurelio Jujuvit killed his wife Tomasa Coroni at San Juan Capistrano, it was Bruno, the mission alcalde, who heard the murderer's admission of guilt and carried the news to Spanish officials.[38] Few alcaldes, however, cooperated as readily as Bruno; in fact, as a group, they exposed very few crimes. For example, in 1779, Francisco, an

36. Hewes and Hewes, eds. and trans., "Indian Life and Customs at Mission San Luis Rey," in Castillo, ed., *Native American Perspectives,* 51. Claudio Ssojorois and Homobono Sumipocsé quoted from testimony of runaway Indians captured by José Argüello, San Francisco Presidio, Aug. 12, 1797, AGN, CA, LXV, expediente 2, 108a–109a. Indian names from Randall Milliken, *A Time of Little Choice: The Disintegration of Tribal Culture in the San Francisco Bay Area, 1769–1810* (Menlo Park, Calif., 1995), 300–301; Ramón Abella and Juan Sainz de Lucio, Nov. 11, 1814, in *APST,* 128.

37. Hugo Reid, [letter no. 19], "New Era in Mission Affairs," in Susanna Bryant Dakin, *A Scotch Paisano; Hugo Reid's Life in California, 1832–1852, Derived from His Correspondence* (1939; rpt. Berkeley, Calif., 1978), 272–273. For a discussion of Anglo-American and foreign views of the Indians and Franciscans in early California, see James J. Rawls, *Indians of California: The Changing Image* (Norman, Okla., 1984); Beechey quoted in Castillo, "The Other Side of the 'Christian Curtain,'" *The Californians,* X (1992), 13.

38. Pedro Poyorena to Antonio Grajera, Mar. 5, 1797, Mission San Juan Capistrano, AGN, CA, LXV, expediente 8, 336a–336b. For a description of some of the police-related duties of the Indian officials as outlined by a former governor of California, see Alvarado, "Historia de California," I, 68–71, C–D 1.

alcalde at Mission San Diego, kept silent after Indians from the mission and the surrounding area attacked the village of Jalò, killing ten or more of its residents.[39] For this, the presidio soldiers arrested him. In 1808, after Indians at Mission San Jose brawled and fled, the alcalde omitted to notify the Spanish authorities, a dereliction of duty that led the governor to brand him a criminal accomplice. Similarly, in 1816, Rosendo, the alcalde at San Juan Bautista, did not alert the authorities about the identities and whereabouts of ten Indians who had taken cattle from the mission herd. His silence earned him a week in jail.[40] More often than not, when called on to explain murders or robberies, alcaldes provided unremarkable testimony, merely echoing accounts offered by others. Again, the willingness of alcaldes to risk punishment and turn a blind eye to some Indian actions or to comply only minimally with Spanish investigations suggests their sense of duty to their fellow Indians over the padres—and their unwillingness to see as criminal many activities that had the Indian community's approbation.

Some actions of Indian officials, such as administering corporal punishment, might not have been the responsibility of pre-mission village leaders, but many of the alcaldes' duties and responsibilities did resemble those of earlier native leaders. Traditional headmen oversaw the production of the community's food while remaining exempt from basic manual labor; similarly, alcaldes participated in the economic activities of the mission as coordinators, not laborers. Village captains made crucial decisions concerning the distribution of food; alcaldes, too, in some instances, decided how to allocate the missions' food and labor. In 1786, for example, Indian officials at Santa Clara took under consideration the Franciscans' proposal to sell the military much of the mission's remaining food, forcing the community to rely on gathering. Although the alcaldes clearly were consulted as unequal partners whose compliance the Franciscans all but expected, the padres' desire for the officials' approval affirmed the alcaldes' status within the Indian community. As Father Tomás de la Peña of Mission Santa Clara recounted, when the military's request for provisions threatened to empty the mission's granaries,

> we called together the principal [Indian] leaders at the mission and we said to them: . . . The soldiers are suffering much from hunger. They have no corn, no wheat, no beans. They are asking us to sell them some of these

39. Letter of Neve, in AGN, CA, LXXI, 1a–17a, esp. 1a–1b.

40. José Joaquín de Arrillaga to commander of San Francisco Presidio, May 12, 1808, Monterey, Archives of California, C–A 26, 503, BL. Father Estevan Tapis requested freedom for Rosendo. Rosendo had been living as an observant Catholic with his wife and four children, and, in his absence, his wife was overwhelmed by their large family. See Tapis to Solá, May 24, 1816, San Juan Bautista, Taylor Coll., doc. 650, HL. Evidently, the governor was convinced by Tapis, since a week later Rosendo was back at the mission as alcalde (Tapis to Solá, June 1, 1816, San Juan Bautista, Taylor Coll., doc. 651, HL).

things so that they can support themselves. . . . If we do sell, there will not be enough on hand to support you until the time of the wheat harvest. If you wish to go away for some weeks to gather nuts, it will be possible to sell them some corn, and there will be that much extra to spend on clothes. You may consult with your own people if you wish.

In less than an hour they returned to say that they would choose life in the open, for the pinole was already getting ripe.

Although De la Peña's proposal was somewhere between an order and a bribe, it clearly worked for all parties involved. Mission Indians got liberty to pursue their traditional harvest and taste again life beyond the mission. Alcaldes demonstrated that they could moderate the mission's demands on Indian labor and secure for neophytes time to pursue customary activities, many of which no doubt would have been condemned had they occurred in the missions. Soldiers filled their bellies. And missionaries, through the sale of foodstuffs to the military, curried favor with the governor and raised extra money to purchase necessities. In a similar accommodation where old leadership roles persisted in new places, Indian captains and then later mission alcaldes presided over annual ceremonies that occurred after harvest. At the end of the gathering season, village leaders at San Carlos customarily gave a feast at which neophytes ate, sang, and danced. This ceremonial leadership continued at Mission San Carlos long into the nineteenth century, when the Indian "*Capitán*" of the mission arranged for a feast and festival on San Carlos Day.[41]

Indian village captains were also important military leaders. So, too, were alcaldes. Customarily, each captain was a skilled archer who "led the van in battle, supplied the bows and arrows, and encouraged his people." These attributes were accommodated into the mission and even put to its defense. Missionaries came to tolerate, even support, Indian displays of martial skill in ways that both acknowledged the Indians' status and buttressed the colonial hierarchy over Indians. When the Franciscans at San Carlos wanted to impress visitors, they allowed Indians to stage hunting exhibitions, thereby suggesting the Indians' skills and the Spaniards' domination over them. French explorer Jean-François de Galaup de la Pérouse visited Mission San Carlos in 1786, and he described one such display:

These Indians are very skilful with the bow; they killed some tiny birds in our presence; it must be said that their patience as they creep towards them

41. Lowell John Bean, "Social Organization," in *HNAI*, VIII, 678; Tomás de la Peña, quoted in Lasuén to Fages, Apr. 7, 1786, in Kenneally, ed. and trans., *Writings of Lasuén*, I, 105; Juan Amorós, in *APST*, 59–60; Sylvia M. Broadbent, "The Rumsen of Monterey: An Ethnography from Historical Sources," in *Miscellaneous Papers on Archaeology*, Contributions of the University of California Archaeological Research Facility, XIV (Berkeley, Calif., 1972), 66.

is hard to describe; they hide and, so to speak, snake up to the game, releasing the arrow from a mere 15 paces.

Their skill with large game is even more impressive; we all of us saw an Indian with a deer's head tied over his own, crawling on all fours, pretending to eat grass, and carrying out this pantomime in such a way that our hunters would have shot him from 30 paces if they had not been forewarned. In this way they go up to deer herds within very close range and kill them with their arrows.[42]

The identities of the Indians involved in this demonstration are unknown, but, given their considerable skill, they might have been village captains or mission alcaldes. Through their participation in these displays, these men affirmed their own status while perhaps sending a message of their own to Franciscans and their guests: We are armed and dangerous and can turn our weapons on you.

As their prowess at hunting suggests, Indian village captains led their people in battle, a responsibility officials subsequently exercised when Franciscans and presidio commanders experimented with using armed parties of Indian auxiliaries to defend the missions from foreign attack. During the 1810s, when the missionaries and Governor Pablo Vicente de Solá feared an English naval invasion—and the military in Alta California was all but cut off from central Mexico because of the beginnings of the revolutionary insurgency—Indians constructed extra bows and arrows for their own use in defending the region. In the fall of 1818, after Spanish officials learned that a South American privateer, Hipólito Bouchard, was headed for the California coast, hundreds of mission Indians armed with bows and arrows helped shore up the region's defenses. Odórico, an ex-alcalde from La Purísima, led twenty-five archers, ten on horseback, to the Santa Barbara Presidio. After Bouchard had sacked the coast and sailed on, the governor feared a second attack, and, in January 1819, he requested hundreds more armed Indians. Mission San Carlos was to provide sixteen of its best Indian archers; larger missions were to send thirty archers. A year later, Father Antonio Ripoll at La Purísima organized an Indian militia—the *Compañía de Urbanos Realistas de Santa Bárbara*—that counted 180 men variously armed with bows and arrows, lances, and machetes. Some went on horseback, and all drilled regularly to the beat of drums. Father President Mariano Payeras soon endorsed a similar plan that created four classes of Indian auxiliaries; mission alcaldes and regidores would command the fourth, the *Flecheros de Reservas*. The Spaniards'

42. Amorós, in *APST*, 126–127; John Dunmore, ed. and trans., *The Journal of Jean-François de Galaup de la Pérouse, 1785–1788*, 2 vols. (London, 1994–1995), I, 169. See also Donald C. Cutter, *California in 1792: A Spanish Naval Visit* (Norman, Okla., 1990), 133. Similarities between both of these accounts strongly suggest that these were staged demonstrations.

PLATE 15. *Indio de Monterey*. By José Cardero. 1791. Courtesy, Museo Naval, Madrid

desire to prevent California Indians from becoming like the Apaches—fearsome mounted warriors who periodically raided Spanish settlements of the southern Great Plains—meant that these Indian auxiliaries were never provided with fire-arms, and their weapons were kept at the mission under lock and key except during drills and times of attack. Further limiting the Indians' access to firearms were several factors: soldiers themselves were short on guns, shot, and powder, and they faced heavy punishments if they traded any firearms to Indians.[43]

If nothing else, the Spanish hoped that armed and mounted Indians, even if they did not have the firepower to repel invaders, might at least look intimidating from a distance and thereby serve as a deterrent. Nevertheless, permitting Indian auxiliaries to arm and drill regularly was the Spaniards' most explosive and risky application of indirect rule, for it bolstered armed, militarily skilled, authority-

43. On the Bouchard attack, see Peter Uhrowczik, *The Burning of Monterey: The 1818 Attack on California by the Privateer Bouchard* (Los Gatos, Calif., 2001); Hubert Howe Bancroft, *History of California*, 7 vols. (San Francisco, Calif., 1884–1890), II, 220–249. On the archers led by Odórico, see Mariano Payeras to José de la Guerra, Oct. 12, 1818, La Purísima, in Donald Cutter, ed. and trans., *Writings of Mariano Payeras* (Santa Barbara, Calif., 1995), 157–158. For the governor's request for reinforce-ments, see Solá to Payeras, Jan. 18, 1819, Mission San Antonio, Taylor Coll., doc. 915, HL; on the Compañía de Urbanos Realistas and the Flecheros de Reservas, see, respectively, Antonio Ripoll to Solá, Apr. 29, 1820, Santa Barbara, Taylor Coll., doc. 1085, HL; Payeras, "Plan para uniforma[n/r] la indiada de las misiónes, de esta California, de modo que sea util á la causa justa," 1821, Taylor Coll., doc. 1257, HL.

holding Indians with European tactics. The Spaniards' plans backfired in 1824, when armed Indians at La Purísima rebelled, built fortifications, and fired a cannon. Those at Santa Barbara joined the fray after the alcalde Andrés Sagimomatsse supplied the rebels with arms previously set aside for the militia. Ultimately, these insurgents proved no match for Spanish soldiers armed with guns, but the precariousness of Spanish authority and indirect rule had been revealed.[44]

Whether alcaldes were organizing laborers or leading warriors, their perquisites of office resembled the advantages that had distinguished village captains. The native elite had constituted a self-perpetuating oligarchy; similarly, in the early years of the elections, only Indian officials cast votes for their successors. Village captains wore "extravagant clothing" and possessed signs of office such as regalia and shell-bead money. Indian officials carried staffs, a customary symbol of leadership, and wore garments that distinguished them from the other neophytes. Officials might also have had special residences at the mission; in 1779, San Antonio Indians constructed houses just for the alcaldes and regidores. Alcaldes also received extra food. At San Carlos in 1783, 1784, 1785, and 1787, alcaldes, mission servants, and the Baja California Indians who had helped to establish the mission all received extra provisions. Twenty-one fanegas of wheat were planted for the mission as a whole; two additional fanegas were sown just for these groups. One of the greatest cultural privileges in Spanish colonial society was riding horseback, and, according to Julio César of Mission San Luis Rey, the alcaldes were among the few Indians allowed this honor.[45]

In pre-mission California, village captains "were usually released from ordinary labor" and "supported by the community," and the same was true for the Indian alcaldes. Anglo-American visitors to Alta California frequently described

44. For Indian auxiliaries as deterrents, see Payeras to padres at missions from Soledad to San Francisco, Feb. 27, 1819, Mission Soledad, in Cutter, ed. and trans., *Writings of Payeras,* 174–175. On Andrés Sagimomatsse, see George Harwood Phillips, *Indians and Intruders in Central California, 1769–1849* (Norman, Okla., 1993), 65; James A. Sandos, "Christianization among the Chumash: An Ethnohistoric Perspective," *American Indian Quarterly,* XV (1991), 65–89, esp. 82.

45. On the village elite, see Lowell John Bean, "Social Organization in Native California," in Bean and Thomas C. Blackburn, eds., *Native Californians: A Theoretical Retrospective* (Ramona, Calif., 1976), 112. For Indian officials' symbols of authority, see Serra to Lasuén, [Mar. 29], 1779, Mission San Carlos, in Tibesar, ed. and trans., *Writings of Serra,* III, 295; Antonio Paterna and José Cavaller, annual report, Feb. 2, 1780, Mission San Antonio de Padua, AGN, AHH, DPHM, 2d Ser., II, doc. 6. On the extra food, see "Libro de cuentas, inventario de la misión," Mission San Carlos, LDS film no. 0913303. Similarly, an itemization of the annual harvest lists the crops that were taken in for these members of the mission community separately from those gathered for everyone else. Lasuén worried that the missions would not have enough food to support officials, who would be entitled to special portions of grain but whose manual labor would be lost to the mission. See Lasuén to Neve, Jan. 25, 1779, in Kenneally, ed. and trans., *Writings of Lasuén,* I, 76–77. On alcades' riding horseback, see Julio César, "Recollections of My Youth at San Luis Rey Mission," trans. Nellie Van de Grift Sanchez, orig. publ. in *Touring Topics,* XXII (1930), 42–43, rpt. in Castillo, ed., *Native American Perspectives,* 13–15.

alcaldes as the laziest Indians in the missions. Hugo Reid noted: "Indian *Alcaldes* were appointed annually by the padre, and chosen from among the very laziest of the community; he being of the opinion that they took more pleasure in making the others work, than would industrious ones! From my own observation this is correct. . . . One of them always acted as overseer on work done in gangs, and accompanied carts when on service." James Pattie, an Anglo-American fur trapper from Ohio, stated that the alcaldes "are very rigid in exacting the performance of the allotted tasks, applying the rod to those who fall short of the portion of labor assigned them." Activities that these Anglo-American visitors interpreted as lazy and domineering might have been an extension of the traditional Indian customs that exempted leaders from manual labor. Despite these perquisites, Indian officials—like village captains—enjoyed only a slight material advantage over their people, and that advantage was never secure, dependent as all Indians were on a fragile mission economy and a suddenly transformed countryside.[46]

Given the Spaniards' desire to use the Indian officials to influence the larger mission population, that many of the early alcaldes and regidores in Alta California were village captains or men who had close blood ties to them is unsurprising. The Franciscans' initial opposition to the elections, after all, had not been a repudiation of the Spanish practice of indirect rule, nor did it reflect a belief that the Indians were without leaders. In a letter discussing events at Mission San Diego, Junípero Serra expressed his preference that Indian officials be recognized Indian leaders:

Let Francisco, with the same staff of office he uses and his coat, be the first alcalde, and it is nothing more than a change of name. Another alcalde might be the captain from one of the rancherías, of those that visit the mission every fifteen days. As for the regidores, who carry no staff, let one be from that ranchería, and the other from another; whether or not they are the captain of it [the ranchería], although it will be more appropriate if they are. In this manner everything will be settled without causing any great novelty.

46. On the labor of village captains, see Bean, "Social Organization," in Bean and Blackburn, eds., *Native Californians*, 112; Bean, "Social Organization," in *HNAI*, VIII, 678. On alcaldes' forcing others to labor, see Reid, [letter no. 19], "New Era in Mission Affairs," in Dakin, *A Scotch Paisano*, 272–273; Ruben Gold Thwaites, ed., *The Personal Narrative of James O. Pattie of Kentucky* . . . , Early Western Travels, XVIII (Cleveland, 1905), 276. James Rawls has pointed out that the majority of the descriptions of Indians and Mexicans by Anglo-Americans were negative. He argues that these portrayals might have been skewed to move public opinion in the United States toward the idea of annexing California (Rawls, *Indians of California*, 44–65).

Serra clearly recognized that the Indians already had their own leaders, and he seems to have viewed the alcalde system as a means of incorporating these leaders into the mission society and its political order. Serra also felt that selecting as alcaldes Indians who were not already recognized as leaders would cause disruption among the Indians and conflict between Indians and Franciscans. Governor Fages stated a similar willingness to recognize native leaders as Indian officials: at Mission San Diego, he also found it convenient and necessary "to continue recognizing those who were captains under native conditions, both at the mission and in the villages." Convenient because the leaders were known to all; necessary because they held the authority the governor wanted to see deployed in his favor.[47]

José María is an example of a local village captain who served as an official at Mission Santa Barbara. When the presidial commander suggested bringing José María along on the search to discover an overland route to New Mexico, the local Franciscans objected, saying that his presence was crucial to the mission's survival. Lasuén recounted to the governor José María's standing in the native villages and the Santa Barbara mission:

> What he [Tapis] stated regarding the Indian, José María, is a tribute to the good judgment and zeal of the missionary. The Mission of Santa Barbara has not been founded many years, and is surrounded by many pagans. It is a very important center, very sensitive, and the focal point of the conquest. For this reason it is only right that it should pain that religious to lose in such circumstances [an Indian with the qualities of] José María.
>
> He is the chief of those Indians. He it is who is in charge of field operations. He collaborates in bringing about the subjection, pacification, and education of those who are Christians, and the conversion of the pagans. He is beloved by the whole nation. I have seen a great part of the Channel in an uproar, and disposed to take up arms, because a rumor had spread that he had been killed at a ranchería in the sierras whither he had gone for a change and a little recreation after he had become a Christian.

José María's selection and service as an Indian official, therefore, reflected the converging designs of the neophytes, the Franciscans, and the governor. It is unclear exactly what made José María so popular with his own people, but Lasuén's suggestion that he was in charge of "field operations" and enjoyed life beyond the missions may provide a clue; perhaps, like the alcaldes at Santa Clara, José María moderated the mission's labor demands and secured for Indians time

---

47. Serra to Lasuén, [Mar. 29], 1779, Monterey, in Tibesar, ed. and trans., *Writings of Serra*, III, 294 (my trans.); Pedro Fages, general report on the missions, [1787], par. 33, Archives of California, C–A 52, 121–151, esp. 144–145, BL.

away from the mission to pursue customary economic and social activities. The Franciscans' willingness to recognize native political leaders such as José María is consistent with their practice of accepting and cultivating those elements of native culture that facilitated their control and conversion of the Indians. Importantly, in native California, village captains did not oversee religious practices. Had Indian societies been theocratic, or had they been seen by the padres as theocratic, the Franciscans would have taken Indian leaders as an affront to Catholicism and prevented them from serving as officials.[48]

As intermediaries between cultures, as men who had defined roles but ambiguous rules, Indian officials were often caught between the conflicting demands of the mission community and of the Franciscans. Men such as Homobono Sumipocsé and Claudio Ssojorois—and surely others who do not appear in the historical record—resisted the alcaldes' enforcement of a labor regime and so resented the alcaldes' use of their authority that they fled their new homes. Conversely, officials' conformity to Indian expectations often invited Franciscan condemnation, which could in turn drive them from the missions. Baltazar, the first alcalde at San Carlos Borromeo, ran afoul of the missionaries when he fathered a child by his wife's sister. The Indian community probably saw Baltazar's sororal polygyny as an emblem of his status and his acceptance of the duties of a good husband; the Franciscans considered it proof of his corruption. When he fled the mission, the Franciscans branded him a deserter and tried to sever his connection to his people. But Baltazar's ties to the Children of Coyote proved resilient for as long as he lived. From his home in the hills, Baltazar sent messages to the Indians at the mission, met with neophytes while they were on paseo, and tried to convince many to abandon San Carlos. In stirring up resistance, Baltazar was clearly relying on his authority as a leader and his notoriety as a defiant Indian official; his tactic was to maintain the trappings of leadership and appeal to individuals beyond the reach and gaze of the padres, both inside and outside the mission. In Baltazar's case, indirect rule had led to direct and calculated resistance; power and authority that the Spaniards could not harness to their own ends had been turned against them.[49]

48. Lasuén to Miguel de la Grúa Talamanca y Branciforte, Apr. 25, 1797, Mission San Carlos, in Kenneally, ed. and trans., *Writings of Lasuén,* II, 18. On José María, see John R. Johnson, "Chumash Social Organization: An Ethnohistoric Perspective" (Ph.D. diss., University of California, Santa Barbara, 1991), 126–127. According to Johnson, José María was the son of a captain, married to the sister of another captain, and had unusually wide-ranging kinship connections. On the degree to which California Indians divided religious, political, and economic authority, see Bean, "Social Organization," and Anna H. Gayton, "Yokuts-Mono Chiefs and Shamans," both in Bean and Blackburn, eds., *Native Californians,* 111–116, 175–224.

49. Serra to Neve, Jan. 7, 1780, Monterey, in Tibesar, ed. and trans., *Writings of Serra,* III, 409; Baltazar, San Carlos bapt. no. 268, Jan. 4, 1775.

Resistance by some alcaldes (such as Modesto and Baltazar) to Franciscan directives and acquiescence by others (such as Francisco Sevilla and Valeriano) suggest the tensions inherent in the alcaldes' role and rule. Even though their behavior at times appeared unpredictable and even unacceptable to Indians or Spaniards, Indian officials occupied a privileged space in the Spanish system as interpreters, mediators, and initiators of the new colonial order. The influence of officials within the Indian community clearly depended not only on the power and authority Spaniards invested in them but on the legitimacy these men brought to their leadership positions. Based on kinship, lineage, native political custom, and affinity for the needs of the Indian community, this legitimacy, in turn, explains both the ability of Spanish officials to orchestrate social, religious, economic, and political change within native communities and the degree to which native officials on occasion kept such initiatives at bay.

THE STAFF OF LEADERSHIP AT MISSION SAN CARLOS

The Indian officials' actions are more easily pulled from the historical record than are their identities. But Indians' names passed to presidio commanders in notifications of election results, and occasionally Indian officials appear in baptismal, marriage, and burial records. Forty-six alcaldes and regidores who served at San Carlos Borromeo from 1779 to 1831, probably about half the officials during those five decades, emerge from these records (see Appendix E). Their family relations, village affiliations, and vital statistics derived from the mission's sacramental registers allow for a composite portrait of the known staff of leadership at San Carlos. Collectively, these men stood at the center of the complex web of kinship and lineage that defined the Indian community. At first, Indians who held power in their own village communities provided the basis for the mission's leadership. Later, new Indian leaders gained promotion through the system. From their ranks came men who instigated rebellions against the Franciscans in the 1820s and reorganized Indian communities after the missions collapsed in the 1830s.[50]

At San Carlos Borromeo, Indian officials had unusual longevity within disas-

50. I uncovered the names of more than 46 officials but identified only 46 in the sacramental registers. During the period 1779–1831, there were a total of 212 leadership spots (53 years × 4 = 212). Of these 212 spots, the identified 46 officials filled at least 101. References by Franciscans at San Carlos Borromeo to fiscales cease at roughly the same time that elections for alcalde and regidor begin. The Franciscans might have continued to appoint fiscales for church-related tasks, but in all likelihood they relied on alcaldes and regidores instead.

trous circumstances. Put simply, they were among those fortunate enough to survive for a period of time amid the tumult of the dual revolutions. Additionally, they were always baptized men who were married or widowed. Women did not achieve recognition as political leaders from the Franciscans, and general studies suggest that political leadership in native California was nearly the exclusive domain of males. Indian officials were usually older and had attained baptism before other men from their villages. Thirteen of fourteen known officials who served during the period 1779–1798 fit this pattern. Of those elected in 1792, Hilario Joseph Holojaue was one of the first adult Esselen men baptized, Athanasio Joseph Huyuramus was older and had been in the mission longer than most Costanoan men, and Sancio Francisco Tepepis and Nicomedes Joseph Unique were older than most of the men from their communities. During the period 1799–1818, the majority of the Indian officials conformed to this pattern.[51]

Indian officials at election ranged in age from eighteen to sixty-four, but most were in their late thirties. Their median age was directly related to their responsibilities and status: Indians in their early twenties or younger would not have held the respect of Franciscans or neophytes, and most men in their fifties or sixties would have been too old for the job. Very few were born and raised at Mission San Carlos; thus nearly all had lived in a ranchería before baptism. During the eighteenth century, for an Indian official to have been born at the mission is almost impossible, since San Carlos was not founded until 1770. Yet, after 1800, only seven of thirty-two officials had lived all their lives under Franciscan supervision. Because of children's susceptibility to diseases at the mission, those born in rancherías might have had a greater chance of living to leadership age and thus of serving as officials. Moreover, men born outside the mission might have been more fluent in a native language and therefore able to cultivate stronger ties to recent recruits than the mission born.

Nevertheless, after 1800, most officials had attained baptism as young children and had spent the majority of their lives at the mission. The Indian officials' increasing mission age—the length of time between their baptism and first election—suggests that, over time, officials had greater knowledge of the Spanish language, Catholic rituals, and the design and workings of the mission system. No official before 1794 had been at San Carlos more than fifteen years when he was first appointed, but, after 1796, most lived at least twenty-five years at San Carlos before selection, and many had been at the mission for more than thirty

51. Richard Levy, "Costanoan," Bean, "Social Organization," and Edith Wallace, "Sexual Status and Role Differences," all in *HNAI*, VIII, 487, 678, 687; Joseph G. Jorgensen, *Western Indians: Comparative Environments, Languages, and Cultures of 172 Western American Indian Tribes* (San Francisco, Calif., 1980), 223–224.

years at their appointment. The main exceptions are three village captains, Nicomedes Joseph Unique, Sancio Francisco Tepepis, and Abrahan Guimesh—all of whom attained baptism as middle-aged men and had mission ages of seven, three, and four. Over the life of the mission, officials had been there for an average of nearly twenty-five years before election.[52]

Although survival to adulthood was a prerequisite for election—and clearly Indian officials had bucked long odds—alcaldes were not the only baptized individuals of leadership age in their respective ethnic-linguistic or village groups. The number of potential officials differed from group to group. In most years, there were 10 to 30 additional men of leadership age (twenty-five to fifty years old) who could have served, had age been the only qualification. For example, in January 1792, Hilario Joseph Holojaue was among 21 Excelen villagers, Nicomedes Joseph Unique was 1 of 5 Sargentaruc, Sancio Francisco Tepepis was 1 of 21 Kalendaruc, and Athanasio Joseph Huyuramus was 1 of 11 Tucutnut villagers and 1 of 25 Indians from the five Rumsen villages who were an appropriate age. Among the whole population, there were 111 men of leadership age.

As noted above, during the early years, Indian officials at San Carlos were likely to have been village captains or their close associates. Sancio Francisco Tepepis and Abrahan Guimesh were village leaders. Nicomedes Joseph Unique, also elected in the 1790s, was the "principal confidant" of the village captain Aristeo Joseph Chilichon. Later, with the death of village leaders and the survival of a cadre of men who spoke Spanish and had familiarity with the Franciscan regime—qualifications that supplanted previous experience as village captains— the mission community tended to produce its own leadership. After the early 1790s, fewer captains lived at the mission; those who came did not attain election. Three latecomers, Joaquín Chato Torres, Agustín Pasay, and Cornelio Siquieis, lived for many years at San Carlos but never became officials. They possibly served during one of the years for which the election results are lost or incomplete. But their lack of service as marriage witnesses suggests that these men were never part of the mission leadership hierarchy, and, to the extent that there was a ladder of leadership at San Carlos, serving as a marriage witness seems to have been an important rung. Although the missionaries might have concluded that the three latecomers did not have the necessary qualifications for election, these three might have retained a measure of influence among their own village groups. These captains, perhaps, were the "chiefs" in 1814 to whom Indians at the

52. If time spent in the mission can be correlated to acculturation, this phenomenon may support the hypothesis that some Indian officials internalized the values of the Franciscans and became harsh disciplinarians.

mission "show more respect and submission . . . than to the alcaldes who have been placed over them for their advancement as citizens."[53]

California Indians customarily passed political leadership from father to son. This practice carried over to San Carlos Borromeo, although it was disrupted by persistently high mortality. Of the thirty-seven baptized sons of identified village captains, only eight saw their mid-thirties. Four of these held positions of responsibility, three as officials, one as an interpreter. Two sons of Marcos Chaulis, Romano and Domicio José, served on the mission cabildo. Nestor José, son of the captain Abrahan Guimesh (who also was an official), became a regidor. And Misael Joseph Apajachiqui, whose father was village captain Felipe de Jesús Jojjoban, served as an interpreter. Low fertility of women and the high death rate among the young meant elite families had difficulty maintaining a direct line of influence. Yet the son of a village leader who lived to adulthood had a far better chance of winning election to the cabildo than others his age.[54]

Long before the coming of missionaries and the onset of the dual revolutions, the Children of Coyote had adopted strategies to offset the crisis of leadership that resulted when disease or warfare wiped out the heirs of leading families: high-born brothers married sisters from important families, or one man might wed several sisters. Baptized Indians pursued these marriage practices, even though abhorrent to the Franciscans, but they could not overcome the high mortality of the younger male neophytes. Indians also seem to have carried into the mission the custom of allowing a captain's eldest daughter to assume political authority if she had no brothers or none capable of leadership. Indians might have transferred authority of a deceased village captain to an eligible son-in-law, perhaps the husband of his eldest surviving daughter. This may explain why five of the Indian officials at San Carlos had fathers-in-law who had held the staff of leadership and another whose father-in-law had been a village captain. In all but one of these six cases, no sons survived, and, in the one case where there was a surviving son, he, too, served as an Indian official. Anthropologists have also suggested that, in native California, leadership could descend to the nephew of the leader. In Mission San Carlos, two Indian officials had uncles who were officials, and two more were the nephews of village captains.[55]

53. For Unique's political status, see Nicomedes Joseph Unique, San Carlos bapt. no. 1074, Mar. 19, 1785. Village captains baptized: Joaquín Chato Torres, San Carlos bapt. no. 2586, May 15, 1806; Agustín Pasay, San Carlos bapt. no. 2665, Aug. 14, 1807; Cornelio Siguieis, San Carlos bapt. no. 2671, Aug. 27, 1807. Juan Amorós, Feb. 3, 1814, is quoted in *APST*, 126.

54. Marcos Chaulis, San Carlos bapt. no. 2581, Apr. 26, 1806; Felipe de Jesús Jojjoban, San Carlos bapt. no. 1381, Nov. 16, 1788.

55. Among the Yokuts, "normally a son followed his father in this office but a younger brother or brother's son might succeed to it." "A chief's daughter or sister occasionally took over" (William J.

Alcaldes who did not have blood ties to former village captains were frequently related to other leading Indians: two were the sons of officials, three pairs were brothers, ten pairs were brothers-in-law, and eleven officials had close ties to mission interpreters. In addition, many alcaldes were related by marriage to soldiers. Longtime alcalde Athanasio Joseph Huyuramus had a daughter whose first and second husbands were soldiers at the Monterey Presidio. Other members of the cabildo had ties to privileged Indians from Baja California who worked closely with the Franciscans during the first years of the missions. Extended leadership families such as these show that, in the face of high death rates, powerful Indian families used marriage to maintain leadership status in the mission.[56]

Native practices of long-term rule and Spaniards' desires to support cooperative local leaders undermined Spanish laws that promoted turnover in office-holding. In the missions of California, Indians and padres pursued a common strategy to assure continuity of leadership: alcaldes and regidores rotated in office each year. Oresio Antonio Sichcon was regidor in 1810, 1812, and 1814 and alcalde in 1811, 1813, and 1815. Other officials sat out a year or two and then returned to office. Because of the rotational system, differences between the responsibilities of alcaldes and regidores faded over time. Important and cooperative Indians, provided they could stay alive, were thus never far from office; some served continuously for up to six years, and others moved in and out over more than fifteen years.

In most years, the elected leadership reflected the mission community; the mission's two language families and four largest village groups could each regularly claim one of the officials. Once Esselen villagers came to the mission after 1776, both Costanoan and Esselen speakers lived at San Carlos Borromeo, although Costanoans enjoyed numerical superiority over the latter throughout the mission's life. If late-eighteenth-century guidelines for the Franciscan missionaries at Mission Nuestra Señora de la Purísima Concepción in San Antonio, Texas, are typical of Franciscan electoral management in northern New Spain, the Franciscans at San Carlos Borromeo worked hard to ensure that officials were drawn from the mission's largest groups. The San Antonio instructions, written by Father José García probably in 1787 or 1788, urged the missionaries to "remind" voters that the

Wallace, "Southern Valley Yokuts," in *HNAI*, VIII, 454). Theopisto Joseph, Facundo Huaclanchi, and Luis Joseph Gergechom had Indian official fathers-in-law; Domicio José twice married the daughters of Indian officials; and Emygdio Joseph married the daughter of the captain Abrahan Guimesh. In some instances, the father-in-law was dead by the time the son-in-law had become an official. Abrahan Guimesh's son Nestor Joseph Unique was also an Indian official; Romano and Domicio José had uncles who were Indian officials, and Landelino José and Francisco de Paula Tiquitiqui were the nephews of village captains.

56. For daughter of Athanasio Joseph Huyuramus, see Cathalina María, San Carlos bapt. no. 29 and San Carlos marr. nos. 154 (May 8, 1780) and 197 (Sept. 30, 1782).

positions of governor and alcalde alternated annually between the most populous groups at the mission, the Pajalache and the Tacame.[57] Similarly, at San Carlos, "to facilitate and make more expedient the government of the mission," the Franciscans considered the mission to be composed of two "nations," each of which spoke a different language.[58] In 1792, the largest village groups at the mission could each claim one official. Since the majority of the neophytes at San Carlos were Costanoan speakers, so were three of four of the Indian officials.[59] In 1796, the largest village groups at the mission were Rumsen, Ensen, Excelen, and Kalendaruc. One official came from each of these groups, and three of four were Costanoan speaking: Athanasio Joseph Huyuramus (Rumsen-Costanoan); Abrahan Guimesh (Ensen-Costanoan); Lucas Antonio Coyyo (Excelen-Esselen); and Jayme Joseph Alcason (Kalendaruc-Costanoan). This correlation between the makeup of officials and the mission population as a whole reflected the needs of Spaniards and Indians alike. Franciscans would have found it difficult to incorporate and control the Indians without assistance from native leaders who could effectively communicate with the mission's most populous groups, and powerful Indian groups might have rebelled had they been excluded from positions of authority.

During the period 1809–1820, the ethnic-linguistic background of the Indian officials continued to reflect that of the mission. Costanoan-speaking Indians still outnumbered Esselen-speaking Indians, and, correspondingly, of the nineteen known officials during this period, only six certainly spoke Esselen. In each of these years, there was always at least one Esselen-speaking Indian official. The composition of the cabildo continued to represent the largest groups in the mission, with the exception of the Kalendaruc, and there were no Indian officials from the smaller village groups.

57. Benedict Leutenegger, trans., *Guidelines for a Texas Mission: Instructions for the Missionary of Mission Concepción in San Antonio, ca. 1760* (1976; rpt. San Antonio, Tex., 1990), par. 18, rpt. in Anne A. Fox, ed., *Archaeology of the Spanish Missions of Texas*, Spanish Borderlands Sourcebooks, XXI (New York, 1991), 81. The Pajalache Indians are also known as the Pajalats; see T. N. Campbell, "Coahuiltecans and Their Neighbors," in *HNAI*, X, 343–358. In Texas, at Mission San Francisco Solano, a similar situation prevailed: each major group was represented by a fiscal. Until the mid-1740s, at Missions San Antonio de Valero and Nuestra Señora de la Purísima Concepción, each major ethnic group was probably represented by an alcalde; see Schuetz, "Indians of the San Antonio Missions," 256–265. For examples of the ethnic distribution of Indian officials in the towns of colonial Mexico, see Haskett, *Indigenous Rulers*, 22, and Chance, *Conquest of the Sierra*, 134–135.

58. Pasqual Martínez de Arenaza and José Francisco de Paula Señán, annual report of Mission San Carlos, Dec. 31, 1789, AGN, AHH, DPHM, 2d Ser., II, doc. 97.

59. By 1792, Mission San Carlos had become linguistically and culturally diverse. Of the 775 Indians of identifiable origin and ancestry at the mission in 1792, 509 were Costanoan speakers: 220 were Rumsen, 112 were Kalendaruc, 88 were Sargentaruc, 73 were Ensen, and 16 were Pagchin. The four Esselen-speaking villages had given up 266 neophytes to the mission, with 156 coming from the ranchería known as "Excelen," or "Santa Clara." From 1792 to 1796, Ensen surpassed Sargentaruc as one of the four largest groups affiliated with the mission. Sargentaruc villagers declined from 88 in 1792 to 71 in 1796, whereas Ensen increased from 73 to 158. In 1792 and 1793, 90 Ensen gentiles attained baptism.

Not until 1810, when twenty-six-year-old Theopisto Joseph became regidor, did a mission-born official serve at San Carlos Borromeo. The paucity of the mission born underscores the practice of drawing the officials from the mission's different village and linguistic groups. Even after Indians born in the 1770s at the mission could have served in the mid-1790s, they did not dominate the leadership positions. And, after 1810, mission-born Indians filled only about one-quarter of the leadership positions; and those baptized before age ten took only slightly more than half. Clearly, the representation of different peoples, some of which did not come to the mission until the mid-1780s, took precedence over the selection of those individuals who, having spent their entire lives in the mission, might have been the most acculturated to Spanish ways and loyal to Franciscan wishes.[60]

INDIRECT RULE: DOUBLE-EDGED SWORD

That Indians rarely mobilized full-scale rebellions in colonial California could be taken as an indication of the Spaniards' effectiveness in establishing indirect rule and the Indians' quick and firm embrace of it. The destabilizing effects of the dual revolutions and the movement of various forms of Indian leadership into the missions blunted most overt insurrection. Through their own efforts and the Spaniards' recognition of their authority, many Indian leaders attained a stake in the evolving system. Indians and missionaries both exerted power through their own means and through each other, leading, most of the time, to relative political stability. When Indians did have grievances, they often pursued remedies short of open and collective rebellion, opting for individual resistance or noncompliance. Also, they could come and go, passing through the porous boundary between mission and countryside, and when necessary they could intimidate Spaniards through rumor and threat of attack. In most instances, when uprisings did occur, they were as much the result of absolute oppression as of accommodations denied. Full-blown rebellions did not occur at Mission San Carlos or most other California missions during the colonial period. Of course, everywhere, individuals like Baltazar challenged the padres' authority, and many resisted the Franciscans' labor regime and their religious teachings, but organized attacks were few and far between.

One of the rare large-scale Indian attacks on the Spanish in Alta California occurred in November 1775, before the institutionalization of indirect rule. For

60. By 1805, the Franciscans at Mission San Carlos could count at least eighteen mission-born men who were at least age twenty-five.

years, many Ipai and Tipai, also known as the Diegueño, had been wary of the Spaniards. Their first assaults had come in the summer of 1769, when scurvy-weakened mariners lay near death on the beach. Six years later, after hundreds of locals had attained baptism at Mission San Diego, they attacked again, but with greater organization and violence. On the night of November 4, 1775, a combined force of as many as one thousand assailants from the mission and the countryside rained arrows down upon Mission San Diego; they set the church, storehouses, and padres' living quarters afire, destroying them. In the onslaught, the Diegueño mutilated and killed one Franciscan and mortally wounded the mission's carpenter and blacksmith.[61]

A confluence of events and circumstances propelled the Diegueño into rebellion. Certainly, the dual revolutions had begun to remake the San Diego region by 1775, as the increase of baptisms and burials at the mission suggests. A year before the attack, the mission had been relocated from the barren coast to its site four miles inland. There, closer to good water and native villages, it encroached directly on Indian settlements and native patterns of land use. Unlike in Monterey, where the mission's agricultural expansion and growing village seemed to offer solutions to the problems of Spanish colonization, the situation at San Diego was altogether different. Arid land rendered it impossible for mission produce to feed many Indians and forced the Franciscans to abandon the policy of congregación in favor of encouraging most of the baptized to remain in their rancherías. Baptized Indians were to come to the mission a day every two weeks to hear Mass and undergo Catholic indoctrination. The fledgling mission, therefore, offered Indians little sustenance or community, and its presence reminded them of the disease and dislocations of Spanish colonization.[62]

A month before the storming of the mission, two village captains, the brothers Carlos and Francisco, had left Mission San Diego and ventured into the countryside with the assent of the padres. While they were on paseo, the two came across a group of elderly, unbaptized women, from whom they apparently confiscated several fish. It is easy to imagine that the two village leaders believed they were entitled to the women's catch; yet the women felt they had been robbed and said so to their fellow villagers, who then complained to the missionaries. In a sense, then, Carlos and Francisco were facing challenges by their own people, some of whom saw in the Franciscans an opportunity to confront a hierarchy that left them at the bottom. When Carlos and Francisco learned that they were

61. Serra to Antonio María de Bucareli y Ursúa, Dec. 15, 1775, Monterey, in Tibesar, ed. and trans., *Writings of Serra*, II, 401–407.
62. On the circumstances at the mission before the rebellion, see Maynard J. Geiger, *The Life and Times of Fray Junípero Serra, O.F.M.; or, The Man Who Never Turned Back (1713–1784)*, 2 vols. (Washington, D.C., 1959), II, 58.

now considered thieves and fugitives, they headed into the hills with five others from the mission and then evaded soldiers sent in search of them.[63]

By charging Carlos and Francisco with thievery and threatening them with arrest, the missionaries not only imperiled the two but undermined the leaders' status over their own people. Perhaps the brothers found particularly galling the Franciscans' attempt to extend Spanish authority into the countryside and interfere with their own customary right to food commoners produced. Widespread resentment of the Spaniards increased late in October, when several baptized Indians suffered a whipping at the mission for having joined in a dance at an outlying ranchería.[64] In the face of the Spaniards' intrusion into economic, political, and cultural affairs far beyond the mission, any fragile foundation for accommodation at San Diego melted away. Francisco and Carlos put together an alliance of some sixty-five to seventy surrounding villages that culminated in the destruction of the mission. Village leaders beyond San Diego no doubt had seen in the mission a growing threat to their own power and hold over their people. They probably grew even more concerned when the Spaniards moved to establish Mission San Juan Capistrano up the coast. Indians, however, also found in this moment of peril an opportunity, for, in mid-October, the military reduced the number of men guarding San Diego from twelve to four, sending the others to build the new mission and leaving San Diego open to attack.

After the rebellion, Francisco eluded capture until late January, and Carlos was arrested in March only after he sought sanctuary in the presidio's makeshift chapel. Military officials called for their execution as murderers and rebels. But the Franciscans pleaded with Spanish authorities to save the Indians' lives and make of them examples of Catholic charity and mercy. Spared death, Francisco remained at the center of Diegueño politics and mission relations, never severing his ties to his people or to the Spaniards. He was so powerful that the padres could not do without him; and he must have come to believe that he should work with the padres, who remained to rebuild the mission. Three years after the deadly rebellion, he and his brother Carlos received the sacrament of confirmation and had deepened their involvement in mission affairs, all in an attempt to maintain their ability to shape their own lives and those of the Diegueño. Serra wrote that the two men were "now such models of loyalty that they are the main support of the Fathers." Francisco formalized his role in mission affairs, becoming in 1779 the first alcalde elected at the mission. But his brother Carlos pursued his own strategy. The same year as Francisco's appointment, Carlos led a deadly

63. According to Serra, Carlos and Francisco were brothers. See Serra to Bucareli, Oct. 4, 1778, San Diego, in Tibesar, ed. and trans., *Writings of Serra*, III, 263. See also José Francisco Ortega to Juan Bautista de Anza, Nov. 30, 1775, San Diego, Archives of California, C–A 15, 2–8, BL.

64. Geiger, *Life and Times of Serra*, II, 60.

assault by baptized Indians on the village of Jalò, prompting the governor to banish him from Mission San Diego and sentence him to years of hard labor. Francisco walked a fine line and suffered arrest for not alerting the padres or soldiers to his brother's violent plans. But, by January 1780, again he had apparently become more compliant with the Spaniards' wishes, or at least he had become more expert at feigning cooperation. Francisco won reappointment to the cabildo in 1780 and served as regidor and fiscal. And he even gained the assignment of scouting the countryside to gather intelligence about another potential attack on the mission, a plum responsibility indeed for a leader never far from those actions that the Spaniards feared most. Clearly, men like Francisco, because of their authority among their people and their skill in working with colonial officials, remained indispensable to Spanish rule and the Indians' ability to shape it.[65]

The Franciscans and the Children of Coyote were soon aware of the San Diego uprising, and the padres anticipated a similar attack on San Carlos. A few days after the destruction of Mission San Diego, an Indian woman came to Carmel with the news that the Ensen were "coming to make war." Serra eagerly anticipated earning a martyr's crown and reportedly declared: "Behold, my Father Companions, now the hour has arrived; the Zanjones [Ensen] are approaching, so they say; there is thus nothing else for us to do but to be courageous and prepare ourselves for whatever God shall decree." The Franciscans' concern must have been heightened by the fact that the Ensen were virtually unknown to them; no Ensen attained baptism until 1777. Rain, not death blows, however, fell upon the mission, and the Franciscans concluded that either foul weather had thwarted the Indians' attack or that it had all been nothing more than "an imaginary tale."[66]

Imaginary tales and false alarms were common in Alta California, and rumors of Indian plots to kill the Franciscans and destroy the missions and presidios proved frequent and intimidating. In late December 1776, a suspicious fire dam-

65. On Francisco's loyalty, see Serra to Bucareli, Oct. 4, 1778, San Diego, in Tibesar, ed. and trans., *Writings of Serra,* III, 263. On Francisco's arrest in 1779, see "Diligencias practicadas . . . ," AGN, CA, LXXI, 1a–17a. On his reappointment in 1780, see Serra to Lasuén, Jan. 12, 1780, Monterey, in Tibesar, ed. and trans., *Writings of Serra,* III, 427; José Francisco Ortega to Neve, Sept. 25, 1781, Mission San Diego, Archives of Monterey, C–A 150, VII, reel 6, doc. 540, BL. On Carlos and sanctuary and the church-state tensions it unleashed, see Geiger, *Life and Times of Serra,* II, 88–98.

66. Quotes are from Francisco Palóu, in Maynard J. Geiger, ed. and trans., *Palóu's Life of Fray Junípero Serra* (Washington, D.C., 1955), 285–286. Palóu, Serra's friend and author of the original Serra hagiography, declared, "Whenever he [Serra] was in any such circumstance and in danger of shedding his blood at the hands of the pagans, his heart, it seems was filled with joy" (ibid). The most zealous of the Franciscan missionaries relished the idea of dying the martyr's death by fulfilling the apostle Mark's injunction: "Whoever loses his life for my sake and the gospel's will preserve it" (Mark 8:35). See also Gutiérrez, *When Jesus Came,* 129.

aged Mission San Luis Rey, and Indians at San Francisco and Santa Clara repeatedly challenged the Spaniards' authority. In March 1781, soldiers at San Diego
braced again for an attack after a village captain's wife married another man at
the mission and was prevented by the padres from returning to her village. In
1795, Indians at San Miguel apparently rumored that they were about to attack in
an attempt to get more food from the padres. And, throughout the mid-1790s,
Indians threatened to destroy Mission Santa Cruz and kill the Franciscans and
soldiers. Again in 1801, the Children of Coyote rumored that they were plotting to
kill the Franciscans and burn San Carlos. No such Indian attack ever occurred at
Carmel, but all these rumors and many others spread by Indians terrified the
padres and soldiers, keeping them all on guard, particularly about offending
native leaders.[67]

As the soldiers and padres at San Diego and elsewhere had discovered, incorporating Indian leaders like Francisco into their orbit was dangerous, but exclud-
ing them held risks greater still. Nicolás José of San Gabriel was another leading
native who used his power to work with and then against Spanish rule. His
actions exemplified the risks inherent for Spaniards in acknowledging Indian
authority while simultaneously clamping down on native sexuality and ceremo-
nialism. Nicolás José was one of the first Indians to enter the Franciscan fold at
San Gabriel and among the most active in the administration of Catholic sacraments. In late September 1774, at the age of twenty-six, he became the first adult
from the village of Sibapet and the third adult male Gabrielino to attain baptism.
Soon thereafter, he married Agustina María, in one of the first marriages at the
mission. In July 1775, their newborn son Cosmé María was baptized.[68]

Whether or not Nicolás José had exercised any sort of religious or political
authority in Sibapet, he did within a few months of his baptism hold a position of
prominence in the religious and political life of the mission. As one of the first
Gabrielino marriage witnesses, he held the early confidence of the Franciscans.
And the identities of the other witnesses with whom he was paired suggest his

67. See Neve to commandant general, Sept. 19, 1771, Monterey, Archives of California, C–A 22, 16–
21, esp. 20–21, BL; José Francisco de Ortega, May 1, 1778, San Diego, Archives of California, C–A 1, 288–
293, BL; Antonio Grajera to Borica, June 13, 1795, San Diego, Archives of California, C–A 7, 429–430,
BL; Hermenegildo Sal to Borica, Feb. 29, 1796, San Francisco, Archives of California, C–A 8, 19–20,
BL; Sal to Pedro Amador, Feb. 28, 1796, San Francisco, Archives of California, C–A 8, 43–44, BL.
Little is known about the rumored 1801 plot against San Carlos; see Bancroft, *History of California*,
II, 146.

68. Nicolás José, San Gabriel bapt. no. 87, Sept. 27, 1774, Mission San Gabriel baptism records, 1771–
1819, LDS film, reel 0002643. Although the page of the manuscript recording Nicolás José's marriage to
Agustina María is lost, the wedding certainly took place before December 1774, and therefore it was one
of the first ten marriages at the mission. Most likely it was the sixth. Agustina María was baptized
alongside Nicolás José; see San Gabriel bapt. no. 88, Sept. 27, 1774. Cosmé María: San Gabriel bapt. no.
161, July 13, 1775.

esteem within the native community. In 1775, for example, Nicolás José served as a witness with the leader of a nearby village. Over the next decade, he was often a marriage witness and a godparent at baptisms, proving his central place within the Indian community and the padres' recognition and affirmation of his elevated status. In 1781, he became the only Gabrielino to serve as a godparent for the child of a Baja California Indian. This Nicolás José almost certainly was the same Nicolás who became the mission's first alcalde in 1778–1779 and aroused the ire of the Franciscans by providing, in Serra's words, "women to as many soldiers as asked for them." For this behavior, Nicolás José was punished, which might have caused him and others to plot a rebellion in the late 1770s.[69]

Years later, in October 1785, Nicolás José again organized Gabrielino neophytes and gentiles from the surrounding area to attack the mission. Given warning, the corporal of the guard on the night of the attack arrested twenty-one Gabrielinos without bloodshed. During an investigation, four leading Indian suspects identified Nicolás José as the prime instigator. Nicolás José, according to his testimony, was upset because neither the padres nor the guards would allow Indians to perform ceremonial dances or practice what the Spaniards termed "gentile abuses." Traditionally, in the fall, the Gabrielino held their annual Mourning Ceremony, which "honored the souls of those who had died in the interval since its [the ceremony's] last performance." It "was the culmination of a series of death rituals, and through its performance the souls of the deceased achieved release from the earth and entrance into the land of the dead."[70]

69. In December 1774, Nicolás José, along with José María Borjino and Antonio Mathias Planes (the future fiscal of the church), served as a witness in the tenth marriage at the mission (San Gabriel marr. no. 10, Dec. 6, 1774; San Gabriel marr. no. 25, Sept. 20, 1775; Matheo María, captain of Ajuibit, San Gabriel bapt. no. 81, June 6, 1774). According to the San Gabriel marriage records from 1774 to 1784, Nicolás José was a participant in the prenuptial investigations at five Catholic marriages, a witness at two weddings, and a *padrino* (godfather) at thirteen baptisms. For details of Nicolás José's participation in the sacraments, see Steven W. Hackel, "Sources of Rebellion: Indian Testimony and the Mission San Gabriel Uprising of 1785," *Ethnohistory,* L (2003), 666 n. 53, 54. Nearly every detail about Nicolás José's life that emerges from the mission's sacramental registers—the comparatively early date of his baptism and marriage, his relatively advanced age when they occurred, and his continual service as godparent and marriage witness—strongly suggests that he would have been a prime candidate to serve as an official when Spaniards introduced the alcalde system into Alta California. The baptism register of Mission San Gabriel records only one other Nicolás before January 1780: Nicolás Sánchez, San Gabriel bapt. no. 178, Nov. 8, 1775. He is not recorded as a godparent or a marriage witness, which suggests that he was not central to the mission hierarchy. On confusions over Spanish names in the sacramental registers, see Appendix A, below. On the alcalde Nicolás's providing women to the soldiers, see Serra to Neve, Jan. 7, 1780, Monterey, in Tibesar, ed. and trans., *Writings of Serra,* III, 414–415. Nicolás José's plot before 1785 emerged in the questions that the governor drafted for the interrogation of the suspects in 1785. For the complete trial transcript, see AGN, PI, CXX, expediente 2, 31a–47b. For mention of the previous rebellion, see Pedro Fages at ibid., 32b, 38a.

70. Testimony of Nicolás José, AGN, PI, CXX, expediente 2, 36a; William McCawley, *The First Angelinos: The Gabrielino Indians of Los Angeles* (Banning, Calif., 1996), 162. On Indian motivations for the rebellion, see Hackel, "Sources of Rebellion," *Ethnohistory,* L (2003), 643–669. See also McCawley,

In 1782, three years before the rebellion, the governor had in fact ordered soldiers not to allow baptized Indians to have dances, a decree that outlawed celebrations such as the Mourning Ceremony. The governor's edict marked a break with Spanish policy in California, and it seems to have been selectively enforced. Throughout Alta California, Indians marked the change in seasons and personal transitions with ritual gatherings and dances to bring the sacred closer to their lives. Dances and ceremonies were quite common at most missions throughout the colonial period. The Luiseño performed dances regularly at Mission San Luis Rey, as did Costanoans at Missions San Jose and San Francisco. At both San Jose and San Francisco, Indians in full regalia danced within the mission courtyard. San Carlos Indians also held dances in their village adjacent to the mission. By the end of October 1785, however, Nicolás José and others at San Gabriel must have found the Spaniards' enforcement of the ban to be intolerable and a threat to the repose of their dead relatives.[71]

What distinguished Nicolás José from other neophytes was, not his frustration with life under Spanish rule, but rather his ability to organize a collective response. Still, in many ways—perhaps to a degree that far surpassed in importance the prestige he garnered through the mission system—his life resembled that of other mission Indians. Although he was baptized and a regular participant in the administration of the Catholic sacraments, he remained faithful to Gabrielino dances, celebrations, and rituals. Although resident at the mission, he remained connected to the unbaptized Gabrielinos of the countryside. And, although at one time a mission alcalde, he, like all mission Indians, struggled against great misfortune. No Indian, no matter how politically or religiously powerful, could escape the diseases that continually ravaged the mission community. By the eve of the rebellion, one-third of the baptized adults from Sibapet, Nicolás José's home village, and one-half of its baptized children were dead.[72] And among these were members of Nicolás José's immediate family. His son Cosmé María perished before the age of two. He buried his wife in June 1783. Within a year of her death, he remarried, but his second wife died just eight months later. If these mounting

---

First Angelinos, 32–33, 189–191; Bernice Eastman Johnston, *California's Gabrielino Indians* (Los Angeles, 1962); Zephyrin Engelhardt, *San Gabriel Mission and the Beginnings of Los Angeles* (San Gabriel, Calif., 1927), 273.

71. For the prohibition on dances, see Fages to José de Zuñiga, Oct. 17, 1782, Monterey, Archives of California, C–A 15, 152, BL; Zuñiga to Fages, 1782, Archives of California, C–A 2, 77–78, BL. On Indian dances at missions, see Pablo Tac, in Castillo, ed., *Native American Perspectives*, 35–58, esp. 47, plate 3; Raymundo Carrillo, Oct. 13, 1802, Santa Barbara, AGN, PI, CCXVI, expediente 1, 104b–111a, esp. 109a–109b.

72. I derived these figures from a database of my own creation that links birth and death records for Indians baptized and buried at Mission San Gabriel. At the time of the rebellion, some forty-seven Sibapet adults had been baptized, of which sixteen were dead. Of fifty-four Sibapet children baptized before the rebellion, by the time of the rebellion, some twenty-seven were deceased.

PLATE 16. *Danse des habitants de Californie à la mission de San Francisco.* By Louis Choris.
1816. Choris et al., *Voyage pittoresque autour du monde*, part 3 (Paris, 1822), plate 3.
Various groups of Indian dancers adorned in regalia perform in front of
the mission church. Missionaries watch from the front of the church, women
dance in the background, and seated men and women make music with
wooden sticks. The Bancroft Library, University of California, Berkeley

personal tragedies shook Nicolás José's faith in Catholicism and the mission
system, he must have largely concealed this growing dissatisfaction from the
Franciscans. He did not flee the mission, and he participated in its religious life
up until the rebellion. In July 1785, he had married again, and in August he served
as a marriage witness.[73]

In the midst of his bereavement and his outward commitment to San Gabriel,
Nicolás José planned the 1785 rebellion. His close work alongside the Franciscans
gave him an understanding of both the strengths and the limits of the Franciscan
program and the soldiers' defenses. It is not clear whether, when faced with the
prohibition on native ceremonial dances, he sought to restore the dynamic equilibrium he had created between his two worlds or whether he sought to destroy
the Spaniards. It is evident, though, that, in organizing the uprising, he tapped
into the fears and frustrations of those inside and outside the mission who were
in a position to help him.

73. Cosmé María, San Gabriel bur. no. 22, Oct. 28, 1775, Mission San Gabriel burial records, 1774–
1855, LDS film, reel 0002646; Agustina María, San Gabriel bur. no. 247, June 5, 1783. Nicolás José
married María Candelaria on Feb. 3, 1784 (San Gabriel marr. no. 192). María Candelaria was baptized
on Jan. 2, 1784 (San Gabriel bapt. no. 953); she died on Sept. 23, 1784 (San Gabriel bur. no. 323). Nicolás
José married Ludgarda María on July 3, 1785 (San Gabriel marr. no. 248) and was a marriage witness at
San Gabriel marr. nos. 252 and 253, both on Aug. 15, 1785.

Nicolás José contacted Toypurina, a twenty-five-year-old unbaptized woman from the village of Japchivit. Her brother was a village leader, and she was considered "very wise" by the villagers of the area. Nicolás José gave her beads to convene a meeting of the leaders of the unbaptized Gabrielino. She, in turn, contacted Temejasaquichí of Juvit village, and he went to the mission to encourage the neophytes to join in the rebellion. Many did. All Indians of the region—baptized and unbaptized—must have seen the abolition of ceremonial dances as a threat to their already imperiled way of being. And they also might have joined the rebellion because of the accelerating effects of the dual revolutions on their lives. In the six years before the rebellion, the mission's population had nearly doubled, increasing from 452 in 1780 to 843 in 1785. Yet this growth was not based on births at San Gabriel but on the increasing number of Indians from greater distances who attained baptism at the mission. This coincided with a steady expansion of the mission's agricultural production and a 300 percent increase in its livestock. The dual revolutions had rearranged the landscape and the human geography of the region, and Indians outside the mission might have attacked San Gabriel in 1785 to block further encroachment on their land by strange animals and unfamiliar Indians: notably, in the attack, insurgents killed sheep and cattle.[74]

Through the haze of time, Nicolás José emerges from the historical record as someone whom the "microhistorians" would consider a "normal exception." He was exceptional in that he was one of the few Indians in colonial California to lead a rebellion against his mission, and, therefore, he left a visible trace in the historical record. But his uniqueness helps us grasp part of what was almost certainly normal about him: the synthesis of his life at the mission with his identity as a Gabrielino, all in the midst of his day-to-day struggle with life and death in the wake of the dual revolutions. For his role in the attack, Nicolás José suffered banishment from San Gabriel and six years of hard labor at the presidio of San Francisco. His separation from his homeland severed him permanently from those who shared the culture he had fought to protect.[75]

74. Testimony of Nicolás José, AGN, PI, CXX, expediente 2, 37a. On his testimony, see Hackel, "Sources of Rebellion," *Ethnohistory*, L (2003), 654 n. 67. See also testimony of Toypurina, AGN, PI, CXX, expediente 2, 34b–35a; on population increases at San Gabriel, see J. N. Bowman, "The Resident Neophytes (Existentes) of the California Missions, 1769–1834," *Historical Society of Southern California Quarterly*, XL (1958), 138–148. In 1780, the mission produced 1,892 fanegas of wheat, barley, corn, beans, peas, lentils, and garbanzos; in 1785, the harvest was 2,725 fanegas. In 1780, the mission counted 1,528 head of cattle, sheep, goats, pigs, horses, and mules; in 1785, the animals numbered 4,945 head. See Engelhardt, *San Gabriel Mission*, 273, 278. On the rebels' killing livestock, see testimonies of Temejasaquichí, Toypurina, and Nicolás José, in AGN, PI, CXX, expediente 2, 34a, 35a, 36b.

75. "Normal exception": see Edward Muir, "Observing Trifles," introduction to Muir and Guido Ruggiero, eds., *Microhistory and the Lost Peoples of Europe* (Baltimore, 1991), xiv. Toypurina was banished from Mission San Gabriel and sent to Mission San Carlos. Temejasaquichí, having already

Rebellions like this one were local in scope, not regional in breadth, and they primarily reinforced the Franciscans' wariness of the Indians upon whom they had become so dependent. Father Gerónimo Boscana, who served in the California missions for a quarter of a century (1806–1831), well understood the risks inherent in relying upon Indian officials. With bitterness, Father Boscana concluded that, since all the intelligent Indians' "operations are accompanied by stratagems and dissimulation, they easily gain our confidence, and at every pass we are deluded." Other Franciscans shared Boscana's skepticism. By 1818, the missionaries had grown so distrustful of the alcaldes that they included in their annual confession questions designed to ferret out rogue or uncompliant officials. To be safe, Father President Vicente Francisco de Sarría instructed his subordinates to specifically ask the "Captains and Alcaldes" at the missions: "Have you ordered the people to do bad things? Or have you consented to let the people you care for do bad things? Or have you failed to advise [the padres] so that they could be corrected?" It seems doubtful that the Franciscans expected alcaldes to reveal their own conspiracies, but the hope that they might further reveals the padres' dependence upon these men whom they could no more trust than do without.[76]

INDIAN OFFICIALS IN MEXICAN CALIFORNIA

Decades before the padres became openly suspicious of Indian officials, Spain had introduced its form of municipal government into the missions to prepare neophytes for the day when they would be self-governing. The protracted struggle of the Mexican independence movement had an enormous impact upon the missions in California and appeared to hasten the arrival of that day. As soon as word of Mexico's independence from Spain reached California in early 1822, Indian officials were called upon to play a new role. Under Mexico's new political system, the territory of California would elect and send a deputy to the new parliament in Mexico. Indians participated in these elections. On April 17, 1822,

---

spent more than two years in jail, was given a stern warning and freed. See opinion of Galindo Navarro confirmed by the commandant general, AGN, PI, CXX, expediente 2, 44a–46a.

76. Gerónimo Boscana, *Chinigchinich: A Historical Account of the Origin, Customs, and Traditions of the Indians at the Missionary Establishment of St. Juan Capistrano, Alta California . . .* , 328, in Alfred Robinson, *Life in California . . .* (1846; New York, 1969). Serra learned this early when one of his "very useful" interpreters was implicated in the San Diego rebellion. And, in 1801, when belief in the Chupu prophecy spread through Mission Santa Barbara, the alcaldes, along with most of the Indians, renounced Christianity. See Robert F. Heizer, "A California Messianic Movement of 1801 among the Chumash," *American Anthropologist,* XLIII (1941), 128–129. For Sarría's instructions, see his confessional, written in June 1818 and circulated in November 1818, SBMAL.

the governor of California ordered "that alcaldes and regidores of the missions, with the assistance of the padres, name in each [mission] an *elector de partido*." Although few records survive today describing the implementation of this law, some missions carried it out. On May 1, 1822, San Antonio Indian officials chose as their elector José Arruz, a mestizo whose father, a soldier, had married an Indian woman. The level of the Indians' participation remains unclear; yet the Indian officials' marks on the certificate of José Arruz's credentials reveal a greater Indian involvement in California's nascent *deputación* than previously suggested by historians.[77]

In a development that held as much, if not more, importance for Indians than these electoral reforms, beginning in 1810 and continuing through the 1820s, the Mexican independence movement shook the hybrid system of indirect and representative rule in the missions of California. Spain's economic and political support for frontier missions evaporated during the Mexican struggle, and, after Mexico won independence in 1821, the new federal government attempted to expel Spanish missionaries, whose loyalty it doubted, and challenged the missions as anachronistic relics of Spanish rule and impediments to economic growth. During these years, soldiers and settlers increasingly relied on the missions for food and laborers just as Franciscan authority was weakening. While politicians at the national level debated the form that the new government would take, Indians also contested political authority in the missions, as they, too, tried to clarify who had the right to rule.[78]

At several missions, Indian officials rejected the colonial order altogether and led their people away. In 1824, Andrés Sagimomatsse, an alcalde at Mission Santa Barbara, joined forces with José Pacomio at La Purísima and rebels at Mission Santa Inés to lead the largest of the Indian uprisings in Mexican California. In

77. On political changes in California after Mexican independence, see Bancroft, *History of California*, II, 450–455; governor of California to father prefect, Apr. 17, 1822, Monterey, Archives of California, C–A 56, 342–345, BL. These men were then to convene and elect a regional representative; see credentials of José Arruz, signed by the Indian officials and Franciscans Juan Bautista Sancho and Pedro Cabot, May 1, 1822, Mission San Antonio, Taylor Coll. (document is misfiled at end of collection), HL. For a similar election, see Pedro Cabot, Nov. 26, 1826, San Antonio, Archives of California, C–A 18, 222–224, BL.

78. On the end of the missions, see Chapter 9 and Epilogue, below, and David J. Weber, *The Mexican Frontier, 1821–1846: The American Southwest under Mexico* (Albuquerque, N.Mex., 1982), 43–68. Municipal electoral reforms instituted elsewhere in Mexico after 1810 did not directly affect the missions. For the revolutionary period, see Roger L. Cunniff, "Mexican Municipal Electoral Reform, 1810–1822," in Nettie Lee Benson, ed., *Mexico and the Spanish Cortes, 1810–1822: Eight Essays* (Austin, Tex., 1966), 59–86. Most Indian communities during this period were subsumed into larger political units, and the Indian cabildo was displaced by an *ayuntamiento* (municipal council), which was usually dominated by non-Indians. In many areas outside of Alta California, these changes spelled the end of Indian political autonomy; see Farriss, *Maya Society under Colonial Rule*, 375–379; Haskett, *Indigenous Rulers*, 197; Cheryl English Martin, *Rural Society in Colonial Morelos* (Albuquerque, N.Mex., 1985), 196–197.

1827, Narciso and two other Indian officials persuaded some four hundred Indians to flee San Jose; another alcalde, Estanislao, joined this resistance the following year; and a fifth San Jose official, Victor, was later implicated and punished. These insurgencies, like those led by Francisco of San Diego and Nicolás José of San Gabriel, dealt hard blows to the missions even though soldiers eventually put them down. Such rebellions did not merely demonstrate Indians' dissatisfaction; taken collectively, they laid bare the dependence of the colonial system on Indian authority, for they showed once again how Indian officials frequently held the fate of the missions in their hands.[79]

At San Carlos Borromeo, worsening economic conditions and declining Franciscan control did not lead to overt rebellion; rather, Indians negotiated and disputed among themselves political control of the mission. As disease, disaffection, and flight greatly reduced the pool of Indians most likely by lineage to assume the staff of leadership, elections began to create, rather than merely reinforce, political authority, and the votes themselves became vulnerable to contestation. When the Franciscan-brokered electoral system failed, one group came to control the vast majority of leadership positions. Their political dominance in the decade 1822–1831 finally provoked open dispute and formal appeals for the intervention of Mexican secular authorities.

By 1831, Indians at San Carlos Borromeo had transformed and adopted a practice that Spaniards had originally considered an emblem of Spanish order. Held on a Sunday after Mass under the scrutiny of the Franciscans, Indian elections in the 1780s and 1790s had been thoroughly infused with Catholic meaning and Franciscan authority. As time passed, however, elections reflected Indian choices more than Spanish procedures. By 1831, Indians had separated the annual election from the Catholic schedule of worship; they held it, not on Sunday, but on Saturday evening when they gathered for their own diversions and discussions. Furthermore, they chose their officials, not in the church or in the shadow of the missionaries, but rather in their own ritual space, their temescal, sheltered from Franciscan intrusion and oversight. In addition to returning the election to an Indian site, they chose two men, Domicio José and Romano Chaulis, who were sons of a village captain.[80]

79. On the Chumash rebellion, see James A. Sandos, "Levantamiento! The 1824 Chumash Uprising Reconsidered," *SCQ*, LXVII (1985), 109–133; Sandos, "Christianization among the Chumash," *American Indian Quarterly*, XV (1991), 65–89; Phillips, *Indians and Intruders in Central California*, 65–69. For Indian insurrections at Mission San Jose, see Ignacio Martínez to José María de Echeandía, May 21, 1827, Taylor Coll., doc. 1936, HL; Jack Holterman, "The Revolt of Estanislao," *Indian Historian*, III (1970), 43–54, 66; Echeandía, Feb. 7, 1829, San Diego, Archives of California, C–A 18, 442–443, BL.

80. On elections as an extension of the church, see Arrillaga to Borica, Apr. 28, 1796, Loreto, AGN, CA, LXV, expediente 7, 307a–308b. Arrillaga describes the election of officials in Baja California missions, procedures that in all likelihood resembled those of Alta California. For indications that

Although this demonstrated a continuity with pre-mission times, the dispute afterward signaled that some of the Children of Coyote had grown accustomed to the representative system that the Franciscans had overseen. In January 1831, four Indians asked that the recent election be invalidated because it had not occurred at the proper time and place and because the winners did not represent different village groups. All of the newly elected officials descended from one group, the Ensens. It was to Antonio Buelna, magistrate at the Monterey Presidio, that Indians brought their objection: "Domicio is the half-brother of Romano, and the first cousin of Francisco. Francisco is the brother-in-law of Agricio José, and furthermore, Agricio José is a distant relative of Domicio; they are one people." Of the four San Carlos Indians who petitioned for a new election, the village ancestry of three has been identified. None was Ensen, and all were from displaced leadership lineages. Gaudín was Rumsen-Costanoan and the grandson of a man who was alcalde in 1786. Landelino José had been regidor in 1827, and he was the nephew of Theodosio Jutis, a captain from the village of Excelen. Martín was also of Esselen descent. His *padrino*, Martín Linquis, was alcalde in 1799 and 1805. Although these men had complained that the four elected Indians were all "one people," they, too, were related: Martín and Landelino José were brothers-in-law, since in 1813 Landelino José had married Martín's sister Serafina.[81]

In their objection, Antonio, Landelino José, Gaudín, and Martín illustrated the Indians' participation in the political system at Mission San Carlos and the importance they placed in the election. In one of the few surviving letters from the colonial period that carries the signature marks of California Indians, they affirmed their right to representation and suggested a remedy for what they perceived as electoral abuses. They proposed a return to the system of drawing officials from the mission's different groups, arguing that "it be made a condition that each direction or tribe will elect only one [official]." Their awareness of the winners' shared family ties and their assertion of diversity within the mission underscore the extent to which mission Indians continued to derive their identities from their places of origin decades after they had left their ancestral village. Furthermore, the protesters implicitly accepted the annual elections as a means of generating and legitimating Indian authority; they denounced the procedures of one election, not the practice of electing officials.[82]

Indians asserted authority over the elections, see letter signed by Antonio with the marks of Landelino José, Gaudín, and Martín to Antonio Buelna, Jan. 18, 1831, Carmel Pueblo, Archives of Monterey, C–A 150, I, reel 1, 266–268, BL. The letter is in the hand of José Joaquín Gómez, the customs officer for Monterey. Buelna did not leave his mark on the document.

81. Ibid.; Theodosio Jutis, San Carlos bapt. no. 896, Dec. 7, 1783.

82. Letter to Buelna signed by Antonio et al., Jan. 18, 1831, Archives of Monterey, C–A 150, I, reel 1, 266–268, BL.

Most Indians in Spanish California experienced disease, dislocation, and an early death; a few, though, also found political opportunity and a chance to shape the colonial system. The prominence of individuals like Francisco, Baltazar, Nicolás José, and Andrés Sagimomatsse and the coherence of the groups they led suggest that the political system the Spaniards relied on to control the missions depended upon and fostered the preservation and creation of native authority. For the most part, Indian officials cooperated with the Spanish, but a crisis could incite them to attack the colonial system. In doing so, they shored up their support among their own people even as they courted dismissal by the Spaniards. Still, it was never in the interest of the Spanish to replace uncooperative officials with Indians whose legitimacy was not recognized by their own people. Nor was it in their interest to level the distinctions of rank among Indians. To have done so would have provoked opposition from the Indians who could most effectively assist in controlling the missions.[83] Doubtless, there were Indian officials whose malleability rather than their kinship or lineage brought them to the attention of the Franciscans. But, for the most part, the alcalde system depended on the extent to which native villages, leadership, and traditions were incorporated into the missions. The authority of Indian officials in colonial California originated from more than brute force, Franciscan missionaries, or the Spanish state. It was carried over from Indian rancherías, legitimated and recreated in annual mission elections, and ultimately strengthened or weakened by the extent to which the officials remained embedded in the shifting family and village relations of the colonial period. Despite all their seeming advantages and connections, mission officials could secure for themselves a life only marginally less difficult than that of their community. But, after the missions were destroyed by the Mexican state in the 1830s, these men often profited from their close associations with missionaries and state officials and became, in an ironic turn, the Indians most likely to gain for themselves independent lives beyond the missions, apart from those who had empowered them.

83. Farriss, *Maya Society under Colonial Rule,* 237.

7

◄ ◄ ► ►

INDIAN LABOR IN THE
MISSIONS, PRESIDIOS, AND PUEBLOS
ECONOMIC INTEGRATION, CULTURAL
RESISTANCE, AND SURVIVAL

In September 1786, the French maritime explorer Jean-François de Galaup de la Pérouse anchored his ships for ten days in Monterey. While Indians from San Carlos worked alongside soldiers from the presidio to load vegetables, animals, grain, and wood into his ships, La Pérouse observed the region. A proponent of individual liberty and the equal rights of man, he likened the mission to a plantation and the Indians to slaves, although ones governed with "gentleness and humanity."[1] Had La Pérouse stayed in California longer, he might have discerned a far more complicated and fluid economy in which Indians took on, even initiated, multiple and overlapping forms of labor.[2] Few California Indians had a singular working identity, such as the one that La Pérouse ascribed to those he saw in 1786. They did labor against their wills for the Franciscans, who believed that work itself played a crucial role in converting them, but they also moderated or evaded those labor demands through steps of their own. Indians

---

1. John Dunmore, ed. and trans., *The Journal of Jean-François de Galaup de la Pérouse, 1785–1788*, 2 vols. (London, 1994–1995), I, 174. Later, La Pérouse continued: "The colour of these Indians is similar to that of negroes; the religious' house, their stores, built of brick and mortar, the threshing floor on which they crush the grain, the cattle, the horses, everything brought to mind a homestead in Sto Domingo or any other colony; . . . the similarity was even greater in that we saw men and women in irons, others were in the stocks and, finally, the sound of whipping could well have reached our ears, this punishment being included, although carried out with little energy" (179–180). Loaded onto the ships of the expedition at Monterey were "44 oxen, 51 lambs, 200 hens, 30 bushels of wheat, 32 of oats, 8 tunny fish, 80 large sacks of vegetables, 1 barrel of milk, wood and dried grass" (193, n. 3).

2. Differing assessments of the nature of Indian labor in the missions are juxtaposed in Rupert Costo and Jeannette Henry Costo, eds., *The Missions of California: A Legacy of Genocide* (San Francisco, Calif., 1987). For an equation of mission labor with all labor in California, see, for example, the important synthesis by Howard Lamar, "From Bondage to Contract: Ethnic Labor in the American West, 1600–1890," in Steven Hahn and Jonathan Prude, eds., *The Countryside in the Age of Capitalist Transforma-*

also worked in various capacities in the presidios for soldiers who found manual labor demeaning and relegated it to Indians in an attempt to elevate their own social status and modify their own racial identities. Moreover, Indians also continued to pursue elements of long-established subsistence economies just as they managed informal economic arrangements and accommodations with soldiers and settlers. In short, California Indians crafted, through their own flexible labor, an active response to European settlement and thereby softened some of the blows of colonization and the dual revolutions.[3] Ultimately, though, the coercive labor systems that ensnared them and the informal work relationships that they entered into with Spaniards not only led soldiers and settlers to depend on others for labor but encouraged Indians to rely more and more on working for Spaniards to improve their own livelihoods. These interdependencies and oppressive labor and social relations continued to characterize Spanish California well after the missions had been secularized in the 1830s.

IMPERIAL CONTEXT OF INDIAN LABOR

In 1769, Spain took possession of Alta California to protect the silver mines of northern New Spain from an encroachment by the Russians or English. By this time, after its defeat in the Seven Years' War, the Crown had become increasingly preoccupied with reducing the expense of its overseas empire and making all of its colonies productive within a framework of mercantilism. Therefore, the economic development of Alta California, the relationships between its missions, presidios, and pueblos, and the colonial labor of Indians all bore the imprint of officials who sought to ensure that soldiers and missionaries could feed, clothe,

tion (Chapel Hill, N.C., 1985), 293–324, esp. 299–300. For an early and still influential study of Indian labor in Alta California, see Sherburne F. Cook, "The Indian versus the Spanish Mission," *Ibero-Americana,* XXI (1943), 1–194, rpt. in Cook, *The Conflict between the California Indian and White Civilization* (Berkeley, Calif., 1976). Cook incorrectly asserted that "subsequent to 1790 the attempt to pay for Indian labor was abandoned and the work was done under unmitigated compulsion" (97). See also Robert Archibald, "Indian Labor at the California Missions: Slavery or Salvation?" *Journal of San Diego History,* XXV (1978), 172–196; Daniel J. Garr, "A Rare and Desolate Land: Population and Race in Hispanic California," *Western Historical Quarterly,* VI (1975), 133–148.

3. David Sweet, "The Ibero-American Frontier Mission in Native American History," in Erick Langer and Robert H. Jackson, eds., *The New Latin American Mission History* (Lincoln, Neb., 1995), 1–48, esp. 31–46. For illustrative examples elsewhere in colonial Latin America of Indians' using their labor to their advantage, see Steve J. Stern, "Paradigms of Conquest: History, Historiography, and Politics," *Journal of Latin American Studies,* XXIV (1992), quincentenary supplement, *The Colonial and Postcolonial Experience: Five Centuries of Spanish and Portuguese America,* 1–34; Cynthia Radding, *Wandering Peoples: Colonialism, Ethnic Spaces, and Ecological Frontiers in Northwestern Mexico, 1700–1850* (Durham, N.C., 1997), 302–310.

and protect themselves with a minimum of royal support. This push for self-sufficiency and productivity permeated an economy that was controlled by the state and reliant upon Indians at almost every level.

In California, at first, the Spanish state provided soldiers and missionaries with purchasing power in the form of salaries or stipends, and it supplied annual shipments of goods they purchased and consumed. Each missionary received an annual support of 350 pesos. Newly established missions were granted an additional 1,000 pesos for agricultural implements, church ornaments, and other necessary goods. These payments largely came from the state-controlled Pious Fund of the Californias, which had been established to support the Jesuit missions of Baja California. Especially during the first years, soldiers, settlers, and padres depended on supplies brought by sea, and they eagerly anticipated the shipments. When the *San Antonio* set sail for Monterey in 1771, it carried ten Franciscans and a wide array of provisions for the missions and presidios: agricultural tools, cooking implements, and, most important, basic foodstuffs and beverages, such as biscuits, ham, sugar, corn, flour, rice, beans, wheat, wine, and brandy. Chickens and pigs even made the journey. But supplies often arrived later than expected, forcing missionaries and soldiers to cut their rations to a minimum and rely on the food reserves of local Indians. Moving men and the tools of colonization to California was expensive, and, by 1773, Alta California had cost the king 250,000 pesos.[4]

Between 1773 and 1781, the *Echeveste reglamento,* named after its author, Juan José Echeveste (the official in charge of forwarding supplies to California), increased the padres' and soldiers' annual salaries, set a standard markup for products imported into the region, and streamlined the purchase and shipment of provisions to California, but it did little to foster the colony's self-sufficiency. In 1781, Governor Felipe de Neve reorganized the finances of California in ways that endured until the advent of the Mexican period. One of the most serious problems Neve confronted in Alta California was the soldiers' poor morale, a condition he partially attributed to their low pay and the inflated prices they were charged for goods. Neve increased their purchasing power by eliminat-

4. For the missionaries' stipends, see the most comprehensive study of the economy of Spanish California: Robert Archibald, *The Economic Aspects of the California Missions* (Washington, D.C., 1978), 3–4. For the California economy in the context of other provinces of northwestern New Spain, see Sergio Ortega Noriega, *Un ensayo de historia regional: El noroeste de México, 1530–1880* (Mexico City, 1993), 101–177. For the goods on the *San Antonio,* see Junípero Serra to Rafael Verger, June 20, 1771, Mission San Carlos, in Tibesar, ed. and trans., *Writings of Serra,* I, 226–235. On the expenses Spain incurred settling Alta California, see Edwin A. Beilharz, *Felipe de Neve, First Governor of California* (San Francisco, Calif., 1971), 34–35. On the Pious Fund, see Charles E. Chapman, *A History of California: The Spanish Period* (1921; rpt. New York, 1939), 174–183.

ing the surcharge on goods and ordering that soldiers receive one-fourth of their pay in coin.[5]

While Spanish officials were worrying about the soldiers' pay and provisions, the missions, through the Indians' labor, were giving the colony its first taste of self-sufficiency. In 1774, Indians at San Carlos, San Gabriel, San Luis Obispo, and San Antonio brought in abundant harvests that satisfied much of the neophytes' need for food. Annual production at individual missions fluctuated, but the exchange of surpluses between them alleviated local shortfalls. More Indian laborers and more careful selection of fields, combined with the padres' realization that wheat, their preferred crop, had a much lower yield than corn, contributed to a steady expansion of agricultural productivity. By 1805, when some twenty thousand neophytes lived in nineteen missions, the Indians' collective harvest of wheat, corn, barley, and beans totaled almost sixty thousand fanegas, nearly a thirtyfold increase in aggregate mission productivity during three decades. Mission livestock also increased quickly, as the small herds of cattle marched overland from Baja California and Sonora in 1769 and, in the early 1770s, multiplied and remade the landscape. By 1805, livestock holdings were so enormous that they had become a nuisance even to Spaniards; in that year, more than 135,000 sheep, 95,000 cattle, 21,000 horses, 1,000 mules, 800 pigs, and 120 goats grazed the lands surrounding the missions.[6] As missions grew to dominate the California economy, they did so within a mercantilist system in which prices were tightly controlled. In general, the colonial governors reduced prices of commodities in California as production of those same goods by mission Indians increased. As prices fell, the Indians' subsidization of the military increased.[7]

5. The *Echeveste reglamento,* dated May 19, 1773, can be found in translation in Francisco Palóu, *Historical Memoirs of New California . . . ,* ed. and trans. Herbert Eugene Bolton, 4 vols. (1926; rpt. New York, 1966), III, 58–77. Under the new regulation, the annual stipend of each mission was set at eight hundred pesos. Double stipends for five years were allocated to padres in charge of establishing new missions. Neve had written the new regulation by June 1779, but it was not formally approved by his superiors until October 1781. See Beilharz, *Felipe de Neve,* 85–96; Archibald, *Economic Aspects,* 10. For Neve's regulation, see John Everett Johnson, trans., *Regulations for Governing the Province of the Californias Approved by His Majesty by Royal Order, Dated October 24, 1781* (San Francisco, Calif., 1929).

6. Archibald, *Economic Aspects,* 179–181.

7. On the expanding agricultural base of the missions, see ibid., 163–164, 167; Ortega Noriega, *Un ensayo de historia regional,* 121. The most concise and informative discussion of cattle ranching in Spanish California is Terry G. Jordan, *North American Cattle-Ranching Frontiers: Origins, Diffusion, and Differentiation* (Albuquerque, N.Mex., 1993), 159–169. On livestock and land use in California, see also Archibald, *Economic Aspects,* 179–181; L. T. Burcham, "Cattle and Range Forage in California: 1770–1880," *Agricultural History,* XXXV (1961), 140–149; R. Louis Gentilcore, "Missions and Mission Lands of Alta California," *Annals of the Association of American Geographers,* LI (1961), 46–72. For Indian protoagricultural practices and their considerable effects upon California's landscape, see Thomas C. Blackburn and Kat Anderson, eds., *Before the Wilderness: Environmental Management by Native Californians* (Menlo Park, Calif., 1993).

The abundance of low-priced, mission-produced foodstuffs fostered the presidios' dependence on the missions. As early as 1774, mission-produced goods fed the soldiers of the mission guard. At first, the Franciscans sold only food to the soldiers, but, after the 1790s, once Indians had mastered new crafts and trades, the missions became veritable general stores. The soap soldiers used to clean themselves, the shoes and boots they pulled on in the morning, the saddles they rode in, the candles they read by, the beds and blankets they slept in, even the coffins in which they were interred—these goods and others were produced by Indians and sold by the Franciscans. The military's dependence on the missions became nearly complete after 1810, when the war for independence undercut Spain's ability to provision California. Mission-presidio exchange was vitally important to the Franciscans, too. For goods they sold to the presidios, the missionaries received credits redeemable in Mexico City, enabling padres to purchase items California Indians could not manufacture, such as prayer books, glass beads, woolen blankets, fine cloth, paper products, cooking spices, wine, chocolate, and rice.[8]

To reduce the military's absolute dependence on the missions at a time when church-state rivalries were boiling over, Spain established the settler communities of San Jose (1777), Los Angeles (1781), and the Villa de Branciforte (1797), near present-day Santa Cruz, intending that their inhabitants would grow enough food to feed the region's soldiers. San Jose produced large surpluses of grain within several years of its establishment and, by 1781, was feeding soldiers at Monterey and San Francisco. Production at San Jose fell after 1796, perhaps as a result of the establishment of Mission San Jose, which gained control of the Indian laborers who had done most of the community's agriculture work. Statistics for agricultural production in Los Angeles are scarce, but it is clear that the pueblo sporadically produced impressive amounts of corn. Productivity in Los Angeles, however, also stagnated after 1800. The Villa de Branciforte was the least productive of the three towns. Although the pueblos were able to sustain themselves and the presidios only in a few years, their surpluses constituted an important supplement to the grain the presidios purchased directly from the missions. After 1790, supply ships no longer needed to bring flour, corn, or beans, the soldiers' most important food staples.[9]

8. On mission food to soldiers, see Archibald, *Economic Aspects*, 83.
9. For agricultural production at San Jose, see Daniel J. Garr, "A Frontier Agrarian Settlement: San José de Guadalupe, 1777–1850," *San José Studies*, II (1976), 93–105, esp. 94–97; Felipe de Neve, September 1782, quoted in Beilharz, *Felipe de Neve*, 165. For annual harvests at Los Angeles: Felipe de Goycoechea, Dec. 31, 1787, Santa Barbara Presidio, and Apr. 24, 1788, San Diego (copy of original), both in AGN, PI, CCXXII, expediente 5, 219a–219b; Francis F. Guest, "Municipal Institutions in Spanish California, 1769–1821" (Ph.D. diss., University of Southern California, 1961), 26–27; Antonio Ríos-Bustamante, "Los Angeles, Pueblo and Region, 1781–1850: Continuity and Adaptation on the North

Just as the region began to be able to feed itself, the Crown transported a group of artisans to Alta California to teach Indians specific trades. Royal officials hoped that these men, through their work with the Indians, could eventually increase the range and number of goods produced in the region. Between 1791 and 1795, roughly twenty artisans worked in California on four- or five-year contracts. Among them were masons, carpenters, potters, and blacksmiths, as well as men skilled in tanning and shoemaking. Even though their numbers were few and their stays brief, these artisans left their mark on California. In the mid-1790s, Indians under their tutelage completed the church at San Carlos, the reconstruction of the Monterey Presidio, and large-scale projects elsewhere, such as water-powered flour mills at San Gabriel and Santa Cruz. More important, though, the artisans proved to be valuable teachers. At San Carlos, eight Indians learned carpentry, two mastered blacksmithing, and another eleven, stone masonry and bricklaying. According to Father President Fermín Francisco de Lasuén, Antonio Domínguez Henríquez successfully taught textile arts in many missions. Men like Henríquez had created the beginnings of an artisanal class of Indians in California. Before long, these Indians would use their skills to mix with and assimilate into the soldier-settler society of California, especially after the mid-1820s, when the state moved against the missions and allowed Indian craftsmen to petition for their separation from the Franciscan establishments.[10]

In fixing prices and supporting the development of the missions, presidios, and pueblos, the Crown intended to make California less of a drain on Spanish coffers. Once California's settlement had been secured and its economy became productive, Spanish officials looked to the colony to support the larger Spanish Empire in ways more direct than simply constituting an impediment to English or Russian expansion. The Crown settled on two valuable industries, the hunting of sea otters and the cultivating of hemp, both of which involved Indians in various forms of production and labor.

As early as the mid-1770s, Spaniards had acquired sea otter pelts from Califor-

---

Mexican Periphery" (Ph.D. diss., University of California, Los Angeles, 1985), 108–120. For the history of Branciforte, see Daniel Garr, "Villa de Branciforte: Innovation and Adaptation on the Frontier," *The Americas,* XXXV (1978), 95–109; Guest, "The Foundation of the Villa de Branciforte," *California Historical Society Quarterly,* XLVI (1967), 307–335; Guest, "Municipal Institutions," 130–192; and "Introduction to the History of the Villa de Branciforte," in Edna E. Kimbro, MaryEllen Ryan, and Robert H. Jackson, *"Como la sombra huye la hora": Restoration Research, Santa Cruz Mission Adobe, Santa Cruz Mission State Historic Park* (Davenport, Calif., 1985).

10. On the artisans who came to California and their projects, see María del Carmen Velázquez, *Notas sobre sirvientes de las Californias y proyecto de obraje en Nuevo México* (Mexico City, 1984), 41–45; Archibald, *Economic Aspects,* 146–152; Edith Buckland Webb, *Indian Life at the Old Missions* (1952; rpt. Lincoln, Neb., 1982), 122–148; Hubert Howe Bancroft, *History of California,* 7 vols. (San Francisco, Calif., 1884–1890), I, 615–618. On Indians and crafts at San Carlos, see Diego de Borica to Miguel de la Grúa Talamanca y Branciforte, Dec. 3, 1795, Monterey, AGN, CA, XLIX, expediente 1, 265–267.

nia Indians. In the mid-1780s, two factors rendered these pelts especially valuable. Their warm and luxurious fur was prized in China, where a prime pelt could fetch a considerable sum or be exchanged for spices and other exotic goods. More important, though, in Canton, furs could be traded for mercury, a metal that was in short supply in New Spain, although it figured prominently in the Crown's plans to maximize silver production. In 1784, Vicente Vasadre y Vega requested royal authority to establish and oversee just such a trade, adding that his plan would prevent the Russians and English from expanding their otter hunting into Spain's waters. The Crown responded enthusiastically, and, by 1786, Vasadre y Vega was in California overseeing the collection of pelts.[11]

Father President Lasuén and Governor Pedro Fages embraced Vasadre y Vega's plan. Both leaders viewed the trade as potentially lucrative, for initially all furs were to be channeled through the presidios and the missions. In just three months, Vasadre y Vega purchased more than one thousand pelts from Baja and Alta California. Had the Indians been more skilled in hunting otter and had the padres been better supplied with goods to barter with them for furs, many more pelts would have been acquired. After 1787, when supplemental trade goods were shipped to the principal missions, the number of skins acquired rose. Between 1787 and 1790, Indians in Alta California provided more than two thousand otter pelts to missionaries. Most came from San Diego and San Juan Capistrano, but Indians at San Francisco, Santa Clara, San Carlos, La Purísima, Santa Barbara, and San Buenaventura also participated in the trade. For their efforts, Indians most likely garnered trade beads from the padres. Missionaries, in turn, sold the skins to the government, acquiring nearly sixteen thousand pesos in credits that they later used to purchase goods in Mexico.[12]

Despite its initial commercial success, bureaucratic obstacles soon thwarted this promising enterprise: Franciscans and soldiers competed with one another for the pelts, Spanish officials felt that Vasadre y Vega had paid too much, and the goods the Franciscans had been promised in return were slow to arrive. In themselves, none of these problems could have doomed Vasadre y Vega's plan, but the powerful Philippine Company, which had been granted certain monopoly rights to trade with China, obstructed Vasadre y Vega's efforts in Canton. In December 1788, Vasadre y Vega abandoned the Far East, and, in 1790, the Crown

---

11. The most authoritative discussion of sea otter hunting in California is Adele Ogden, *The California Sea Otter Trade, 1784–1848* (Berkeley, Calif., 1941). See also Archibald, *Economic Aspects,* 116–118.

12. Ogden, *California Sea Otter Trade,* 16–20. On the magnitude of the trade in skins between 1787 and 1790, see accounts for years 1787–1790, Archivo del Colegio de San Fernando account books, XVI–XXI, AGN, DPHM, and annual reports of Mission San Francisco, 1789 and 1790, AGN, AHH, DPHM, 2d Ser., III, docs. 107, 118.

terminated Spanish California's first export industry. After 1790, padres and soldiers occasionally shipped pelts to San Blas; most skins in the future, however, were either purchased or gathered by Anglo-American traders or Russian hunters, who increasingly ventured into California's waters after the mid-1790s.[13]

A year after the Crown withdrew its support for the export of otter pelts, Indians under the Franciscans' guidance began to cultivate a second and briefly more successful commodity, hemp. Production of hemp in Spain fell short of domestic needs, and the fiber was essential for the rigging materials required by the Spanish navy. To spur production, the Crown in 1777 dispatched experts to several American colonies and selected Alta California as one province in which hemp cultivation would be especially promoted. As early as 1791, Indians at some of the northern missions planted small quantities of hemp but with unimpressive results. Production took a more serious turn after 1795, when special instructions were sent from Mexico on how to grow the crop. In December, Governor Diego de Borica ordered the settlers at San Jose to begin farming it and authorized them to hire Indians from the surrounding region to help. The following fall, Indians and settlers harvested 560 pounds of hemp. Cultivation increased dramatically after the harvest of 1805, when Spanish officials focused their efforts on the Los Angeles region, where Indian laborers did the field work. In 1810, the province produced a whopping 220,000 pounds, a total that alone probably exceeded the previous two decades' production. The Crown and colonists had finally found an export staple that could be abundantly produced in Alta California; but, within a year, the industry was finished, an early victim of Mexico's struggle for independence. With no way to transfer the harvested hemp to San Blas, Governor José Joaquín de Arrillaga restricted cultivation to the needs of the province, which were minimal. Following the collapse of the trade in sea otter pelts and hemp, California's economy would remain without a valuable export commodity, and therefore largely cut off from external markets until the rise of the hide-and-tallow trade in the 1820s and 1830s. Indians, however, would continue to work throughout the colonial province in a variety of capacities.[14]

13. Ogden, *California Sea Otter Trade*, 20–24.

14. On the development of the hemp industry in California, see Sanford A. Mosk, "Subsidized Hemp Production in Spanish California," *Agricultural History*, XIII (1939), 171–175; Archibald, *Economic Aspects*, 118–120. Indians labored to plant and harvest hemp; see Fermín Francisco de Lasuén to Tomás Pangua, Dec. 16, 1793, Mission San Diego, and Jan. 26, 1795, Mission San Carlos, both in Kenneally, ed. and trans., *Writings of Lasuén*, I, 295–297, 327–329; Diego de Borica to comisionado of San Jose, Dec. 23, 1795, Monterey, Archives of California, C–A 23, 517, BL; José de Iturrigaray to [José Joaquín de Arrillaga], Dec. 4, 1805, Mexico, Archives of California, C–A 12, 74, BL. On the end of the commercial cultivation of hemp in California, see Arrillaga to Joaquín Sánchez, Feb. 22, 1811, Monterey, Archives of California, C–A 26, 12, BL.

INDIAN LABOR IN THE MISSIONS

Indian labor made possible Spain's exploitation of the riches of the Americas, and in this regard Alta California did not prove exceptional. Few Spaniards or Mexicans emigrated to California; those who did looked to natives to do their heavy manual labor. Thus, nearly everything grown, manufactured, or consumed in the region's missions, presidios, and pueblos was to a great extent produced by laboring Indians. Baptized Indians worked principally at missions where, from the Franciscans' perspective, their labor constituted a morally enriching disciplinary activity that hastened their conversion from savagery to civilization. To the Franciscans, Indians outside the missions lived as wild animals, at the whim of nature, without comfort or recourse to work. "The wild countryside supplies their manner of living," Father President Lasuén claimed, "which differs little from that of beasts. . . . After grazing on grasses when they are in season, they gather seeds for the winter. . . . In satiating themselves today, they take little care of tomorrow." Franciscans like Lasuén, therefore, saw the transformation of savage Indians into industrious Christians as a wrenching process that was quite literally unnatural for the Indians. The recitation and memorization of the catechism and doctrina might have prepared the Indians' souls for salvation, but it was the missions' regimented daily work schedule that would provide the structure and discipline the padres believed the Indians lacked. Thus, once they had baptized an Indian, the Franciscans believed it was their responsibility to oversee not only the spiritual life of that individual but the economic life as well. The Franciscans further believed that Indians, in accepting baptism, had given themselves over to the padres' complete management.[15]

The Franciscans' critique of Indians as lazy and undisciplined was especially pointed and firmly anchored in the padres' passionate misinterpretation of Indian culture. Their views, although tailored to the natives of Alta California,

15. Fermín Francisco de Lasuén, "Refutation of Charges," June 19, 1801, Mission San Carlos, AGN, PI, CCXVI, expediente 1, 68a. In colonial California, despite the rapid decline in the native population, the population of the gente de razón never approached that of the Indians. In the coastal portion of Alta California that Spain controlled, Indians outnumbered the soldiers and settlers 59,700 to 150 in 1770; 57,000 to 480 in 1780; 43,600 to 1,060 in 1790; 35,850 to 1,800 in 1800; 25,900 to 2,300 in 1810; and 21,750 to 3,400 in 1820 (Peter Gerhard, *The North Frontier of New Spain,* rev. ed. [Norman, Okla., 1993], 309). On the padres' belief that they would not restrict themselves to the management of the Indians' religious lives, see Lino Gómez Canedo, *Evangelización y conquista: Experiencia franciscana en hispanoamérica,* 2d ed. (Mexico City, 1988), 208–214. According to Father Ramón Olbés, at Mission Santa Barbara, the "missionary fathers supervise planting and harvesting at the proper seasons[,] for the Indians are not capable of doing this alone for in such undertakings they are like children." "They would prefer going to the sierras or to their own rancherias rather than busy themselves in this way" (see *APST,* 109).

emerged from a larger elite critique during the early modern era directed at traditional peoples, be they craft workers, peasants, enslaved Africans, or Indians. Throughout Spain during the eighteenth century, priests condemned Spaniards for resisting work and for falling victim to vices bred by idleness. And, throughout the Atlantic World, preindustrial peoples who resisted new forms and regimens of labor were branded as backward and culturally deficient. Although worlds apart, Spanish agriculturalists, English laborers, and California Indians all were tarred with the same brush during the eighteenth century.[16]

Motivated by their view that Indians needed to be put to work to achieve salvation, Franciscans often resorted to violence, intimidation, and coercion. Indian laborers at the missions were neither enslaved nor indentured servants: in essence, they were a semicaptive labor force, held in place by both their own needs for food and community life and by the Spaniards' willingness to make them work and remain at the missions. Franciscans or Indian alcaldes frequently took roll to make sure that laborers were present and not shirking their assigned tasks. Those who avoided work were first scolded; then, if they did not mend their ways, they were whipped or imprisoned. Consequently, many fled. At the request of the Franciscans, soldiers occasionally attempted to force runaways back to the mission. This effort succeeded haphazardly and perpetuated a cycle of coercion and violence that contributed to the Indians' already high levels of despair and illness, further reducing their willingness and ability to work. Neophytes did not earn a daily wage. Missionaries insisted Indians were compensated, albeit indirectly, for their labor, since they gained food, housing, and an occasional change of clothing at places like San Carlos Borromeo.[17]

Despite the padres' attempt to fill the Indians' days with a routine of work and prayer and their stomachs with mission-produced *atole* and *pozole*, the Children of Coyote never allowed the Franciscan regime to completely displace their indigenous economic activities or food procurement. As we saw earlier, baptized Indians continued to gather roots, acorns, and grasses and hunt fowl, game, and fish even as they worked in the missions' fields and workshops, thereby interweaving Indian and Spanish technologies, work rhythms, and productive processes. During the early years of Mission San Carlos and other missions as well,

---

16. Charles C. Noel, "Missionary Preachers in Spain: Teaching Social Virtue in the Eighteenth Century," *AHR*, XC (1985), 866–892.

17. On the likelihood that the oppressive conditions of the missions exacerbated the Indians' health problems, see Cook, *Conflict*, 91–134; Robert H. Jackson and Edward Castillo, *Indians, Franciscans, and Spanish Colonization: The Impact of the Mission System on California Indians* (Albuquerque, N.Mex., 1995), 44; Jackson, *Indian Population Decline: The Missions of Northwestern New Spain, 1687–1840* (Albuquerque, N.Mex., 1994), 126, 165–166.

Indians worked in the fields, wove fabrics on looms, and pursued Spanish techniques of building construction, but only when doing so did not conflict with their seasonal labor and food gathering.

The annual cycle of work at the missions reflected an accommodation between the Indians' subsistence economy and the seasonal work of the planting and harvesting of mission crops, the breeding, shearing, and slaughter of introduced livestock, and the manufacture of woolen and leather goods. Laborers spent seven or eight months of the year, primarily from midwinter to late summer, engaged in the agricultural and pastoral economy of the missions. For example, at Mission Santa Barbara, beginning in mid-December, Chumash laborers devoted a few days to planting barley. Then, from mid-December through mid-January, they would sow wheat, the mission's primary crop. In February, the neophytes would plant garbanzo beans, peas, and *havas* (lima beans). Corn followed in mid-March; kidney beans, in April. In the spring, the men turned their attention to livestock. In mid-April, they sheared the sheep and castrated and branded the cattle. As the mission's herds grew, shearing took up more and more time. In 1797, this required about three weeks, but, by 1803, laborers devoted almost six weeks to shearing the mission's flock of eight thousand sheep. That same year, workers spent a month branding and castrating cattle. After the completion of the shearing and branding, usually by mid-June, Indians harvested the small crop of barley over a few days. By late June or early July, they commenced with the wheat harvest, a task that often stretched over a month. Corn did not ripen until the end of August or early September, when Indians would harvest it in two or three days. The remaining months of the year would be devoted to the maintenance of the fields or less structured work.[18]

The Chumash at Mission Santa Barbara pursued other tasks at the mission throughout the year, irrespective of season. They watched the fields for infestations of rodents and insects, protected the herds from predators, and shepherded livestock from field to field so as to prevent overgrazing. The winnowing of grain and the slaughter of stock continued year-round, dictated by the number of individuals to feed at the mission and the presidios. Workers operated the mission's tannery, soapworks, and looms all year, unless extra laborers had to be diverted to complete the harvest, the shearing, or the branding. By 1800, Mission

18. Father Estevan Tapis, who was assigned to Mission Santa Barbara from 1793 to 1804, meticulously recorded the economic life of the mission. Those farther north or south would have followed different programs, depending on local climate and soil conditions. This schedule is drawn from an analysis of Tapis, "Book of Planting and Harvesting," Mission Santa Barbara, SBMAL. This account book is also known as "Book of Accounts of Seeds and Harvests; Records of Masses, Mission Santa Barbara, 1787–1807," in Maynard J. Geiger, *Calendar of Documents in the Santa Barbara Mission Archives* (Washington, D.C., 1947), 252.

Santa Barbara had three *telares* (weaving shops) where sixty Chumash men and women produced enough sackcloth to clothe the mission's inhabitants and provide blankets for many of the soldiers and their families.

Mission Indian laborers followed a steady daily routine and endeavored to incorporate Spanish tools, technologies, and schedules into their own worldviews. Had they not proved so adept at European technologies and patterns of labor, Alta California would have remained a colony dependent on imported grains, where Franciscans, soldiers, settlers, and Indians lived and prayed in thatched huts.[19] Each morning, a bell or an alcalde summoned the community—except those whose work was done by assignment—to gather in the mission quadrangle, and there the laborers received their daily tasks. Then the Indians returned briefly to their homes just outside the mission. The able-bodied would begin working about two hours after sunrise and continue until around 11:15 A.M. After a midday meal and a break, labor would resume. According to the padres, work concluded an hour or so before sunset, in time for communal prayers; soldiers asserted that Indians started earlier and worked a bit longer, from sunrise until sunset. But both soldiers and padres agreed that Indians worked at the missions five to eight hours a day, five or six days a week. Indians did not work for the missions on Sundays or religious holidays, which numbered as many as ninety-two days in the calendar of Catholic worship. The average workload in the missions was not so onerous as to damage the Indians' health unless they were already ill. But the Franciscans' coercive measures proved psychologically debilitating and, in the long run, likely physically damaging to the neophytes.[20]

19. Incorrectly, scholars have argued that Indian laborers suffered incapacitating psychological disorientation when they confronted unfamiliar methods and modes of production at the missions. See Cook, *Conflict*, 101; Douglas Monroy, *Thrown among Strangers: The Making of Mexican Culture in Frontier California* (Berkeley, Calif., 1990), 52, 54, 58. Serra noted how San Carlos Indians had begun to work with Spanish tools: "Our adult new Christians in this mission, inspired by the example of the few workmen I have thus far succeeded in getting, are beginning to apply themselves diligently to work: some with hoes in hand, levelling the ground to increase our crops, others digging in the garden, others making adobe bricks, others again sawing. These last weeks all have been busy with the wheat harvest, carrying the sacks to the storehouse, and doing anything they are told." See Serra to Antonio María de Bucareli y Ursúa, Aug. 24, 1774, Monterey, in Tibesar, ed. and trans., *Writings of Serra*, II, 143–145.

20. For general descriptions of Indian labor in the missions, see the responses to an investigation of conditions in the missions initiated by Governor Borica in the mid-1790s, excerpts of which are reprinted in Cook, *Conflict*, 91–94. See also the responses of the Franciscans of Missions San Miguel and San Antonio to the 1812 questionnaire in *APST*, 82–83. Lasuén argued that Indians normally worked five to six hours in the summer and four to five hours in the winter ("Refutation of Charges," June 19, 1801, Mission San Carlos, AGN, PI, CCXVI, expediente 1, 69b, and in Kenneally, ed. and trans., *Writings of Lasuén*, II, 207–208). For historians' discussion of the difficulty of the labor regime, see Cook, *Conflict*, 94; Monroy, *Thrown among Strangers*, 65; Sylvia L. Hilton, *La Alta California española* (Madrid, 1992), 314–327. On the number of feast days observed in the missions of Alta California, see Maynard J. Geiger, *The Indians of Mission Santa Barbara in Paganism and Christianity* (Santa Barbara, Calif., 1982), 32; Richard Steven Street, "'We Are Not Slaves': A History of California Farmworkers, 1769–1869—The Formative Years" (Ph.D. diss., University of Wisconsin, Madison, 1995), 165–166.

Although the padres professed a great fear that idleness would lead the Indians to vice, Indians performed most of the nonagricultural work around the mission as piecework, and, according to the Franciscans, they often completed the daily quota in less than a day. At Santa Barbara and elsewhere, the padres seemed more concerned with the intensity of the Indians' labor than its duration. During periods of construction, men worked as labor crews, and each had a specific daily production quota. Nine men were to make 360 adobes a day, and a crew of sixteen, 500 tiles a day. Women who did not work in the telar or alongside the men making tiles ground two *almudes* of wheat each day for the mission's atole. The largest number of laborers toiled in the telar, and there, too, workers had specific daily assignments. Each day from March through October, Chumash carders at Santa Barbara produced three to four pounds of wool; spinners, one pound of yarn; and weavers, ten varas of sackcloth for the neophytes' clothes. In November through January, perhaps because the days were shorter and colder, the padres reduced the expected productivity of the telar by 20 percent. Leather workers also had daily production allotments. Shoemakers, for example, were given two days to manufacture a pair of simple shoes. In demanding a steady amount of daily labor even during the winter, the padres' regime contravened the native custom of far less regular work from the late fall to the early spring.[21]

Nevertheless, Indians apparently easily attained these quotas, and some earned premiums for surpassing them. Those who completed the daily allotment of adobes and tiles by 11:00 A.M. took the afternoon off; Indians who filled their weekly requirement of adobes or tiles by Thursday gained Friday and Saturday for their own purposes. Although the mission could use only so many adobes and tiles, it always needed cloth for clothes and blankets, so weavers earned the equivalent of two reales in beads or wheat for every ten varas of cloth they produced beyond the daily requirement. One Chumash man who most likely collected this bounty was Tiburcio, a weaver at Mission Santa Barbara who, Father Estevan Tapis noted with pride, "completed 100 varas of cloth in 3 days and 2 hours, making each day 30 varas."[22]

All able-bodied Indians, regardless of age, performed some sort of task. The type of work, however, depended on the season, the mission's level of economic

21. Estevan Tapis and Juan Cortés to Lasuén, Oct. 30, 1800, Mission Santa Barbara, AGN, PI, CCXVI, expediente 1, 81a–81b.
22. Ibid. It is not exactly clear how many beads or how much wheat two reales amounted to. A "bundle" of beads was valued at seven reales, and a fanega of wheat sold for two pesos. Thus two reales would purchase one-third of a bundle of beads and one-eighth of a bushel of wheat. For the work of Tiburcio, see Tapis, "Book of Planting and Harvesting," notes indicating what Indians wove at the mission in the years after May 1800.

development, and the age, gender, and skills of the individual. Most men eventually were trained in trades, such as masonry, carpentry, or leather working, or they performed basic manual labor around the mission or in the fields. Women worked in domestic activities: sewing, washing, culling wheat, and grinding pinole. But not all of the jobs in the missions were segregated by sex. At Mission Santa Cruz in 1825, for example, forty men and forty-six women labored in the telares. Just as with linguistic and catechistic instruction, the Franciscans placed their greatest hopes for Indian economic advancement in children, who they believed could be taught "with ease and without violence to grow accustomed to work." Children, therefore, worked at simple chores, such as ensuring that weeds and birds did not damage vegetable gardens. Privileged young men and boys worked directly for the Franciscans as pages, acolytes, and sacristáns. And a select group of men held the supervisory positions of alcalde and regidor.[23]

The survival and productivity of the mission, as with most agricultural communities, depended upon the flexibility of its labor. When it came time to sow the fields or harvest the crops, bricklayers would put down their tools, weavers would leave their looms, and all of the mission's able-bodied laborers would take to the fields. Shearing sheep, branding livestock, and other indispensable seasonal work, such as producing lime and salt, preparing the tannery, and making tiles so that the mission would have a reserve of roofing material for the soaking winter rains—all of these required a concentration of workers in one industry for a limited amount of time. During these periods of communal work, specialized or gendered notions of labor were displaced by the immediate needs of the mission community.

After the mid-1790s, when the handful of artisans from Mexico began to teach specific trades at the missions, skilled Indians comprised an increasingly large proportion of the mission labor force. By 1825, for example, 31 percent of the 277 laborers present at Mission Santa Cruz toiled on textile looms, and nearly 10 percent worked as artisans or apprentices: carpenters (7), shoemakers (4), masons (4), gunsmiths (3), soapmakers (3), and blacksmiths (2). During the 1820s, mission masons, bricklayers, and carpenters frequently maintained and reconstructed the presidios at the military's insistence. For a few Indians at the

23. Historians have yet to fully examine the implications of the differences between indigenous and Spanish gender divisions of labor in the California missions. For a discussion of some of the work performed by Indian women in the missions, see Virginia Marie Bouvier, *Women and the Conquest of California, 1542–1840: Codes of Silence* (Tucson, Ariz., 2001), 82–87, 104–107. Labor at Santa Cruz is clearly described by Luís Gil y Taboada, Dec. 31, 1825, Mission Santa Cruz, Documentos Para la Historia de California, IV, part 2, 607–609, BL (hereafter cited as DPHC). On the need for children to work in the missions, see Lasuén, "Refutation of Charges," June 19, 1801, Mission San Carlos, in Kenneally, ed. and trans., *Writings of Lasuén*, II, 210–211.

end of the mission period, the acquisition of such specialized skills would provide a measure of liberation and independence.[24]

For most Indians, the Franciscan labor regime remained simply oppressive, and, to moderate its demands, many resorted to absenteeism or feigned illness. Large-scale exoduses occasionally depleted a mission's workforce, but more common, especially in the later years of the mission period, was the staff's slow disintegration. For example, in December 1825, of the 235 men who should have been available for work at Mission Santa Cruz, 28 had fled, another 28 were "actually or habitually" sick, and 3 were blind. Only 3 of 127 women had absconded, but 22 more were ill, and another was blind. Thus, late in the mission period, nearly a quarter of the adult population at Santa Cruz was unable to work because of flight or illness.[25] In all likelihood, the number of workers at other missions was similarly reduced. Clearly, many of these Indians were indeed ill, as high mortality rates had to have been accompanied by even higher rates of morbidity. But Indians sick and well realized that, in a world overcome by disease, illness—feigned and real—was their most credible excuse to avoid unwanted labor. Franciscans participated in this charade, acknowledging that "the healthy [Indians] are clever at offering as a pretext chronic ailments and they know that they are generally believed, and that even in cases of doubt the missionary dispenses them from work."[26] Although the missionaries could not have been pleased that Indians were shirking labor, the padres must have been gratified to hear Indians at least pay homage to what they were taught: illness was the only justification for avoiding labor. And inherent in the Indians' feigned illness and the padres' reprieves was a recognition that a return to health would bring a resumption of work.

Beyond the Franciscans' tolerance of assertions of illness, Indians had also won a grudging acceptance of their intent to absent themselves from mission labor for days or weeks on end at various times during the year. They had gained this concession by insisting upon it time and time again, sometimes as a condition of accepting baptism. At times, the proportion of available workers at the mission could drop to half or less of the adult population, which often meant seeing the fruits of the Indians' labor spoiled. In 1799, Mission San Carlos lost more than three hundred fanegas of harvested corn because Indians had gone to the countryside. Earlier, they had brought the crop in from the fields and put it to dry in the mission's plaza, but rain saturated and ruined the corn while they were away.

24. Gil y Taboada, Dec. 31, 1825, Mission Santa Cruz, DPHC, IV, part 2, 607–609; Pablo Vicente de Solá to Mariano Payeras, Mar. 25, 1820, Taylor Coll., doc. 1075, HL.

25. Gil y Taboada, Dec. 31, 1825, Mission Santa Cruz, DPHC, IV, part 2, 607–609.

26. Lasuén, "Refutation of Charges," June 19, 1801, Mission San Carlos, AGN, PI, CCXVI, expediente 1, 69b.

Franciscans feared that letting the baptized return to native villages would undermine the mission and their attempt to civilize Indians, but there was no choice,
given the Indians' repeated insistence.

SOLDIERS AND MANUAL LABOR IN ALTA CALIFORNIA

Indians sought more than simply to balance work in the missions with older
patterns of subsistence and production. Had Indians worked only at the missions, they would have been more desperate, soldiers would have been more
miserable, and the colony would have been more volatile. Throughout the colonial period, Indians toiled at the presidios of San Diego (1769), Monterey (1770),
San Francisco (1776), and Santa Barbara (1782) in a wide spectrum of arrangements and statuses ranging from coerced and uncompensated to independent
and paid. These extensive and multiple relationships emerged in Alta California
for several principal reasons: building the presidios necessitated a huge amount
of labor, soldiers and settlers were few and especially averse to certain forms of
manual labor, and Indians pushed to the edge often found that working for
soldiers allowed them to improve their daily subsistence.[27]

Only a fraction of the forty-five to sixty men usually assigned to each garrison
were available for manual labor. In 1784, for example, when Santa Barbara Presidio was under construction, only eighteen of the sixty men on its muster roll
were available to work on the fort: fifteen were assigned to guard the garrison and
its herd, fifteen served at Mission San Buenaventura, six were posted in the
pueblo of Los Angeles, four were carrying mail to San Diego, one was cutting
timbers in Monterey, and another soldier was away from the presidio, "on the
frontier." Similarly, four years later, merely thirteen of fifty-nine soldiers were
actually able to work at the presidio. When the few available men were put to

27. Overviews of the presidios as colonial institutions are Leon G. Campbell, "The Spanish Presidio
in Alta California during the Mission Period, 1769–1784," *Journal of the West*, XVI (1977), 63–77; John
Phillip Langellier and Katherine Meyers Peterson, "Lances and Leather Jackets: Presidial Forces in
Spanish Alta California, 1769–1821," *Journal of the West*, XX (1981), 3–11; Philip Wayne Powell, "Genesis
of the Frontier Presidio in North America," *Western Historical Quarterly*, XIII (1982), 124–141; Sidney B.
Brinckerhoff and Odie B. Faulk, *Lancers for the King: A Study of the Frontier Military System of Northern
New Spain, with a Translation of the Royal Regulations of 1772* (Phoenix, Ariz., 1965); Thomas H. Naylor
and Charles W. Polzer, eds., *The Presidio and Militia on the Northern Frontier of New Spain: A Docu-
mentary History*, 2 vols. (Tucson, Ariz., 1986–1997); Christon I. Archer, *The Army in Bourbon Mexico,
1760–1810* (Albuquerque, N.Mex., 1977). For discussions of the men who served in the presidios of
California, see Joseph P. Sánchez, *Spanish Bluecoats: The Catalonian Volunteers in Northwestern New
Spain, 1767–1810* (Albuquerque, N.Mex., 1990); Leon G. Campbell, "The First Californios: Presidial
Society in Spanish California, 1769–1822," *Journal of the West*, XI (1972), 583–595. The most com-
prehensive study of presidios in northern New Spain omits California (Max L. Moorhead, *The Presidio:
Bastion of the Spanish Borderlands* [Norman, Okla., 1975]).

work on the construction or maintenance of the forts, they complained that such labor was beneath them, and their superiors' responses to this griping shaped the labor relations of the province.[28]

In central New Spain, during the sixteenth and seventeenth centuries, Spanish explorers, soldiers, and settlers had forced Indians to work under the systems of captive slavery, encomienda, and repartimiento. Whereas these institutions endured into the eighteenth century in many of the peripheral and frontier areas of northern New Spain, they played next to no role in Alta California.[29] Moreover, in the Southwestern Borderlands, the construction of presidios never depended upon these coercive systems to mobilize laborers. Throughout the borderlands, troops had built presidios as Spain moved north.[30]

In California, the soldiers' discontent with this all-too-predictable work requirement emerged early and most clearly in letters by two men who found this labor, and all that it entailed, most distasteful. In June 1770, during the early construction of the Monterey Presidio and the adjacent Mission San Carlos, Miguel Periquez became embittered with work that he believed was unending and demeaning. Later, Periquez went as far as to accuse Governor Pedro Fages of being an abusive and demanding taskmaster:

> There was nothing we were not told to do: felling trees, building houses, carrying poles, mixing clay, making adobe, digging and carrying off the soil, cleaning up, making toilets—slaves could not have been treated worse. They gave us so much to do that we had to work all day from dawn to dusk. And without a stop, not even for meals. Most days we went without eating

28. On the allocation of the soldiers at Santa Barbara, see Felipe de Goycoechea, July 1, 1784, Santa Barbara, AGN, Obras Publicas, XV, expediente 1, 2a–2b; Richard S. Whitehead, *Citadel on the Channel: The Royal Presidio of Santa Barbara, Its Founding and Construction, 1782–1798* (Santa Barbara, Calif., 1996), 138.

29. The best guide to the vast literature on the establishment and abolishment of these labor institutions is Russell M. Magnaghi, *Indian Slavery, Labor, Evangelization, and Captivity in the Americas: An Annotated Bibliography* (Lanham, Md., 1998). Classic studies on the encomienda are Lesley Byrd Simpson, *The Encomienda in New Spain: The Beginning of Spanish Mexico* (Berkeley, Calif., 1950); and Lewis Hanke, *The Spanish Struggle for Justice in the Conquest of America* (Philadelphia, 1949). For a synthetic overview of labor systems in New Spain, see Murdo J. MacLeod, "Aspects of the Internal Economy of Colonial Spanish America: Labour; Taxation; Distribution and Exchange," in Leslie Bethell, ed., *The Cambridge History of Latin America*, II (Cambridge, 1984), 219–264. On these institutions and the borderlands, see Peter Alan Stern, "Social Marginality and Acculturation on the Northern Frontier of New Spain" (Ph.D. diss., University of California, Berkeley, 1984); Susan M. Deeds, "Rural Work in Nueva Vizcaya: Forms of Labor Coercion on the Periphery," *HAHR*, LXIX (1989), 425–449; Radding, *Wandering Peoples*, 37–39. For a discussion of these labor institutions by one California father president, see Tapis to Arrillaga, Oct. 5, 1810, Taylor Coll., doc. 369, HL.

30. In the late 1750s, Seri men and women were forced to construct the presidio of San Miguel de Horcasitas. See Charles W. Polzer and Thomas E. Sheridan, *The Californias and Sinaloa-Sonora, 1700–1765* (Tucson, Ariz., 1997), 395, vol. II, part 1 of Naylor and Polzer, eds., *Presidio and Militia*. On soldiers' building presidios, see Moorhead, *The Presidio*, 167.

so as to get through the work. If we did not finish it, he [Fages] told us we would have to finish it on Sunday. This was when we had Sundays free. But for the first seven or eight months we had neither Sundays nor feastdays free; we had only the time it took for Mass to be said; the rest was for work. . . .

And if from time to time we stopped to roll a cigarette he [Fages] let out a flood of oaths—that we were traitors to the King, that we were cheating in our work, that none of us amounted to a row of beans, and that all we thought of was drinking and eating.

Believe it or not, we were in such dire straits that we ate vipers, rats, snakes, sea skates, coyotes, crows—any animal whatever except only black beetles. And of what grew in the fields, we ate everything raw which we knew positively would not harm us, worse than so many horses, until most of the men became poisoned. And I was one of the number.[31]

The discontented Periquez had come to California as part of the Catalonian Volunteers, a small army recently organized in Spain and intended to serve as harbor guards in Havana.[32] Periquez must have been shocked and disappointed by the drudgery of his work in frontier California. In the summer of 1770, Mariano Carrillo, a soldier of a more humble station, who was born in Loreto and enlisted in 1756, also recoiled from the heavy labor Fages required from him. He seemed especially put off by Fages's insistence that the soldiers build a warehouse for the as-yet-unbuilt presidio in addition to performing their standard duties as soldiers:

We were . . . told that since there were no other men for the task, we soldiers would have to undertake it. At once the work of cutting timber and transporting it on mules was begun. We soldiers acted as woodsmen and muleteers, without any of us being excused, and although there were two muleteers at hand, everyone did a like share of the work. . . .

[We labored] from sun-up to sun-down, without any more rest during the day than the time we spent for our meals. Since at night the soldiers still had guard duty to perform, their daily tasks proved most burdensome to them, and their plight became all the more distressing when they realized that the following day would bring no let up in their work.

31. "Report of Corporal Periquez to Captain Callis," n.d., in Tibesar, ed. and trans., *Writings of Serra,* I, 402–406, esp. 404–405.

32. The Catalonian Volunteers were organized in Spain and sent to northwestern New Spain in the wake of the Seven Years' War. Born in Spain, Periquez came to America in 1767 and served briefly in Sonora before his unit was sent to California under the command of Pedro Fages. Periquez was present when Portolá claimed Monterey for Spain in June 1770, and he served in California until 1774, when the Catalonian Volunteers were pulled from the region (Sánchez, *Spanish Bluecoats,* 49).

This heavy regimen quickly led to a souring of labor relations in Monterey, and Carrillo noted that "the men became so disgruntled that there was not one among them who did anything cheerfully." He continued: "If the *Comandante* found any one resting or late in coming out to work he would say to him: 'What is the matter with you? Why aren't you at work? Is this the way you earn the king's money? Man, have you no conscience? The king supplies you with rations, pays you wages and supports you. All you care to do is to sleep, rest and get your belly full.'" According to Carrillo, Fages became so disgusted with the slow pace of the soldiers' work that he "decided to set the amount of work to be done daily at the different tasks." Tasks left incomplete would have to be taken up on Sunday. And authorities would deny rations of food to soldiers who did not complete their work.[33]

Most soldiers, like Carrillo and Periquez, who were literate and therefore perhaps especially upset with menial labor, grumbled and complained but eventually submitted to this grinding work. A few, however, refused to do so. In a pointed and revealing exchange, one soldier told Fages that "it was not part of his duty to work, and that he would not work." As a result, Fages placed the recalcitrant in irons for two days and locked him up in a cell. Only after the man had knuckled under did he win release and return to the arduous work of building the Monterey Presidio.[34]

At several points in his letter, Carrillo implied that the work necessary to build the presidio was intolerable, suggesting that soldier-laborers were on the verge of desertion. And Carrillo proved prescient, for, in the early 1770s, at least eight soldiers asked to be transferred out of the province on account of the heavy labor, and this was during a time when there were fewer than seventy soldiers assigned to the region. Others pleaded with Junípero Serra to intercede on their behalf and secure either their transfer or the removal of their boss, Pedro Fages. An unspecified number actually deserted. When Serra traveled to Mexico City in 1773 to argue for radical changes in the administration of Alta California, one of his chief complaints was that Fages's harsh labor regime and abusive manner was driving soldiers to desert. To prove this point, Serra carried with him copies of the letters by Periquez and Carrillo. The viceroy took Serra's criticisms seriously and eventually recalled Fages. Yet to see these soldiers' complaints as simply an indictment on Fages's character as Serra did would be a mistake. For the letters of Periquez

33. Mariano Carrillo, in "Three Early California Letters," in Thomas Workman Temple II, ed. and trans., *Historical Society of Southern California Quarterly*, XV, part 4 (1933), 28–50, esp. 32. By 1772, when Carrillo wrote his letter, he had been promoted to corporal, or squad leader.

34. Ibid., 40. The man who drew Fages's ire was most likely Ignacio Estavenel, a member of the Catalonian Volunteers (ibid., 49 n. 18).

and Carrillo were first and foremost criticisms of the work regimen soldiers in Alta California were compelled to adhere to in the early years of colonization.[35]

The first decade or so of Spanish colonization in Alta California saw numerous accusations of desertion and insubordination leveled against soldiers. They justified their rebellious acts by pointing to the excessive and degrading manual labor. Most of those who deserted were arrested and put on trial, and surviving records from these legal proceedings provide insight into the frustrations soldiers endured in California. In November 1778, less than a decade after the complaints of Periquez and Carrillo, four soldiers and two servants deserted Monterey during one of the periodic construction projects at the presidio. One of the accused, Antonio Alegre, a military man since 1766, left because of a combination of boredom and overwork. On the day that he fled, Alegre had been put to work "cutting pieces of wood, cleaning the corral, gathering reeds, and other assigned tasks." He was further upset that he had not been given his complete ration of food. Another of the accused, José Beltrán, abandoned the presidio because he considered the work improper for a soldier. Like Alegre, Beltrán was especially affronted that he had been obliged to clean the corral. Most important, Beltrán argued "that it was not the obligation of the troops to work in the tasks of the presidios and their construction, and that he had never heard it said that those tasks were the obligation of the troops."[36]

Monterey was not the only presidio where the morale of the troops was dangerously low from too much heavy manual labor. In January 1780, during the building of the San Francisco Presidio, Captain José Moraga ordered two of his men to go to a local quarry and return with four wagonloads of rocks for the presidio's foundation. Soldiers Mariano Cordero and Ignacio Soto spent the better part of the morning on the first trip. But, once they had brought the first load to the presidio, Soto informed Captain Moraga that he was done, because such work was not the responsibility of a soldier. Moraga wasted no time putting Soto in irons. A second soldier, Ignacio Higuera, sided with Soto and tried to

35. For reports of soldiers' wanting out of California, see Palóu, May 19, 1773, Mexico, in Palóu, *Historical Memoirs,* ed. and trans. Bolton, III, 59–60; Sánchez, *Spanish Bluecoats,* 63. Serra had numerous disputes with Fages and was glad when Fages's own troops faulted their superior's leadership. See Serra to Antonio María de Bucareli y Ursúa, Mar. 13, 1773, Mexico City, in Tibesar, ed. and trans., *Writings of Serra,* I, 299–301.

36. Declaration of Antonio Alegre, Dec. 23, 1778, Monterey Presidio, in "Causa criminal militar contra José Beltrán, Antonio Alegre, Francisco Villagomes y Francisco María Ruiz, soldados de la compañia del presidio de Monterrey . . . ," AGN, CA, II, part 1a, expediente 11, 352a–352b; declaration of José Joaquín Beltrán, ibid., 350b–351a. In April 1780, the soldiers were ordered back to their posts, but, as punishment, they forfeited all of the time that they had already served (decision of Pedro Galindo Navarro, Apr. 16, 1780, Arispe, agreed to by Teodoro de Croix, May 1, 1780, ibid., 371a–373a). There have been no studies of soldiers' desertion rates in Alta California or anywhere in the Spanish Borderlands.

persuade others at the presidio to cease their labors. Higuera, too, soon found himself in irons, and both men were charged with disobedience and encouraging other soldiers to resist orders.[37]

Within a day of their arrest, both men were on trial. Military trials such as these were designed to prove, rather than determine, guilt. In fact, José Moraga, the officer whose orders had been ignored, oversaw the trial and interrogated Soto, Higuera, and some five other men who had worked alongside them at the presidio. Moraga appointed his squad leader, José Antonio Sánchez, to serve as the proceedings' scribe. Sánchez did his work carefully: for the three days of the men's testimony, he recorded their indignation as they recounted their work on the construction of the presidio.

Soto, a twenty-six-year-old recruit from Sonora, asserted the commonly held belief among the soldiers that defending the presidio—rather than building it— was a soldier's duty. And Higuera, a twenty-five-year-old recruit from Sinaloa, left no doubt why he had deserted his post: he testified that "he had entered into the service of his sovereign for the matters of service, and not to be a *pedrero* [rock-carrier], hod carrier, or [laborer at] the other tasks" that the soldiers had to do at the presidio. When asked if he knew whether he could be forced under the military regulations to do such work at the presidio, Higuera became unsure of himself, but he remained certain that one day the sergeant had told him that "the king did not need soldiers here" and that the soldiers would earn their money by building the presidio.[38]

For soldiers like Soto and Higuera and many others in Alta California, the work required of them was not only strenuous but made a mockery of their responsibilities and what they took to be their personal exemptions from some types of work, in particular the *trabajos mecánicos* (manual labor) required to build the presidio. *Trabajos mecánicos* is a phrase that appears frequently in the soldiers' testimony; in the eighteenth century, it referred to work that was manual, as opposed to intellectual, and menial, without dignity or honor. In the soldiers' defense, José Raymundo Carrillo argued that the men simply did not understand their obligation as soldiers to work in that capacity.[39]

Soldiers powerfully articulated their belief that they were exempt from tra-

---

37. José Moraga to Neve, Jan. 31, 1780, in "Proceso formado contra Ignacio Soto e Ignacio Higuera soldados del presidio de San Francisco por inobediencia a travajar en la fábrica del mismo presidio." This document has neither an expediente number nor actual page numbers (AGN, CA, LXXI, 2–3).

38. Declarations of Ignacio Soto, Feb. 1, 1780, and Ignacio Higuera, Feb. 2, 1780, both at San Francisco, in AGN, CA, LXXI, 18, 21–22. For the assumptions and procedures that guided these investigations and trials, see Chapter 8, below.

39. José Raymundo Carrillo to Neve, Feb. 16, 1780, Monterey, AGN, CA, LXXI, 25–26.

bajos mecánicos, but only officers of high rank and a very few of the lowest-ranking men could escape this work. To gain exemption from trabajos mecánicos, low-ranking soldiers had to demonstrate noble ancestry and pure Spanish descent or have fathers who had achieved at least the rank of captain. All the rest had to do whatever work came their way. The presidial regulations of 1772 stated that a common soldier should give his "blindest obedience and subordination to his corporals, sergeants, and officers" and made no exception for menial labor of any kind. Furthermore, the regulations suggested that construction work on the presidios was in fact the soldiers' responsibility: the labor was "to be done in common since it redounds to the benefit of all." Few soldiers in Alta California, however, understood or accepted this belief.[40]

Upon the conclusion of Soto and Higuera's trial, both were sent to the Monterey Presidio for imprisonment until higher authorities decided their punishments. The task of transporting the two men fell to the *cabo* (squad leader) and scribe José Antonio Sánchez. But an unusual thing happened on the road. Soon after Sánchez had left San Francisco with his prisoners, before they had even made it to Mission Santa Clara, Sánchez—apparently activated by sympathy—tried to persuade both Soto and Higuera and the other three soldiers in the military escort to desert. He suggested they would somehow make their way back to Sonora and ask the commandant general of the Interior Provinces whether it was the obligation of the soldiers to build the presidio's ramparts. Several of the men refused to go along with him, and, instead of returning to Sonora, Sánchez soon found himself incarcerated next to Soto and Higuera.[41]

In his own trial, Sánchez argued that he and others rejected the harsh labor their superiors required because they considered it a betrayal of the faith they had invested in their commanders and an obligation not required of them under Spanish military regulations. Sánchez further added that he had deserted because his superiors had not lived up to the promises made to him when he enlisted for duty. He had been part of a large group of soldiers recruited in 1775 to found San Francisco; Juan Bautista de Anza had said the king was offering 350 pesos per year and "five horses, a mule, and a mare" to soldiers who would bring their families to Alta California. How much pay Sánchez received is not clear—cabos were paid

40. For Spanish military regulations and exemptions from trabajos mecánicos, see *Ordenanzas de S.M. para el régimen, disciplina, subordinación, y servicio de sus exércitos* (1768; rpt. Cádiz, 1810), tratado 2, título 18, articles 1–7, 126–127. In article 7, the exemption is from "servicios mecánicos de quarteles." For specific regulations relating to men in the presidios, see Brinckerhoff and Faulk, *Royal Regulations of 1772*, title 13, article 12, 43, and title 11, article 1, 35.

41. Declaration of Clemente Castro, Mar. 6, 1780, AGN, CA, LXXI, 3–6, esp. 5; declaration of Ignacio Higuera, Mar. 15, 1780, ibid., 36–40, esp. 36.

only slightly more than the soldiers they supervised—but, when he deserted four years and eleven months after he enlisted, he claimed he was still owed "three horses and the mare."[42]

During his trial, a dozen soldiers cursed their labor and made it apparent that Sánchez had done more than encourage Higuera and Soto to desert. Before then, he had counseled men that they did not have to do the heavy work Captain Moraga asked of them. One soldier, Juan José Peralta, had even heard Sánchez mumble something to the effect that the soldiers need not do the work since the king and God loved the men and would provide "2,000 pesos and Indians" for the work on the presidio. For encouraging insubordination, Sánchez was sentenced to six years of hard labor in California. Soto and Higuera endured a year under arrest while awaiting the disposition of their case, but their punishment was light: one month of hard labor in public works.[43]

In their desertions and acts of insubordination, men like Ignacio Soto, Ignacio Higuera, and José Antonio Sánchez staged what might be termed one of California's earliest and most important labor rebellions. Theirs was a strike against both the limited social mobility dictated by their own racial and cultural origins as much as it was a rebellion against the hard labor they were compelled to perform in the presidios. In Spanish America, menial tasks ordinarily fell to people of color: Indians, mestizos, or enslaved Africans. With only a few exceptions, nearly all the soldiers and settlers of early California—the very men who resisted trabajos mecánicos—fitted the particulars of this bill: they were a mixed group, born of Indians, Africans, and Spaniards who themselves had performed manual labor on the ranches and in the mines of northern central Mexico.[44] This was almost certainly true of Soto, Higuera, and Sánchez and most of the men from borderland communities who claimed that their jobs as soldiers put them above heavy manual labor. Despite their own origins and mixed ancestry, there was little doubt in the minds of these men that, compared to California's Indians, they themselves were Spanish. Men like them clearly saw their own enlistment and service in the military and their work in California as a way of transcending

42. Declaration of José Antonio Sánchez, Mar. 8, 1780, AGN, CA, LXXI, 19. On the Anza expeditions, see Herbert E. Bolton, ed. and trans., *Anza's California Expeditions,* 5 vols. (Berkeley, Calif., 1930). Many of the Indians who came from Baja California with the Franciscans also felt that they had not received what they had been promised. Lasuén wrote that many "were disconsolate, with good reason. . . . Despite [their efforts on behalf of the Franciscans] they are treated like stepchildren. Not only do they fail to receive the big returns they were promised when they were recruited, but they work much harder and receive less in return than in their own country." See Lasuén to Francisco Pangua, Aug. 3, 1775, Monterey Presidio, in Kenneally, ed. and trans., *Writings of Lasuén,* I, 49.

43. Declaration of Juan José Peralta, Mar. 19, 1780, AGN, CA, LXXI, 56–58, esp. 57; order of Galindo Navarro, Apr. 6, 1781, assented to by Croix, Apr. 13, 1781, ibid., 101–105.

44. See Chapter 2, above, and William Marvin Mason, *The Census of 1790: A Demographic History of Colonial California* (Menlo Park, Calif., 1998), 67–69.

their own origins and crafting new identities. Their superiors, who themselves were usually native-born Spaniards, saw things differently. But they soon realized that they could not afford to force their soldiers into trabajos mecánicos, and they adjusted their policies accordingly.

Bowing to the pressures of griping, balking, and deserting soldiers and hoping to restore order to the ranks, the governors at first attempted to secure extra pay for soldiers who labored on the construction and maintenance of the presidios. In April 1779, Governor Felipe de Neve requested bonus pay for the soldiers who worked on the presidios of Monterey, San Francisco, and San Diego. And, in 1780, Neve asked for a total of 12,000 pesos of goods for the troops, 4,000 for each presidio. His successor Pedro Fages submitted a similar request in 1787 and 1788, and he prepared a detailed list of items to be sent to each of the presidios. Fages, who had seen his first turn as governor undone by his harsh labor demands, came to understand that he had to respect the soldiers' view of what constituted proper duty. In 1797, soldiers who worked on the expansion of the San Francisco Presidio requested and received bonus pay. Depending on their rank, the soldiers' extra pay ranged from 6 reales a day for sergeants down to 2 reales a day for the lowest-ranking man. For the twenty-six weeks that these men worked on the presidio—from the middle of May through the middle of November—the military incurred an added charge of some 1,520 pesos.[45]

But extra pay was just a stopgap measure, and military leaders soon moved beyond paying soldiers more and looked for ways to relegate trabajos mecánicos to Indians. Men like Soto, Higuera, and Sánchez alone were not responsible for the ultimate employment and coerced labor of thousands of Indians in California's presidios, but their discontent did hasten the day when Indians were typically hired to do manual labor and domestic chores. Because the military and individual soldiers were short on funds and could no longer simply compel Indians to work as in other regions and previous centuries, Indian labor took numerous forms and stages between freedom and unfreedom. Not all Indian labor was solely a result of the soldiers' aversion to it; in many instances, Indians sought work to gain access to food and other material goods. In all, Indian labor

45. The governors made numerous requests for extra pay for the soldiers, all found in AGN, PI, CCXVI, expediente 8: Neve to Croix, June 22, 1780, Monterey, 363a–363b; Fages to Jacobo de Ugarte y Loyola, Feb. 18, 1787, San Diego, 371a–372b; Fages to Ugarte y Loyola, Dec. 11, 1788, Monterey, 374a; Fages, copy of Neve's letter with attached memorandums, 375a–378b; and conde de Revillagigedo, Oct. 26, 1791, Mexico, 384a–385a. The funds or goods requested in 1780 were not sent until the 1790s, and by that time the figure had been reduced to 5,200 pesos, the number of presidios had increased from three to four (Santa Barbara was founded in 1782), and many of the soldiers who had done the work had died or retired (Arrillaga to conde de Revillagigedo, Oct. 1, 1792, AGN, PI, CCXVI, expediente 8, 422a–422b). On soldiers' extra pay at San Francisco Presidio for work performed in 1797, see AGN, CA, LIII, expedientes 16, 17.

PLATE 17. *Vue du presidio San Francisco.* By Louis Choris. 1816. Choris et al., *Voyage pittoresque autour du monde,* part 3 (Paris, 1822), plate 2. This print of Choris's sketch shows various scenes of Indian labor at the presidio. On the far left, three men appear to be convict laborers, driven as they are by a mounted soldier. In the middle, gentile laborers gather by a fire. In the foreground, a soldier leads a group of laborers to the presidio. The Bancroft Library, University of California, Berkeley

in the presidios can be divided into many categories; in its various forms and settings, it involved both baptized and unbaptized Indians and relied upon physical coercion and economic incentives.

INDIAN CONVICT LABOR AT THE PRESIDIOS

To contemporary observers and modern historians, the most notable Indian laborers at the presidios were those who were coerced and exploited, the most visible of which were often convicts. Spanish authorities routinely condemned both baptized and unbaptized Indians they accused of everyday crimes to hard labor at one of the presidios. The military did not pay these men, known as *presidarios;* it merely provided a meager subsistence. Indian presidarios were commonplace in colonial California. In fact, their labor was so prevalent that missionaries charged that the military used the Indians' minor crimes as a pretext to seize their labor. As Father Lasuén explained, the soldiers' "greedy desire to obtain free labor" led them to hold Indians suspected of cattle rustling or flight from the missions "as prisoners, but in reality as peons." The military's use of presidarios peaked in the mid-1790s, when Indians were put to work overhauling the garrisons and forts in preparation for the arrival of additional troops. In one instance, groups of fourteen to forty-six Indian convicts labored continuously at the San Diego Presidio during 1796. In January through mid-February and mid-August through December, these Diegueños built a barracks, a kitchen, and two complete houses; in between, from mid-February through mid-August, they constructed fortifications. Governor Borica boasted to his superiors that expenses were so low for much of this work because most of the heavy labor had been done by "Indians who were given a daily ration but no salary because they had killed livestock, fled from their missions, or [committed] other crimes." Clearly, the military had found one way to exact labor from local Indians even in the face of the Crown's elimination of encomienda and repartimiento.[46]

NEOPHYTE CONTRACT LABOR AT THE PRESIDIOS

The impressment of gangs of presidarios supplied neither as many laborers as the military needed nor the skilled workers it increasingly depended upon. Thus, even as missionaries condemned the military's extraction of labor from Indian convicts, the Franciscans increasingly supplied the presidios with Indian contract or day laborers. Under this system, military officials requested from the mission a specific number of laborers for a period of days, weeks, or months. First in large groups and later as individuals, these Indians performed a host of tasks at the presidios, from building and patching walls to cooking soldiers' meals. Thus, in 1796, the presidarios at work at San Diego Presidio found themselves toiling alongside a mix of skilled and unskilled day laborers from Missions San Diego and San Miguel.[47]

Neophytes at first had little role in setting the terms of their presidial labor or even in agreeing to provide it. Because the military had no legal claim to Indians' labor in colonial California, it had to pay the mission a fixed rate per day for each laborer it employed. Common laborers generally earned the missions one and a half reales per day; carpenters and masons cost the presidios slightly more.[48] The

46. Lasuén to Ugarte y Loyola, Oct. 20, 1787, Mission San Carlos, in Kenneally, ed. and trans., *Writings of Lasuén*, I, 168. For the presidarios' work, see Antonio Grajera and Pablo Grijalba, Dec. 31, 1796, San Diego, AGN, PI, XVII, expediente 15, 398a–398b; Borica to Branciforte, Mar. 23, 1797, San Diego, AGN, CA, LXV, expediente 11, 411a–411b. The savings that accrued to the Spanish treasury through the use of Indian convicts were not insignificant; had their work at the San Diego Presidio in 1796 been performed by mission Indians whose labor did not come free, the government would have run up a bill of thousands of pesos. By putting to work Indians under arrest, the military's only labor-related expenses were food. See accounts signed by Antonio Grajera and Pablo Grijalba, Dec. 31, 1796, San Diego, AGN, PI, LXVII, expediente 15, 395a–443a, esp. 398a–398b.

47. Grajera and Grijalba, Dec. 31, 1796, San Diego, AGN, PI, LXVII, expediente 15, 399a, 400a.

48. In 1824, Indian carpenters, masons, and blacksmiths earned four reales a day (for their missions); axmen and hod carriers were paid three reales a day (Taylor Coll., doc. 1212, HL). In *Economic Aspects,*

Franciscans steadily furnished workers even though they believed that the soldiers' behavior could corrupt the Indians, and they were aware that the military routinely overworked Indians. Through their work at the presidio, Indians often became unwilling and uncompensated partners in the military's efforts to shore up the region's defenses. Moreover, through their coerced labor, Indians improved the soldiers' morale by sparing them from a good measure of the arduous *trabajos mecánicos* that were so necessary to build and maintain the forts. Furthermore, because the missions themselves profited from the Indians' labor, these day laborers added hundreds, if not thousands, of pesos to the missions' coffers annually.

As in so many areas of the Franciscans' relations with the military that concerned Indians, the system of sending neophytes to work at the presidios was one of uneasy cooperation, born out of mutual need but colored by mistrust and rivalry. No mission accounts survive for Serra's years at San Carlos, but his correspondence reveals a steadfast opposition to Indians' laboring for the presidios. In July 1775, he refused to send several laborers to unload the supply ship *San Carlos*. The ship's crew could have done it, Serra maintained, but, he charged, they were so tired, lazy, or ornery that they would not even "throw it [the cargo] into the water," much less unload it properly. The cargo in question was significant: 700 fanegas of corn to feed the troops stationed at Monterey. Soldiers also refused to empty the ship, apparently choosing hunger over labor. This dispute over who would take on the task—sailors, soldiers, or Indians—and the military's desire to have Indians pick up the slack reinforce the conclusion that Alta California's presidios suffered not from a shortage of laborers but rather a lack of willing ones.[49]

Archibald discusses how Indian labor was valued at one and a half reales a day. Sherburne F. Cook erred in asserting that Indian labor after 1790 was compulsory and not compensated (Cook, *Conflict*, 97). Edward D. Castillo similarly argued that "the presidios, like the missions and most other buildings in colonial California, were built with free native labor provided by the neophytes and prisoners" (Castillo, "The Impact of Euro-American Exploration and Settlement," in *HNAI*, VIII, 102).

49. Serra to Fernando Rivera y Moncada, July 6, 1775, Mission San Carlos, in Tibesar, ed. and trans., *Writings of Serra*, IV, 423. This abundance of corn was of great importance to the military. In 1774, Indians at San Carlos harvested only 150 fanegas of corn. See Zephyrin Engelhardt, *Mission San Carlos Borromeo (Carmelo): The Father of the Missions* (1934; rpt. Ramona, Calif., 1973), 244. Historians have found similar resistance to many forms of labor by military men and colonists elsewhere in the New World, especially in British North America. Edmund S. Morgan discusses how expectations of easy wealth colored attitudes toward labor in the early days of colonial Virginia in *American Slavery, American Freedom: The Ordeal of Colonial Virginia* (New York, 1975), 44–70. See also Morgan, "The Labor Problem at Jamestown, 1607–18," *AHR*, LXXVI (1971), 595–611. For a general overview of labor in early Anglo-America, see Richard S. Dunn, "Servants and Slaves: The Recruitment and Employment of Labor," in Jack P. Greene and J. R. Pole, eds., *Colonial British America: Essays in the New History of the Early Modern Era* (Baltimore, 1984), 157–194; Stephen Innes, ed., *Work and Labor in Early America* (Chapel Hill, N.C., 1988), 3–47.

Serra refused to send Indians to unload the ship for a variety of reasons. He preferred that Indians spend their time storing away the mission's harvest in one of its granaries, and he believed that sending laborers from a newly established mission to work for the military broke Spanish law and undercut the Franciscans' efforts at conversion. "I desire to have many Indians strong in the faith," Serra retorted, "but why should they be strong for filling [military] storehouses and unloading ships?" Serra counseled Lasuén at San Diego that, if the governor insisted on obtaining neophytes for work at the presidio, he should "be sure to ask the Lieutenant, as tactfully as possible, to take those [Indians] who, because they live at some distance, are to come less frequently or not at all to work at the mission." In such a way, the missionaries could agree to policies Serra found objectionable, but their compliance would be nearly meaningless. Later, Serra even counseled Lasuén that it was "contrary to law, to try to force Indians of this category [recently converted neophytes] to work" at the presidio.[50]

In the early years at San Carlos and other missions, the Indians' pursuit of their own subsistence economies complicated the military's employment of Indian day laborers. From late spring to early fall, comparatively few Indians would have been present at the missions; many, as we know, congregated by the seashore to catch sardines and gather shellfish or dispersed to the hills to collect grasses, acorns, and other wild seeds. And, frequently, those who remained at the mission accepted assigned work like soldiers and sailors, "with such haughtiness that at times," Serra complained, "out of a group of more than fifty, we do not succeed in gathering together more than a dozen." Even tasks that gave Indians the opportunity to leave the mission and were necessary for the preparation of food often went unfilled over the summer. Serra lamented, "We often find ourselves without firewood to cook the pozole for them, even though it is so easy to collect it." In the context of the missionaries' challenges in engaging an Indian labor force for their own purposes, Serra's resistance to creating one for the soldiers is understandable.[51]

Beyond the Indians' reluctance to accept labor on the padres' terms, the Franciscans had another reason to claim that the recently established missions suffered from labor shortages. In the early years, most of the baptized were women and young children. In July 1775, of the several hundred Children of Coyote affiliated with San Carlos, only fifty-four were men between the ages of fifteen and forty. The majority of these had attained baptism fairly recently, and, most likely, not all were healthy or remained at the mission. Therefore, sending only a

---

50. Serra to Rivera y Moncada, July 6, 1775, Mission San Carlos, in Tibesar, ed. and trans., *Writings of Serra*, IV, 421–423; Serra to Lasuén, Apr. 6, 1778, and Aug. 16, 1779, both in Monterey, ibid., III, 181, 367.
51. Serra to Rivera y Moncada, July 6, 1775, Mission San Carlos, ibid., IV, 421–423.

few laborers to the presidio would have severely reduced the supply of the mission's ablest and most willing laborers, especially since the governor had a habit of requesting the strongest and most skilled workers. Serra's reluctance might also have been a result of the mission's low productivity: he needed in the fields during the harvest all the laborers he could find. In fact, from the early 1770s through the early 1780s, so short was the supply of labor at San Carlos that gentiles from the surrounding areas were recruited to bring in the harvest.[52]

Under the administration of Lasuén (1785–1803), Serra's successor as father president, San Carlos became securely established with greater agricultural output and an ability to attract and sustain more laborers. And it was only then that neophyte contract labor at the Monterey Presidio expanded and became routine. In contrast to 1775, when only fifty-four men of peak working age (fifteen to forty) were affiliated with the mission, by 1789, the mission population had increased to 732, 158 of whom were men between the ages of fifteen and forty. During the 1780s, the mission's agricultural fields were now productive and yielded a surplus that padres consistently sold to the presidio. In 1789, Indians at the mission harvested approximately 3,180 fanegas, whereas, in 1774, the year before Serra had refused the military's request, they had harvested only 282 fanegas. Nearly every year after 1785, San Carlos Indians were sent to work at the presidio, and, in certain years, their labor was so extensive that it amounted to the equivalent of nine or ten workers toiling six days a week all year (Table 35).[53]

Most of these laborers went to the presidio after winter storms or the soldiers' folly had taken their toll on the fort. When, in August 1789, a supply ship and the presidio exchanged cannon salutes, a spark landed on the thatched roof of the presidio, igniting a fire that consumed storehouses and the troops' and officers' quarters. Wary of putting his own men to work rebuilding the presidio, Governor Fages requested fifteen or twenty Indians from San Carlos. Fages pledged to feed the workers and credit the mission for their labor. Lasuén embraced the

52. Women were crucial to the mission economy, but the Franciscans would have directed the heaviest manual labor to the men, and they only sent men to the presidio as contract day laborers. I estimate male laborers from my database linking all baptisms to burials at the mission. Engelhardt lists 244 Indians "existent" at Mission San Carlos in 1774 (Engelhardt, *Mission San Carlos Borromeo*, 243). J. N. Bowman lists the mission population at 250 in 1775 (Bowman, "The Resident Neophytes [Existentes] of the California Missions, 1769–1834," *Historical Society of Southern California Quarterly*, XL [1950], 138–148).

53. For population at the mission, see Engelhardt, *Mission San Carlos Borromeo*, 243. The estimated number of men aged fifteen to forty at the mission comes from my database of Mission San Carlos. The agricultural harvest at San Carlos in 1775 is not known. For other years, see Engelhardt, ibid., 244. He has incorrectly totaled the figure for 1774 agricultural output; it should read 282 fanegas, not 182. For the 1789 harvest, see Pasqual de Arenaza and José Francisco de Paula Señán, annual report of Mission San Carlos, Dec. 31, 1789, AGN, AHH, DPHM, 2d Ser., II, part 2, doc. 97. The number of days of Indian labor equals the total of reales charged (eight reales to a peso) divided by one and a half (the daily rate for a laborer).

TABLE 35. Mission San Carlos Neophyte Contract Labor at the Monterey Presidio, 1785–1810

Year	Pesos Mission Charged Presidio	Equivalent Days of Labor
1785	7	37
1786	49	261
1787	102	544
1788	26	139
1789	133	709
1790	0	0
1791	0	0
1792	83	443
1793	0	0
1794	18	96
1795	127	677
1796	4	21
1797	346	1,845
1798	6	32
1799	30	160
1800	131	699
1801	252	1,344
1802	—	—
1803	—	—
1804	—	—
1805	0	0
1806	—	—
1807	0	0
1808	540	2,880
1809	536	2,859
1810	0	0
Total	2,390	12,746
Avg. per year	109	579

Note: Values rounded to the nearest peso. There are eight reales to a peso and twelve granos to a real. Labor days are calculated at a daily labor rate of 1.5 reales. Averages are calculated using only years where information is available.

Source: Taylor Coll., docs. 2445, 2447–2458, 2462–2468, 2470, 2474, HL; Archives of California, C–A 21, 133, 167.

governor's request. "It is not only a duty I owe," he told the governor, "but, in addition, a source of personal satisfaction." That year, San Carlos Indians worked more than seven hundred labor days at the presidio, earning for the mission 133 pesos in credits.[54]

During the mid-1780s, Indian day laborers also began to build and maintain the Santa Barbara fort and its soldiers' barracks. But, in Santa Barbara, the financial arrangements were different. In 1784, when construction began on adobe buildings, the military did not have enough money to hire large crews of mission day laborers, nor was there as yet a mission adjacent to the Santa Barbara Presidio from which it could hire contract workers. The governor overcame these problems, not by putting grumbling soldiers like Miguel Periquez to work, but by holding back a small percentage of the troops' salaries, which he then used to hire laborers from Mission San Gabriel, located eighty-five miles away in the Los Angeles basin. By this plan, each soldier in the Santa Barbara presidial company gave up three to six pesos a year. For the men, this was a good deal; the small sum came out of salaries that most probably thought they would never receive, and it freed them from the trabajos mecánicos they detested. By May 1786, the Gabrielino had helped manufacture twenty thousand adobes for the Santa Barbara Presidio, and, in June, they began to raise the walls of the soldiers' quarters. In the late 1780s, the presidial company again contributed part of its salary for the hire of day laborers, but these workers came from Mission Santa Barbara, which, by 1789, had a population of more than four hundred.[55]

Between 1794 and 1805, the years when records are most complete, Chumash laborers worked nearly 4,000 days at the presidio (Table 36). Indians completed the majority of this work before 1797, during the presidio's construction. In 1796,

54. Fages to Ugarte y Loyola, Aug. 14, 1789, Monterey, AGN, CA, XLVI, expediente 2, 30a–31a; Fages to Lasuén, Aug. 14, 1789, Monterey, CMD 152, SBMAL; Lasuén to Fages, Aug. 14, 1789, Mission San Carlos, in Kenneally, ed. and trans., *Writings of Lasuén*, I, 196. For the record of the Indians' labor, see José Francisco Ortega, "Account between Monterey Presidio and Mission San Carlos," Dec. 31, Oct. 20, 1789, Monterey, Taylor Coll., docs. 2450, 2451, HL. Robert Archibald discusses how neophyte contract labor was an important part of mission-presidio economic relations in *Economic Aspects*, 102–104.

55. Holding back a portion of the soldiers' pay was common throughout the borderlands. Soldiers had wages withheld not only to pay for goods they had purchased for their military service but to allow them to build up a reserve fund of some one hundred pesos to cover any future purchases. Soldiers' pay also often was held back to create a common fund that the presidio could devote to outfitting new recruits or to funding any unforeseen expenses. For labor of Gabrielinos, see Goycoechea to Fages, May 28, 1786, Archives of California, C–A 3, 319–320, BL. For the soldiers' pay at Santa Barbara, see Goycoechea, Dec. 30, 1782, Archives of California, C–A 7, 62, BL. This plan continued into the 1790s; in June 1790, Goycoechea, the presidial commander, asked the troops to contribute to the Indians' pay during the construction of the presidio walls (Goycoechea to Fages, July 6, 1790, Santa Barbara, Archives of California, C–A 5, 170, BL). In the early 1790s, the soldiers successfully petitioned for repayment of the money that had been deducted from their wages (José Thadeo Sanchez and José Miguel Flores, n.d., and Arrillaga, Aug. 20, 1793, San Francisco, both in AGN, PI, CCXVI, expediente 8, 379a–379b, 426a–429b).

TABLE 36. Mission Santa Barbara Neophyte Contract Labor at
the Santa Barbara Presidio, 1794–1805

Year	Pesos Mission Charged Presidio	Equivalent Days of Labor
1794	269	1,435
1795	108	576
1796	180	960
1797	0	0
1798	62	331
1799	9	48
1800	3	16
1801	0	0
1802	22	117
1803	22	117
1804	31	165
1805	40	213
Total	746	3,979
Avg. per year	62	332

Note: Values rounded to the nearest peso. There are eight reales to a peso and twelve granos to a real. Labor days are calculated at a daily labor rate of 1.5 reales.

Source: "Book of Accounts of Mission Santa Barbara with the Presidio from 1794 through 1805," SBMAL.

a year when reliance on Indian labor was particularly heavy, Indians manufactured ten thousand adobes to build a pottery kiln. Beyond Santa Barbara and Monterey, day laborers worked on the presidios of San Francisco and San Diego after damaging storms, and they expanded both to accommodate more soldiers and their families. Once the buildings were essentially completed in the late 1790s, Indian labor tapered off. Subsequently, hired Indians performed chores, such as cleaning plazas and working in gardens. [56]

By the 1790s, the military was taking mission day laborers for granted.[57] But

56. On the construction of the pottery kiln, see Whitehead, *Citadel on the Channel,* 147–148.

57. When Spanish naval engineers concluded that the presidios were poorly constructed and would be unable to protect the coast from an English invasion, they called for forty Indian *peones* to work for thirty days at two reales a day per Indian; see Juan Francisco del Bodega y Quadra, Feb. 23, 1793, Tepic, AGN, CA, IX, expediente 3, 36a–143a, esp. 46a–47b. In 1795, they planned on fifty Indian laborers for two years to reconstruct San Francisco Presidio (Alberto de Cordova, July 30, 1796, San Francisco, AGN, PI, CCXVI, expediente 6, 243a–244a). At San Francisco, large groups of Indian contract laborers worked on the construction of the fort in 1796 and 1797. In those years, they worked well over 3,500 and 5,500 days respectively (Raymundo Carrillo, Apr. 16, 1796, San Francisco Presidio, AGN, PI, XVII, expediente 15, 426a–426b). See also Magín Matías Catalá, Oct. 7, 1797, Mission Santa Clara, for 1,170 labor days worked by mission Indians at the presidio; Martín de Landaeta, Oct. 10, 1797, Mission San

the heavy demands soldiers placed on laborers created tensions between Indians and the missionaries. In 1795, Mission Santa Barbara sent ten laborers to the presidio to make tiles for a week. By the fourth day, the Indians "complained that they could not tolerate the work, [and] that their hands and arms were very sore." When the Franciscans inquired as to the nature of their work, the Indians explained they had had to make 500 tiles, "which required them to dig up mud, carry it to a trough, get water from a well 15 varas deep or from a distant lake, [and] bring sand from the beach a ¼th of a league away." Initially, the Franciscans did not believe this, and they encouraged the Indians to continue their work. But, the next day, the laborers "repeated the complaint with more urging, adding that that day they had been forced to make 525 tiles." Finally, at the end of the week, when the Franciscans charged the soldiers with overworking the Indians, the presidial commander responded that he would have required the same of his soldiers.[58] True enough. But that, after all, was the whole point of the military's employing Indians: they performed loathsome work the soldiers had rejected. Although the Indians' complaints registered with the Franciscans, they did not lead to an end of mission-presidio contract labor. And the Franciscans' continued insistence that neophytes work at the presidios further undermined Indians' faith in them and tolerance of life at the missions. According to Lasuén, "It cost the missionaries a great deal to induce their neophytes to go and serve as peons at the presidios. . . . The fact is, that while we know that the Indian wishes to do what the Father orders, he would not wish to go to the presidio." However much the Franciscans overestimated what they interpreted as the Indians' attempts to please them, the Indians' complaisance was just a thin cover for their frustration with being sent to work at the presidio.[59]

The Franciscans seemingly did little to moderate the soldiers' treatment of mission laborers, but the Indians' continued resistance to work at the presi-

Francisco, for 1,214 days of labor worked by mission Indians at the presidio; Catalá, Mission Santa Clara, Dec. 28, 1797, for 830 more labor days by Santa Clara neophytes at the presidio; and Landaeta, Dec. 30, 1797, for 1,276 labor days by San Francisco neophytes at the presidio, all in AGN, CA, LIII, expediente 16; and see reports in AGN, CA, XLVIII, part 2, expediente 13, 383a–397b. In 1796, Indian presidarios and day laborers from Mission San Diego bolstered the neighboring presidio and its fortifications (Grajera and Grijalba, Dec. 31, 1796, San Diego, AGN, PI, XVII, expediente 15, 399a, 400a).

58. Tapis and Cortés to Lasuén, Oct. 30, 1800, Mission Santa Barbara, AGN, PI, CCXVI, expediente 1, 81b.

59. In 1801, when he was defending the missions against the military's charges that the Franciscans overworked the Indians, Lasuén countered that the soldiers worked mission contract laborers very hard. At the presidios, the soldiers set an overseer over the Indians, who worked them "from an early hour until midday, and from very soon after that until almost nightfall." Sometimes the soldiers gave the Indians a certain task to complete, but early completion did not hasten the end of the working day: "If [the soldiers] assign a task, and the Indians by making greater effort than usual in order to gain a little time off for relaxation, complete it early, another job is given them." See Lasuén, "Refutation of Charges," June 19, 1801, Mission San Carlos, in Kenneally, ed. and trans., *Writings of Lasuén*, II, 208.

dios compelled the padres to provide incentives. By 1801, Father Lasuén recommended that each neophyte who worked at the presidio be given, "in addition to the prescribed ration, his day's wages in any form in which he wished to have it, without indemnifying the mission to the extent of even half a real." The military commander agreed, and Indians then worked at the presidio over several months at a time. Elsewhere, Indians at Santa Barbara earned one real in corn, wheat, or flour for each day they worked at the presidio. By collecting such payments, Indians might have found the work more acceptable, even though the load remained the same.[60]

As Indians acquired different skills and the needs of the presidios evolved, the composition of day laborers changed. In the 1780s, laborers from Mission San Carlos had done most of the heavy menial work at the presidio, but, in March 1820, eleven missions from Santa Inés to San Jose sent some fifty-five masons, adobe makers, tile makers, and axmen to Monterey; just twelve general manual laborers made the journey. All of these men remained at the presidio for months. In October, having had more than enough, they asked to return to their homes and threatened to flee if their wish was not granted. Governor Pablo Vicente de Solá or his subordinate Mariano Estrada, who was supervising the work at Monterey, released the workers soon thereafter.[61] The following spring, Solá requested sixty-six more artisans from Payeras. Six (three from Mission San Carlos and three from Mission San Antonio) had been working at the Monterey Presidio since January. Twenty of the neophytes were to report to the presidio in March, and the remaining forty were to go after the rains had subsided. As in 1820, these laborers came from eleven missions, and, the more skilled the worker, the higher his wage. Carpenters, masons, and blacksmiths earned their respective missions four reales a day; the axmen and hod carriers, three reales a day; and the common laborers earned one and a half reales a day. What compensation, if any, these men took for themselves through this work is not known. But their enhanced skills almost certainly gained them greater flexibility in work routines and an artisanal identity, something that would become invaluable during the era of secularization.[62]

60. Ibid., 209; Tapis and Cortés to Lasuén, Oct. 30, 1800, Mission Santa Barbara, AGN, PI, CCXVI, expediente 1, 81b.

61. Solá to Mariano Payeras, Mar. 25, 1820, Mission San Carlos, and Payeras to the ministers of the missions from Santa Inés to San Jose, Apr. 7, 1820, Mission La Purísima, both in Taylor Coll., docs. 1075, 1079, HL. Later, Payeras noted that the neophytes would work better "if they have full bellies," and he asked Governor Solá that the Indians be treated well—in particular, that they be given atole in the mornings and evenings if possible, even if it was necessary to designate one of the sixty-seven workers as the cook. See Payeras to Solá, Apr. 18, 1820, Mission La Purísima, Taylor Coll., doc. 1180, HL. For the Indians' release, see Payeras to Solá, Oct. 24, 1820, Mission La Soledad, Taylor Coll., doc. 1183, HL.

62. Payeras to the missionaries in the jurisdiction of Monterey with the exception of San Carlos, Mar. 3, 1821, Taylor Coll., doc. 1205, HL; Payeras to missions from Soledad to Santa Inés, Apr. 28, 1821, Mission La Soledad, Taylor Coll., doc. 1212, HL. Payeras's circular letter lists what type of workers each

TABLE 37. Neophyte Contract Labor for Individual Soldiers,
Mission Santa Barbara Presidio, 1794–1807

Year	Pesos Mission Charged Presidio	Days of Labor
1794	79	423
1795	74	396
1796	75	398
1797	50	268
1798	89	476
1799	106	566
1800	9	50
1801	23	123
1802	16	85
1803	157	837
1804	142	757
1805	237	1,262
1806	389	2,075
1807	6	30
Total	1,452	7,746
Avg. per year	104	553

Note: For this table, original values were in days of labor, not pesos the presidio owed the mission, and I
have rounded my calculations to the nearest peso. The daily rate for labor was 1.5 reales, with eight reales
to the peso.
Source: "Book of Accounts of Mission Santa Barbara with the Presidio from 1794 through 1805," SBMAL.

At the same time that the presidios began increasingly to rely on skilled Indian
laborers, individual soldiers turned to mission day laborers at adjacent presidios
to cook their meals, wash their clothes, and shore up their own lodgings. The
scope of this labor is most evident at Santa Barbara, where, between 1794 and
1806, an average of two to three Chumash each day worked for individual soldiers
(Table 37).[63] Sometimes, up to fifteen mission day laborers carried out domestic

---

mission was to provide. Requests for large numbers of neophytes were probably a regular occurrence
during the late Spanish colonial period and the early Mexican period, for, in May 1821, the governor
again requested that Payeras provide a large contingent of neophytes to work on the presidio at San
Francisco (Solá to Payeras, May 18, 1821, Monterey, Taylor Coll., doc. 1217, HL); see also Payeras's
circular letter to the missions from Santa Cruz to San Rafael requesting laborers and the signatures of
the missions and descriptions of what they will provide, May 18, 1821, Mission San Carlos, Taylor Coll.,
doc. 1218, HL.

63. "Book of Accounts of Mission Santa Barbara with the Presidio from 1794 through 1805," SBMAL.
See also the account books at the BL for Missions Soledad, 1810–1819, San Francisco, 1805–1825, and La
Purísima Concepción (BANC film 2244, original at SBMAL).

chores for soldiers and their families. As was the case with day laborers who performed the trabajos mecánicos, the Indians' wages at first accrued directly to the mission. Accordingly, neophytes shunned this work as well. At San Juan Bautista, Indians forced the Franciscans into providing incentives, and some Indians kept half of the wages that accrued to the mission.[64]

Indians worked for individual soldiers in a wide range of activities. They often labored over a day or two, fetching wood, water, and salt, making soap, grinding corn, and cooking meals.[65] Vaqueros, muleteers, shearers, and shepherds tended the soldiers' growing herds of horses, sheep, and cattle. And, when individual soldiers needed construction crews, they turned to the missions not only for the men and women who would make adobes and tiles but for the skilled masons, bricklayers, and carpenters who could soundly construct a house. Thus, in 1803, when Mariano Cota needed a home built, he hired mission laborers for weeks at a time to clear the land and make adobes and tiles for his walls, floor, and roof. Seste, an Indian mason from Mission Santa Barbara, supervised the final construction of Cota's adobe.[66] Indians worked for those who found themselves without manpower. In 1806, two men labored three days in the house of a soldier's mother. Similarly, the widow Agueda Lopes hired groups of Indians by the week for two months. For her, these men performed numerous activities: some worked with picks, axes, and hatchets; others drove oxen; two more dug a well.[67]

Not surprisingly, Indians worked more for presidial officers than soldiers. Officers employed Indians on major construction projects or as cooks or gardeners for weeks or months at a time. By contrast, Indians toiled for low-ranking soldiers for just a day or two per year. Only officers had the money or credit to regularly hire laborers directly from the mission. Privates had little cash, were rarely paid in pesos, and usually received their salaries in supplies and food. But, because privates were as reluctant to perform domestic chores and heavy labor as were their superiors, they devised other means to hire and pay Indians.[68]

Soldiers were increasingly interested in hiring female domestic servants, but the Franciscans hesitated to provide the presidios with women laborers, fearing that soldiers would coerce or force women into sexual relations. Nevertheless, Indian girls baby-sat soldiers' children, and some Indian women even served as

64. Tapis to Luís Argüello, July 13, 1823, San Juan Bautista, Taylor Coll., doc. 1529, HL.

65. "Book of Accounts of Mission Santa Barbara with the Presidio from 1794 through 1805," 40, SBMAL.

66. Ibid., 61. Similarly, when Ignacio Lugo needed a skilled woodworker, he looked no farther than the mission, where he hired "one Carpenter with instruments from the mission" (ibid., 139).

67. Ibid., 44, 189–190.

68. On the soldiers' pay, see Felipe de Neve, *Reglamento para el gobierno de la provincia de Californias, 1781*, ed. Salvador Bernabéu Albert (Madrid, 1981).

wet nurses at the presidio.[69] Older women carried wood to the presidios and washed the soldiers' clothes. Over decades, and in many capacities, the labor of Indian men and women, children as well as adults, proved crucial to the household economy of the soldiers. Less clear, though, is the degree to which these coercive and exploitative economic relations fostered other relations between Indians and the gente de razón.

By the 1830s, as some mission Indians were facing depopulation and all missions were approaching secularization, resident Franciscans grew reluctant to allocate laborers to the military. In June 1833, Governor José Figueroa requested two or three neophytes from San Carlos, *maestros tejeros* (master tile makers), to help rebuild the Monterey Presidio after an especially rainy winter. Compared to the previous requests of the military, this one was minimal. But Father President Rafael de Jesús Moreno quickly wrote Figueroa that he could not comply. Old age or illness had left half of the neophytes incapacitated. A good number of others had fled, and the remainder "did not want to work unless they were threatened with punishment." In an indication of the reduced state of Franciscan authority over the Children of Coyote a half century after the outset of colonization, Moreno offered Figueroa a yoke of oxen, but not one laborer.[70]

NEOPHYTE INFORMAL LABOR AT THE PRESIDIOS

During the half century before the Monterey Presidio received a team of draft animals in place of laborers, Indians had come to resent and resist working for soldiers on the padres' and military commanders' terms. But that never precluded them from toiling for soldiers on their own initiative to gain food and other material goods. Indians made time to work at the presidio before or after their daily labor and especially during seasons when their workload was reduced. And many Indians on leave from the missions chose to work at the presidio rather than pursue more customary economic activities in the countryside. In their spare time, Indians entered into "the service of anyone who employs them," according to the padres, who also claimed that Indian "cooks, laundrymen, millers, water-carriers, and woodcutters" were often found in the soldiers' quarters in neighboring presidios. These laborers were compensated with the same currency in which the soldiers often were paid: handfuls of corn and wheat and

69. Lasuén, "Refutation of Charges," June 19, 1801, Mission San Carlos, in Kenneally, ed. and trans., *Writings of Lasuén*, II, 212.
70. José María Figueroa to Vicente Francisco de Sarría, June 12, 1833, Monterey, and Rafael de Jesús Moreno to Figueroa, June 14, 1833, San Carlos, both in Taylor Coll., docs. 2137, 2138, HL.

strips of cloth and beef. Their labor—which can be termed overt neophyte informal labor—is impossible to quantify because Indians and soldiers did their best
to keep it outside the recorded economy. Nevertheless, correspondence of Franciscans and soldiers suggests that this labor was prevalent and involved men and
women of all ages and skills.[71]

Neophytes did not perform informal labor at the presidios just on their free
time. Many worked for soldiers on the sly, when they still had incomplete work at
the mission. With a small piece of leather or a handful of corn, soldiers hired
Indians to gather wood, grind corn, and wash clothes. Again, by necessity, Indians and soldiers hid these transactions from the Franciscans, since the padres
had Indians whipped when they evaded their labor at the mission. Yet, even
within the bounds of the missions, soldiers in the guard furtively contracted with
Indians for their labor.[72]

Men with special skills—weavers, shoemakers, tanners, and deerskin workers—frequently slipped away to the presidio. Sometimes the Franciscans would
go to a mission workshop only to find one of the spinners, carders, or weavers
was absent. Such was the case in 1797, when Agapito left Mission Santa Barbara's
workshop to run the presidial commander's loom. For each day's labor at the
presidio, Agapito probably earned eighteen inches of cloth. Five days after he had
begun working at the presidio, Agapito was brought back to the mission and
given eight lashes, not, the padres explained, because he worked for the military,
but rather because he had left without permission. For countless Indians like
Agapito, covert informal labor for soldiers provided an opportunity to supplement their meager rations and, when caught, to show contempt for Franciscans'
control over their labor. Women also stole away from the mission to work at the
presidio. From time to time, therefore, the missionaries would send an Indian
official to make sure that no women had gone to work in the house or garden of a
soldier. By the late 1790s, informal neophyte labor, both overt and covert, had
become so common that soldiers, in paying the Indians for their work, often
exhausted their weekly rations shortly after they received them.[73]

71. On mission Indians' working at the presidios, see Arrillaga, Nov. 3, 1804, Loreto, AGN, PI,
CCXVI, expediente 1, 117b. On the tasks they performed there, see Lasuén, "Refutation of Charges,"
June 19, 1801, Mission San Carlos, in Kenneally, ed. and trans., *Writings of Lasuén*, II, 211–212.

72. Raymundo Carrillo, Oct. 13, 1802, Santa Barbara, AGN, PI, CCXVI, expediente 1, 110a.

73. On mission laborers' heading to the presidio, see Lasuén, "Refutation of Charges," June 19, 1801,
Mission San Carlos, in Kenneally, ed. and trans., *Writings of Lasuén*, II, 213. For Agapito, see Tapis and
Cortés to Lasuén, Oct. 30, 1800, AGN, PI, CCXVI, 83a–84a. According to Tapis, Agapito was paid in
cloth worth two reales. I checked a price list for those years and from it calculated the length of the
cloth. For the soldiers' payments to informal laborers, see Señán to Lasuén, Oct. 2—, 1800, Mission San
Buenaventura, AGN, PI, CXXVI, expediente 1, 96a.

GENTILE LABOR IN SAN JOSE AND LOS ANGELES

Unbaptized Indians also found, in their own labor for soldiers and settlers, a means to retain independence and an opportunity to better manage their lives in the wake of the dual revolutions. The Indians' desires for work fitted well with the needs of the majority of settlers and retired soldiers, most of whom, of course, eschewed heavy manual labor and looked to local Indians to perform many of their tasks. In San Jose, soon after the pueblo was established in 1777, Costanoans of the Santa Clara Valley began to work for its settlers. Significantly, the establishment of the pueblo and the granting to its founders of various animals and livestock created familiar pressures on native peoples that impelled them to work for the Spaniards in their midst. By 1782, Indians near Mission Santa Clara had complained that the settlers' cattle were making scarce the herbs and acorns they gathered from the countryside.[74] That same year, the military issued strict guidelines for the employment of local unbaptized Indians in an attempt not just to regularize their labor but to manage the emerging social relations. Settlers' requests for Indian laborers were to be channeled through a ranking military officer, who would contact a village leader. Indians then were to be paid for work done; coercion would not be tolerated in their recruitment. Indian women, whom settlers frequently employed to mill grain or perform other domestic tasks, were no longer to enter into the *pobladores'* (settlers') homes because such "familiarity" had led to "grievances against both populations." The author of these laws was in all likelihood not just referring to potential conflicts between Indians and settlers in San Jose but to the Yumas' uprising a year earlier that destroyed two Spanish settlements and killed four padres and some thirty soldiers.[75]

As in the Santa Clara Valley, the Gabrielino of southern California began to work for settlers in the recently established pueblo of Los Angeles (1781). Yet they would work for the settlers only when doing so did not conflict with their own subsistence economy. In 1784, Lieutenant José Francisco de Ortega must have felt that he alone cared about the pueblo's corn and wheat; with great concern, he reported to the governor that the settlers were "few and useless" as laborers. Indians, who had tilled the land and planted the crop, had offered to help with

74. José Murguía and Tómas de la Peña, Nov. 2, 1782, Mission Santa Clara, in Tibesar, ed. and trans., *Writings of Serra*, IV, 400.

75. On the laws governing the employment of Indians by the settlers of San Jose, see the guidelines José Joaquín Moraga sent to the corporal of the guard at the pueblo of San Jose, December 1782, Archives of California, C–A 2, 160–166, esp. 162–163, BL. Governor Fages incorporated these regulations into those he issued for the comisionado of San Jose (Fages to [Ignacio] Vallejo, July 18, 1785, Monterey, Archives of California, C–A 22, 338–341, BL). For an overview of the Yuma rebellion, see John Francis Bannon, *The Spanish Borderlands Frontier, 1513–1821* (1963; rpt. Albuquerque, N.Mex., 1974), 227–228.

the harvest, but only after they had finished their own seasonal gathering. That fall, after completing their own harvest, the Gabrielino reaped from the pobladores' fields more than 1,800 fanegas of corn, 340 fanegas of kidney beans, and 9 fanegas each of wheat, lentils, and garbanzos.[76]

Within less than a decade of the establishment of Los Angeles, the expansion of the pobladores' and vecinos' fields and the steady increase in their livestock must have imperiled the Gabrielino economy and made their full-time work for the settlers an imperative. Thus, in January 1787, Governor Fages modified for Los Angeles the San Jose guidelines regulating the recruitment and employment of gentile laborers. Here, too, the governor sought to end the "pernicious familiarity" that resulted from the presence of so many Indian laborers: Indians were not to live in town or enter the settlers' homes, and they were to sleep under the watch of the sentry if they spent the night. Under these restrictions, Indians worked in the settlers' fields, where they earned a third to half of the crops they harvested. Gabrielinos also toiled in Los Angeles as vaqueros, cooks, muleteers, water carriers, and domestic servants. By the mid-1790s, the presence of so many Indian laborers had led to considerable acculturation between the Indian and Spanish communities. Many Indian workers spoke Spanish and dressed like their employers, "clad in shoes, with sombreros and blankets." Moreover, many settlers spoke the Indians' language; a few even married Indian women.[77]

In fostering and maintaining labor relations with settlers, the Gabrielino of Los Angeles and the Costanoan of the Santa Clara Valley had to overcome some of the Spaniards' official hostility and wariness. Governor Fages tried to limit contacts to the realm of labor, and the Franciscans sought to block them altogether. The settlers offered the same material incentives the missions used to attract Indians: food, clothing, and beads. But, in the missions, Indians would chafe under Franciscan oversight, live in overcrowded housing, and encounter rampant disease. The pobladores, by comparison, cared little about changing the Indians' religion or sexuality and required laborers to return to their own homes

76. José Francisco de Ortega to Fages, Apr. 18, 1784, Los Angeles, Archives of California, C–A 22, 176–177, BL. On Indian labor in Los Angeles, see William Mason, "Indian-Mexican Cultural Exchange in the Los Angeles Area, 1781–1834," *Aztlán: International Journal of Chicano Studies Research,* XV (1984), 123–144. See also George Harwood Phillips, "Indians in Los Angeles, 1781–1875: Economic Integration, Social Disintegration," *Pacific Historical Review,* XLIX (1980), 427–451. For Los Angeles harvests, see Ríos-Bustamante, "Los Angeles, Pueblo and Region," 110.

77. Los Angeles labor regulations: Fages to Vicente Féliz, Jan. 13, 1787, Mission San Gabriel, Archives of California, C–A 4, 148–155, BL, partially trans. in William Marvin Mason, "Fages' Code of Conduct toward Indians, 1787," *Journal of California Anthropology,* II (1975), 90–100. For compensation of Indian fieldworkers, see response of the Franciscans of Mission San Gabriel, in *APST,* 129. On Indian-settler cultural exchanges, see Vicente de Santa María, 1795, quoted in Mason, "Indian-Mexican Cultural Exchange," *Aztlán,* XV (1984), 129, and Ríos-Bustamante, "Los Angeles, Pueblo and Region," 90–96.

at the end of the day. The inability of the missions to compete with the attractions of the pueblos led Father Lasuén to conclude that the towns and their inhabitants were "an immense hindrance to the conversion of the pagans, for they give them bad example, they scandalize them, and they actually persuade them not to become Christians, lest they would themselves suffer the loss of free labor." More frustrating to Franciscans like Lasuén was the disaffection of those who had previously professed their allegiance to the mission. Baptized Indians also sought work and refuge in the pueblos, even though neophytes who were repeatedly found in town without permission risked a flogging of ten lashes. Lasuén clearly understood the unbaptized Indians' motivations for working in the pueblos, but time and the dual revolutions were on the Franciscans' side, and, before long, most Indian groups who had retained a measure of independence by laboring for soldiers and settlers eventually found themselves drawn into the missions, unable to live beyond them.[78]

GENTILE LABOR AT THE PRESIDIOS

Perhaps a measure of the Santa Clara Costanoans' strain under the dual revolutions and resourcefulness in attempting to stay free of the missions was their willingness during the 1790s to make themselves available as laborers at the Monterey Presidio. They did so because it involved only a short-term commitment and was perhaps their best way of obtaining European goods without becoming entangled in the Franciscans' web. Working at the presidio also guaranteed them a large supply of food, which was a powerful incentive during the mid-1790s, when severe drought stunted the production of the region's wild seeds. For the military, the employment of these experienced Indian laborers had advantages over day laborers contracted from the mission: a reliance upon the Franciscans for neophyte contract laborers was expensive and involved an agreement to feed the neophytes adequately and not treat them harshly. Furthermore, relations between the military and the Franciscans were always tense, and the governors resented the missionaries' control of the neophytes' labor. When possible, the military sidestepped the Franciscans and contracted directly with gentile laborers. Thus, both the military and unbaptized Indians had strong motivations in working outside the Franciscan system.[79]

78. Lasuén to Ugarte y Loyola, Oct. 20, 1787, Mission San Carlos, in Kenneally, ed. and trans., *Writings of Lasuén*, I, 168; Fages to Féliz, "Instruction for the Cabo of the Escolta of the Pueblo of Los Angeles," Jan. 13, 1787, Mission San Gabriel, Archives of California, C–A 4, 148–155, esp. 155, BL.

79. In some instances, when a presidio was built in advance of neighboring missions, the military had no choice but to look to gentile laborers. Such was the case in Santa Barbara, where, from 1783

In 1789, after the soldiers carelessly sparked the destruction of half of the Monterey Presidio, Governor Fages, as we have seen, hired neophyte contract laborers to rebuild the presidio and construct a new church inside its quadrangle. But he also employed unbaptized Costanoans from the Santa Clara Valley who were prepared to meet the military's urgent labor needs. By 1790, they were familiar with Spanish work routines, had proved themselves to be a reliable work force, and had frequently found employment in the homes and fields of San Jose Pueblo. For seven years, from April 1790 to September 1796, crews from the Santa Clara Valley worked one-month shifts at the Monterey Presidio. Ranging in size from eighteen to ninety-seven laborers, at least fifteen groups toiled at Monterey in these years. Collectively, these teams worked approximately 14,550 days at the presidio, almost twelve times more days of labor than Indians contracted from San Carlos (Tables 35, 38). In 1794, groups of Santa Clara Valley gentiles also worked briefly on the fortifications of the San Francisco Presidio.[80]

Governor Fages, having been undone previously by the soldiers' unwillingness to perform *trabajos mecánicos*, proved instrumental in steering the military toward gentile laborers. It was he who developed a system of incentives and protections to recruit Indians from the Santa Clara Valley, seventy miles distant from Monterey. Fages first called together the Indians' "captains and leaders" and proposed "that they send groups of five, ten, fifteen, or twenty [men to Monterey,] according to the number of people that they had and could do without for the protection of their lands." In return for their labor, Fages promised food, "blankets, shirts, beads, and seashells." Before departing for Monterey, the Spaniards would gather up and hold each Indian's "bows and arrows to avoid all problems." The Indians' main concern was for the safety of villagers left behind.[81]

---

through 1786, local Chumash not yet affiliated with one of the missions helped construct the presidio. For their labor, they were paid in wheat. See Croix to Fages, Apr. 19, 1783, Archives of California, C–A 2, 372, BL; Ortega to [Ugarte y Loyola], June 8, 1786, Archives of California, C–A 3, 430, BL. See also Maynard J. Geiger, ed. and trans., *The Life and Times of Fray Junípero Serra, O.F.M.; or, The Man Who Never Turned Back (1713–1784)*, 2 vols. (Washington, D.C., 1959), II, 289–290.

80. The most thorough discussion of the Santa Clara Valley Indians during the precontact and mission period is by Randall Milliken, *A Time of Little Choice: The Disintegration of Tribal Culture in the San Francisco Bay Area, 1769–1810* (Menlo Park, Calif., 1995). On these Indians' work for settlers, see Lasuén to Ugarte y Loyola, Oct. 20, 1787, Mission San Carlos, in Kenneally, ed. and trans., *Writings of Lasuén*, I, 168. Fages said that each crew of Indians should work at the Monterey Presidio for one moon (Fages to Macario de Castro, Apr. 23, 1790, Monterey, Archives of California, C–A 44, 31–32, BL). For these Indians' work at the San Francisco Presidio, see Milliken, *A Time of Little Choice*, 122–123.

81. On Fages's plan for the employment of Indians from the Santa Clara Valley at Monterey, see Fages to Branciforte, Aug. 12, 1793, Mexico, AGN, PI, CCXVI, expediente 7, 335a–337b. This copy was written by a scribe and signed by Fages. See also Branciforte to Borica, Dec. 12, 1795, Mexico, Archives of California, C–A 7, 405–413, BL; Donald C. Cutter, *California in 1792: A Spanish Naval Visit* (Norman, Okla., 1990), 133–134, for similar descriptions of the labor exchange by a Spanish naval officer who visited Monterey in 1792.

TABLE 38. Gentile Contract Labor Groups, Monterey Presidio and Church, 1790–1796

| | LABOR CREWS | | | |
Year	Number of Workers	Estimated Labor Days	Workers' Combined Estimated Labor Days	Equivalent Pesos
1790	21	36	756	142
	24	30	720	135
	26	24	624	117
1791	97	48	4,656	873
	21	30	630	118
1792	40	30	1,200	225
1793	33	30	990	186
	29	24	696	131
1794	29	35	1,015	190
	24	21	504	95
	19	11	209	39
1795	18	48	864	162
1796	26	24	624	117
	20	24	480	90
	24	24	576	108
Total	451	439	14,544	2,727

Note: For 1794, estimated days of labor are exact, since sources indicate the number of days laborers worked in that year. All other estimates assume six days of labor per week. The equivalent pesos are calculated at a daily labor rate of 1.5 reales per worker.

Source: Archives of California, C–A 44, 31, 39–40, 42, BL; AGN, CA, XXI, 412a–412b; Archives of San Jose, C–A 283, reel 2, 593–595, 608–609, 614, BL; ibid., reel 4, 388, 390–391, 418; AGN, PI, CCXVI, 467a–478a.

Despite Fages's repeated injunctions that the laborers not be forced to come to Monterey and that those who remained behind be protected, Indians suffered abuses. The group that arrived in July 1790 apparently had not been contacted "with delicacy" but had been "surprise[d] at their dance." Fages scolded Macario de Castro, the comisionado of San Jose: "That is not what I ordered you to do, but just the opposite. . . . In no way did I desire these outrages, and much less when they are at their fiestas." Fages again told Castro to arrange the work parties through the Indians' captains "and to make them see that the King" needed their labor. Indians of the Santa Clara Valley probably attached little significance to the needs of a remote Spanish monarch. Fages's oversight, however, seems to have put an end to these sorts of "outrages," and groups of Indian laborers traveled to Monterey for many years. For the most part, these Indians were recruited, fed, and paid according to Fages's plan. Years later, though, one local village captain complained that, when the men had gone to Monterey, other Indians had attacked their villages, insulted their wives, and stolen their food.[82]

Indian village captains worked with Fages to organize labor crews and to control the payments they received. After the Indians had completed their work at the presidio, Governor Fages usually gave all of the goods that the crew had earned to the Indians' village captain, thereby allowing him to distribute rewards as he felt appropriate. Perhaps the captains themselves insisted on this system as the price of facilitating access to laborers from their communities. On other occasions when the governor paid each worker his remuneration, captains earned twice as much as the laborers. And, when the military was having trouble recruiting gentile laborers, the presidial commander of Monterey told the comisionado in San Jose to give the Indian captains one or two blankets to facilitate the formation of a work party.[83]

While they traveled to and from San Jose and during their time in Monterey, Indians enjoyed substantial food supplies from the military. In 1791, for example, ninety-seven Indians from the Santa Clara Valley, the largest such crew to go to Monterey, worked at the presidio for two months, from May 27 until July 28. For their trip to Monterey, the Indians had a food allotment of 2 fanegas and 6 almudes of grain and 4 almudes of corn. This food came in addition to the provisions they brought with them: "pinole, rabbits, fish, fruits, wild seeds, and other nourishments." The Indians' supplying much of their own provisions not only suggests the degree to which they sought to balance the old and the new, but it raises the possibility that they took the food the Spanish supplied with the intent to barter or stockpile it. At the presidio, the workers received a total of 26 fanegas and 3 almudes of corn in their pozole, and the meat from 12 sheep, 93

82. Fages to Castro, July 22, 1790, Archives of California, C–A 44, 39–40, BL; Gabriel Moraga to José Argüello, Aug. 20, 1794, California File, HM, doc. 26186, HL; Fages to Castro, Aug. 3, 1790, Archives of California, C–A 44, 41, BL. For provisions given to these Indians, see José Argüello's accounts, Oct. 31, 1791–Dec. 31, 1793, AGN, PI, CCXVI, expediente 6, 467a–477a; Argüello, Dec. 31, 1795, AGN, CA, XXI, expediente 12, 408–411. Itemized expenses have not survived for all of the years 1790–1796. On the attack on the village while the men were at Monterey, see Ignacio Vallejo to Borica, Aug. 20, 1797, San Jose, Archives of California, C–A 8, 335, BL.

83. Hermenegildo Sal to comisionado of San Jose, May 18, 1796, Archives of San Jose, reel 2, 604, BL. In June 1790, Governor Fages wrote three letters during a period of eleven days to the comisionado asking why the next group had not yet arrived (Fages to Castro, June 8, 12, 18, 1790, Archives of California, C–A 44, 38, BL). By redoubling their efforts, the Spaniards were able to cobble together a group of twenty-six Indians, who arrived in Monterey in mid-June; see Sal to Gabriel Moraga, July 19, 1796, Monterey, Archives of San Jose, reel 2, 608–609. See also Fages to Castro, Aug. 3, 1790, Archives of California, C–A 44, 41, BL. Fages and his successors frequently supplied blankets to their subordinates in San Jose to facilitate the recruitment of Indians; see Moraga to José Argüello, Aug. 20, 1794, California File, HM, doc. 26186, HL; Sal to Moraga, June 26, 1796, Archives of San Jose, reel 2, doc. 45, 613–614, BL.

bulls, and 96 calves. For sustenance on their return home, the group was given 2 bulls and 2 fanegas of corn. Other groups received similar provisions for their work at the presidio during these years.[84]

Indian subsistence patterns and seasonal cycles—not just the work schedule of the Spaniards—determined when the gentile Indians would work at Monterey, and, in times of bad weather or in the cold of winter, Indians made themselves scarce. As José Joaquín de Arrillaga complained, because of the "intensely cold" winter, it "was not in 1793–[17]94 easy to find Indians to work on the construction of the church at the presidio." Santa Clara Valley Indians chose not to work at Monterey from November through March. The rainy, cool winters made transportation often difficult over muddy roads, and Indians of the region generally did not undertake intensive labor during these months. In some years, workers did not arrive at the presidio until late May or early June.[85]

Fages boasted to his superiors that his employment of gentile Indians had saved "the major expense of paying the daily wages of the Indians from the missions." The cost-conscious Spaniards believed that gentile laborers were less expensive than neophytes, and they were right. If gentiles and neophytes were given equal amounts of food while they worked, then the main difference in the cost of their labor was in the wages or payments in kind that they received. For a month's work at the presidio, each gentile laborer earned one *frezada pastora* (blanket), valued at between five and nine reales. By comparison, one neophyte laborer garnered the mission thirty-six reales in wages for the same amount of time. Thus, at least four gentiles worked at the presidio for the cost of one neophyte.[86]

84. For provisions given to these ninety-seven laborers, see José Argüello, Oct. 31, 1791, Monterey, AGN, PI, CCXVI, expediente 9, 467a–467b, 474a; Argüello, [September 1798, Monterey,] AGN, CA, XXI, expediente 12, 412a–412b. On Indians' bringing their own food to Monterey, see Fages to Branciforte, Aug. 12, 1793, Mexico, AGN, PI, CCXVI, expediente 7, esp. 336a. For their provisions on their return, see Argüello, Dec. 31, 1795, AGN, CA, XXI, expediente 12, 412a–412b. Fages had ordered that only the "useless," old, sick, or skinny bulls be slaughtered for the Indians (Argüello to governor, Sept. 24, 1798, AGN, CA, XXI, expediente 12, 413a–413b).

85. Arrillaga to conde de Revillagigedo, Jan. 8, 1794, AGN, PI, CCXVI, expediente 8, 436a–436b. On the seasonality of the Indians' work at Monterey, see Hermenegildo Sal, "Account between Monterey Presidio and Mission San Carlos," June 30, 1797, Monterey, Taylor Coll., doc. 2448, HL. During the fall of 1793, because gentile Indians were not available for work at Monterey, the military employed two groups of neophytes from neighboring Mission San Antonio (José Argüello, Dec. 31, 1795, AGN, CA, XXI, expediente 12, 412a–412b).

86. Fages to Ugarte y Loyola, June 2, 1790, Monterey, AGN, CA, XLVI, expediente 2, 31a–31b. On occasion, the laborers received cigars to encourage their work. The military paid one and a half reales per day for a neophyte contract laborer, who would work six days a week. I could have used twenty-six days a month as a base figure, but, for comparative purposes, it did not seem consistent with the gentiles' working four weeks, or twenty-four days. It is possible, however, that gentiles worked seven days a week. A neophyte would cost the military, on average, thirty-six reales for four weeks of labor; the presidio paid according to the number of days contract laborers worked. Gentiles were paid one

In all, for their nearly 14,550 days of work at the presidio, Indians received 451 blankets valued at 9 reales apiece for a total of 507 pesos. Had these 451 Indians been mission day laborers, who each cost the military 1 ½ reales a day, the corresponding charges would have been 2,727 pesos—nearly five and a half times as great. A factor that contributed to the economy of gentile labor was that many groups worked for more than a month, and this extra effort was not compensated. In 1793, for example, thirty-three gentiles worked at the presidio for five weeks, from June 9 until July 16. Assuming the weather was good and they were all healthy, these Indians would have worked a minimum of six days a week, putting in among them a total of 990 days of labor. Had they been neophytes, the presidio would have owed the mission 185.5 pesos for the five weeks of work. The military, however, paid the gentile laborers only 37.1 pesos in blankets valued at 9 reales apiece. In this case, the San Jose Indians took home one-fifth the wages the presidio would have had to pay for mission labor.[87] Although these gentiles and others who worked at the presidio were in a sense underpaid for their labor, at least their earnings flowed into their hands rather than mission coffers. Fages's superiors enthusiastically supported his reduction of expenses by employing gentile laborers. Upon reviewing the amount spent on the reconstruction of the Monterey Presidio, Jayme Beltrán, one of the Spanish officials who had to approve the expenditures for the rebuilding of the presidio, commended the "ingenious method with which señor governor don Pedro Fages arranged the construction of the presidio" and its "great economy," which benefited the Royal Treasury.[88]

In addition to obtaining food and blankets—both of which could be used or exchanged—gentile contract laborers who came to Monterey also gained access to two scarce and valuable commodities: trade beads and seashells. Indian captains routinely received from Fages four to six strings of beads upon completion of the crew's work, and they also gathered heaps of shells from the shoreline. Indians, in fact, collected so many shells that two mules were required to transport them back to the Santa Clara Valley. These shells and the beads made from them were among the most important forms of wealth and economic exchange in native California. For centuries, Indians had traded beads and shell ornaments

blanket even if they worked at Monterey for more than a month. For purposes of comparison, however, it is safe to assume that, for four weeks of work, a gentile laborer would be paid with a blanket worth between five and nine reales but occasionally as high as twelve reales. Stays could range from four to eight weeks, though most of the groups worked in Monterey for four.

87. For the account of what was provided to these workers, see José Argüello, Dec. 31, 1793, Monterey, AGN, PI, CCXVI, expediente 9, 474a.

88. Jayme Beltrán, Sept. 10, 1795, AGN, PI, CCXVI, expediente 7, 342a–343b. In 1796, Governor Borica noted that the San Jose gentiles had been paid the smallest wages (Borica to Branciforte, Mar. 12, 1796, Monterey, AGN, PI, CCXVI, expediente 8, 444a–446a).

made from olivella, a small marine snail, from the coastal regions all the way into the Great Basin. Most coastal groups participated in this trade, but Indians of the Monterey region had manufactured shell beads since at least 200 B.C.E. The gathering, manufacturing, and export of these units of exchange and items of aesthetic value must have been disrupted by the dual revolutions and the establishment of the coastal missions of San Carlos (1770) and Santa Cruz (1791) and others farther inland. Through their work at the Monterey Presidio, the Santa Clara Valley Indians might have regained their access to this important commodity, thereby enabling them to temporarily stitch together one patch of an increasingly frayed native economy.[89]

The last documented movement of Indian laborers from San Jose to Monterey occurred in September 1796, and it seems evident that, by then, most of the Santa Clara Valley Indians who had worked at Monterey had attained baptism at Mission Santa Clara. Others would most likely soon join that mission or Mission San Jose, founded in May 1797. Even though Indians from San Jose continued to work at the presidio through 1796, that March, Governor Borica told his superiors that large construction projects in Alta California would no longer be feasible. Most of the artisans who had supervised the work had returned to Mexico; and, since most of the Indians who worked at the presidio had attained baptism and affiliated with a local mission, the military could no longer hire them without the agreement of the Franciscans. Beyond that matter, the very few unbaptized Indians of the Santa Clara Valley sought better economic opportunities closer to their homes.

By 1796–1797, Santa Clara Valley Indians who still resisted baptism found it more advantageous to work for settlers in San Jose than for soldiers in Monterey. Although they forfeited their access to an abundance of shells, the value of the beads manufactured from them might have been in decline, given the enormous disruption of Indian trading relationships during the colonial era. By 1796, just as the work at the Monterey Presidio was winding down, one observer noted that, in San Jose, gentiles were working everywhere: they "cultivate the fields, do

---

89. On the Indians' collecting shells, see Fages to Branciforte, Aug. 12, 1793, Mexico, AGN, PI, CCXVI, expediente 7, 337b. For the Indians' production and exchange of shell beads, see James A. Bennyhoff and Richard E. Hughes, *Shell Bead and Ornament Exchange between California and the Western Great Basin*, Anthropological Papers of the American Museum of Natural History, LXIV, part 2 (New York, 1987), 80–175. Brooke S. Arkush studied Yokuts trade networks, in "Yokuts Trade Networks and Native Culture Change in Central and Eastern California," *Ethnohistory*, XL (1993), 619–640. For a discussion of prehistoric Indian trade routes in California, see James T. Davis, "Trade Routes and Economic Exchange among the Indians of California," *Reports of the University of California Archaeological Survey*, LIV (1961). Davis notes that Costanoan Indians (most likely affiliates of those in the Santa Clara Valley) traded mussels, abalone shells, salt, and dried abalone to the Yokuts (Tulare Yokuts) of the San Joaquín Valley for piñon nuts (19). See also L. L. Sample, "Trade and Trails in Aboriginal California," *Reports of the University of California Archaeological Survey*, VIII (1950), 1–30.

the planting, and harvest the crops; in short they do almost everything that is done."[90] In 1797, the comisionado of San Jose asked a local Indian captain, Pala, for two children so that they could be taught how to grow hemp. Instead of his children, Pala offered more: his villagers' labor, perhaps in the hope that they could sell their labor without traveling overland and putting their families at risk. Ultimately, these people chose to stay closer to home, where they worked for San Jose settlers, since only by participating in the region's ascendant Spanish labor economy could they continue outside of the mission.

By the late eighteenth century, no Spaniards in Alta California challenged the belief that heavy, manual labor was indeed the province of Indians. What made this belief so strong was the soldiers' and settlers' own insistence—made incrementally over time, although without evident foundation—that they, as gente de razón, were not in fact suited to manual labor even though, by the norms and conventions of the day, they were. In a sense, it was the close intermingling of mestizo soldiers and settlers with California Indians, the fact that together they were creating a new economic life in the presidios and expanding pueblos and ranchos of the region, that led the so-called gente de razón to insist upon their superiority over the California Indians who often came to live and work alongside them.

The early soldiers' assertion that they were above most forms of manual labor and the later soldiers' and settlers' practice of employing Indians in so many work activities were related developments that emerged from the specific context of Spanish settlement in California and Indians' responses to it. Over time, mestizo soldiers and settlers—and most certainly their children—adjusted their own racial and caste origins to conform to their novel sense that they were above trabajos mecánicos and above those they employed to work for them. As such, these people were involved in a double self-creation, one that entailed not just a reinvention of what sort of work they would do as soldiers and settlers but what sort of people they in fact were. As stated earlier, only five out of central Mexico's more than two dozen caste terms appeared consistently in Alta California (español, mestizo, mulato, coyote, and indio), and, as of 1790, nearly half of the non-Indian adults in the region were identified as "español."[91] But this figure dramati-

90. Señán to Branciforte, May 14, 1796, College of San Fernando, Mexico City, in Lesley Byrd Simpson, ed., *The Letters of José Señán, O.F.M., Mission San Buenaventura, 1796–1823*, trans. Paul D. Nathan (San Francisco, Calif., 1962), 2.

91. Table 2, based on a retabulation of data in Mason, *Census of 1790*, 77–105. In this sense, California resembled the rest of the Spanish Borderlands West. Very few of the presidial soldiers in the eighteenth century were born in Spain, and about half descended from Spanish parents. Of the 911 officers and men of the sixteen garrisons outside California between 1773 and 1781, 50 percent were of direct European lineage *(europeos,* españoles, or *criollos)*; 37 percent were mixed bloods (mestizos, *castizos,*

cally overstates the "whiteness" of the soldiers and settlers of California; over time, they simply moved themselves to lighter and higher castes. By deriving their own race and caste identities from their occupations rather than vice versa, they upended the cultural and racial norms of their society even as they endorsed them through complaints and actions that accelerated the consignment of the heaviest manual labor to California Indians. And Indians had little choice but to take up this burden. Faced with a declining population and the steady collapse of their subsistence networks, the best they could hope for was a moderate compensation and an ability to integrate this new work into their increasingly complex and multiple laboring lives, even though, in shoring up the soldiers' and settlers' communities, they ensured that their own survival would be purchased at increasingly unfavorable terms.

Thus, during the colonial period, Indian labor became indispensable in California not just to the domestic economy of soldiers and Indians but to the emerging social and racial identities of the soldiers and settlers, most of whom were themselves mestizo or mulato. As early as 1800, one Franciscan, Father José Francisco de Paula Señán, noted the social import of the Indians' labor for the soldiers: "It is common that the soldiers, and their wives, when they take Indians [as laborers], begin to act like nobles [*Damas y Caballeros*]." And, in 1815, twenty years before the missions were secularized, two decades before Mexican soldiers gained control of the missions' lands and laborers and began to proudly call themselves *californios*, Father Ramón Olbés of Santa Barbara observed that the "people who live in this province known as the gente de razón are so lazy and so given to idleness that they know nothing else than to ride horseback and consider all work as dishonorable." "To them it seems that only Indians ought to work."[92]

mulatos, moriscos, coyotes, *lobos,* and *castos).* The remaining 13 percent were classified as Indians; see Moorhead, *The Presidio,* 182–183.

92. Vicente de Santa María and Señán to Lasuén, Oct. 2—, 1800, Mission San Buenaventura, AGN, PI, CCXVI, expediente 1, 95b–96a. For Olbés, see *APST,* 130. There is an extensive literature on the californios. For modern approaches to the study of californio identity, see Monroy, *Thrown among Strangers;* Rosaura Sánchez, *Telling Identities: The Californio Testimonios* (Minneapolis, 1995).

8

◄ ◄ ▶ ▶

PUNISHMENT, JUSTICE, AND HIERARCHY

All mission Indians lived under the threat of Spanish violence, and, in time, many who flouted the padres' plans found themselves imprisoned, flogged, hobbled, or forced to do labor. Beyond backing up the missionary program with force, soldiers also policed the countryside and imposed their own system of criminal justice, through which they harshly punished Indians who committed robbery, rebellion, assault, or homicide. Spanish officials went to some lengths to bring order and consistency—and therefore what they saw as a measure of fairness—to the administration of justice in Alta California. But Spanish systems of law and justice by design fostered and enforced a social hierarchy with Indians at the bottom. As such, these systems bred Indians' resentment, proving consistent only in their asymmetrical treatment of natives and the gente de razón.

Like any people who live in stable communities, California Indians had laws that prohibited certain behaviors. They considered theft, assault, rape, and murder as threats to family, village, and community. How the Children of Coyote responded to acts of violence by their own is not known. But, across and up and down California, Indians held to a common set of practices: the guiding belief was that criminals owed a debt to their victims or to their victims' families. Chiefs, headmen, shamans, or the aggrieved worked to ensure that criminals compensated victims for losses they suffered. Thus miscreants were punished, not on behalf of the larger community or village, but for the individuals who were wronged. Corporal punishment, imprisonment, or forced labor was not a standard part of California Indians' disciplinary repertoire. In only a few instances could the aggrieved carry out a death sentence, and, in these rare situations, murderers might be killed as they had killed their victims. Usually, those deprived of a family member by murder could extract payments from the guilty. Indians reinforced these beliefs and practices through "ritual, story, anecdote, and action." Elders and parents taught and counseled and, if necessary, scolded and reprimanded disobedient children. Parents rarely, if ever, beat their offspring. As we shall see, the Spaniards' very different ideas and practices regarding corporal punishment and the correction of criminals rendered life under Spanish rule increasingly difficult for Indians and added one more layer of strife and turmoil to their lives.[1]

CORPORAL PUNISHMENT AND THE MISSIONS

Since the days of Hernán Cortés, missionaries and secular officials in New Spain had held that the rod and lash were integral to colonial rule, and the Franciscans were firmly committed to their use in Alta California. The padres sought to lead Indians to Christ by example and exhortation. But, when neophytes did not follow their teachings, the Franciscans punished them to compel them to mend their ways. Accordingly, missionaries or their Indian assistants routinely flogged or beat neophytes who skipped Mass, shirked assigned labor, engaged in premarital sex, committed adultery, or ran from the missions. Although the overwhelming majority of whippings went unrecorded at the time they were administered, the Franciscans' correspondence and the testimony of California Indians from the colonial period indicate that corporal punishment was quite common, so routine that it was indeed an inescapable part of life at San Carlos for the Children of Coyote.

The seventeenth-century missionary manual California Franciscans most commonly consulted, Alonso de la Peña Montenegro's *Itinerario para párrocos de indios*, endorsed the beating of Indians and asserted that the whip was essential for the Indians' good behavior and ultimate conversion. The California Franciscans claimed that, without flogging, Indians would never live as Christians. And, like their Catholic predecessors elsewhere in New Spain, missionaries claimed their authority to punish Indians was natural and divinely sanctioned and likened the floggings to those with which "natural parents punished their legitimate and beloved children." In 1800, Fathers Estevan Tapis and Juan Cortés defended their right to punish mission Indians by asserting that they—like natural parents—had, in a sense, given the Indians life: "We have conceived of these neophytes by means of the efforts to seek them and reduce them so that they embrace Christianity. It was we who baptized them, through which they received lives of grace. We minister to them with the Holy Sacraments, and we endeavor to instruct them in the maxims of moral Christianity. We therefore use that authority, that God concedes to parents, for the good education of their children: to exhort them, to

1. On California Indian concepts of crime and punishment, see, for example, T. R. Garth, "Atsugewi," in *HNAI*, VIII, 239. For the reinforcement of these beliefs and practices, see, for example, Lowell John Bean, "Cahuilla," ibid., 582; Bean, *Mukat's People: The Cahuilla Indians of Southern California* (Berkeley, Calif., 1972), 120–122.

reprimand them, as well as to punish them when necessary." Toward the end of the colonial period, Father José Francisco de Paula Señán, the fourth president of the California missions, echoed this belief and the beliefs of his predecessors: "The missionary father attends to the correction and suitable chastisement [of the neophytes] and he applies the punishment like a natural father on his sons." (Missionaries, it should be noted, often turned this violence on themselves, scourging their own flesh to demonstrate their piety and sinfulness.) Such practices of corporal punishment were without counterpart in Indian society.[2]

The Franciscans intended the corporal punishment of Indians to be exemplary and humiliating, and they probably succeeded, given that most Indians had little or no experience with floggings, either in public or private. Whether these beatings were relatively mild or meant to inflict physical injury, the dynamic they created must have rendered them especially demeaning. In Alta California, Indian men—like many criminals in Europe—suffered their beatings in public for maximum humiliation, to serve, the Spaniards believed, as a potent deterrent. Believing that women suffered more from shaming and humiliation, the Franciscans had Indian women flogged by other women away from public view, in the barracks set aside for young girls or older single women.[3] Father President

2. José Francisco de Paula Señán, in *APST*, 144. On the *Itinerario* and the punishment of Indians, see William B. Taylor, *Magistrates of the Sacred: Priests and Parishioners in Eighteenth-Century Mexico* (Stanford, Calif., 1996), 215–216, 642 n. 62, esp. 216. On Franciscans as the "natural parents" of the Indians, see Estevan Tapis and Juan Cortés, Oct. 30, 1800, Mission Santa Barbara, AGN, PI, CCXVI, expediente 1, 85a. See also Serra to Teodoro de Croix, Aug. 22, 1778, Monterey, in Tibesar, ed. and trans., *Writings of Serra*, III, 252–253. Serra also argued that the belief that "spiritual fathers should punish their Indian children with whippings appears to be as old as the conquest of these kingdoms; so general, in fact, that the saints do not seem to be any exception to the rule" (Serra to Felipe de Neve, Jan. 7, 1780, Monterey, ibid., 412–413 [my trans.]). The Bible contains statements supporting parental corporal punishment, but the padres did not mention any of these directly in their correspondence. Perhaps they saw no need to cite scriptural injunctions that were widely held. See Prov. 13:24, 22:15, 29:15. 1 Cor. urges more restraint with the rod.

3. The manner in which Cortés had allowed himself to be whipped in public by the Franciscans inspired Serra (Serra to Neve, Jan. 7, 1780, Monterey, in Tibesar, ed. and trans., *Writings of Serra*, III, 412–413). The classic condemnation of the Franciscans' use of physical punishment is Sherburne F. Cook, "The Indian versus the Spanish Mission," *Ibero-Americana*, XXI (1943), 1–194, rpt. in Cook, *The Conflict between the California Indian and White Civilization* (Berkeley, Calif., 1976). For Franciscan arguments sympathetic to the missionaries, see Francis F. Guest, "An Examination of the Thesis of S. F. Cook on the Forced Conversion of the Indians in the California Missions," *SCQ*, LXI (1979), 1–77; Guest, "Cultural Perspectives on California Mission Life," *SCQ*, LXV (1983), 1–65; Guest, "An Inquiry into the Role of the Discipline in California Mission Life," *SCQ*, LXXI (1989), 1–68; Guest, "The California Missions Were Far from Faultless," *SCQ*, LXXVI (1994), 255–307. Guest focuses on the beatings' physical, rather than emotional, pain and argues that the padres' corporal punishment was rarely worse than a parental spanking.

On where missionaries punished Indians, see Tapis and Cortés, Oct. 30, 1800, Mission Santa Barbara, AGN, PI, CCXVI, expediente 1, 85a; Fermín Francisco de Lasuén, "Refutation of Charges," June 19, 1801, Mission San Carlos, in Kenneally, ed. and trans., *Writings of Lasuén*, II, 217. The women who administered these floggings are not known. Some of the punishments they administered could be

Lasuén believed that private beatings helped to instill in women the "modesty, caution, and uprightness that belongs to their sex." Unlike the Indians of central Mexico or the woodlands of eastern North America, the Children of Coyote did not ritually torture or sacrifice captives. Thus they did not glorify the stoic endurance of pain as did other native societies, and they had no experience administering or receiving the public punishments that became so common in the California missions.[4]

The Franciscans could claim royal support for their right to "correct" their spiritual children with beatings, but that support was becoming more tenuous all the time. In 1773, the viceroy and a Mexican royal council, at Serra's urging, had declared that, "just as a father of a family has charge of his house and of the education and correction of his children," in Alta California, "the management, control, and education of the baptized Indians pertains exclusively to the missionary fathers." Yet Mexican officials had granted the Franciscans this authority primarily because Alta California was an unsettled frontier, and they did so in the face of a rising tide of regalism that intended to circumscribe clerical authority over Indians and parishioners in New Spain. At the same time that California missionaries formalized their right to whip mission Indians, royal officials and leading Catholics in central Mexico campaigned against the use of the lash by parish priests and missionaries. As a result, church leaders increasingly emphasized that priests should be "gentle teachers," and Bourbon officials, seeing missions as anachronisms, denounced and prohibited whippings by members of the clergy as usurpations of state authority. The Franciscans in California, however, distanced themselves from such beliefs and reforms, asserting that their use of corporal punishment was appropriate since they were not parish priests but apostolic missionaries charged with civilizing and converting a primitive people. By the 1770s, therefore, the beatings that California Indians routinely endured would, in central Mexico, have been inflicted by only the most brutal and old-fashioned parish priest. These punishments, then, were not only alien to the Indians who suffered them but offensive to a growing sector of colonial society as well.[5]

---

brutal. See Diego de Borica to Mariano Apolinario, Sept. 26, 1796, Monterey, Archives of California, C–A 24, 496–497, BL. Apolinario was a Dominican of Baja California who officiated at San Diego from 1791–1800 (see *California Pioneer Register and Index, 1542–1848 . . . Extracted from The History of California by Hubert Howe Bancroft* [1884–1890; rpt. Baltimore, 1964]).

4. Lasuén, "Refutation of Charges," June 19, 1801, Mission San Carlos, AGN, PI, CCXVI, expediente 1, 72b.

5. For the order clarifying missionaries' control over California Indians, see Francisco Palóu, "Decision of His Excellency and the Royal Council in regard to the Petitions of the Reverend Father President," May 6, 1773, in Palóu, *Historical Memoirs of New California . . .*, ed. Herbert Eugene Bolton, 4 vols. (1926; rpt. New York, 1966), III, 37–56, esp. 50. On Bourbon reforms and parish priests, see Nancy M. Farris, *Crown and Clergy in Colonial Mexico, 1759–1821* (London, 1968); Taylor, *Magistrates of the Sacred*, 215–221.

As we have seen, disputes between the governors and the Franciscans over the election of Indian officials in the missions had been central to church-state struggles in the region, and, predictably, during the 1770s, Governor Felipe de Neve insisted that only the military—not the Franciscans—could punish Indian officials. Father Serra countered that "the alcaldes are also children" under the care of the padres and therefore not exempt from punishment at the missionaries' hands. In the 1790s, Governor Diego de Borica decreed that paternal authority did not allow the padres to administer more than twenty-five lashes. Only the military, he insisted, could give more severe floggings. These orders stood until 1826, when, as the missions were first being secularized, Governor José María de Echeandía decreed that Franciscans were not to whip married or adult Indians and were to limit their correction of Indian children to fifteen lashes a week.[6]

In addition to flogging Indians, the padres, with the help of alcaldes and the soldiers stationed at the missions, punished Indians by placing them in stocks or by shackling or hobbling their feet or legs. In 1786, La Pérouse left no doubt that the stocks at San Carlos were both secure and punishing: "These stocks consist in a heavy beam, sawn crosswise, in which a hole has been made large enough to take a leg; a hinge links one of the ends of this beam, which has been cut in half; it is opened up at the other side in order to let the prisoner's leg pass through, and it is closed with a padlock; he is forced to lie down in a rather uncomfortable position." Another restraining device known as a *corma* caught the eye of the second lieutenant and paymaster of the San Francisco presidial company, José Pérez Fernández, who sent a sketch of one to Governor José Joaquín de Arrillaga in 1794. The apparatus, which closed around the prisoner's feet, was formed of two pieces of wood hinged together, twenty-four inches long and about ten inches wide. Rags were placed around the prisoner's feet to prevent abrasions and permanent injury. According to Pérez Fernández, the corma could be used to punish Indians and allow them to perform simple tasks, such as cleaning wheat or grinding corn. Pérez Fernández thought the corma especially appropriate to chastise Indian women who were "guilty of adultery or other serious faults." Fernando Librado, a Chumash man born in 1838, recalled the use of a similar instrument at Mission San Buenaventura during his childhood. The hobble "was shaped of wood to cover the foot like a shoe." "It was made from two pieces of

6. Serra to Neve, Jan. 7, 1780, Monterey, in Tibesar, ed. and trans., *Writings of Serra*, III, 412 (my trans.); Borica to Apolinario, Sept. 26, 1796, Monterey, Archives of California, C–A 24, 496–497, BL; José María de Echeandía, circular letter to presidial districts of San Diego, Santa Barbara, and Monterey, July 25, 1826, Monterey, copy made by Echeandía, August 1826, Taylor Coll., unnumbered, at end of box 9, HL. Eventually, a compromise was worked out: missionaries would punish Indian officials in missions far removed from one of the presidios, and, at missions like San Carlos that were adjacent to one of the presidios, the "correction" of the Indian alcaldes would be entrusted to the governor and his soldiers.

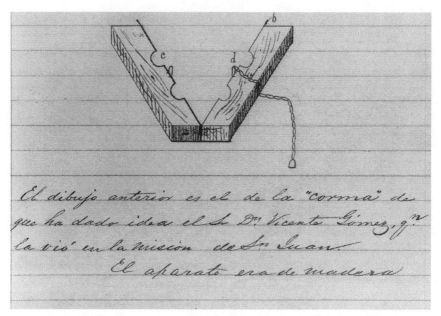

PLATE 18. Sketch of a *corma,* or wooden hobble, placed around the legs of mission Indians who defied Franciscan authority. Copy of original by José Pérez-Fernández. 1794. Archives of California, C–A 7, 55, BL. The offender's legs would have been placed between the two pieces of wood. Once closed, the hobble would have been secured with a chain. The Bancroft Library, University of California, Berkeley

wood which opened, and the entire foot was placed into it from the toe to heel. These pieces of wood were joined to a ring which went about the knee, and from this ring straps were attached to a belt that went around the waist of a person. Weights were fastened to the straps. As punishments, the missionaries would work men and women in the fields with these weighted wooden shoes." Again, Indians encumbered by this device would not have to sit idle, a state that the padres considered conducive to vice and that detracted from productivity. Missions did not have regular prison cells, so, at night, Indian offenders were placed in stocks, confined in the guardhouse, or secured in the mission's kitchen or one of its workshops.[7]

That the Franciscans considered violence toward Indians integral to their missionary approach is best illustrated by their own words and deeds. In 1786, two Baja California Indians and fifteen neophytes at Mission Santa Clara accused

7. John Dunmore, ed. and trans., *The Journal of Jean-François de Galaup de la Pérouse, 1785–1788,* 2 vols. (London, 1994–1995), I, 180 n. 1; [José] Pérez Fernández to José Joaquín de Arrillaga, Feb. 1, 1794, San Francisco, Archives of California, C–A 7, 55–56, BL. On the use of the corma, see also Tapis and

Father Tomás de la Peña of assault and murder. To the soldiers who first reported the Indians' accusations to the governor, the charges seemed credible because they knew De la Peña's fiery temperament and heavy-handedness. Governor Pedro Fages deemed the accusations of sufficient merit to warrant an investigation that took weeks, involved dozens of individuals, and required his travel from Monterey to San Jose and San Francisco. For the governor, who directed the main inquiry, as well as for Father President Lasuén, who conducted his own investigation, the appropriateness of De la Peña's punishments was determined by whether they had drawn blood or caused notable bruises.[8]

In their testimony during the investigations, Indians did not simply complain that De la Peña had beaten them. Doing so would have got them nowhere, given the general (although waning) acceptance of corporal punishment. Rather, they stated that De la Peña had punished them abusively and excessively for minor or careless mistakes. On several occasions, they claimed, his beatings had drawn blood. In detail, they described how the padre had kicked and mortally wounded Sixto, a fourteen-year-old boy, who had inadvertently flooded part of a field while irrigating the mission's crop of beans. Some Indians claimed to have seen De la Peña break the neck of an old man because he was wearing only a blanket, not the cotton shirt provided by the missionaries. And they testified that De la Peña had also beaten to death another old man who was too sick and too weak to work.

De la Peña's own handwritten defense and account of his actions underscore that the Spanish colonial system in Alta California endorsed and even promoted the casual striking of Indians for a range of actions, including seemingly innocent mistakes and minor acts of disobedience. De la Peña never denied hitting Indians. But he insisted that he had not mistreated any of them and that the Indians in question had died from illness, not from his blows. He admitted that twice he

---

Cortés, Oct. 30, 1800, Mission Santa Barbara, AGN, PI, CCXVI, expediente 1, 84b, 85a. On Librado's complicated genealogy, see John R. Johnson, "The Trail to Fernando," *Journal of California and Great Basin Anthropology,* IV (1982), 132–138. For Librado's recollections, see Travis Hudson, ed., *Breath of the Sun: Life in Early California as Told by a Chumash Indian, Fernando Librado to John P. Harrington* (Banning, Calif., 1979), 17. Franciscan imprisonment of Indians: Señán and Vicente de Santa María, San Buenaventura, Oct. 2–, 1800, AGN, PI, CCXVI, expediente 1, 97a. This practice was technically in keeping with laws that forbade priests from operating jails. See Taylor, *Magistrates of the Sacred,* 209, 213.

8. For the Indians' declarations in the initial inquiry of April 1786, see AGN, PI, I, expediente 6, 150a–151b. For the judicial proceedings overseen by Lasuén in late May 1786 and the Indians' testimony, see Kenneally, ed. and trans., *Writings of Lasuén,* I, 109–137. For the testimony of the Indians during Fages's inquiry of July and August 1786, see AGN, PI, I, expediente 6, 163a–189a. On punishments that the father president deemed excessive, see Lasuén, "Refutation of Charges," June 19, 1801, Mission San Carlos, in Kenneally, ed. and trans., *Writings of Lasuén,* II, 221. The Indians who testified before the governor were asked only whether De la Peña's punishments had drawn blood, not whether De la Peña or anyone else at the mission had whipped or beaten them or other Indians. Thus, to Fages and Lasuén, punishments in general were acceptable.

had struck and injured Indians at Santa Clara. This was undeniable because Spaniards had witnessed the blows. De la Peña acknowledged that, one afternoon in July 1783, he and Father Diego Noboa had gone to see the recently sowed fields of the mission where the Indian Ybon was supposed to have been watering. But Ybon had already left, according to De la Peña, either because he did not want to irrigate the land or because he did not understand what De la Peña had told him to do. Later, as punishment, De la Peña hit Ybon over the head with a cane. Although the blow drew blood, De la Peña dismissed the injury as insignificant. Ybon's wound, De la Peña sarcastically noted, "was so great that a little dust stanched the flow, and it healed immediately." De la Peña also explained that, on July 31, 1784, after he offered Mass and performed a marriage at which the governor was present, he had observed a commotion in the mission church. Two boys were pushing and shoving one another, fighting instead of chanting the *Alabado* as De la Peña had ordered. Upset, the missionary hit the scuffling boys in the ears. Later that day, when he was back in his quarters with Governor Fages, the padre was told that one of the boys' ears was bleeding. De la Peña had the boy brought to him, and, in the presence of Fages, he sprinkled tobacco powder on the wound and applied a bandage. De la Peña characterized the wound as nothing more than a bloody scab. Upon reading De la Peña's defense and admission that he had injured two Indians, Father President Lasuén declared the padre innocent of all charges and free from all suspicion. Lasuén's superiors at the College of San Fernando also backed De la Peña's actions and character. Given the missionary's matter-of-fact attitude and the complete support his actions elicited from his superiors, his deeds reveal not just the behavior of one man but the acceptable behavior of many.[9]

The Indians' accusations against De la Peña had rested upon their own credibility. And their case collapsed when cross-examination revealed that many had possibly not seen the events they had initially claimed to have witnessed. Ultimately, the Indians' accusations were found to be calumnious and motivated by the resentments of Plácido, a Baja California Indian whom De la Peña had recently stripped of some of his special access to food stores at the mission because he had lost some cloth. Fages, however, had seen firsthand De la Peña's "fiery temperament," how the padre had "broken the ear" of one Indian and hit another in the face and how, "instead of treating the Indians as a father would, he

9. Tomás de la Peña to Lasuén, Nov. 21, 1786, San Carlos, AGN, PI, I, expediente 4, 45a–62b; De la Peña to Lasuén, Dec. 2, 1786, San Carlos, AGN, PI, I, expediente 4, 63a–65b (Ybon's wound at 56a; the child's bloody ear at 55b); Lasuén, summary of findings, May 31, 1786, Santa Clara, and Lasuén to José Antonio Rengel, July 3, 1786, San Carlos, both in Kenneally, ed. and trans., *Writings of Lasuén,* I, 117, 119. Lasuén's defense of De la Peña came after his own inquiry, in advance of Fages's investigation and before De la Peña's own letters to Lasuén in which he responded formally to the accusations.

had given them severe punishments from his own hand until some bled." Fages concluded that De la Peña's character was ill suited for missionary work. Years later, Fages remained convinced that De la Peña had committed violent excesses with Indians; in accusing him of crimes, Indians had committed calumny "in name only."[10]

The continuing struggle between the Franciscans and the governors over the padres' corporal punishment of Indians erupted again in 1798 when Father Antonio de la Concepción Horra of Mission San Miguel wrote the viceroy that the Franciscans poorly administered the missions and treated Indians with cruelty. To his fellow missionaries, Horra appeared to be mentally imbalanced, but, in a climate of deep suspicion between church and state, the governor took the accusations seriously and investigated them thoroughly. The result was another clear case of the padres' beating Indians. In the course of their own defense, Franciscans asserted that the punishments they administered were, on the whole, "gentle and mild," never surpassing twenty-five lashes in a day and neither drawing blood nor leaving notable bruises. Again, in downplaying their punishments of Indians, the Franciscans left no doubt that the floggings were common and violent.[11]

In the formal investigations prompted by Horra's accusations, the region's presidial commanders provided dramatic accounts at odds with the missionaries'. They asserted that Indians often took up to fifty blows at a time and that the most serious offenders endured a *novenario*: twenty-five lashes on nine separate days.[12] They also charged that the Franciscans flogged neophytes without

10. Pedro Fages to commandant general, Aug. 3, 1786, Monterey, AGN, PI, I, expediente 6, 202b–205b; Fages to José Antonio Roméu, Feb. 26, 1791, Monterey, Archives of California, C–A 6, 152–169, esp. 168, BL. According to one of the Indians who testified in the investigation, after Plácido lost the cloth, he had to get his food just like everyone else. Plácido had previously been the highest-ranking Indian at Santa Clara, a fact exemplified by his name's appearing first in *padrónes* for the mission in 1782 and 1783. See DPHM, 2d Ser., II, reel 3, BL; declaration of Anacleto Valdez, AGN, PI, I, expediente 6, 171b. See also Randall Milliken, *A Time of Little Choice: The Disintegration of Tribal Culture in the San Francisco Bay Area, 1769–1810* (Menlo Park, Calif., 1995), 93–95. The battle between De la Peña and his detractors continued to the highest levels of the colonial bureaucracy. In September 1791, the viceroy declared De la Peña unfit as a missionary and ordered him recalled (conde de Revillagigedo, Aug. 27, 1791, Mexico, AGN, PI, I, expediente 6, 222a–226a). Yet De la Peña's superiors at the College of San Fernando appealed the judgment and ordered a subsequent investigation that found De la Peña of good character. By then, the controversial missionary had been declared mentally unbalanced by Spanish officials. He returned to Mexico City in the summer of 1794.

11. For the investigation into Horra's allegations, see AGN, PI, CCXVI, expediente 1, 5a–134b; Lasuén, "Refutation of Charges," June 19, 1801, Mission San Carlos, AGN, PI, CCXIV, 74a, and in Kenneally, ed. and trans., *Writings of Lasuén*, II, 221. The original reads "suaves y dulces."

12. Antonio Grajera, commander of San Diego Presidio, Mar. 21, 1799, San Diego, AGN, PI, CCXVI, expediente 1, 31a; Raymundo Carrillo, commander of San Diego Presidio, Oct. 13, 1802, AGN, PI, CCXVI, expediente 1, 110a–110b. Beatings the presidial commanders described were far in excess of those endured by Indians in Mexican parishes at the same time, where punishments above twenty-five lashes were considered extreme, cruel, and grounds for a criminal investigation against the *cura* (Taylor, *Magistrates of the Sacred*, 217–218).

first informing the presidial commanders or asking for their permission, a practice that was increasingly at odds with customs in central Mexico, where, in the
eighteenth century, parish priests customarily asked for the assistance *(auxilio)* of
civil authorities in the enforcement of laws.[13] Despite their indignant and accusa-
tory tone, a hollowness characterizes the soldiers' charges that the padres over-
stepped their authority; presidial commanders sought to erase the difference
between parish priests and apostolic missionaries and thereby reduce the Franciscans' power. Crucially, the soldiers—like the Franciscans—never questioned
that recalcitrant or erring Indians should be whipped. Concern for the Indians'
welfare was secondary to the contest for authority in colonial California.

The Franciscans' unapologetic beating of Indians drew down upon the missions the government's scrutiny and criticism. It served as a visible and convenient reminder that the California missions were out of step with late colonial
society and the priorities of the Bourbon state and offered critics of the Franciscans another reason why the missionaries had to be replaced by more compliant
secular parish priests. The lesson the padres took from these controversies was to
moderate slightly their punishments of Indians and, more important, to conceal
evidence from critics. Ultimately, Lasuén had urged De la Peña to refrain from
"giving an ear-pulling, a punch, a rap on the head, or a slap with the hand," not
because these were cruel or inappropriate punishments, but because they could
give the missionaries' enemies "an excuse for similar false charges." And, in the
wake of the controversy over Horra, the father guardian of the California missionaries ordered them never to punish a baptized Indian in the presence of
anyone not affiliated with the mission and never to tell anyone outside the order
how they punished Indians, lest such information create political troubles.[14]

On rare occasions, Indians complained to soldiers of their rough treatment at
the Franciscans' hands, but most Indians silently endured their beatings or imprisonment. Everywhere, however, the Franciscans' use of force brought added

13. Charges that the padres punished Indians without asking for the military's approval: Hermenegildo Sal, commander of Monterey Presidio, Dec. 1, 1798, Monterey, AGN, PI, CCXVI, expediente
1, 15b; [Felipe de Goycoechea], commander of Santa Barbara Presidio, in Tapis and Cortés, Oct. 30,
1800, Santa Barbara, AGN, PI, CCXVI, expediente 1, 84b. After the sixteenth century, according to
Taylor, "Royal auxilio was required for crimes that fell entirely within the priest's jurisdiction (such as
absence at mass and ignorance of the catechism), as well as for those in the gray area of jurisdiction
shared by civil and religious authorities (such as drunkenness and illicit sex)." After the mid-eighteenth
century, Taylor continues, "the right of royal auxilio was claimed by the audiencias and district
governors with growing frequency" *(Magistrates of the Sacred,* 210–211). Predictably, the missionaries
denied that they had to ask for the soldiers' assistance or approval before they punished Indians for
moral offenses or for failing to abide by their orders.
14. Lasuén, summary of findings, May 31, 1786, Santa Clara, in Kennealy, ed. and trans., *Writings of
Lasuén,* I, 117; circular letter from José Gasol to the California missionaries, "Libro patente," Oct. 1,
1806, Mission San Carlos, LDS film no. 0913303.

turmoil to mission communities. Indians resented the blows to their bodies and the missionaries' threats that discouraged and even prevented them from pursuing familiar and important activities. Some Indians, those who were already discontented with life in the missions, fled from lashings or ran away after they had been punished. Magin Llucal, a forty-three-year-old Huchiun, testified that he had fled Mission San Francisco because "of his hunger, and when he was sick, they put him in the stocks on orders of the alcalde." Timoteo Guecusia declared that he left the mission "because when he was very sick, the alcalde Luís came to get him and whipped him, and afterward Father Antonio Dantí cudgeled him." And Otolon Eunucse asserted that he, too, had abandoned the mission because, after his wife had sinned with Salvador the vaquero, "Father Antonio ordered him whipped because he was not taking care of his wife." For these men, the physical punishments and humiliations they endured at the Franciscans' hands made a difficult situation intolerable.[15]

Some Indians chose not to flee but rather to strike back. In 1808, three Diegueños killed Pedro Miguel Alvarez, the mayordomo at Mission San Diego, in part because he had repeatedly beaten them. In 1811, Nazario, an Indian cook at San Diego, poisoned Father José Pedro Panto for giving him 124 lashes over a day and a half. Nazario explained that he "was tormented by the multitude of lashes" and "found no other way to revenge myself." Public punishment and humiliation of Indians not only sparked individual acts of resistance but at least one collective rebellion as well. The hundreds, if not thousands, of Chumash from Missions Santa Inés, La Purísima, and Santa Barbara who joined in rebellion in 1824 rose in part because of the flogging of a La Purísima neophyte by a soldier at nearby Mission Santa Inés. Actions such as these, however, did not lessen the extent to which missionaries relied on the lash. In fact, as Indians grew more resistant, the Franciscans might have brandished their canes and lashes with greater regularity as they sought to maintain control.[16]

15. Testimony of runaway Indians, Aug. 12, 1797, San Francisco Presidio, AGN, CA, LXV, expediente 2, 108a–109a. Indians' names and basic information are in Milliken, *A Time of Little Choice*, 299–303. Soldiers also testified that the Franciscans' harsh punishments of the Indians had contributed to the Indians' flight from the missions. See declarations of Raymundo Carrillo, Pedro Amador, Alejo Miranda, and Diego Olivera, Sept. 12, 1796, San Francisco Presidio, AGN, CA, LXV, 111a–118b. Indians' motivations for fleeing the missions are discussed in Chapter 3.

16. "Causa criminal contra tres indios neófitos de la misión de San Diego por la muerte que dieron a su mayordomo," 1809, AGN, CA, LXII. The page numbers for this case are to the internal documents, not the whole volume. For a translation of the trial of Nazario, see Doyce B. Nunis, Jr., "The 1811 San Diego Trial of the Mission Indian Nazario," *Western Legal History*, IV (1991), 47–58, esp. 51. Panto survived the poisoning but died seven months later. Father Gerónimo Boscana believed that Panto had died from the lingering effects of the poison, but Nunis suggests that was not possible. Nazario was sentenced to eight months' hard labor at the presidio. On the Chumash rebellion, see James A. Sandos, "Levantamiento! The 1824 Chumash Uprising Reconsidered," *SCQ*, LXVII (1985), 109–133.

In the late 1820s, during the onset of secularization, the Franciscans' dependence upon threats of violence to make Indians work and pray came back to haunt them. As the governors stripped away the missionaries' power to punish Indians with blows, Franciscans everywhere found themselves unable to have their way. At Mission San Diego, half of the laborers refused to participate in the harvest, and another group refused to transfer mission-produced tallow to port. Throughout the province, Franciscans protested the governors' limitation of physical punishment as a "trampling" of their "paternal authority." Some padres held to their lashes as the only means to fend off what they saw as chaos and ruin. At Mission San Francisco, Father José María Gutiérrez asserted that Indians had neither reason nor shame and could only be motivated through fear of a whipping. It was not until the edict of Father Prefect Francisco García Diego in July 1834 that the Franciscan leadership in California acted to end corporal punishment of Indians. But, by then, the missions were well on their way to secularization, and missionary rule was nearing its close. In abolishing beatings, García Diego decried the now-forbidden practice as inhumane. But much of his reasoning centered on the Franciscans: he asserted that the whipping of Indians had driven many from the missions, a tragedy that could cause the padres themselves to be punished for the loss of so many souls. Ever mindful of the missionaries' reputations, he called on them to abandon corporal punishment and other "infamous and obnoxious" methods. But he did not expect the Franciscans to completely let go of their control over the Indians' bodies. If gentle means were not sufficient to correct insolence, García Diego advised his fellow Franciscans to lock up recalcitrants.[17]

While retaining for themselves the responsibility of disciplining Indians who challenged their authority within the missions, Franciscans depended on soldiers to reclaim and punish those who fled from their authority. Although the fugitives' overall numbers constituted only a small percentage of the missions' population, absent Indians set a bad example and, if left unchallenged, could induce others to abandon the missions. Thus, throughout the colonial period, leading missionaries repeatedly tried to enlist the Spanish military to search for runaways. Yet the governors found it impolitic and dangerous to send soldiers to help the Franciscans track down fugitives. Although they believed they had superior weapons, the military knew they were undermanned and therefore feared operating from a position of weakness, especially in the hilly backcountry,

17. Narciso Durán to José María de Echeandía, Nov. 29, 1830, Taylor Coll., doc. 2090, HL; José María Gutiérrez to governor, June 16, 1833, San Francisco, Archives of California, C–A 15, 132–134, BL; García Diego to the northern missions of Alta California, July 4, 1833, Santa Clara, Taylor Coll., doc. 2151, HL.

PLATE 19. *Modo de pelear de los yndios de Californias (How California Indians Fight)*. By Tomás de Suria. 1791. This image might also have been titled *How Spanish Soldiers Fight*, for it depicts the Spaniards' reliance on horses and lances instead of firearms, which were often in short supply and ill-repair, to intimidate and defeat California Indians. Here, the soldier seeks protection from the Indians' arrows behind a small leather shield as he charges forward. Courtesy, Museo Naval, Madrid

where soldiers were forced to dismount their horses and proceed on foot. Felipe de Neve, who was governor of Alta California from 1777 to 1782, resisted sending soldiers to capture absent neophytes or to punish gentile Indians who harbored them. He concluded that such raids were ineffective, could easily result in fatalities among the soldiers and Indians, and would allow the Indians to grasp quickly the limits of the few soldiers in Alta California. At the end of his term, Neve instructed his successor, Pedro Fages, to avoid using the military to retrieve fugitive neophytes, and he stressed that, for the successful colonization of the region, it was "highly useful" that the gentiles "do not learn to kill soldiers." "This rule," Neve insisted, "overrides all other rules."[18] A decade later, Fages told his own successor that maintaining the Indians' fear of the Spaniards was crucial, for it "advantaged the conquest" of the region.[19]

During his second governorship (1782–1791), Fages tried to rely on diplomacy, negotiation, and alliances to reclaim fugitive Indians and prevent villagers from harboring them. Early in December 1782, Mission San Carlos neophytes who

18. Neve to Fages, Sept. 7, 1782, in Edwin A. Beilharz, *Felipe de Neve, First Governor of California* (San Francisco, Calif., 1971), 160–162.

19. Fages to Roméu, Feb. 26, 1791, Monterey, Archives of California, C–A 6, 152–169, esp. 156, BL.

were seeking refuge in the rancherías of Eslenajan and Ensen prompted him to dispatch a military expedition. Apparently, Eslenajan was harboring mission Indians who had fled several times, and no method had persuaded them to remain at the mission more than a few months.[20] In addition to capturing these runaways, Fages's goal was to establish a loose understanding between the Spaniards and the non-Christian Indians at Ensen and Eslenajan, and thereby render future military action unnecessary. Fages requested two interpreters from Mission San Carlos, one for the Esselen-speaking Eslenajan and a second for the Costanoan-speaking Ensen. He ordered the interpreters to explain to the village captains that the soldiers had come in peace bearing presents to show them the "rebelliousness" of the neophytes they were harboring and to state that they were prepared to use force to reclaim fugitives. Despite their own limited number, the soldiers also offered to protect the Indians against their enemies. In return, the Indian villagers were to help them retrieve runaway neophytes. Fages instructed his lieutenant, Diego Gonzales, to explain to the village captains that, when a neophyte sought refuge in their villages, they were to "secure him without causing injury and take him to a mission or presidio," where they would receive "corn, dry goods, or beads."[21] Thus, in essence, the overextended Spanish soldiers offered bribes to persuade Indian villagers to turn in fugitive neophytes. How the Esselen responded to Gonzales's expedition is not recorded, but they probably resisted. By late February, Theodosio Jutis, captain of Excelen Village, was under arrest in the presidio of Monterey, perhaps because of conflict during Gonzales's military expedition. And there seems to have been a violent clash around that time between soldiers and the Esselen in which at least one villager was killed.[22]

20. Neve to Fages, Sept. 7, 1782, in Beilharz, *Felipe de Neve,* 161.

21. Fages to [Diego Gonzales], Dec. 11, 1782, Monterey, Archives of California, C–A 23, 153–154, BL; Fages to Serra, Dec. 18, 1782, Monterey, Archives of California, C–A 23, 158, BL. Fages provided detailed instructions for Lieutenant Diego Gonzalez and the eight soldiers under his command to follow during the expedition.

22. There is no record of why Theodosio Jutis was arrested; we know of his arrest only through a note in his son's baptismal entry. See Modesto (San Carlos bapt. no. 773, Feb. 24, 1783). A baptismal entry dated July 24, 1783, for Juan Luciano (San Carlos bapt. no. 806), also of Excelen Village, states that his father was recently killed by soldiers; see also the marriage entry of Juan Luciano's mother, Euprepia María (San Carlos marr. no. 352).

The Franciscans continued to request assistance in reclaiming fugitives. In September 1787, the Indian Bruno returned after spending twelve days on the run from soldiers, having left San Carlos without the padres' permission. See Lasuén to Fages, Sept. 6, 1787, Mission San Carlos, in Kenneally, ed. and trans., *Writings of Lasuén,* I, 152; Bruno (San Carlos bapt. no. 193). In 1798, Father Mariano Payeras appealed to the governor for aid in recovering neophytes who had fled San Carlos and returned to the villages of Kalendaruc and Mutsun. And, in April 1799, Father Francisco Pujol notified Borica that nine neophytes were missing from the mission. A military expedition was dispatched in June 1799, and at least ten Indians from San Carlos accompanied Sergeant Macario de Castro. See Borica, "Instructions for Travel to Villages of the Gentiles," June 7, 1799, Monterey, Archives of California, C–A 10, 327–330, BL; Pujol and Baltasar Carnicer to Borica, Apr. 3, 1799, Mission San Carlos, Taylor Coll., doc. 207, HL.

The Indians' refusal to relinquish baptized fellow villagers and the military's hesitation to send soldiers after them led some padres to take matters into their own hands. In July 1797, missionaries at San Francisco sent out Raymundo, a Baja California Indian, along with thirty neophytes, to reclaim a large group of runaways. On the shore of the East Bay, a group of Huchiuns attacked Raymundo and his men. Soon thereafter, a follow-up reprisal party of Spanish soldiers also came under attack. In the ensuing battle, seven gentiles died, one cavalry horse was killed and two injured, and scores of gentiles and neophytes were taken captive by the Spaniards.[23]

Bloody incidents such as these reinforced the military's wariness of mounting sorties against fugitive Indians. Trying a different tack, Spanish soldiers aggressively punished those few Indians who repeatedly fled and were easily recaptured, perhaps hoping that making examples out of a small number of unfortunates could prevent others from running away. Most Indians who left the missions and were later brought back faced terms of hard labor at the presidios; the governor usually determined their sentences case by case because fugitivism was often coupled with other crimes. In 1797, Cristiano, a San Francisco neophyte, served four months' hard labor at the presidio with a shackle on his leg not just for running away but for doing so with several married women.[24] When Indians fled and also stole cattle, they usually faced especially severe beatings: in 1811, ten Chumash neophytes who had attacked some of Mission San Buenaventura's livestock received a novenario and hard labor at the presidio.[25] Despite these and other heavy punishments, Indians determined to leave the missions continued to do so. As mentioned above, to the consternation of the Franciscans, Indians not only left the missions to return to their ancestral villages or to supplement their diets, but they did so to work at the presidios or the pueblos of San Jose or Los Angeles. As early as 1786, the governor ordered that Indians who repeatedly left Mission San Buenaventura for informal labor at the local presidio receive a dozen lashes and be forcibly returned to the mission. Ultimately, however, regulations such as these, designed as they were to restrict Indians' actions and speed their adoption of Spanish lifeways, testified to the limitations of Spaniards' power in relation to Indians' ability to maneuver around it.[26]

23. For translated documents relevant to Raymundo's expedition, see Milliken, *A Time of Little Choice*, 289–299.

24. Borica to commander of San Francisco Presidio, Dec. 2, 1789, Monterey, Archives of California, C–A 24, 98, BL.

25. Arrillaga to presidial commander at Santa Barbara, Feb. 19, 1811, Monterey, Archives of California, C–A 26, 11, BL. These Indians' crimes are not fully specified. The record, which is only a paraphrase of the now-lost original, says that the fugitives had caused damage *(hacían daño)* at San Buenaventura. The construction *hacían daño* usually referred to Indians who stole or killed livestock.

26. Fages to José Francisco de Ortega, Jan. 2, 1786, San Gabriel, Archives of California, C–A 22, 225, BL.

SOLDIERS AS POLICE

Even though they were stretched thin along a remote colonial frontier, the Spanish intended to extend their authority over all Indians in Alta California, not just those in the missions. Soldiers policed the territory between and around the missions and punished Indians with great frequency, as Indians, in attempting to survive the dual revolutions and balance the old and the new, often ran up against Spanish boundaries of authority and behavior. Stealing cattle, horses, or mules from mission or presidial herds, setting fire to fields, riding horseback, or obtaining access to firearms—the Spanish saw all of these activities as threatening. Indians accused of these acts encountered an intermediate level of Spanish authority and force, one that stood beyond the Franciscans' correction of neophytes for immorality and minor offenses.

California Indians so regularly stole, injured, or killed livestock belonging to the mission that, on at least two occasions before 1800, Spanish officials were forced to decree ever harsher penalties for Indians caught rustling. Those who acted against Spanish livestock commonly received increasing combinations of lashes, imprisonment, hard labor, and time in the stocks. By 1787, first-time offenders received a week in the stocks and twenty lashes on release. Repeat offenders went into the stocks for twenty days and took fifteen lashes upon their arrest and fifteen more upon release. Those caught a third time suffered imprisonment and a penalty to be decided upon by the governor himself.[27]

Despite the increasing severity of these punishments, Indians continued to kill Spanish cattle, especially from the royal herds at Monterey and Santa Barbara. Clearly, even with the padres' constant oversight and the threats of corporal punishment hanging over all Indians, the Spanish could not stop Indians from taking livestock. As discussed in Chapter 3, Indian attacks on Spanish herds during the 1790s resulted from a combination of factors, in particular the pressure that the severe drought and Spanish livestock had placed on native sources of food. In 1795, Governor Borica issued a new regulation in the midst of this crisis. Upon arrest, Indians got fifteen lashes, a month in prison, and hard work at the presidio. Once released, they received fifteen more lashes and a warning that next time the punishment would be more severe. Second-time offenders were given fifteen lashes upon arrest and release, two months of hard labor, and twelve lashes every Sunday. Third-timers earned six months' hard labor and

27. Fages to commander of Monterey Presidio, Jan. 11, 1787, San Gabriel, Archives of California, C–A 4, 156–157, BL. Presidial commanders and cabos of the mission guards punished Indians who attacked the herds. They did so without delay, formality, trial, or consultation with higher officials, generating little or no documentation.

twelve lashes every Sunday. Yet even in the face of these retributions, Indians continued to attack the royal herd pastured near Monterey.[28]

In response to the dual revolutions, Indians had first killed stock to prevent the destruction of their lands; later, they did so to nourish themselves. Many paid a heavy price. In 1796, Juan Nepomuceno, an "incorrigible" cattle thief from San Francisco, was sentenced to three years' labor at the presidio. This Costanoan did not live out his sentence; he drowned in a well—perhaps one that he was assigned to clean—near the presidio before completing his term. In 1802, three cattle thieves from San Juan Bautista endured two months of hard labor at the presidio and twenty lashes every two weeks. That same year, Cornejo of San Carlos suffered his punishment at the mission, perhaps to remind others that cattle theft was a dangerous business. For stealing a cow, Cornejo was shackled and forced to work during the day, and at night he was placed in the stocks at the mission guardhouse. These punishments still did not deter others from attacking livestock. In fact, the sheer number of Indians punished for rustling cattle prompted one soldier in 1831 to remark that nearly all Indians bore signs of floggings.[29]

The struggle between Indians and Spaniards over food sources extended from animals to crops and the management of the countryside as well, leading Spaniards to punish other Indian subsistence activities. Given the extreme distance of Alta California from other regions of New Spain, the infrequent arrival of supply ships from Mexico, the cost of shipping goods to the region, and the shortage of provisions for the soldiers, the military intended to protect the fledgling agricultural development of the missions and pueblos from Indian incursions. In 1782, five years after the pueblo of San Jose was founded to supply soldiers with food, Indians were stealing or damaging the pueblo's crops enough to cause a military order stipulating arrest, imprisonment for several days, and twenty-five lashes. A decade later, Governor Arrillaga criminalized Indians' customary practice of setting fire to their fields, a strategy long used in native hunting and protoagriculture. No longer permitted to burn the grasses of the countryside and thereby promote the germination and growth of specific seed-bearing plants, Indians

28. Punishments for Indians who killed or stole cattle: Diego de Borica, Nov. 1, 1795, Monterey, Archives of California, C–A 23, 417–418, BL.

29. Punishment of Juan Nepomuceno: Borica to presidial commander at San Francisco, 1796, Monterey, Archives of California, C–A 24, 85, BL; Rodríguez to Borica, Sept. 12, 1799, San Diego, Archives of California, C–A 10, 257–258, BL. Cornejo: governor to commander at Monterey, Feb. 10, 1802, Loreto, Archives of California, C–A 26, 166, BL. The claim that nearly all Indians showed signs of flogging might have been an exaggeration, for it was offered in the defense of a soldier who was on trial for whipping to death an Indian cattle thief. Nevertheless, even if it is an exaggeration, that the defender thought it would be convincing suggests the ubiquity of these punishments and Indian cattle rustling. Excerpt of trial of Hilario García: Gómez, asesor del territorio, Mar. 11, 1831, San Carlos, Archives of California, C–A 19, 136–140, esp. 139, BL.

must have found themselves increasingly unable to check the advance of European plants and extract a subsistence from the land. After this decree, simply preparing cooked food outside the missions became risky. In November 1816, Agustín of Mission San Juan Bautista was arrested after his wife accidentally set fire to a field near Monterey. The two had been on paseo when an unexpected wind caused their campfire to spread uncontrollably. Fearing a harsh punishment, Agustín fled into the hills and hid for three days; overcome by sickness and hunger, he returned to the mission, where he sought protection from the Franciscans. Only the intervention of Father Estevan Tapis, who explained to the governor that the fire was accidental, saved Agustín from a beating at the hands of the military.[30]

Although the introduction of livestock damaged the native economy and provoked conflict between Indians and Spaniards, over time many mission Indians found new livelihoods in the expanding pastoral economy. From the earliest days of the colonial period, many learned to handle horses as they became involved in the herding and slaughter of cattle at missions and ranchos. The Indians' attempts to become skilled equestrians and adapt to the changing economy, however, ran up against one of the Spaniards' overriding concerns: ensuring that California Indians did not become a serious military threat to their rule. High-ranking Spanish officials in central Mexico feared that California Indians would become skilled horsemen like the Apaches, and, from the dawn of the colony, they intended that soldiers restrict Indian equestrianism to a few select individuals. Beyond posing a potential military challenge to the soldiers, mounted Indians were an affront to Spanish notions of social status, for, in Iberian culture, horseback riding was the preserve of the elite. However, since Indians performed most of the manual labor in California and could accomplish some of their tasks only on horseback, Indians—both gentiles and neophytes—quickly became proficient riders. In fact, soldiers and settlers, it seems, tended to promote, rather than prevent, Indian equestrianism. Placing their own personal economic advancement and their desire to have Indians work for them above the social pretensions of their superiors and the security of the region, soldiers and settlers often hired gentiles and neophytes on horseback to work their fields, herd their animals, and perform other labor-intensive tasks. By 1796, gentiles on horseback evidently were common enough for the governor to issue a standing order mandating the punishment of soldiers who employed them. An outright ban on

30. José Moraga, "Instructions to the Cabo of the Guard of the Pueblo of San Jose," December 1782, San Francisco, Archives of California, C–A 2, 160–166, esp. 164, BL; Estevan Tapis to governor, Nov. 15, 1816, San Juan Bautista, Taylor Coll., no. 613, HL; Tapis to Pablo Vicente de Solá, Nov. 16, 1816, San Juan Bautista, Taylor Coll., doc. 662, HL.

mission Indian laborers' riding horses was impractical, but the military in 1818 restricted the privilege at each mission to an approved list of vaqueros. Indians and missionaries, however, ignored this, prompting the governor in 1819 to order twenty-five lashes for any Indian found on horseback who was not an approved vaquero.[31]

Although Indians continued to ride horses in the face of punishment, few, if any, ever obtained any firearms, so Spanish fears of an Apache-like resistance in Alta California proved unwarranted. Soldiers were threatened with heavy retributions for trading guns and shot to Indians; moreover, Spanish soldiers in California were so poorly armed themselves that they had no guns or shot to spare. The trade of firearms to California Indians during the colonial period, therefore, was seemingly nonexistent. Yet the danger of Indians' fashioning metal into daggers or other weapons worried Spanish authorities so that they prohibited soldiers and their families from selling Indians knives, "bits of swords, lances, or other instruments." This seems to have been exceptionally effective not only because soldiers did not want to arm potential enemies but because they themselves had few of these items to begin with. So rare was the trade of metal objects to California Indians that, in 1807, soldiers went to great lengths to recover a single hatchet that Indians had acquired near the pueblo of San Jose. Spanish officials briefly relaxed this prohibition in the early 1820s, when a select group of Indians from each mission were armed with machetes to help defend the presidios from foreign attack.[32]

Although Spaniards interpreted these aforementioned Indian acts as threats to their rule, most of these actions were, in fact, Indian attempts to carve out a place for themselves in the new order. On rare occasions, though, Indians did rise up in overt and coordinated attempts to push back or overthrow Spanish rule. At these moments of conflict, Spanish officials called upon soldiers to quell any resistance,

31. Officials' fears that California Indians could become effective mounted warriors: Croix to Neve, Apr. 22, 1780, Arispe, Archives of California, C–A 55, 256, BL; Fages to Lasuén, Aug. 20, 1787, CMD 126, SBMAL. Regulation of 1796: Sal to comisionado of San Jose, Apr. 29, 1796, Monterey, Archives of San Jose, reel 2, doc. 83, 684–685, BL. Restriction of 1818: Solá to Vicente Francisco de Sarría, Jan. 2, 1818, CMD 714, SBMAL; José María Estudillo, Jan. 18, 1818, Archives of San Jose, reel 1, doc. 14, 135–139. Order of 1819: Solá to Guerra, July 19, 1819, San Carlos, Archives of California, C–A 17, 222 (MS does not specify which Guerra), BL.

32. The prohibition on selling metal implements to Indians was included in most of the regulations directed at the mission guards. See Fages to Diego Gonzalez, interim commander of the Monterey Presidio, Mar. 1, 1783, Monterey, Archives of California, C–A 2, 428–438, par. 3, BL; Neve, "Instructions to the Commander of the Presidio of Santa Barbara and the Sergeants of the Escorts of Purísima Concepción and San Buenaventura," Mar. 6, 1782, San Gabriel, AGN, CA, LXI, 106a–116b; Diego de Borica, "Instruction for the Escolta of Mission San Juan Bautista during Its Establishment," May 18, 1797, Monterey, Archives of California, C–A 10, 138–144, par. 9, BL. Spaniards and hatchet: José María Estudillo to Macario de Castro, Oct. 9, 1807, Monterey, Archives of San Jose, reel 1, doc. 29, 98–100, BL.

investigate the rebels' motivations and punish their insolence. Because rebellions were, by definition, serious challenges to Spanish authority, the military acted quickly. After they had restored order, soldiers and officers from the nearest presidio conducted preliminary investigations and arrested and flogged those they considered ringleaders. Only then did presidial commanders begin more deliberate inquiries, attempting to ferret out the rebels and their motivations. Sometimes the governor himself would take on this responsibility, leading the investigation or specifying the questions put to the accused.

Spanish investigations into Indian rebellions were not full-blown criminal inquiries; they involved a minimum of legal formality and were speedy, lasting only a day or so. Indian suspects and witnesses gave testimony, often through interpreters.[33] Next, presidial commanders wrote a summary of the case and perhaps punished with additional whippings those believed to be guilty. Then the governor would examine the trial record and forward it to his superiors in Mexico for their review and their determination of a final punishment of the accused. At no point could accused rebels defend or exonerate themselves other than through their own testimony. They could not cross-examine witnesses, rebut testimony, or mount a defense. Clearly, in these instances, the Spaniards' goal was to reestablish their authority as quickly as possible, and they no doubt feared that delaying all punishments twelve to eighteen months until final word came from Mexico would only encourage others to revolt. Eventually, high-ranking Mexican authorities usually ordered that Indian rebels be punished with additional lashes, hard labor, and banishment. Indians observing the public flogging and hard labor of the accused were to learn the costs of rebellion. Banishment prevented influential Indians from reorganizing rebellions among their followers, and it deprived rebel Indians of living among those who shared

33. Indian testimony from the Spanish colonial period raises important evidential issues. In nearly all instances, especially in the first years of Spanish colonization, Indian testimony was solicited with the assistance of an interpreter, who was usually a presidial soldier. These frontier interpreters largely were self-taught, and their ability to move back and forth accurately between Spanish and local Indian dialects is uncertain. Furthermore, the men who recorded testimony in California were soldiers whose principal qualification was basic literacy. Although they were aware of their responsibility to record faithfully the testimony they heard, they were not professional scribes. California Indian testimony, therefore, is a highly mediated source. Finally, the possibility of coercion in eliciting Indian testimony may also give rise to debate about the accuracy of Indian responses: many of the Indians who testified in criminal cases, notably those accused of crimes, suffered confinement and might have testified while shackled. Judicial torture, however, although considered a legitimate procedural step available to Spanish officials, does not seem to have been used to extract testimony or confessions from Indians in Alta California or elsewhere in the Spanish Borderlands during the late colonial era. In a review of hundreds of cases from colonial New Mexico and Texas, Charles R. Cutter did not find one case of torture (*The Legal Culture of Northern New Spain, 1700–1810* [Albuquerque, N.Mex., 1995], 123). Similarly, in a review of dozens of cases that took place in Alta California, I found no instance of torture.

their culture. Capital punishment, even of rebels, was extremely rare in California as it was throughout all of colonial Mexico.

Immediately after soldiers had put down the uprising at Mission San Gabriel in 1785, organized by Nicolás José, suspect neophytes from the mission and gentiles from the surrounding area suffered arrest and twenty to twenty-five lashes. A speedy trial then ensued. Four Gabrielinos the Spaniards identified as the instigators testified and then endured imprisonment over two years, until the governor finally received notification from Mexico as to their punishments. One of the leaders, the woman named Toypurina, was banished from San Gabriel and sent to San Carlos; Nicolás José was banished to a distant presidio and punished with six years of hard labor. Two men found guilty of being accomplices were freed after serving more than two years in prison. Some forty years later, for leading a far more effective and bloody challenge to Spanish authority that led to the deaths of four Spaniards, seven Chumash leaders faced execution, four suffered banishment and ten years' hard labor, and seven more earned terms of eight years' hard labor.[34]

Indian assaults on individual soldiers or Franciscans were almost as rare as collective rebellions. Those who attacked Spaniards faced rigorous punishment, often, it seems, without a formal trial. For throwing a stone at one missionary, Hilario endured the novenario, and then, on nine consecutive Sundays, he was given an additional thirty-five or forty lashes. Onesimo, Prospero, and José Reyes of Mission San Jose received sentences of three to six years' labor at the presidio of San Francisco for injuring Father Pedro de la Cueva. The handful of Indians who actually killed missionaries suffered punishments more severe still, just short of death. In 1816, five Indians accused of murdering Father Andrés Quintana were sentenced by the viceroy to two hundred lashes and from six to ten years of hard labor in chains.[35]

34. On the rebellion at San Gabriel, see Steven W. Hackel, "Sources of Rebellion: Indian Testimony and the Mission San Gabriel Uprising of 1785," *Ethnohistory*, L (2003), 643–669. For the punishment of the leaders of the Chumash rebellion: José de la Guerra, Mar. 23, 1824, Mission La Purísima, "Sentencia contra indios rebeldes," Archives of California, C–A 18, 188–189, BL. Two other Indian rebels were sentenced to death in absentia.

35. Hilario: this may have occurred in Baja California (Arrillaga to Rodríguez, Feb. 16, 1805, Loreto, Archives of California, C–A 26, 260–261, BL). De la Cueva, according to Maynard Geiger, "was a sick man, a genuine alcoholic, whom neither counsel nor confinement could cure" (*Franciscan Missionaries in Hispanic California, 1769–1848: A Biographical Dictionary* [San Marino, Calif., 1969], 61). De la Cueva sailed from California in November 1806. Onesimo, Prospero, and José Reyes are listed as being at the presidio of San Francisco from 1809 through 1812. It seems unlikely that the punishment of the three would have commenced three years after De la Cueva's departure from the province (Documentos Para la Historia de California: Archivo Particular de la Familia Estudillo, 1874, 4 vols., I, fol. 98a, 218, BL [hereafter cited as DPHC, Estudillo). At first, Quintana's death was considered the result of natural occurrences, but, two years later, details surfaced of a plot against the padre's life in revenge for his cruel treatment of Indians at Mission Santa Cruz (Geiger, *Biographical Dictionary*, 205–206). For attackers' punishments, see Arrillaga to De la Cueva, Mar. 28, 1816, Monterey, Archives of California, C–A 26, 34, BL.

Occasionally, when baptized Indians assaulted gentiles, Spanish officials doled out punishments, fearing, no doubt, that the mission Indians could antagonize the as-yet-unbaptized and thereby undermine Spanish colonization.[36] In 1780, near San Diego, Carlos, Luis, and Rafael led an attack on the village of Jalò that resulted in the deaths of at least ten of its inhabitants. These three Diegueño *cabecillas* (ringleaders) had been involved in numerous acts of resistance and violence dating from the 1775 attack on the mission. After reviewing the transcript of the investigation, one that involved no recorded Indian testimony, officials in Mexico recommended banishment of the three to a distant presidio; the governor sent them to Loreto in Baja California.[37] Two decades later, when a Santa Clara neophyte assaulted an unbaptized Costanoan who was working in San Jose, Spanish soldiers moved quickly to make amends with the gentile Indians before the incident was allowed to jeopardize the labor relations of the pueblo and impede the harvest of wheat and hemp. The governor, through the comisionado of San Jose, assured the unbaptized Costanoans that the offender would receive the strongest necessary punishment "short of execution," even though the Indian who allegedly had been beaten had not "been brought forth to clarify exactly what had happened." Spanish officials believed that twenty-five lashes on three or four consecutive days was enough to "compensate" the gentiles for the neophyte's "transgression." Left to their own devices, local Indians certainly would have pursued another means of punishment, but the Spaniards' actions seem to have prevented an outbreak of hostilities. Whether they did so by compensating or intimidating the aggrieved is unknown.[38]

Clearly, Indians who threatened the colonial order invited quick and harsh punishments. But, when mission Indians assaulted one another, they were usually left to settle these scores on their own, as soldiers and their superiors were loath to involve themselves in disputes between Indians, especially when their own authority and the colonial hierarchy were not jeopardized. Most likely, native forms of retribution and compensation came to the fore. Only in exceptional cases, when colonial officials were compelled into action by Indians at the missions or by their need to regulate relations between Indian groups, did Spaniards investigate Indian assaults on neophytes and punish their assailants. In an unusual case from late in the colonial period, José of Mission San Fernando

---

36. Punishments of gentiles for attacking neophytes: Arrillaga to commander of San Diego Presidio, Apr. 4, 1812, Monterey, Archives of California, C–A 26, 312, BL; José Antonio Carrillo, Sept. 20, 1828, Los Angeles, Archives of California, C–A 18, 388–389, BL.

37. Felipe de Neve, July 12, 1781, San Gabriel, AGN, CA, LXXI, 14a–14b.

38. Arrillaga to comisionado of San Jose, Aug. 17, 1807, Soledad, Archives of San Jose, reel 1, 114–115, BL, trans. in Milliken, *A Time of Little Choice*, 317–318; Arrillaga to Macario de Castro, Sept. 5, 1807, San Antonio, Archives of California, C–A 26, 211, BL.

stabbed another neophyte during a dispute over money lost in a game of chance; he ended up with a sentence of two years at the Monterey Presidio. The Indians of San Fernando, however, had forced the Spaniards' involvement, since, after the stabbing, a group seized José, tied him up, and carried him off to the mission guardhouse.[39]

The military rarely prosecuted Indian-on-Indian assaults that appeared to be of a personal nature, just as it shied away from settling disputes between soldiers unless they involved challenges to superiors and therefore threatened the hierarchy of authority. And prosecuting soldiers, settlers, or missionaries for assaulting neophytes was near to an impossibility, given that Spaniards generally accepted the corporal punishment of Indians for a host of behaviors. Not until the 1830s, when Mexican authorities began to restrict corporal punishment, were soldiers and settlers in fact pursued for assaulting Indians, but even then those found guilty incurred only a very light punishment of just several months' hard labor.[40]

Centuries of colonization in New Spain had taught Spanish administrators that structuring society and controlling Indians properly required authority over soldiers. Only laws and clearly stated punishments could dissuade unmarried, unruly, and poorly paid soldiers from fraternizing with and taking advantage of Indians and thereby provoking conflicts. Thus soldiers were not just to police Indians' behavior but also their own. No general instructions to the commander of the Monterey Presidio or the soldiers posted at San Carlos survive. However, in all likelihood, their behavior would have been restricted by instructions similar to those given to the military guard of San Diego, a mission also established at the outset of Spanish rule in Alta California. Predictably, the regulations created boundaries between Indians and soldiers even as colonization brought them together: soldiers were not to be "familiar" with the gentiles or let them enter the mission guardhouse, nor were they to go in search of gentiles or enter their rancherías. Soldiers who defied these directives could be punished with up to eight days of guard duty wearing four *cueras* (leather jackets). Those who had sex with Indians, even if the women consented, would have to perform duty for nine consecutive days wearing five cueras.[41]

39. "Summary of Proceedings against José, a Neophyte of San Fernando Mission, Accused of Wounding the Indian Meliton, of the Same Mission," Apr. 25–June 7, 1821, Mission San Fernando, DLG, box 20, folder 885, HL.

40. For instances of soldiers punished for assaulting Indians, see Agustín V. Zamorano, Feb. 7, 1832, Monterey, Archives of California, C–A 19, 233, BL; Teodoro Gonzalez to Juez de Paz of San Jose Pueblo, May 12, 1843, Archives of San Jose, reel 2, 37, BL.

41. "Instructions for the Escolta of Mission San Diego," n.d., AGN, PI, CCXI, 341a–344b. This document is not dated, but its context and surrounding documentation suggest that it was written in 1773 or before, perhaps in 1770.

A similar set of regulations restricted the access of gentile Indians to the presidios and missions. Only unarmed gentiles were allowed to come, and only five or six could stay overnight. The instructions to the mission guards did not outlaw trade with unbaptized Indians; they merely stated that exchange had to be concluded in the presence of military superiors.[42] All of these regulations, then, tended toward a segregation of soldiers, neophytes, and gentiles and tight control over their interactions. The Spaniards' fears of intermixing proved overblown and wrongheaded, and, in fact, these regulations probably only exacerbated tensions by heightening suspicions and obstructing trade and exchange that actually could have eased the Indians' accommodation to life under Spanish rule. Eventually, sooner rather than later, a host of imperatives drove both Indians and soldiers together, more often than not in unequal economic relationships that strengthened, rather than weakened, the emerging colonial hierarchy.

INDIANS AND SPANISH MILITARY JUSTICE

As noted above, when Spaniards saw threats to their rule, they wasted little time in deciding Indians' guilt and punishing neophytes and gentiles according to local Spanish regulations that outlawed a wide variety of Indian activities. Yet not all Indians accused of crimes met this sort of justice. When charged with serious crimes not specific to the colonial frontier, such as theft or murder, Indians came under the jurisdiction of the Spanish judicial system and found themselves before a frontier version of a military court. In this venue, quick informality gave way to a time-consuming adherence to formal procedure and process.[43]

42. For example, see Neve, "Instructions to the Commander of the Presidio of Santa Barbara and the Sergeants of the Escorts of Purísima Concepción and San Buenaventura," Mar. 6, 1782, San Gabriel, AGN, CA, LXI, 106a–116b.

43. Until relatively recently, historians had not closely examined either the criminal justice system or the legal culture of the northern Spanish frontier. Cutter's *Legal Culture* explores Texas and New Mexico. Scholars of other regions of New Spain have made good use of judicial records. Among the most important studies are William B. Taylor, *Drinking, Homicide, and Rebellion in Colonial Mexican Villages* (Stanford, Calif., 1979); Steve J. Stern, *The Secret History of Gender: Women, Men, and Power in Late Colonial Mexico* (Chapel Hill, N.C., 1995). See also Gabriel Haslip-Viera, *Crime and Punishment in Late Colonial Mexico City, 1692–1810* (Albuquerque, N.Mex., 1999).

With the exception of studies of a few celebrated crimes, there has been little scholarship on how Spain administered criminal justice in Alta California. See Richard L. Carrico, "Spanish Crime and Punishment: The Native American Experience in Colonial San Diego, 1769–1830," *Western Legal History,* III (1990), 21–33; Nunis, "The 1811 San Diego Trial," *Western Legal History,* IV (1991), 47–58; David J. Langum, "The Legal System of Spanish California: A Preliminary Study," *Western Legal History,* VII (1994), 1–23. Most scholars have erroneously concluded that the necessary primary source documents simply do not exist to support a study of criminal justice in colonial California. See David J. Langum, *Law and Community on the Mexican California Frontier: Anglo-American Expatriates and the Clash of Legal Traditions, 1821–1846* (Norman, Okla., 1987), 1–2. Sherburne F. Cook provided a pioneering study

Indian thieves and murderers fell under the jurisdiction of Spanish military law for several reasons: the military held control of the province, and its law was the law in Alta California; theft and homicide were crimes covered in military codes of justice; and, with the notable exception of the Franciscans, nearly the entire Spanish population of the region was composed of military officers, soldiers, and their families, all of whom were entitled to be tried in the legal jurisdiction known as a *fuero*.[44] Thus, although California Indians did not technically fall under the *fuero militar,* Indians accused of robbery and homicide were prosecuted according to the same rules that governed the trials of soldiers and settlers accused of similar crimes.[45] Indians and the gente de razón, however, were far from equal before the bar, since the judicial system itself helped to create and maintain status and race distinctions between these groups. Differences between how Spanish colonial society and its judiciary viewed Indians and the gente de razón meant that their punishments for seemingly similar crimes often

---

of how the Franciscans and the military punished Indians *(Conflict,* 113–134). Most subsequent studies of Spanish criminal justice in California have relied on his categorization and compilation of Indian crimes and Spanish punishments.

44. As the size and influence of the Spanish army expanded under Bourbon rule, so, too, did the military fuero. By the time Alta California was settled, the Crown had extended the fuero militar beyond the officers and men of the regular army to include their wives and dependent children, their widows and surviving children, and their domestic servants; see Lyle N. McAlister, *The "Fuero Militar" in New Spain, 1764–1800* (Gainesville, Fla., 1957), 7. McAlister notes that there were some thirty-four separate privileged jurisdictions in New Spain (ibid., 6). Colonial California had only military courts that were convened as need arose. In 1768, the year before the establishment of the first missions and presidios in Alta California, the essential elements of the fuero militar were codified and published in the *Ordenanzas de S.M. para el régimen, disciplina, subordinación, y servicio de sus exércitos* (1768; rpt. Cádiz, 1810). Tratado 8, título 5, articles 1–71 provided a very brief explanation of the rules of military justice and outlined proper procedures for the investigation of crimes and the prosecution and punishment of criminals who came from the ranks of the military. Título 10, articles 1–121 listed criminal acts and recommended commensurate punishments. I examined an 1810 edition held by UCLA. For more on the *Ordenanzas,* see McAlister, *Fuero Militar,* 7. In Alta California, during the colonial period, there was nothing like the general Indian court or a *protector de indios.* For discussion of these legal institutions, see Woodrow Borah, *Justice by Insurance: The General Indian Court of Colonial Mexico and the Legal Aides of the Half-Real* (Berkeley, Calif., 1983); Charles R. Cutter, *The Protector de Indios in Colonial New Mexico, 1659–1821* (Albuquerque, N.Mex., 1986). On military justice in Alta California, see also Carlos Antonio Carrillo, "Speech of Carlos Antonio Carrillo in the Mexican Chamber of Deputies, Requesting Adequate Courts for the Administration of Justice in Alta California, [October 18,] 1831," in John Galvin, ed., *The Coming of Justice to California: Three Documents,* trans. Adelaide Smithers [San Francisco, Calif., 1963], 52).

45. The *auditor de guerra* (military adviser) of the viceroy made this clear in 1795 after reviewing a case from Baja California in which an Indian had been accused of murder. The case had not been tried according to military regulations, and the viceroy therefore would not impose a severe sentence on the offender. The viceroy stated that, for California, "there were no other laws [for criminal justice] than the Military Ordinances, which supplied sufficient light for the investigation of crimes . . . and were adaptable to the circumstances" of the frontier region. He continued that the trials of Indians must be conducted in the same manner as in the investigations of soldiers in the presidios "without dispensing with any of the requirements of the [military] Code" (signed by Miguel de la Grúa Talamanca y Branciforte, June 16, 1795, Mexico, AGN, PI, CXXXIV, expediente 24, 47a–48a).

varied. In Alta California, the murder of a soldier was not the same crime as the murder of an Indian, and an Indian who murdered was not the same sort of criminal as a soldier who murdered. Furthermore, Spanish notions of Indians as holding no private property of value meant that, although Indians could be seen as thieves, they were rarely considered victims of theft. Of course, Spanish definitions of murder or robbery—the unlawful taking of another's life or property— completely ignored Indian understandings of what constituted a crime and its appropriate punishment. One Spaniard's idea of murder might have been an Indian's ideal of compensatory justice, and an Indian's notion of the fair appropriation of goods from colonists might have been a Spaniard's conception of robbery.

In New Spain, military justice differed little in substance or procedure from Spanish civic justice, except that the men who presided over it were military officers. Spanish law classified Indians as "poor and wretched" "minors," which suggested that natives were unable to defend themselves and required special legal protections, much like orphans or indigent youths. However, despite their special status, Indians in frontier regions like Alta California regularly offered testimony in trials of other Indians, Spaniards, and on their own behalf. From local presidial commanders to viceregal counselors, Spanish officials consistently viewed this testimony as reliable and admissible, and they depended on it when they assigned guilt and determined appropriate punishments for Indians and Spaniards alike.[46]

Indians were often the sole witnesses to murders and thefts that occurred in the missions, and their testimony therefore was nearly indispensable to the determination of guilt and an elaboration of the judicial process. Spanish officials could have tried to assign guilt and mete out punishments without taking the testimony of Indians. To have done so, however, would not only have been impracticable, but it would have been an abdication of one of the primary responsibilities of the Crown's representatives: to discover the truth, to dispense justice, and to demonstrate the legitimacy, fairness, and procedural consistency of the Spanish legal system.[47] Although these lofty ideals did not always animate the actions of lesser officials in frontier regions like California, they nonetheless were taken seriously by the highest-ranking royal officials in Mexico City. To

46. McAlister, *Fuero Militar*, 10; Cutter, *Legal Culture*, 54–55, especially 167 n. 37. On Indians under the law, see Cutter, *Protector de Indios*, 6–9. Some Spanish jurists warned that, although Indian testimony was admissible in criminal proceedings, it was "prone to falsehood" and "not worth that of 'one proper witness.'" This belief, however, pervasive in central Mexico during the colonial period, had only a marginal impact on judicial process in frontier areas such as New Mexico, Texas, or Alta California during the eighteenth and nineteenth centuries. See Cutter, *Legal Culture*, 117.

47. Throughout the colonial period, Spanish jurists insisted that "the true occupation of the king is to do justice in his kingdom" (Lorenzo Guardiolo y Sáez, quoted in Cutter, *Legal Culture*, 31).

them, trials of Indians accused of homicide and robbery served not only to punish the guilty but to educate the Indian community at large and, in some cases, even the military officers who administered Spanish justice. In that sense, the trials of California Indians and the Indian participation and testimony they elicited functioned as extended civics lessons, secular counterparts to the Indians' religious education. What these trials taught Indians, however, was contradictory: the Spanish judicial system ensured that Indians accused of certain crimes would be prosecuted according to the same well-defined procedures as soldiers and settlers. But any sense of equality or fairness ended there. The Spaniards' invidious assumptions about Indian culture could only lead them to dismiss Indian motivations, and the unequal punishments of Indians and the gente de razón reinforced the social structure that placed California Indians on the bottom.

In New Spain, a hierarchy of officials sought to ensure the administration of justice. At the pinnacle was the king, who delegated his immediate authority to dispense justice in the New World to the Council of the Indies, the various viceroys, and numerous courts of appeal (*audiencias*), provincial governors, and their subordinates.[48] The most powerful Spanish judicial authority in California was the governor, who, as the king's magistrate, was to provide impartial justice "to all, with no exceptions." Despite their considerable judicial responsibilities, none of the nine governors of Spanish California had any specific training in the law or benefited from the ready services of a legal adviser. They were first and foremost military men who had won promotion through patronage, martial skills, leadership, and valor, and their principal responsibilities were to oversee

---

48. During the initial period of Spanish settlement and conquest of the New World, Spain's overseas colonies belonged to Castile, and therefore the laws of the Spanish colonies were Castilian. Over time, as local circumstances dictated the need for new laws and the modification of older ones, a distinct body of law emerged that was specifically relevant to the Spanish New World. Collectively, these laws were known as the *Derecho indiano* (Cutter, *Legal Culture*, 31–43). Laws that held sway during the colonization of Alta California were consolidated and published as the *Recopilación de leyes de los reynos de las Indias . . .*, 4 vols. (Madrid, 1681).

After 1776, the Crown created an administrative division for the provinces of the northern borderlands, the Interior Provinces, which was overseen by a commandant general. Until 1785, the commandant general existed independently of the viceroy of New Spain and reported directly to the king, but after 1785, the Interior Provinces and its head became subordinate to the viceroy. The office of the commandant general often functioned as the final arbiter of criminal investigations in colonial California. For discussions of these administrative changes, see Bernard E. Bobb, *The Viceregency of Antonio María Bucareli in New Spain, 1771–1779* (Austin, Tex., 1962); María del Carmen Velázquez, "La comandancia general de las Provincias Internas," *Historia Mexicana*, XXVII (1977), 163–176; Lillian Estelle Fisher, *The Intendant System in Spanish America* (Berkeley, Calif., 1929); Oakah L. Jones, Jr., *Nueva Vizcaya: Heartland of the Spanish Frontier* (Albuquerque, N.Mex., 1988); Noel M. Loomis, "Commandants-General of the Interior Provinces: A Preliminary List," *Arizona and the West*, XI (1969), 261–268; Alfred Barnaby Thomas, *Teodoro de Croix and the Northern Frontier of New Spain, 1776–1783* (Norman, Okla., 1941); Marc Simmons, *Spanish Government in New Mexico* (1968; rpt., Albuquerque, N.Mex., 1990).

the military and to ensure its preparedness to defend the region. Only Felipe de Neve (1777–1782) and Diego de Borica (1794–1800) had extensive administrative experience before assuming the governorship of Alta California. Neither had legal training.[49]

It was the governor himself who usually oversaw trials of soldiers and settlers accused of murder or robbery. Yet, in another important sign of how the implementation of the judicial system shaped and reflected the emerging society, the governors delegated to presidial commanders (who held the rank of lieutenant) and their immediate subordinates (at the rank of second lieutenant or sergeant) the implementation of Spanish criminal justice as it first pertained to Indians. Thus low-ranking officers most often presided as judges in criminal investigations of Indians, and to them fell the responsibility of overseeing the procedures of Indians' trials, initially determining the guilt or innocence of the accused, and recommending an appropriate punishment. Like the governors they served, these men had no training in military law.[50]

Military officers who presided as judges learned by doing and depended heavily on legal manuals written expressly for men in their circumstances. The most widely circulated late-eighteenth-century procedural guidebook for military justice was Félix Colón de Larriátegui's four-volume *Juzgados militares de España y sus indias*, first published in Madrid in 1787. One appears in the 1834 inventory of Mission San Carlos, and this set likely belonged to the presidio decades earlier.[51]

49. Quote is from the *Recopilación de leyes,* libro 5, título 2, law 7, in Cutter, *Legal Culture,* 75. Although it is certain that, at the higher levels of the colonial bureaucracy, the judicial system was an adjunct of the political system, at the lower levels of Alta California where judicial proceedings were actually carried out, the legal system was an adjunct of the military. As Colin M. MacLachlan has argued, "In New Spain the needs of justice were served by political institutions that exercised various judicial functions as an adjunct to their political authority" (Colin M. MacLachlan, *Criminal Justice in Eighteenth Century Mexico: A Study of the Tribunal of the Acordada* [Berkeley, Calif., 1974], 21). On the governors' experience, see Donald A. Nuttall, "The Gobernantes of Spanish Upper California: A Profile," *California Historical Quarterly,* LI (1972), 253–280. When they initiated or reviewed criminal proceedings, the governors relied upon the firsthand knowledge of judicial procedures they had acquired during their military careers. They also consulted the multivolume *Recopilación de leyes* (Serra to Rafael Verger, Aug. 15, 1779, San Carlos, in Tibesar, ed. and trans., *Writings of Serra,* III, 353). And they kept in the capital of Monterey copies of laws decreed by the king or issued by previous governors as well as an archive of criminal proceedings that could guide them through investigations and suggest appropriate sentences. No record of the legal books that the California governors might have had at their disposal exists. For a discussion of the law books held by other governors in the Spanish Borderlands, see Joseph W. McKnight, "Law Books on the Hispanic Frontier," *Journal of the West,* XXVII (1988), 74–84.

50. In the eight cases I examined most closely of Indians charged with murder, the post of *juez fiscal* was held by the presidial commander five times, the second lieutenant twice, and a sergeant once.

51. José María del Refugio del Reál and José Joaquín Gómez, inventory of San Carlos, Dec. 10, 1834, San Carlos, SBMAL. There is a striking difference in detail between Félix Colón de Larriátegui's full discussion of military judicial procedures and the spare presentation of the laws of military justice in the *Ordenanzas.* The *Ordenanzas* devote seven pages to the *sumaria* and *plenario* (tratado 8, título 5,

This authoritative and exhaustive work explained all aspects of Spanish military justice and left little to chance or imagination. *Juzgados militares* provided military officials with a step-by-step procedural guide to the trial of a soldier for any number of crimes. Colón de Larriátegui's text alternates between an explanation of legal principles, a citation of legal authorities, and an annotated discussion of a sample trial of a soldier accused of homicide. A frontier official could thus learn the proper administration of oaths, the circumstances under which a criminal could take asylum in a church, the legal definitions of hundreds of offenses, and various penalties that the king had prescribed. *Juzgados militares* even recommended the questions judges were to ask witnesses and those accused of crimes. Scribes could also find the specific form in which to record the proceedings of the trial and even a discussion of how the pages of the case file were to be sewn together upon the completion of the inquiry.

Colón de Larriátegui described ten essential procedures that were required for a proper military trial, and all of these applied to prosecutions of California Indians. Omission or misordering of any step could jeopardize the case. The first five steps of the criminal proceeding, known together as the *sumaria,* were by far the most important phase of any criminal prosecution. In theory, the sumaria—the investigative part of the trial—was merely a fact-finding inquiry; the objective was to investigate the crime, not convict the accused. In reality, though, the presiding official presumed and almost always established the guilt of the accused during the sumaria. The case began with a letter from the governor or presidial commander authorizing a criminal investigation and appointing a *juez fiscal.* The first act of the sumaria itself was naming the scribe who would record testimony and document procedures followed in the trial. Next, any witnesses to the crime testified, experts weighed in, and, finally, the accused would either confess to the crime or profess his or her innocence. Thus only at the very end of the sumaria did the accused participate, and, by then, several witnesses had already suggested the defendant's guilt.[52]

---

articles 1–26). Colón de Larriátegui, by contrast, devoted more than one hundred pages to a discussion of how those same procedures should be applied (*Juzgados militares de España y sus indias,* III, sects. 1–151, 1–101). The viceroy specifically recommended Colón de Larriátegui's manual for those not familiar with military law. See Branciforte, June 16, 1795, Mexico, AGN, PI, CXXXIV, expediente 24, 47a–48a; see also Joseph W. McKnight, "Law Book on the Hispanic Frontier," 74–84; McKnight, "Law without Lawyers," *West Texas Historical Association Year Book,* LVVI (1990), 51–65.

52. Colón de Larriátegui, *Juzgados militares,* III, sects. 1–151, 1–101. Here I am simplifying drastically. These ten steps were only the most essential. Any trial was composed of hundreds of possible questions, procedures, and forms, and all cases were slightly different. The genius of *Juzgados militares* was its ability to anticipate such a tremendous range of circumstances. On the origins of the sumaria, see Cutter, *Legal Culture,* 105–124. The investigation of the San Carlos neophyte Estanislao Joseph Tupag (San Carlos bapt. no. 459) for the murder of his wife provides an example of a sumaria that removed the presumption of guilt and led to the dismissal of charges. See Taylor Coll., unnumbered doc., 63-2a–

Upon the conclusion of the sumaria, the *plenario* ensued. This might stretch over days or weeks. At the outset of the plenario, the accused would be granted a *defensor* (defender) and, if necessary, receive an interpreter. (Soldiers served as defenders and interpreters without any special training in Spanish law.) Then, in a process known as the ratification, all of the witnesses' declarations and the suspect's confession or assertion of innocence would be read back in the presence of the defensor. The witnesses and the defendant would be given the opportunity to verify, supplement, or withdraw any part of their testimony. Discrepancies would be reconciled through a *careo,* in which individuals who gave contradictory testimony confronted one another, underwent simultaneous cross-examination under oath, and swore that they did not have a grudge against the defendant. After the careo, the presiding officer would review the case, render a finding, and, if necessary, propose a punishment. Finally, the defensor would review the case file and offer a written defense of the accused. At that point, the presidial commander would send the written record of the trial to the governor for review. If the governor concluded that the presiding officer had neglected to perform any of the important steps, he could order the case reopened so that it might be completed in conformity with Spanish law.[53]

In cases of homicide, sentences could be severe and capital punishment an option. Therefore, in those instances, the governor forwarded completed cases to his superiors in Mexico for review by legal experts. The commandant general had a staff of two principal advisers (an *asesor general* and an *auditor de guerra*). The asesor would summarize the case, write an opinion, propose a punishment, and then pass the case on to the commandant general, who seems in nearly all instances to have concurred with the asesor. If the asesor found defective procedures in the case, he would advise the commandant general to instruct the governor to correct the problem and resubmit the case. Finally, the case would be passed on to the viceroy and his advisers for their opinion or assent. Although such reviews were intended to ensure an adherence to legal procedures, they added years to the administration of criminal justice in Alta California.

63-10a, HL; Hubert H. Bancroft, *History of California,* 7 vols. [San Francisco, Calif., 1884–1890], I, 687–688). Cases that demonstrated the innocence of the accused would not have been sent to higher officials for review, so they are less likely to exist in the historical record for California.

53. On the plenario, see Cutter, *Legal Culture,* 125–146. *Sanar* (to make whole) was the verb most commonly used to describe the process in which defective cases were reopened and completed in full compliance with standard procedures. In most military jurisdictions, after the sumaria and plenario, a military court *(consejo de guerra)* convened to decide the guilt or innocence of the accused. Ideally, this was composed of seven to fifteen officers, but, in isolated areas, that was not always possible. Thus the determination of guilt or innocence could be made, not by a military court, but by the military tribunal of the province or, as in the case of Alta California, by the military officer who acted as judge in the criminal investigation (Colón de Larriátegui, *Juzgados militares,* III, sect. 4, 3–5, by order of the king, Nov. 10, 1781).

If one hallmark of justice in Spanish California was the concern with process—at least at the higher levels of judicial administration—another was equitable solutions and punishments that would preserve or restore tranquility and benefit the community. Colonial magistrates were to consider each case as distinct and arrive at a solution that balanced the legitimate interests of all parties. Spanish laws, therefore, did not prescribe a rigid formula for meting out justice; sentences outlined in the military regulations represented only maximum permissible punishments, not ones necessarily imposed. Colonial magistrates exercised personal discretion *(arbitrio judicial)* in sentencing as they sought to balance the need to punish offenders and larger goals. Such was clearly the case in Alta California, where governors and presidial commanders imposed so wide a variety of sentences on Indian murderers and thieves that there was no such thing as a standard punishment. Certainly arbitrio judicial created the possibility that military judges might sentence Indians in a capricious fashion, but the variability in punishments meted out seems to have emerged from military officials' attempts to tailor the punishment to the nature of the crime and the status of its perpetrator. This, of course, does not mean that Spanish punishments were not arbitrary in the Indians' eyes. In fact, given the assumption of Indian inferiority and backwardness embedded in Spanish culture, it is hard to conclude that Indians could have seen them any other way. Furthermore, although this system might have been flexible in sentencing, it rarely, if ever, acknowledged Indians as having legitimate interests or motivations, and it afforded them few chances to present or explain their own intentions or actions. To the extent that accused Indians had an opportunity to offer a defense, Spanish defenders made their cases for them, and their words only reinforced Indians' subordinate status. Moreover, the community that benefited through sentencing of Indians was nearly always that of the gente de razón; the larger goals of the colonial magistrates were always stability of the colonial hierarchy, not conformity to native understandings of justice, criminality, and punishment.[54]

HOMICIDE AND ROBBERY—PROSECUTION, DEFENSE, AND PUNISHMENT

The Spanish belief that justice was advanced through fair and regular process is evident in trials of Indians accused of homicide and stealing, which were among the most thoroughly investigated crimes in Alta California. Notably, murder was

54. On the ideological representation of Spanish judicial goals, see Charles R. Cutter, "Judicial Punishment in Colonial New Mexico," *Western Legal History,* VIII (1995), 115–125.

the only Indian-on-Indian crime regularly prosecuted by the Spaniards. Murders by neophytes of neophytes were infrequent and hardly ever challenged Spanish control of the region, but their violent nature forced Spanish authorities into action. As a result, murders in the missions spawned lengthy investigations, especially if the case was a spousal homicide. A recently discovered infidelity, a desperate desire to be free from an unhappy marriage, or a dispute over money, in particular over the strings of beads that frequently changed hands during games of chance, were at the center of many deadly disputes in the missions. In most cases of Indian homicide, officials followed Colón de Larriátegui's elaborate procedures. Take, for example, the trial of four Chumash at Mission San Buenaventura—Junípero, Bonifacio, María Bernarda, and Alhuynaiuhit, an unbaptized Indian—all of whom were accused of killing María Bernarda's husband, Marcos. On October 29, 1795, Francisco María Ruiz, a sergeant at the Santa Barbara Presidio who was stationed at nearby San Buenaventura, was alerted that the head and decapitated corpse of Marcos, a gardener at the mission, had been discovered in a nearby creek. On November 2, at nine o'clock in the morning, Felipe de Goycoechea, the Santa Barbara presidial commander and juez fiscal in this case, opened the inquiry. On November 2, 3, and 4, seven Indians at the mission gave declarations to Goycoechea, and, on the fifth, four who had been implicated by the previous witnesses made confessions. The next day, José Francisco de Ortega agreed to defend the suspects and attended the ratifications of the witnesses' declarations. A day later, each defendant cross-examined and confronted the witnesses in Ortega's presence. On November 10, Goycoechea concluded that the Indians were guilty and could be hanged "in accordance with the Royal Ordinances, Article sixty-four, Title ten, Treatise eight." Two weeks had elapsed since the body of Marcos had been found in the creek, and the scribal record of the proceedings approached ninety pages. Almost every word, phrase, sentence, and paragraph, indeed, nearly every question posed by the presidial commander conformed to military code and procedures outlined by Colón de Larriátegui. Governor Borica reviewed the transcript, found no deficiency, and forwarded the case to the viceroy, who found it consistent with standard procedures.[55]

Although the trial of Marcos's killers exemplifies how military officials on the California frontier could prosecute a case according to the Spanish code of military justice, records of other trials show that this was not always the situation.

55. For the complete case, see "Criminal contra los reos Junípero, Bonifacio, el gentil Alhuynaiuhit, y la complice María Bernarda . . . ," AGN, PI, CXXXIV, expediente 24, 1a–45a. Preliminary finding of guilt: Felipe de Goycoechea, Nov. 10, 1795, Santa Barbara Presidio, ibid., 41a–41b. For procedurally complete trials of Indians conducted in conformity with military laws and customs, see AGN, CA, LXV, expediente 8, 335a–370a, and expediente 6, 241a–301b.

And, in some instances, Indians suffered dearly because of a complete breakdown of judicial procedure. The 1801 case against the neophytes Primo, Bentura, and Eulalia for the murder of Eulalia's husband (described in Chapter 5) deviated from standard procedure in many ways. The scribal record is sloppy, and numerous procedures were skipped or not recorded. Most important, none of the accused had a defender. Neither the governor nor the viceregal officials who reviewed the case commented upon this omission. That the undefended Primo and Bentura were among the handful of California Indians executed for their crimes, then, is not surprising. They, in fact, were the first California Indians put to death for murder during the colonial period.[56]

When judicial procedure collapsed at the local level, higher legal authorities sometimes intervened and forced California officials to follow military code, even when there must have been exceptional local pressures to move to a swift and merciless punishment. Such was the case in the trial of Aurelio of Mission San Francisco for the rape and murder of Guadalupe Galindo, the eight-year-old daughter of a Spanish soldier. One morning in May 1805, Guadalupe had been left alone to play in a field adjacent to the presidio. When Guadalupe's mother noticed her daughter's absence, she summoned help. Before long, several soldiers found the girl's body hidden nearby under some bushes. Aurelio was arrested soon thereafter as he ran up a nearby hillside attempting, in his words, to take sanctuary in the chapel at Mission San Francisco. Presidial commander José Argüello ordered his younger brother to oversee the trial, but, when he declined because of bad health, the responsibility fell to Sergeant Luis Peralta, perhaps the only man of so low a rank to oversee a homicide trial in Alta California.[57]

Early in the trial, Guadalupe's parents described the morning of her death, two

56. "Proceso contra los neófitos de la misión de San Antonio llamados Primo, Bentura y Eulalia . . . ," AGN, PI, VI, expediente 3, 44a–85b. The three were charged with treacherous homicide, a more serious crime than premeditated murder (Colón de Larriátegui, *Juzgados militares*, III, sect. 434, 262–267). According to military justice, if a defendant would not or could not choose a defender, the presiding judge was to appoint one for him (sects. 51–53, 39–44, and royal ordinance of Oct. 11, 1723, 44). Once selected, an officer or a soldier could not decline to serve as a defensor (sect. 51, 39–41). The defendants' confessions in this case do not have the carefully worded language that usually characterized an admission of guilt; the confession of the accused was usually the single most important factor in a conviction, and military officials were urged to take extreme care to shape it so as to remove any doubt about the nature of the crime and the defendant's guilt (sects. 54–55, 44–50). Primo and Bentura were executed by firing squad and buried at Mission San Antonio on Dec. 31, 1801 (Raymundo Carrillo, Jan. 3, 1802, AGN, PI, VI, expediente 3, 67b–68b).

57. For the complete case, see "Causa formada contra Aurelio indio neófito de la misión de San Francisco por homicidio y estupro ejecutado contra niña Guadalupe Galindo de edad de ocho años de la mañana del 9 de mayo de dho año," AGN, CA, LIX (page numbering is irregular). Peralta was himself no exemplar of good behavior. In September 1783, he had been transferred to a different post as a punishment for adultery (Fages to Moraga, Sept. 17, 1783, San Fernando, Archives of California, C–A 23, 202, BL).

midwives explained the girl's injuries, and three soldiers recounted the search for Aurelio and his arrest. Aurelio confessed to the rape and murder, although he claimed that he had never intended to kill the girl but only to prevent her from calling out to her mother. Sergeant Peralta concluded the trial by proclaiming Aurelio's guilt, asking for the death penalty, and candidly admitting that he had no training in judicial procedures.[58] To those involved, the case must have seemed wrapped up. But it was actually just beginning. Peralta had failed to administer an oath to Aurelio before extracting a confession, and Aurelio had not had a defender. Moreover, although Peralta had ratified all the declarations, he had completely omitted the careo, believing that it was not necessary because Aurelio had confessed, and none of the witnesses had actually seen him commit the crime.[59]

Governor José Joaquín de Arrillaga reviewed the case and sent it back to San Francisco so that Aurelio could choose a defender who would witness the ratifications of the declarations and provide for his defense. Four months after he had first closed the trial of Aurelio, Peralta reconvened all the witnesses, administered an oath to Aurelio's defender, and ratified all the declarations anew. Several days later, after examining the case file, Ramón Lasso de la Vega submitted a thorough defense on Aurelio's behalf. With the procedural defects seemingly corrected, Peralta passed the file to the governor, who sent it on to the viceroy.[60]

But the viceroy's asesor found even more procedural omissions. There was no doubt, one of the viceroy's legal counselors concluded, that Aurelio had raped and killed "the unsuspecting innocent and poor little eight-year-old girl" with "his brutal claws." These "horrifying events demanded punishment," the asesor acknowledged, but he observed that, "even in cases as grave as these, one cannot dispense with the essential formalities . . . which are missing here and must be undertaken." First and foremost, the trial would not be valid until Aurelio's confession had been taken under oath in the presence of his defender; this was an "indispensable formality." During the confession, Aurelio was to be asked about "all the particulars of the deed, about the violence with which the little girl's leg was dislocated, the proof of the rape, the perpetration of the death; whether the rape was a matter of circumstance or had been premeditated; why Aurelio had dragged her across the ground instead of satisfying his appetite where he had encountered the girl; why he fled immediately to the hills, and whether he

58. Luis Peralta, "Conclusión de la causa," May 11, 1805, AGN, CA, LIX, 14a.

59. The language of the trials always describes Indians as selecting their own defense counsel, but this probably reflects the form the scribes copied, not the way defenders were chosen. Most likely, presiding officers appointed defensores for California Indians, and the appointment could not be refused.

60. Ramón Lasso de la Vega, Sept. 12, 1805, San Francisco Presidio, AGN, CA, LIX, 21a–22a. Because Aurelio was considered a minor in age and status, his defender was a curador adlitem (Cutter, Legal Culture, 126).

wanted to take refuge in the church; and whether he knew the enormity of his crime, and the capital punishment that it warranted." Peralta also was to examine all those who knew Aurelio to determine if he was, in fact, insane and if his madness was "permanent or transitory." To that end, the soldiers who arrested Aurelio were to be asked what Aurelio said and how he acted when he had been captured. Finally, to verify the death of the girl and her age, the asesor wanted copies of her baptismal and burial records. What must have first looked to Peralta and the girl's family like an open-and-shut case had been transformed into a protracted trial and an opportunity for the viceroy's office to instruct its frontier subordinates in the fundamentals of military justice and in the hierarchy of power.[61]

So, on May 13, 1806, more than a year after he had first concluded the trial, Peralta opened the case against Aurelio for a third time. Two soldiers and the girl's uncle explained that they had known Aurelio since he was a little boy. Aurelio had worked around the presidio and was sane, although he had a terrible stutter. Peralta then proceeded to take Aurelio's confession. After making the sign of the cross and swearing to tell the truth, Aurelio answered the questions the asesor had outlined. Lasso de la Vega then wrote out another defense and another plea for mercy. Peralta again stated that he had no training in the law and forwarded the case to his superiors for review. On June 2, 1806, once the governor had received certified copies of the girl's baptism and burial records, he sent the case to the viceroy.[62]

While Aurelio sat in prison or performed hard labor at the San Francisco Presidio, adjacent to where the family of the slain girl lived, his case moved slowly through the colonial bureaucracy. After numerous legal counselors had examined the trial, the viceroy issued his ruling in late February 1807. A month later, the viceroy sent a copy of his decision to California's governor, who must have received it around the second anniversary of the crime. After three trials, two years, and one final sentence, Spanish justice had run its course. Aurelio was guilty of rape, but the murder had been unintended as he and his defender had asserted. The death penalty was waived. Instead, Aurelio was to receive two hundred lashes in front of the assembled neophytes of San Francisco mission, and he was to serve ten years of hard labor in shackles wherever the governor determined.[63]

Only on rare occasions did mission Indians commit murder; more frequently, they took food or provisions from mission and presidial stores in an attempt to

---

61. Opinion of the *auditor*, Dec. 16, 1805, AGN, CA, LIX, 22a–23a.

62. Peralta noted that he was unable to locate a surgeon who could provide a more expert opinion of Aurelio's mental capacity (Peralta, AGN, CA, LIX, 27b).

63. Opinion of auditor José Antonio del Cristo, Feb. 19, 1807, AGN, CA, LIX.

better their own lot. And thus robbery became commonly and thoroughly prosecuted in California. Yet, where Indians were involved, robbery was a crime committed by Indians against the institutions of colonization. Indians appear never
to have been prosecuted for stealing from one another, nor were soldiers punished for stealing from Indians. Of course, such thefts must have occurred, but
Spanish officials did not see any material goods in native society of enough value
to warrant full trials and investigations. In a typical case of robbery during the
Spanish period, some eleven Indians at Mission San Francisco stole money,
chocolate, shoes, string, knives, and other items from the presidio. In the lengthy
investigation and trial that followed, the military determined the guilt of the
Indians and calibrated their punishments according to their ages and level of
involvement in the crime. The principal instigators received thirty lashes on three
separate days; several others suffered twenty lashes. And two Indians who had
concealed the crime were sentenced to a month of hard labor at the presidio.
Aniceto, who had also kept quiet, received a lesser sentence because he was only
thirteen years old.[64]

THE ARGUMENTS OF INDIANS' DEFENSORES

One of the most important and revealing aspects of trials of Indians for homicide
or robbery is the arguments put forward by defensores. In California, defenders
were appointed because they were literate, not because they had experience with
the law or sympathy for the accused. They constituted the only opportunity
accused criminals—Indian or gente de razón—had to call attention to legal im-
proprieties or to explain circumstances that might justify a moderation of punishment. Thus the presence of a defender added a measure of fairness to the
process, at least in theory and in the eyes of the Spanish. Yet, in nearly every
instance, defenders and their words were double-edged. Most of their arguments
were grounded in, and supported, dismissive assumptions about Indians and
their social, political, and religious development. To a remarkable degree, the
concepts they invoked were the same ones that the Franciscans used when they
characterized Indians as uncivilized simpletons immersed in the errors of their
ancestors. To be sure, though, at the moment of their sentencing, Indians gained
from being seen in such a negative light, but they did so at the expense of a
reinforcement of the emerging social order.[65]

64. Diego de Borica, Jan. 16, 1799, Monterey, Archives of California, C–A 16, 115, BL.
65. In some instances, defenders offered only perfunctory arguments, often nothing more than a
one-paragraph summation of the case against the defendant sandwiched between a florid preamble

Most defenders described Indians as depraved individuals whose ignorance demanded moderate punishments. Silverio, who had killed his wife, merited mercy because of his absolute "ignorance." Fifteen years after his baptism, he still was not well "civilized" and had hardly learned how to cross himself. Aurelio, who had raped and killed young Guadalupe Galindo, was probably insane, his defender argued, suggesting that his "lack of sense" had "extinguished the rays of light that we call reason." Aurelio therefore quite literally, in the eyes of his defender, was without reason, certainly not a member of the gente de razón. The viceroy and his legal counselor completed the picture, attributing Aurelio's attack to his being raised among "barbarous pagans" steeped in "brutal customs." A few years later, the defender of the three men charged with the murder of the San Diego mayordomo argued that the killers were essentially boys of scant ability, who, as neophytes, had little knowledge of divine laws. They were "simple" and of "limited reach," and their quick confession to a crime that no one else had witnessed proved their minimal intelligence and that they conducted themselves like "*muchachos*" (boys).[66]

During the 1820s and 1830s, the increasing hostility of the Mexican government and liberal elements within California to the missionaries, coupled with the growing material impoverishment of mission Indians, fueled the critique that neophytes were mired in backwardness and seemed to offer defensores added justification for Indian crimes. In 1831, when Pedro, a Diegueño serving time as a convict laborer in San Francisco, stood trial for theft, the juez fiscal José Sánchez asked for a punishment of six months' labor in public works. Sánchez, in justification of this light sentence, argued that Pedro was by nature ignorant and not aware of the seriousness of his crime. But Sánchez went even further and blamed

---

and a conclusion cribbed from Colón de Larriátegui. Colón de Larriátegui presented sample defense arguments to show the range of possibility; but, unlike the procedural forms he presented, these defense arguments were not intended to be copied verbatim by the defender. See Colón de Larriátegui, *Juzgados militares*, III, sects. 98–128, 68–88. Surely, the eyes of a seasoned high-ranking legal official must have glazed over when he was confronted with yet another plea to not "spill the blood" of such an "unfortunate wretch" (ibid., III, sect. 123, 75–86). For an example of the formulaic defenses occasionally offered on behalf of California Indians, see those presented by Mariano Cota and José Antonio Rodríguez, Oct. 20, 1796, AGN, CA, LXV, expediente 6, 285a–288a. When these two took their oaths in this case, the scribe took the unusual step of noting that both had been selected and had agreed to serve "only because there were no officials, nor gente de razón capable of doing it within fifty leagues of the mission" (AGN, CA, LXV, expediente 6, 270b–271a). Formulaic appeals from California officials must have proved especially unconvincing, given that they were often entirely out of context and inappropriate. Colón de Larriátegui was suggesting how defensores might appeal to the sympathies of a full-blown military court, which, in California, was never convened.

66. Defense of Silverio: Mariano Cota, October [date of month illegible], 1796, Mission San Luis Obispo, AGN, CA, LXV, expediente 6, 285a–286b. Aurelio: Opinion of the auditor, Feb. 19, 1807, Mexico City, signed by the viceroy, Feb. 23, 1807, AGN, CA, LIX. Murderers of San Diego mayordomo: José de la Guerra, Dec. 22, 1808, San Diego Presidio, AGN, CA, LIX, 66–69.

the missionaries for not properly teaching the Indians how to be peaceful and productive members of society. According to Sánchez, neophytes "received absolutely no education" and lived "submerged in the ultimate level of ignorance and servitude." Given their oppression, Sánchez asked, "What can be expected of these poor unfortunates?" That same year, the defender of Atanasio, an eighteen-year-old who had stolen from a *comisaria*, asked for mercy because the accused was rough, uncivilized, or *"rudo."*[67]

It was only on the rarest of occasions that defenders actually presented arguments rooted in an understanding and explanation of Indian motivations, and, even then, their arguments were overwhelmed by prevailing views that Indians were backward. The killers of Marcos had been charged with treacherous homicide, and their defender, José Francisco de Ortega, set out to prove that the murder fell short of this standard. Ortega was at the end of a long and illustrious military career, and he brought to his task decades of experience with frontier law and California's Indians. He was born in Celaya (Guanajuato), enlisted in the military in 1755 as a private, and came north in 1769 with Portolá and Serra, who took a liking to him and tried to secure for him the appointment of gobernante to replace Fages in 1773. Ortega established the Santa Barbara Presidio in 1781, was commandant there until 1784, and headed the Monterey Presidio from 1787 to 1791. In 1795, when he defended the Indians charged with murder, he was retired and attached to the Santa Barbara Presidio at half pay.[68]

Ortega understood that treacherous homicide required the victim to be caught unaware that his life was in danger and attacked in such a manner that he could not have defended himself from the assault. Thus Ortega pointed out that Marcos's wife, María Bernarda, previously had acquired herbs with which she had tried to poison Marcos; once Marcos had become aware of his wife's intentions, he had wisely refrained from eating any food she made for him. Furthermore, the day before his death, Marcos had refused to return some beads to María Bernarda, and she had warned him ominously that "it would be the last time" he gambled with her money. The poison and the warning, Ortega concluded, should have made Marcos highly suspicious. Nevertheless, late one evening, María Bernarda enticed him into the mission garden where the other assailants were lying in wait. Ortega had provided a convincing argument that the murder did not meet the definition of treachery, since Marcos must have realized that his life was in danger. Then, in arguing against capital punishment, Ortega sought to justify the Indians' motivations and thereby lessen the enormity of their crime.

67. Manuel Victoria, Aug. 27, 1831, Monterey, Archives of California, C–A 19, 236–239, BL. The governor rejected Sánchez's argument and imposed a longer sentence. Atanasio: Juan María Ibarra, Apr. 26, 1831, Monterey, Archives of California, C–A 19, 321–325, BL.

68. Bancroft, *History of California,* I, 670–672.

Marcos had repeatedly beaten María Bernarda. And it was normal, claimed Ortega, for a wife to try to free herself from an abusive husband, especially one who gambled. Furthermore, beads were important in the Indian exchange economy and particularly valuable to the Chumash women of the Santa Barbara region. Marcos's behavior had violated the standards of his own culture, Ortega claimed. In denying María Bernarda the beads, Ortega concluded, Marcos had taken "from her that which could serve to feed her children, that which regularly was left under the care of the wife, not the father."[69]

Having seen the murderers' motivations for what they were, Ortega still felt obliged to fall back on a plea for mercy rooted in the argument that the accused were "a simple, uncivilized people, of little capacity." Three were "ignorant" neophytes, and the fourth was "blind with the errors of his *gentilidad*" (heathenism). Goycoechea, the juez fiscal, offered the same view, stating in his case summary that the Indians had acquired only a small element of civilization and were a *gente rústica*. As punishment for decapitating the gambling and abusive Marcos, the Indians of San Buenaventura received, not the death penalty, but a severe flogging and four years in prison. Ortega had drawn upon his knowledge of military law, and, in an attempt to cast the offenders' crimes in a more favorable light, he had based his arguments upon insights into native American culture. But, although this defense stands out as highly skilled, there is no evidence to suggest that it was any more or less effective than a standard assertion of Indian backwardness. In fact, to officials in Mexico, that is all it amounted to. After reading the case record and Ortega's detailed defense, the viceroy ruled that the Indians' lives should be spared because of their "*rusticidad*."[70]

PUNISHMENT

That Marcos's killers escaped a death sentence is hardly shocking, given the Spaniards' reluctance to impose capital punishment anywhere in New Spain. Premeditation and treachery had to be established for a death penalty to stand,

69. Defense by José Francisco de Ortega, Dec. 11, 1795, Santa Barbara Presidio, AGN, PI, CXXXIV, expediente 24, 43a–45a, esp. 44a. On the legal definition of treacherous homicide, see Colón de Larriátegui, *Juzgados militares*, III, sects. 434–440, 262–267. For María Bernarda's warning to Marcos, see declaration of Pedro Nolasco, Nov. 4, 1795, Santa Barbara Presidio, AGN, PI, CXXXIV, expediente 24, 11b.

70. Defense by José Francisco de Ortega, Dec. 11, 1795, Santa Barbara Presidio, AGN, PI, CXXXIV, expediente 24, 43a–45a, esp. 45a; Felipe de Goycoechea, Nov. 10, 1795, Santa Barbara Presidio, AGN, PI, CXXXIV, expediente 24, 41a–41b. By November 1796, the governor had been informed by the viceroy of the Indians' punishments: Junípero, María Bernarda, and Alhuynaiuhit were to receive fifty lashes and four years in prison. Bonifacio, who slit Marcos's throat, was to receive an additional fifty lashes (governor to commander of Santa Barbara Presidio, Nov. 18, 1796, Monterey, Archives of California, C–A 23, 360, BL).

and most of the accused could argue that their crime had been unintentional or impulsive. Moreover, the Crown wanted to put criminals to work rather than to death. Throughout late colonial New Spain, convict labor was the most frequent punishment meted out for both trivial and serious offenses. State mobilization of convict labor had a long precedent in European society, and it proved especially useful and profitable to the Crown in New Spain following Indian epidemics and shortages of soldiers and settlers. And, of course, the Indians' status as uncivilized newcomers to Catholicism encouraged Spanish officials to moderate sentences and spare Indians execution.[71]

In Alta California, in some twenty homicide cases involving thirty-four Indians accused of murdering other Indians between 1770 and 1834, only three of the accused were sentenced to death and executed. In another ten cases involving some forty-nine Indians who rebelled against the missions, killing Franciscans, soldiers, or settlers, only seven were executed; all of these executions occurred in 1824, in the wake of the Santa Barbara Chumash rebellion that left four Spaniards dead. Even for the premeditated and "outrageous" murder of Pedro Miguel Alvarez, the mayordomo at San Diego, Fermín, Fernando, and Francisco were sentenced to ten years of labor at the presidio in 1808. Similarly, for the rape and murder of Guadalupe Galindo, the "depraved" minor Aurelio was brutally whipped and then put to work for ten years. In most cases, the religious status of the murderer seems to have been a determining factor in the severity of the punishment. Unbaptized Indians who murdered were likely to get fifty lashes and less than a year in jail. Baptized Indians who committed murder were occasionally whipped and almost always faced four to ten years' labor at a presidio far from their mission.[72]

In determining sentences in homicide cases, Spanish officials sought to balance the need to punish murderers with the effect a sentence might have on the larger colonial effort. In 1798, Governor Borica claimed that the imposition of

71. On the rarity of capital punishment in New Mexico, see Cutter, *Legal Culture*, 138–140; Cutter, "Judicial Punishment," *Western Legal History*, VIII (1995), 126. For the punishment of murderers in central Mexico late in the colonial period, see Taylor, *Drinking, Homicide, and Rebellion*, 97–106. On the prevalence of convict labor and the rarity of the imposition of the death penalty in late colonial central Mexico, see Haslip-Viera, *Crime and Punishment*, 102, 134.

72. Murder of Alvarez: José de la Guerra, Dec. 2, 1808, San Diego, AGN, CA, LXII, 66–69 (page nos. cited are to trial). Sentence of Aurelio: José de Iturrigaray, Feb. 23, 1807, Mexico City, AGN, CA, LIX. Aurelio is listed is having been freed in 1816 (DPHC, Estudillo, I, fol. 108, 233). If a killing by a neophyte was considered accidental and spontaneous or fell into the context of justifiable violence, the sentence was much shorter, usually two years or less of labor at a presidio. Such was the case in 1813, when Francisco Javier, the alcalde of Mission San Fernando, threw a piece of wood at a man he thought was shirking labor. For inadvertently killing him, Javier was sentenced to just two months of labor at the presidio; see José Joaquín Maitorena, Dec. 7, 1813, San Fernando, Archives of California, C–A 17, 175, BL.

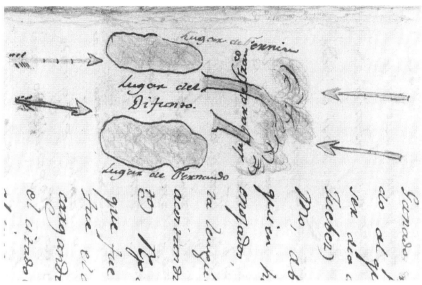

PLATE 20. Sketch in the margin of a *sumaria* illustrating how three Diegueño men attacked
and mortally wounded Mission San Diego's abusive labor foreman. Dec. 2, 1808, San
Diego, AGN, CA, LXII, 66–69. Fermín, Francisco, and Fernando took cover behind
rocks and trees as they shot their arrows at Pedro Miguel Alvarez, whose location
is shown by the words "Lugar del Difunto" ("location of the deceased").
Courtesy, Archivo General de la Nación, Mexico

capital punishment against Silverio, a neophyte who had murdered his wife,
would severely disrupt the colonization and tranquillity of the region. "I firmly
believe," Borica told the viceroy, "that, if we carry out the death penalty with the
culprit Silverio, it will cause such dread and shock to the countless gentiles who
live in the Tulares and the region near San Luis [Obispo] that they will withdraw
from coming to the missions, and it will infinitely retard their spiritual conquest."[73] Conversely, when Toribio of San Diego, who had killed two gentiles in a
village near the mission, was sentenced to eight years' labor, not death, Spanish
officials feared that the offended gentiles, who might have considered the sentence too lenient, would revenge themselves against the soldiers or the mission.
Pedro Galindo Navarro, the asesor, sought to fashion a sentence that would
mollify the gentiles and thereby safeguard the mission from attack. He ordered
that the presidial commander explain to the aggrieved Indians that eight years'
labor was the maximum penalty permitted under Spanish law in this case, and he

73. Borica to Branciforte, Apr. 19, 1798, Monterey, 396a–396b. Silverio was sentenced to eight years'
labor at the San Diego Presidio (Borica to ——, Nov. 30, 1798, Monterey, AGN, CA, LXV, expediente 6,
298a–298b).

required that Toribio perform his labor in shackles and in a place located near the gentiles, so that they constantly could witness the rigor of his enduring punishment.[74]

As shipments of supplies to Alta California became more infrequent and goods stored at the presidio became more difficult to replace, the punishments of Indians for theft—unlike those meted out against murderers—became steadily more rigorous, overriding defenders' arguments that Indians so undeveloped deserved mercy. When a group of baptized and unbaptized Indians stole from the San Diego Presidio in 1811, they received punishments considerably more severe than when the thirteen-year-old Aniceto and others had committed a similar crime in San Francisco a decade earlier. This time, the three neophytes and three gentiles endured eighty lashes over four days and terms of four to five years' labor at the presidio. Two Indians who had hidden the stolen goods received fifty lashes and two months' hard labor, and two others who had purchased the stolen goods served two months' hard labor. In 1826, when Valerio and several others were found guilty of stealing from Mission Santa Barbara, a crime for which Valerio had been punished previously, he suffered ten years of labor at the Loreto Presidio and perpetual banishment from Alta California. An accomplice was sentenced to six years' labor at the Santa Barbara Presidio. By the 1830s, some unfortunates caught stealing ran out of chances to repeat their crime. In 1831, when Atanasio was found guilty of stealing on several occasions from the Monterey comisario, he was shot by a firing squad, even though his defender pointed out that he was less than eighteen years old and therefore too young to understand the seriousness of his crime. That same year, Andrés, an eighteen-year-old neophyte from Mission San Carlos, committed a similar crime. As a first-time offender, his life was spared. But he suffered a public whipping of one hundred lashes and then had to spend the next six months working at the mission, his feet hobbled in a corma. Andrés had not acted alone, and Simón Aguilar (a convict laborer at the presidio) and Eduardo Zagarra (a local settler) were shown no mercy and executed as habitual criminals. Executions such as these made powerful impressions: forty-five years later, Estévan de la Torre remembered how Atanasio, Aguilar, and Zagarra had been put to death as they kneeled and begged for their lives in the estuary of Monterey.[75]

74. Opinion of [Pedro] Galindo Navarro, May 3, 1783, Arispe, AGN, CA, LXXV, 6a–9a.

75. Ignacio Martínez, Apr. 19, 1811, San Diego, Archives of California, C–A 17, 198–199, BL; José Joaquín Maitorena, Mar. 29, 1826, Santa Barbara, Archives of California, C–A 18, 225, BL; Juan María Ibarra, Apr. 26, 1831, Monterey, Archives of California, C–A 19, 321–325, BL; Rodrigo del Pliego, May 28, 1831, Monterey, Archives of California, C–A 19, 240–243, BL; Estévan de la Torre, "Reminiscencias, 1815–48," 23–26, BL. For the burial records of these men, see San Carlos bur. nos. 2784 (Atanasio), 2792 (Simón Aguilar), and 2793 (Zagarra).

TOWARD A HIERARCHICAL SOCIETY

Clearly, defenses offered on behalf of accused Indians fostered and supported ideological distinctions between groups within California colonial society. The differential punishments that followed put those distinctions to work most often to the detriment of Indians, making painfully clear to them the nature of the social order in colonial California. As we have seen, Indians often suffered long terms of hard labor for murder and heavy floggings for robbery. Soldiers who committed murder—whether the victims were Indians or soldiers—received sentences of hard labor of a similar duration as Indian murderers. Yet, as gente de razón, soldiers and settlers were exempted from corporal punishment, a form of reprimand almost completely restricted to Indians and one that marked them as low and different. Typical was the punishment of the soldier Eduardo Garnica: for killing another soldier, he was sentenced to six years' labor at the presidio but not flogged. Similarly, when Hilario García was found guilty of whipping cruelly and excessively an Indian leader—the beating was so severe that it was said García broke three canes in administering it—he was sentenced to five years of labor and imprisonment but given no lashes. Children of the gente de razón, however, who committed murder, were judged and punished like Indians; they were seen as unable to understand their crimes and then flogged. In 1784, when two teenagers murdered a gentile near San Jose, the "muchachos" and an unbaptized Indian who accompanied them were all given punishments of twenty-five lashes in the presence of the aggrieved gentiles.[76]

The gente de razón committed their share of robberies in Alta California, but again the sentences they received, especially early in the colonial period, were usually shorter than those given Indians who committed similar crimes. For instance, in 1780, four soldiers stationed at the presidio of San Francisco were found guilty of stealing, on numerous occasions, a wide range of goods from the presidio storehouse that they later sold to other soldiers. Because of the severity of the crime, officials sent the case to Mexico for review. Pedro Galindo Navarro, one of New Spain's highest-ranking legal officials, suggested that two of the soldiers be sentenced to two hundred lashes and ten years' labor and that the other two suffer four years' labor. Teodoro de Croix, the commandant general, however, shortened the soldiers' sentences and eliminated the corporal punishment. Similarly,

76. Punishment of Garnica: Luís Antonio Argüello and others, Sept. 24, 1824, Monterey, Archives of California, C–A 18, 113, BL. García: Gómez, asesor of the territory, Mar. 11, 1831, San Carlos, Archives of California, C–A 19, 136–140, BL. It was not clear whether the Indian leader had been killed by the beating or died from other causes brought on by the assault. Punishment of teenage killers: decision of Galindo Navarro approved by Neve, commandant general, Apr. 3, 1784, AGN, PI, CXX, expediente 8, 163a–178a. The youths were ages sixteen and seventeen.

when Tomás Olivera stole items worth 160 pesos from the house of the Santa Barbara Presidio commander Juan Antonio Carrillo, his punishment was simply six years of hard labor at the presidio. And, when José Antonio Robles and his son Nieves broke into a trunk owned by Franciscan Ramón Olbés and stole some of his possessions, the son was given four years' labor at the presidio and the father only two years because of his bad health. In 1809, Governor José Joaquín de Arrillaga wrote to the presidial commander of Monterey that he did not approve punishing with blows the attempted adultery of soldier Pedro García, emphasizing that "such punishment is rarely used in the province with soldiers and that there are others [punishments] that do not degrade them so much."[77]

Throughout the colonial period, Spanish officials relied on corporal punishment, military justice, and unequal punishments to help uphold the colonial order and to rebuke Indians who challenged it. As a result, many Indians no doubt concluded that openly opposing the Franciscans' and soldiers' authority was dangerous and that justice dispensed by the military was unfair. Coming from different cultural backgrounds, Indians and Spaniards did not criminalize the same behaviors or employ similar punishments. There is nothing in the historical record to suggest that the Children of Coyote had inflicted whippings and floggings on criminals. Certainly, though, California Indians must have used their laws and systems of justice to uphold social differences and inequities. Only in unusual instances, where Indians were accused of murdering one another or stealing from the presidio, was the Spanish legal system consistently restrained by high-ranking officials' concern with process, order, and a compulsion to grant mercy so that it worked to the benefit of Indians. Yet, in these cases, Indians often spent years imprisoned or laboring at a presidio awaiting their merciful sentence from Mexico, and those lenient sentences often had been won only by their own defenders' characterization of them as primitives. Given all of these factors, it is hard to imagine how Indians could have seen Spanish justice—whether doled out by padres or soldiers—as anything other than one more means through which missionaries, soldiers, and settlers could dominate them and the region.

77. Soldiers sentenced for theft from presidio: Galindo Navarro, June 5, 1783, Arispe, and Teodoro de Croix, June 7, 1783, Arispe, both in AGN, CA, LXXI (incomplete page numbering; case begins on 76a). Olivera: Francisco María Ruíz, July 9, 1805, Santa Barbara, Archives of California, C–A 16, 252–253, BL. Father and son Robles: letter to Captain Argüello from unknown source, June 7, 1819, Monterey, Archives of California, C–A 54, 235, BL. See also Governor Solá to José Estrada, Mar. 23, 1819, San Antonio, Archives of California, C–A 17, 285–291, BL. When Teodoro Silvas and Tomás Cañedo stole items from Patricio Pico, they were sentenced to five and three years of labor, respectively. For soldiers sentenced to six and eight years for theft, see José Antonio de la Guerra, July 24, 1810, Santa Barbara, Archives of California, C–A 17, 31–32, BL. García: governor to commandant of Monterey, Nov. 14, 1809, Mission Soledad, Archives of California, C–A 26, 218, BL.

Even though Indians must have rejected as unjust most elements of the Spanish judicial system, they at least sought to understand it. And many came to believe that they understood enough to turn it to their own advantage. More often than not, though, they knew too little and miscalculated. Such was the case with Junípero and Bonifacio, who murdered Marcos outside Mission San Buenaventura. They testified that they did not expect a harsh punishment because, five years earlier, an unbaptized Indian had spent only two years in prison for the murder of two soldiers.[78] They had reasoned that the Spaniards would punish an unbaptized Indian more severely than they would punish a baptized Indian, and that the murder of a soldier would warrant a more severe punishment than the killing of an Indian. Their argument was logical; as such, it reflects a recognition that not all people would be equal before the law. But Junípero and Bonifacio evidently did not understand that a gentile—because he was considered completely uncivilized—would merit more mercy, and hence a lighter punishment, than they would as neophytes. And they had no way of knowing that their own trial would not unfold in accordance with military justice, leaving them open to execution. Similarly, in the mid-1780s, a handful of neophytes at Mission Santa Clara miscalculated when they attempted to have the abusive Father Tomás de la Peña removed. After their case fell apart, they suffered long terms of hard labor for giving false testimony.

Ironically, the clearest indication that California Indians understood some elements of Spanish criminal justice is found in the actions of some of the most violent offenders. Throughout Alta California, Indians like Aurelio and Eulalia realized that the easiest way to soften the penalties of Spanish criminal justice was to take sanctuary in a mission church after they had committed their crimes. Indian murderers took asylum in just about half of all reported homicides in colonial California. Doing so had benefits: they were more likely to have a procedurally correct trial and less likely to be flogged than those who did not claim sanctuary. And they would be exempted from capital punishment.[79]

These brief glimpses of Indian attempts to use the Spanish judicial system to their advantage are not intended to demonstrate that Indians embraced or even accepted as legitimate judicial processes that had been imposed on them. Yet they do suggest that some Indians grappled with the rules and attempted to turn them

78. The murderer spent two years in jail awaiting final judgment of his case from central Mexico. For this earlier case, see AGN, CA, XLVI, expediente 1, 1a–28a.

79. The issue of church asylum for Indian criminals was hotly debated in Alta California and often led to confrontations between the military and the missionaries. The dispute between the missionaries and Governor Fernando de Rivera y Moncada is the most noteworthy example of these tensions. See Langum, "Legal System of Spanish California," *Western Legal History*, VII (1994), 13 n. 36. An informative article on the subject of asylum is Elizabeth Howard Fast, "The Right of Asylum in New Mexico in the Seventeenth and Eighteenth Centuries," *HAHR*, VIII (1928), 357–391.

to their advantage, just as they or others tried to make the best of the annual elections in the missions and the opportunities for labor and trade that missions and presidios offered. After 1850, however, the Children of Coyote and other California Indians who survived into the American period found that the lessons they had learned about Spanish and Mexican criminal justice were of little use in a legal system that denied them, or anyone who was not "white," the right to testify against the Anglo-Americans who had initiated a new conquest of California.[80] In the years leading up to California statehood, Indians began to get a sense of the injustices that would occur with frequency under Anglo-American rule and its discriminatory codes of law. After 1850, the harsh punishment that befell one Indian in 1847 during military rule would become a commonplace. Accused of stealing a hat and then denied the opportunity to testify in his own defense, the Indian Hosea was condemned to twenty-four lashes with a cat-o'-nine-tails and ordered to pay court costs of $6.75, a fine that, if not paid immediately, would have led to months, if not years, of forced labor, either in public works or for a private citizen who had purchased his labor from the court.[81] Perhaps, then, the most important lessons Indians like Hosea could have taken with them into the American period was an awareness of the degree to which legal systems—be they Spanish, Mexican, or American—can nurture inequitable societies.

80. Robert F. Heizer and Alan J. Almquist, *The Other Californians: Prejudice and Discrimination under Spain, Mexico, and the United States to 1920* (Berkeley, Calif., 1971), esp. 120–132. There has been little investigation of how Indians used and understood the Mexican legal system during the 1830s. For an essay that suggests the rich possibilities of such an inquiry, see Miroslava Chavez, "Pongo Mi Demanda': Challenging Patriarchy in Mexican Los Angeles, 1830–1850," in Valerie J. Matsumoto and Blake Allmendinger, eds., *Over the Edge: Remapping the American West* (Berkeley, Calif., 1999), 272–290.

81. John Burton, ca. Jan. 14, 1847, Archives of San Jose, reel 2, 514, BL.

COLLAPSE OF THE COLONIAL ORDER

9

THE ERA OF SECULARIZATION

LAND AND LIBERTY

By 1847, when Hosea was facing his harsh sentence at the hands of an increasingly discriminatory society, the California missions were in ruins, their Indians dispersed, their buildings crumbled, and their power eclipsed. All of these dramatic changes had their origins in the 1820s and 1830s, when the Mexican state began to wash away the political and economic relationships that held the missions together and kept Indians in them. After winning independence from Spain in 1821, politicians in Mexico initiated an era of reorganization that surpassed anything the architects of the Bourbon reforms had implemented. Like their Spanish predecessors, these Mexican-born liberals considered Franciscan rule anachronistic and Indian land use inefficient. California's soldiers and settlers agreed and hungered for control over the land, livestock, and laborers that missionaries controlled. The result was mission secularization, a drawn-out and contested process in which parish priests replaced missionaries; Indians won gradual emancipation and small plots of land; soldiers, settlers, and even some Indians secured "surplus" mission lands; and secular administrators oversaw and at times plundered remaining mission property and assets. Collectively, these redistributions of wealth and power ushered in a new political and economic order in which Indians enjoyed new rights and opportunities even as they confronted persistent challenges and restrictions. At San Carlos during the early 1830s, continuing depopulation further threatened its people while the onset of these changes held out the hope of a new beginning.

During secularization, Indian laborers remained as integral to the new and evolving economic order as they had been during the Spanish colonial era. But the men who ended Franciscan rule saw Indians as laborers only, not as objects of conversion. Therefore, leading californios did not replace the Franciscans' religious program with one of their own, and Indians regained a good deal of their personal autonomy during secularization. Select Indians—namely, craftsmen, former mission officials, survivors with political and economic ties to the Fran-

ciscans or influential californios, and those with large and extended family networks—found opportunities in the midst of the upheavals of the 1820s and
1830s. Some quickly gained independence from the Franciscans; they relocated to
towns or presidios, where they plied trades they had learned in the missions.
Others obtained ranchos of significant size and integrated themselves into the
local economy. Most ex-neophytes, however, toiled on very small plots of newly
acquired land or remained landless and were forced to work for the gente de
razón, who now commanded large estates and needed their labor. A small number of San Carlos Indians began to work as domestic servants in the nearby
pueblo of Monterey, where they attracted little notice from their contemporaries.
Those who remained at the mission enjoyed greater self-determination than
under Franciscan rule, although amid deteriorating material circumstances. For
nearly all Indians during the era of secularization, marketable skills, ties to key
californios and Franciscans, and networks of family support provided the difference between economic independence and servitude, between a reasonable subsistence and abject poverty.

After secularization, no matter what their circumstances, Indians had more
freedom than in the preceding decades. Perhaps to a greater degree than they had
ever known, emancipated Indians came and went as they pleased, decided for
themselves whether and how they wanted to practice Catholicism, and lived
without missionaries' or soldiers' monitoring the most intimate aspects of their
lives. As more Indians left the missions, they began to spread out. And, as the
great flood of colonialism retreated from Alta California only to be replaced by
another wave of change, Indians lived scattered throughout the Monterey region
and coastal California. Occasionally, they came together to work and socialize,
but new patterns of landholding and economic organization rooted in privately
held domains combined to keep most dispersed. By the 1840s, the communal
ways that had characterized Mission San Carlos and the villages of the Children
of Coyote were of the past. Two events of that decade—an epidemic of smallpox
and the influx of Anglo-Americans culminating in the United States' takeover in
1846—helped to finish off bygone patterns of life and work.[1]

REGIONAL ISOLATION AND THE SEEDS OF CHANGE

During the final decade of Spanish rule in Alta California, revolutionary movements in Spain and Mexico ruptured virtually all state support for California's
missions and presidios, rendering the region's ties to central Mexico increasingly

1. The epidemic and the United States takeover are treated at greater length in the Epilogue, below.

flimsy. Neither padres nor soldiers could count on annual salaries or the goods bought with them, and promising industries, such as the export of hemp and grain, collapsed. The colonial project survived mainly through Indian labor and the productivity of the missions, which continued to feed and clothe the padres and Indians while providing soldiers and pobladores with food, basic commodities, and manufactured goods. Father President Mariano Payeras estimated that, after 1810, the missions provided 500,000 pesos in unreimbursed assistance to the presidios and the pueblos. The extraction of so much surplus labor and production took an enormous toll on mission Indians. "These poor people," lamented Payeras, "will be the most unfortunate and wretched in the world, if they alone, many only recently baptized and uncivilized, have to support so many troops for so long a time."[2]

Between 1810 and 1821, although only one official supply ship arrived from San Blas, a minimum of twenty Spanish merchant ships called in Alta California, and this maritime trade helped to buoy up the local economy. Most of the legal trade was carried on between missionaries and Lima traders, who largely took over the function of the San Blas supply ships. The Limeños purchased tallow—a fat rendered from slaughtered cattle—from the Franciscans and, in return, conveyed goods from Mexico bought specifically for the missions. The presidios also participated in this trade, although only through the assistance of the missions, which provided the cash and tallow that presidial commanders used to purchase goods from visiting ships.[3]

Clandestine trade with Anglo-American, British, and Russian traders also helped padres and soldiers obtain imported necessities after 1810. Governors José Joaquín de Arrillaga (1800–1814) and Pablo Vicente de Solá (1815–1822) publicly condemned this illegal exchange, but, in private, they orchestrated it. José Darío Argüello (acting governor 1814–1815) probably spoke for most soldiers, settlers, and padres in Alta California when, in regard to this contraband trade, he wryly observed: "Necessity makes licit what is not licit by law." Although the governors and Franciscans applauded their ingenuity in trading with foreign nationals, the isolation of Alta California from the economies of Spain and central Mexico steadily increased. And, although this illicit trade met many of the immediate needs of the gente de razón, it fostered a dependence on foreign markets that most californios would eventually regret.[4]

---

2. Mariano Payeras to reverend father guardian [José Gasol], June 18, 1821, Mission San Antonio de Padua, in Donald C. Cutter, ed. and trans., *Writings of Mariano Payeras* (Santa Barbara, Calif., 1995), 299.

3. Robert Archibald, *The Economic Aspects of the California Missions* (Washington, D.C., 1978), 124.

4. On clandestine trade in Alta California, see ibid., 132–141; Argüello quoted in David J. Weber, *The Mexican Frontier, 1821–1846: The American Southwest under Mexico* (Albuquerque, N.Mex., 1982), 125.

Independent Mexico did little to integrate California into the national economy or support soldiers stationed in its presidios. By most accounts, after Mexican independence, the economic well-being of the region's colonists, soldiers, and Indians further deteriorated. Don José María Herrera, the deputy commissioner of finances whom Mexico sent to Monterey in 1825, failed to ensure the effective fiscal administration of Alta California. Soldiers remained unpaid for years, refused to serve, or simply abandoned the disintegrating presidios. Disgruntled soldiers mounted a spectacular, yet unsuccessful, mutiny in Monterey in 1829. They seized the presidio and railed against the central government for sending them leaders who ignored their plight. The revolt did little to improve the conditions of the rebels, and it proved something of a temporary setback for Deputy Commissioner Herrera. In May 1830, having been accused by Governor José María de Echeandía of playing a central role in the uprising, Herrera found himself imprisoned on the American ship *Volunteer* and bound for Mexico.[5]

California politicians complained that the central government neglected their basic needs, and the governor's new economic policies alienated soldiers and settlers alike. Independent Mexico dispensed with Spain's restrictive mercantile policies and opened California to foreign trade, but import and export taxes remained high, and, after 1826, Monterey remained the sole official port of entry. The inadequacy of Mexican coastal patrols and customs officials left most Californians to practice the free trade they preached; yet a host of forced contributions, fee assessments, and taxes on everything from otter pelts to cattle brands threatened to whittle away at the pobladores' and soldiers' meager incomes. Additionally, the settlement policy of the central government infuriated many californios. With the important exception of the Híjar-Padrés colony, which brought artisans and teachers to California in 1834, the only colonists the Mexican Republic sent to California were foundlings and convicts. In large measure, because of these policies, many californios came to view the central government in Mexico and its representatives with skepticism or outright hostility.[6]

Yet, despite the provincials' own frustrations with the local economy, during

---

5. On soldiers' going unpaid, see Jessie Davies Francis, "An Economic and Social History of Mexican California, 1822–1846: Chiefly Economic" (Ph.D. diss., University of California at Berkeley, 1935), I, 344–348, 364–368; Weber, *Mexican Frontier,* 112. The mutiny in Monterey is described in Hubert Howe Bancroft, *History of California,* 7 vols. (San Francisco, Calif., 1884–1890), III, 67–86.

6. On foreign trade in Alta California and californios' views of the central government, see Weber, *Mexican Frontier,* 149, 151, 156–157, 255–260; Francis, "An Economic and Social History of Mexican California," 265–289. In 1826, Mexico had only five vessels to patrol ten thousand miles of coastline. Immigration to California during the Mexican era is discussed in C. Alan Hutchinson, *Frontier Settlement in Mexican California: The Híjar-Padrés Colony and Its Origins, 1769–1835* (New Haven, Conn., 1969), 267–351.

the Mexican period, a great and rapid economic transformation took place in Alta California. Most important, with the opening up of California to international trade, the region's reliance on foreign markets for the sale of its surplus goods accelerated dramatically. A host of foreign companies quickly vied for access to the region's developing hide-and-tallow industry.[7] In June 1822, months before the Spanish flag was officially lowered in Monterey, the English trading concern of McCulloch, Hartnell and Company negotiated a three-year monopoly on the purchase of the province's surplus hides and tallow. Both the Franciscan father president and the Mexican governor could hardly contain their optimism about the expansion of the hide-and-tallow trade. "If things go as planned the poverty of the Province will disappear and the Missions will be provisioned," wrote Father Mariano Payeras, "and it will be even less necessary to order items from Mexico City." To his secular counterpart, Governor Pablo Vicente de Solá, who had previously relied on *contrabandistas* to provision his troops, this legalized trade was the opportunity for which the region had been waiting.[8]

In addition to opening California to international trade, the Mexican government transferred control over the most important economic resources in the region—land, livestock, and Indian laborers—from the missionaries to the settlers. The Colonization Act of 1824 and the supplemental regulations of 1828 created mechanisms through which private individuals—Mexican nationals, foreign immigrants, and even a select number of Indians—could obtain land. Under the terms of the 1824 act, no one person could obtain title to more than "one square league of irrigable land, four leagues of land dependent upon the seasons, and six for the purpose of raising cattle." Although the supplemental regulations

---

7. Through the early 1830s, the missions dominated the production of hides and tallow in California; the extent to which the Franciscans reoriented the mission economy to supply foreign demand for hides and tallow, however, remains a matter of debate. Some scholars have suggested that the padres maximized production of livestock by diverting surplus labor from other agricultural pursuits and additional measures that could have arrested the decline of the neophyte population. See David Hornbeck, "Economic Growth and Change at the Missions of Alta California, 1769–1846," in *CC*, I, 423–433, esp. 426–429. See also Julia G. Costello, "Variability among the Alta California Missions: The Economics of Agricultural Production," in *CC*, I, 435–449. Douglas Monroy notes a similar shift in the outlook of the Franciscans, although he suggests that, as early as 1810, missionaries became more concerned with "buying and selling (in other words, money) than with souls" (*Thrown among Strangers: The Making of Mexican Culture in Frontier California* [Berkeley, Calif., 1990], 69). For a different view, see Robert H. Jackson, "The Changing Economic Structure of the Alta California Missions—A Reinterpretation," *Pacific Historical Review*, LXI (1992), 387–415.

8. Mariano Payeras to José Gasol, June 26, 1822, Mission Soledad, in Cutter, ed. and trans., *Writings of Payeras*, 322–323. Bancroft states that the Spanish flag came down in Monterey in late September or early October (*History of California*, II, 458). For more on these negotiations and the governor's enthusiasm for this trade, see Adele Ogden, "Hides and Tallow: McCulloch, Hartnell and Company, 1822–1828," *California Historical Society Quarterly*, VI (1927), 254–264; and Bancroft, *History of California*, II, 475–477.

of 1828 gave "governors of the territories the authority to grant vacant land, and specified the procedure to be followed," its final provisions stipulated that mission lands, by far the most valuable and accessible, could not be colonized "at present." Six years later, the Secularization Act of 1834 swept this qualification aside, opening up prime mission lands for settlement. Taken together, these laws ushered in the greatest transfer of land and resources in California since Portolá had claimed the region for Spain in 1770. And, as a result, by the 1840s, the private rancho had replaced the mission as the dominant economic institution in California, rendering the majority of former mission Indians landless, if not homeless.[9]

Although California Indians could not have envisioned the political and economic changes ushered in by Mexico's independence, many certainly attached meaning to the wane of Spanish authority and immediately felt an affinity for the new government, especially Governor José María de Echeandía (1825–1833). Indians marked the onset of Mexican rule in Monterey with a raucous celebration at which they danced, ran footraces, and played music. Decades later, General Mariano Guadalupe Vallejo remembered that, "when the neophytes saw that the Mexicans had lowered the flag upon which the lions were depicted and in its place had run up one in the middle of which there was an eagle perched on a nopal cactus, they were greatly delighted, because, before the arrival of the Reverend Father Serra, the eagle had been the emblem of their religious beliefs." Paulino Joseph Soletasay, also known as Paulino Serra, who had lived his whole life under Franciscan rule at San Carlos, exemplified this belief. Upon seeing the Mexican flag raised, he told Vallejo: "Nowadays, you think [the] same as we, now that [the] eagle, worth a lot, is up and [the] lion, worth nothing, is down. . . . Now anybody [may] dance when [he] want[s] to, also sell Brandy on Sunday." Soletasay proved too optimistic, but his response shows his frustration with life under Spanish rule. Vallejo would later recall that, during the era of secularization, "the Indians did not receive at our hands the treatment they deserved, for their property was, to a certain extent, wasted and devoted to uses very different from those to which it should have been applied." A gulf separated the two men's understandings, suggesting the alternate meanings Indians and californios attached to secularization: Soletasay anticipated greater personal freedoms following the transformation of the region; Vallejo, looking back, simply regretted

9. On the Colonization Act of 1824 and the supplemental regulations of 1828, see Weber, *Mexican Frontier*, 162, 180–181; Hutchinson, *Frontier Settlement in Mexican California*, 112–113, 137; Robert H. Becker, *Diseños of California Ranchos, Maps of Thirty-seven Land Grants (1822–1846)* . . . (San Francisco, Calif., 1964), xii–xiii. For a brief summary of the provisions of this legislation, see Bancroft, *History of California*, II, 515–516 n. 8, III, 34–35 n. 7; and David Hornbeck, "Land Tenure and Rancho Expansion in Alta California, 1784–1846," *Journal of Historical Geography*, IV (1978), 371–390, esp. 378.

economic injustices and did not comment on the Indians' regained personal liberties.[10]

MISSION SECULARIZATION AND POLITICAL CHANGE

The changes that Soletasay anticipated and Vallejo regretted unfolded slowly and incrementally as leaders in Mexico struggled over plans to convert California's missions into parishes, a step they agreed was long overdue.[11] Missions in central Mexico had been secularized long before California's had been founded, and reformers emphasized that ten years was the maximum any mission should be in existence.[12] The reformers intended to replace missionaries with priests who would be in charge only of the Indians' religious obligations and observances. Indians themselves would control their own economic and political affairs, and some of their labor would be overseen by an appointed administrator. Predictably, the Franciscans countered that California Indians could not live without their supervision, and they fiercely opposed all attempts to remove the Indians from their direct control. Because the wars of independence had depleted the resources with which the state formerly had supported the Franciscan missions, lack of adequate means gave added impetus for some Mexican leaders to call for a

10. On Indians' enthusiasm for the end of Spanish rule and for Echeandía, see Juan Bautista de Alvarado, "Historia de California" (1876), 5 vols., I, 168, 173, C–D 1, BL (English trans.). Indians celebrate the beginning of Mexican rule and Vallejo's recollections: Mariano Guadalupe Vallejo, "Recuerdos históricos y personales tocantes a la Alta California, 1769–1849 . . . ," 5 vols. (1875), I, 221–222, IV, 18, C–D 17, 20, BL (English trans.). See also Paulino Joseph Soletasay, San Carlos bapt. no. 1172.

11. As early as 1813, the Mexican government had passed laws ordering the secularization of the missions. See Daniel J. Garr, "Planning, Politics and Plunder: The Missions and Indian Pueblos of Hispanic California," *SCQ*, LIV (1972), 291–312, esp. 297. Weber, *Mexican Frontier*, 60–68, takes a wide-ranging look at the secularization of the missions in California and the Southwest. See also a useful summary of the historical antecedents to mission secularization in California in Gerald J. Geary, *Secularization of the California Missions (1810–1846)* (Washington, D.C., 1934). Hutchinson provides a thorough analysis of the local proponents of secularization in *Frontier Settlement in Mexican California*. He examines the Mexican government's role in secularization in "The Mexican Government and the Mission Indians of Upper California, 1821–1835," *The Americas*, XXI (1965), 335–362. Bancroft summarizes the main events of secularization in *History of California*, III, 301–355. Edward D. Castillo has examined one Indian's narrative of the years after secularization in "An Indian Account of the Decline and Collapse of Mexico's Hegemony over the Missionized Indians of California," *American Indian Quarterly*, XIII (1989), 391–408. See also Manuel P. Servín, "The Secularization of the California Missions: A Reappraisal," *SCQ*, XLVII (1965), 133–149. On mission secularization throughout the borderlands, see Robert H. Jackson, *From Savages to Subjects: Missions in the History of the American Southwest* (New York, 2000), 116–125; James E. Ivey, "Secularization in California and Texas," *Boletín: The Journal of the California Mission Studies Association*, XX (2003), 23–36.

12. The origin of the ten-year rule is explored by Geary, *Secularization of the California Missions*, 17–18. According to Geary, arguments that all of the missions should have been secularized ten years after their establishment relied upon an inherited misinterpretation of a tithing exemption granted to Indians.

sale of the properties of the Pious Fund and breaking up the Franciscan establish-ments.[13] The padres' claim that Indians remained a backward people went un-challenged and even reinforced the newly empowered liberals' ideology that placed faith in the industriousness of the individual and the transformative power of private property. A report that the secretary of state presented to the Mexican Congress on November 8, 1823, noted that the missions could "do no more than establish the first principles of society." To truly elevate the Indians, it would be necessary to affix them "to society by the powerful bond of property." Early proposals for mission secularization, therefore, called for the redistribution of some mission lands among the neophytes. This would have been good news, indeed, to California Indians, especially those of the Santa Barbara missions who rose up in 1824. A Mexican government council in 1825 even went so far as to recommend secularization of the missions, but the realization that the mis-sions were still the economic backbone of Alta California led to a scuttling of any initial plans.[14]

It was in the midst of a debate unresolved and fears of new Indian insurrec-tions that José María de Echeandía took over the governorship of Alta California in 1825. The central government urged him to dismantle the missions yet denied him the power to simply close them down. As governor, Echeandía maintained an active interest in promoting the welfare and aspirations of Indians, and he gained popularity among them, especially those of the south who saw in him their best chance for greater independence. As a first step toward seculariza-tion, Echeandía curtailed the authority of the Franciscans and created a means through which the most acculturated could free themselves from Franciscan control. Echeandía's Decree of Emancipation in Favor of the Neophytes, pub-lished on July 25, 1826, granted Indians the right to separate themselves from the missions, "provided they had been Christians from childhood or for fifteen years, were married, or at least not minors, and had some means of gaining a liveli-hood." Indians desiring to leave the mission would have to gain the approval of the local presidial commander and the Franciscans. Echeandía's mandate also limited the Franciscans' authority over those Indians who remained at the mis-sions by barring Franciscans from flogging married or adult Indians and from punishing Indian children with more than fifteen lashes a week. These orders quickly had a wide and immediate effect by increasing Indians' leverage over the Franciscans. Once Indians learned that they could be freed, they balked at the padres' orders. In an example of increasingly common defiance, one man at San

13. Spain had previously relied upon the Pious Fund to maintain the missions at Baja and Alta California.

14. The reports of the secretary of state and the government council of 1825 are discussed in Geary, *Secularization of the California Missions,* 88, 94–95.

Carlos responded to Father Ramón Abella's request that he yoke up the oxen by saying that he would petition for his emancipation. Indians refused to work for Abella, and those Abella wanted to punish threatened to leave.[15]

Upon learning of Echeandía's plan to allow certain Indians liberty, most of the Chumash men at Mission San Buenaventura requested their freedom. In three letters and a memorandum addressed to Echeandía, Pacifico, a Buenaventura neophyte, gave voice to the Indians' grievances with mission life and their hopes for the future. The documents Pacifico produced reveal to an extraordinary degree that many Indians believed a transitional moment had arrived for them. Pacifico's handwriting and command of the Spanish language demonstrate that he had a higher degree of literacy than many of the gente de razón Mexican society had placed over him. The way Pacifico folded his completed letters neatly in half and then again to form an envelope and addressed them in careful writing to "señor general don José María Echeandía en el puerto de S. Diego" suggests that he had corresponded with government officials before. It is easy to imagine that Pacifico was trained as a scribe by one of the Franciscans, and, from that experience, he had learned how to frame and construct a formal letter to someone to whom he owed obedience. How he acquired his literacy skills and pen, ink, and paper remain unclear, but he put them all to good use.

Pacifico's first letter to Echeandía, dated October 23, 1826, shows a mind at work within a Spanish culture and a tradition of submission and subjection, yet one that was all the while envisioning new freedoms within a less restrictive order. Well versed in the language of the colonial vassal, Pacifico appealed to Echeandía, his "respected and venerated leader." Begging for mercy and placing himself metaphorically at Echeandía's feet, Pacifico hoped that the governor would look upon the San Buenaventura Indians with "eyes of pity" and "place in liberty" 125 men listed on an attached memorandum. Pacifico closed the letter with a variant of the familiar abbreviation "B.L.M.," short for "Besa la mano," or "Kissing the hand of Your Excellency." Then, in writing his name, he inscribed a beautiful and personal rubric that resembled an object of great import in California Indian society, a woven basket.[16]

15. For background on the 1826 decree, see Bancroft, *History of California*, III, 102–103. For the decree itself, see José María de Echeandía, circular letter to presidial districts of San Diego, Santa Barbara, and Monterey, July 25, 1826, Monterey, copy made by José María Estudillo, August 1826, Taylor Coll., unnumbered, at end of box 9, HL. It is not clear why this decree was not also directed to the San Francisco presidial district. Earlier in the decade, the Franciscans had been instructed not to discipline the Indians with corporal punishment, but flogging had continued nevertheless. For Indians' responses to the decree, see Ramón Abella to José María Herrera, Jan. 30, 1827, San Carlos, Taylor Coll., doc. 1953, HL; Abella, "Contestación al alcalde de el presidio José Castro," Taylor Coll., box 7, 298a, 299a–299b, HL.

16. Pacifico, Mansueto, and Francisco Xaviel to Echeandía, Oct. 23, 1826, San Buenaventura, AGN, CA, XVIII, expediente 33, 458a–458b. Pacifico wrote "B.S.M." in place of the standard "B.L.M."

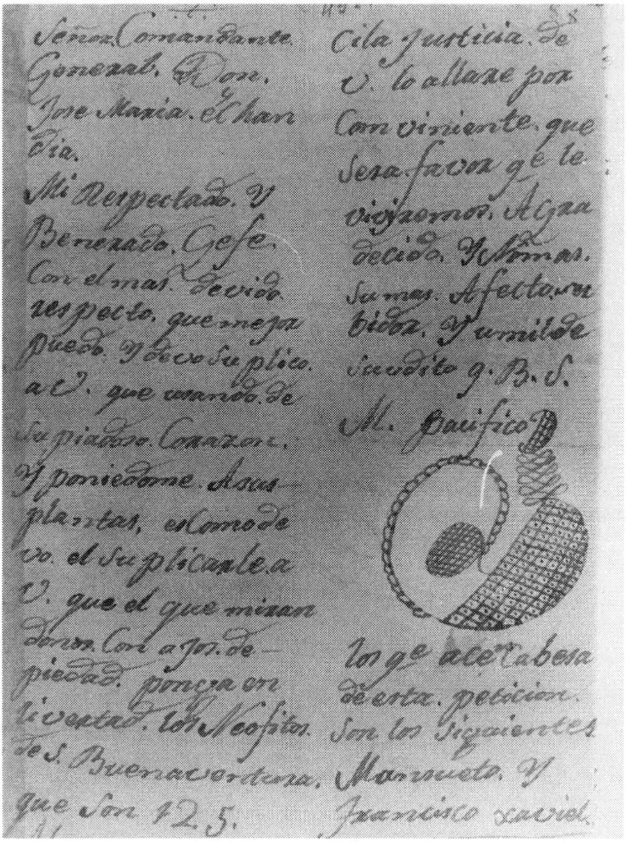

Señor Comandante
General. Don
Jose Maria. Echan
dia.
Mi Respectado. Y
Benerado. Gefe.
Con el mas. devido
respecto, que mereze
puedo. Y devo Suplico.
a V. que cuando de
Su piadoso. Corazon.
Y poniendome. Asus
plantas, eslomode
vo. el Suplicarle. a
V. que el que mesean
donos. Con a Jos. de
piedad. poncra en
livertad. los Neofitos.
de S. Buenaventura,
que son 125.
Cila justicia. de
V. lo allare por
Conviniente. que
Sera favor q e le
viviremos. Agra
decidos. Y Somos.
Su mas. Afecto. su
bidor. Y umilde
suudito q. B. S.
M. Pacifico
los q e ace Cabesa
de esta. peticion.
Son los Siguientes
Mansueto. Y
Francisco xaviel.

PLATE 21. Letter of Pacifico, Mansueto, and Francisco Xaviel to Governor José Maria de Echeandía requesting freedom for themselves and other neophytes from Mission San Buenaventura, Oct. 23, 1826, AGN, CA, XVIII, expediente 33, 458a–458b. Note the flourish after Pacifico's signature, which resembles a woven basket (see Plate 22). Courtesy, Archivo General de la Nación, Mexico

The memorandum from the San Buenaventura neophytes deftly straddles two worlds. Its very title, "Memorandum of the Neophytes Who Have Presented Themselves with All Submission Asking for Their Departure," speaks of an awareness of colonial power and a desire to limit it. In form, the petition mimics the countless lists and statistical reports that missionaries and other colonial officials generated for their superiors. Pacifico structured the document in response to Echeandía's principal requirement that liberated Indians be able to support themselves and their families. Thus he grouped the men by their occupations: as

PLATE 22. Chumash coiled rush *(juncus)* basketry bowl, most likely collected near Santa Barbara in 1793 by Archibald Menzies, a botanist on the expedition of Captain George Vancouver. © The Trustees of The British Museum

masons, tilemakers, carpenters, muleteers, laborers, weavers, vaqueros, and soapmakers. At the end of the list, just as was true for censuses constructed by Spanish officials, came the widowed and unmarried. So constituted, the memorandum must have represented nearly all the adult men at the mission, and since, with freedom, these men would have left the mission with their wives and children and others in their family, it seems clear that Pacifico and others had in mind the end of San Buenaventura.[17]

Less than a week after sending the memorandum to Echeandía, Pacifico, Gervasio, and Peregrino María respectfully wrote a second note to the governor that justified their desire for freedom and made three demands. They called for the mission to be converted into a pueblo so they could work for themselves. Wisely, they added that doing so would not prevent them from continuing to provision the military. Second, they wanted a different missionary, one who cared for them and therefore "would not punish them and who would always provide them food and clothing." Here they were criticizing Father Francisco Suñer, a man of broken health who served at the mission from 1823 to 1831. Suñer was generally considered to be irritable and unpleasant. And, third, they requested that soldier Juan Lugo be installed as their overseer. In doing so, they revealed the limits of

17. Pacifico et al., "Memorandum of the Neophytes Who Have Presented Themselves with All Submission Asking for Their Departure," Oct. 23, 1826, San Buenaventura, AGN, CA, XVIII, expediente 33, 459a–459b. At the time of the petition, there were some 850 Indians at the mission.

their vision, or the limits of what they thought attainable; they wanted to improve their lot but still imagined themselves living within a colonial situation, under Catholicism, and supervised by a Spaniard.[18]

Hopeful that Echeandía would act on their behalf, or desperate that he would not, Pacifico, Gervasio, and Peregrino María traveled to San Diego, evidently to appeal directly to the governor. There, most likely at the presidio, the three delivered to Echeandía a final articulation of what they needed to achieve economic independence. The trio asked that the mission's money, land, seed, rakes, axes, cattle, horses, and mules be distributed among the Indians at San Buenaventura. They closed their letter by assuring Echeandía that they wanted nothing more and that "these were their final voices and words." So they were, at least as far as this matter was concerned. Pacifico and his signature appear nowhere else in the historical record.[19]

The men of San Buenaventura had responded to the aspirations that Echeandía had engendered in them, but Pacifico and his fellow petitioners had asked for more than Echeandía and the missionaries were prepared to give. Echeandía's response to the petition and to Pacifico's letters is not known, but it is clear that he did not meet the demands, even though he certainly sympathized with them. The padres' disparaging response must have given Echeandía pause. Father President Narciso Durán urged caution on Echeandía and expressed shame that Indians under Franciscan tutelage could propose what he saw as unrestrained freedom. Father Suñer dismissed out of hand the idea that Indians could live on their own. In response to Pacifico's pleas, Suñer penned a letter that easily could have come from Father Serra's hand six decades earlier. Lazy by nature and "more animal than rational," Indians, Suñer believed, could never support themselves. He warned that, once released from the structure of mission life, Indians would idle away their time, end up as domestic servants for the californios, and perhaps even resort to crimes to feed themselves. Invoking the rhetoric of centuries of Franciscan missionaries who had come before him, Suñer went as far as to suggest that neither an Indian's words nor deeds could be accepted at face value: "Sometimes he comes dressed in sheep's clothing, but within he is a rapacious wolf; his voice is that of Jacob and his hands are those of Esau. Not all Indians are like this, but there are many who are, who bless what they would like to curse and kiss the hand that they would like to burn." Given that Echeandía would not emancipate any Indians at San Buenaventura without the approval of Durán and

18. Pacifico, Gervasio, and Peregrino María, Oct. 28, 1826, San Buenaventura, AGN, CA, XVIII, expediente 33, 457a–457b. On Francisco Suñer's reputation, see Maynard Geiger, *Franciscan Missionaries in Hispanic California, 1769–1848: A Biographical Dictionary* (San Marino, Calif., 1969), 252–253.

19. Pacifico, Gervasio, and Peregrino María, Nov. 23, 1826, San Diego, AGN, CA, XVIII, expediente 33, 460a–460b.

Suñer, Pacifico and his fellow petitioners would not be freed yet. Their petition, however, was not lost on government officials and might even have influenced policymakers. Two years later, when Echeandía submitted his own plan to convert the missions into pueblos, he included Pacifico's letters as proof that Indians were ready to be liberated from the missions.[20]

Beyond Mission San Buenaventura, Echeandía's decree elicited a response that officials considered more manageable than Pacifico's, as men and women individually began to initiate their own emancipation. They did so in short appeals of a paragraph in length, in which they identified themselves and argued for their freedom. Most of their appeals were written for them, but some are clearly in the Indians' own writing. Again, when viewed collectively, these short documents reveal Indians' discontent with the missions and their hopes for a better life elsewhere. In one typical request, Gil Ricla, who might have been the first California Indian to take advantage of the decree, identified himself as a *ciudadano* of Mission San Diego and stated that, as a carpenter, he would be able to support his family. Not knowing how to write or sign his name, Gil Ricla had found someone to pen the petition for him. Upon its receipt, Echeandía asked the padres at San Diego to verify that Gil Ricla was a Christian of good conduct. They replied that he was Christian since birth, twenty-nine years old, married, the father of three, well behaved, and a carpenter of sufficient skill to maintain his family in comfort. With the padres' endorsement in hand, the governor's secretary promptly approved Gil Ricla's request. Without such support, Indians could not separate from the mission, as in June 1827, when Father Felipe Arroyo de la Cuesta advised Echeandía that Epifanio, Pedro Bautista, and two others simply were not ready for emancipation from San Juan Bautista because they were not well grounded in Catholicism.[21]

Gil Ricla's desire for liberation should not have come as a surprise, as he was one of the most acculturated Diegueños at the mission and the sort of individual whom Echeandía had in mind when he envisioned emancipations. Ricla's father came to San Diego from Baja California to build the mission, and Ricla himself

20. Narciso Durán, Feb. 16, 1827, Mission San Jose, AGN, CA, XVIII, expediente 33, 463a–464a; Suñer, Dec. 19, 1826, Mission San Buenaventura, ibid., 461a–462b. Echeandía's plan: ibid., 453a–456b.

21. [Gil Ricla], Apr. 4, 1826, San Diego, Taylor Coll., doc. 1817, HL. Franciscan approval of request: Fernando Martín and Vicente Pasqual Oliva, Apr. 30, 1826, Mission San Diego, ibid. Governor's approval: Agustín V. Zamorano, ibid. Arroyo de la Cuesta advises against emancipation of certain Indians: June 20, 1827, Monterey, Archives of California, C–A 18, 282, BL. Gil Ricla's petition of Apr. 4, 1826, preceded Echeandía's decree. Before Echeandía's order, missionaries at San Diego had agreed to some emancipations. Gil Ricla's request came in the midst of these discussions (Bancroft, *History of California,* III, 102). On early emancipations, see also Lisbeth Haas, "Emancipation and the Meaning of Freedom in Mexican California," *Boletín: The Journal of the California Mission Studies Association,* XX (2003), 11–22.

became one of the Franciscans' most trusted assistants. Although he was not yet thirty when he petitioned for freedom, he had already served at least twenty-one times as a godparent and fourteen times as a marriage sponsor. After his emancipation, Ricla retained his religious ties to the mission and moved to the San Diego Presidio, where his wife, Pia, gave birth to another three children, all of whom were baptized. Ricla's transition from neophyte to ciudadano was so extensive that, upon the baptism of his last child, Ricla was described as a "gente de razón del presidio." His own loyalty to the padres, his trade, and his work at the fort were the expression and means of his entrance into presidial society.[22]

Ricla's passing into soldier-settler society was uncommon, but his petition and subsequent emancipation were not. For years after the decree of July 25, 1826, as secularization and the granting of freedoms slowly moved forward, Indians continued to petition for liberty from Franciscan rule. María Jacinta of Mission San Luis Rey directed her appeal to officials in Los Angeles. A widow with responsibility for two unmarried daughters, María Jacinta believed that she could better support herself and her family away from San Luis Rey, even though she did not specify exactly how she could do so. After more than thirty years of mission life, she characterized San Luis Rey as a place where she had experienced "naught but work and sufferings." By leaving the mission, she hoped to "alleviate the few remaining days" of her life. Not knowing how to write, she closed her appeal with a scribbled cross mark. Juan Santos wrote his own petition and offered more details about the life he envisioned away from Mission Santa Clara. He was working in San Jose as a mason, and in the future he intended to do so "as a settler of the pueblo, not as a neophyte of the mission." The change of status would have allowed him, not the mission, to be paid his wages. But more than his economic status seemed to be at stake. He hoped to move to San Jose with his family to "enjoy the civil liberty that the laws granted to all citizens." By that, he most likely meant freedom from a life under Franciscan supervision.[23]

Only one emancipation petition put forward by a San Carlos Indian survives. In September 1828, Manuel Ventura placed his mark on his request to separate from the mission. His petition consisted of one short paragraph that offered no specifics about his family or means of support beyond the mission. Whether Manuel Ventura won his liberation is not known, but certainly many other Indians from San Carlos did after Echeandía's decree of 1826. Twenty-three had left before the end of that year, a period when the mission's population had

22. Mariano de Jesús, Mission San Diego bapt. no. 6547, Apr. 21, 1833, in CMRC, San Diego Baptisms, MSS film 528:16, reel 2, HL.

23. María Jacinta, May 12, 1839, Los Angeles County (Prefecture) Records, MSS film 382A:324, HL (English trans.); Juan Santos to prefect, July 27, 1839, San Jose Pueblo, Archives of Monterey, C–A 150, IX, reel 9, doc. 1560, 475, BL.

already dipped below three hundred. Many moved to the Monterey Presidio or ranches in the neighborhood of the Pajaro River, north of the mission.[24]

A year after the decree, Father Ramón Abella despaired that "the Indians [at the mission] are very few, and each day there are fewer because they are leaving." They were happy to leave the mission, in Abella's view, for, "in the first place, they go wherever they like." "If they work, they get paid a daily wage, and if they don't work, they are not paid, but they are still at liberty." By 1831, another twenty-five San Carlos Indians "had gone wherever they desired in the area, with their families." When Abella tried to coax them back, "they said they were *'licenciados,'*" legally emancipated Indians. Powerless, Abella admitted that "those that wanted to leave I allowed to do what they wished." "I had no means to attract them." Abella, in an echo of Suñer's argument against the San Buenaventura petitioners, ridiculed the idea that Indians would be able to live independently beyond the mission: he believed they thought only of the present and were content that tomorrow would take care of itself as long as there were clams to be gathered on the coastline. He acknowledged, however, that San Carlos Indians had rejoined that they would be fine as "cultivators" and just wanted to be left alone. In their now lost petitions, many had also maintained that, as weavers, they would earn a living in Monterey. By the end of 1832, more than seventy had left Carmel, some with the permission of the government, but many had liberated themselves. The mission was beginning to disintegrate much as it had come together, as individuals and families managed their lives in response to change.[25]

Although no extant records detail exactly who obtained permission to leave San Carlos after July 1826, a list of the mission population in 1833 and information gleaned from the sacramental registers indicate many who took advantage of the decree or simply left on their own. Virtually all of the adults the padres listed as licenciados were like Gil Ricla: married, resident at the mission for at least fifteen years, and skilled at a trade, such as masonry or carpentry. With the

24. Manuel Ventura to Echeandía, Sept. 24, 1828, Monterey, Taylor Coll., doc. 2034, HL; Mission San Carlos biennial report, 1825–1826, SBMAL.

25. Ramón Abella to José María Herrera, Jan. 30, 1827, San Carlos, Taylor Coll., doc 1953, HL; Abella, Mission San Carlos annual report for 1831, Dec. 31, 1831, SBMAL. Abella admits powerlessness: Abella, Mission San Carlos annual report for 1832, quoted in Zephyrin Engelhardt, *Mission San Carlos Borromeo (Carmelo): The Father of the Missions* (1934; rpt. Ramona, Calif., 1973), 172. Abella echoes Suñer and recounts Indians' responses: Abella, "Contestación al alcalde de el presidio José Castro," Taylor Coll., box 7, unnumbered doc., 298a, 299a–299b, HL. The Franciscans could usually determine the approximate number of Indians at any mission by applying the difference in births and deaths during the current year to the previous year's total population. At the end of 1828, the Franciscans at Mission San Carlos explained that this process no longer worked because, after these early emancipations, there were so many Indians who had been born or who had died in the presidio or on the local ranchos that they were unsure how many Indians were at the mission or in the area (Abella and Vicente Francisco de Sarría, Mission San Carlos biennial report, 1827–1828, Dec. 31, 1828, SBMAL).

withdrawal of so many of the most acculturated, the mission was increasingly home only to "children, old folks, the ill, and the helpless and destitute." All of this left the aged Abella in despair. He bemoaned that those remaining refused to work and that those granted emancipation, in his view, remained idle. In his words, the departure of so many had left him overwhelmed by additional responsibilities. In exasperation, as Indians took their liberty, Abella could only write: "Yo soi el que estoi esclavo" ("I am the one who is enslaved"). Among those whose departure and freedom contributed to Abella's growing sense of enslavement were former alcaldes and regidores, such as Amadeo Yeucharom and Baldomero José. Baldomero José would secure a rancho of his own and live for years beyond the mission with his wife and children. Amadeo Yeucharom, however, would die in 1835 having lived just five of his sixty-one years beyond Franciscan rule. Many of his descendants, though, most notably his son Onesimo Antonio (a shoemaker at Carmel), his granddaughter María Loreta, and his great-grandchildren Isabel Meadows and Manuel Onesimo, would live long lives outside the mission.[26]

The 1826 emancipation decree initiated the liberation of many Indians from San Carlos, but it was only the first of many proclamations that broke down the missions and men like Ramón Abella. In March 1829, the central government expelled all Spaniards and therefore all missionaries from California. Echeandía did not enforce the expulsion, but soon a plan was worked out to replace the resident friars with Mexican-born Franciscans. In January 1833, missionaries from the Missionary College of Guadalupe, Zacatecas, arrived in Monterey, and, when José María del Reál was assigned to San Carlos, Abella, who had served there since 1819, moved to San Luis Obispo, located just north of Santa Barbara. Despite changes in mission leadership, the missions had not yet been turned into parishes, and the fate of their lands remained unresolved. Further unresolved was whether these issues would be decided by politicians in California or by the National Congress of Mexico. In the early 1830s, the governor, Franciscans, and other local interested parties—virtually everyone but California Indians—put forward different written plans for the alienation and distribution of the missions' lands. In January 1831, Governor Echeandía moved forward with his revised attempt to convert missions into towns, arguing that Indians at missions like San Buenaventura were ready and that a Spanish law of 1813 authorized such changes. Indians at San Gabriel and San Carlos were to elect officials who

26. Abella, "Contestación al alcalde de el presidio José Castro," Taylor Coll., box 7, unnumbered doc., 298a, 299a–299b, HL; Amadeo Yeucharom (San Carlos bapt. no. 249); Baldomero José (San Carlos bapt. no. 1572). Theopisto Joseph (San Carlos bapt. no. 1001) was another former mission official who gained his freedom. On Onesimo Antonio, see San Carlos bapt. no. 2105 and San Carlos marr. no. 871.

would govern along with an appointed administrator. Neophytes over age eighteen, if married, and twenty-five, if single, would gain possession of land. Similar changes were to follow at other missions. Indians spread word of this plan, and, in some areas, they heard about it directly from Mexican officials, but growing political turmoil and the advent of Manuel Victoria's 1831 governorship in northern Alta California prevented its full implementation.[27]

Mexico's independence from Spain and continuing debates over the status of the missions had emboldened Indians who anticipated greater autonomy and control over mission resources. In the 1820s, many Indian officials had led rebellions against Mexican authority and Franciscan rule: in 1824, of course, the Chumash of the Santa Barbara missions had launched their insurrection, and, three years later, Narciso, Estanislao, and Victor had led rebellions against Mission San Jose. In the spring and early summer of 1833, some Gabrielinos and Diegueños grew impatient and worried that they might never control the lands they worked. They were radicalized in their belief that Echeandía, who was now in charge of only the southern portion of Alta California, was soon to be replaced, and they feared that his successor might not look favorably upon their cause. Tomás Tajochí, a literate Indian who exchanged letters with Echeandía, emerged as their leader. Tajochí's attempt to piece together a rebellion across southern California prompted authorities to seek his capture; by July, he was under arrest and the rebellion, over. The actions and expectations of men like him, however, were not lost upon the leadership of the province, and they might have added impetus to the finalization of plans already under discussion.[28]

Just as Tajochí's rebellion was coming undone, newly arrived Governor José Figueroa (1833–1835) issued his Provisional Regulations for the Emancipation of Mission Indians. This was a gradualist plan that built upon Echeandía's earlier efforts: it envisioned partial freedom for Indians more than twelve years in the missions who were married or widowed, had children, and could support themselves. Ex-neophytes were to live in newly established pueblos adjacent to the

27. On the arrival of the Zacatecans in California, see Engelhardt, *Mission San Carlos Borromeo*, 162–165, 181. Echeandía's plan to convert missions to pueblos is discussed in Bancroft, *History of California*, III, 304–308. Ramón Abella's final years were marked by poverty and infirmity, his eyes and nostrils chronically inflamed after years of using snuff. He died in 1842, just four days short of his seventy-eighth birthday, having spent forty-four years—longer than any other Franciscan—in California (Geiger, *Franciscan Missionaries in Hispanic California*, 3–6). The governorship of Alta California was extremely unstable in the 1830s. See Bancroft, *History of California*, III, 327, 359; Weber, *Mexican Frontier*, 255–261.

28. Tajochí and several of his supporters were placed on trial, found guilty, and sentenced to several years' hard labor. Their punishments would have been more severe had Mexican officials not sympathized with the Indians' frustrations and believed that the rebels lived in "imbecility" and "ignorance" at the missions. See José Figueroa, "Sentence of Seditious Indians," Nov. 22, 1833, Monterey, Archives of California, C–A 19, 370–373, BL.

missions. Yet the emancipated could be called back for work by the parish priest or the alcalde so that "neither the mission work nor that of private individuals shall suffer." Ex-neophytes were to receive small plots of land, livestock, and farming implements, "according to the circumstances of the mission." They could not sell their land or slaughter or sell their animals as they wished. Carried out only in a limited fashion at San Diego and San Luis Rey and more extensively at San Juan Capistrano, the plan went no further. Figueroa had exceeded his authority in issuing the regulations, Indians were less than enthusiastic at being required to work at the mission and not being able to profit from their land and cattle after emancipation, and the gente de razón, who wanted mission lands, got none.[29]

A month after Figueroa promulgated his plan, the Mexican National Congress legislated the secularization of the missions of Baja and Alta California by simply ordering the conversion of the missions to parishes overseen by secular administrators. The congress said nothing about the Indians and their relationship to the missions, nor did it offer a mechanism for the alienation of mission lands. But the act itself removed any doubt that secularization would occur, thereby forcing the governor and local officials to craft a plan before one was crafted for them. After wrangling over weeks and then months, on August 9, 1834, Figueroa issued provisional guidelines for the distribution of mission land, tools, and livestock and the creation of secular communities. Each Indian head of a family who was over twenty years old would receive a small parcel of land between one hundred and four hundred varas square. Distributed among these heads of families would be one-half of each mission's livestock and not more than half of the mission's tools and seeds. Abolished were the monjerías, the dormitories for unmarried women and widows. Surplus property was to be placed under the care and responsibility of a mayordomo and left at the disposal of the government, which would then be able to grant land to petitioners under the terms of the Colonization Act of 1824 and the supplemental regulations of 1828. Emancipated Indians faced severe limitations. They could never sell their land or livestock, and they would be required to aid in the cultivation of lands and fields not distributed and "render to the padre the necessary personal service." The Secularization Act of 1834, therefore, sought to balance contradictory aims: it freed some Indians from the priests' control, thereby providing laborers for ranchos and a measure of economic independence for Indians. But it also ensured that missions, long the economic foundation of the region, remained minimally productive and that Indians, considered unused to independence, enjoyed only limited liberty. Six

29. José Figueroa, "Provisional Regulations for the Emancipation of Mission Indians," July 15, 1833, in Bancroft, History of California, III, 328–330 n. 50.

decades after they came into existence, the California missions were on the chopping block, and Indians and the gente de razón would begin to struggle over what remained of their material wealth.[30]

In accordance with the Secularization Act, Father Réal and a government commissioner, José Joaquín Gómez, performed an inventory of San Carlos. They set the value of Mission San Carlos and its properties at 46,022 pesos, but, in many ways, the value of the mission remained unquantifiable, for the boundaries of the mission's lands had never been formally established, since Mission San Carlos had, in fact, never assumed formal possession of them. Like all California missions, it claimed—as a sort of trustee for the neophytes—all surrounding territory that neophytes put to use or might need in the future. When the missionaries had held the upper hand in the control of the region's resources, their claim to enormous tracts of land on behalf of the Indians had gone largely uncontested. Yet, when the Franciscans lost power, the informality of these previous understandings and customs hastened the missions' despoliation. To the Spanish state, missions were a temporary yet expedient instrument that allowed the organization of regions for defense, the control and assimilation of local populations, and a measure of frontier self-sufficiency. Once these needs had been met or supplanted, secularization typically followed, and missionaries moved on or retired. In Alta California, when the Mexican state no longer needed or wanted the missions, it legislated them out of existence, rendering obsolete the missionaries' control over Indians and null their claims to land on behalf of the natives.[31]

Although the land used by the mission went unspecified in the inventory, such was not the case for other assets. Clearly, on the eve of secularization, San Carlos retained some of its productive capacity. It held several hundred cattle, horses,

30. "Decree of Mexican Congress Secularizing the Missions, August 17, 1833," in Bancroft, *History of California,* III, 336–337 n. 61; José Figueroa, "Provisional Rules for the Secularization of the Missions of Alta California," Aug. 9, 1834, in Bancroft, *History of California,* III, 342–344 n. 4.

31. José María del Refugio del Reál and José Joaquín Gómez, inventory of San Carlos, Dec. 10, 1834, San Carlos, SBMAL. The closest missionaries came to a formal description of the lands of San Carlos was in 1828, when Ramón Abella and Vicente Francisco de Sarría responded to Governor Echeandía's request for a report on the lands missions claimed. The padres explained that the mission occasionally grazed sheep and cattle on the southern portion of the Monterey peninsula. They had found the lands of the upper Carmel Valley largely useless for grazing cattle; the valley was too narrow and its surrounding hills too craggy and overgrown. The flatland immediately south and east of the mission, essentially the bottom of the Carmel Valley, was heavily used to cultivate crops and graze sheep, horses, cattle, oxen, and mules. The mission also kept cattle some twenty-five miles east, up the Salinas Valley, at a place known as Sanjones, the ancestral home of the Ensen. It pastured an additional herd of sheep at Las Salinas, some thirteen miles north of San Carlos, where the Salinas River meets the ocean. But all of these animals grazed and took water throughout the area surrounding the mission, even as far south as San Francisquito Springs, above what is now Robinson Canyon and the original site of the Indian village Echilat. See Sarría and Abella, Jan. 22, 1828, Monterey, trans. in Engelhardt, *Mission San Carlos Borromeo,* 167–170.

and mares, and its outlying ranches counted some 3,000 sheep and 1,500 head of cattle. The mission orchard produced pears, apples, peaches, and olives. Of physical structures, there were storerooms, a mill, a bakery, and a granary. The carpentry shop remained equipped with hatchets, hammers, and planes. The tannery had its vats and some 35 deerskins. And the blacksmith's works held bellows, anvils, hammers, files, borers, and bevels. There were oxen and plows to till the fields, sickles to cut the grain, and wagons to bring in the harvest. There were even some 77 shearing scissors, 21 pairs of wool cards, and 132 fanegas of uncleaned wool. Yet most of these workshops stood empty, and their tools remained idle.[32]

By secularization, disease and emancipation had left few people to toil in workshops and fields, shear sheep, clean wool, or tend the mission's animals. In San Carlos's final years, especially after 1826, as Indians left, harvests from mission fields grew increasingly irregular. In 1827, 1829, and 1831, Indians brought in just 3.1, 2.0, and 2.3 fanegas per person, far below the average of 3.6 over the life of the mission. The population of San Carlos had peaked at 876 in 1795, and then it declined steadily, falling on average between 3 and 5 percent per year. The decreases would have been more pronounced had not a final 43 villagers from the adjacent area joined the mission in the early 1800s. By 1833, only about 220 Indians lived at San Carlos. The most skilled and independent had left or died. An untold number had never been born because of the sterility of many San Carlos residents. Of those at the mission, nearly half were under age twenty and a third were over forty, leaving just about two dozen men between the ages of twenty and thirty-nine. Too small to be an economically productive community, the mission had become a decaying congregation of families and dependents, an increasingly dilapidated place where people often competed with one another for food.[33]

INDIAN LAND TENURE IN THE ERA OF SECULARIZATION

The architects of the August 9, 1834, secularization plan intended the placement of Indians on small plots of land and the redistribution of millions of acres of "surplus" mission lands to men like themselves. This privatization of landholding in California proceeded at a dizzying pace during the 1830s and 1840s. In the Spanish period, fewer than thirty soldiers received usufruct rights to land; in

32. Réal and Gómez, inventory of San Carlos, Dec. 10, 1834, San Carlos, SBMAL.
33. The figures used to determine per capita agricultural production are from Engelhardt, *Mission San Carlos Borromeo,* 244. On the population of the mission in 1833, see "Padrón de los neófitos de esta misión de San Carlos." n.d., Taylor Coll., doc. 2353, HL.

the first decade of Mexican rule, fewer still gained title. But, after 1833, Mexican governors approved some seven hundred petitions for land, most after 1840. By the late 1830s, the governors of California had already given away nearly all the land near San Carlos, having been very generous to a select minority: fewer than twenty grantees collectively received more than ninety thousand acres in the Monterey area. This process was repeated throughout Alta California, and, by 1846, californios controlled virtually all the best land along the coast, the interior valleys near the sea, and the Napa and Sacramento valleys situated farther inland. Overall, some ten million acres of land, or 10 percent of the surface area of present-day California, had passed into private hands by the close of the Mexican period.[34] With that enormous transfer of landed wealth came an entirely new political structure. Under the new system, the Catholic Church was nearly powerless and the governors had to contend with the rise of a class of powerful landowners who could challenge their authority. During this great land giveaway, some Indians did secure ownership, but their holdings were dwarfed by those of the californios. Nevertheless, a new pattern of Indian land tenure emerged during the 1830s and 1840s, with ex-mission Indians on small holdings scattered among Mexican rancheros who often controlled vast expanses of territory. Despite the often meager size of the plots, these allotments gave Indians greater independence than they had since they began moving to San Carlos in the early 1770s.

Often, the only glimpse of Indian landholding during the Mexican period comes from documents produced decades later, when the United States required claimants to prove the legitimacy of their title before accepting it as valid under the law. For example, in 1859, when José Castro was trying to establish his ownership of the Rancho San José y Sur Chiquito, a narrow strip of land along the coast south of the mission, he produced testimony from Gil Sánchez, a

34. From 1784 to 1834, the governors confirmed some fifty-one land grants (Paul W. Gates, ed., *California Ranchos and Farms, 1846–1862* [Madison, Wis., 1967], 3). On the total number of land grants in Alta California, see Robert Glass Cleland, *The Cattle on a Thousand Hills: Southern California, 1850– 1880* (San Marino, Calif., 1969), 23; Weber, *Mexican Frontier*, 196; Francis, "An Economic and Social History of Mexican California," 478–483. Most grants issued during the Mexican period were for between ten thousand and twenty thousand acres, but some individuals or families, such as the Yorbas and the Castros, amassed several hundred thousand acres. For acreage granted and who got the best land, see Hornbeck, "Land Tenure and Rancho Expansion," *Journal of Historical Geography*, IV (1978), 383–388; Terry G. Jordan, *North American Cattle-Ranching Frontiers: Origins, Diffusion, and Differentiation* (Albuquerque, N.Mex., 1993), 166; Gates, *California Ranchos*, 7–9. At least sixty-six women— mostly single or widowed—received grants after 1821 (Lisbeth Haas, *Conquests and Historical Identities in California, 1769–1936* [Berkeley, Calif., 1995], 83). Although exact figures remain elusive, approximately one-third of all grants in the 1840s went to settlers with non-Spanish, mostly British or American, surnames (Weber, *Mexican Frontier*, 205–206, 350 n. 89). These ranchos were, on average, slightly larger than those granted to Mexicans. Most non-Hispanic immigrants came late to California and had to settle for less desirable property farther inland.

regidor at Monterey in the mid-1830s. Sánchez testified that the rancho "was given by myself, by order of the governor, to three Indians" from Mission San Carlos. According to Sánchez, these three unknown Indians cultivated the land for several years. Another claimed that, before 1844, the land in question was owned by an Indian woman. A woman's presence on the land could explain why Father José María del Reál of the mission stated dismissively in 1839 that the land was deserted and useless for cultivation. Hints of Indian landownership in the Monterey region surfaced during the inquiry into the title for the very small Rancho el Tucho, located along the banks of the Salinas River, several miles inland from Monterey Bay. In 1843, José Joaquín Buelna had declared that two Carmel Indians were granted land there in 1840. Apparently, though, soon there-after, one grantee had moved to Santa Cruz, the other to San Jose. Similarly, San Carlos Indians also seem to have been granted land they later abandoned on Rancho los Laureles, located east of the mission up the Carmel Valley. In all of these instances, Carmel Indians at some time held parts, if not all, of these ranchos, but the Indians' identities are lost, as are the circumstances of their use and abandonment of their land.[35]

Reconstruction of a portion of the Indian landownership in the Monterey region during the era of secularization suggests that, of the nearly three hundred Indians who lived at San Carlos in the mid-1820s, probably around one hundred received land in the vicinity of the mission or settled on land that was granted to a family member. Nearly all who acquired land during the Mexican period did so through two principal means: Indians who were acculturated and connected to Franciscan and Mexican officials petitioned for ranchos just like any other citizen; most neophytes, however, if they gained land at all, did so as a direct result of secularization, when mission administrators granted them parcels of land. There were meaningful differences between these processes. Indians who petitioned for land gained ownership and held title to it. They also generally received ranchos of hundreds, perhaps thousands, of acres. Those who received land during the allotment of mission lands gained far less: modest plots and no title.[36]

35. Testimony of Gil Sánchez, deposition of Florencio Serrano, both June 9, 1863, Rancho San José y Sur Chiquito, SDC 373, 132–134, 149, BL; José María del Reál, Feb. 7, 1839, Monterey, unclassified expediente, Rancho San José y Sur Chiquito, Spanish Archives (English trans.), III, 264, California State Archives, Sacramento (hereafter cited as CSA); José Joaquín Buelna, refugio, Dec. 1, 1843, Rancho el Tucho, SDC 300, reel 35, 38, HL.

36. That non-Indians received the overwhelming majority of land grants has obscured the fact that so many former mission Indians held or received title to land in the era of mission secularization. For some who did, see Monroy, *Thrown among Strangers*, 124–125; Haas, *Conquests and Historical Identities*, 53–56. San Juan Capistrano Indians received 9,775 varas in small plots in 1841 (Agustín Olvera, July 12, 1841, Los Angeles, Archives of California, C–A 33, 141, BL). Although most land did not go to Indians, the land that did generally went to a very select few. In 1838, Governor Alvarado gave Rancho Milpitas, which comprised more than 43,000 acres, to Ignacio Pastor of San Antonio (Augusta Fink, *Monterey*

All Indian property holders struggled against others who wanted their land or their livestock. Two californios in particular, José Antonio Romero and his son Mariano, repeatedly challenged the landholdings of San Carlos Indians after secularization. Why these men preyed so upon Indian landholders is unclear, but they obviously did not have the contacts necessary to gain legitimately the land they so desired. José Antonio Romero was an early administrator of the secularized mission who seems to have helped himself to mission cattle, horses, and sheep. Mariano Romero would serve as mayordomo and be denounced by San Carlos residents for cruelty. The Romeros' predatory behavior reveals many of the perils Indians faced during the era of secularization as they sought to negotiate new lives for themselves beyond the missions.[37]

Among the earliest San Carlos Indians granted land were those who gained emancipation in the late 1820s. Interestingly, the first San Carlos–affiliated Indian to achieve formal and state-sanctioned landownership in the Monterey region was a woman, Cristina Salgado. Her attempts to secure title to land north of San Carlos reveal a complicated process that a select group of Indians mastered. Born at San Luis Obispo in 1777, Salgado married Gaspar María Talatis, an Esselen from San Carlos, in 1819. She had been previously married. Her father and mother had come to San Luis Obispo from Mission San Borja in Baja California as part of a small group of acculturated Indian families who moved north with the Franciscans between 1769 and 1773. The padres intended that these transplanted Indians would help organize new missions. Salgado's parents would have brought a commitment to Catholicism, an understanding of Spanish, and a willingness to follow and assist the Franciscans. It seems quite likely, then, that Salgado herself was quite comfortable with Spaniards, Catholicism, and the workings of the colonial system.[38]

County: The Dramatic Story of Its Past [Santa Cruz, Calif., 1972], 77). At Santa Clara, more than 66,000 acres were distributed after secularization. Eight grants totaling 54,282 acres went to non-Indians, and just under 12,000 acres were given in three grants to a total of six mission Indians. Notably, in 1834, the population of Santa Clara mission stood at eight hundred. Of the Santa Clara Indians who did receive land, Lope Inigo, a former official, got 3,042 acres (Laurence H. Shoup and Randall T. Milliken, *Inigo of Rancho Posolmi: The Life and Times of a Mission Indian* [Novato, Calif., 1999], 110–113). In the Santa Barbara missions, only one man received a sizable grant; perhaps thirty received small plots to raise vegetables and grains (John R. Johnson, "The Chumash Indians after Secularization," in Howard Benoist and María Carolina Flores, eds., *The Spanish Missionary Heritage of the United States: Selected Papers and Commentaries from the November 1990 Quincentenary Symposium* [San Antonio, Tex., 1993], 143–164).

37. On José Antonio Romero's confiscating mission property, see Estévan de la Torre, "Reminiscencias, 1815–48," 38, BL. For Mariano Romero's baptism, see Santa Clara bapt. no. 4066. I thank Sheila Ruiz Harrell for calling this record to my attention.

38. For her birth, see San Luis Obispo bapt. no. 272, Nov. 3, 1777, San Luis Obispo de Tolasa, Baptisms, 1772–1821, LDS film no. 0913300. For her parents' movement to Alta California, see E. Moisés Coronado, *Descripción e inventarios de las misiónes de Baja California, 1773* (Palma de Mallorca, 1987),

With the padres' permission, Salgado and Talatis left San Carlos soon after their marriage. Evidently, Talatis's skill as a carpenter and his Catholic faith, at least in the eyes of the Franciscans, had given the padres confidence that the couple could do well on their own. In 1825, they lived in the pueblo of San Jose. The following year, they moved to the Salinas Valley, first to the rancho known as Natividad, then farther west to Las Salinas, where the mission pastured sheep. After Talatis's death in 1827, Salgado remained at Las Salinas on land that became her own. In her final years, she showed a remarkable degree of industriousness, political savvy, and community involvement.[39]

In 1833, Salgado requested from Governor Figueroa title to the land upon which she resided, the Rincón de las Salinas, a rancho of 2,200 acres along the coast at the mouth of the Salinas River. The initial report on the merits of her petition pointed out that Salgado had devoted "great personal expense" to the improvement of the land. Through her efforts, but also, one suspects, through Talatis's, she had built a house and a small mill. Denying her petition would not only injure a "poor" widow, "respected" and "industrious," but would also "inconvenience the population of this capital who are supplied from the products of her industry." Clearly, she had developed her land in accordance with reigning Mexican liberal notions of economic progress and cultivated the political support necessary to secure and work a rancho.[40]

Figueroa granted provisional approval to her request and, as required by Mexican law, initiated another investigation, in which Salgado provided witnesses to support her petition. She called three respected californios, José de Jesús Vallejo, Simeón de Castro, and Ramón Amezquita, all of whom held various municipal posts in Monterey in the 1830s. Castro, a native of Santa Barbara, owned a rancho just to the north of the Rincón de las Salinas. So, too, did Vallejo, who might have known Salgado from her days in San Jose, his place of birth. All three offered supportive testimony, but Amezquita—also a native of San Jose—provided the most detailed description of her industriousness. Now a widow

215. Gaspar Talatis was baptized in 1790 at San Carlos at age eight (San Carlos bapt. no 1461, Jan. 6, 1790). For Salgado's marriage to Talatis, see San Carlos marr. no. 876, Apr. 24, 1819. Cristina Salgado is identified in the land records as Christina Delgado. Talatis's first wife, Casta Josefa, whom he married in 1796, had died in 1800 (San Carlos bapt. no. 2077, San Carlos marr. no. 534, and San Carlos bur. no. 1652).

39. Gaspar Talatis was a carpenter at the time of his marriage to Cristina Salgado (San Carlos marr. no. 876). For the padres' sense of Gaspar Talatis's religious convictions, see his death record (San Carlos bur. no. 2612). Talatis's burial record suggests that the couple moved to Las Salinas in 1826, but her petition for the land says they moved there in 1825 (Cristina Salgado, May 18, 1833, SDC 215, Rincón de las Salinas, reel 26, 10–11, HL).

40. José Avila and Pedro del Castillo, May 31, 1833, Monterey, SDC 215, Rincón de las Salinas, reel 26, 25–26, HL. The process through which individuals attained land is discussed in Becker, *Diseños of California Ranchos*, xiii–xv.

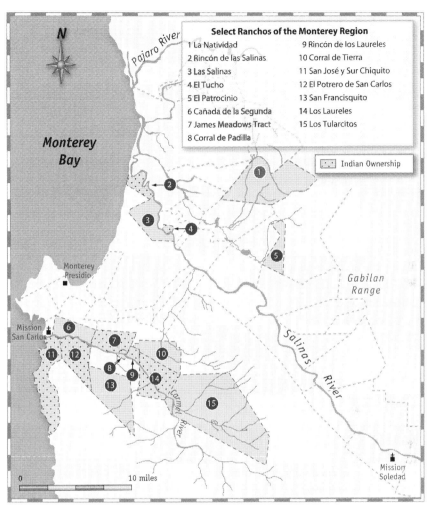

MAP 4. Ranchos and Indian Landholding in the Monterey Region, ca. 1833–1850. Drawn by Gerry Krieg. All boundaries and locations are approximate. *Sources:* SDC cases; Augusta Fink, *Monterey County: The Dramatic Story of Its Past* (Santa Cruz, Calif., 1972); Donald Thomas Clark, *Monterey County Place Names: A Geographical Dictionary* (Carmel Valley, Calif., 1991); "Lower Salinas Valley circa 1840," Miscellaneous Maps, Rarebook 458975, HL

with no children of her own, Cristina Salgado had raised four orphans, one of whom was a San Carlos Indian boy, Vicente Guajox, who was orphaned in 1818 at age two. Salgado ran a mill and now had two houses. She cultivated six hundred varas of land and grazed seventy head of cattle, twenty-five to thirty mares, and some tame horses. Most likely, Vicente Guajox helped her run this diversified rancho after Talatis's death. Figueroa approved the petition, and Salgado gained title by May 1834. A year later, she attained juridical possession of the Rincón de las Salinas. This was the means through which landowners formalized and made known to others the boundaries of their possessions. Recipients of land grants could gain juridical possession only after they had fulfilled any conditions set forth in the original grant and measured and demarcated the land's limits. Thus Salgado must have engaged a team of *cordeleros,* men who, on horseback, measured her property with cords some fifty varas in length.[41]

By 1836, the year of her sixtieth birthday, Salgado had been joined on her rancho by another widow from the ex-mission, María Bernarda Panna, whose husband had died in February 1835. María Bernarda Panna was forty-two years old and had come to the Rincón de las Salinas with seven children, four of whom were her own. On the Rincón, this mixed group apparently raised cattle for their hides and tallow. In the spring and early summer of 1844, Panna's son, Manuel, and Salgado registered, sold, and shipped from the port of Monterey hides carrying the "mark of señora Cristina." That same year, a decade after she had secured ownership of her land, Salgado sold it to Rafael Estrada, a caretaker of the Monterey customs house. Theirs was a transaction that solidified what might have been more than an economic partnership. For two hundred dollars, to be delivered in partial payments, Estrada was to take care of Salgado's small property while she retained the right "to remain in her house and [on her] rancho so long as she may live." Moreover, the contract between the two stated that "he will not molest her, but on the contrary that he will get along well with her." Apparently, Estrada moved to the Rincón before her death, built his own house on the property, and eventually brought his own family and cattle to the land. Cristina Salgado was unusual in holding her land so long and incorporating herself into the region's community and economy; no doubt all were of a piece, with landownership, economic integration, and ties to local officials all reinforcing one another and allowing this woman to achieve a remarkable level of economic independence. Clearly, though, as with all landholding ex-neophytes, her independence was made possible only by the support of others.[42]

41. Vicente de Avila Guajox, San Carlos bapt. no. 3010; "Padrón de los neófitos de esta misión de San Carlos," n.d., Taylor Coll., doc. 2353, HL; testimony of Ramón Amezquita, June 13, 1833, Monterey, SDC 215, Rincón de las Salinas, reel 26, 28–29, HL; Figueroa, Dec. 2, 1833, SDC 215, Rincón de las Salinas, reel 26, 21, HL. On her receipt of juridical possession, see deposition of David Spence, June 28, 1853, San Francisco, SDC 215, Rincón de las Salinas, reel 26, 5–8, HL. For cordeleros, see Becker, *Diseños of California Ranchos,* xiv–xvii.

42. For the residents of the rancho, see José Ramón Estrada, "Padrón general que manifiesta el número de havitantes que ecsisten en la municipalidad de Monterrey, 1836," Apr. 14, 1836, Vallejo Papers, LXXXVI, doc. 190, 35, BL (hereafter cited as "Monterey Census of 1836"); María Bernarda Panna, San Carlos bapt. no. 2204. Her husband, Luis Gonzaga: San Carlos bapt. no. 1761, San Carlos bur. no. 2882. Her children: Manuel, San Carlos bapt. no. 3464; Benito de Palermo, San Carlos bapt. no. 3609; María de Pilar, San Carlos bapt. no. 3143; Marcelino, San Carlos bapt. no. 3943. Account of hides

Most of the San Carlos men who acquired their own land did so after they distinguished themselves as political leaders at the mission and cultivated connections to missionaries and californios. Once they had land, though, they, too, struggled to prevent others from dispossessing them. A case in point is Baldomero José, who had served as regidor in 1815 and 1817 and alcalde in 1816 and 1819. Baldomero José had come to San Carlos with his parents in 1791 at age ten. He probably obtained his emancipation in the late 1820s or early 1830s; by 1832, he and his family were living in the town of Monterey. Like Gaspar María Talatis, Baldomero José did not acquire his land as an allotment after secularization. Just before the mission was secularized, he received as a "conditional loan" a plot measuring some two thousand square varas up the Carmel Valley, perhaps seven or eight miles from the mission. He petitioned for ownership after secularization, desiring the land "for his personal benefit" and his family. In March 1836, he secured title to this rancho, which by then was known as the Corral de Padilla. There, he raised crops and grazed his animals. But, just a year after he received title, he traveled to Monterey and told the town's alcalde, Estévan Munrás, that José Antonio Romero—the second secular administrator of the mission—was rustling and slaughtering cattle at a place known as Los Laureles, east of the Corral de Padilla. Almost certainly, Romero was stealing cattle from Baldomero José, too, but Baldomero José's lack of a registered brand rendered it impossible for him to make that charge stick.[43]

Romero had moved to Los Laureles with several others, including three Indian servants, Diego Onesimo of San Carlos, Arsenio, and Arsenio's wife. Baldomero José had long remained quiet about Romero's thievery. In his own words, "Since he was an Indian, he was afraid that Romero would kill him." In bringing charges against Romero, he gambled that Romero would not take revenge upon him and asked Munrás to keep his visit confidential. Munrás determined that Romero had no right to be in Los Laureles and that he had, in fact, been killing cattle bearing the marks of other rancheros, including Munrás himself. Romero denied the charges, but Munrás ordered him and his livestock out of the Carmel Valley. Any doubt of Romero's guilt was removed when the jailed Arsenio revealed that Romero had, in fact, killed stock bearing the brands of Munrás and Rafael Gómez, as well as some that carried no markings. Perhaps the unbranded cattle

registered at and shipped from the port of Monterey: Gabriel de la Torre, Feb. 10–June 1, 1844, Monterey Coll., doc. 383, entries for Mar. 14, Apr. 3, May 26, HL. On Estrada, see Salgado's sale of her land, Mar. 3, 1847, Monterey, SDC 215, Rincón de las Salinas, reel 26, 49–50, HL. See also deposition of David Spence, June 28, 1853, San Francisco, SDC 215, Rincón de las Salinas, reel 26, 5–8, HL.

43. Baldomero José, San Carlos bapt. no. 1572; José Aguila, "Padrón de las familias del cuartel número 1.o," Jan. 26, 1833, Monterey, Archives of Monterey, C–A 150, XII, reel 7, 732, BL; Nicolás Gutiérrez, Mar. 7, 1836, Monterey, SDC 160, Corral de Padilla, reel 20, 12, HL; Estévan Munrás, Mar. 10, 1837, Monterey, Archives of Monterey, C–A 150, II, reel 2, 649–657, BL.

belonged to Baldomero José. Baldomero José spoke Spanish and knew where to take his complaint and how to bide his time so as to maximize the chance that Mexican officials would act against Romero. He needed all those skills to protect himself and his property from destruction.[44]

Upon the death of Baldomero José, his widow, Beata Rosa, endeavored to hold the Corral de Padilla, and her struggle to do so demonstrates the connections between Indians and californios, the precariousness of Indians' positions through these relations, and the long shadow population pressures cast over surviving Mission San Carlos Indians, often forcing them to rely on others only distantly related to them. In January 1840, Mariano Romero petitioned for a rancho that would have been carved out of the Corral de Padilla. Apparently, Romero had been cultivating a corner of the Corral de Padilla for some time, and, upon Baldomero José's death, he tried to lay claim to the widow's portion, arguing that she was not using it and that he wished to graze his livestock on it. The governor rejected that plan, and, when Marcelino Escobar, a Mexican official, gave Romero the tough news, Romero became "haughty" and began to mutter what Escobar considered to be "foolish things." To protect Beata Rosa's property from future encroachment, Escobar then set out to formalize her land's boundaries. Representing the widow's interest in the measurement of the Corral de Padilla was Domingo de Guzmán, her seventeen-year-old godchild, who was a son of the alcalde Amadeo Yeucharom and one of the brothers of Onesimo Antonio. Documents in the land case referred to Domingo de Guzmán as Beata Rosa's son, but he was the son of her half sister, María Desamparados.[45] Making the story even more complicated, Guzmán's younger sister, María Cleofas, had married Mariano Romero. Thus Romero seemed to be trying to dispossess his wife's aunt and was being blocked by his brother-in-law. Seen another way, Beata Rosa was facing dispossession at the hands of her niece, and she turned to her nephew for protection.

Beata Rosa depended on Domingo de Guzmán because she had no choice. Her husband had been widowed four times at San Carlos. He had fathered five children; three died in infancy, one died in childhood, and one lived to his early teen years but was probably dead by the time of Beata Rosa's struggles. Beata Rosa's marriage to Baldomero José was her third. All were childless. Help and heirs to the Corral de Padilla, therefore, would have had to come from collat-

44. Diego Onesimo, San Carlos bapt. no. 3147; Arsenio José de Calasas, San Carlos bapt. no. 2821. Arsenio's wife was Ursula Hajäxom, San Carlos bapt. no. 2845. For Baldomero José's charges against Romero, see Estévan Munrás, Mar. 10, 1837, Monterey, Archives of Monterey, C–A 150, II, reel 2, 649–657, BL.

45. Beata Rosa, San Carlos bapt. no. 613; Marcelino Escobar, Jan. 9, 1840, San Carlos Pueblo, unclassified expediente, Rancho Palo Escrito, Spanish Archives (English trans.), VII, 368, CSA.

eral lines. But, between them both, they had only one surviving sibling—María Desamparados. Her first marriage yielded six children, at least two of whom died in childhood. A third, Toribio, was not counted in the 1836 census of the mission.[46] One of the survivors was Domingo de Guzmán, and it was this Domingo who acted as agent on behalf of his aunt and godmother in 1840 when the Corral de Padilla was measured, bounded, and clearly identified as Beata Rosa's. With the land thusly marked off, all of the Corral de Padilla was temporarily beyond Romero's reach. However, in March 1843, he succeeded in selling the Corral to Simeón de Castro for two hundred dollars, and somehow by 1850 he had ended up possessing some 711 acres on the rancho.[47] It is easy to see Romero as trying to deprive an Indian widow of her land, but, in ultimately acquiring 711 acres on the rancho, he gave his Indian wife access to land that would not otherwise have been hers. Also, perhaps, Romero was not so much taking advantage of the situation as helping his wife hang on to family land, given the tenuous standing of Indians and their property rights after the United States' takeover of California. The one deprived of land, however, must have been Domingo de Guzmán, who might have stood to inherit the Corral de Padilla after Beata Rosa's death, had Romero not sold it to Simeón de Castro.

Cristina Salgado and Baldomero José acquired their ranchos through their own petitions, not through the general allotment of mission lands. Securing their land involved letters and official inquiries and generated an extensive historical record. Such was the intent of the Colonization Act of 1824 and the supplemental

46. María Desamparados, San Carlos bapt. no. 1856; Domingo de Guzmán, San Carlos bapt. no. 3300. Baldomero José's San Carlos marriages: 539, 573, 706, 787, 960. Baldomero José's children: Clara de los Reyes, San Carlos bapt. no. 2686, San Carlos bur. no. 1815; Jacinto, San Carlos bapt. no. 2751, San Carlos bur. no. 1878; Ygnacio de Loyola, San Carlos bapt. no. 2960, San Carlos bur. no. 2137; Santiago, San Carlos bapt. no. 3203, San Carlos bur. no. 2352; Lucas, San Carlos bapt. no. 3325. Beata Rosa's San Carlos marriages: 505, 555, 960. María Desamparados's children: Toribio, San Carlos bapt. no. 2915; Firmina, San Carlos bapt. no. 3015, San Carlos bur. no. 2226; María Cleofas, San Carlos bapt. no. 3115; Pedro Martir, San Carlos bapt. no. 3488; Vicente Abaquilla, San Carlos bapt. no. 3746, San Carlos bur. no. 2912.

These complex family relationships confounded the priests who came to California during the period of secularization. Father José María del Reál arrived at San Carlos in 1834 and, in the marriage register, he confused the name of Mariano Romero's bride, María Cleofas, with that of her mother, María Desamparados (San Carlos marr. no. 1057 [June 6, 1834]).

47. William E. P. Hartnell, "Listing of Property of Citizens and Count of Those Qualifying for Poll Tax," June 14, 1850, Río del Carmelo, 473, Archives of the Monterey County Historical Society, Monterey, Calif. (hereafter cited as Hartnell, "Listing of Property"). In 1843, Romero had claimed to be acting as Beata Rosa's agent, and court records from the transaction refer to her as his aunt; but the legitimacy and motivations behind his sale of her land remain suspect (Mariano Romero, Mar. 15, 1842, SDC 160, Corral de Padilla, reel 20, 7, HL). In fact, it was the sketchiness of this deal that would later prevent Castro's descendants from having their claim to the Corral de Padilla ratified by the United States Land Claims Commission.

regulations of 1828. Without such a clear and incontrovertible record of their landownership, their land, or anyone else's, would have had little value, for it could not have been reasonably developed, sold, or transferred. But the lands allocated to Indians through secularization were of an entirely different status. The Secularization Act prevented Indians from selling or transferring their allotments, and thus Indians did not gain title or clear ownership. Mexican officials might have recorded the specifics of these land distributions, but not with the care that they devoted to documents generated during the granting of ranchos. What remains, then, are the outlines of policies pursued and small bits of evidence showing that San Carlos Indians did receive land through the Secularization Act. But who gained allotments cannot be fully determined.

Governor Figueroa's order that his decree granting land to Indian heads of household be applied to San Carlos was carried out in May 1835. Most likely, before Figueroa's death in late September 1835, secular administrators gave four hundred square varas of land to each of the Indian families at the mission. Donato, a blacksmith, received his plot of land at that time, on the southern bank of the Carmel River. But the details of other allotments are unclear. Officials in charge of secularization originally envisioned that most of these grants would be made from the lands just south and east of the mission, where animals had long grazed. José Joaquín Gómez, the first administrator of the ex-mission, argued that other lands need not be set aside for the Indians, because El Potrero de San Carlos, the pasture near the mission, was sufficient "on account of the great extent of that place and the small number" of Indians. After secularization, some Indians certainly got allotments on El Potrero, but to whom these grants went and how large they were is unclear. Beyond El Potrero, on the productive lands to the south of the mission along the coast and to the east in the Carmel Valley, many Indians did obtain small plots of land of around four hundred by four hundred varas. Although there is no record of Indians' obtaining lands in the Carmel Valley in the four miles immediately to the east of San Carlos, Indians apparently settled there on parcels set aside for them to sow crops and reap their "wealth." In 1839, Marcelino Escobar, the Mexican official who oversaw the ex-mission, unsuccessfully tried to protect them from a retired soldier, Lazaro Soto, who requested a grant comprising their lands. In spite of Escobar's appeal, Governor Juan Bautista de Alvarado (1836–1842) gave the lands immediately to the east of the mission to Soto, even though ex-mission Indians already cultivated them. Soto held these lands at least through 1850. Where the displaced Indians went is uncertain.[48]

48. On the implementation of Figueroa's order, see De la Torré, "Reminiscencias, 1815–1848," 36. Land to Donato: Gil Sánchez, July 18, 1841, Monterey, unclassified expediente, Spanish Archives (En-

Up the valley, east of the lands taken from Indians by Soto, at least sixteen families, two widowers, and two widows had better luck holding their assigned plots. They cultivated small fields along a narrow strip of land about three miles long and between a quarter- and a half-mile wide on both banks of the Carmel River. Together, they probably numbered between fifty and sixty Carmel Indians. Thus they constituted about one-quarter of the Children of Coyote who lived to see the end of San Carlos. Most of the men in whose name the plots were assigned had been at Carmel their whole lives, and all had been married. Of those born outside the mission, two came from villages in the Carmel Valley. How these people were assigned specific plots of land is unknown, but family members seem to have cultivated plots adjacent to one another. Sabas María farmed land next to his son Juan de Mata, and the brothers Bonaventura and Pasqual worked neighboring fields along the river. Some of these Indians had their own horses, as both Constancio and Romano Chaulis on occasion lent mounts to the local militia. Less clear is whether these Indians lived year-round on these plots or whether they continued to inhabit their adobes at the mission.[49]

At the end of the 1830s, Alvarado upheld their right of possession and recognized their claims as valid. When, in November 1839, none other than José Antonio Romero applied for a land grant that would have displaced these families, the governor said no, because ex-mission Indians occupied and worked the land. Given permission to restate his request in a manner less prejudicial toward the occupants, Romero quickly did so, submitting in support of his petition two *diseños* (sketch maps) showing the location of Indians who had settled near the lands he desired. One map depicts the individual plots of land along the Carmel

---

glish trans.), IV, 556–557, CSA; José Joaquín Gómez, Nov. 20, 1834, Monterey, SDC 3, Los Tularcitos, reel 1, 40, HL; Marcelino Escobar, Mar. 16, 1839, Monterey, SDC 356, Rancho Cañada de la Segunda, reel 43, 19–20, HL; Hartnell, "Listing of Property," June 14, 1850, Cañada de la Segunda, 475.

49. These *diseños* were submitted along with José Antonio Romero's land petition (see SDC 159, Meadows Tract, reel 20, 17–18, HL). The original diseños are in California Private Land Claims, complete expediente 193 (Meadows Tract), 2 sketch maps (diseños), RG 49, National Archives at College Park, College Park, Md. By matching names on the detailed diseño for the Meadows Tract with the census of the mission (Taylor Coll., doc. 2353, HL) and the information in my database, I conclude that the following men (bapt. nos. cited in parentheses) and their families had settled east of the mission on allotments received during secularization: Maximiano Joseph (540), Benjamin Joseph (961), Leandro Joseph (1070), Constancio Joseph (1161), Telesforo María (1694), Sabas María (1734), Landelino José (1779), Odorico Antonio (1919), Romano (2267), Ancelmo (2389), Gaudin (2453), Firmín (2784), Arsenio José de Calasani (2821), Juan de Mata (2871), Pasqual (2883), Hermenegildo (2990), Bonaventura (2998), and Macedonio (3005). The diseño also indicates land held by two unnamed widows and an "Alipio," who, most likely, was from Mission Soledad. On Indians and horses, see Marcelino Escobar, July 26, 1840, San Carlos, Archives of Monterey, C–A 150, IX, reel 9, doc. 1698, 907–909, BL, and Escobar to José María Villavicencio, July 28, 1840, San Carlos, ibid., doc. 1704, 931–933.

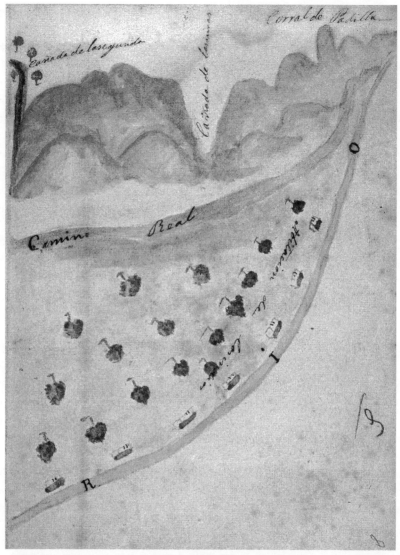

PLATE 23. *Diseño*, or sketch map, submitted by José Antonio Romero in support
of his petition for land in the Carmel Valley. 1839. These diseños were intended to
show the boundaries and key features of potential ranchos. Here, the Royal Road,
or the *Camino Real*, runs from left to right at the base of a set of hills. The Carmel
River is marked *R I O*. Along the river in the valley are houses constructed by
Indians (marked *Abitacion de los indios*) on plots of land they received
during mission secularization. Courtesy, National Archives at College
Park, College Park, Md.

River; the other is more representational, but it illustrates that Indians had built houses on their land by 1839.[50]

When Governor Alvarado assented to Romero's revised request in January 1840, he set as the southern boundary of the grant the lands cultivated by the Indians. Moreover, since Romero intended to graze 150 cattle, 70 horses, and 50 lambs on this land, the governor also inserted terms indemnifying Indians' property against damage by Romero's livestock; Indians could secure Romero's wayward stock until they had obtained adequate compensation. Each time Romero's original grant changed hands during the 1840s, its southern boundary was always the same: "the lands cultivated by the Indians." Indians held this strip of land well into the 1850s. In the summer of 1850, William E. P. Hartnell found fourteen Indians, one of whom was a woman, in possession of some 125 acres along the Carmel River.[51]

Whereas these Indian families made do with the small plots of land they gained during secularization, another San Carlos Indian, Fructuoso José, had so prospered on lands he had been allotted that he took action to increase his holdings. Born at the mission in 1785, Fructuoso José, like Baldomero José, had served as a mission official. He had received a small parcel of land in 1835 during secularization. Two years later, in October 1837, Fructuoso José told the governor that his 400 varas of enclosed land did not allow adequate pasturage for his increasing herd: he had five yoke of oxen, twelve cows, and eighteen horses. He petitioned for El Potrero—the pasture, just southeast of the mission, that had been parceled out to Indians such as Fructuoso José at the time of secularization. Now it was nearly vacant, having been abandoned by all but Fructuoso José. The governor granted these 4,307 acres to him, and, at that time, he had a small wooden house on his rancho, where he lived with his wife and possibly his three daughters, all of whom were married. By 1838, Fructuoso José had replaced his wooden house with one of adobe, increased his horse herd to twenty-five, acquired sheep and milk cows, and enclosed his land. Two years later, Fructuoso José received juridical possession of his rancho. On that day, in a sure sign of his awareness of the norms and expectations of Mexican laws and society, Fructuoso José measured and walked the boundaries of his rancho with Marcelino Escobar, the alcalde from San Carlos. Then, in an echo of the ritual Portolá carried out when he claimed Alta California for Spain, Fructuoso José would have pulled up

50. José Antonio Romero, Nov. 30, 1839, Monterey, SDC 159, Meadows Tract, reel 20, 7, HL. Denial of Romero's claim and invitation to resubmit: José Amesti, Dec. 10, 1839, San Carlos, ibid., 8–9; Alvarado, Dec. 30, 1839, ibid., 9.

51. José Antonio Romero, Nov. 30, 1839, ibid., 7; Alvarado, Jan. 7, 1840, ibid., 10–11; Hartnell, "Listing of Property," May 29, June 11, 1850, 470, 474. Quote: SDC 159, Meadows Tract, reel 20, 23–27, HL.

grass, scattered handfuls of earth, and broken branches, all to demonstrate that he was the "true lord" and "possessor" of El Potrero de San Carlos.[52]

Fructuoso José lived on El Potrero with his wife until his death in 1845 and, like Cristina Salgado, was involved in the hide-and-tallow trade. In 1835, he registered with the municipality of Monterey for the use of a cattle brand, thereby allowing him to differentiate his cattle and hides from those of others and permitting him and only him to sell hides he produced.[53] His widow, Hyginia María, worked the rancho until 1852, when she sold a portion of El Potrero to Joaquín Gutiérrez, an emigrant from Chile. Hyginia María, like Cristina Salgado, remained on the land in her own home, and Gutiérrez, like Rafael Estrada, agreed to take care of the woman he had purchased land from for "as long as she lived." She might have been joined on the land in 1850 by her eldest daughter, María Estefana, by then a widow, who retained some twenty-nine acres of the rancho.[54]

In 1853, Hyginia María and her two younger daughters sold more of the rancho's land to Gutiérrez. Soon thereafter, Gutiérrez was listed on the Monterey County tax roll as the owner of El Potrero and its more than 4,300 acres. Gutiérrez had property assessed at more than six thousand dollars: 4,347 acres of pasture, 100 acres of arable land, 2 houses, 200 head of wild cattle, 10 mares, 7 horses, and 1 yoke of bullocks.[55] Possibly around that time, Joaquín Gutiérrez married María Estefana. A decade later, when the United States challenged the validity of all land grants in California conferred during the Spanish and Mexican periods, Gutiérrez and María Estefana professed their ownership; remarkably, the land claims commission upheld it. Although Fructuoso José's daughter, through marriage and an awareness of both the Mexican and American land systems, had kept hold of the rancho, this family's private landholding marked a significant departure from the practices of their grandparents, who had held land communally in the days before the arrival of the missionaries and Spanish soldiers and then lost it in the eyes of the Spaniards when Portolá took possession of Monterey in 1770, and Mission San Carlos was founded soon thereafter.

52. Fructuoso José was baptized Fructuoso de Jesus (San Carlos bapt. no. 1048). For particulars of his land petition and his use of the Potrero, see SDC 333, El Potrero de San Carlos, reel 40, 4–57, HL. On California rituals of possession, see Becker, *Diseños of California Ranchos,* xv. Quotes from juridical possession of William E. P. Hartnell, witnessed by José Castro and Manuel Butrón, Dec. 18, 1834. See also SDC 254, Rancho el Alisal (el Patrocinio), reel 30, 39, HL.

53. José María Maldonado, Oct. 12, 1835, in "Libro de registro de fierros . . . , 1835–1836," in Archives of Monterey, C–A 150, XV, reel 15, doc. 3565, 242, BL.

54. Hyginia María, San Carlos bapt. no. 1700; María Estefana, San Carlos bapt. no. 2753; Hartnell, "Listing of Property," June 14, 1850, San Carlos, 476. On the 1852 sale, see SDC 333, Potrero de San Carlos, reel 40, 31, HL.

55. "Assessment List of Taxable Property in the County of Monterey, Year, 1852," 27 (corrected entry), Monterey County Historical Association, Salinas, Calif. For contract for 1853 sale, see SDC 333, Potrero de San Carlos, reel 40, 38, HL.

Although most San Carlos Indians settled on land they acquired through the petition process or secularization, a few secured ranchos of possibly thousands of acres through other avenues. By 1837, Agricio Joseph, an official at San Carlos in 1824, 1825, 1826, and 1831, and Neomesia, his wife of three decades, had built a house and established a farm on land previously held by the mission, some six or seven miles to its east up the Carmel Valley, on what became known as Rincón de los Laureles. Seemingly, they merely settled on the ex-mission land before they had official permission to do so. Although Agricio Joseph did not hold a deed for his land, he had secured written assurances from officials in Monterey that the land was, in fact, his. He was recognized as the legitimate owner of the land, for, when two californios petitioned for the lands east of Agricio, known as Los Laureles, the diseño they submitted identified the western boundary as the Rincón del Neófito Agricio.[56]

In March 1839, however, Agricio Joseph's hold on his homestead was imperiled by José Antonio Romero himself, who petitioned for a grant encompassing his settlement. Agricio Joseph's use of the land, his general good conduct, and his ongoing responsibilities as alcalde at the ex-mission led Mexican officials to initially deny Romero, but they eventually granted him another parcel of land that came very close to overlapping Agricio Joseph's. They did so on the condition that Romero not impinge upon Agricio Joseph's land and use of it.[57]

Romero seems not to have bothered Agricio Joseph, for doing so surely would have cost him his own land, and he hired several Indians to help him run his fledgling rancho. But, before long, his old ways got him into serious trouble. Quirino, one of the Indians in his employ, accused him of stealing cattle, just as Baldomero José had, and Diego Onesimo of San Carlos substantiated the charge. Apparently, Romero had stolen six old horses and fed them to his dogs. Found guilty of the additional crime of cattle rustling, on July 30, 1841, Romero was banished for a year to the Santa Barbara Presidio.[58] Clearly, for years, Romero had been a thorn in the side of many San Carlos Indians. But, just as Indians' landholding often depended on ties to californios, the fortunes of californios like Romero often were determined by their relations with Indians. Romero never

56. Agricio Joseph, San Carlos bapt. no. 2004; Neomesia, San Carlos bapt. no. 1551; José Antonio Romero to prefect of 1st District, Apr. 17, 1839, Archives of Monterey, C–A 150, IX, reel 8, doc. 1463, 117, BL; José Castro to Romero, Apr. 9, 1839, Archives of Monterey, C–A 150, IX, reel 8, doc. 1465, 125–128, BL. For the diseño, see SDC 240, reel 28, 54, HL.

57. José Antonio Romero to governor, Mar. 3, 1839, Archives of Monterey, C–A 150, IX, reel 8, doc. 1460, 113, BL; Marcelino Escobar, Mar. 16, 1839, ibid., doc. 1461, 114. The boundaries were poorly identified, roughly between the Corral de Padilla, the Carmel River, and Los Laureles. The crude map that accompanied Castro's document granting Romero the land gave only a rough approximation of the land's boundaries. See ibid., doc. 1466, 132.

58. "Información sumaria contra José Antonio Romero por abigeato, 1841," Archives of Monterey, C–A 150, III, reel 3, 276–306, BL.

seems to have had difficulty finding Indians to work for him. But those very same Indians, and others he troubled, complicated his acquisition of land and exposed his criminality with an eye toward bringing him down.

Agricio Joseph might have breathed a sigh of relief after the banishment of Romero, but his troubles continued. In 1844, he complained to Mexican officials that two of his neighbors, José Manuel Boronda and Blas Martínez, had "intruded" on his land. Apparently, Agricio Joseph had earlier received a document granting him the land, but he had lost it and needed another document to prove to Boronda and Martínez that the land was truly his. Agricio Joseph explained that he had put the property to good use and needed it for his family: "I am a poor Indian supporting myself of my personal labor tanning hides and skins, making my sowing for the subsistence of my family, for I have already grandchildren."[59] At the time, he lived with his wife Neomesia and most likely their two sons, a daughter-in-law, and four grandchildren. He and Neomesia had had ten children together at Mission San Carlos, but only two survived childhood. By his own account, Agricio Joseph had ventured into the profitable hide-and-tallow trade that had largely become the economy of Mexican California. Having demonstrated his use of the land, Agricio Joseph gained title to his 718 acres in March 1844 but with the provision that he could never sell or transfer it to another. A year later, Agricio Joseph sold the Rincón de los Laureles to José María Escobar for "two tame milk cows with their calves, one domesticated horse, a gun and thirty dollars." Why he did so is unclear, but Agricio Joseph had traded his land for what amounted to food, income, transportation, protection, and cash. He had also secured for himself and his family a good deal. Five years later, a parcel of land nearly five times greater had sold for less per acre, or a total of eight horses, one mare, and six milk cows and calves. Where Neomesia, the children, and the grandchildren went just after the land sale is not clear, but before long she was living on another parcel of land to the west down the Carmel Valley.[60]

Most Indians of the Monterey region sold or abandoned their land within a decade of receiving it. At least one family, however, purchased a rancho and then held it for many decades. In 1848, after the close of the Mexican period, María Loreta Onesimo and her English husband, James Meadows, bought more than 4,000 acres immediately west of Agricio Joseph's former rancho for $1,500.[61]

59. Agricio Joseph, Feb. 22, 1844, Monterey, SDC 187, Los Laureles, reel 23, 4, 12–13, HL. Agricio Joseph seems to have signed his petition himself.

60. For Agricio Joseph's sale of the rancho, see contract dated June 24, 1845, Monterey, SDC 187, Los Laureles, reel 23, 22, HL. Terms for the sale of part of Rancho los Laureles (Boronda) in Donald Thomas Clark, *Monterey County Place Names: A Geographical Dictionary* (Carmel Valley, Calif., 1991), 453.

61. James Meadows was born in England in 1817, came to California as a crewman on board the

María Loreta's grandfather, Amadeo Yeucharom, was among the first Indians at San Carlos; he attained baptism in 1774 and emancipation in the early 1830s. His son and María Loreta's father, Onesimo Antonio, was born at San Carlos in 1796. María Loreta Onesimo came into the world in 1817, the first of twelve children. She married Meadows in 1842, and, six years later, they bought approximately the same tract of land granted to José Antonio Romero in January 1840. In the intervening period, Romero had sold it to William Garner for some $700; Garner had passed it on to Thomas O. Larkin, who, in a little more than a year, sold it to Meadows. Before long, Meadows had placed on the rancho an adobe house with a thatched roof, sixty head of cattle, four bulls, fifteen mares, three mules, and a wagon. Impressively, he held cash reserves of some $8,000.[62] In 1853, Meadows petitioned the United States courts for ratification of his claim, and, in 1866, he won approval and was officially patented 4,592 acres of land in the heart of the Carmel Valley. On this land, which became known as the Meadows Tract, María Loreta lived for decades with her husband, children, father, and aged grandmother, long after all the other San Carlos Indians had seemingly sold or lost their lands. Together, this small group spoke their native language, told tales about mission life and before, and shared rituals and songs passed down from their ancestors. That the Onesimo clan survived to do so was in no small measure due to initiative and even luck, but also certainly to María Loreta's marriage to Meadows, a man who had what no Carmel Indians had: sufficient money to purchase a rancho and then the ability to hold it for decades. María Loreta Onesimo lived to 1900; James Meadows died in 1906.

The fragmentary but compelling record of Indian land tenure in the Monterey region during the 1820s, 1830s, and 1840s reveals the struggles of many San Carlos Indians who achieved, if only briefly, economic independence. Clearly, many who obtained land, such as Baldomero José and Agricio Joseph, were among those few who had established themselves as leaders or persons of authority in the mission's final years. They profited from the formal relationships they had created with Franciscans or californios who were now in a position to help them. Others who obtained and held land relied heavily on family networks, first to make the case that they needed acreage and then both to work the land that they gained and to hold on to it over time. For some women—María Loreta Onesimo, María Cleofas, and María Estefana—marriage to non-Indians sealed their owner-

whaling ship *Indian,* and jumped ship in Monterey in 1837. He was exiled to San Blas in 1840–1841 as a result of his political activities but returned to Monterey in 1842, and in that year he married María Loreta Onesimo (Clark, *Monterey County Place Names,* 305). Record of the marriage in the San Carlos book of marriages has not been found.

62. Hartnell, "Listing of Property," June 13, 1851, Monterey, 434.

PLATE 24. James Meadows. Photo by C. W. J. Johnson. ca. 1881-1885. Monterey.
Johnson Collection, HP 1136, California History Room Archives, Monterey
Public Library, Monterey, Calif.

ship. But, in so many other instances, relations with non-Indians, such as José
Antonio Romero, proved only a hindrance. Nevertheless, Mexican officials during the era of secularization typically upheld the rights of emancipated Indians to
hold land, and Indians understood and pursued their rights as citizens to the best
of their abilities. In so doing, they succeeded in ways unimaginable to missionaries who had so resisted secularization and had argued that Indians could not
survive without Franciscan guardianship.

Carmel Indian landowners' achievements in securing property and incorporating themselves into the local economy were to a large degree made possible

by the tragedy that so few survived to see the dissolution of San Carlos and the privatization of its lands. Simply put, there seems to have been enough vacant territory to accommodate the small number of Carmel Indians who qualified for land under secularization or petitioned for it on their own. Providing Carmel Indians with lands might have caused problems for José Antonio Romero and his son Mariano, but the aspirations of most Monterey californios certainly were not frustrated by the needs of so few Indians. Elsewhere, though, at missions that had populations of more than 1,000 in 1834, such as San Diego (1,382), San Gabriel (1,323), Santa Clara (1,108), San Jose (1,795), and San Luis Rey (2,848), far more ex-mission Indians endured poverty, homelessness, and landlessness during and after secularization. Some resorted to petty crimes or stole cattle or horses from ranchos to feed themselves or gain cash to purchase what they could not live without. Many of the rancheros of the Monterey region, in fact, increasingly felt besieged by Indian raiders, some of whom came from the more populous missions of southern California as well as California's interior valleys. A number of Indians from larger missions also plotted rebellions to reclaim mission lands or to protest what they took to be the despoliation of their resources. Such was the case in the pueblo of San Jose, where displaced Indians, driven by hunger and growing desperation, tried in 1842 to organize an attack to regain access to mission lands. Most landless Indians, though, had no choice but to move to distant towns like Monterey or Los Angeles or to settle on remote ranchos, where they competed with others for work and a meager subsistence.[63]

INDIANS AT SAN CARLOS AFTER SECULARIZATION

Indians who obtained land were the most fortunate of those who lived through mission secularization; they had the skills and connections to make the most out of the new order, and they secured a degree of independence previously unknown to them in the missions. But not all Indians left San Carlos for lands outside of it. Many stayed behind, perhaps even after they had been allotted land, and tried to ride out this period of transformation. Around them, the mission declined and its buildings decayed, with settlers and citizens from Monterey scavenging for materials. The ruination accelerated in 1835, when thousands of tiles were first taken from the mission for the roof of the town hall in Monterey.

63. For the plans of the San Jose Indians, see "Informaciónes contra los indígenas de San José," Archives of Monterey, C–A 150, III, reel 3, 471–505, BL. On Indian horse thieves, see George Harwood Phillips, *Indians and Intruders in Central California, 1769–1848* (Norman, Okla., 1993), 109– 116, 130– 150, 158–165. See also Sylvia M. Broadbent, "Conflict at Monterey: Indian Horse Raiding, 1820–1850," *Journal of California Anthropology*, I (1974), 86–101.

The declining importance to Mexican officials of the mission itself and the Indians it had served, as well as the increasing attention the Catholic Church now granted to the gente de razón of Monterey, were underscored by the dedication of a *campo santo*, or burial ground, at the Monterey Presidio on July 31, 1839. Henceforth, Catholic interments would be performed only at the town's cemetery and not at the mission. Similarly, after the summer of 1839, nearly all baptisms and sacraments occurred in the chapel of Monterey. It was around this time, too, that the ex-mission's resident priest moved to town, leaving no doubt that the days of the Indians' formal religious indoctrination and Catholic supervision were over.[64]

Indians who remained at the mission disappear from view, except at moments of crisis. On occasion, fights broke out at San Carlos while men gambled and drank. One night in 1836, the Indian Estevan was mortally wounded after he had had too much *aguardiente* and had broken up a game of chance. If the killing itself was shocking, so, too, was the identity of the assailant: town council regidor Gil Sánchez stood accused of the crime. Apparently, Sánchez had gone to the mission for drinks and a game of monte, as he often did. There, he had attacked Estevan, hitting him in the head with a bone. Sánchez's absence undermined the trial, and no record of its resolution exists. That he could be a brutal man is not in doubt, for, in 1842, he was found guilty of killing another man. Although violent and disorderly episodes such as Estevan's murder suggest that residents of the ex-mission were at risk and under stress, the very presence of alcohol and open gambling reveals just how much the site had changed. For better or worse, it had become a meeting place where Indians and californios socialized, gambled, and drank, all activities that the padres had tried to prevent.[65]

It was perhaps this new openness that led to San Carlos's brief population increase in the years just after secularization. Clearly, though, the mission's resources had become too limited to support those who lived there. In March 1839, the mayordomo, Mariano Romero, counted 321 people, 55 of whom were gente de razón. Food shortages led some Indians to pool their supplies and even pilfer wheat from communal stores. In 1835, José Josesillo broke into the granary and stole several bushels. The theft seems to have been committed by him alone, but his whole extended family was soon implicated, and their close and confusing relations—as well as their custom of sharing and storing food together—made

64. Removal of tiles: George Allen, "Account of Receipts and Disbursements [of the Monterey Municipal Funds]," January–December 1835 and 1836, Monterey Coll., MR 41 and MR 43, box 2, HL; José María del Reál, July 31, 1839, note after San Carlos bur. no. 2206.

65. "Causa seguida en averiguación de la muerte del neófito Estevan del pueblo de San Carlos," 1836, Archives of Monterey, C–A 150, II, reel 2, 554, 571, BL. On Sánchez's violent acts, see Bancroft, *History of California*, IV, 653–663.

solving the case nearly impossible. As José Antonio Romero, who was charged with investigating the theft, stated about the Indians who had given accounts of the crime: "The Indian alcalde Romano [Chaulis] is the son-in-law of José [Josesillo], who committed the crime, Sabas [María] the shepherd is the father of Vicenta, wife of the thief, and Vicenta is the mother of the alcalde's wife, Eulalia." Romero could only conclude: "Their kinship is common knowledge and notorious." Further complicating the matter was the close alliance of Romano Chaulis's family with the Onesimo clan, for, apparently, Onesimo Antonio's wife, María Ygnacia, was also keeping her wheat in the same large container that the wives of Romano Chaulis and José Josesillo were. The Onesimo clan's seeming ubiquity emerged out of the fact that Onesimo Antonio had eleven siblings, and he himself would father twelve children of his own at San Carlos. These complicated webs of kinship might have been notorious and frustrating to men like Romero, but they help explain how and why certain Indians survived the dissolution of the mission and later established themselves in the Monterey countryside.[66]

Faced with declining circumstances, Indians did not hesitate to take their complaints about the management of the ex-mission directly to the seat of government in Monterey. In 1834, elected officials Guillermo Mentico and Martín Linquis, along with three others, asked for the removal of Mariano Romero, claiming that he had beaten them and several pregnant women and that he had prevented them from their customary gathering of leftover grain after the threshing. Romero was only rebuked and told he did not have the authority to punish Indians. In the summer of 1840, others at San Carlos complained daily to the Mexican alcalde in Monterey about the gente de razon's use of their land. And, that fall, they protested the surveying of the mission's dwindling lands, leading the government to suspend the activity and thereby temporarily preventing the granting of mission lands to non-Indians. But encroachment probably continued, for, by the summer of 1840, the mission was home to only twenty Indian families.[67]

Within a few years of the Indians' final attempts to protect their resources, San Carlos was almost completely abandoned and its buildings in shambles. In the 1840s, an epidemic of smallpox thinned the ranks of local Indians, many of whom

---

66. "Criminal contra el indio Josesillo (el carpintero) por roba de semillas en la misión del Carmelo," Archives of Monterey, C–A 150, II, reel 2, 63–76, BL. José Josesillo was baptized Juan José (San Carlos bapt. no. 2347). See also María Ygnacia, San Carlos bapt. no. 2323.

67. Guillermo Mentico, Martín, Anselmo, Juan de Mata, and Valentín, July 21, and Manuel Jimeno Casarin, July 22, 1834, Monterey, Archives of California, C–A 39, 39–41, BL; Marcelino Escobar, July 26, José María Villavicencio, Aug. 14, and José Z. Fernández, Nov. 10, 1840, all in Archives of Monterey, C–A 150, IX, reel 9, docs. 1698, 1822, and 1824, 907–909, 1296–1297, 1302, BL.

had frequented the mission, and the arrival of numerous Anglo-Americans in Monterey heralded the ascent of legal and racist pressures against Indians and their places of congregation. Romano Chaulis and his extended family stayed at or around San Carlos through at least 1850, even though he had been allotted land in the Carmel Valley during secularization. Romano Chaulis had served as an official at the mission in 1830 and 1831, and, in 1835, he was elected alcalde for the Indian community living at the site. In 1844, the Monterey municipal government appointed him *juez de campo* for the lands neighboring San Carlos. His responsibility seems to have been to report cattle rustling to the authorities in Monterey. In the spring of 1852, Romano Chaulis, who was at that time fifty-four years old, was working as a day laborer for David Jacks, a Scotsman, who was attempting to grow beans, barley, and potatoes on several acres of land he had purchased in the Carmel Valley. By then, Chaulis and his family had left the mission and might have been living with his son Juan Bautista and his wife's eighty-eight-year-old grandfather, Sabas María. All were identified in the 1852 California census as living on the James Meadows Tract, most likely in the vicinity of the plot of land Sabas María himself had received during secularization. Also living on the Meadows Tract in 1852 were María Loreta's father, Onesimo Antonio, his son Diego Onesimo (the young man who had helped to reveal José Antonio Romero's thievery), and Onesimo Antonio's mother-in-law, Lupicina Francisca Unegte, who was by then eighty years old. Seven other Indians—all under age seventeen— lived on the Meadows Tract. The mission seems to have come apart and been abandoned completely by the early 1850s, but this family cluster had remained intact elsewhere on lands owned by María Loreta Onesimo and James Meadows.[68]

INDIANS IN MONTEREY DURING THE ERA OF SECULARIZATION

As discussed earlier, from the first decade of Spanish settlement in Alta California, Indians had found work in a variety of capacities for the soldiers and settlers of California's presidios and towns. This Indian labor often had been informal and furtive, since the Franciscans did their utmost to keep the baptized in the missions

68. Romano Chaulis's son: Juan Bautista, San Carlos bapt. no. 3509. Onesimo Antonio's mother-in-law: Lupicina Francisca Unegte, San Carlos bapt. no. 1725. For a sense of the mission as it neared ruin, see Abel Du Petit-Thouars, *Voyage autour du monde sur la frégate la Vénus, pendant les années 1836–1839* (Paris, 1840–1855), relation 2, 116–121. On Romano Chaulis as juez de campo: testimony of Romano, in "Criminal contra el indio Josesillo," Archives of Monterey, C–A 150, II, reel 2, 63–76, BL. See also "Libro de actas," Jan. 3, 1844–Mar. 9, 1844 (passage cited is dated Jan. 9), Proceedings of the Monterey Ayuntamiento (hereafter cited as Monterey Ayuntamiento), Monterey Coll., MR 255, box 3, HL. On responsibilities of juez de campo, see José Fernández, Mar. 15, 1843, Archives of Monterey, C–A 150, XI, reel 11, doc. 2340, BL; cash book, 1852, David Jacks Coll., HL.

PLATE 25. *Harbor and City of Monterey, California 1842.* By H. E. ca. 1850. BANC PIC 1963.002:1473, The Bancroft Library, University of California, Berkeley

and far from the gente de razón. Upon Echeandía's emancipation decree in 1826, many Indians left the missions for the pueblos, as did an increasing number after the Secularization Act of 1834. By 1836, Monterey was home to approximately seven hundred people who lived in eighty-seven households and three military barracks. Soldiers, sixty-four of whom were posted at the presidio, formed the most common occupational group, but they comprised a declining percentage of the town's population. Twenty-nine heads of household declared they worked the land for a living, and a wide and growing assortment of artisans, among them carpenters, blacksmiths, painters, tailors, and shoemakers, plied their trades in the town. More than a dozen merchants—half were Anglo-Americans who had recently come to California—resided in the capital. A smaller group of lawyers, scribes, and civil administrators also worked in Monterey. About one-third of Monterey households had domestic servants, roughly three-fourths of whom were former mission Indians.[69]

The Monterey labor force became increasingly diverse during the 1830s, as Indian domestic servants worked alongside individuals from as far away as Boston, France, and Arabia. Of the eighty-one servants enumerated as living in the town in 1836, almost all were male, forty-one were Indians, and only six were from San Carlos. Indian servants worked for only the wealthiest families, and

69. "Monterey Census of 1836." This census contains ninety households, not including ranchos. I include here only population figures for the ranchos close to Monterey and Mission San Carlos, not those also included in the census but situated closer to Missions Santa Cruz, San Juan Bautista, or San Antonio.

nearly all lived with merchants. Lawyers, scribes, and civil servants also had domestic servants, but most were not Indian. Although Indian domestic servants were incorporated into their employers' households, their work was temporary. A comparison of the Monterey household census of 1836 with a more fragmentary one taken just three years earlier shows a nearly complete turnover of live-in Indian domestic servants in those few years. Doubtless, scores, if not hundreds, of additional Indians were not recorded on household census lists, for these men and women worked simply as day laborers in Monterey households and businesses. The ubiquity of these Indian laborers prompted some observers to claim that Indians did all the work in the town. This casual labor by Indians was a vital part of the economy of Monterey and a tested survival strategy for Indians. Anglo-American businessmen like John B. R. Cooper often mediated and facilitated the hiring and compensation of Indian laborers. The ledger of Cooper's general store includes entries for individuals, such as "Indian cook," "Esteban the Indian," and "Carlos the Indian." These men worked for other local merchants, such as Nathan Spear, but received credit for their labor at Cooper's store.[70]

By 1836, a small number of Indians from outside the region had set up independent households in Monterey. Most prominent among these was José Pacomio Pogui, who a dozen years earlier had led the Chumash in rebellion at Mission La Purísima. Banished from Santa Barbara for his crimes and having served out his punishment at the Monterey Presidio, he had settled in the town. José Pacomio was an extraordinary man: he first distinguished himself as a boy at La Purísima, and the Franciscans taught him to read and write. At age eighteen, missionaries apprenticed him to a Spanish carpenter, and, within four years, he had mastered the craft. When he chafed at Franciscan rule, he helped put together the most inclusive anticolonial rebellion in the history of the region, involving hundreds of Indians at several missions. A decade afterward, he was again a carpenter, living in Monterey with his wife and seven other Indians, at least three of whom were from the Santa Barbara region. José Pacomio also owned livestock, for he registered his own cattle brand with the municipality of Monterey. He seems to have taken an active and public role: in 1833, he was one of ten ciudadanos in town to respond to a call for an expedition against horse

70. For the 1833 census, see Archives of Monterey, C–A 150, VII, reel 7, docs. 720, 725, 673–678, 725–733, BL. When Richard Henry Dana, Jr., author of *Two Years before the Mast* (1840), visited Monterey in January 1835, he observed, "The Indians . . . do all the hard work, two or three being attached to the better house; and the poorest persons are able to keep one, at least, for they only have to feed them, and give them a small piece of coarse cloth and a belt for the men, and a coarse gown, without shoes or stockings, for the women" (80) (1869 ed.; rpt. New York, 1964). Cooper's ledger: John Walton, *Storied Land: Community and Memory in Monterey* (Berkeley, Calif., 2001), 71–72.

thieves preying on the region's ranchos. In 1836, he won appointment by the Monterey town council as a *comisario de policía*. And, in 1833, 1839, and possibly the intervening years, he voted in municipal elections. Of this public service, General Mariano Guadalupe Vallejo recalled that he acted with "judgement and perspicacity." José Pacomio's skill as a tradesman, his Spanish literacy, and his ties to Mexican officials help explain the arc of his life as he moved from outlawed resistance leader to accepted Mexican citizen. He pursued his rebellion and took advantage of his new rights with uncommon skill and vigor.[71]

Needless to say, many Indians who lived in Monterey, whether or not they were from San Carlos, frequented the mission in the years before and immediately after its secularization. Many did so, until its resident priest moved to Monterey, because they desired baptism for their children or the sacrament of marriage for themselves. Also, for years after secularization, San Carlos held the largest concentration of Indians in the area and remained a center of Indian activity. One San Carlos man who lived in Monterey but went often to the mission was José *el cantor*, who had gained his emancipation in 1831. José el cantor and his wife lived in town with a lawyer, Rafael Gómez, and his wife, Josefa Estrada. Literate, a mason, and a very fine singer and musician, he tutored the local Spanish children in Catholic songs. On more than one occasion, though, in the evenings and on weekends, he went back to the mission to meet other Indians and play games of chance. Returning to San Carlos, whether for licit or illicit activities, allowed Indians to recover—if only temporarily—some of the companionship and connections they lost when they moved to Monterey and became aggregated to families of the gente de razón.[72]

Unlike Monterey, Los Angeles had an Indian *pueblito* that quickly became home to hundreds of Indians freed and displaced by secularization. In 1830, fewer than 200 Gabrielinos lived in the town; in 1836, some 252 resided there; and, by 1844, the pueblo was home to at least 377 Indians. As in Monterey, many worked

71. Pacomio Pogui, La Purísima bapt. no. 1600, identified in Glenn J. Farris and John R. Johnson, *Prominent Indian Families at Mission La Purísima Concepción as Identified in Baptismal Marriage and Burial Records,* California Mission Studies Association Occasional Papers, no. 3 (California[?] 1999). Pacomio in Monterey: "Monterey Census of 1836," 15. His brand: doc. 3567, in "Libro de registro de fierros . . . , 1835–1836," in Archives of Monterey, C–A 150, XV, reel 15, 243, BL. Office holder: Monterey Ayuntamiento, Nov. 18, 23, 1833, Monterey Coll., MR 251, box 1, 93–97, HL; Libro borrador, Monterey Ayuntamiento, 1836, Jan. 5–Dec. 31, at Jan. 5, 1836 (5) and May 18, 1876 (45), Monterey Coll., MR 253, HL. Voter: Elections for deputados, Mar. 3, 1839, Archives of Monterey, C–A 150, IX, reel 8, 134–136, BL; Vallejo, "Recuerdos históricos," I, 290, C–D 17, BL (English trans.). For more details on Pacomio's life, see Mardith K. Schuetz-Miller, *Building and Builders in Hispanic California, 1769–1850* (Tucson, Ariz., 1994), 106–107.

72. Joaquín Castro to alcalde of San José, Aug. 1, 1831, Branciforte, Archives of San José, C–A 283, reel 5, 788, BL; "Monterey Census of 1836," 22; Alvarado, "Historia de California," I, C–D 1, 59.

as domestics for the gente de razón, but here their large numbers made them the object of increasingly oppressive and segregationist legislation. In January 1844, the Los Angeles town council ordered the arrest of "vagrant" Indians. A year later, municipal officials approved an ordinance proposing to prevent "dirty" Indians from hearing Mass with non-Indians. Town leaders then condemned the Indians' village as a center of gambling and drinking, and, in December 1845, they voted to move it across the river. Two years later, they intended to do away with the settlement altogether and prohibited "persons other than Indians," from taking part in the Indians' diversions and warned them not to "mingle" with Indians. Soon thereafter, though, the town council deemed it impractical to remove the native settlement but ordered the Indians to cease their gatherings by eleven at night and "to not allow any white people to mix with them." Subsequently, Indians could have "diversions" only if they requested a permit through their alcaldes, and any whites found present would incur a fine of twelve reales. Clearly, the Los Angeles town council was as concerned about the behavior of non-Indians as it was of Indians drawn to the pueblito, but the nature of the town's economy and its reliance upon Indian laborers dictated the steady intermingling of both groups after hours, just as had often happened during the Spanish period.[73]

INDIANS AND THE RANCHOS

Beyond Monterey and San Carlos, on the burgeoning ranchos carved out of mission lands, landless Indians who had worked in the missions' pastoral economy found employment and sometimes even a place to live. Ranchos themselves became pasturage for the large herds required for the hide-and-tallow trade; in all likelihood, California produced and exported more than six million hides and seven thousand tons of tallow between 1826 and 1847. Virtually all of this trade was orchestrated by New England–based merchant houses and made possible by Indian labor. Although the rise and fall of the trade owed much to Anglo-American entrepreneurs, recently emancipated Indians were crucial to the rancheros' production of these export goods. On the ranchos, former mission Indi-

73. For Indian labor in Los Angeles during this transitional period, see George Harwood Phillips, "Indians in Los Angeles, 1781–1875: Economic Integration, Social Disintegration," *Pacific Historical Review*, XLIX (1980), 427–451. The Indian population of Los Angeles is discussed in Steven W. Hackel, "Land, Labor, and Production: The Colonial Economy of Spanish and Mexican California," in Ramón A. Gutiérrez and Richard J. Orsi, eds., *Contested Eden: California before the Gold Rush* (Berkeley, Calif., 1998), 111–146, esp. 136. For legislation restricting Indians in Los Angeles, see Los Angeles Common Council Minutes, in Archives of the City of Los Angeles: Jan. 1, 1844, III, 165–166; Jan. 11, 1845, II, 760; Dec. 22, 1845, II, 854–855; Mar. 13, 1847, IV, 282–284; June 3, 1847, IV, 327–329; July 3, 1847, IV, 366–371.

ans performed the same basic tasks that had allowed the Franciscans to dominate the trade until 1834: they herded and slaughtered cattle, preserved hides, and rendered tallow.[74]

The demand for hides was greatest in the eastern United States, where manufacturers turned them into shoes and other leather products. Traders from Boston purchased the hides outright or, more commonly, bartered for them with a wide array of manufactured products, which they sold at three to four times their New England value. Shipped to Peru, tallow was made into soap and candles and then sold to silver miners. Tightening their monopoly on the trade, maritime traders encouraged rancheros to go deep into debt.[75] Anglo-American merchants like Thomas O. Larkin and Abel Stearns, who purchased hides and sold Boston goods from their stores in California, controlled a large portion of the trade. Once a fall in the price of hides on the Boston market rendered the trade unprofitable and the deterioration of relations between the United States and Mexico in the mid-1840s made Boston traders wary of sending their ships into California's waters, decisions in the eastern United States, not in central Mexico or in California, precipitated the collapse of the hide-and-tallow trade. By the time gold was discovered at Sutter's Mill in 1848, the heyday of the trade had already passed, and most remaining hide droghers quickly abandoned their ships for the goldfields.[76]

Only a handful of Indians worked on the smallest ranchos, but the largest employed hundreds of workers to raise and slaughter livestock and dozens more to attend to domestic chores. On these enormous ranchos, men and women often divided the labor by gender, with men in the fields and women in the adobes, where they sewed, washed, and cooked. But the slaughter of animals—like the harvest of crops at the missions—was an orchestrated activity that involved both men and women. General Mariano Guadalupe Vallejo described in graphic detail how skilled Indians rapidly slaughtered and processed cattle. Six mounted horsemen, knives in hand, rode at full speed and, with great skill, passing near a cow or a steer, "drove the point of a large knife into the spinal cord at the back of the neck." "The animal fell dead instantly," and the men "continued

74. On the very largest ranchos, Indian ranch hands usually lived in clusters of makeshift dwellings, where they continued to practice many elements of their culture. See Roberta S. Greenwood, "The California Ranchero: Fact and Fancy," in CC, I, 451–465. On hides and tallow produced in Mexican California and the role of American firms in the trade, see Francis, "Economic and Social History of Mexican California," 525–526, 532; Weber, *Mexican Frontier,* 138–139. The most important American firm, Bryant, Sturgis and Company, which exported some 500,000 hides from California between 1822 and 1842, is the focus of Adele Ogden, "Boston Hide Droghers along California Shores," *California Historical Society Quarterly,* VIII (1929), 289–305.

75. Ogden, "Boston Hide Droghers," *California Historical Society Quarterly,* VIII (1929), 302; Francis, "Economic and Social History of Mexican California," 524.

76. Ogden, "Boston Hide Droghers," *California Historical Society Quarterly,* VIII (1929), 299–300.

PLATE 26. *California Rancho Scene, Monterey.* By Alfred Sully. ca. 1849. In this watercolor, Sully shows *californios* as an elevated social class above the Indians, who work on the ground, butchering cattle or preparing food. Courtesy, Oakland Museum of California, Oakland Museum Kahn Collection

right on killing to right and left in this manner." Next came a dozen men who skinned the dead animals. Then the cutters butchered the carcasses, cutting the flesh "into pieces and strips for jerking." "The death parade was finally closed by a flock of Indian women who [were] provided with hampers of heavy tanned leather in which they gathered up the fat and tallow which they then rendered out in large iron kettles or copper vats." To Vallejo, these scenes of slaughter "presented to the eyes of the passerby a worse aspect than that presented by the field of Waterloo after the defeat of the dreaded and haughty guard of Napoleon I."[77]

During the earliest years of the secularization period, few Indians lived on the ranchos of the Monterey region, but no doubt as many as hundreds worked there. Probably typical of this sort of informal labor was that performed by

77. Vallejo, "Recuerdos históricos," IV, 81–82, C–D 20, BL (English trans.). For a discussion of Indian laborers on Mariano G. Vallejo's enormous Rancho Petaluma, see Stephen W. Silliman, *Lost Laborers in Colonial California: Native Americans and the Archaeology of Rancho Petaluma* (Tucson, Ariz., 2004). On the largest ranchos' laborers, see Tomás Almaguer, *Racial Fault Lines: The Historical Origins of White Supremacy in California* (Berkeley, Calif., 1994), 48–49. See also the firsthand description of rancho life in José del Carmen Lugo, "Life of a Rancher," *Historical Society of Southern California Quarterly,* XXXII (1950), 185–236.

Quirino of San Carlos. A skilled vaquero, he broke horses for the local gente de razón, apparently taking care of the animals until they were tame. In the mid-1830s, there were some fourteen private ranchos in the vicinity of Monterey. Of the 318 or so people on them, according to the 1836 census, about three dozen were Indian servants; californios who owned, operated, or lived on the ranchos made up the rest. The largest group of enumerated Indian servants—twelve in all—resided on William E. P. Hartnell's Rancho el Patrocinio. Six other neophytes from missions San Diego, San Fernando, and San Gabriel lived and worked on Hartnell's rancho as well. These young men, ages twelve to sixteen, were all students in Hartnell's fledgling and short-lived seminary. They studied alongside Pablo de la Guerra, Joaquín de la Torre, Rafael Estrada, José Suñol, and Salvador Osio, youths from leading californio families.[78]

Indian ranch hands rarely received cash for their services, and their informal work was poorly compensated. As throughout the colonial period, when both gentiles and neophytes had combined elements of their traditional subsistence economies with Spanish practices, Indian ranch hands participated in multiple economies. Most were involved in a complicated set of reciprocal obligations that scholars have variously described as "peonage," "seigneurialism," or "paternalism."[79] Laborers worked for basic supplies and a daily ration of food, which they supplemented themselves through their own vegetable gardens or any stray stock they could pilfer from herds. One San Carlos Indian, José Cupertino (son of Paulino Joseph Soletasay, the man who had been so optimistic the day the Spanish flag came down in Monterey), stood accused of stealing thirteen mules and a mare from the herd of Rafael Gómez, the employer of José el cantor. Although his guilt was in no way certain, he was sentenced to a month in public works for his knowledge of the crime.[80] Some ranch hands, like their own employers, accepted goods in advance of their labor and then found themselves bound until they had repaid their debt. Although by no means the dominant labor institution on the

78. Quirino, San Carlos bapt. no. 2993; testimony of Quirino, in "Información sumaria contra José Antonio Romero por abigeato, 1841," in Archives of Monterey, C–A 150, VIII, reel 3, 276–279, BL. For residents of Hartnell's rancho, see "Monterey Census of 1836," 31–32.

79. Numerous scholars have attempted to characterize the labor systems on the ranchos. Sherburne F. Cook and others have described the ranchos as a peonage system; see Cook, "The Indian versus the Spanish Mission," *Ibero-Americana*, XXI (1943), 1–194, esp. 51, rpt. in Cook, ed., *The Conflict between the California Indian and White Civilization* (Berkeley, Calif., 1976); Weber, *Mexican Frontier*, 211. Monroy concludes that the ranchos were "seigneurial" (*Thrown among Strangers*, 100–103), and Almaguer sees the Indian-rancho ties as "paternalism" (*Racial Fault Lines*, 49–50). Even though most scholars do not categorize labor relations on the ranchos as slavery, scholarship on Indian-ranchero relations owes much to the historiography on slave plantations, especially the work of Eugene D. Genovese.

80. José Cupertino, San Carlos bapt. no. 2965; accusation of Gómez, May 6, 1836, Archives of Monterey, C–A 150, II, reel 2, 524–535, BL; decision of Marcelino Escobar, May 9, 1836, Archives of Monterey, C–A 150, II, reel 2, 531, BL.

ranchos, enslavement of Indians who had been captured on punitive raids occurred on a few disreputable ranchos. Most rancheros, however, combined aspects of these different labor arrangements to ensure the availability and compliance of Indian workers. Few ranch owners became rich off the profits they derived from the Indians' labor, but most made enough money to acquire some of life's comforts, such as fine cloth, extravagant garments, and other luxury goods, and thereby further distinguish themselves from their workers as they sought to define themselves as an elevated social class.[81]

During the era of secularization, Indians faced uncertainties and hardships whether they stayed at the mission, cultivated their own land, or worked and lived in Monterey or on a rancho. But many seem to have done so with hopes for a better future once Mexico took control of the region, removing many of the oppressions of Spanish and Franciscan rule and opening up new opportunities for personal independence. Paulino Joseph Soletasay believed that greater liberties were afoot for Indians once the eagle rose and the lion fell. Gil Ricla, María Jacinta, Juan Santos, and others who initiated their own emancipation could feel within their grasp a better life marked by less suffering and greater economic independence. And Indian petitioners for land, such as Cristina Salgado, Baldomero José, Fructuoso José, and Agricio Joseph, all pursued ranchos because they could imagine independent lives for themselves and their families in the Monterey countryside. Yet, as is so often the situation in human history, paradoxes and disappointments abound. The Indians' move toward independence revealed their dependence upon others, their freedoms came within restraints, and their autonomy bred isolation. Whether it was in submitting appeals for their own emancipation or obtaining possession of their own land, Indians depended on others who were literate and connected to men of influence in the local Mexican government. If and when they achieved independence, limitations persisted. Agricio Joseph, for example, secured land and then defended it from encroachments by californios, but he could not even travel to nearby Mission San Juan Bautista without a written passport from local Mexican authorities.[82] Nor did he

81. Monroy, *Thrown among Strangers*, 136–138. On slavery on the ranchos, see Francis, "Economic and Social History of Mexican California," 505–509. The most thoroughly documented example of the variability of labor relations on the ranchos occurred on the periphery of Mexican California, in John A. Sutter's inland rancho, New Helvetia. See Albert L. Hurtado, *Indian Survival on the California Frontier* (New Haven, Conn., 1988), 55–71. For a comparative study of the variability of rancho labor relations, see Ricardo D. Salvatore, "Modes of Labor Control in Cattle-Ranching Economies: California, Southern Brazil, and Argentina, 1820–1860," *Journal of Economic History*, LI (1991), 441–451.

82. Marcelino Escobar, Apr. 12, 1839, Archives of Monterey, C–A 150, IX, reel 8, doc. 1488, 195, BL. The passport was granted to Agricio, Miguel, Bono José, Tiburcio, and "three of four others," so that they would not be impeded in their travels.

have the right to sell his own land. Once separated from the mission, many who lived in Monterey or its surrounding ranchos often felt the need to return; they valued the sacraments administered by church officials, and they missed the conversation, the games of chance, and the after-hours drinking of aguardiente common following secularization. Despite the drawbacks of their new lives, most Indians of the Monterey region by the early 1840s could probably look back on their struggles and the recent past and conclude that, for the first time in their lives, they had gained more than they had lost.

◀◀ ▶▶

EPILOGUE

The coming to California of missionaries, soldiers, and settlers, and the flood of plants, animals, microbes, and institutions they brought with them, ushered in dual revolutions that over decades and generations imperiled the Children of Coyote's culture and very existence. Eventually, Spanish colonial institutions gave way, and surviving Indians once again adjusted to their new surroundings as they reclaimed autonomy and independence during the era of secularization. Yet, for too many, that autonomy would prove short-lived, as Indians were forced to confront new calamities in the mid-1840s. They suffered terribly as smallpox ravaged the Monterey region in 1844. Their political and civil rights and sense that society could accommodate them were increasingly undermined at the beginning of the Mexican-American War (1846–1848), when the United States seized California. And Indians' economic futures grew increasingly uncertain as city dwellers and ranch owners headed to the goldfields, then returned as the Monterey region developed local industries and grew as a center of commerce and trade. By the early 1850s, more than 2,600 residents lived in Monterey, about one-fourth of whom were Indian. In search of work as vaqueros, farmhands, or domestic servants, most had come from the secularized missions of the south or the interior valleys of the east. A small, unknown number of San Carlos Indians, probably fewer than two hundred, survived at midcentury. Among these were a handful who lived extremely long lives, almost, one can imagine, in defiance of the crippling mortality that had cut short the lives of so many of their children, siblings, spouses, and parents. They would persevere and provide the Children of Coyote with a bridge to the future and a memory of the past.[1]

1. Population of Monterey: "Inhabitants in the County of Monterey," 1852 California special census, schedule 1, film 73/03, roll 2, 59, microfilm, BL.

VIRUELAS

After secularization, Indians endeavored to carve out independent lives but remained powerless to combat diseases that undermined their survival. Smallpox
had attacked California in the 1830s and earlier but spared Monterey and Mission
San Carlos until 1844. The epidemic of that year might have been the most deadly
of California's historic period. The contagion was carried to the region by ship
and apparently spread to the town through the crew's soiled laundry. Through
the late spring and summer, the plague afflicted Indians and gente de razón. A
minimum of 125 of the town's residents died, at least 85 of whom were Indian. As
many as hundreds more succumbed without their deaths' being recorded in local
Catholic Church records. In June and July, a day hardly passed without another
burial in Monterey's campo santo.[2]

Ironically, the recorded deaths and burials of so many in such a brief time
reveal the diverse origins of Indians in Monterey by the mid-1840s. At least eight
of the epidemic's victims were from San Carlos. Among these was Bernarda,
younger sister of María Loreta Onesimo, the woman who in 1848 would purchase
a tract of land in the Carmel Valley with her husband, James Meadows. Five of the
dead had lived at nearby Mission Soledad. Landless and out of work, twenty
victims had come to Monterey from southern California, with eight emigrating
from Mission San Luis Rey alone. Four originated in Baja California. And nine
Indians from the interior valleys had only recently arrived in the town. The
largest number of those buried by church officials during the epidemic were
identified simply by name, not origin. Such were the exigencies of the time.[3]

Town leaders responded slowly to the epidemic, even though they saw its fury.
Thomas O. Larkin, the American consul in Monterey, wrote that, in mid-April,
an American settler, Joseph Harner, had died of smallpox in town. Larkin told
Harner's mother that, although her son was "of a stout and healthy frame, the

2. The source of the epidemic cannot be determined with certainty, but some pointed the finger at
United States consul Thomas O. Larkin. Apparently, the *California* had arrived from Mexico with the
disease. The men on board recovered, but "the contagion was carried in laundry sent by Consul
Thomas Larkin from the ship to the town of Monterey" (Sherburne F. Cook, "Smallpox in Spanish and
Mexican California, 1770–1845," *Bulletin of the History of Medicine,* VII [1939], 153–191, esp. 188). True
or not, Larkin did not dwell on this fact or the outbreak and its devastating effects on the Indians of
Monterey. Two years later, he wrote: "The Indians who were taught by the Spanish Padres the different
mechanical arts are now dead, and no more of their Tribe will ever take their places" ("Description of
California," Apr. 20, 1846, in George P. Hammond, ed., *The Larkin Papers: Personal, Business, and
Official Correspondence of Thomas Oliver Larkin, Merchant and United States Consul in California,* 11
vols. [Berkeley, Calif., 1951–1968], IV, 305).

3. In San Carlos bur. no. 4425, July 3, 1844, the padres identified Bernarda as the daughter of Onesimo
Antonio, but there is no corresponding baptism record for a Bernarda whose father was Onesimo
Antonio. Having moved from the mission, Catholic priests knew the Indians less well and even under
normal circumstances could confuse their names.

sickness soon took strong hold of him and gave us no hopes." Less than two weeks after Harner's death, Father José María del Reál buried María of Mission San Luis Rey, the first Indian victim said to have died of *viruelas*. Three weeks later, the disease claimed José Pacomio Pogui, the remarkable Chumash man. Not until late May, after the epidemic had already killed dozens, did the Monterey Board of Health draw up precautionary measures. Their first act was to rent the house of the recently deceased Pacomio for use as a hospital. Thirty-one town residents soon pledged some $250 per month to supply and staff the facility. The board of health also requested the services of five men to dispose of the dead and ordered the citizens to whitewash their houses.[4]

Some of the town's residents, perhaps afraid and desperate, showed no empathy for the Indians' sufferings. Three decades after the epidemic, Estévan de la Torre, who was a regidor in Monterey in 1844, bitterly recounted how the board of health came to respond to the outbreak:

> Before the establishment of the hospital many of the Indian domestic servants had gone away by night into the fields where presumably they succumbed without anyone helping them. I saw this with my own eyes in the case of an Indian whom I met on the street one night while I was on patrol with eight of my neighbors. . . . The Indian was in a ditch by a wall where he had been moved to get him out of the way. On hearing the groans I approached the place from which they proceeded. I asked him who was there. He replied that he was the cook of Mr. David Spence and was called Alejo. He said a cowboy had come from the ranch, taken him, and placed him in a cowhide, dragged him away, and thrown him in that ditch. After consulting with my companions, we wrapped him up in two of our blankets and had him brought to my own house, in which there was another Indian seriously stricken with smallpox. This was about midnight and the unlucky man died at four in the morning. I reported this to the *Ayuntamiento*, but since Mr. Spence and the other members were associates and friends, the affair had no serious consequences for him. As to the deceased, I had him taken to the cemetery and given burial. I made use of this occurrence to arouse sentiment in favor of doing something for these unfortunates and from this resulted the establishment of the hospital.

4. Thomas Oliver Larkin to Dolly Harner, Apr. 23, 1844, Monterey, in Hammond, ed., *Larkin Papers*, II, 105; San Carlos bur. nos. 4353, 4367; Junta de Sanidad, May 28, 1844, Monterey, Monterey Coll., MR 268, box 3, HL; Manuel Micheltorena et al., "Lista de subscriptores que subscribi mensualmente por la manutencion de un hospital in Monterey durante la presente enfermedad," May 31, 1844, in Hammond, ed., *Larkin Papers*, II, 132–133. Cook, "Smallpox in Spanish and Mexican California," *Bulletin of the History of Medicine*, VII (1939), 187–188, says that the epidemic began in Monterey in May.

The creation of the hospital perhaps reduced the spread of contagion and congregated the ill, but it would have done little to alleviate their suffering. The epidemic had claimed most of its victims by early July and run its course by October.[5]

The scourge cast a long shadow. It wiped out many who had so remarkably adapted to life first in the missions and then again beyond them, and it almost certainly killed or weakened those who had settled lands of their own after secularization. Those who survived found their ranks further thinned and their struggles magnified. The smallpox outbreak also affected those who had tended to the dying and buried the dead. For years afterward, church officials, when recording a death occasioned by neither disease nor violence, often noted that the individual had died a "natural death," a phrase not found in Monterey's burial records before the epidemic and a circumstance perhaps to be at once appreciated and mourned, especially since it so rarely characterized the final moments of Indians in the region after 1769.

U.S. RULE

Two years after they endured smallpox, Indians suffered a more lasting blow when the United States seized Monterey in July 1846. Thus began an interim period of United States military rule that ended in California's admission to the Union in September 1850. In the Treaty of Guadalupe Hidalgo (signed February 2, 1848, approved in May 1848), the United States took formal ownership of California and pledged to protect the rights and privileges of the region's Mexican citizens, a group that by then included Indians. But Anglo-American politicians in California had other ideas. Meeting in Monterey in 1849, the California Constitutional Convention denied Indians voting rights and requested their removal from the territory. The following year, the state legislature barred Indians from testifying in any case where a white person was a party. Refused citizenship and the right to sue or testify in a court of law, California Indians were rendered defenseless just as they were overrun by tens of thousands of Gold Rush settlers and fortune hunters. Despite their paternalistic, destructive policies, the Spanish and Mexican governments had felt an obligation to protect Indians and incorpo-

5. Alejo, an Indian from Santa Barbara, did cook for Spence. See José Ramón Estrada, "Padrón general que manifiesta el número de havitantes que ecsisten en la municipalidad de Monterrey, 1836," Apr. 14, 1836, Vallejo Papers, C–E 86, doc. 190, 19, BL. Estévan de la Torre quoted in Cook, "Smallpox in Spanish and Mexican California," *Bulletin of the History of Medicine,* VII (1939), 190–191 (emphasis added). San Carlos bur. no. 4469 (Oct. 3, 1844) is the last Carmel burial where the deceased was identified as dying of smallpox.

rate them into society. Mid-nineteenth-century Anglo-Americans labored under no such compulsion.[6]

The United States Congress, motivated by racism and exclusionism, authorized the president to negotiate treaties through which Indians would cede forever all land in California. Officials envisioned removing Indians from areas of white settlement and placing them on reserves, where ostensibly they would be given food, education, and protection from settlers. Spanish and Mexican policies toward Indians had been conceived by remote officials but implemented locally by missionaries or others working with individuals; by contrast, agents of United States policy in nineteenth-century California never directly engaged the overwhelming majority of California Indians. Three Indian agents were given the task of making treaties with all California Indians and then provided with only $25,000 to support their efforts. Knowing next to nothing about the diversity of Indian groups, negotiators produced a mere eighteen treaties carrying the marks of some 139 signatory groups. Hundreds of peoples were left out. Many of the signatories signed more than once, whereas others represented only villages or themselves. Most of the land set aside for Indians was in the foothills of the Sierras. Indians of Monterey were never party to any treaty negotiations with the United States, even though, under agreements signed by others, they would have relinquished all claims to their lands. It was the greed of settlers, however, not these absurdities, that doomed the treaties. In July 1852, the Senate refused to ratify the agreements, convinced by California politicians that they set aside too much land for Indians. Under this American system, in which Indians had no way to assert rights or landownership, the only Monterey Indians to retain access to land were those very few who had family ties to californios or Anglo-Americans.[7]

The refusal to ratify the treaties absolved the United States of any explicit obligations toward California Indians. Yet the federal government did recognize a moral and legal responsibility to protect native Americans and compensate them for lands illegally seized, and, through the mid-twentieth century, it established scores of reservations in California by executive order. None, however, covered the Monterey region. Given the attitudes of the federal government, state

6. On California laws' discrimination against Indians, see Robert F. Heizer and Alan J. Almquist, *The Other Californians: Prejudice and Discrimination under Spain, Mexico, and the United States to 1920* (Berkeley, Calif., 1971), 92–119.

7. For the men who negotiated the treaties and their contacts with Indians, see George Harwood Phillips, *Indians and Indian Agents: The Origins of the Reservation System in California, 1849–1852* (Norman, Okla., 1997), 68–182. On these treaties and the Senate's failure to ratify them, see Robert F. Heizer, "Treaties," in *HNAI*, VIII, 701–704; George E. Anderson, W. H. Ellison, and Robert F. Heizer, *Treaty Making and Treaty Rejection by the Federal Government in California, 1850–1852* (Socorro, N.Mex., 1978); Heizer, *The Eighteen Unratified Treaties of 1851–1852 between the California Indians and the United States Government* (Berkeley, Calif., 1972).

officials, and the hordes of gold seekers, it is not surprising that, under Anglo-American rule, Indians' circumstances deteriorated. In the area of the Mother Lode, Indians faced extermination; in the coastal regions, they were pushed aside or overrun. As one descendant from Mission San Carlos remembered: "The government never helped the Carmel people. . . . The American government[,] instead of caring for them like they cared for the other Indians in the other parts, seemed like it didn't know these Carmeleños existed." Most "scattered" and lived as the "most poor"; many fell victim to "vices and drinking."[8]

GENERATIONS TOGETHER AND RANCHERÍA DISPERSAL

Travelers to the Monterey region in the late 1840s and 1850s often noted the disappearance of visible reminders of California's Spanish period. Mission San Carlos itself continued to crumble, a casualty in more ways than one to expanding Monterey. After mission secularization, the town's residents scavenged the buildings and grounds for bricks, tiles, and timbers for their own houses and businesses. Nevertheless, into the 1850s, several Indian families still made San Carlos their home. Some lived in brush huts near the water and eked out a living taking in laundry from the town's residents. By the winter of 1852, the roof of the church had begun to collapse, and all remaining items of value were relocated to the presidio chapel in Monterey. At that point, Catholic religious services were limited to one annual mass, which was held on November 4, the feast of the mission's patron saint, San Carlos Borromeo. A decade later, geologist William H. Brewer found rubble and trash strewn about the church. Birds nested in its exposed eaves and a dead pig lay at the foot of the baptismal font.[9]

After 1848, when the mission had little to offer, the Onesimo clan settled on what would be known as the Meadows Tract. It was there that Neomesia had moved after her husband, Agricio Joseph, had sold the Rincón de los Laureles for cattle, a horse, a gun, and thirty dollars. Born at the mission in 1791, she had had ten children with Agricio Joseph. In the fate of those children, one can glimpse

8. On the implications of the treaties' nonratification, see Omer C. Stewart, "Litigation and Its Effects," in *HNAI*, VIII, 705–712. Isabel Meadows quoted in "Profile: Isabel Meadows," in Linda Yamane, ed., *A Gathering of Voices: The Native Peoples of the Central California Coast*, Santa Cruz County Historical Journal, no. 5 (Santa Cruz, Calif., 2002), 14 (hereafter cited as Yamane, ed., *A Gathering of Voices*).

9. William R. Garner, *Letters from California, 1846–1847*, ed. Donald Munro Craig (Berkeley, Calif., 1970), 98; Martin J. Morgado, *Junípero Serra's Legacy* (Pacific Grove, Calif., 1987), 112; Francis P. Farquhar, ed., *Up and Down California in 1860–1864: The Journal of William H. Brewer, Professor of Agriculture in the Sheffield Scientific School from 1864 to 1903* (1930; rpt. Berkeley, Calif., 1949), 2d ed., 106–107.

PLATE 27. Isabel Meadows, ca. 1865. From a daguerreotype. The occasion of this photograph is unknown. She was a young woman at the time she sat for it. Historic Photograph File, HP 1139, California History Room Archives, Monterey Public Library, Monterey, Calif.

the depth of California Indians' suffering under Spanish and Mexican rule. Seven of her offspring died in infancy or early childhood. One lived to age fourteen. Another, Macedonio, lived only long enough to secure a plot of land after the mission was secularized. The last surviving child, Sebastian, was hanged for murdering a Monterey merchant. With her own children gone, Neomesia devoted herself to a youngster in her midst: Isabel Meadows, daughter of María Loreta Onesimo and James Meadows and, eventually, the living repository of much of her people's culture and history. To Isabel Meadows, Neomesia was "Omesia." Born the same year the United States took Monterey, Isabel learned

Rumsen, the local Indian language, while absorbing the beliefs of her female ancestors, elements of which predated the Spanish period. Her accumulated knowledge and collected memories suggest just how much Indian culture was lost in the maelstrom of the mission and the Mexican and American periods— and how much miraculously survived. Her memories reveal a strong gender connection and a female genealogy stretching back to mission days. But her world seems to have been the world of the women around her, and the *mentalité* of the men of the Onesimo clan appears dimly, if at all, in her recollections.[10]

In 1872, the *Monterey Democrat* noted the death of Isabel Meadows's great-grandmother, "Lupecina, an Indian woman aged 116 years, a native of the peninsula between Monterey and Carmelo bays, living and dying within a short distance of the place of her birth. . . . 'Ancient of the days' she had been, ever since the American flag was hoisted at Monterey, she was herself constituted one of the chief relics of the bygone." Although something of a curiosity to local settlers, Lupicina Francisca Unegte connected Monterey Indians' past with their present. She was 100 years old at the time of her death (not 116), having been baptized in 1792 as a young adult, along with nearly eighty others who came to San Carlos from a village near the Salinas River. In the year of her baptism, more than eight hundred Indians lived at San Carlos. During her life, she and the world around her had been dramatically transformed, and certainly that transformation had begun during her childhood with the arrival of the Spaniards. Lupicina, long into her life, still practiced elements of a culture that predated the arrival of the Spanish. She attributed her longevity to something she had learned from her elders: with each new moon, she took an ember and burned a small cross into her hair. This was a practice she said those younger than she had mocked and disparaged but one that had allowed the "people of before" to live more than a hundred years.[11]

A decade after Lupicina Francisca Unegte's death, Helen Hunt Jackson, the American poet and novelist best known for *Ramona,* visited a settlement known as "the Indian hamlet up the Carmel Valley." In her book *Glimpses of California,* Jackson described a village hidden away, up a stream, that could be reached only by a narrow, hard-to-find path. Following the trail, Jackson eventually came to a "lovely spot,—half basin, half rocky knoll,—where, tucked away in nooks and hollows, are the little Indian houses, eight or ten of them, some of adobe, some of

10. Neomesia, San Carlos bapt. no. 1551; Felipe y Santiago, San Carlos bapt. no. 3613; Isabel Meadows, John P. Harrington Papers, reel 80, frames 342b (n.d.), 364b (October 1934), National Anthropological Archives, Smithsonian Institution, Washington, D.C.

11. *Monterey Democrat,* Dec. 21 (in *Sacramento Union,* 1872), in Stephen A. Dietz, Thomas L. Jackson, et al., *Final Report of Archaeological Excavations at Nineteen Archaeological Sites for the Stage 1 Pacific Grove–Monterey Consolidation Project of the Regional Sewerage System,* I (Berkeley, Calif., 1981), 120; Lupicina Francisca Unegte, San Carlos bapt. no. 1725, Feb. 17, 1792. Lupicina's recollections: Isabel Meadows, Harrington Papers, reel 80, frame 400a (April 1935).

tule reeds." The little houses were surrounded by small patches of "corn, barley, potatoes, and hay." The men were away cutting wood, farming, or fishing. This little village, a remnant group of Carmel Indians, raised crops to feed themselves and their animals and sold their labor or goods the land produced, in an attempt to survive apart from Monterey society. Their lodgings, like their lives and livelihoods, blended old and new. Several women at the village were startled by Jackson and those who accompanied her. One of the older women laughed at first when Jackson asked her age, but then she revealed that she had been born at the mission, most likely before its secularization. The old woman stated that she never thought about when she was born, but "it was written down once in a book at the mission." Although this woman's identity is unknown, certainly her baptism is among those thousands listed in the surviving mission register. Perhaps she was Omesia, for she lived until 1883.[12]

By 1875, the land southeast of the mission, consisting of two former Mexican land grants—El Potrero de San Carlos (once granted to Fructuoso José) and the Rancho San Francisquito—had been purchased by Bradley Varnum Sargent and his three brothers. Sargent was one of the dominant landholders in Monterey County; he and his brothers eventually owned eighty thousand acres in central California. Sargent had made his money in the goldfields and later went into the livestock business. Moving to Monterey in 1857, he became supervisor of the county and in 1886 was elected a state senator from Monterey and San Benito counties. He was a powerful man and, like José Antonio Romero before him, a persistent thorn in the side of the Indians of Carmel Valley. He pressured them to leave even when they were not on his land. At least one woman, Isabel Díaz, granddaughter of Onesimo Antonio and a cousin of Isabel Meadows, confronted Sargent, asking him why he wanted more land and telling him that her people were not a hindrance to anyone. Such protests fell on deaf ears. Some Indians simply moved away from their homes in the Carmel Valley, so offended and threatened were they by Sargent's bullying attitude. Those who tried to stay were eventually run off when Sargent placed one of his men on the land and insisted that he had purchased it. A half-century earlier, during the Mexican period, to the chagrin of men like José Antonio Romero, Monterey Indians engaged agents of the law to block others from dispossessing them. Under the American system, however, Indians had no such recourse. Isabel Meadows remembered that, after the Indians had been run off, they "gathered together camping at the river—and from there the Indian people dispersed."[13]

12. Helen Hunt Jackson, *Glimpses of California and the Missions* (Boston, 1903), 154–158. Omesia: author's conversation with Linda Yamane, Sept. 16, 2002.

13. On Sargent, see Augusta Fink, *Monterey County: The Dramatic Story of Its Past* (Santa Cruz, Calif., 1972), 196; "Bradley," in Donald Thomas Clark, *Monterey County Place Names: A Geographical Dictio-*

PLATE 28. *Carmel Mission on San Carlos Day—1875*. By Jules Tavernier. In these years, the exterior walls of the mission church were more or less preserved, whereas the inside was a ruin. Courtesy, William A. Karges Fine Art, Carmel, Calif.

THE ONESIMOS, SAN CARLOS DAY, AND REMAKING THE MISSION

Long after the era of secularization and the arrival of the Americans, many of the dispersed and perhaps others throughout the Carmel Valley and the Monterey region maintained emotional and religious ties to the mission. On San Carlos Day, they returned to the chapel's ruins. In 1879, Robert Louis Stevenson attended San Carlos Day Mass and was impressed not only with the number of Indians in attendance but with their knowledge of Catholic liturgy: "An Indian, stone-blind and about eighty years of age, conducts the singing; other Indians compose the choir; yet they have the Gregorian music at their finger-ends, and pronounce the Latin so correctly that I could follow the meaning as they sang. The pronunciation was odd and nasal, the singing hurried and staccato. 'In saecula saeculo-ho-horum,' they went, with a vigorous aspirate to every additional syllable." These men and women added their own cadences and melodies to the Mass, and in so doing made it their own, perhaps more fully than they ever could have under Franciscan supervision. The man who led the singing is often

---

nary (Carmel Valley, Calif., 1991), 50–51. Recollections of Isabel Diaz: Isabel Meadows, Harrington Papers, reel 80, frame 362b (April 1935). Quote: "Profile: Isabel Meadows," in Yamane, ed., *A Gathering of Voices*, 14.

PLATE 29. *The Day of San Carlos.* By J. D. Strong. 1879. On the far left is Jules Simoneau, a Monterey restauranteur who hosted Robert Louis Stevenson and the artists Tavernier and Strong. To Simoneau's left is María Loreta Onesimo, and next to her is her husband, James Meadows. The altar boy is unknown. Reverend Angel Delfino Casanova leads the religious service. The elderly man with the cane is "Old Ventura," about whom little is known. California Historical Society; FN–08402

referred to as Ramón, but this might very well have been Romano Chaulis, the former mission alcalde and juez de campo who frequented the mission long after its collapse. Stevenson took from his encounter with the Indians of San Carlos more than a sense of their Catholic piety: when he contracted a serious illness during his stay in Monterey in 1879, he was cured by an herbal concoction given to him by Jacinta Gonzalez, an Indian whose parents were born at the mission.[14]

Through the early decades of the twentieth century, the Onesimo clan regularly came to San Carlos. In the 1920s, descendants of Onesimo Antonio partici-

14. Robert Louis Stevenson, *From Scotland to Silverado* . . . , ed. James D. Hart (Cambridge, Mass., 1966), 166. In the 1870s, the Reverend Angelo Delfino Casanova, the pastor at the presidio in Monterey, reroofed the sacristy at the mission so that Mass could be said there on San Carlos Day. The mission church would remain roofless until the early 1880s. For Ramón the blind Indian at San Carlos, see Anne B. Fisher, *No More a Stranger* (Stanford, Calif., 1946), 250–251.

PLATE 30. Onesimo family laying the cornerstone for the reconstructed Mission San Carlos, Oct. 2, 1921. Photographer unknown. Manuel Onesimo holds the cornerstone with his son Berthold as it is blessed by Reverend R. M. Mestres. Photo courtesy of Pat Hathaway, California Views Historical Photo Collection, Monterey, Calif.

pated in the early restoration of San Carlos and attempts to preserve and commemorate the remains of Father Serra, who had been buried there. Manuel Onesimo, grandson of Onesimo Antonio and cousin of Isabel Meadows, helped to lay the cornerstone of the reconstructed mission with his own son Berthold in October 1921. On that same day, Monterey's Spanish-born priest, R. M. Mestres, baptized Alejandro, Berthold, and Juan Onesimo, all sons of Manuel Onesimo and the great-grandchildren of Onesimo Antonio. The Indians' participation in San Carlos Day was central to the continuing celebrations of these years. Indians in attendance would select one of their own as captain of the fiesta, much as they had elected their own officials at the mission during the colonial period. Alfonso Ramirez, born in 1852 and descended on his mother's side from San Carlos Indians, was for many years in the early 1930s elected captain of the fiesta. At that time, Ramirez was living in Carmel, and his home was a gathering place for mission descendants. He had long known this celebration as one in which Indians took part. He recounted in a 1932 letter that, long ago, when he first came to help at the church, "Roman [perhaps Romano] and his wife Ventura use[d] to sing." "And the son's of Roman use[d] to play the violin."[15]

Indians ventured to the mission on special occasions, but Father Mestres envisioned making their presence permanent. As he worked to restore the mission in the 1920s, the priest envisioned a village for Indian families descended from those who had lived at San Carlos. He proposed to bring together some fifty men, women, and children whom he identified as full-blooded descendants of the original San Carlos neophytes. Many of these were living in the mountains south of Carmel "in rude huts on land that is not their own." The men made their living cutting wood and working at other odd jobs, and they could occasionally be seen riding in and around Monterey on old, broken down, horse-drawn "buckboards." The Onesimo clan, so prominent in laying the cornerstone of the rebuilt mission church, was central to Mestres's plan. He hoped to coax to the mission "Onesimo Bernabé," who lived with seven others in a small hut in a canyon on the Meadows Tract. Mestres also intended that another Onesimo, José Bernabé, a fixture in town, commonly seen "sunning himself on the main street of Carmel," be the patriarch of the village. These local survivors would then be joined by six families of Carmel Indians who lived together at Tejon Indian reservation, southeast of Bakersfield. Apparently, these families had moved to the interior of California nearly a century earlier, during secularization.[16] Each family was to inhabit a suitable home on two to three acres of fertile land, and in turn they would be expected to earn at least a part of their living from the soil. Indians would now be brought back to the mission and turned into agriculturalists, even though for generations they had lived elsewhere and pursued other means of economic independence. Predictably, property set aside for the Indians' use would be held in trust by a board so that they could not sell it.

Mestres's plan went nowhere. Most likely, it was too expensive, and local property owners opposed it. One also imagines that those barred from the com-

15. Applications to the 1928 California Judgment Enrollment, nos. 8131 (Alfonso Ramirez), 8132 (Laura P. Ramirez), RG 75, I–32, reel 24, Records of the Bureau of Indian Affairs, National Archives and Record Administration (hereafter cited as Applications); Beverly R. Ortiz, "Chocheño and Rumsen Narratives: A Comparison," in Lowell John Bean, ed. and comp., The Ohlone Past and Present: Native Americans of the San Francisco Bay Region (Menlo Park, Calif., 1994), 127–130; Dietz, Jackson, et al., Stage 1 Pacific Grove–Monterey Consolidation Project, I, 115–119.

16. "Restoration of Indian Village Sought, Carmel Priest Launches Plan to Aid Pure Blood Aborigines," Post Enquirer (Oakland), Nov. 21, 1923, "Newspaper Clippings Pertaining to California Indians," in C. Hart Merriam Papers, reel 75, frames 00082–00083, BL; John Walton, Storied Land: Community and Memory in Monterey (Berkeley, Calif., 2001), 215; Marie Celeste Pagliarulo, "The Restoration of Mission San Carlos Borromeo, Carmel, California, 1931–1967" (master's thesis, University of San Francisco, 1968); Sydney Temple, The Carmel Mission (Santa Cruz, Calif., 1980); Morgado, Junípero Serra's Legacy, 195–196.

PLATE 31. *Manuel Onesimo—"Panoche," Carmel, August 26, 1934.* Photograph by L. S. Slevin. This image was most likely taken at Mission San Carlos during events commemorating the sesquicentennial of Father Junípero Serra's death. Serra died on August 28, 1784. The Bancroft Library, University of California, Berkeley

PLATE 32. *Onesimo's Home, Carmel Valley, 1924.* Photograph by L. S. Slevin. Home of one group of the Onesimo family, tucked away in an overgrazed canyon on the Meadows Tract of the Carmel Valley. The Bancroft Library, University of California, Berkeley

munity would have resented Mestres's desire to restrict membership to people who could demonstrate a pure San Carlos Indian descent. Certainly, Indians descended from San Carlos must have felt some sort of tie to one another. But the notion of full-blooded San Carlos Indians was a creation of European intervention. Moreover, Indians' oral traditions emphasized family lineages and groupings at variance with such circumstantial alignments.

Long before Mestres's plan had foundered, most San Carlos descendants had moved on and married others outside the mission. With the demographic horrors of the mission and smallpox behind them, their numbers gradually increased. In the years immediately after 1928, San Carlos descendants numbered nearly four hundred. They made themselves known to state officials after all California Indians won the right to sue for compensation, a consequence of the United States Senate's failure to ratify the eighteen treaties. The state, like Mestres, saw these men, women, and children simply as Indians of Mission San Carlos Borromeo, not as descendants of a particular group or lineage. They lived in all regions of the state, but most resided in central California. Of these, twenty-eight were fully descended from San Carlos Indians; seventeen had three out of four grandparents from San Carlos; and another twenty-three each had one parent who was a mission descendant. Many had lived their whole lives in the Monterey region. Only a few, those who had served in the military, had left Monterey for an extended period of time. Most of the men with occupations stated that they were general laborers. Few held property. They were, as Isabel Meadows had suggested, among the "most poor." Charles F. Post and Joseph W. Post, however, were notable exceptions. Their father, William Brainerd Post, had married Anselma, a daughter of Onesimo Antonio and María Ygnacia; Anselma, like her older sister María Loreta, had married an Anglo-American with the means to acquire and retain lands formerly encompassed by Mission San Carlos. In 1928, Charles, the older son, held five hundred acres and a homestead property jointly valued at some four thousand dollars, and Joseph had taken over his father's property, a ranch of some twelve thousand acres in Big Sur valued at fifteen thousand dollars. Also among the applicants were Salvador Espinosa, the son of María Viviena Soto, and Guadalupe Martínez, a cannery worker and the granddaughter of Jacinta Gonzalez; both María Viviena Soto and her niece Jacinta Gonzalez had recounted to Alfred Kroeber in the first years of the twentieth century the story of the creation of Coyote's Children.[17]

LIVING MEMORY

As the world changed around the descendants of Mission San Carlos, so, too, did they change. Yet many retained a commitment to their ancestral beliefs and to their distinct history. Isabel Meadows, in her late eighties, recalled Omesia's account of a time long, long ago, before cattle ate the land's seeds and the seeds came no more. She learned from her mother that, when Indians held dances at San Carlos, singers with beautiful voices would often come from Mission Soledad. She also knew how her ancestors gathered acorns, the words they said when they did so, and how her grandfather Onesimo Antonio, when he lived at the mission, carried wood gathered in a strap of oiled rawhide. She held to her family's understanding of secularization: when the mission "was run down and most of the Indians had moved away," the padre gave the Indians land so that he himself could live in Monterey. "*Se licenciaron*," the people used to say of his act. After that, Meadows recalled, "Roman[o], the old man Manjarés and his family, Mariano Romero and a few other people were all that remained living at the river

17. Applications, nos. 8127 (Charles F. Post), 8128 (Joseph W. Post), 8070 (Salvador Espinosa), and 8106 (Guadalupe Martínez). Indians living in California in May 1928 who had descended from those in ˋe state in 1852 would be eligible for compensation. This was made possible by an act of Congress of ˋ18, 1928 (45 Stat. 602), that authorized the attorney general of California to bring a suit in the U.S. ˋof Claims on behalf of Indians. All Indians had to apply for admission onto a roll of those ˋr compensation. See "Indians of California Census Rolls Authorized under the Act of May 18, ˋnded, Approved May 16–17, 1933," M–1853 (microfilm), National Archives.

[the mission]." She remembered how, as a child, she went on foot, with her grandparents and aunts, past the mission and to the shore in search of pebbles. And she fondly recalled a time during her youth when Indians in the Carmel Valley had gathered manzanita berries and made a drink better than any lemonade. "They would say: '*vamos a las manzanas.*'" Perhaps most important, Meadows not only spoke Spanish but had learned her people's language and continued to speak it until she died in 1939 at age ninety-three.[18]

All of these memories and experiences meant that Meadows and other surviving Monterey Indians lived in a world rich with associations and meanings that were perhaps unique to themselves. At times, they could have felt alienated from and oppressed by the larger society surrounding them, especially as they made sense of it on their own terms. Such might have been the case for Meadows when she attended the San Francisco Panama-Pacific Exposition in 1915, which was devoted to demonstrating the triumph of Western ideas and peoples over the "primitive." Millions attended. Meadows must have been among the throngs to walk through halls where Indians and their cultures were on display as artifacts and exemplars of vanquished peoples. She would have seen whole pavilions given over to showcasing the agricultural "progress" of the state and the nation under American leadership. Two decades after the exposition, Meadows vividly recalled the live animals on display. She remembered a coyote, in chains, "his cheeks all stained with streaks from the tears running down where he had cried so much." Perhaps because of the cumulative effect of experiences like these, Isabel Meadows spent her last years sharing her language and memories with Smithsonian anthropologist John P. Harrington and hoping that, one day, the Carmel people would recover their lost land. In her words, doing so would allow them to "put their ranchería like before, to revive their language, and to be counted again in the world."[19]

The Children of Coyote would never be able to "put their ranchería like before." But it is doubtful that many wanted to do so. In the twentieth century, most descendants of those at San Carlos married non-Indians, and they made lives for themselves, holding with them always their own understandings of their past and present identity. More than three-quarters of a century after Isabel Meadows encountered her chained coyote in San Francisco, the earlier days she longed for lived on in the memories of Alex Ramirez, Onesimo Antonio's great-great-grandson, when he recalled his childhood in Monterey. As a boy growing up in

18. Isabel Meadows, Harrington Papers, reel 80, frames 343a (n.d.), 356a, 356b, and 361a (all April 1935), 362a (April 1936), 363a (n.d.), and 495a (n.d.).
19. Robert W. Rydell, *All the World's a Fair: Visions of Empire at American International Expositions, 1876–1916* (Chicago, 1984). Coyote: Isabel Meadows, Harrington Papers, reel 80, frame 345b (October 1934). Ranchería: "Profile: Isabel Meadows," in Yamane, ed., *A Gathering of Voices,* 14.

PLATE 33. Isabel Meadows. Courtesy, National Anthropological Archives,
Smithsonian Institution (91–30298)

the house of his grandfather during the Depression, he saw a man dancing at
their home in buckskin with a large hat over his hair and coffee can lids dangling
from his outfit. The lids had been saved by Alex's mother, and perhaps they took
on a semblance of the same meaning in this dance as had the shells or bone rattles
that once had adorned the regalia of the Indians before Spaniards, Mexicans, and
Anglo-Americans had taken control of California and sought to deprive the
ⁿhildren of Coyote of their culture and lifeways.[20]

ⁿnerations before Alex Ramirez saw reminders of ancient dances in his

"*Chocheño* and *Rumsen* Narratives," in Bean, ed. and comp., *The Ohlone*, 99–163, esp. 128.

grandfather's home, the glare of California's Gold Rush and the transformation of the region into the thirty-first state of the Union obscured California's colonial past to most observers. Moreover, the men whose efforts and writings helped to promote California's statehood and economic expansion were often anti-Catholic, Hispanophobic, and quick, therefore, to dismiss the inhabitants of Spanish and Mexican California as primitive. To Alfred Robinson, author of *Life in California* (1846), the californios were "generally indolent, and addicted to many vices." Of their use of the land and the economy, Englishman Sir George Simpson scoffed: "Nature doing everything, man doing nothing." Less still was said about the Indians who had lived in and around the missions and had built much of Spanish California. By this time, their numbers had been greatly reduced, and those who remained worked on the margins of society or had married into californio families. These mid-nineteenth-century writings rendered remote and seemingly insignificant much of the history of Monterey and its early peoples and those who survived the missions.[21]

These days, a few Indian artifacts and the imperfectly restored ruins of the chapel and the Franciscans' rooms at Mission San Carlos are the most visible reminders of the Indian and Spanish presence during Monterey's colonial era. Fortunately, evidence of this period's important past survives elsewhere, reminding us that, long before California's colonial history became a tool of commerce—converted as it was into a valuable tourist commodity and a form of mass architecture—Indians and Spaniards interacted in complex ways. Within the mission, Indians could do little to withstand the diseases that undermined their culture and community, but they consistently struggled against religious indoctrination, unfamiliar marriage and sexual practices, and restrictions of their freedom of movement. And they sought opportunities within Spanish political, legal, and economic systems, even when those very systems furthered their oppression. Following mission secularization, many Indians regained their autonomy, acquired rights, and achieved independent lives, either on former mission lands, in Monterey, or beyond. Through it all, they endured enormous setbacks while fashioning survival strategies and sustaining narratives of their culture and historical identity. That they did so stands in opposition to their near-erasure from the historical consciousness of contemporary America and the scholarly academy. And, today, in defiance of the weight of history but in accordance with their past struggles, California Indians are reviving their languages, resurrecting their unique cultures, and individually and collectively recovering from the flood.

21. Robinson and Simpson quoted in Leonard Pitt, *The Decline of the Californios: A Social History of the Spanish-Speaking Californians, 1846–1890* (Berkeley, Calif., 1966), 15–16. For an exploration of the negative stereotypes Anglo-Americans used to describe the californios, see James Rawls, *Indians of California: The Changing Image* (Norman, Okla., 1984), esp. 60–65.

GLOSSARY

Alabado: Catholic hymn, usually sung in praise of the consecrated Host

Alcalde: Spanish municipal official; here, almost always an Indian official in a mission

Almud: Unit of grain measure; one-twelfth of a *fanega*

Arras: Traditional gift of thirteen coins given by the bridegroom to the bride

Audiencia: Royal high court with expansive jurisdiction, organized by region

Ayuntamiento: Municipal council; here, of Mexican California, superseding the *cabildo*

Cabildo: Municipal council, annually elected

Californios: *Gente de razón* of Alta California

Careo: Judicial procedure involving confrontation between defendant and witnesses; cross-examination

Comisionado: Town commissioner

Congregación: Resettlement by Spaniards of dispersed Indian settlements into one community; also known as *reducción*

Coyote: Spanish caste category; offspring of Spanish or *mestizo* and Indian parents

Crude birth rate (CBR): Live births in year ÷ population at midyear × 1,000

Crude death rate (CDR): Deaths in year ÷ population at midyear × 1,000

Cura: Parish priest

Defensor: Defense counsel in a judicial proceeding

Doctrina: Prayers, lessons, and hymns constituting daily religious instruction, also known as the *rezo;* a protoparish of Indians under the authority of a bishop, not the *regular clergy*

Encomendero: Possessor of an *encomienda*

Encomienda: Grant carrying the right to assess Indians' tribute (and, often, the obligation to indoctrinate them in Catholicism)

Español: Spanish caste category; offspring of Spanish parents born in the Old or New World

Fanega: Unit of grain measure; about 1.5 bushels

Fecundity: Physiological ability to bear children; opposite of sterility

Fertility: Number of live births, usually measured over the duration of a woman's married life or a five-year period of her adulthood

Fiscal: Church steward appointed by the missionaries; legal counsel to an *audiencia*

Fuero: Special judicial privileges enjoyed by a particular group

Gente de razón: "People of reason"; a cultural category referring to non-Indians

Gentil: "Gentile"; Spanish term for an unbaptized Indian, often suggesting primitiveness or savagism

Habilitado: Presidial supply master and paymaster; elected by the presidio company

Indio: "Indian"; Spanish social, ethnic, and caste category; offspring of Indian parents (distinguished from *gente de razón*)

Infant mortality rate: Deaths under age one in year ÷ live births in year × 1,000

Juez: Spanish official with judicial responsibilities

Licenciado: A graduate or one who has been discharged from the military; here, a *neófito* given legal permission by Mexican officials to separate from a mission and live independently

Mayordomo: Supervisor or labor foreman at a mission; here, always a *gente de razón*

Mestizo: Spanish caste category; offspring of Spanish and Indian parents

Monjerío: Barracks in which California Franciscans confined unmarried Indian women and widows overnight

Mulato: Spanish caste category; offspring of African and Spanish parents

Neófito: "Neophyte"; here, a baptized Indian affiliated with a mission

New Spain: Spanish viceroyalty that encompassed territory of modern Mexico and parts of the states of Arizona, California, New Mexico, and Texas

Novenario: A flogging administered over nine separate days

Padrino: Godfather

Peso: Spanish monetary unit. A silver peso was worth eight *reales* of silver, or ninety-six granos of silver

Plenario: Second phase of Spanish judicial proceeding, involving the weighing of evidence and the determination of guilt

Poblador: Settler; here, always a *gente de razón*

Precepto anual: Catholic Easter duty of confession and Communion

Presidario: Convict laborer at a *presidio;* here, almost always an Indian

Presidio: Frontier military fort or garrison

Ranchería: Small settlement; here, an Indian village

Ranchero: Ranch owner

Rancho: Ranch

Real: Monetary unit valued at one-eighth of a *peso*

Recopilación: Short title for *Recopilación de leyes de los reynos de las Indias,* a compilation of Spanish colonial law; first published in 1681

Regidor: An elected Spanish municipal official; here, almost always an Indian official in a mission

Regular clergy: Members of a religious order, such as the Franciscans; cf. *secular clergy*

Repartimiento: Labor draft

Requerimiento: Spanish statement read to Indians before battle urging acceptance of Christianity and allegiance to the Spanish Crown

Rudeza: Rudeness, roughness; here, a term Spaniards applied to Indians, suggesting primitiveness and lack of civilization

Sacristan: Church official selected by a missionary; here, always a *neófito*

Secular clergy: Priests under authority of a bishop; cf. *regular clergy*

Secularization: Here, the process through which missions were converted to parishes, missionaries replaced by priests, mission property redistributed, and Indians granted freedom

Soltera/soltero: Woman or man who has never been married

Sumaria: First phase of a Spanish judicial proceeding involving the investigation of the crime and the gathering of sworn testimony

Trabajos mecánicos: Manual labor; here, the arduous work required to build and maintain the California presidios

Vaquero: Ranch hand; here, almost always an Indian; usually a job that involves horsemanship

Vara: Rod or staff held by missionaries, Indian *alcaldes,* or government officials symbolizing political authority; unit of length measuring about 33 inches, or .836 meters

Vecino: Spanish civil category denoting a householder or resident of a municipality; here, almost always a *gente de razón*

Viático: Catholic sacrament of Communion administered to the dying; a last rite

Viruelas: Smallpox

CHRONOLOGY

1513	Vasco Núñez de Balboa discovers the Pacific Ocean
1519–1521	Spain conquers Mexico
1528–1536	Alvar Núñez Cabeza de Vaca travels overland from Florida to Mexico
1533	Expedition of Fortún Jiménez sails to Baja California and names the Bay of La Paz
1535	Hernán Cortés renames the Bay of La Paz Santa Cruz and establishes settlement
1539–1540	Expedition of Francisco de Ulloa proves California is not an island; expedition of Fray Marcos de Niza
1540–1542	Expedition of Francisco Vásquez de Coronado
1542–1543	Expedition of Juan Rodríguez Cabrillo and Bartolomé Ferrer sails up Pacific to Cape Mendocino
1565	Fray Andrés de Urdaneta discovers route from Philippines to Mexico
1579	Francis Drake claims New Albion on the Pacific Coast for England
1587	Expedition of Pedro de Unamuno makes landfall in central California
1595	Expedition of Sebastián Rodríguez Cermeño anchors at Drake's Bay
1598	Juan de Oñate initiates colonization of New Mexico
1602–1603	Expedition of Sebastián Vizcaíno names Monterey Bay and explores region
1610	Juan de Oñate establishes Santa Fe
1680	Pueblo Indian revolt
1697	Father Juan María de Salvatierra founds Mission Nuestra Señora de Loreto, Baja California
1728–1729; 1741–1742	Expeditions of Vitus Bering in the North Pacific
1756	Beginning of Seven Years' War
1762	England seizes Manila and Havana from Spain

1763	Treaty of Paris concludes Seven Years' War: Spain loses Florida and gains control of Louisiana west of the Mississippi, New Orleans, and Havana; France relinquishes to Great Britain all territory in North America
1765	José de Gálvez named *visitador general* of New Spain
1767–1768	Jesuits expelled from New Spain
1768	Naval base of San Blas founded; Father Junípero Serra named father president of Baja California missions
1768–1771	Father Francisco Garcés explores the Gila and Colorado rivers
1769	Land and sea expeditions depart for Alta California; establishment of mission and presidio at San Diego
1770	Gaspar de Portolá takes possession of Monterey for Spain; establishment of Mission San Carlos and Monterey Presidio
1771	Establishment of Missions San Antonio and San Gabriel
1772	Establishment of Mission San Luis Obispo
1772–1773	Serra in Mexico City to consult with viceroy
1773	*Reglamento* of Juan José Echeveste establishes guidelines for economy of California
1774–1776	Juan Bautista de Anza brings colonists and livestock to California from Sonora
1775	Indian rebellion at Mission San Diego
1776	Establishment of Mission San Francisco and San Francisco Presidio; establishment of Mission San Juan Bautista; creation of the position of commandant general of the Interior Provinces
1776–1783	American War of Independence
1777	Establishment of Mission Santa Clara; establishment of the pueblo of San Jose
1779	*Reglamento* of Governor Felipe de Neve reorganizes price and wage structure of California economy
1781	Establishment of pueblo of Los Angeles; Yuma rebellion cuts overland route between Mexico and California
1782	Establishment of Mission San Buenaventura and Santa Barbara Presidio
1784	Serra dies in Monterey; Fermín Francisco de Lasuén becomes father president
1785	Indian rebellion at Mission San Gabriel
1786	Jean-François de Galaup de la Pérouse visits Monterey; establishment of Mission Santa Barbara

1787	Establishment of Mission La Purísima Concepción
1791	Expedition of Alejandro Malaspina explores Monterey; establishment of Missions Santa Cruz, La Soledad
1792	First visit of George Vancouver's expedition at Monterey
1794	Final visit of Vancouver expedition at Monterey
1797	Establishment of Missions San Jose, San Juan Bautista, San Miguel, and San Fernando and the Villa de Branciforte
1798	Establishment of Mission San Luis Rey
1804	Establishment of Mission Santa Inés
1810	Start of Mexican War for Independence
1817	Establishment of Mission San Rafael
1818	South American privateer Hipólito Bouchard attacks settlements along California coast
1821	Mexico gains independence from Spain
1823	Establishment of Mission San Francisco Solano
1824	Colonization Act of 1824 authorizes private citizens to obtain land from the government
1826	José María de Echeandía's Decree of Emancipation in Favor of the Neophytes grants certain Indians the right to separate from missions
1828	Supplemental regulations allow governor to grant vacant lands not held by missions
1833	José Figueroa's Provisional Regulations for the Emancipation of Mission Indians outline a plan of partial freedom for select Indians; decree of Mexican Congress orders conversion of California missions to parishes
1834	Figueroa's Provisional Rules for the Secularization of the Missions of Alta California establishes plan for the distribution of mission property to Indians
1844	Outbreak of smallpox in Monterey
1846	Start of Mexican-American War; United States takes possession of California
1848	Treaty of Guadalupe Hidalgo ends Mexican-American War; Mexico cedes Alta California and New Mexico to the United States; gold discovered at Sutter's Mill
1849	California constitution written and approved
1850	California becomes thirty-first state of the Union

| 1851 | Congress passes Land Act of 1851, creating a commission to review land titles in California |
| 1852 | United States Senate fails to ratify eighteen treaties negotiated between U.S. and representatives of California Indian groups |

Note: The Jiménez expedition began under the command of Diego Becerra de Mendoza. After he was killed in a mutiny, Jiménez, as first pilot, took over.

APPENDIX A

Methodological Comments

To standardize and regulate the administration of Catholic sacraments, the Council of Trent (1545–1563) required all priests and missionaries to record in separate books the sacraments they administered. These registers made it far less likely that baptism would be granted to the same individual more than once, and they helped church officials prevent closely related individuals from marrying. Priests found the registers indispensable as they tried to keep track of the names and identities of those whose spiritual life they oversaw. For all of these reasons, missionaries and then parish priests kept meticulous records of all sacraments they administered at Mission San Carlos between 1770 and 1839 and at the Monterey Presidio chapel in subsequent years.

MISSION REGISTERS

This study makes extensive use of those records to examine Indian recruitment to San Carlos, the demographic structure of the villages incorporated into the larger mission community, life histories and family relationships of baptized Indians, family formation and reproduction in the mission, mortality and population decline, and the administration of Catholic sacraments. After a summary of the content of each of the registers, this appendix discusses their value as ethnographic sources, the creation of a database based upon them, tests to determine and ensure the database's accuracy, and the methods of analysis used to study population change at San Carlos.[1]

The San Carlos registers contain consistent information. Franciscans always noted a unique number for each Indian baptized, starting with 1 for the first baptism at the mission; the date, type (regular or conditional), and site (native village or mission) of the baptism; the Indian's sex, estimated age, Spanish name, native name, and political group or village of birth; the Indian's godparents, family relations (parents, siblings, and children), and birth status (legitimate or illegitimate) if the child was born at the mission; and the name of the Franciscan who administered the sacrament. Occasionally, the Franciscans would record a person's political or occupational status, and they also noted the first and last individuals they baptized from a particular region or village.

Burial records consist of a unique number, the date and site of the burial, the deceased's

---

1. The original sacramental registers are in the Archive of the Diocese of Monterey in California. Microfilm copies of the registers are owned by the Genealogical Society of the Church of Jesus Christ of Latter-Day Saints, Salt Lake City, Utah. The film numbers are as follows: baptismal register (1770–1896), 0913159; burial register (1770–1915), 0913162; and marriage register (1772–1908), 0913161.

sex, estimated age, Spanish name, native name if known, baptism number if known, and familial relationships to other baptized Indians. The padres also noted any last rites they administered. If illness or an act of violence led to a sudden death, one that prevented the granting of final sacraments, the Franciscans would leave a special notation in the burial entry.

For marriages, Franciscans recorded the marriage number, date, type (renewal or standard), and witnesses. They also specified the number of times the banns were read and the identity of the officiating Franciscan, as well as the bride's and groom's status (widowed or never before married), mission of baptism, baptism number, Spanish and native names, parents' names if known, and the name of a previous spouse if the bride or groom was widowed. Missionaries further indicated when they bestowed the nuptial blessing on the bride and noted anything of special interest, for example, if the groom was an alcalde, interpreter, or sacristan. Periodically, from the 1770s to the mid-1790s, the father president was empowered to perform confirmations, and these are recorded in a separate register. Confirmation records contain no information not listed in the other registers, but they can be used to verify when certain individuals were alive and present at the mission.

MISSION REGISTERS AS ETHNOGRAPHIC SOURCES

Sacramental registers provide ethnographic evidence not available elsewhere, but, like any source, they must be studied with care. The Franciscans' occasional clerical errors, cross-cultural misunderstandings, and underregistration of vital events pose challenges. Record keeping was difficult for Franciscans who were new to San Carlos, and clerical omissions were more frequent during times of food scarcity and epidemic disease, when Indians left the mission or died in great numbers. Furthermore, the Spanish names of some Indians changed over their lives, or different missionaries simply recorded variants over time. Elzeario could become Eleutario, Elisio, or Elisco. Franciscans commonly used as equivalents names such as Francisco Antonio, Antonio Francisco, Antonio, or Francisco. Multiple references to individuals and family relations in the mission's registers permit an awareness of these inconsistencies and allow for correct record linkage.[2]

Cross-cultural confusion often created problems for missionaries as they sought to identify Indians they baptized, married, and buried. Indians might not have understood European kin classifications, and the Franciscans probably did not always understand those of the Indians. Among some Costanoan groups, the terms for "nephew" and "grandson" apparently were the same. If a variation of this classification system was used by the Indians of the Monterey region, it may explain why some men are listed as being cousins and brothers and why there is conflicting evidence regarding some individuals' genealogy. In his confessional aid for Mission San Buenaventura, Father José Francisco de Paula Señán provided the best discussion by a Franciscan of the missionaries' attempts to avoid these confusions. Señán noted the problems he encountered and offered his strategy for clarifying native kinship:

> It is extremely difficult to unravel the blood relationships among these people, who call brother and sister, without any distinction, any first or second cousins, even distant

2. For an exploration of these issues, see John R. Johnson, "Mission Registers as Anthropological Questionnaires: Understanding Limitations of the Data," *American Indian Culture and Research Journal*, XII (1988), 9–30.

relatives, and perhaps even those whose blood relationship is neither real nor true. So, in order to get clear even such an obvious relationship as that of brother and sister, the question which is marked with a [hand] is important, and (in order) to find out whether they are cousins, even first cousins, the next question—so indecently worded—will serve: Is your aunt the mother of your "sister?"

Franciscans at Mission San Carlos must have used similar tactics to clarify family relations. Again, multiple references to individuals and their relatives over many years and in different registers allow the identification of individuals and correct record linkage.[3]

In some instances, it was the Indians' cultural conventions that limited the information available to the Franciscans. Many San Carlos neophytes had prohibitions against stating the name of a deceased relative or friend. The French explorer Jean-François de Galaup de la Pérouse, who visited Monterey in 1786, observed that Indians at San Carlos "feel offended if one should inadvertently pronounce [the deceased's] names in their presence." And, in 1814, Father Juan Amorós elaborated on the Indians' practice of not speaking of the dead:

> These natives consider it very disrespectful to talk about their deceased parents and relatives. Thus a boy whose parents died when he was quite young has no one to tell him the names of his father, grandfather or kinsfolk. In the course of a quarrel for greater vituperation they exclaim: "Your father is dead," and the flame of their fury grows greater. So they have no means of remembering their ancestors. When someone dies his clothing and belongings are burned. If an animal such as dogs, horses, hens, etc., are among their possessions, they are killed. If they had plants, they are uprooted. When asked the reason for this procedure, they answer: "it is to obliterate the memory of the dead."

These beliefs explain why the Franciscans, when they recorded the baptism of an adult whose own parents had not been baptized, could only note that his or her parents were deceased. Naming taboos limited the gathering of information on the parents of Indians born outside the mission but had little effect on the family reconstitution of Indians born at the mission.[4]

As stated above, missionaries always recorded the age of an individual at baptism. But, because the Indians either did not measure time in the same manner as the Franciscans or did not understand Spanish words for numbers, all ages of adults baptized are the guesses of the Franciscans. In 1777, Serra noted this problem:

> In most cases, with the exception of a few children, the age at the time of Baptism is unknown. . . . Concerning the age of the Indian neophytes, . . . it may be remarked that since most of them were baptized in adult age, we cannot know exactly how old they are because they themselves cannot give us the information. Accordingly, the age is put down at what they appear to be—no exact figures being possible—as has always been our practice in census and baptismal records.

3. Madison S. Beeler, ed., *The Ventureño Confesionario of José Señán, O.F.M.*, University of California Publications in Linguistics, XLVII (Berkeley, Calif., 1967), 41. On Rumsen kinship terms and classifications, see Sylvia M. Broadbent, "The Rumsen of Monterey: An Ethnography from Historical Sources," in *Contributions of the University of California Archaeological Research Facility*, XIV (Berkeley, Calif., 1972), 45–94, esp. 69.

4. John Dunmore, ed. and trans., *The Journal of Jean-François de Galaup de la Pérouse, 1785–1788*, 2 vols. (London, 1994–1995), I, 185; Juan Amorós, in *APST*, 59–60.

When the missionaries guessed an adult Indian's age, they almost always picked a multiple of five. Thus ages for adults at baptism cluster around estimates such as fifteen, twenty, twenty-five, thirty, thirty-five, etc.[5]

CREATING THE DATABASE

When I embarked on this project in the early 1990s, I was the beneficiary of work begun in the 1970s by Randall Milliken. To study village locations and marriage patterns in the Monterey region through 1790, Milliken created two separate and well-designed databases to capture information in the San Carlos registers. One matched baptisms to burials and the other contained information on marriages. Over more than a decade, I verified, modified, and supplemented data gathered by Milliken, who was primarily interested in gleaning information on the gentiles baptized at the mission. My focus largely has been on the Indian community at San Carlos through the period of secularization, and I required a whole new set of fields and a broadening of the database. I completed information on baptisms, burials, and marriages through 1850 and integrated all fields into one relational database. New linkages between baptism, marriage, and burial records and the merging of marriage-related fields with the database on births and deaths allowed for family reconstitution and a study of population change at San Carlos. The linked database of all three registers contains nearly four thousand records and involves some sixty-eight fields. These records pertain to some three thousand Indians who lived at the mission between 1770 and 1850.[6]

RECORD LINKAGE AND ACCURACY

Family reconstitution involves linking individuals' burial records to their baptism records, children's baptism records to their parents' marriage records, and parents' marriage records back to their own baptism and burial records. In essence, it is the creation of life histories for families. In the years between 1770 and 1850, the Franciscans recorded the deaths of more than 2,300 San Carlos Indians. Of these, more than 95 percent have been matched to their corresponding baptismal record.[7]

---

5. Junípero Serra to Miguel Pieras, Sept. 6, 1777, Monterey, in Tibesar, ed. and trans., *Writings of Serra,* III, 171.

6. Randall Milliken, *Ethnohistory of the Rumsen,* Papers in Northern California Anthropology, no. 2 (Berkeley, Calif., 1987), orig. publ. as "Ethnohistory of the Rumsen: The Mission Period," in Stephen A. Dietz, Thomas L. Jackson, et al., *Final Report of Archaeological Excavations at Nineteen Archaeological Sites for the Stage 1 Pacific Grove–Monterey Consolidation Project of the Regional Sewerage System,* I (Berkeley, Calif., 1981), 10–102. For a full discussion of Milliken's database, see Milliken, "An Ethnohistory of the Indian People of the San Francisco Bay Area from 1770 to 1810" (Ph.D. diss., University of California, Berkeley, 1991), 345–369. See also Milliken, *A Time of Little Choice: The Disintegration of Tribal Culture in the San Francisco Bay Area, 1769–1810* (Menlo Park, Calif., 1995).

7. Sherburne F. Cook and Woodrow Borah, who also worked with the records of San Carlos, were only able to identify 70.9 percent of Indians buried at the mission. See Cook and Borah, "Mission Registers as Sources of Vital Statistics: Eight Missions of Northern California," in Cook and Borah, eds., *Essays in Population History,* III, *Mexico and California* (Berkeley, Calif., 1979), 190. Johnson, in his work in the Santa Barbara–area missions to 1822, could not match "burial entries with baptismal entries for 8.4 percent of Chumash baptisms at Mission Santa Barbara, 4.0 percent at Mission La

Cross-checking the database with three mission censuses helped to ensure the basic reliability of the database. The first two censuses are simple lists of Indians, one dated December 31, 1796, the other January 3, 1798. The third document, a household census, was compiled by the missionaries at mission secularization.[8] Most discrepancies I uncovered involved the small number of Indians who transferred to other missions or fled; these individuals show up as alive in the database but do not appear on the censuses.[9]

Standard tests caught errors that might have been introduced when the Franciscans created the registers or when information was transferred to the database. On all individuals in the database, I verified that the date of birth is earlier than or on the date of baptism and that the date of death is no more than 105 years after the date of birth. On all husbands and wives, I verified that the marriage occurred before or on the date of death. On all children, I checked that the date of birth is later than or on the date of the marriage of the child's parents; that the date of birth is earlier than or on the wife's date of death; and that the date of birth is not later than nine months after the father's death.[10]

FAMILY RECONSTITUTION AND HISTORICAL DEMOGRAPHY

The study of population change at Mission San Carlos contained herein relies on the technique of family reconstitution pioneered and refined by historical demographers over recent decades. Family reconstitution involves linking various records of information about individuals found scattered throughout the mission's sacramental registers. Other documents, namely aggregate sources (annual totals of baptisms, marriages, or deaths), can be used to show population trends, determine crude annual birth and death rates, and, through various mathematical operations, estimate reproduction ratios that suggest the rate of population growth or decline. The study of aggregate sources, and the results it generates, contribute greatly to an understanding of population change. But crude birth and death rates (the number of people born or buried divided by the midyear population and multiplied by a constant, usually one thousand) do not in themselves explain population change; rather, they are the products of other dynamics, namely the rates of mortality and fertility of various age groups. And age-specific mortality and fertility rates can best be arrived at through family reconstitution, a process that requires thousands and thousands

Purísima, and 9.6 percent at Mission Santa Inés" ("Mission Registers as Anthropological Questionnaires," *American Indian Culture and Research Journal,* XII [1988], 18).

8. Macario de Castro, Dec. 31, 1796, San Carlos, LDS film no. 0909228, and Macario de Castro, Jan. 3, 1798, San Carlos, Archives of the Missions, folder 20, BL; "Padrón de los neófitos de esta misión de San Carlos," n.d., Taylor Coll., doc. 2353, HL.

9. Father Lasuén wrote about some of these problems: "In regard to the missions in whose midst the five additional ones were founded: various native neophytes from districts adjoining them were added to these latter [missions], and as a consequence, in their case, the number in residence will be found to exceed the number baptized; and in the others it will be less than when the number of the deceased is deducted, for some who are living were transferred to new foundations." See Fermín Francisco de Lasuén, "Biennial Report for the Years 1797 and 1798," Feb. 20, 1799, San Carlos, in Kenneally, ed. and trans., *Writings of Lasuén,* II, 386; see also Zephyrin Engelhardt, *Mission San Carlos Borromeo (Carmelo): The Father of the Missions* (1934; rpt. Ramona, Calif., 1973), 172. By 1798, some fifty San Carlos Indians had been transferred to help found other missions. See James Culleton, *Indians and Pioneers of Old Monterey* (Fresno, Calif., 1950), 262 n. 144.

10. These tests were used to identify potential problems, not to automatically exclude any records. Thus I excluded no records where children were born before the marriage of their parents.

more hours than an analysis of the same population using aggregative methods. Although family reconstitution yields precise figures, one should keep in mind that these numbers are estimates, rates based on numerators (events) and denominators (populations at risk), and therefore only an approximation of the past based on the best documentation and most revealing methodology. Yet because it is the standard method of a great number of historical demographers, family reconstitution allows for comparisons between the population dynamics in San Carlos and other communities of the early modern period.[11]

Rarely has family reconstitution been applied to communities in colonial Latin America. Scholars have believed that high rates of illegitimacy, an underregistration of births and deaths, and Indians' lack of surnames have prevented the reconstitution of Indian families living under Catholic priests.[12] In important respects, though, the records of San Carlos closely resemble those of the European communities that family reconstitution was designed to study, and thus it meets the general criteria for analysis. Its baptism, marriage, and burial records are intact, there was very little migration out of the community, underregistration of births and deaths was rare, and illegitimacy was low. The detailed baptism, marriage, and burial records compensate for the Indians' lack of family names.[13]

11. On the technique of family reconstitution, see Louis Henry, *Techniques d'analyse en démographie historique* (Paris, 1980), 65–147; Henry, *Manuel de démographie historique* (Geneva, 1967); E. A. Wrigley, "Family Reconstitution," in Wrigley, ed., *An Introduction to English Historical Demography: From the Sixteenth to the Nineteenth Century* (New York, 1966), 96–159; Wrigley and Roger Schofield, *The Population History of England, 1541–1871: A Reconstruction* (Cambridge, Mass., 1981), 1–32; Wrigley, R. S. Davies, J. E. Oeppen, and Schofield, *English Population History from Family Reconstitution, 1580–1837* (Cambridge, 1997), 3–18. Also useful are David S. Reher and Schofield, *Old and New Methods in Historical Demography* (Oxford, 1993); Henry, *Population: Analysis and Models*, trans. Etienne van de Walle and Elisa F. Jones (New York, 1976). For the application of mathematical models to aggregate data, see Robert H. Jackson's use of the technique of inverse projection in Jackson, *Indian Population Decline: The Missions of Northwestern New Spain, 1687–1840* (Albuquerque, N.Mex., 1994).

12. On why historians have not successfully applied the technique of family reconstitution to colonial Latin America, see Robert McCaa, "The Peopling of Mexico from Origins to Revolution," in Richard Steckel and Michael R. Haines, eds., *A Population History of North America* (Cambridge, 2000), 241–304, esp. 269; see also Claude Morin, "Los libros parroquiales como fuente para la historia demográfica y social novohispana," *Historia mexicana*, XXI (1972), 389–418; Cecilia Andrea Rabell, *La población novohispana a la luz de los registros parroquiales: Avances y perspectivas de investigación* (Mexico City, 1990), esp. 7–10, 27–30. Three family reconstitution studies have been published for Mexico, and two are, for the most part, studies on non-Indians: Tomás Calvo, "Familles mexicaines au XVIIe siècle: Une tentative de reconstitution," *Annales de démographie historique* (1984), 149–174; Herbert S. Klein, "Familia y fertilidad en Amatenango, Chiapas (1785–1816)," in Elsa Malvido and Miguel Angel Cuenya, comp., *Demografía histórica de México: Siglos XVI–XIX* (Mexico City, 1993), 112–122. See also David Robichaux, "La formación de la pareja en la Tlaxcala rural . . . ," in Robichaux, comp., *El matrimonio en Mesoamérica ayer y hoy: Unas miradas antropológicas* (Mexico City, 2003), 205–236.

13. Since the pioneering work of Sherburne F. Cook, mission registers have been used to study population change in the missions, but all of this work falls short of family reconstitution. For example, Cook and Borah went so far as to link burials to baptisms at eight missions, but they did not link children to their parents or brides and grooms to their respective baptism and burial records. See Cook and Borah, "Mission Registers as Sources of Vital Statistics," in Cook and Borah, eds., *Essays in Population History*, III, *Mexico and California*, 177–192. In recent decades, anthropologists have mined mission records to reconstruct the settlement geography and political and social structures of Indians baptized at the missions. For studies on California Indians that use sacramental registers, see Johnson, "Mission Registers as Anthropological Questionnaires," *American Indian Culture and Research Journal*, XII (1988), 28 n. 1. On the completeness of California's sacramental registers, see Jackson, *Indian Population Decline*, 10–11.

This inquiry has followed the standard techniques of family reconstitution pioneered by Louis Henry. The statistical analysis was carried out at the Centre Roland Mousnier, Université Paris IV–Sorbonne, under the guidance of Professor Jean-Pierre Bardet and Jacques Renard. A computer program—CASOAR (Calculs et Analyse sur Ordinateur Appliqué à la Reconstitution des Familles)—developed jointly by Bardet and Renard made this work possible. Robert McCaa of the University of Minnesota provided crucial assistance in interpreting the statistics generated by CASOAR.[14]

The records of the reconstituted families fall into several categories, depending upon whether there are known dates for when a couple may be said to have entered observation (the date of marriage) and exited observation (the date of death of one of the spouses). This classification system was outlined by Henry.[15] Records where the date of marriage is known are category M. If the date of marriage cannot be determined, the record is classified as E. Records where the end of observation of the couple is known are F. If there is no date for the end of observation, the record is classified as O. These distinctions are most important in the study of fertility (live births per woman), or what the French know as *fécondité*, for, to analyze the number of children a woman bears in a marriage, one has to know the beginning and end of that marriage. Studies of fertility, therefore, involve only records that are in the group MF. If less than half of all married couples under study are MF, then the statistics generated in an analysis of fertility may not be considered representative of the larger community. For this study of the period 1770 to 1839, there were a total of 805 Indian couples. Of these couples, 163 came to the mission already married; they are classified as E and excluded from studies of fertility. Of the remaining 642 couples formed at Mission San Carlos, fully 77 percent (493 out of 642) are MF. Analyses of mortality and seasonality of births and burials are not restricted to records classified as MF and encompass some 1,144 births and 2,235 deaths recorded at San Carlos between 1770 and 1839.

The fruits of this analysis are presented in Chapter 3 in my discussions of Indian mortality and fertility at San Carlos. Preliminary study of data obtained through the family reconstitution of two additional missions, San Diego and San Gabriel, yields levels of mortality and fertility roughly equal to those found at San Carlos. Data for this additional mission-register research was compiled at the Huntington Library under my supervision by the staff of the Early California Population Project.

14. See Henry, *Techniques d'analyse en démographie historique,* 65–147. On the origins of CASOAR, see Michael Hainsworth, Jean-Pierre Bardet, Louis Henry, and Pierre Chaunu, *Logiciel C.A.S.O.A.R.: Calculs et analyses sur ordinateur appliqués aux reconstitution* (Paris, 1981).

15. See, for example, Henry, *Techniques d'analyse en démographie historique,* 65–147.

APPENDIX B

Father Presidents of the Alta California Missions, 1769–1833

Name	Dates of Service
Junípero Serra	1769–Aug. 28, 1784
Francisco Palóu	Aug. 28, 1784–Feb. 6, 1785 (interim)
Fermín Francisco de Lasuén	Feb. 6, 1785–June 26, 1803
Estevan Tapis	June 26, 1803–Dec. 8, 1812
José Francisco de Paula Señán	Dec. 8, 1812–Nov. 22, 1815
Mariano Payeras	Nov. 22, 1815–Oct. 9, 1819
José Francisco de Paula Señán	Oct. 9, 1819–Aug. 24, 1823
Vicente Francisco de Sarría	Aug. 24, 1823–Apr. 2, 1825 (interim)
Narciso Durán	Apr. 2, 1825–June 9, 1827
José Bernardo Sánchez	June 9, 1827–June 16, 1831
Narciso Durán	June 16, 1831–1833

Note: The date of Serra's appointment as president of the Alta California missions is unclear. In 1767, after the expulsion of the Jesuits, he was appointed president of the Baja California missions. In 1768, José de Gálvez and Serra worked to plan the conquest of Alta California, and Serra was father president when he founded Mission San Diego on July 16, 1769. Durán's rule continued after mission secularization.

Source: Maynard Geiger, *Franciscan Missionaries in Hispanic California, 1769–1848: A Biographical Dictionary* (San Marino, Calif., 1969).

APPENDIX C

Gobernantes of Spanish Alta California

Name	Dates of Service
Gaspar de Portolá	Mar. 9, 1769–July 9, 1770 (1)
Pedro Fages	July 9, 1770–May 25, 1774 (2)
Fernando de Rivera y Moncada	May 25, 1774–Feb. 3, 1777 (2)
Felipe de Neve	Feb. 3, 1777–Sept. 10, 1782 (3)
Pedro Fages	Sept. 10, 1782–Apr. 16, 1791 (3)
José Antonio Roméu	Apr. 16, 1791–Apr. 9, 1792 (3)
José Joaquín de Arrillaga	Apr. 9, 1792–May 14, 1794 (4)
Diego de Borica	May 14, 1794–Jan. 16, 1800 (3)
José Joaquín de Arrillaga	Jan. 16, 1800–Mar. 26, 1804 (4) Mar. 26, 1804–July 24, 1814 (5)
José Darío Argüello	July 24, 1814–Aug. 30, 1815 (6)
Pablo Vicente de Solá	Aug. 30, 1815–Nov. 10, 1822 (5)

1 = Military commander of the colonizing expedition
2 = Military commandant of Alta California
3 = Governor of the Californias
4 = Interim Governor of the Californias
5 = Governor of Alta California
6 = Interim Governor of Alta California

Source: Donald A. Nuttall, "The Gobernantes of Spanish Upper California: A Profile," *California Historical Quarterly*, LI (1972), 253–280.

APPENDIX D

Governors of Mexican Alta California

Name	Years of Service
Luis Argüello	November 1822–November 1825 (interim)
José María de Echeandía	November 1825–January 1831
Manuel Victoria	January 1831–December 1831
José María de Echeandía	December 1831–January 1833 (south)
Agustín Vicente Zamorano	February 1832–January 1833 (north)
José Figueroa	January 1833–September 1835
José Castro	September 1835–January 1836 (interim)
Nicolás Gutiérrez	January 1836–May 1836 (interim)
Mariano Chico	May 1836–July 1836
Nicolás Gutiérrez	August 1836–November 1836
José Castro	November 1836–December 1836
Juan Bautista de Alvarado	December 1836–December 1842
Manuel Micheltorena	December 1842–February 1845
Pío Pico	February 1845–August 1846
José María Flores	October 1846–January 1847
Andrés Pico	January 1847

Note: Alvarado was revolutionary governor from December 1836–July 1837; interim governor from July 1837–November 1839; and governor from November 1839–December 1842.

Sources: Thomas C. Barnes, Thomas H. Naylor, and Charles W. Polzer, *Northern New Spain: A Research Guide* (Tucson, Ariz., 1981), 99–100; *California Pioneer Register and Index, 1542–1848 . . . Extracted from The History of California by Hubert Howe Bancroft* (1884–1890; rpt. Baltimore, 1964).

Identified Mission San Carlos Indian Officials, 1779–1831

Spanish Name/Indian Name (Village)	Bapt. No.	Age at Baptism	Birth	Years Served
Baltazar (Ichxenta)	0268	40	1735	1779, 80
Carlos Juan (Achasta)	0079	25	1748	1783, 84, 88
Athanasio Joseph/Huyuramus (Tucutnut)	0278	42	1733	1783, 84, 92, 96, 97
Miguel Joseph/Uycparis (Achasta)	0011	9	1762	1785
Rafael Francisco (Tucutnut)	0117	6	1767	1785
Vicente Marinero (Tucutnut)	0271	20	1755	1786
Hilario Joseph/Holojaue (Excelen)	0473	20	1757	1792
Nicomedes Joseph/Unique (Sargentaruc)	1074	30	1755	1792
Sancio Francisco/Tepepis (Kalendaruc)	1456	37	1752	1792
Silvestre Joseph/Cheml (Excelen)	0486	20	1757	1794
Lucas Antonio/Coyyo (Excelen)	0433	30	1746	1796, 97
Jayme Joseph/Alcason (Kalendaruc)	0921	40	1743	1796, 97
Abrahan/Guimesh (Ensen)	1748	49	1743	1796, 97
Augusto Joseph/Chumges (Sargentaruc)	0724	14	1768	1798, 99, 1807, 09
Martín/Linquis (Excelen)	0843	7	1776	1799, 1805
Thadeo/Tutach (Socorronda)	0255	5	1769	1799, 1806, 07, 09, 13, 14
Luis Joseph/Gergechom (Tucutnut)	0746	13	1769	1799
Celestino Joseph/Aschistchaschi (Excelen)	0455	10	1767	1808, 09, 13, 14
Facundo/Huaclanchi (Excelen)	0872	10	1773	1808, 09, 10
Emydgio Joseph (Sargentaruc)	0725	13	1769	1810, 11
Theopisto Joseph (Mission)	1001	0	1784	1810, 11
Oresio Antonio/Sichon (Eslenajan)	1509	7	1783	1810, 11, 12, 13, 14, 15
Nestor José (Ensen)	1729	12	1780	1811

Spanish Name/Indian Name (Village)	Bapt. No.	Age at Baptism	Birth	Years Served
Faustino Jovita/Gilpina (Ichxenta)	0297	1	1774	1812
Mathias Antonio (Ensen)	0771	6	1777	1812, 13
Eusebio Joseph/Saueyom (Ensen)	0731	18	1764	1812
Raphael Joseph (Mission)	1270	0	1787	1814, 15, 16, 17, 18
Jacome de la Marca (Mission)	0595	0	1779	1815
Baldomero José (Excelen)	1572	10	1781	1815, 16, 17, 19
Phelipe de Jesus (Excelen)	1053	0	1785	1816, 17
Francisco de Paula/Tiquitiqui (Ensen)	1877	12	1781	1816, 17, 24, 30
Rosendo/Atoch (Ensen)	0863	17	1766	1818, 19, 21, 23
Amadeo/Yeucharom (Echilat)	0249	3	1771	1819
Fileto José/Eyeshmas (Excelen)	1593	14	1777	1819
Pacífico (Mission)	0178	0	1774	1822, 23
Pacomio José (Pagchin)	1554	10	1781	1823, 24
Ambrosio/Guelohs (Echilat)	0204	3	1771	1824
Agricio Joseph (Excelen-Ensen)	2004	5	1790	1824, 25, 26, 31
Salvador (Sargentaruc)	2631	11	1796	1826
Ynnocencio Joseph/Asiemis (Ensen)	0827	7	1776	1826
Severo José/Palacp (Ensen)	1574	7	1784	1826
Domicio José (Ensen)	1871	4	1789	1827, 31
Fructuoso de Jesus (Mission)	1048	0	1785	1827, 30
Landelino José (Mission)	1779	0	1792	1827
Romano Chaulis (Ensen)	2267	1	1798	1830, 31
Francisco/Huechirremis (Ensen)	2487	16	1790	1823, 31

Note: This table contains only identified officials. From 1779 to 1831, there were a total of 212 leadership positions. Of these 212 spots, 46 identified officials are known to have filled at least 101.

Source: Mission San Carlos bapt. nos. 827, 1114, 1964, 2521, 2627, 2670, 2695, 2974, 3075, 3133; San Carlos marr. nos. 143, 319, 337, 569, 906, 933, 989; San Carlos bur. nos. 605, 2356, 2754; San Carlos confirmation no. 566; Taylor Coll., docs. 173, 334, 348, 374, 391, 394, 401, 414, 457, 696, 1574, 1591, 1816, 1930, HL; AGN, CA, LXV, expediente 7, 305a; Archives of California, C–A 24, 501, BL; Fermín Francisco de Lasuén to Diego de Borica, Jan. 1, 1797, Mission San Carlos, in Kenneally, ed. and trans., *Writings of Lasuén,* II, 5; Archives of Monterey, C–A 150, I, reel 1, 266–268, BL.

INDEX

Abella, Ramón: on gentile Indians' low fertility, 118; on secularization, 383–384

Abortion, 226

Abrahan Guimesh (San Carlos), 254, 255, 257

Achasta, 1, 76, 138

Adult mortality. *See* Mortality

Agapito (Santa Barbara), 309

Agreda, María de Jesús de, 133–134

Agricio José (San Carlos), 270, 403–404, 418,
426–427

Agriculture: at Mission San Carlos, 72–74, 78,
300, 388; at Mission San Diego, 259; and
mission surpluses, 275; and pueblos, 276.
See also Mission San Carlos Borromeo

Aguilar, Simón, 362

Agustín (San Juan Bautista), 338

Agustina María (San Gabriel), 262, 264

Agustín Pasay (San Carlos), 254

Alcaldes. *See* Indian officials

Alegre, Antonio, 291

Alegre, Antonio María, 221

Alhuynaiuhit, 352, 358–359

Almirante (vessel), 35

Alvarado, Juan Bautista de, 398, 399, 401

Alvarez, Pedro Miguel: murder of, 178–179,
331, 357, 360, 361

Alvitre, Sebastian, 198–199

Amadeo Yeucharom (San Carlos), 384, 396,
405

Amezquita, Ramón, 392

Anastacia María (San Carlos), 207

Andrés (San Carlos), 362

Andrés Sagimomatsse (Santa Barbara), 248,
268

Aniceto (San Francisco), 356, 362

Anselma (San Carlos), 436

Anselmo Lapiquia (San Luis Obispo), 211

Antonio (San Carlos), 270

Antonio Pablo (San Juan Capistrano), 204

Anza, Juan Bautista de: and recruits to Alta
California, 56, 57, 59, 293–294; and overland route to Alta California, 57; and syphilis, 115–116

Archangel Raphael (painting), 168–170

Argüello, José Darío, 55, 353; on foreign trade,
371

Aristeo Joseph Chilichon (San Carlos), 184,
189 n. 11, 254

Arrillaga, José Joaquín de, 279, 316, 354; and
prohibition on Indian agricultural burning,
337; on corporal punishment of *gente de
razón*, 364; on foreign trade, 371

Arroyo de la Cuesta, Felipe, 143–144 n. 31, 145–
146, 200 n. 32; on Indian emancipation,
381

Arruz, José, 268

Arsenio (San Carlos), 395

Art. *See* Liturgical art

Artisans, 277

Asia trade, 277–279

Aspasniajan, 78

Atanasio, 362

Athanasio Joseph Huyuramus (San Carlos),
253, 254, 256, 257

Audiencias, 29

Aurelio (San Francisco), 353–355, 357, 360, 365

Aurelio Jujuvit (San Juan Capistrano), 207–
209, 223

Avila, Francisco, 221

Baja California: exploration of, by Spain, 29–
32; missions of, 40, 74; population of, 41;
expulsion of Jesuits from, 42, 236; art from,
148; Indian *cabildos* in, 233–234

Baldomero José (San Carlos), 384, 395–396,
418

Baltazar (San Carlos), 251

Banns. *See* Marriage: rituals of

Made in the USA
Las Vegas, NV
20 April 2021